System Design on AWS
Building and Scaling Enterprise Solutions

Jayanth Kumar and Mandeep Singh
Foreword by Swami Sivasubramanian

System Design on AWS

by Jayanth Kumar and Mandeep Singh

Copyright © 2025 Jayanth Kumar and Mandeep Singh. All rights reserved.

Published by O'Reilly Media, Inc., 1005 Gravenstein Highway North, Sebastopol, CA 95472.

O'Reilly books may be purchased for educational, business, or sales promotional use. Online editions are also available for most titles (*http://oreilly.com*). For more information, contact our corporate/institutional sales department: 800-998-9938 or *corporate@oreilly.com*.

Acquisitions Editor: Megan Laddusaw
Development Editor: Melissa Potter
Production Editor: Katherine Tozer
Copyeditor: Shannon Turlington
Proofreader: Piper Content Partners

Indexer: nSight, Inc.
Interior Designer: David Futato
Cover Designer: Karen Montgomery
Illustrator: Kate Dullea

February 2025: First Edition

Revision History for the First Edition
2025-02-14: First Release

See *http://oreilly.com/catalog/errata.csp?isbn=9781098146894* for release details.

The O'Reilly logo is a registered trademark of O'Reilly Media, Inc. *System Design on AWS*, the cover image, and related trade dress are trademarks of O'Reilly Media, Inc.

The views expressed in this work are those of the authors and do not represent the publisher's views. While the publisher and the authors have used good faith efforts to ensure that the information and instructions contained in this work are accurate, the publisher and the authors disclaim all responsibility for errors or omissions, including without limitation responsibility for damages resulting from the use of or reliance on this work. Use of the information and instructions contained in this work is at your own risk. If any code samples or other technology this work contains or describes is subject to open source licenses or the intellectual property rights of others, it is your responsibility to ensure that your use thereof complies with such licenses and/or rights.

978-1-098-14689-4

[LSI]

Table of Contents

Foreword. xiii

Preface. xv

Part I.   System Design Basics

1. System Design Trade-offs and Guidelines. 5
    System Design Concepts   6
        Communication   6
        Consistency   8
        Availability   13
        Reliability   19
        Scalability   20
        Maintainability   21
        Fault Tolerance   22
    Fallacies of Distributed Computing   24
    System Design Trade-offs   26
        Time Versus Space   27
        Latency Versus Throughput   27
        Performance Versus Scalability   28
        Consistency Versus Availability   28
    System Design Guidelines   31
        Guideline of Isolation: Build It Modularly   31
        Guideline of Simplicity: Keep It Simple, Silly   32
        Guideline of Performance: Metrics Don't Lie   32
        Guideline of Trade-offs: There Is No Such Thing as a Free Lunch   33

Guideline of Use Cases: It Always Depends	33
Conclusion	34

2. Storage Types and Relational Stores 35
Data Storage Format	36
File-Based Storage	36
Block-Based Storage	37
Object-Based Storage	38
Relational Databases	39
Relational Database Concepts	42
Relational Database Management System Architecture	47
Optimizing Relational Databases	50
Scaling Relational Databases	54
Open Source Relational Database Systems	63
Conclusion	65

3. Nonrelational Stores 67
Nonrelational Database Concepts	68
Schema Flexibility	68
Data Models	68
Scalability	69
High Availability and Fault Tolerance	69
BASE	69
Key-Value Databases	71
Data Model	71
Data Access and Retrieval Operations	73
Scaling Key-Value Stores	73
Availability in Key-Value Stores	76
Advantages, Trade-offs, and Considerations	77
Dynamo: Key-Value Database	78
Document Databases	79
Data Model	79
Availability in Document Stores	80
Advantages, Trade-offs, and Considerations	81
MongoDB: Open Source Document Database	82
Columnar Databases	83
Data Model	83
Consistency Levels	84
Columnar Store Architecture	86
Advantages, Trade-offs, and Considerations	88
Apache Cassandra: Open Source Columnar Database	88
Graph Databases	90

Data Model	90
Data Access and Retrieval	90
Advantages, Trade-offs, and Considerations	91
Neo4j: Open Source Graph Database	91
Conclusion	93

4. Caching Policies and Strategies... 95

Benefits of Caching	96
Cache Eviction Policies	97
Belady's Algorithm	97
Queue-Based Policies	97
Recency-Based Policies	98
Frequency-Based Policies	98
Allowlist Policy	99
Cache Invalidation	100
Caching Strategies	102
Read-Intensive Strategies	102
Write-Intensive Strategies	104
Cache Deployment	105
In-Process Caching	105
Interprocess Caching	106
Remote Caching	106
Choosing a Cache Deployment Approach	106
Caching Mechanisms	107
Content Delivery Networks	108
Push CDNs	109
Pull CDNs	109
Open Source Caching Solutions	111
Memcached	111
Redis	113
Conclusion	118

5. Load Balancing Approaches and Techniques................................. 119

Networking Components	120
Benefits of Load Balancing	122
LB Deployment and Placement Strategies	123
Global Server Load Balancing	123
Local Load Balancing	123
Load Balancing Algorithms	125
Static Load Balancing Algorithms	125
Dynamic Load Balancing Algorithms	126
Session Persistence in LBs	127

Stateful Load Balancers	127
Stateless Load Balancers	128
Types of Load Balancers	129
LB Types Based on Functionality	129
LB Types Based on Configuration	132
Nginx: Open Source Load Balancer	133
Conclusion	135

6. Communication Networks and Protocols. 137

Communication Models and Protocols	137
OSI Model	138
TCP/IP Model	139
Communication Types	150
Pull Mechanism: HTTP Polling	151
Push Mechanism: WebSockets	151
Push Mechanism: Server-Sent Events	153
Common Communication Protocol Standards	154
Remote Procedure Call	154
REST	155
GraphQL	157
Web Real-Time Communication	159
Conclusion	160

7. Containerization, Orchestration, and Deployments. 163

Evolution of Application Deployment	164
Containerization	166
Docker	166
Container Orchestration	174
Container Deployment Strategies	178
CI/CD Pipeline with Gitflow and Automated Deployment Strategies	180
Gitflow Workflow for Branch Management	180
Continuous Integration	181
Continuous Deployment	182
Monitoring and Incident Management	182
Conclusion	183

8. Architectural Designs and Patterns. 185

Change Data Capture	186
Publisher-Subscriber Architecture	188
Message Brokers	188
Message Queues	189
Choreography and Orchestration	190

Choreography	190
Orchestration	191
Deciding Between Choreography and Orchestration	193
Big Data Architecture	193
Lambda Architecture	193
Kappa Architecture	194
Data Lake Architecture	195
Solution Architecture	196
Monoliths	196
N-tier Architectures	197
Microservices	198
Event-Driven Architecture	199
EDA Concepts and Implementations	199
Paradigms of Event-Driven Implementations	200
Common Cloud Architecture Patterns	202
Event-Based Patterns: CQRS and Saga	202
Failure-Tolerant Patterns: Circuit Breaker, Retry with Backoff, and Rate Limiter	203
Domain-Based Patterns: Domain-Driven Design and Decompose by Subdomains	203
API Routing Strategies and Patterns	204
Other Cloud Architecture Patterns	205
Open Source Distributed Systems Architecture	206
HDFS	206
Apache Kafka: Distributed Message Queue	211
Comparing HDFS and Kafka	215
Conclusion	215

Part II. Diving Deep into AWS Services

9. AWS Network Services. 221

Getting Started with AWS	222
AWS Regions	223
AWS Availability Zones	223
AWS Local Zones	224
AWS Edge Locations	224
Introduction to AWS Networking Services	225
Amazon VPC	225
Subnets	231
Internet Connectivity	233
Route Tables	233

Security Groups	234
Network Access Control Lists	236
Amazon VPC-to-Internet Connectivity	237
Connectivity Between Amazon VPCs	239
Hybrid Connectivity	243
Amazon Route 53	246
AWS Elastic Load Balancer	248
Amazon API Gateway	250
Amazon CloudFront	251
Conclusion	253

10. AWS Storage Services.. 255

Cloud Storage on AWS	256
Amazon Elastic Block Store	256
Amazon Elastic File System	257
Amazon Simple Storage Service	259
AWS Databases	262
Amazon RDS	263
Amazon DynamoDB	265
Amazon DocumentDB	268
Amazon Neptune	270
Amazon ElastiCache	272
Amazon OpenSearch	275
Amazon Timestream	276
Amazon Keyspaces	276
Conclusion	277

11. AWS Compute Services.. 279

Amazon Elastic Compute Cloud	279
Amazon Machine Image	281
Instance Type	282
Autoscaling	284
AWS Lambda	286
Containerization Services	289
Amazon Elastic Container Service	290
Amazon Elastic Kubernetes Service	293
Conclusion	295

12. AWS Messaging, Orchestration, Monitoring, and Access Management Services.... 297

Amazon Managed Streaming for Apache Kafka	297
Amazon Kinesis	299
Amazon Kinesis Data Streams	299

Amazon Kinesis Data Analytics	302
Amazon Kinesis Data Firehose	303
Amazon Kinesis Video Streams	304
Amazon Simple Queue Service	305
Amazon Simple Notification Service	307
Workflow Orchestration	309
AWS Step Functions	310
Amazon Managed Workflow for Apache Airflow	313
Amazon CloudWatch	315
Application Logs	315
Metrics and Alarms	316
AWS Identity and Access Management	320
Amazon Cognito	323
AWS AppSync	326
Conclusion	328

13. Big Data, Analytics, and Machine Learning Services...... 329

AWS Big Data and Analytics	329
Amazon Elastic MapReduce	330
AWS Glue	334
Amazon Athena	338
Amazon QuickSight	339
Amazon Redshift	340
Machine Learning on AWS	344
Amazon SageMaker	344
AWS ML Application Services	346
AWS ML Infrastructure	348
Conclusion	349

Part III. System Design Use Cases

14. Designing a URL Shortener Service...... 355

System Requirements	355
Functional and Nonfunctional Requirements	356
System Scale	357
Storage Space	358
Starting with the Design	360
URL Shortening Algorithm	360
System APIs	365
System Considerations	367
Database Selection	368

        Custom Domain Support 369
    Launching the System on AWS 371
        Day Zero Architecture 371
        Scaling to Millions and Beyond 376
        Day N Architecture 379
    Conclusion 383

15. Designing a Web Crawler and Search Engine. 387
    System Requirements 388
        Functional and Nonfunctional Requirements 388
        System Scale 389
    Starting with the Design 391
        Designing the Web Crawler 393
        Designing the Search Engine 398
    Launching the System on AWS 404
        Day 0 Architecture 405
        Scaling to Millions and Beyond 407
        Day N Architecture 409
    Conclusion 414

16. Designing a Social Network and Newsfeed System. 415
    System Requirements 415
        Functional and Nonfunctional Requirements 416
        System Scale 417
    Starting with the Design 417
        Handling New Posts 418
        Managing User Connections 424
        Search Service 425
    Launching the System on AWS 427
        Day 0 Architecture 427
        Scaling to Millions and Beyond 428
        Day N Architecture 436
    Conclusion 440

17. Designing an Online Game Leaderboard. 441
    System Requirements 442
        Functional and Nonfunctional Requirements 442
        System Scale 444
    Starting with the Design 446
        Concepts and Principles 446
        A Rough System Design 448
    Launching the System on AWS 451

        Day 0 Architecture   451
        Scaling to Millions and Beyond   454
        Day N Architecture   460
    Conclusion   463

18. Designing a Hotel Reservation System... 465

    System Requirements   465
        Functional and Nonfunctional Requirements   466
        System Scale   467
    Starting with the Design   469
        Property Onboarding Architecture   469
        Property Search Architecture   471
        Property Booking Architecture   478
        Property Reviews Architecture   488
    Launching the System on AWS   490
        Day 0 Architecture   490
        Scaling to Millions and Beyond   493
        Day N Architecture   497
    Conclusion   498

19. Designing a Chat Application... 501

    System Requirements   501
        Functional and Nonfunctional Requirements   502
        System Scale   503
    Starting with the Design   503
        Messaging Architecture   504
        WhatsApp Architecture with Erlang   511
    Launching the System on AWS   516
        Day 0 Architecture   516
        Scaling to Millions and Beyond   517
        Day N Architecture   520
    Conclusion   522

20. Designing a Video-Processing Pipeline for a Streaming Service.................. 525

    System Requirements   525
        Functional and Nonfunctional Requirements   526
        System Scale   527
    Starting with the Design   528
        Video Encoding   529
        Video-Quality Validation   531
        Content Indexing   531
        Content Distribution   532

Launching the System on AWS	534
Day 0 Architecture	534
Scaling to Millions and Beyond	536
Day N Architecture	540
Conclusion	542

21. Designing an Online Stock-Trading Platform........................... 543

System Requirements	544
Functional and Nonfunctional Requirements	544
System Scale	545
Starting with the Design	545
Designing a Stock Tick System	546
Designing the Order Management System	550
Designing Ultra-Low-Latency Systems	553
Building the P&L Dashboard	555
Launching the System on AWS	557
Day 0 Architecture	557
Scaling to Millions and Beyond	559
Day N Architecture	562
Conclusion	566

Index.. 569

Foreword

Systems design is one of the most important aspects of building apps that are scalable, available, performant, and secure, even when your usage increases by an order of magnitude or two. That's why I found the topic of this book to be so important. I like that this book starts with covering the basics of trade-offs in distributed systems, such as the CAP theorem, units of blast radius, and other common trade-offs in systems design, and then moves to how to apply these principles in practice. I found this approach—going from core principles to actually putting them into practice on critical design decisions (such as "What is the best database for running my workload?" and "What's the best caching strategy for my workloads?" and "Which storage service should I choose?")—to be especially helpful as it teaches people how to think about these problems even as new capabilities from AWS emerge, making the concepts in this book more durable.

Personally, reading this book reminded me so much of the early days of AWS, when we spent a lot of time discussing these trade-offs. At that time, concepts like CAP theorem, blast radius, and seamless scalability were not well understood, and we had robust discussions around these topics and the inherent trade-offs they come with. However, those discussions led to some incredibly robust AWS services, such as S3, DynamoDB, and many others that millions of AWS customers love. I hope the you grasp these concepts and are inspired to build similarly amazing products and services that delight their customers.

Congratulations to the authors for writing such an excellent book, and best of luck to all who embark on this journey!

— Swami Sivasubramanian,
Vice President, AI and Data at AWS

Preface

System design is a disciplined art, so let's create some large-scale masterpieces.

System Design on AWS is a comprehensive guide to helping software architects and engineers understand, build, and scale complex systems on the Amazon Web Services (AWS) cloud. The book provides a structured approach to tackling real-world system design challenges on AWS in a continuously evolving cloud landscape. The material focuses on fundamental principles, architectural trade-offs, and practical use cases, guiding you from Day 0 (minimum viable product) to Day N (most valuable product). Through detailed chapters, this book demystifies AWS's wide-ranging services and how they can be strategically leveraged to address both technical and business requirements.

How This Book Is Organized

Organized into three core parts, this book begins by establishing a foundation in system design, then dives into the essential AWS services for building resilient architectures, and concludes with practical system design use cases. Foundational system design patterns, scaling mechanisms, caching strategies, network protocols, and deployment strategies are covered. By exploring these elements in a cloud context, the book offers a toolkit for approaching and solving large-scale design problems in any industry. Each part opener breaks down the chapters included in that part, so take a look at those openers for details. This book aims to equip you with:

- A solid understanding of fundamental system design principles and trade-offs
- Proficiency in key AWS services and their roles in building large-scale systems
- Insight into real-world use cases that illustrate how to structure and deploy scalable architectures on AWS
- Strategies to balance performance, scalability, and cost in AWS cloud environments

What This Book Isn't

This book does not provide detailed code implementations for deploying the infrastructure or application business logic. Instead, it emphasizes the architecture and design process, helping you understand how to break a system down into manageable components and make informed architectural decisions.

Who Should Read This Book

This book is ideal for software architects, developers, DevOps engineers, and system architects who want to build or scale applications on AWS. It is especially useful for professionals transitioning from on-premises to cloud infrastructure or aiming to leverage AWS for large-scale applications. A basic understanding of software implementation and familiarity with one programming language are recommended.

This book is also recommended for people holding leadership positions in software development and DevOps. The guidance and principles in the book will help you remove team blockers while building systems and making informed decisions.

While this book is titled *System Design on AWS* and the focus is on the AWS cloud, we recommend it to everyone who loves to build systems on any of the cloud providers' platforms or for on-premises data centers as well as anyone who is just curious about building systems. The design and scaling principles discussed in the book are agnostic of cloud providers.

Conventions Used in This Book

The following typographical conventions are used in this book:

Italic
: Indicates new terms, URLs, email addresses, filenames, and file extensions.

`Constant width`
: Used for program listings, as well as within paragraphs to refer to program elements such as variable or function names, databases, data types, environment variables, statements, and keywords.

`Constant width bold`
: Shows commands or other text that should be typed literally by the user.

`Constant width italic`
: Shows text that should be replaced with user-supplied values or by values determined by context.

 This element signifies a general note.

Many of the tools and services discussed in these pages are abbreviated on repeated mentions for your convenience. For example, *Amazon Elastic Compute Cloud* is sometimes called *Amazon EC2* or just *EC2*.

O'Reilly Online Learning

 For more than 40 years, *O'Reilly Media* has provided technology and business training, knowledge, and insight to help companies succeed.

Our unique network of experts and innovators share their knowledge and expertise through books, articles, and our online learning platform. O'Reilly's online learning platform gives you on-demand access to live training courses, in-depth learning paths, interactive coding environments, and a vast collection of text and video from O'Reilly and 200+ other publishers. For more information, visit *https://oreilly.com*.

How to Contact Us

Please address comments and questions concerning this book to the publisher:

> O'Reilly Media, Inc.
> 1005 Gravenstein Highway North
> Sebastopol, CA 95472
> 800-889-8969 (in the United States or Canada)
> 707-827-7019 (international or local)
> 707-829-0104 (fax)
> *support@oreilly.com*
> *https://oreilly.com/about/contact.html*

We have a web page for this book, where we list errata, examples, and any additional information. You can access this page at *https://oreil.ly/SystemDesignOnAWS*.

For news and information about our books and courses, visit *https://oreilly.com*.

Find us on LinkedIn: *https://linkedin.com/company/oreilly-media*.

Watch us on YouTube: *https://youtube.com/oreillymedia*.

Acknowledgments

This book is the culmination of insights, experience, and feedback from numerous collaborators and industry experts. We thank our colleagues, reviewers, and readers for their contributions and dedication to advancing cloud-based system design.

We extend our sincere gratitude to the entire O'Reilly team, both visible and behind the scenes, for their contributions and feedback on this book. We would not have met with the O'Reilly team without an introduction from John Culkin and his expert review of our early proposal of this book. We would like to thank Megan Laddusaw for support on the book proposal and getting the chapters outline ready. A special thanks to Melissa Potter, our development editor, for her patience and support. Her initial reviews were incredibly helpful in structuring the content and helped make the book more valuable.

A big thanks to Swami Sivasubramanian for taking the time to write a wonderful foreword; his words perfectly set the stage, and we couldn't have asked for a better introduction. Thank you to Harshit Bangar, Rakesh Kumar, Neha Shetty, Dinesh Chittibala, Alankrit Kharbanda, Kristina Manukyan, and Rohn Arya for reviewing the book and providing many helpful suggestions and insightful comments.

We would also like to thank the Dragonfly DB team for sponsoring the two early-release chapters on their website and making them freely available for the tech community. Special thanks to all the companies out there publishing detailed engineering blogs and sharing the innovations and deep dives.

Mandeep Singh

I would like to thank my wonderful wife, Priyanka, for her patience and encouragement and for putting up with me spending long hours writing. I am forever grateful to my parents for enabling me to achieve my dreams and always putting my interests before theirs. Thanks to all my family members for their support and guidance.

Thanks to my college, Army Institute of Technology, for introducing me to computer science and helping me become a disciplined individual. Thanks to all the amazing opportunities I had working at different organizations: AWS, Amazon, Jupiter, and Skytap (a Kyndryl company). I met a lot of amazing folks, and they have greatly shaped my thinking around decision making and systems building. I would also like to thank my friends, teachers, and professional connections for suggestions and discussions along the way.

The idea of writing a book would never have originated without my coauthor, Jayanth. Thanks for sharing the opportunity with me—the entire writing of this book has been entirely a new experience and learning for me.

Jayanth Kumar

This book is a heartfelt expression of gratitude to my family and all the teachers who have guided me throughout my life. I am forever grateful for their support, encouragement, and wisdom that have profoundly shaped who I am. I got the inspiration to author such a technical book from my professors, Pushpak Bhattacharya and George Varghese, who infected me with their enthusiasm for the music of systems and algorithmics.

I owe much of my journey to the institutions that nurtured my curiosity and skills: my alma maters IIT Bombay and the University of California, Los Angeles. These environments were instrumental in developing my foundation and pushing me to explore new horizons in technology and system design.

My career has been a canvas of experiences, shaped by incredible mentors and colleagues at SAP, Goodhealthapp, Delhivery, Amazon, and Turl Street Group. Each role allowed me to build and scale systems through various growth stages, from 0 to 1 at Goodhealthapp (startup), 1 to 10 at Delhivery (unicorn), 10 to 1,000 at SAP (enterprise), and 1,000+ at Amazon (FAANG), and each taught me invaluable lessons in resilience, adaptability, and innovation.

This book could not have come to life without the dedication of my coauthor, Mandeep Singh, who tirelessly worked alongside me, often burning the midnight oil to cover ground where I left off. His commitment and attention to detail have been invaluable in bringing this work to completion.

There are a lot of folks whom I wish I could mention individually, whose contributions, guidance, and shared knowledge shaped this book, but I am constrained by space, so please know that your impact is felt and appreciated. I am also indebted to the broader tech community, whose inspiration fuels my dedication to this field. It is my hope that this book will add value to our shared pursuit of innovation and learning.

PART I
System Design Basics

Perfection is finally attained not when there is no longer anything to add but when there is no longer anything to take away.
—Antoine de Saint-Exupéry

The first part of this book will give you a solid foundation in system design, offering insights into the fundamental principles that underpin all types of software systems, ranging from trade-offs to the criteria for picking the right tools and technologies and thus, the right architecture patterns.

In Part I, you will:

- Grasp the system trade-offs inherent in large-scale distributed systems and know how to balance conflicting demands like scalability, reliability, and maintainability
- Develop a clear understanding of options for data storage, including file, block, and object stores, alongside relational and nonrelational databases and methods for scaling them
- Master techniques to achieve low latency and high throughput in storage and compute through caching and content delivery networks (CDNs)
- Learn to horizontally scale systems with load balancers, API gateways, and reverse proxies
- Navigate the choices among communication and network protocols at different layers of the Open Systems Interconnection (OSI) and TCP/IP models and know how to choose when to use what

- Familiarize yourself with the system design architecture patterns that are commonly used in the industry and learn how to adapt them to various system requirements
- Gain insight into the AWS services that map to different system design paradigms, which we will explore further in later chapters

Chapter 1 will delve into the world of trade-offs in large-scale distributed systems. We'll explore essential concepts like reliability, scalability, and maintainability, shedding light on why these trade-offs emerge. We'll tackle common misconceptions through the fallacies of distributed computing and address pivotal choices such as space versus time, latency versus throughput, performance versus scalability, and consistency versus availability. We'll also offer practical guidelines and strategies that have emerged from years of system design wisdom, providing tangible approaches to enhance system performance and efficiency.

Chapter 2 will introduce you to different types of data storage, including file, block, and object stores. We'll cover relational databases, their concepts, and their architecture in this chapter. You'll gain insights into the intricacies of scaling and optimizing relational databases, including techniques like partitioning, indexing, replication, federation, sharding, and denormalization.

Chapter 3 will unveil the architecture of nonrelational databases, such as key-value, wide-column, document, and graph databases, and discuss how leaderless architectures enable scalability through mechanisms like quorum-based replication, consistent hashing, and eventual consistency.

Chapter 4 will introduce you to caching, where we will explore diverse caching strategies spanning different tiers, from client and server to application and database levels. We'll dissect core caching approaches like write-through, read-through, refresh-ahead, write-back, and cache-aside. Moreover, we'll unravel the potential of both push and pull CDNs in reducing latency and improving the efficiency of content delivery.

Chapter 5 will explore load balancers, API gateways, and reverse proxies, and includes discussions on Layer 4 (L4) network scaling and Layer 7 (L7) application layer scaling. Concepts like sticky sessions, forward proxies, and reverse proxies will come to life as we delve into the nuances of creating scalable, resilient architectures.

Chapter 6 will demystify network protocols, unraveling the intricacies of TCP/IP and User Datagram Protocol (UDP), as well as HTTP, SMTP, Extensible Messaging and Presence Protocol (XMPP), and their suitable applications. You'll gain a comprehensive understanding of synchronous and asynchronous service design and delve into standards like REST, WebRTC, and GraphQL. Mastering these communication concepts will better equip you to make informed choices for different use cases.

Chapter 7 is all about containerization: the creation, management, and orchestration of Docker containers. You'll also be introduced to modern strategies for container deployment, enabling you to manage the complexity of modern cloud native applications.

Chapter 8 will cover different architectural designs and patterns, starting with choreography and orchestration in detail, where we explore asynchronous architectures, message brokers, message queues, and publisher-subscriber patterns. As you delve deeper into large-scale software engineering design, you'll compare microservices with monolithic designs, serverless architecture, the saga pattern, the event-sourcing pattern, big data architectures, and domain-driven design.

After this comprehensive journey through the nuances of system design in Part I, you'll be well prepared to wield these principles and technologies in creating effective and efficient large-scale systems. Part II will cover the AWS services in detail, bringing these concepts to light in their use and trade-offs in cloud architecture.

CHAPTER 1
System Design Trade-offs and Guidelines

Today's modern technological revolution is happening because of large-scale software systems. Big enterprise companies like Google, Amazon, Oracle, and SAP have all built large-scale software systems to run their (and their customers') businesses. Building and operating such large-scale software systems requires first-principles thinking to design and develop the technical architecture before actually putting the system into code. This is because we don't want to be in a state where these systems will not work or scale as more users need them.

If the design is right in the first place, the rest of the implementation journey becomes smooth. This requires looking at the business requirements, understanding the needs and objectives of the customer, evaluating different trade-offs, thinking about error handling and edge cases, and contemplating future changes and robustness while worrying about basic details like algorithms and data structures. Enterprises can avoid the mistake of wasted software-development effort by carefully thinking about systems and investing time in understanding bottlenecks, system requirements, users being targeted, user access patterns, and many such decisions, which, in short, is *system design*.

This chapter covers the basics of system design with the goal of helping you understand the fundamental concepts, the trade-offs that naturally arise in such large-scale software systems, the fallacies to avoid in building such systems, and the guidelines of system design—those lessons that have been learned from building large-scale software systems over the years. This chapter is intended to introduce you to the essentials—we'll dig into the details in later chapters, but we want you to have a good foundation to start. Let's begin with the basic concepts of system design.

System Design Concepts

To understand the building blocks of system design, we should understand the fundamental concepts around systems. We can leverage *abstraction* here: the concept in computer science of obfuscating the inner details to create a model of these system design concepts, which can help us grasp the bigger picture. The concepts in system design, be it any software system, revolve around communication, consistency, availability, reliability, scalability, system maintainability, and fault tolerance. We will go over each of these concepts in detail, creating a mental model while also exploring how they are applied in large-scale system design.

Communication

A large-scale software system is composed of small subsystems, known as *servers*, that communicate with one another—that is, they exchange information or data over the network to solve a business problem, provide business logic, and compose functionality. Communication can take place in either a synchronous or an asynchronous fashion, depending on the needs and requirements of the system. Figure 1-1 shows the differences in the sequence of actions in synchronous and asynchronous communication.

> We will cover the communication protocols as well as mechanisms for asynchronous communication in detail in Chapter 6.

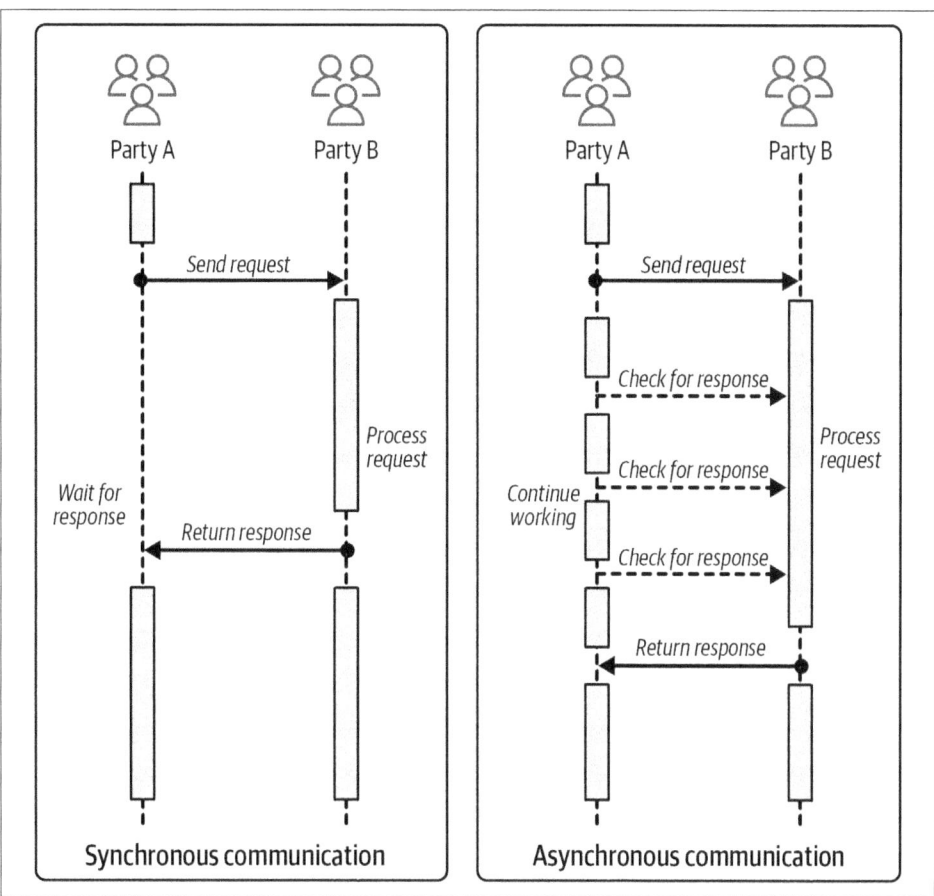

Figure 1-1. Sequence diagram for synchronous versus asynchronous communication

Synchronous communication

Imagine having a phone conversation with your friend: you hear them and speak with them at the same time and use pauses in between to allow the conversation to complete. This is an example of *synchronous communication*: a type of communication in which two or more parties communicate with one another in real time. This type of communication is more immediate and allows for quicker resolution of issues or questions.

In system design, a communication mechanism is synchronous when the sender will block (or wait) for the call or execution to return before continuing. This means that until a response is returned by the receiver, the application will not execute any further, which could be perceived by the user as latency or performance lag in the application.

System Design Concepts | 7

Asynchronous communication

Now, imagine that instead of a phone conversation, you switch to email. As you communicate over email with your friend, you send the message and wait for the reply to come at a later time (but within an acceptable time limit). You also follow a practice to follow up if there is no response after this time limit has passed. This is an example of *asynchronous communication*: a type of communication in which two or more parties do not communicate with one another in real time. Asynchronous communication can also take place through messaging platforms, forums, and social media, where users can post messages and responses may not be immediate.

In system design, a communication mechanism is asynchronous when the sender does not block (or wait) for the call or execution to return from the receiver. Execution continues in your program or system, and when the call returns from the receiving server, a *callback* function is executed. Asynchronous communication is often used in system design when an immediate response is not required or when the system needs to be more flexible and tolerant of delays or failures.

In general, the choice of synchronous or asynchronous communication in system design depends on the specific requirements and constraints of the system. Synchronous communication is often preferred when real-time response is needed (such as the communication between the frontend UI and the backend), while asynchronous communication is often preferred when flexibility and robustness are more important (such as checking the status of a long-running job).

Consistency

Consistency—being consistent or in accordance with a set of rules or standards—is an important requirement when it comes to communication between servers in a software system. Consistency can refer to a variety of concepts and contexts in system design.

In the context of distributed systems, consistency can be the property of all *replica* nodes (more on this in a moment) or servers having the same view of data at a given point in time. This means that all replica nodes have the same data, and any updates to the data are immediately reflected on all replica nodes.

In the context of data storage and retrieval, consistency refers to the property of each read request returning the value of the most recent write. This means that if a write operation updates the value of a piece of data, any subsequent read requests for that data should return the updated value. Let's discuss each of these in more detail.

Consistency in distributed systems

Distributed systems are software systems that are separated physically but connected over the network to achieve common goals using shared computing resources.

Ensuring consistency—that is, providing the same view of the data to each server in a distributed system—can be challenging because multiple replica servers may be in different physical locations and may be subject to different failures or delays.

To address these challenges and ensure data consistency in distributed systems, we can use various techniques:

Data replication
　In this approach, multiple copies of the data are maintained on different replica nodes, and updates to the data are made on all replica nodes simultaneously through blocking synchronous communication. This ensures that all replica nodes have the same view of the data at any given time.

Consensus protocols
　Consensus protocols ensure that all replica nodes agree on the updates to be made to the data. They can use a variety of mechanisms, such as voting or leader election, to make sure all replica nodes are in agreement before updating the data.

Conflict resolution
　If two or more replica nodes try to update the same data simultaneously, conflict resolution algorithms are used to determine which update should be applied. These algorithms can employ various strategies, such as last writer wins or merge algorithms, to resolve conflicts.

Consistency in data storage and retrieval

Large-scale software systems produce and consume a large amount of data, and thus, ensuring consistency in data storage and retrieval is important for maintaining the accuracy and integrity of the data in these systems. For example, consider a database that stores the balance of a bank account. If we withdraw money from the account, the database should reflect the updated balance immediately. If the database does not ensure consistency, it is possible for a read request to return an old balance, which could lead to incorrect financial decisions or even financial losses for us or our banks.

To address these challenges and ensure read consistency in data storage systems, we can use various techniques:

Write-ahead logging
　In this technique, writes to the data are first recorded in a log before they are applied to the actual data. This ensures that if the system crashes or fails, the data can be restored to a consistent state by replaying the log.

Locking
   Locking mechanisms are used to ensure that only one write operation can be performed at a time. This ensures that multiple writes do not interfere with one another and that reads always return the value of the most recent write.

Data versioning
   In this technique, each write operation is assigned a version number, and reads always return the value of the most recent version. This allows for multiple writes to be performed concurrently while still ensuring that reads return the value of the most recent write.

We will discuss some of these techniques for ensuring consistency in detail in Chapters 2 and 3.

Consistency spectrum model

Since consistency can mean different things, the *consistency spectrum model* helps us reason about whether a distributed system is working correctly when it's doing multiple things at the same time, like reading, writing, and updating data. The consistency spectrum model represents the various consistency guarantees that a distributed system can offer, ranging from eventual consistency to strong consistency. The consistency guarantee chosen depends on the specific requirements and constraints of the system. Let's walk through the consistency levels in the consistency spectrum model:

Strong consistency
   At one end of the spectrum, strong consistency guarantees that all replica nodes have the same view of the data at all times and that any updates to the data are immediately reflected on all replica nodes. This ensures that the data is always accurate and up to date, but it can be difficult to achieve in practice as it requires all replica nodes to be in constant communication with one another.

We will cover the strong consistency requirements of relational databases as part of the ACID model in Chapter 2.

Monotonic read consistency
   Monotonic read consistency guarantees that once a client has read a value from a replica node, all subsequent reads from that client will return the same value or a more recent value. This means that a client will not see "stale" data that has been

updated by another client. This provides a stronger consistency guarantee than eventual consistency because it ensures that a client will not see outdated data.

Monotonic write consistency
   Monotonic write consistency guarantees that once a write operation has been acknowledged by a replica node, all subsequent reads from that replica node will return the updated value. This means that a replica node will not return outdated data to clients after a write operation has been acknowledged. This provides a stronger consistency guarantee than eventual consistency because it ensures that a replica node will not return outdated data to clients.

Causal consistency
   Causal consistency works by categorizing operations into dependent and independent operations. Dependent operations are also called *causally related operations*. Causal consistency preserves the order of the causally related operations. It guarantees that if two operations are causally related in dependent and independent operations, then they will be seen in the same order by all processes in the system. This means that if operation A must happen before operation B, then all processes in the system will see A before they see B. This provides a stronger consistency guarantee than eventual consistency because it ensures that the order of related operations is preserved.

Eventual consistency
   At the other end of the spectrum, eventual consistency guarantees that, given enough time, all replica nodes will eventually have the same view of the data. This allows for more flexibility and tolerance of delays or failures but can result in temporary inconsistencies in the data.

 We will cover the tunable consistency feature of some of the nonrelational columnar databases like Cassandra in Chapter 3.

Figure 1-2 shows the difference in the results of performing a sequence of actions under either strong consistency or eventual consistency. As you can see on the left showing strong consistency, when *x* is read from a replica node after updating it from 0 to 2, it will block the request until replication happens and then return 2 as the result. On the right illustrating eventual consistency, you can see that when the replica node is queried, it will give a stale result of *x* as 0 before replication completes.

The consistency spectrum model therefore provides a framework for understanding the trade-offs between consistency and availability in distributed systems and helps system designers choose the appropriate consistency guarantee for their specific needs.

System Design Concepts | 11

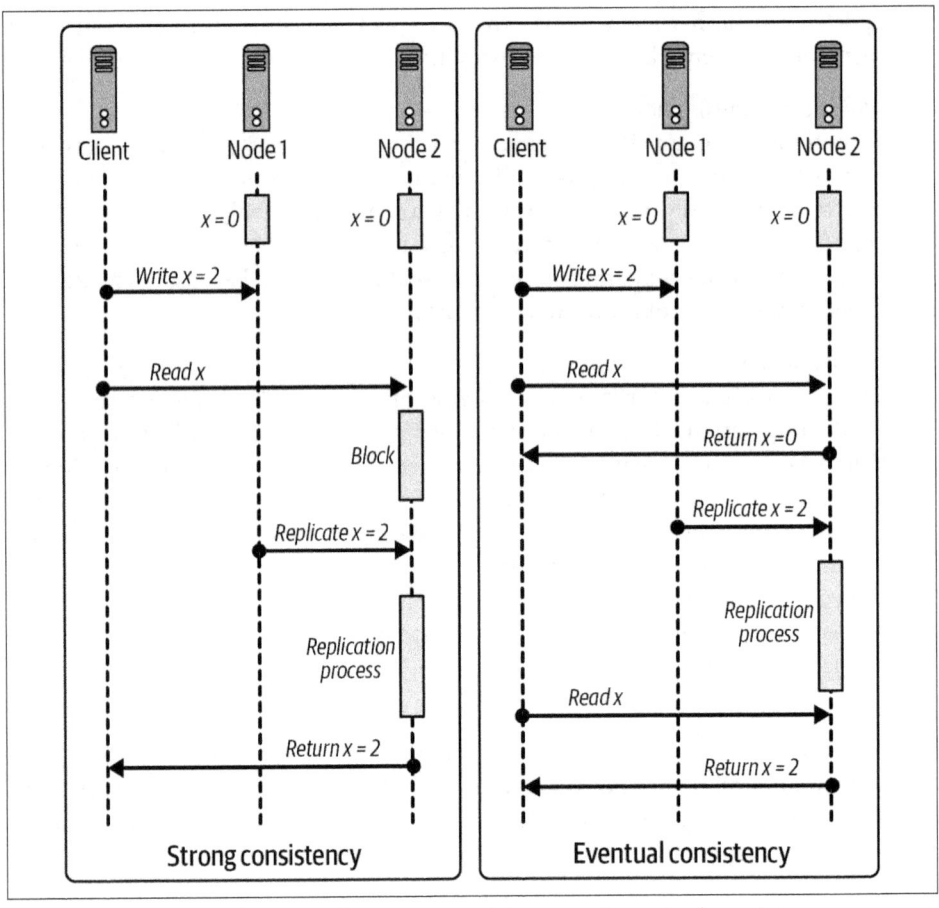

Figure 1-2. Sequence diagrams for strong consistency and eventual consistency

The level of consistency that a distributed system aims to achieve directly affects its complexity: stricter consistency models (like strong consistency) require extensive coordination, synchronization, and consensus across nodes, increasing latency and operational costs and making failure handling more challenging. This complexity is especially pronounced in geographically distributed systems, where network latency and scalability constraints complicate synchronization of global data. Conversely, relaxing consistency requirements (as in eventual consistency) reduces system complexity, enabling higher scalability and availability at the cost of allowing temporary data inconsistencies. Ultimately, there's a trade-off between data accuracy and system simplicity, with each choice tailored to the specific needs and tolerance for latency, availability, and correctness in the application.

Availability

In a large-scale software system, subsystems or servers can go down and may not be fully available to respond to the client's requests; this is referred to as the system's *availability*. A system that is highly available can process requests and return responses in a timely manner, even under heavy load or when there are failures or errors. Let's try to quantify the measurement of availability of the system.

Measuring availability

Availability can be measured mathematically as the percentage of the time the system was up (total time − time system was down) over the total time the system should have been running:

$$\text{Availability \%} = \frac{(\text{Total Time} - \text{Sum total of time system was down})}{\text{Total Time}} \times 100$$

Availability percentages are represented in nines based on this formula over a period of time. You can see a breakdown of what these numbers really work out to in Table 1-1.

Table 1-1. Availability percentages represented in nines

Availability percentage	Downtime per year	Downtime per month	Downtime per week
90% (1 nine)	36.5 days	72 hours	16.8 hours
99% (2 nines)	3.65 days	7.2 hours	1.68 hours
99.5% (2 nines)	1.83 days	3.60 hours	50.4 minutes
99.9% (3 nines)	8.76 hours	43.8 minutes	10.1 minutes
99.99% (4 nines)	52.56 minutes	4.32 minutes	1.01 minutes
99.999% (5 nines)	5.26 minutes	25.9 seconds	6.05 seconds
99.9999% (6 nines)	31.5 seconds	2.59 seconds	0.605 seconds
99.99999% (7 nines)	3.15 seconds	0.259 seconds	0.0605 seconds

The goal for availability usually is to achieve the highest level possible, such as "five nines" (99.999%) or even "six nines" (99.9999%). However, the level of availability that is considered realistic or achievable depends on several factors, including the complexity of the system, the resources available for maintenance and redundancy, and the specific requirements of the application or service.

Achieving higher levels of availability becomes progressively more challenging and resource intensive. Each additional nine requires an exponential increase in redundancy, fault-tolerant architecture, and rigorous maintenance practices. It often involves implementing redundant components, backup systems, load balancing, failover mechanisms, and continuous monitoring to minimize downtime and ensure rapid recovery in case of failures.

While some critical systems, such as financial trading platforms or emergency services, may strive for the highest levels of availability, achieving and maintaining them can be extremely difficult and costly. In contrast, for less critical applications or services with a lower level of availability, such as 99% or 99.9%, may be more realistic and achievable within reasonable resource constraints.

Ultimately, determining what level of availability is realistic and achievable depends on a careful evaluation of the specific requirements, resources, costs, and trade-offs involved in each case.

Availability in parallel versus in sequence

The availability of a system that consists of multiple subsystems depends on whether the components are arranged in sequence or in parallel with respect to serving the request. Figure 1-3 shows the arrangement of components in the sequential system on the left, where the request needs to be served from each component in sequence, and the parallel system on the right, where the request can be served from either component in parallel.

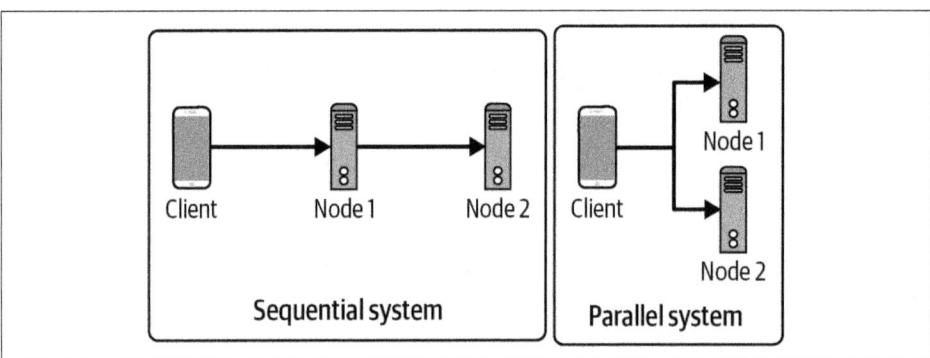

Figure 1-3. Sequential system versus parallel system

If the components are in sequence, the overall availability of the service will be the product of the availability of each component. For example, if two components with 99.9% availability are in sequence, their total availability will be 99.8%:

Availability of two components in sequence
= Availability of component 1 × Availability of component 2
= .999 × .999 = .998001 ~ 99.8%

On the other hand, if the components are in parallel, the overall availability of the service will be the sum of the availability of each component minus the product of their unavailability. For example, if two components with 99.9% availability are in parallel, their total availability will be 99.9999%. This can lead to significantly higher availability compared to the same components arranged in sequence (from 3 nines to 6 nines in the example):

Availability of two components in parallel
= 1 − Unavailability of both components
= 1 − (P(Component 1 going down) × P(Component 2 going down))
= 1 − (.001 × .001) = 1 − .000001
= .999999 ∼ 99.9999 %

The arrangement of components in a service can have a significant impact on its overall availability, so it is important to consider this when designing a system for high availability.

Ensuring availability

Ensuring availability in a system is critical for maintaining the performance and reliability of the system. There are several ways to increase the availability of a system:

Redundancy
    When a system has multiple copies of critical components or subsystems, it can continue to function even if one component fails. This can be achieved by using redundant load balancers, failover systems, or replicated data stores.

Fault tolerance
    Systems designed to be resistant to failures or errors can continue to function even when there are unexpected events. This can be achieved by using error-handling mechanisms, redundant hardware, or self-healing systems.

Load balancing
    By distributing incoming requests among multiple servers or components, a system can more effectively handle heavy loads and maintain high availability. This can be achieved by using multiple load balancers or distributed systems.

We will cover load balancing in detail in Chapter 5 and explore the different types of AWS load balancers in Chapter 9.

Availability patterns

There are two major complementary patterns to support high availability: failover and replication.

Failover patterns. *Failover* refers to the process of switching to a redundant or backup system in the event of a failure or error in the primary system. The failover pattern chosen depends on the specific requirements and constraints of the system, including the desired level of availability and the cost of implementing the failover solution. The two main types of failover patterns are active-active and active-passive:

Active-active failover
> In an active-active failover pattern, as shown on the left in Figure 1-4, multiple systems are used in parallel, and all systems are actively processing requests. If one system fails, the remaining systems can continue to process requests and maintain high availability. This approach allows for more flexibility and better utilization of resources but can be more complex to implement and maintain because it requires more sophisticated load balancing and failover mechanisms.

Active-passive failover
> In an active-passive failover pattern, as shown on the right in Figure 1-4, one system is designated as the primary system and actively processes requests while one or more backup systems are maintained in a passive state. If the primary system fails, the backup system is activated to take over processing of requests. This approach is simpler to implement and maintain because data only needs to be replicated in one direction: from the active server to the passive server. It also avoids the complexities of data conflicts and the synchronization issues that can occur in an active-active setup. However, this can result in reduced availability if the primary system fails, as there is a delay in switching to the backup system.

Failover patterns can require additional hardware and can add complexity to the system. There is also the potential for data loss if the active system fails before newly written data can be replicated to the passive system. The choice of failover pattern depends on the specific requirements and constraints of the system, including the desired level of availability and the cost of implementing the failover solution.

> These failover patterns are employed in relational data stores, non-relational data stores, caches, and load balancers, which we will cover in Chapters 2, 3, 4, and 5, respectively.

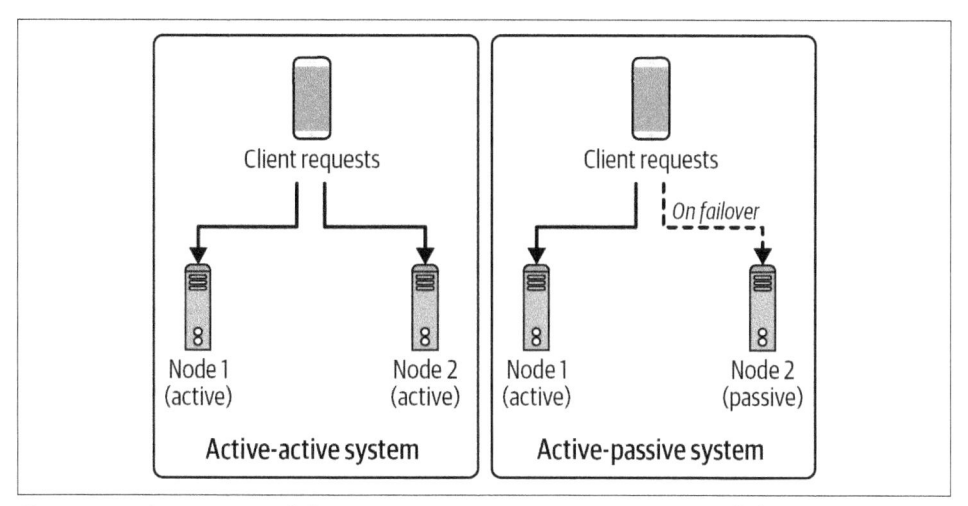

Figure 1-4. Active-active failover system setup versus active-passive failover system setup

Replication patterns. *Replication* is the process of maintaining multiple copies of data or other resources to improve availability and fault tolerance. The replication pattern chosen depends on the specific requirements and constraints of the system, including the desired level of availability and the cost of implementing the replication solution. The two main types of replication patterns are multileader and single leader:

Multileader replication
  In a multileader replication pattern, as shown on the left in Figure 1-5, multiple systems are used in parallel, and all systems can read and write data. This allows for more flexibility and better utilization of resources because all systems can process requests and updates to the data simultaneously. A load balancer is required or application logic changes need to be made to support multiple leaders and identify on which leader node to write. Most multileader systems either are loosely consistent or have increased write latency for synchronization to remain consistent. Conflict resolution comes more into play as more write nodes are added, leading to increases in latency. This approach can become complex to implement and maintain because it requires careful management of conflicts and errors.

Single-leader replication
  In a single-leader replication pattern, as shown on the right in Figure 1-5, one system is designated as the leader system and is responsible for both reading and writing data while one or more follower systems are used to replicate the data. The follower systems can be used only for reading data; updates to the data must be made on the leader system. Additional logic is required to be implemented to promote a follower to the leader. This approach is simpler to implement and

maintain but can result in reduced availability if the leader system fails because updates to the data can be made only on the leader system and there is a risk of losing the data updates.

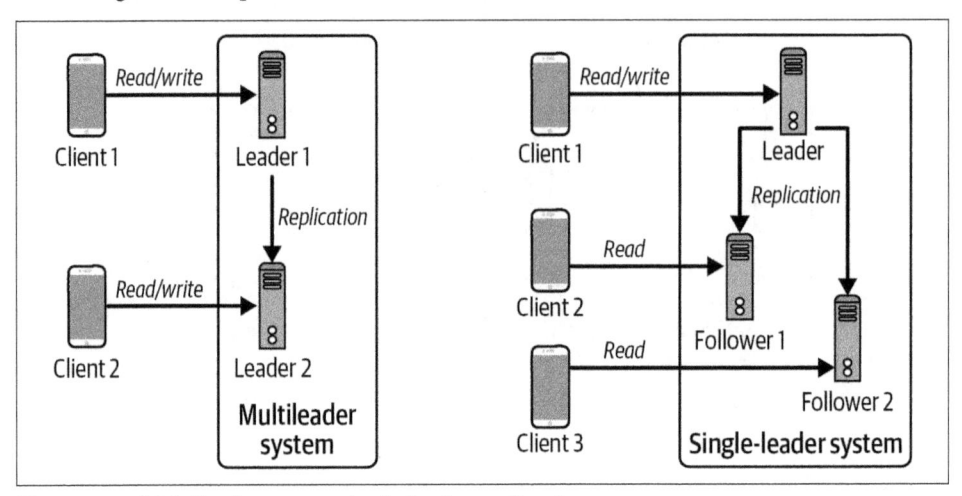

Figure 1-5. Multileader versus single-leader replication system setup

There is a risk of data loss if the leader system fails before newly written data can be replicated to other nodes. The more read replicas that are used, the more writes need to be replicated, which can lead to greater replication lag. In addition, using read replicas can affect the performance of the system because the system may get bogged down with replaying writes and become unable to process as many reads. Furthermore, replication can require additional hardware that can add complexity to the system. Finally, some systems may have more efficient write performance on the leader system since it can spawn multiple threads to write in parallel, while read replicas may only support writing sequentially with a single thread. The choice of replication pattern depends on the specific requirements and constraints of the system, including the desired level of availability and the cost of implementing the replication solution.

> We will cover how relational and nonrelational data stores ensure availability using single-leader and multileader replication in Chapters 2 and 3. Do look out for leaderless replication using consistent hashing to ensure availability in nonrelational stores like key-value stores and columnar stores in Chapter 3.

Reliability

In system design, *reliability* refers to the ability of a system or component to perform its intended function consistently and without failure over a given period of time. It is a measure of the dependability or trustworthiness of the system. Reliability is typically expressed as a probability or percentage of time that the system will operate without failure. For example, a system with a reliability of 99% will fail only 1% of the time. Let's try to quantify the measurement of reliability of the system.

Measuring reliability

One way to measure the reliability of a system is by using mean time between failures (MTBF) and mean time to repair (MTTR).

Mean time between failures. MTBF is a measure of the average amount of time that a system can operate without experiencing a failure. It is typically expressed in hours or other units of time. The higher the MTBF, the more reliable the system is considered to be:

$$\text{Mean time between failures (MTBF)} = \frac{(\text{Total Elapsed Time} - \text{Sum total of time system was down})}{\text{Total Number of Failures}}$$

For mission-critical systems, an MTBF of tens of thousands of hours or more is generally desired, while consumer electronics may have lower MTBF values. For example, high-reliability servers typically aim for an MTBF of 50,000 hours or more; consumer-grade laptops may have an MTBF of around 5,000–10,000 hours.

MTBF helps estimate the frequency of failures, allowing for better planning and budgeting of maintenance activities. If MTBF is low for a critical component, redundancy can be implemented to minimize downtime. In high-availability setups, multiple servers or components with lower MTBFs may be clustered to achieve overall reliability. As MTBF increases with design changes, you can quantitatively assess reliability improvements, ultimately leading to fewer failures and reduced operational costs.

Mean time to repair. MTTR is a measure of the average amount of time it takes to repair a failure in the system. It is also typically expressed in hours or other units of time. The lower the MTTR, the more quickly the system can be restored to operation after a failure:

$$\text{Mean time to repair (MTTR)} = \frac{(\text{Total Maintenance Time})}{\text{Total Number of Repairs}}$$

Together, MTBF and MTTR can be used to understand the overall reliability of a system. For example, a system with a high MTBF and a low MTTR is considered to be more reliable than a system with a low MTBF and a high MTTR as it is less likely to experience failures and can be restored to operation more quickly when failures do occur.

Reliability and availability

It is important to note that reliability and availability are not mutually exclusive. A system can be both reliable and available, or it can be neither. A system that is reliable but not available is not particularly useful since it may be reliable but not able to perform its intended function when needed. A system that is available but not reliable is also not useful since it may be able to perform its intended function when needed, but it may not do so consistently or without failure.

To achieve high reliability and availability to meet agreed service-level objectives (SLOs), it is important to design and maintain systems with redundant components and robust failover mechanisms. Performing maintenance and testing regularly also ensures that the system is operating at its optimal level of performance. In general, the reliability of a system is an important consideration in system design because it can affect the performance and availability of the system over time.

> SLOs and goals, including change management, problem management, and service request management, of AWS Managed Services (which will be introduced in Part II) are provided in the AWS documentation (*https://oreil.ly/oex3G*).

Scalability

In system design, we need to ensure that the performance of the system increases with the resources added based on the increasing workload, which can be either request workload or data storage workload. This is referred to as *scalability* in system design, which requires the system to respond to increased demand and load. For example, a social network needs to scale with the increasing number of users as well as the content feed on the platform that it indexes and serves.

The two major complementary patterns to scale a system are vertical scaling and horizontal scaling:

Vertical scaling
 Vertical scaling involves meeting the load requirements of the system by increasing the capacity of a single server by upgrading it with more resources (CPU, RAM, graphics processing units, storage, etc.), as shown on the left in Figure 1-6. Vertical scaling is useful when dealing with predictable traffic since it allows

for more resources to be used to handle the existing demand. However, there are limitations to how much a single server can scale up based on its current configuration. The cost of scaling up is also generally high as adding more higher-end resources to the existing server will require a greater investment.

Horizontal scaling

Horizontal scaling involves meeting the load requirements of the system by increasing the number of the servers by adding more commodity servers to serve the requests, as shown on the right in Figure 1-6. Horizontal scaling is useful when dealing with unpredictable traffic because there is increased capacity to handle more requests, and if demand arises, more servers can be added to the pool cost-effectively. Although horizontal scaling provides a better cost proposition for scaling, the complexity of managing multiple servers and ensuring that they work collectively as an abstracted single server to handle the workload is the catch here.

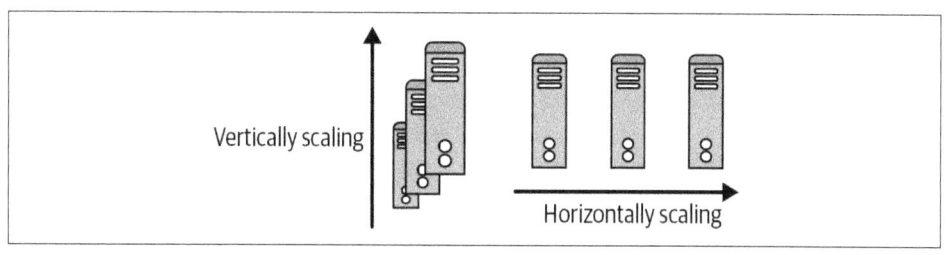

Figure 1-6. Vertical scaling versus horizontal scaling

> We will cover both scaling approaches and mechanisms in detail in Chapter 5.

In early-stage systems, you can start scaling up by vertically scaling the system and adding better configurations to it. Later, when you hit the limitation in scaling up, you can move to horizontally scaling the system.

Maintainability

In system design, *maintainability* is the system's ability to be modified, adapted, or extended to meet the changing needs of its users while ensuring smooth operations. For a software system to be maintainable, it must be designed to be flexible and easy to modify or extend. Maintainability involves these three underlying aspects of the system:

Operability
> This requires the system to operate smoothly under normal conditions and even return to normal operations within a stipulated time after a fault. When a system is maintainable in terms of operability, that reduces the time and effort required to keep the system running smoothly. This is important because efficient operations and management contribute to overall system stability, reliability, and availability.

Lucidity
> This requires the system to be simple and clear to understand, to extend by adding features, and even to fix bugs. When a system is lucid, that enables efficient collaboration among team members, simplifies debugging and maintenance tasks, and facilitates knowledge transfer. It also reduces the risk of introducing errors during modifications or updates.

Modifiability
> This requires the system to be built in a modular way to allow it to be changed and extended easily, without disrupting the functionality of other subsystems. Modifiability is vital because software systems need to evolve to adapt to new business needs, technological advancements, or user feedback. A system that lacks modifiability can become stagnant, resistant to change, and difficult to enhance or adapt to future demands.

By prioritizing maintainability, organizations can reduce downtime, lower maintenance costs, enhance productivity, and increase the longevity and value of their software systems.

Fault Tolerance

Large-scale systems generally employ a large number of servers and storage devices to handle and respond to user requests and store data. *Fault tolerance* requires the system to recover from any failure (either hardware or software failure) and continue to serve the requests. This means avoiding single points of failure in a large system and being able to reroute requests to functioning subsystems to complete the workload.

Fault tolerance needs to be supported at hardware as well as software levels while ensuring data safety—that is, making sure the data is not lost. The two major mechanisms to ensure data safety are replication and checkpointing.

Replication

Replication-based fault tolerance ensures both data safety and serving the request by replicating the service through multiple replica servers and replicating the data as multiple copies across multiple storage servers. During a failure, the failed node is swapped with a fully functioning replica node. Similarly, data is served again from a replica store in case the data store has failed. We discussed replication patterns in "Availability" on page 13.

Checkpointing

Checkpointing-based fault tolerance ensures that data is reliably stored and backed up, even after the initial processing is completed. It allows for a system to recover from any potential data loss by restoring a previous system state and preventing data loss. Checkpointing is commonly used to ensure system and data integrity, especially when dealing with large datasets. It can also be used to verify that data is not corrupted or missing because it can quickly detect any changes or issues in the data and then take corrective measures. Checkpointing is an important tool for data integrity, reliability, and security.

> Recovery managers of databases use checkpointing to ensure the durability and reliability of the database in the event of failures or crashes. This will be covered in detail in Chapter 2.

Checkpointing can be done using either synchronous or asynchronous mechanisms:

Synchronous checkpointing
　　Synchronous checkpointing in a system is achieved by stopping all the data mutation requests and allowing only read requests while waiting for the checkpointing process to complete for the current data mutation. This always ensures a consistent data state across all the nodes.

Asynchronous checkpointing
　　Asynchronous checkpointing in a system is done by checkpointing asynchronously on all the nodes while continuing to serve all the requests (including data mutation requests) without waiting for the acknowledgment of the checkpointing process to complete. This mechanism suffers from the possibility of having an inconsistent data state across the servers.

In checkpointing-based fault tolerance, recovery time objective (RTO) and recovery point objective (RPO) are key metrics that help define the effectiveness of data recovery and system reliability:

Recovery point objective
　　RPO defines the maximum acceptable amount of data loss measured in time. It represents how much data a system can afford to lose before that significantly affects operations. In checkpointing, RPO determines how frequently checkpoints should be created. For instance, if the RPO is set to 15 minutes, the system should take a checkpoint every 15 minutes to ensure that no more than

System Design Concepts | 23

15 minutes' worth of data is lost during recovery. A smaller RPO (more frequent checkpoints) provides better data protection but can increase system load and storage requirements. For large datasets, achieving a low RPO requires efficient data storage and fast checkpointing.

Recovery time objective
RTO specifies the maximum acceptable downtime following a failure, indicating how quickly the system should be restored to operational status. Checkpointing helps reduce RTO by allowing the system to resume from the most recent checkpoint rather than restarting from scratch. Faster recovery time is critical when handling large datasets or processing real-time data, where any downtime can impact users or services. The effectiveness of checkpointing on RTO depends on the ease of restoring data from the checkpoint and the system's ability to resume operations quickly without extensive reprocessing.

You should now understand the basic concepts and requirements of a large-scale system. We strive toward building a performant and scalable system—one that is also highly available, reliable, maintainable, and fault tolerant. Before getting into how to build such systems, let's go through the inherent fallacies as well as the trade-offs in designing them.

Fallacies of Distributed Computing

Because a large-scale software system involves multiple distributed systems, it is often subject to certain fallacies that can lead to incorrect assumptions and implementations. These fallacies (*https://oreil.ly/Byb-U*) were introduced by L. Peter Deutsch (*https://oreil.ly/rKk8M*). They cover the false assumptions that software developers commonly make when implementing distributed systems. The eight fallacies are as follows:

Reliable network
The first fallacy is assuming that "the network is reliable." Networks are complex, dynamic, and often unpredictable. Small issues like switch or power failures can bring the entire network of a data center down, making the network unreliable. Thus, it is important to account for the potential of an unreliable network when designing large-scale systems, ensuring network fault tolerance from the start. Given that networks are inherently unreliable, to build reliable services on top we must rely on protocols that can cope with network outages and packet loss.

Zero latency
The second fallacy is assuming that "latency is zero." Latency is an inherent limitation of networks, constrained by the speed of light—that is, even in theoretically perfect systems, the data can't transfer between the nodes faster than the speed of light. To account for latency, the system should be designed to bring

clients close to the data through edge computing and even by choosing the servers in geographic data centers nearer to the clients and routing the traffic wisely.

Infinite bandwidth

The third fallacy is assuming that "bandwidth is infinite." When a high volume of data is flowing through the network, there is always network resource contention, leading to queuing delays, bottlenecks, packet drops, and network congestion. To account for finite bandwidth, build the system using lightweight data formats for the data in transit that will preserve the network bandwidth and avoid network congestion.

Secure network

The fourth fallacy is assuming that "the network is secure." Assuming a network is always secure when there are multiple ways it can be compromised (including software bugs, OS vulnerabilities, viruses and malware, cross-site scripting, unencrypted communication, malicious middle actors, etc.) can lead to system compromise and failure. To account for insecure networks, build systems with a security-first mindset and perform defense testing and threat modeling on the built system.

Fixed topology

The fifth fallacy is assuming that "topology doesn't change." In distributed systems, the topology changes continuously because of node failures or node additions. Building a system that assumes a fixed topology will lead to system issues and failures due to latency and bandwidth constraints. Hence, the underlying topology must be abstracted out, and the system must be built oblivious to the underlying topology and tolerant to its changes.

Single administrator

The sixth fallacy is assuming that "there is one administrator." This can be a fair assumption in a very small system like a personal project, but this assumption breaks down in large-scale distributed computing, where multiple systems have separate OS, separate teams working on them, and thus, multiple administrators. To account for this, the system should be built in a decoupled manner, ensuring that repair and troubleshooting become easy and distributed, too.

Zero transport cost

The seventh fallacy is assuming that "transport cost is zero." Network infrastructure has costs, including the costs of network servers, switches, routers, other hardware, the OS of that hardware, and the team cost to keep it all running smoothly. Thus, the assumption that the cost of transporting data from one node to another is negligible is false and must consequently be noted in budgets to avoid vast shortfalls.

Homogeneous network
> The eighth fallacy is assuming that "the network is homogeneous." A network is built with multiple devices with different configurations and using multiple protocols at different layers. Taking into consideration the heterogeneity of the network as well as focusing on the interoperability of the system (i.e., ensuring that subsystems can communicate and work together despite having such differences) will help to avoid this pitfall.

> The AWS Well-Architected Framework (*https://oreil.ly/_4X-y*) consists of six core pillars that provide guidance and best practices for designing and building systems on the AWS cloud to avoid these fallacies and pitfalls. The Operational Excellence pillar avoids the fallacy of single administrator and homogeneous network. The Security pillar avoids the secure-network fallacy. The Reliability pillar avoids the fallacy of a reliable network and fixed topology. The Performance Efficiency pillar avoids the fallacy of zero latency and infinite bandwidth. The Cost Optimization and Sustainability pillars avoid the fallacy of zero transport cost. We won't cover the Well-Architected Framework in detail here.

These fallacies cover the basic assumptions we should avoid when building large-scale systems. Overall, neglecting the fallacies of distributed computing can lead to a range of issues, including system failures, performance bottlenecks, data inconsistencies, security vulnerabilities, scalability challenges, and increased complexity of system administration. It is important to acknowledge and account for these fallacies during the design and implementation of distributed systems to ensure their robustness, reliability, and effective operation in real-world environments.

Now, let's go through the trade-offs that are generally encountered when designing large-scale software systems.

System Design Trade-offs

System design involves making a number of trade-offs that can have a significant impact on the performance and usability of a system. When designing a system, you must consider factors like cost, scalability, reliability, maintainability, and robustness. These factors must be balanced to create a system that is optimized for the particular needs of the user. Ultimately, the goal is to create a system that meets user needs without sacrificing any of these important factors.

For example, if a system needs to be highly reliable but also have scalability, then you need to consider the trade-offs between cost and robustness. A system with a high level of reliability may require more expensive components, but these components may also be robust and allow for scalability in the future. On the other hand, if cost is a priority, then you may have to sacrifice robustness or scalability to keep the system within budget.

Trade-offs in addition to cost and scalability must be taken into account when designing a system. Performance, security, maintainability, and usability are all important considerations that must be weighed. In this section, we will discuss some theoretical trade-offs that arise in system design.

Time Versus Space

Time-space trade-offs or time-memory trade-offs arise inherently in implementing algorithms in computer science for the workload, even in distributed systems. These trade-offs are necessary because system designers need to consider the time limitations of the algorithms and sometimes use extra memory or storage to make sure everything works optimally. One example of such a trade-off is using look-up tables in memory or data storage instead of performing recalculations and thus serving more requests by just looking up precalculated values.

Latency Versus Throughput

Another trade-off that arises inherently in system design is latency versus throughput. Before diving into the trade-off, let's make sure you understand these concepts.

Latency, processing time, and response time

Latency is the time that a request waits to be handled. *Processing time*, on the other hand, is the time taken by the system to process the request once it is picked up. Hence, the overall response time is the duration between the request that was sent and the corresponding response that was received, accounting for network and server latencies. Mathematically, it can be represented by the following formula:

Response Time = Latency + Processing Time

Throughput and bandwidth

Throughput and bandwidth are metrics of network data capacity and are used to account for network scalability and load. *Bandwidth* refers to the maximum amount of data that could theoretically travel from one point in the network to another in a given time. *Throughput* refers to the actual amount of data transmitted and processed throughout the network. Thus, bandwidth describes the theoretical limit, and throughput provides the empirical metric. The throughput is always lower than the bandwidth unless the network is operating at its maximum efficiency.

Bandwidth is a limited resource because each network device can handle and process only a limited capacity of data before passing it to the next network device, and some devices consume more bandwidth than others. Insufficient bandwidth can lead to network congestion, which slows connectivity.

Since latency measures how long the packets take to reach the destination in a network, while throughput measures how many packets are processed within a specified period of time, they have an inverse relationship. Higher latency causes packets to queue up in the network, slowing packet processing and ultimately reducing throughput.

Because the system is being gauged for lower latency under high throughput or load, the metric to capture latency is through percentiles, such as p50, p90, p99, and so on. For example, the p90 latency is the highest latency value (slowest response) of the fastest 90% of requests. In other words, 90% of requests have responses that are equal to or faster than the p90 latency value. Note that average latency of a workload is not used as a metric because averages as point estimates are susceptible to outliers.

Because of the latency versus throughput trade-off, the latency will also increase as the load is increased on the system for higher throughput. Hence, systems should be designed with an aim for maximal throughput within acceptable latency.

Performance Versus Scalability

As discussed in "Scalability" on page 20, *scalability* is the system's ability to respond to increased demand and load. On the other hand, *performance* is how fast the system responds to a single request. A service is scalable if it results in increased performance in a manner proportional to resources added. When a system has performance problems, it is slow for a single user (p50 latency = 100 ms), but when the system has scalability problems, the system may be fast for some users (p50 latency = 1 ms for one hundred requests) but slow under heavy load for the users (p50 latency = 100 ms under one hundred thousand requests).

Consistency Versus Availability

Strong consistency in data storage and retrieval is the guarantee that every read receives the most recent write, while *high availability* is the requirement of the system to always provide a nonerror response to the request. In a distributed system where the network fails (i.e., packets get dropped or delayed due to the fallacies of distributed computing leading to partitions), there emerges an inherent trade-off between strong consistency and high availability. This trade-off is called the *CAP theorem*, also known as *Brewer's theorem*.

CAP theorem

The CAP theorem, illustrated as a Venn diagram in Figure 1-7, states that it is impossible for a distributed system to simultaneously provide all three of the following guarantees: consistency (C), availability (A), and partition tolerance (P). According to the theorem, a distributed system can provide at most two of these guarantees at any given time. Systems need to be designed to handle network partitions because networks aren't reliable, and hence, partition tolerance needs to be built in. So the CAP theorem implies that in the presence of a network partition, one has to choose between consistency and availability.

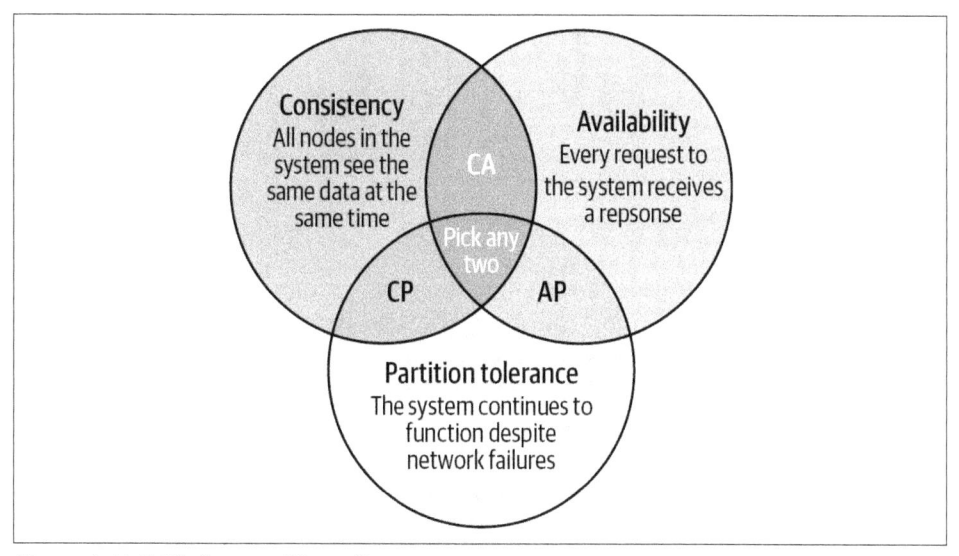

Figure 1-7. CAP theorem Venn diagram

However, the CAP theorem is frequently misunderstood to mean that one has to choose to abandon one of the three guarantees at all times. In fact, the choice is really between consistency and availability only when a network partition or failure happens; at all other times, the trade-off has to be made based on the PACELC theorem.

PACELC theorem

The PACELC theorem, illustrated as a decision flowchart in Figure 1-8, is a more nuanced version of the CAP theorem. It states that in the case of network partitioning (P) in a distributed computer system, one must choose between availability (A) and consistency (C) as per the CAP theorem, but otherwise (E), even when the system is running normally in the absence of partitions, one has to choose between latency (L) and consistency (C). This trade-off arises naturally because to handle network partitions, data and services are replicated in large-scale systems, leading to the choice between the consistency spectrum and the corresponding latency.

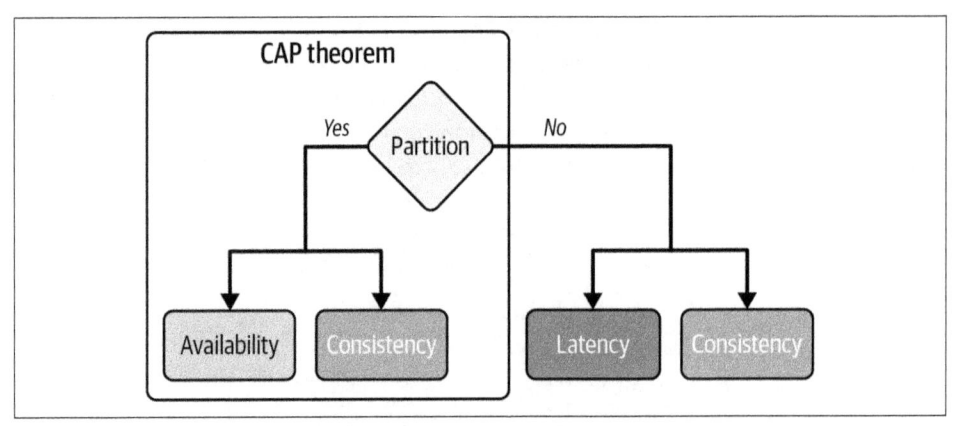

Figure 1-8. PACELC theorem decision flowchart

If the system tries to provide for strong consistency at one end of the consistency spectrum model, it has to do replication with synchronous communication and blocking to ensure that all the read replicas receive the most recent write, waiting on the acknowledgment from all the replica nodes, which adds to high latency. On the other hand, if the system does asynchronous replication without waiting for acknowledgment from all nodes, it will end up providing eventual consistency (i.e., the read request will eventually reflect the last recent write) when the replica node has acknowledged the data mutation change for serving the requests.

The CAP and PACELC theorems are important concepts in distributed systems design that provide a framework for understanding the trade-offs involved in designing highly available and strongly consistent systems.

> We will cover how nonrelational stores navigate the CAP theorem trade-off by discussing BASE properties in detail in Chapter 3.

Given such requirements, fallacies, and trade-offs in system design, to avoid repeating mistakes of the past, we should adhere to a set of guidelines that the previous generation of software design practitioners learned. Let's dig into those now.

System Design Guidelines

System design will always present the most interesting and challenging trade-offs, and a system designer should be aware of the hidden costs and be well equipped to get it right—though not perfect! These guidelines, which have emerged over years of practicing system design, help us avoid pitfalls and handle trade-offs when designing large-scale systems. These guidelines aren't just vague generalities but rather virtues that help us reflect on why the system was designed and implemented the way it was and why that was the right thing to do.

Guideline of Isolation: Build It Modularly

Controlling complexity is the essence of computer programming.
　—Brian Kernighan

The first guideline is to build the system modularly—that is, break a complex system down into smaller, independent components or modules that can function independently yet also work together to form the larger system. Building a large-scale system modularly helps improve all its requirements:

Maintainability
　Modules can be updated or replaced individually without affecting the rest of the system.

Reusability
　Modules can be reused in different systems or projects, reducing the amount of new development required.

Scalability
　Modules can be added or removed and even scaled independently as needed to accommodate changes in requirements or to support growth.

Reliability
　Modules can be tested and validated independently, reducing the risk of system-wide failures.

Modular systems can be implemented in a variety of ways, including through the use of microservice architecture, component-based development, and modular programming, which we will cover in more detail in Chapter 7. However, designing modular systems can be challenging as it requires careful consideration of the interfaces between modules, data sharing and flow, and dependencies.

Guideline of Simplicity: Keep It Simple, Silly

Everything should be made as simple as possible, but no simpler.
—attributed to Albert Einstein

The second guideline is to keep the design simple by avoiding complex and unnecessary features and overengineering. To build simple systems using the KISS (Keep It Simple, Silly) guideline, designers can follow these principles:

Identify the core requirements
Determine the essential features and functions the system must have and prioritize them.

Minimize the number of components
Reduce the number of components or modules in the system, making sure each component serves a specific purpose.

Avoid overengineering
Don't add unnecessary complexity to the system, such as features that are not necessary for its functioning.

Make the system easy to use
Ensure that the system is intuitive and straightforward for users to use and understand.

Test and refine
Test the system to ensure that it works as intended, and make changes to simplify the system if necessary.

By following the KISS guideline, you as a system designer can build simple, efficient, and effective systems that are easier to maintain and less prone to failure.

Guideline of Performance: Metrics Don't Lie

Performance problems cannot be solved only through the use of Zen meditation.
—Jeffrey C. Mogul

The third guideline is to measure, then build, and rely on the metrics since you can't cheat the performance and scalability. Metrics and observability are crucial for understanding the behavior and performance of large-scale systems and for identifying potential issues before they become problems.

Metrics are quantitative measures that are used to assess the performance of a system. They provide a way to track key performance indicators, such as resource utilization, response times, and error rates, and to identify trends and patterns in system behavior. By monitoring metrics, engineers can detect performance bottlenecks and anomalies and take corrective actions to improve the overall performance and reliability of the system.

Observability refers to the degree to which the state of a system can be inferred from its externally visible outputs. This includes being able to monitor system health and diagnose problems in real time. Observability is important in large-scale systems because it provides a way to monitor the behavior of complex systems and detect issues that may be affecting their performance.

Together, metrics and observability provide the information needed to make informed decisions about the operation and management of large-scale systems. By ensuring that systems are properly instrumented with metrics and that observability is designed into the system, you can detect and resolve issues more quickly, prevent outages, and improve the system's overall performance and reliability.

Guideline of Trade-offs: There Is No Such Thing as a Free Lunch

> *Get it right. Neither abstraction nor simplicity is a substitute for getting it right.*
> —Butler Lampson

The fourth guideline is "there is no such thing as a free lunch" (TINSTAAFL), or the realization that all decisions come with trade-offs and that optimizing for one aspect of a system often comes at the expense of others. There are always trade-offs and compromises that must be made when designing a system. For example, choosing a highly optimized solution for a specific problem might result in reduced maintainability or increased complexity. Conversely, opting for a simple solution might result in lower performance or increased latency.

The TINSTAAFL guideline highlights the need for careful consideration and balancing of competing factors in system design, such as performance, scalability, reliability, maintainability, and cost. Designers must weigh the trade-offs between these factors and make informed decisions that meet the specific requirements and constraints of each project. Ultimately, you need to realize that there is no single solution that is optimal in all situations and that, to build the right system, you as the system designer must carefully consider the trade-offs and implications of your design decisions.

Guideline of Use Cases: It Always Depends

> *Not everything worth doing is worth doing well.*
> —Tom West

The fifth guideline is *design always depends* because system design is a complex, multifaceted process that is influenced by a variety of factors, including requirements, user needs, technological constraints, cost, scalability, maintenance, and even regulations. By considering these and other factors, you can develop systems that meet the needs of the users, are feasible to implement, and are sustainable over time. Since there are many ways to design a system to solve a common problem, this guideline indicates a stronger underlying truth: there is no one "best" way to design the system. In other words, there is no silver bullet. Thus, we settle for something reasonable and hope it is good enough.

Conclusion

This chapter has given you a solid introduction to how we design software systems. We've talked about the main concepts underlying system design, the trade-offs we must make when dealing with big software systems, the fallacies to avoid in building such large-scale systems, and smart guidelines for avoiding such fallacies.

Think of system design as like balancing on a seesaw: you must find the right equilibrium between different trade-offs. As an overall guideline, system design is always a trade-off between competing factors, and you as a system designer must carefully weigh these factors to create systems that are effective and efficient.

In the rest of Part I, we're going to explore the basic building blocks of systems. We'll talk about important topics like where we store data, how we speed things up with caches, how we distribute work with load balancers, and how different parts of a system talk to one another through networking and orchestration.

Once you've got a handle on those basics, we'll dive into the world of AWS systems in Part II. This will help you understand how to make big and powerful systems using Amazon Web Services. All this knowledge will come together in Part III, where we'll put everything into practice and learn how to design and build large-scale systems on AWS for specific use cases.

Before we get there, our next stop is exploring different ways to store data and introducing you to relational databases.

CHAPTER 2
Storage Types and Relational Stores

Data storage is an essential component of modern computing systems that plays a vital role in system design. As businesses and organizations grow, they generate and store vast amounts of data, which makes it important to have a scalable, reliable storage infrastructure that can keep up with the increasing demands. Efficient, reliable storage of data is necessary to ensure that applications and services can function effectively and provide optimal performance to end users. Various types of data storage solutions are available, ranging from traditional file-based systems to more modern block and object stores. Databases also play a significant role in storing and managing structured data, making them a critical aspect of system design.

In this chapter, we will explore different types of data storage solutions in the context of system design. We will start by discussing traditional file-based storage systems and their limitations before moving on to block and object stores, which have become increasingly popular in recent years because they can handle large amounts of unstructured data.

We also cover the different types of relational databases in this chapter. (We will look at nonrelational stores in Chapter 3). As we examine the challenges of scaling relational databases, we'll cover various techniques, such as indexes, SQL tuning, denormalization, federation, partitioning, sharding, and replication, that can improve performance and meet the demands of large-scale applications.

By the end of this chapter, you will have a solid understanding of the available data storage solutions as well as the strengths and weaknesses of different relational database types and how they can be used to design efficient, reliable, and scalable systems. This chapter will serve as the foundation for the concepts we'll use to compare and select AWS relational database offerings, including flavors of Amazon Relational Database Service (RDS) and Amazon Aurora, which are covered in Chapter 10.

Data Storage Format

The evolution of data storage hardware over the years has posed a challenging problem: how to store the data in a particular format that obscures the underlying storage hardware and can be read, written, and modified across different hardware, even as they evolve. This has led computer scientists and engineers to come up with device drivers, specifically *storage drivers*, which are installed on different OS to enable working with the data on that particular storage hardware; the data is stored in a specific *format* that is agnostic to the underlying hardware.

Three different formats, shown in Figure 2-1, have emerged based on how the data is logically arranged on the storage hardware: file-based, block-based, and object-based. Each has its own capabilities and limitations. *File-based storage* organizes and represents the data as a hierarchy of files and folders. *Block-based storage* chunks data into arbitrarily organized, fixed-size blocks. And *object-based storage* organizes data as objects linked with the associated metadata. Let's go through each of these storage formats in detail.

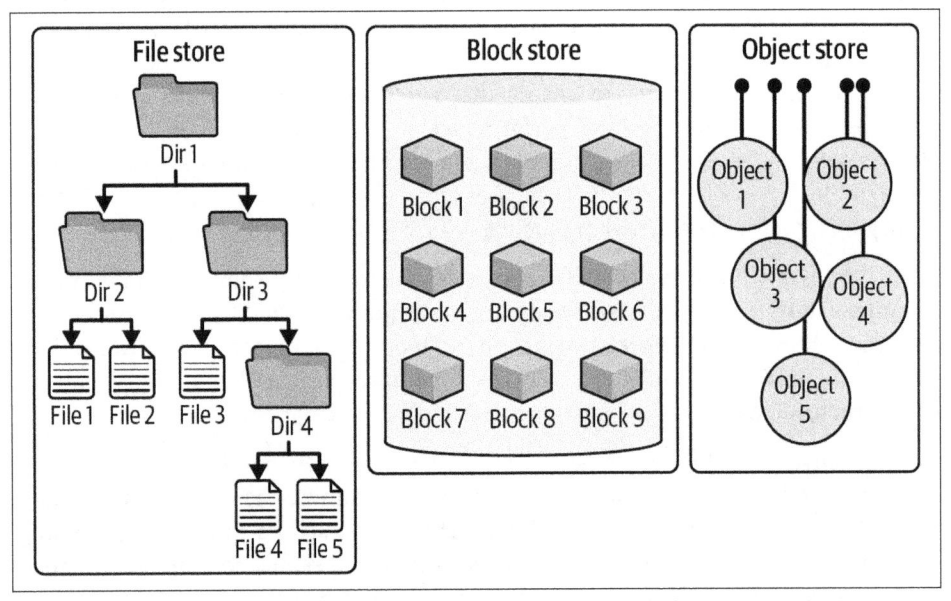

Figure 2-1. Storage abstraction in a file store, block store, and object store

File-Based Storage

File-based storage refers to the storage of data in a folder, just like how paper documents are kept in a filing cabinet. When the data is needed, the computer must know the path to find it, which can be a long, arduous path string. File-based storage is commonly used for storing structured data, such as documents, images, videos, and audio files.

Data in files is organized and retrieved using metadata, like in a library card catalog. Imagine a closet full of file cabinets. Every document is arranged in some form of logical hierarchy: by cabinet, by drawer, by folder, by file, and then by paper. The filesystem provides a similar hierarchical structure to organize electronic files, and data is stored in blocks or pages on disk.

This is the oldest and most widely used data storage system for direct and network-attached systems. It's great for storing complex files and easier to navigate than other formats because of the logical hierarchy. When you access files on your personal computer, you leverage the file storage as when a file store instance is mounted to a computer or virtual machine, it is seen as a local directory.

The caveat with file-based storage is, just like with your filing cabinet, the virtual drawer can open only so far. File-based storage systems must scale out by adding more systems, rather than scale up by adding more capacity.

> Amazon Elastic File System (EFS) is a scalable, fully managed file storage service offered by AWS that provides shared file storage for Amazon Elastic Compute Cloud (EC2) instances, enabling multiple instances to access the same data concurrently, which makes it suitable for applications requiring shared access to files. We will cover it in more detail in Chapter 10.

Block-Based Storage

Block-based storage organizes data into fixed-size blocks or pages, which are stored on disk or flash memory. Each block is assigned a unique address, and data can be read or written to individual blocks. Block-based storage is designed to separate the data from the user's environment and distribute it across multiple environments that are better suited to serve the data. This means that some block data can be on a Windows environment, some on a Linux environment, and so on. When data is requested, the storage software reassembles the data blocks from these environments and delivers them to the user. Typically used in storage area network (SAN) environments, block-based storage requires a functioning server to operate.

Unlike file-based storage, block-based storage doesn't rely on a single path to data, so it can be retrieved quickly. Each block lives on its own and can be partitioned so that it can be accessed in a different OS, which gives the user complete freedom to configure their data. It's an efficient and reliable way to store data, and it is easy to use and manage. It works well for enterprises that perform big transactions and those that deploy huge databases—meaning the more data you need to store, the better off you'll be with block-based storage.

The caveat with block-based storage is that it can be expensive. It has limited capability to handle metadata, which means it needs to be dealt with at the application or database level, adding more complexity for a developer or systems administrator to worry about.

Block-based storage is commonly used in enterprise storage systems, such as SAN and network-attached storage (NAS). It provides better performance, reliability, and scalability than file-based storage because each block can act as an independent disk, giving administrators flexibility to configure and allocate storage volumes as needed. This makes block-based storage ideal for large, dynamic enterprise environments, where storage needs to grow or be reconfigured on demand.

> Amazon Elastic Block Store (EBS) offers scalable block storage volumes on the AWS cloud that can be attached to EC2 instances, providing durable, high-performance storage for applications that require low-latency access to data, such as databases and applications that need block-level storage. We'll cover it in Chapter 10.

Object-Based Storage

Object-based storage is a type of storage architecture where unstructured data is broken down into discrete units called *objects* and kept in a single repository, rather than in traditional file and folder structures or server blocks. These objects are stored across distributed hardware and are accessed using a unique identifier and metadata that describes the data, including information such as age, security and access contingencies, and even details like the location of equipment used to create a video file.

Object storage volumes function as modular units, with each one being a self-contained repository of data. Retrieval of this data is done using the unique identifier and metadata, which distributes the workload and enables administrators to apply policies for more efficient searches. Object-based storage is also known for its scalability, cost efficiency, and suitability for static and unstructured data. It has a simple HTTP API that is used by most clients in all programming languages.

However, there are limitations to object-based storage. Objects cannot be modified, meaning that data must be written entirely at once. Also, object-based storage does not work well with traditional databases because writing objects is a slow process, and programming an app to use an object storage API is not as straightforward as using file-based storage.

Choosing a data storage format depends on the type of data being stored as well as the performance, reliability, and scalability requirements of the system. File-based storage is best suited for structured data while block-based and object-based storage are more appropriate for unstructured data. Block-based storage provides better performance and reliability than file-based storage while object-based storage offers better scalability and cost-effectiveness.

> Amazon Simple Storage Service (S3) is an object storage service offered by AWS that provides highly scalable and durable storage for a wide range of data types, accessible via APIs. It is suitable for storing and retrieving large amounts of data, backups, and static website content as well as a data lake for analytics. See Chapter 10 for more detail.

We have looked at different data storage formats and compared them in terms of usage, cost, performance, and scalability. Next, let's discuss how data is stored and structured in databases for easy retrieval and processing.

Relational Databases

A *database* is a structured collection of data that is organized and stored in a computer system for easy access and management. It is designed for efficient storage, retrieval, and manipulation of large volumes of data. A database typically consists of one or more tables, which are organized into rows and columns. Each row represents a unique record in the database and each column represents a specific attribute or piece of information about the record.

A *database management system (DBMS)*, on the other hand, is a collection of software systems that sits on top of a database, acting as a bridge between the database and users, as shown in Figure 2-2. A DBMS offers multiple interfaces or APIs that enable users to store, retrieve, and manipulate data. The DBMS also provides a range of features related to transactions, recovery, backups, concurrency, authentication and authorization, metadata catalog, and other capabilities.

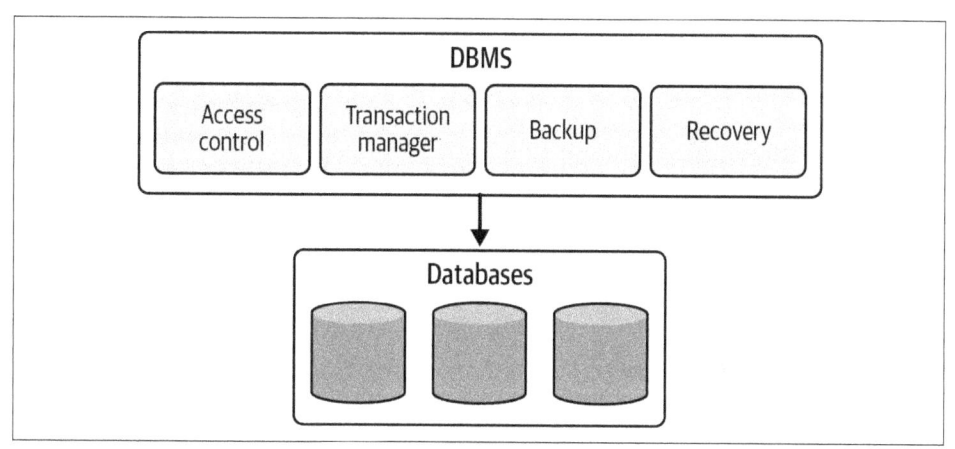

Figure 2-2. Databases versus a database management system

Databases can be classified into two major types based on their structure, usage, and functionality: relational and nonrelational. We'll go through relational databases in detail in this chapter. We'll cover nonrelational databases in Chapter 3. *Relational databases* use a set of tables with relationships between them to organize data.

Designed to store and manage large amounts of structured data, relational databases are the most common type of database. They are based on the relational model (*https://oreil.ly/kPo_3*), which was introduced by Edgar F. Codd in the 1970s. This model organizes data into tables, which can be related to one another using keys. Examples of open source relational databases include MySQL, PostgreSQL, and MariaDB. Oracle, Microsoft SQL Server, IBM Db2, and SAP HANA are preferred as enterprise relational databases.

Tables in a relational database are organized into rows and columns, like a spreadsheet. Each row represents a record, and each column represents an attribute or a piece of data about the record. The columns are defined by a data type, which specifies the type of data that can be stored in that column. Figure 2-3 shows a sample implementation of a logical schema design of a database for storing customer orders.

The logical components of a database schema design are:

Tables
> The fundamental units of a relational database, tables store and organize data in rows and columns. Each table represents a specific entity or concept, and each row in the table represents an individual instance of that entity; each column represents a specific attribute or property.

Rows
> Rows, also known as *records* or *tuples*, represent individual instances of data stored in a table. Each row contains data values that correspond to the attributes defined by the table's columns. Rows are unique within a table and are typically identified by a primary key.

Columns
> Columns, also known as *fields* or *attributes*, represent the specific properties or characteristics of the data stored in a table. Each column has a defined data type that determines the kind of data it can store, such as integers, strings, dates, or binary data.

Relationships
> One of the key features of a relational database is the ability to create *relationships*: associations between tables. This is achieved using *keys*, which are columns that uniquely identify each record in a table. The most common types of relationships are one-to-one, one-to-many, and many-to-many. These relationships help maintain data consistency and enable efficient retrieval of related information.

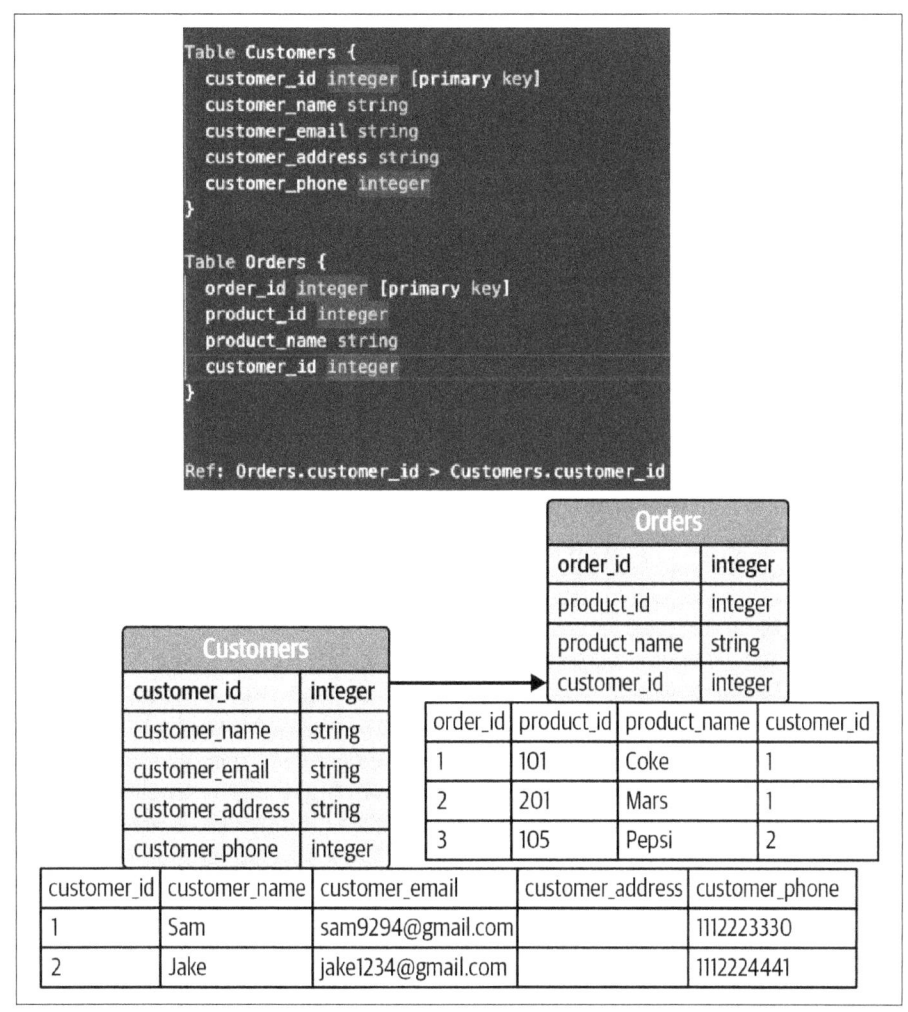

```
Table Customers {
  customer_id integer [primary key]
  customer_name string
  customer_email string
  customer_address string
  customer_phone integer
}

Table Orders {
  order_id integer [primary key]
  product_id integer
  product_name string
  customer_id integer
}

Ref: Orders.customer_id > Customers.customer_id
```

Figure 2-3. Logical schema design of an orders database

Keys

Keys are used to establish relationships between tables and ensure data integrity. The *primary key* identifies each row in a table, and it must have a unique value for each record. *Foreign keys* are used to establish relationships between tables by referencing the primary key of another table. Establishing these relationships between tables using keys enables data to be easily retrieved and updated across multiple tables. We will cover keys in more detail later in this section.

Indexes
> Indexes are data structures that enhance the performance of queries by providing quick access to specific data within a table. They are created on one or more columns of a table, allowing faster search and retrieval operations based on the indexed values.

Constraints
> Constraints enforce rules and conditions on the data stored in a database. Common constraints include primary key constraints, foreign key constraints, unique constraints, and check constraints. They ensure data integrity, enforce referential integrity, and prevent the insertion of invalid or inconsistent data.

Views
> Views are virtual tables derived from the data stored in one or more tables. They are created based on predefined queries and provide a way to present data in a customized or simplified manner without altering the underlying tables. Views can be used for security purposes, for data abstraction, or to simplify complex queries.

Transactions
> Relational databases use transactions to keep their state consistent. In the context of DBMS, a *transaction* is a logical unit of work that represents a series of operations performed on a database as a single, indivisible unit. These operations may include inserting, updating, or deleting data from one or more tables in the database. Transactions ensure data consistency and integrity by allowing multiple operations to be executed together. The ACID (atomicity, consistency, isolation, and durability) properties govern the behavior of transactions, which we will cover in more detail later in this section.

These logical core components work together to form the foundation of a relational database schema, providing a flexible and efficient way to store, organize, and retrieve structured data.

Relational Database Concepts

Now let's look at the basic concepts, including structured query language (SQL), ACID, and the entity-relationship (ER) model, that form the foundations of modern relational databases.

SQL

Relational databases use SQL to manipulate and retrieve data. SQL allows users to create, modify, and query databases with a set of commands. Some common SQL commands include `SELECT`, `INSERT`, `UPDATE`, and `DELETE`. The query language serves as a programming language that establishes the syntax, structure, and semantics governing interactions with the database. It provides a standardized way to store, access, and manipulate data within the database.

SQL can be categorized into these four types, each serving a distinct purpose:

Data definition language (DDL)
   DDL is a query language used to create and modify the structure and framework of database objects. It encompasses operations like creating tables, defining indexes, dropping tables, and removing indexes.

Data manipulation language (DML)
   DML is a query language employed to create, update, delete, and retrieve information from the database. It involves operations like inserting rows into tables, updating existing rows, deleting rows, and querying data.

Data control language (DCL)
   DCL is a query language designed to grant or revoke access to entities and operations within the database for clients. It includes commands like granting privileges to users, revoking privileges, and managing security permissions.

Transaction control language (TCL)
   TCL is a query language dedicated to managing and ensuring the consistent execution of a group of database operations as a single unit. It encompasses commands like committing transactions to make changes permanent or rolling back transactions to discard changes.

Collectively, these query languages form the set of SQL query types, providing the necessary tools to define, manipulate, control access to, and manage transactions within a database system.

ACID

The *ACID model* is a set of properties ensuring that database transactions are processed reliably and accurately. ACID stands for:

Atomicity
   A transaction must be all or nothing.

   Atomicity ensures that a sequence of operations is treated as a single logical unit of work. Either all the operations within the unit of work are successfully completed or none of them are applied at all. This guarantee prevents partial updates to the database. When all operations are successfully executed, it is known as a *commit*. In case of failure, all the operations are rolled back, reverting the database to its original state. Atomicity provides application developers with the confidence that the database will always be in a consistent state, even in the event of failures. It also enables safe retrying of operations without concerns about creating duplicate data.

Consistency
> A transaction must maintain the consistency of the database.

> Consistency guarantees ensure that the database transitions from one valid state to another. During the transition, the database enforces rules and constraints defined by the application to maintain data integrity. Consistency is a user-controlled property, meaning that the application must define the valid rules and constraints that lead to a consistent final state. For example, an application may define a rule that the balance of a bank account should always remain positive. The database itself does not enforce these rules but ensures that any changes made to the data adhere to the defined consistency constraints.

Isolation
> Transactions must be isolated from one another to ensure that they do not interfere with one another.

> Isolation ensures that concurrent transactions do not interfere with one another, maintaining data integrity and preventing conflicts. Multiple transactions can run simultaneously, and the isolation guarantee dictates how they should interact. If the result of concurrently executing transactions is the same as if they were executed sequentially, then the database supports isolation. Isolation levels, such as Read Uncommitted, Read Committed, Repeatable Read, and Serializable, define the degree of isolation provided by the database. Each level offers different trade-offs between concurrency and data integrity, so the appropriate level should be chosen based on the application's requirements.

Durability
> Once a transaction is committed, its changes must be permanent and survive any subsequent failures.

> Durability guarantees that once a transaction is committed, its changes are permanently stored and will survive system failures, such as crashes or power outages. Typically, this involves persisting the data to nonvolatile storage like a disk. Durability ensures that critical data remains safe and accessible in the long term. Even in the face of catastrophic events, the database will retain the committed changes and recover them when the system is restored.

The ACID properties ensure that database transactions are processed in a reliable and consistent manner, even when there are failures or concurrent operations. By enforcing these properties, the DBMS can maintain the integrity and reliability of the data stored in the database.

ER model

The *ER model* is a conceptual model used in relational database design to describe the relationships between entities (objects or concepts) and their attributes. It provides a graphical representation of the database schema, which can be used to design, communicate, and understand the structure of the database.

The ER model, shown in Figure 2-4, represents entities as rectangles, attributes as ovals, and relationships between entities as diamonds. Relationships can be one-to-one, one-to-many, or many-to-many. The ER model is a useful tool for designing and communicating the structure of a database because it enables designers to visualize the relationships between entities and the attributes that describe them.

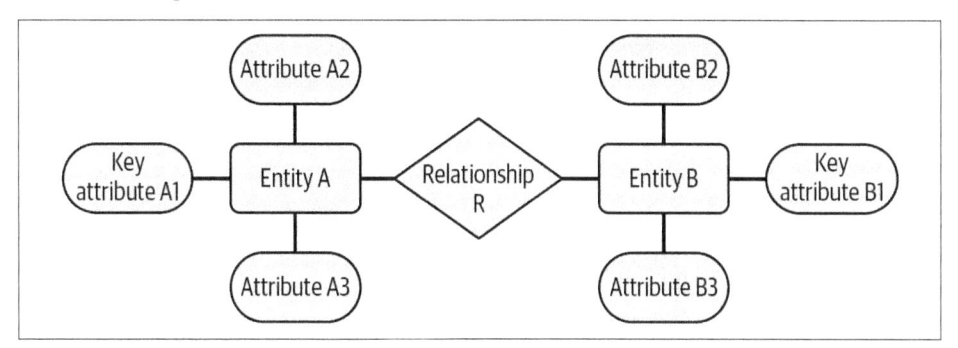

Figure 2-4. ER model representation

Schema normalization

Schema normalization is the process of organizing data in a database to reduce redundancy and improve data integrity. It involves breaking down a large table into smaller, more manageable tables, each with its own unique purpose and set of attributes. The goal of schema normalization is to minimize data duplication and ensure that each piece of data is stored in only one place in the database.

Let's take an example of a table called Customers in our Orders database that has the following columns: customer_id, customer_name, customer_email, customer_address, and customer_phone. In this table, the customer_name, customer_email, customer_address, and customer_phone are repeated for each customer.

To normalize this schema, as shown in Figure 2-5, we can decompose the Customers table into two tables: CustomerInfo and CustomerContact. The CustomerInfo table will contain customer_id and customer_name, while the CustomerContact table will contain customer_id, customer_email, customer_address, and customer_phone.

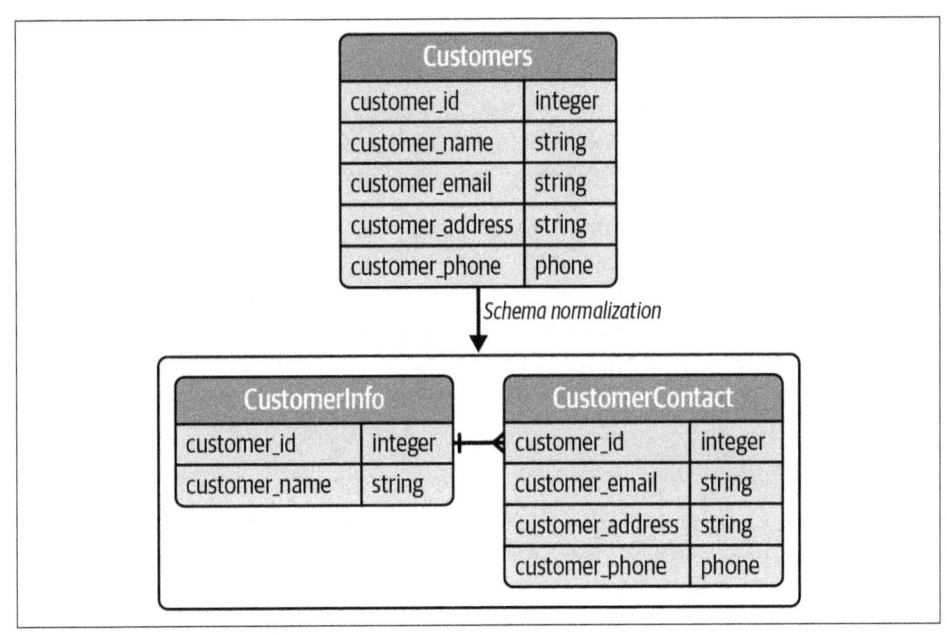

Figure 2-5. Schema normalization of the Customers table

By doing this, we have eliminated the redundancy of customer information in the Customers table and stored it only once in the CustomerInfo table. This normalization reduces the storage space required for the database, eliminates data inconsistencies that may arise from redundant data, and makes it easier to update customer information without having to change it in multiple places.

Keys

Keys are used in relational databases to establish relationships between tables. A *key* is a column or set of columns that uniquely identifies each row in a table. There are several types of keys:

Candidate key
   A candidate key is a column or set of columns in a table that can uniquely identify each record in that table. It is called a "candidate" key because it is a potential primary-key "candidate" for the table. For example, in a table of customers, the customer_email could be a candidate key because each customer has a unique email address.

Primary key
   A primary key is a candidate key that has been chosen as the main key for the table. It uniquely identifies each record in the table and is used as a reference by other tables that have relationships with this table. For example, in a table of orders, the order ID could be the primary key.

Foreign key
A foreign key is a column or set of columns in one table that refers to the primary key of another table. It is used to establish relationships between tables and ensure data integrity. For example, in a table of orders, there could be a foreign key that references the customer ID in the Customers table to link each order to the customer who ordered it.

Now, let's discuss the core components required for a DBMS architecture. The exact architecture may vary from one implementation to another, but the core components generally remain the same.

Relational Database Management System Architecture

The architecture of a relational database management system (RDBMS) is shown in Figure 2-6.

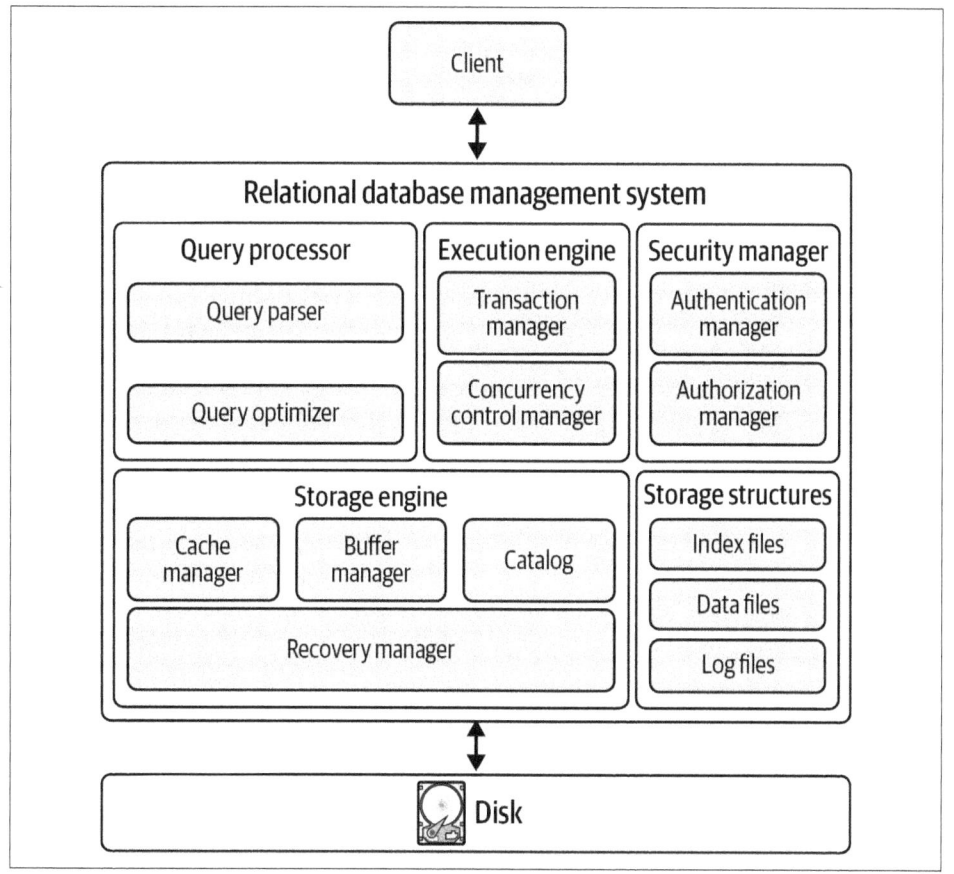

Figure 2-6. RDBMS architecture block diagram

Let's go over the components one by one:

Query processor
　The query processor translates the user query into an execution format suitable for the underlying execution engine. It has two main submodules: the query parser and the query optimizer:

- The query parser parses the query given by the user into an *abstract syntax tree (AST)*, which serves as an intermediate representation of the query for execution. The query parser performs parsing, tokenization, syntax validation, semantic analysis, and tree construction in the process of generating the AST.
- The query optimizer uses the AST generated by the query parser to generate an optimized plan for executing the user's query. By considering internal statistics like data cardinality, placement, and costs associated with local and remote execution, the optimizer evaluates multiple execution plans.

Execution plan
　An execution plan represents a series of steps organized in a directed dependency graph, which must be executed in a specific order to fulfill the user's query. Leveraging the internal statistics, the query optimizer selects the most cost-effective execution plan among the alternatives. It then forwards the chosen plan to the execution engine for processing.

Execution engine
　The execution engine is responsible for executing the query plan generated by the query optimizer. It interacts with the storage engine to retrieve data; performs any necessary joins, filtering, and sorting operations; and returns the result set to the user. The execution engine is also responsible for orchestrating the execution plan across distributed nodes in a distributed relational database.

Storage engine
　The storage engine manages the physical storage and retrieval of data, including access and manipulation of data in the database. It handles tasks such as data page management, file allocation, data compression, and indexing. The storage engine interacts with the execution engine to fetch and store data efficiently.

Buffer manager
　The buffer manager handles the management of data buffers in memory. It controls the movement of data between disk and memory, optimizes disk I/O operations, and ensures that frequently accessed data is kept in memory for faster access. The buffer manager minimizes disk access by caching data pages in memory.

Cache manager

The cache manager handles the management and optimization of data caching. It stores frequently accessed data in memory to improve query performance by reducing disk I/O operations. The cache manager ensures that the most frequently used data is readily available in memory for faster retrieval.

Transaction manager

The transaction manager plays a vital role in coordinating and overseeing operations on the data structures within the storage structures module. Its primary responsibility is to ensure that a sequence of operations either executes successfully as a whole or gets rolled back entirely, leaving no partial updates behind. This crucial guarantee provides end users with the confidence that the database will consistently maintain its integrity before and after executing any database operations. To achieve this, the transaction manager collaborates closely with the concurrency control manager and the recovery manager. By leveraging these components, the transaction manager ensures that the visible data in the database remains consistent and aligns with the expectations of end users.

Concurrency control manager

The concurrency control manager handles concurrent access to the database by multiple users or transactions. It ensures that transactions are executed in an isolated and consistent manner, preventing conflicts and maintaining data integrity. It manages locking, transaction isolation levels, and conflict-resolution mechanisms.

Recovery manager

The recovery manager ensures the durability and reliability of the database in the event of failures or crashes. It manages transaction logging, checkpointing, and crash-recovery mechanisms to maintain data integrity and consistency. The recovery manager ensures that the database can be restored to a consistent state after a failure.

The recovery manager ensures durability by maintaining an immutable data structure known as a *log file* within the DBMS. This log file diligently records every write operation applied to the database to facilitate recovery processes. Essentially, the recovery manager acts as a reliable and persistent intermediate storage for all write requests.

Each written page is meticulously preserved in the primary memory, designated as a "dirty page." To ensure durability, the recovery manager batches all the dirty pages and asynchronously synchronizes them with the disk. Once the dirty pages have been successfully flushed to disk, they are considered "clean pages." In addition, before a write request is acknowledged as completed by the client, it is appended to a disk-resident append-only data structure. This step provides a safeguard against data loss of dirty pages in the event of a crash or system restart.

The log file serves as a valuable checkpoint, allowing the recovery process to restore data for the dirty pages. On system restart, the OS flushes all remaining dirty pages to disk and discards any uncommitted transactions. This ensures that the system begins in a clean state, ready to process subsequent writes and reads without the risk of incomplete or inconsistent data.

Security manager
The security manager enforces data security and access controls. It authenticates users, manages user permissions and privileges, and ensures data confidentiality, integrity, and availability. The security manager protects the database from unauthorized access and maintains data privacy.

Catalog
The catalog, also known as the *data dictionary* or *metadata repository*, stores the metadata about the database schema, tables, columns, indexes, constraints, and other database objects. It provides information about the structure and organization of the database, allowing the RDBMS to interpret and manipulate the data accurately.

These core components work together to provide the necessary functionality for managing and manipulating data in an RDBMS. They ensure efficient query processing, data storage, concurrency control, data recovery, and data security.

In the next section, we will explore the different ways of optimizing query performance in RDBMSs using index types, including primary and secondary indexes, SQL tuning, denormalization, and query federation.

Optimizing Relational Databases

Optimizing relational databases is an essential task for any database administrator or developer to improve the performance of the queries that run on top of it. Let's look at the various ways to optimize databases.

Indexes

One way to optimize SQL queries is by using indexes. An *index* is a data structure that improves the speed of data retrieval operations on a database table. By creating indexes on frequently used columns, the optimizer can quickly find the data needed to execute the query, resulting in faster query execution times than when performing a full table scan. Columns that you are querying (SELECT, GROUP BY, ORDER BY, JOIN) could be faster with indexes. Indexes are usually represented as self-balancing B-trees that keep data sorted and allow searches, sequential access, insertions, and deletions in logarithmic time. The following are the two types of indexes that can be created in an RDBMS:

Primary indexes
> A primary index is an index that is created on a table's primary key (a column or set of columns that uniquely identifies each row in the table). By creating a primary index on the primary key, the database can quickly find the location of a specific row in the table, resulting in faster retrieval times for the data.

Secondary indexes
> A secondary index is an index that is created on a nonprimary key column or set of columns. A secondary index can be used to improve the performance of queries that involve filtering or sorting data based on a specific column or set of columns. For example, if a query frequently filters data based on a customer's phone number, creating a secondary index on the phone number column can significantly improve the query's performance.

B+ trees are widely used in RDBMSs as an indexing structure for facilitating fast data retrieval and efficient query processing. The B+ tree data structure provides efficient key-based searching and range queries on large amounts of data. A *B+ tree* is a self-balancing tree data structure that stores data in a sorted manner, as shown in Figure 2-7. It consists of internal nodes and leaf nodes, where leaf nodes contain the actual data records or pointers to the data records. Each node in the B+ tree has a fixed number of keys and pointers. The keys in the internal nodes act as separators, guiding the search process, while the leaf nodes store the data records or pointers to the data records in sorted order.

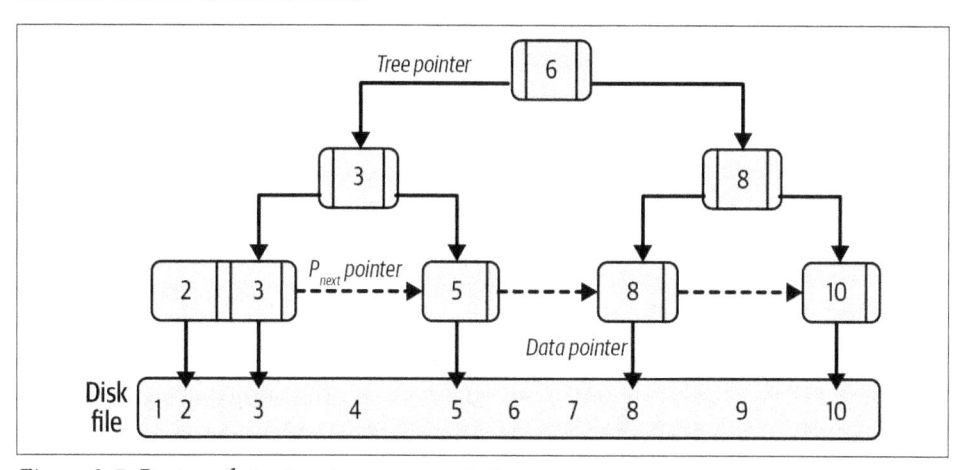

Figure 2-7. B+ tree data structure representation

When an index is created on a column, a B+ tree index is constructed where each node in the tree corresponds to a range of values from the indexed column. The leaf nodes of the B+ tree contain the values of the indexed column along with the corresponding pointers to the actual data records. B+ trees can also be used to create multicolumn indexes in RDBMSs. In this case, each node in the B+ tree contains multiple keys, allowing for efficient searching and querying based on multiple columns. Composite and multicolumn indexes are beneficial for queries that involve complex conditions or join operations on multiple columns.

B+ trees provide efficient key-based searching and range queries, which are crucial for improving query performance in RDBMSs. When a query involves searching for a specific value or a range of values, the B+ tree index allows the database system to navigate the tree quickly to find the desired data records. The balanced nature of the B+ tree ensures that the height of the tree remains relatively small, resulting in faster search operations with logarithmic time complexity.

B+ trees also enable efficient sequential and range scans in RDBMSs. The leaf nodes of the B+ tree are linked together, allowing for scanning of the entire index or a specific range of values. Sequential or range scans are often performed for queries involving sorting or aggregations or when a subset of data needs to be retrieved based on specific conditions.

Finally, B+ trees efficiently handle update and insert operations in RDBMSs. When a new record is inserted, the B+ tree index is updated in a way that ensures the tree's balance and sorted order are maintained. Similarly, when a record is updated, the corresponding entry in the B+ tree index is adjusted accordingly. This ability to handle dynamic updates and inserts without significant performance degradation makes B+ trees suitable for transactional systems.

Using a lot of indexes comes with its own caveats as placing an index can keep the data in memory, requiring more space. Writes could become slower since the index also needs to be updated. When loading large amounts of data, it might be faster to disable indexes, load the data, and then rebuild the indexes.

SQL tuning

As prescribed in the section "Guideline of Performance: Metrics Don't Lie" on page 32 in Chapter 1, to improve the performance of SQL queries, it is first important to benchmark and profile your queries to uncover bottlenecks. *Benchmarking* involves simulating high-load and high-throughput situations, while *profiling* requires measuring the p90 latency of the query and analyzing the slow query log to identify performance issues. Based on these metrics, *SQL tuning* is improving the performance of SQL queries by removing the bottlenecks and optimizing query plans.

One way to optimize SQL queries is to minimize large write operations because performing operations like writing, modifying, deleting, or importing extensive amounts of data can have a significant impact on the performance of queries. These operations may even result in table blocking when tasks involve updating and manipulating data, adding indexes or check constraints to queries, processing triggers, and similar actions. Moreover, the act of writing a substantial volume of data will inevitably lead to an increase in the size of log files.

Another technique to optimize SQL performance is to schedule query execution during off-peak hours. This approach is particularly beneficial when dealing with multiple `SELECT` queries involving large tables or executing complex queries with nested subqueries, looping queries, and the like. When executing resource-intensive queries in a database, the RDBMS applies locks to the tables involved, preventing simultaneous access by different transactions. Consequently, other users are unable to work with those tables, leading to limited access to specific data. Running heavy queries during peak times not only strains the server but also restricts other users' data access.

Adding multiple tables to a query and performing joins can potentially burden the query and lead to performance issues. Moreover, having a large number of tables to retrieve data from may result in an inefficient execution plan. `JOIN` elimination is one of the many techniques employed to achieve efficient query plans. Dividing a single query into several separate queries that can be joined later can eliminate unnecessary joins, subqueries, and tables. This approach helps streamline the query and enhance its performance by removing redundant and extraneous elements.

Enhancing RDBMS performance and optimizing SQL queries are critical tasks for both database developers and administrators. They must meticulously evaluate various factors, such as the selection of specific operators, the number of tables involved in a query, the query's size, its execution plan, statistics, resource allocation, and other performance metrics. These considerations play a pivotal role in determining whether query performance improves or deteriorates. By carefully analyzing and addressing these factors, developers and administrators can effectively tune and improve query performance.

Denormalization

In most systems, read operations significantly outnumber write operations by a ratio of 100:1 or even 1,000:1. Performing a complex database join during a read can be resource intensive, particularly due to disk operations.

Denormalization is the technique aimed at improving read performance, although it may come at the cost of reduced write performance. It involves duplicating data across multiple tables to avoid costly joins. Some RDBMSs offer materialized views, which handle the task of storing redundant information and maintaining consistency among redundant copies.

When data is distributed through methods like federation and sharding, managing joins across different data centers adds further complexity. Denormalization can help alleviate the need for complex joins in such scenarios. However, denormalization has its disadvantages because of data duplication, which can lead to redundancy. Maintaining consistency among redundant copies requires the use of constraints, which further adds complexity to the database design. If multiple tables store redundant copies of a customer's email address—for instance, in the Customers and Orders tables—a unique constraint on the email in the Customers table helps prevent duplicate email entries. Additionally, setting a trigger or cascading update constraints can ensure that updates to the email in the Customers table are automatically reflected in the Orders table, preventing inconsistent copies. Therefore, a denormalized database under heavy write load may perform worse than its normalized counterpart.

Overall, denormalization can provide performance benefits for read-heavy workloads, but it introduces trade-offs in terms of data redundancy and increased complexity in database management.

Query federation

Query federation is a technique that involves splitting a large query into smaller queries that can be executed independently on different database servers. This technique requires schema federation—that is, functional partitioning of the database across multiple database servers. Executing smaller queries on different servers can reduce the overall query execution time, resulting in faster query results. Query federation is useful for optimizing queries that involve large amounts of data or complex joins.

By using these techniques to optimize relational databases, database administrators can improve performance and provide faster, more efficient access to data. Next, we'll cover the techniques used to scale relational databases in practice.

Scaling Relational Databases

As businesses grow and their data needs increase, it becomes necessary for them to scale their databases to handle the increased workload. *Scaling* refers to the process of increasing the capacity of a database to accommodate more data, users, and transactions. Let's explore scaling relational databases using partitioning, sharding, and replication.

Partitioning

Partitioning is the process of dividing a large database table into smaller, more manageable parts called *partitions*. Each record within the database is assigned to a specific partition, ensuring that every record belongs to one and only one partition. Each partition operates as an independent database, capable of executing read and write operations autonomously. As a result, database queries can be directed toward a single partition to focus on specific data or distributed across multiple partitions for broader processing. The client can direct the query either to a specific partition or to a coordinator node, which then forwards the query to the right set of partitions, thus orchestrating the partitions. The two types of partitioning, shown in Figure 2-8, are vertical and horizontal, with two possible approaches to horizontal partitioning.

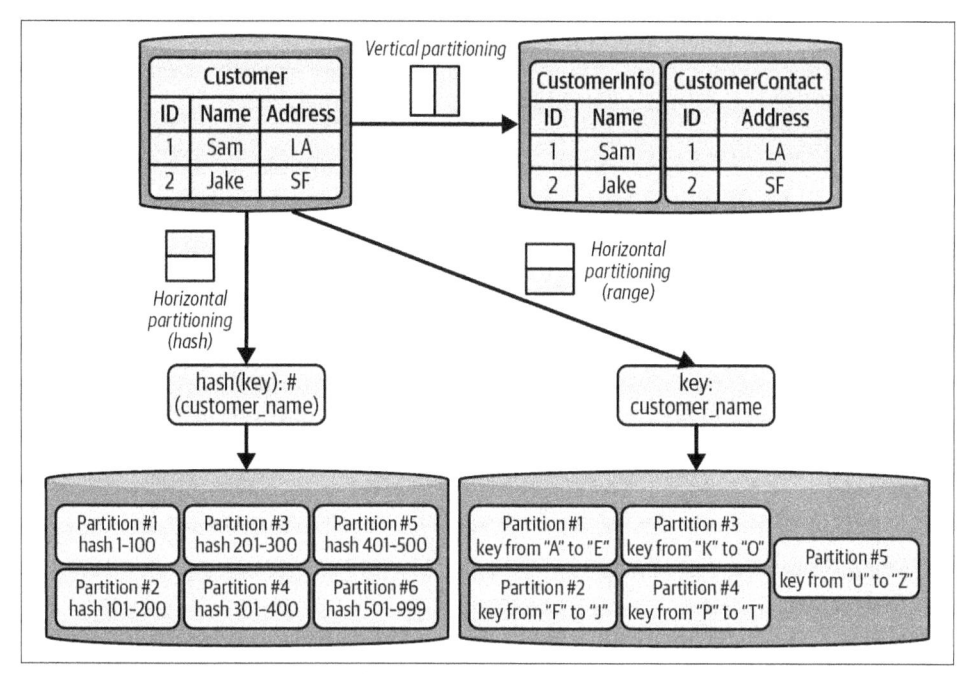

Figure 2-8. Partitioning approaches in a database

Vertical partitioning involves splitting a table by columns. For example, a customer table might be split into two tables, one containing customer information and another containing customer contact data.

Horizontal partitioning involves splitting a table by rows. For example, a large customer table might be split into smaller tables, each containing a specific range of customer records based on their last name or zip code. Horizontal partitioning can have two approaches: hash partitioning and range partitioning.

Hash partitioning. The strategy of partitioning by key hash involves generating a hash of the key and evenly distributing it among the partitions. In this strategy, a hash function (such as MD5 or SHA-256) is applied to the input key of the table. The hash ranges are then divided into buckets, with each bucket assigned to a specific partition. It's important to note that a single host instance can accommodate multiple partitions.

For this strategy to work effectively, the hash function must be deterministic, meaning that the same key should always produce the same hash value and be directed to the same partition. Additionally, each key should resolve to a unique hash value, ensuring a balanced distribution of data across the partitions.

The advantage of hash partitioning is that it eliminates the problems of hot spots and skewed partitions that can occur with range partitioning by using a unique,

Relational Databases | 55

deterministic hashing strategy. However, since the partitioning is on the key's hash, this strategy can't do range queries. We need to query all the partitions if we want to fetch a set of keys, making the DBMS do a scatter and gather pattern.

Range partitioning. In *range partitioning*, we partition a continuous range of keys into separate buckets, which are then assigned to specific partitions. It is important to note that a single host instance can accommodate multiple partitions. The key range assigned to each bucket may or may not be continuous, allowing flexibility in the distribution of data.

Within each partition, the keys are stored in a sorted order. This organization of data enables efficient range scan queries because it simplifies the process of retrieving data within specific key ranges. The system can swiftly access and retrieve data that falls within a given range. In the example shown in Figure 2-8, it becomes easy to retrieve all customers having emails starting with *P* in lexicographic order. Additionally, the range-partitioning strategy is relatively straightforward to implement.

However, if the access patterns on partitions are uneven or unfair, certain partitions may end up with more data or queries than others, leading to skewed partitions and placing a heavier load on specific partitions, which can potentially cause congestion. Such imbalanced partitions that experience a disproportionately high workload are called *hot spots*. For example, in Figure 2-8, if a significant majority of customers have emails beginning with *A*, that can result in the choking of Partition 1 because of the overwhelming amount of data and queries concentrated in that partition.

Partitioning a database offers advantages for large datasets as well as enables high throughput capability. Partitioning enables data to be distributed across multiple machines via sharding, allowing for the handling of datasets that exceed the capacity of a single machine. By spreading the data across multiple partitions, the database can accommodate and manage large-scale data requirements.

With data distributed across multiple partitions, read and write queries can be processed independently by each partition. This parallel processing capability enables the database to handle a higher overall throughput compared to what a single machine can handle. By leveraging the collective power of multiple machines, partitioning enhances the system's ability to process concurrent queries and transactions efficiently. Thus, partitioning can improve query performance by reducing the amount of data that needs to be scanned to execute a query. This results in faster query response times and better scalability.

Sharding

Sharding is the process of distributing a large database across multiple servers. Each server contains a subset of the data, and queries are distributed across all servers. Sharding is useful for scaling databases that have become too large to be managed on a single server. For example, in a "customers" database, as the number of customers grows, more shards are added to the cluster to accommodate the increasing load. Common approaches to sharding a customer table include using the customer's last name, initial, or geographic location.

There are two types of sharding, as shown in Figure 2-9: vertical and horizontal, with different possible approaches to horizontal partitioning, including hash-based, range-based, and round-robin sharding.

Sharding offers similar advantages to federation, including reduced read and write traffic, decreased replication, and improved cache utilization. It also helps reduce the size of indexes, leading to faster query performance. In the event of a shard failure, the other shards remain operational, although implementing replication is crucial to prevent data loss. Sharding eliminates the need for a central master for write serialization, enabling parallel writes and increasing overall throughput.

However, sharding comes with its disadvantages. Application logic needs to be updated to handle shard-specific operations, potentially resulting in complex SQL queries. Data distribution can become unbalanced, particularly if a shard has a subset of power customers, leading to increased load on that particular shard. Rebalancing shards adds complexity, although using a consistent hash-based sharding function can minimize data transfer. Joining data from multiple shards becomes more challenging, and overall, sharding introduces additional hardware requirements and increased system complexity.

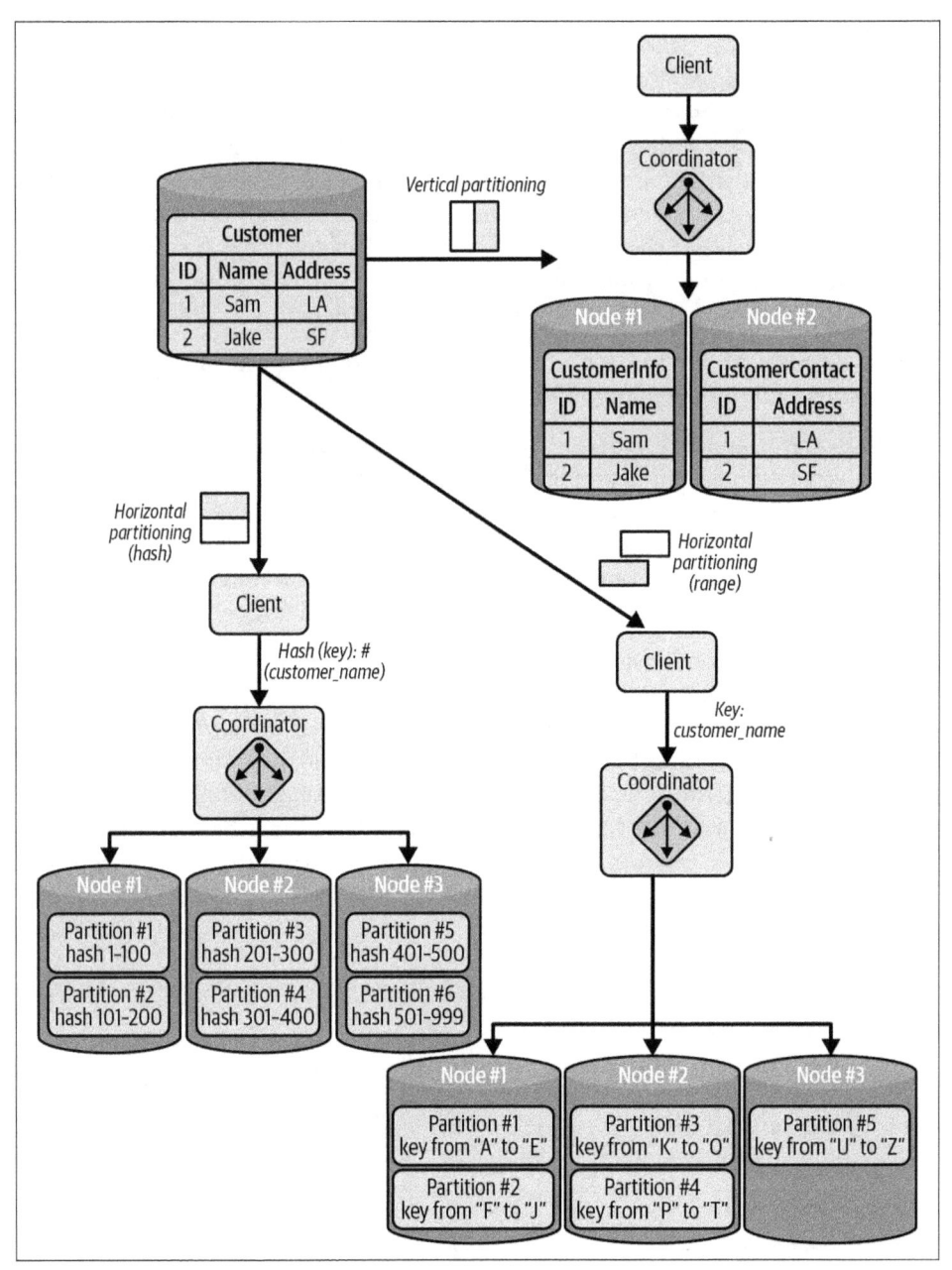

Figure 2-9. Sharding approaches in a database

Replication

Replication is the process of copying data from one database server to another. Every node that stores a copy of the data is called a *replica*. Replication is a key feature in distributed databases that offers several advantages in enhancing availability, load distribution, and latency reduction. By maintaining multiple copies of data across different host machines, replication provides the following benefits:

High availability
  Replication ensures high availability by storing copies of data on multiple host machines. In the event of a failure or downtime of one host machine, the database can seamlessly redirect read and write operations to other live machines that hold replicated data. This fault-tolerance mechanism prevents service disruptions and ensures continuous access to data, enhancing the overall availability of the system.

Load distribution
  With replication, the database can distribute read and write queries across multiple host machines. This load-distribution strategy prevents overburdening of individual machines, thereby improving overall system performance and scalability. By spreading the workload, replication enables efficient utilization of computing resources and better handling of concurrent user requests, resulting in enhanced throughput and responsiveness.

Reduced latency
  Replicating data across geographically distributed host machines allows for placing the replicated copies closer to end users. This proximity reduces the network latency experienced by users when accessing the database. By minimizing the distance between the data and the user, replication improves response times and enhances the user experience, especially in scenarios where low latency is critical, such as real-time applications or distributed systems with users located in different regions.

Disaster recovery and data resilience
  Replication serves as a foundation for disaster-recovery strategies. By maintaining multiple copies of data, distributed databases can withstand catastrophic events, hardware failures, or natural disasters. In case of data loss or unavailability on one host machine, the replicated copies can be used for data recovery and system restoration. Replication ensures data resilience and minimizes the risk of data loss, contributing to the overall reliability and robustness of the database.

Scalability and performance
  Replication plays a crucial role in scaling distributed databases. As the data size or user load increases, additional host machines can be added to the system, each hosting a replicated copy of the data. This horizontal-scaling approach allows the

database to handle larger workloads and accommodate growing user demands. By distributing data and queries, replication contributes to improved system performance, enabling efficient parallel processing and reducing response times.

The two types of replication for RDBMSs are single-leader and multileader, both of which are illustrated in Figure 2-10.

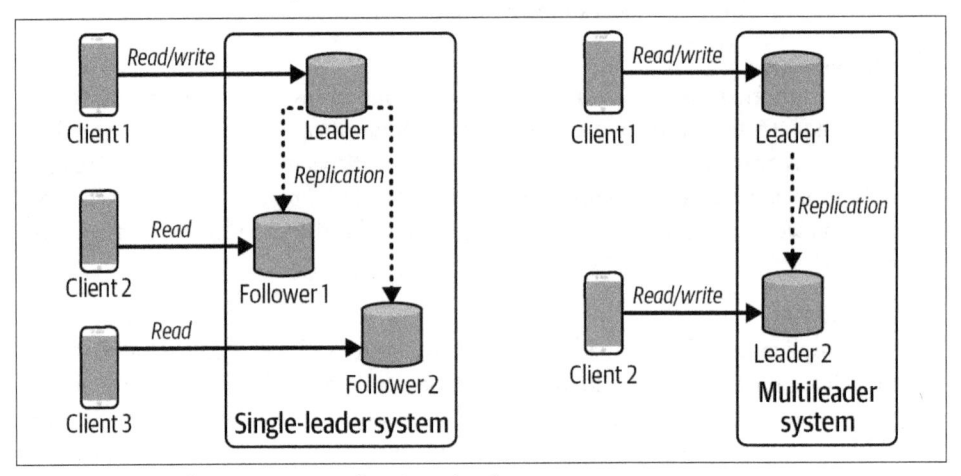

Figure 2-10. Replication approaches in a database

In *single-leader replication*, one database server serves as the leader, and the other servers serve as followers. The leader server handles all write operations while the follower servers handle read operations. Changes made to the leader server are replicated to the follower servers, ensuring that all servers contain the same data either synchronously or asynchronously. This type of replication is useful for scaling read-heavy databases.

In *multileader replication*, each database server can both read and write data. Changes made to one server are replicated to the other server either synchronously or asynchronously, ensuring that all servers contain the same data. This type of replication is useful for scaling databases that require high availability. In single-leader, there will be a lag in leader election and promotion, but in multileader, failure will be opaque, leading to a high-availability setup. However, this comes with a trade-off: conflict resolution, which we discussed in Chapter 1. Since writes can occur on multiple leaders independently, conflicting updates may arise when the same data is modified in different locations simultaneously.

For these replication types, replication can be done on follower nodes as full replication, snapshot-based replication, transactional replication (i.e., replicating the transactional updates), or key-based incremental replication (i.e., scanning the database for modified keys and only replicating data for those keys). The replication can be done either synchronously or asynchronously, each with its own caveats.

Synchronous replication. In distributed databases, *synchronous replication* provides a mechanism for replicating data from a leader replica to follower replicas using synchronous communication, keeping data always up to date across all replicas. By maintaining synchronous replicas that are always in sync with the leader replica, this replication mechanism offers several advantages:

Consistent writes
With synchronous replication, the client considers a write operation successful only when it is acknowledged by both the leader replica and the synchronous follower replica. This strict synchronization ensures that the data remains consistent across replicas. By waiting for confirmation from both replicas, the system guarantees that the write has been durably committed and is available for subsequent read operations. Though it increases latency, this consistency is vital for applications that require strict data integrity and accuracy.

Immediate failover
One significant advantage of synchronous replication is its ability to facilitate immediate failover in the event of a leader-replica crash. Since the synchronous replicas are always up to date with the leader, any of these replicas can be immediately promoted as the new leader without any data loss. This seamless transition ensures continuous availability of the system even when there are failures. By eliminating downtime and minimizing data loss, synchronous replication enhances the overall resilience and reliability of the distributed system.

Data durability
Synchronous replicas guarantee that data is durably stored across multiple replicas. When a write operation is confirmed by both the leader and the synchronous follower replicas, that ensures that the data is safely persisted on multiple machines. This redundancy provides data durability, protecting against data loss in the event of a replica failure or system crash. By maintaining multiple synchronized copies, synchronous replication ensures that critical data remains intact and recoverable, enhancing the overall data resilience of the system.

Consistency in read operations
Synchronous replication ensures consistency not only in write operations but also in read operations. As the synchronous replicas are always up to date with the leader, read operations can be performed on any of the replicas with the guarantee of accessing the most recent and consistent data. This feature enables load balancing and improves the system's ability to handle read-intensive workloads.

In summary, synchronous replication in distributed databases provides the benefits of consistent writes, immediate failover, data durability, and consistency in read operations. By maintaining synchronous replicas that are always in sync with the leader, this replication mechanism ensures data integrity, continuous availability, and reliable access to up-to-date information. Synchronous replication is particularly valuable in scenarios where strict consistency and high availability are paramount, such as in financial systems, real-time applications, and mission-critical environments.

Asynchronous replication. In distributed databases, *asynchronous replication* provides a mechanism for replicating data from a leader replica to asynchronous replicas. This replication approach has specific characteristics and considerations:

Near real-time updates
Asynchronous replicas apply changes from the leader replica in near real time, albeit with a potential delay. This means that the asynchronous replicas may not be immediately up to date with the latest changes made on the leader. The time lag between the leader and asynchronous replicas results in a temporary inconsistency in data across the replicas. However, over time, the asynchronous replicas converge as they catch up with the leader's updates.

Data lag and potential staleness
Due to the asynchronous nature of replication, the asynchronous replicas can lag the leader replica. The extent of this lag depends on various factors, such as network conditions, system load, and the volume of changes being replicated. As a result, the asynchronous replicas may not reflect the most recent state of the data. This potential staleness can affect applications or use cases that require access to the most up-to-date information. It's essential to consider this trade-off between near real-time updates and potential data lag when employing asynchronous replication.

Risk of data loss
Because asynchronous replicas can be lagging or stale, promoting an asynchronous replica as the new leader in the event of a leader-replica crash can introduce the risk of data loss. Since the asynchronous replica may not have received or applied all the changes made on the previous leader, promoting it prematurely can result in missing or inconsistent data. To mitigate this risk, careful considerations and measures, such as monitoring the replication lag and ensuring that the asynchronous replica has caught up sufficiently, should be taken before promoting it as the new leader.

Scalability and performance
Asynchronous replication is often favored in distributed systems that prioritize scalability and performance over strict consistency. By allowing some flexibility in the replication process and tolerating temporary data inconsistencies, asynchronous replication can handle high write throughput and accommodate systems with large-scale deployments. This approach enables the system to distribute the workload and scale horizontally while maintaining acceptable response times.

In summary, asynchronous replication in distributed databases provides near real-time updates but introduces the possibility of data lag and potential staleness. While it offers scalability and performance advantages, the risk of data loss exists when promoting an asynchronous replica as a new leader. Careful planning, monitoring, and appropriate fallback mechanisms are necessary to ensure data integrity and minimize the impact of data inconsistencies when employing asynchronous replication.

Scaling distributed relational databases is an important task for businesses that need to handle increasing amounts of data and traffic. Partitioning, sharding, and replication are all useful techniques for scaling databases. Partitioning can improve query performance by reducing the amount of data that needs to be scanned to execute a query. Sharding is useful for scaling databases that have become too large to be managed on a single server. Replication is useful for scaling databases that require high availability or have heavy read traffic.

To conclude the chapter, let's go over the most popular open source RDBMS choices.

Open Source Relational Database Systems

Open source RDBMSs are popular choices for businesses and developers because of their affordability, flexibility, and community support. Two widely used open source RDBMSs are MySQL and PostgreSQL. In this section, we will compare MySQL and PostgreSQL.

MySQL

MySQL (*htttps://dev.mysql.com/doc*) is an open source RDBMS that was first released in 1995. It is one of the most popular RDBMSs in the world, with a large user community and a broad range of features. MySQL is known for its speed and scalability, making it an ideal choice for businesses that need to handle high volumes of data and traffic.

Features of MySQL include:

- Support for SQL and NoSQL queries
- Scalable architecture
- High performance
- Simplicity and ease of use
- Ability to handle read-heavy workloads
- Strong support for clustering and replication

PostgreSQL

PostgreSQL (*https://postgresql.org/docs*) is an open source RDBMS that was first released in 1996. It is known for its robustness, reliability, and feature-richness. PostgreSQL is a popular choice for businesses that require advanced data management capabilities and powerful query processing.

Features of PostgreSQL include:

- Support for SQL and NoSQL queries
- ACID-compliant transactions
- Strong support for stored procedures and triggers
- Support of JSON and XML data types
- Ability to handle write-heavy workloads
- Advanced data management features

MySQL and PostgreSQL are compared in Table 2-1. Both are open source RDBMSs, are ACID-complaint, and support SQL and NoSQL queries. Both offer strong support for replication and clustering. However, MySQL has a simpler and more straightforward syntax, while PostgreSQL offers more advanced features and capabilities. MySQL is better suited for read-heavy workloads; PostgreSQL is better suited for write-heavy workloads.

Table 2-1. MySQL versus PostgreSQL

Property	MySQL	PostgreSQL
Summary	Open source RDBMS.	Object-relational database management system (ORDBMS). It provides all the facilities of an RDBMS with additional support of object-oriented concepts like classes, objects, and inheritance.
Data type support	Supports standard SQL types.	Supports standard SQL types along with many advanced types, such as array, jsonb, and user defined types.
JSON support	Supports JSON documents to be stored in a column by converting to an internal format that permits quick read access to document elements. JSON columns cannot be indexed directly. To create an index that references such a column indirectly, you can define a generated column that extracts the information that should be indexed, then create an index on the generated column.	Supports two data types related to JSON: • The JSON data type stores an exact copy of the input text whose processing functions must reparse on each execution. • The jsonb data type is stored in a decomposed binary format that makes it slightly slower to input, due to added conversion overhead, but significantly faster to process since no reparsing is needed. It also supports indexing, which can be a big advantage.

Property	MySQL	PostgreSQL
Indexes	Types of indexes include primary key, foreign key, unique index, single column, multicolumn (up to 16 columns), and spatial.	Types of indexes include primary key, foreign key, unique index, single column, and multicolumn (up to 32 columns). It also supports the following two types: • Expression indexes can be created with an index of the result of an expression or function, instead of simply the value of a column. • Partial indexes index only a part of a table.
Replication	One-way, asynchronous replication where one server acts as a primary and others as secondaries. You can replicate all databases, selected databases, or even selected tables within a database.	Synchronous replication (called *2-safe replication*) that utilizes two database instances running simultaneously where the primary database is synchronized with a secondary database. Unless both databases crash simultaneously, data won't be lost.
Performance	Implements concurrent connections by spawning a thread per connection, which is relatively low overhead.	Uses a process-per-connection design, which is significantly more expensive than a thread-per-connection design. Also seems to have poor support for handling large connection counts even when there is sufficient memory available.
Speed	By not including certain SQL features, MySQL stays light to prioritize speed and reliability. MySQL's speed is especially apparent when it comes to highly concurrent read-only operations.	PostgreSQL supports query plans that can leverage multiple CPUs to answer queries with greater speed. This, coupled with strong support for multiple concurrent writes, makes it a great choice for complex operations like data warehousing and online transaction processing (OLTP).

Both MySQL and PostgreSQL are powerful open source RDBMSs that offer a broad range of features and capabilities. MySQL is known for its speed and scalability, while PostgreSQL is known for its robustness and advanced data management capabilities. When choosing between them, it's important to consider the specific needs of your organization and the requirements of your application.

> Amazon RDS offers multiple options by providing various database engine versions (commonly referred to as "flavors"), instance classes, and storage types. These flavors are essentially different configurations of managed database engines, each optimized for specific use cases and workloads. RDS supports several popular relational database engines, including MySQL, PostgreSQL, Oracle, SQL Server, and MariaDB. We'll cover RDS in Chapter 10.

Conclusion

This chapter has provided a comprehensive overview of relational databases and their underlying concepts, architectures, and strategies for scalability. We began by delving into various types of storage mechanisms, including file, block, and object stores, laying the foundation for understanding how data is managed and accessed. From there, we transitioned into a thorough examination of relational databases, elucidating the key principles that govern their design and operation.

The focal point of the chapter revolved around addressing the challenges of database scalability. We uncovered a range of advanced techniques, such as partitioning, indexing, replication, federation, sharding, and denormalization, each offering unique solutions to accommodate growing datasets and increasing user demands. In exploring these strategies, you have gained valuable insights into how to effectively optimize performance and maintain the integrity of relational databases as their usage expands.

To further enrich your understanding, we introduced two prominent open source databases, MySQL and PostgreSQL, to acquaint you with the practical implementations of the concepts covered in this chapter. These databases are powerful tools that showcase the real-world application of the theoretical knowledge we have presented.

As we conclude this chapter on relational databases, we open the door to the exciting realm of nonrelational databases. The next chapter will embark on an exploration of alternative database paradigms that have gained prominence in recent years. Nonrelational databases, with their diverse models and unique features, present a compelling alternative to traditional relational systems. Delving into this subject will deepen your understanding of the evolving landscape of database technologies.

CHAPTER 3
Nonrelational Stores

In the ever-evolving landscape of modern data management, traditional relational databases have long been the stalwarts of structured data storage and retrieval. However, the rise of new technologies, diverse data formats, and the need for high-performance, scalable solutions has led to the development of a new class of databases known as *nonrelational* or *NoSQL* databases. These databases have gained popularity for their ability to handle the challenges posed by today's data-intensive applications and their capacity to adapt to various data models while offering unprecedented scalability and performance.

Relational databases have traditionally been the cornerstone of data management, providing a structured, standardized approach to organizing and retrieving information. As the digital universe continues to expand exponentially, though, traditional relational models face inherent limitations when confronted with the demands of modern web applications, real-time analytics, and large-scale distributed systems.

Nonrelational databases break away from the rigid constraints of the relational paradigm and introduce novel data models and storage mechanisms that challenge the status quo. These databases prioritize scalability, fault tolerance, and low-latency access, enabling organizations to effectively handle massive volumes of data and support dynamic, rapidly evolving data requirements.

In this chapter, we will discover the fundamental principles, key concepts, and various types of nonrelational databases, shedding light on their strengths, weaknesses, and ideal use cases. Our exploration will encompass a range of popular NoSQL database models, including document stores, key-value stores, columnar databases, and graph databases, each tailored to address specific challenges in data management. We'll also discuss their architecture and how leaderless architecture supports scaling using quorums, optimistic replication, consistent hashing, and hinted handoff.

Throughout this chapter, we will delve into the intricacies of data modeling, query languages, and consistency models associated with nonrelational databases. We will examine the core architectural principles that underpin their design, such as horizontal scalability, distributed data storage, and decentralized control. We will also explore the trade-offs that come with nonrelational databases in data consistency, data integrity, and the impact on application development.

By the end of this chapter, you will have gained a comprehensive understanding of nonrelational databases, empowering you to make informed decisions when choosing the right data storage solution for your organization's needs. Whether you are a seasoned data professional or a curious enthusiast, prepare to embrace the world of nonrelational databases and discover the remarkable possibilities they offer in the era of big data and beyond.

> AWS offers a range of nonrelational database services, such as Amazon DynamoDB, Amazon DocumentDB, Amazon Neptune, Amazon ElastiCache, Amazon OpenSearch, Amazon Keyspaces, and more, to meet customer requirements for different business use cases. We will cover these in more detail in Chapter 10.

Nonrelational Database Concepts

This section introduces the fundamental concepts that characterize nonrelational databases.

Schema Flexibility

Unlike relational databases that enforce a fixed schema, nonrelational databases allow for dynamic and flexible schema designs. This means that data can be stored without the need to predefine a strict structure, making it easier to accommodate varying data formats and evolving application requirements.

Data Models

Nonrelational databases support various data models, each optimized for specific use cases. The most common data models include:

Document stores
　　These databases store and manage data in flexible, semistructured documents, often in formats like JSON or Binary JSON (BSON). This approach is ideal for applications dealing with complex or dynamic data.

Key-value stores
> These databases store data in a simple key-value format, making them highly efficient for read and write operations. They are commonly used for caching and high-speed data retrieval.

Column-family stores
> These databases organize data into column families, allowing efficient storage and retrieval of large volumes of data, especially in analytical and data-warehousing scenarios.

Graph databases
> These databases focus on relationships between data entities, making them well suited for applications that require complex querying and analysis of interconnected data.

Scalability

Nonrelational databases are designed to scale horizontally, distributing data across multiple nodes or servers. This enables them to handle massive datasets and high levels of concurrent traffic. Scaling is achieved through techniques like sharding and replication, allowing applications to grow seamlessly as demand increases.

High Availability and Fault Tolerance

Many nonrelational databases prioritize high availability and fault tolerance. They are often designed to handle hardware failures, network partitions, and other disruptions without compromising data integrity or accessibility.

BASE

In the realm of nonrelational databases, the acronym *BASE* stands for "Basically Available, Soft state, Eventually consistent." BASE is an alternative approach to data consistency and availability as per the CAP theorem, compared to the ACID properties traditionally associated with relational databases. BASE is particularly relevant in distributed, large-scale systems where high availability and scalability are key requirements, often at the expense of strict strong consistency.

> Refer to Chapter 1 to review the CAP theorem, a trade-off that naturally arises in distributed systems. Also, refer to Chapter 2 for more information about ACID properties, which are fundamental properties of relational databases.

The principles of BASE include:

Basically available
　The "basically available" aspect of BASE emphasizes that a nonrelational database should always ensure some level of availability, even when there are network partitions, hardware failures, or other issues. The database system is designed to respond to client requests even if that means sacrificing some level of consistency in the data. Availability is a critical requirement for modern applications that cannot afford downtime or unresponsiveness.

Soft state
　"Soft state" implies that the state of the system can change over time due to various factors, such as node failures, network delays, or concurrent updates. This contrasts with the traditional ACID principle of maintaining a hard or rigid state consistency at all times. In a BASE system, it's acknowledged that the system's state might be fluid, and applications need to be designed to handle such variability gracefully.

Eventually consistent
　Perhaps the most distinctive characteristic of BASE is the principle of "eventually consistent." Unlike ACID, which enforces strict consistency at all times, BASE allows for a temporary lack of consistency between replicas in a distributed system. In other words, it recognizes that updates to the database may take some time to propagate across all nodes, and there might be a brief period during which different nodes have slightly different views of the data. However, as the system resolves conflicts and synchronizes updates, the data will eventually converge to a consistent state.

BASE principles are particularly suitable for scenarios where rapid scalability and high availability are paramount, such as in modern web applications, real-time analytics, and large-scale data processing. It's important to note that while ACID properties provide strong guarantees of data integrity and consistency, they can potentially hinder performance and scalability in distributed environments. BASE, on the other hand, offers availability at the expense of strong consistency, allowing applications to maintain responsiveness and continue functioning despite network partitions or hardware failures.

It's worth mentioning that the choice between ACID and BASE depends on the specific requirements of an application. Some applications, like financial systems or traditional relational databases, may prioritize the strict consistency provided by ACID—hence the need to use relational databases. Meanwhile, others, like social media platforms or content delivery networks (CDNs), may benefit more from the availability and scalability offered by BASE principles.

Now, let's go over the different types of nonrelational databases based on these data models, starting with key-value databases.

Key-Value Databases

Key-value databases are a type of nonrelational database that offer a simple yet powerful data model for enabling efficient storage and retrieval of data based on unique keys using distributed hash tables. This design principle, which revolves around mapping keys to their corresponding values, provides a highly scalable, flexible approach to data management. In this section, we will delve into the architecture and design considerations of key-value stores, uncovering the inner workings of these streamlined databases.

Data Model

The fundamental concept of a key-value store revolves around a basic data structure: the key-value pair. The data is stored in tables similar to RDBMS, but the table abstraction is built over the key-value store. Each key is associated with a corresponding value, forming a unit of data storage called an *item*. The keys are typically unique within the database and are used to access and retrieve their associated values. The values in a key-value store can be of various types, including strings, numbers, binary data, or even complex structures like JSON objects. Let's look at the data-model characteristics of key-value stores: schemaless design and key implementation.

No fixed schema or indexes

Unlike traditional relational databases, key-value stores do not enforce a fixed schema. This means that different key-value pairs can have varying structures, allowing for dynamic data models. So some item records can have attributes that other records don't have.

Key-value stores typically lack complex indexing mechanisms because they rely heavily on the efficiency of key-based lookups for data retrieval. Indexing, if present, is often limited to the keys themselves, optimizing the process of locating the desired values.

Keys

In a key-value store, the primary key, partition key, and sort key are fundamental concepts for efficiently organizing and retrieving data, as shown in Figure 3-1.

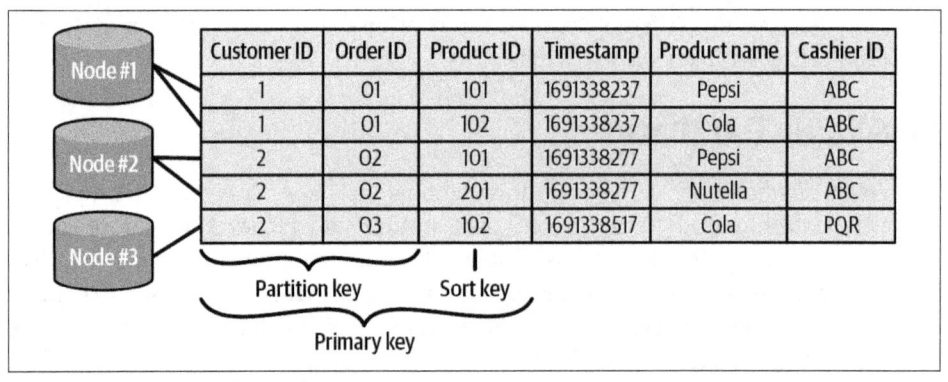

Customer ID	Order ID	Product ID	Timestamp	Product name	Cashier ID
1	01	101	1691338237	Pepsi	ABC
1	01	102	1691338237	Cola	ABC
2	02	101	1691338277	Pepsi	ABC
2	02	201	1691338277	Nutella	ABC
2	03	102	1691338517	Cola	PQR

Figure 3-1. Keys in a key-value store

Let's explore each of these concepts in more detail:

Primary key
　　The primary key is a unique identifier associated with each key-value pair in the key-value store. It serves as the primary means of accessing and retrieving data. The primary key provides a direct mapping to the corresponding value, allowing for fast retrieval operations. Typically, the primary key is a simple data element, such as a string, an integer, or a combination of multiple fields. By ensuring uniqueness, the primary key guarantees that each key-value pair is identifiable within the store.

Partition key
　　The partition key is a subset of the primary key and is responsible for data distribution across multiple storage partitions in a distributed key-value store. It determines the storage location of the data within the store. The partition key is used to partition the dataset into smaller, more manageable subsets that can be distributed across different physical or virtual storage nodes. Each partition operates independently, allowing for horizontal scaling and improved performance. Selecting an appropriate partition key enables data to be evenly distributed and balanced across the partitions, avoiding hot spots and ensuring efficient storage and retrieval operations.

Sort key
　　The sort key, also known as a *range key*, is an optional attribute used to order or sort the data within a partition. While the primary key uniquely identifies each key-value pair, the sort key allows for efficient range queries and data retrieval in a specific order. The sort key is particularly useful when you want to query a range of data based on a specific criterion, such as retrieving all records with timestamps within a range or retrieving data in alphabetical or numerical order. Organizing data based on the sort key enables the key-value store to perform efficient range-based queries and optimizes retrieval performance.

In summary, the primary key uniquely identifies each key-value pair in a key-value store. The partition key determines the distribution of data across multiple storage partitions, enabling horizontal scalability and load balancing. The sort key, while optional, facilitates efficient sorting and range-based queries within each partition. Understanding and appropriately utilizing these key concepts in a key-value store helps optimize data storage, data retrieval, and query performance.

Data Access and Retrieval Operations

In a key-value store, several operations are commonly used to manipulate data associated with specific keys:

GetItem
: The GetItem operation retrieves the attributes that describe an item associated with a given primary key. If no item exists for the provided key, the GetItem operation returns an empty result.

PutItem
: The PutItem operation is used to insert an item into the store. If there is no existing item with the specified key, the operation creates a new item and associates it with the key. If an item already exists for the given key, the PutItem operation replaces the existing item with the new item.

UpdateItem
: The UpdateItem operation is employed to modify an existing item. If an item with the specified key exists, the operation updates the attributes of that item. It allows for adding new attributes, modifying existing ones, or removing attributes from the item. If no item exists for the given key, the UpdateItem operation adds a new item instead.

DeleteItem
: The DeleteItem operation is used to remove an item from the key-value store. By providing the primary key of the item, the DeleteItem operation deletes the corresponding item. If no item exists for the specified key, no action is taken.

These operations form the basic set of functions used to interact with the items in a key-value store based on the associated keys. Using these operations, developers can manage and manipulate the data within a key-value store.

Scaling Key-Value Stores

Key-value stores are designed to handle massive volumes of data and to support horizontal scalability. To achieve this, they often adopt a distributed architecture, where data is partitioned across multiple nodes or servers. Each node is responsible for storing a subset of the data, allowing the system to handle high loads and provide fault tolerance. Distributed key-value stores employ techniques like leaderless replication using consistent hashing or partitioning algorithms to evenly distribute the data across the nodes. Let's go through these techniques in detail.

Leaderless replication

Leaderless replication is a technique used in distributed systems, including key-value stores, to achieve high availability and fault tolerance without relying on a single designated leader node. Instead of having a dedicated leader responsible for coordinating read and write operations, all nodes in the system are equal and can accept client requests independently, as shown in Figure 3-2.

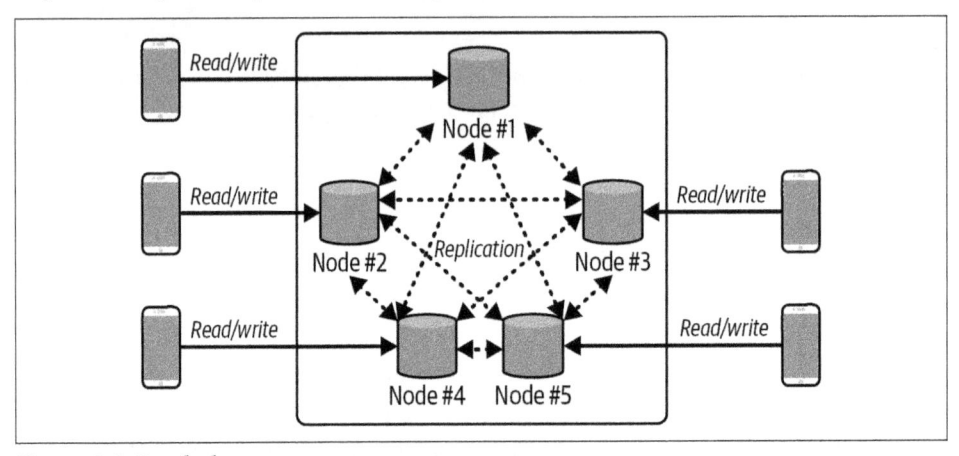

Figure 3-2. Leaderless system setup

In leaderless replication, data is typically divided into smaller partitions or shards, and each shard is replicated across multiple nodes in the system using peer-to-peer replication. This replication ensures data redundancy and fault tolerance. When a client wants to read or write data, it can send the request to any node in the system without needing to know which node is the leader. Each node can handle read and write operations, eliminating the bottleneck and single point of failure associated with a dedicated leader.

To ensure consistency, leaderless replication often employs techniques like quorums and conflict-resolution mechanisms. *Quorums* define the minimum number of successful responses required for an operation to be considered successful. For example, a quorum of N/2 + 1 nodes may be required to acknowledge a write operation to ensure that a majority agrees on the state change. A typical quorum model requires that the sum of the write quorum (W) and the read quorum (R) is greater than the total number of nodes (N). This is often represented as: W + R > N.

Conflict-resolution tools, such as vector clocks and Merkle trees, help resolve conflicts that may arise when different nodes receive conflicting updates for the same data. Merkle trees, for example, efficiently identify the specific differences between two versions of a dataset. By comparing the root hashes of these trees, one can pinpoint the exact branches where discrepancies occur, simplifying the process of identifying and reconciling conflicting data.

Leaderless replication provides high availability and fault tolerance because the system can continue operating even if some nodes become unavailable. Clients can send requests to any available node, and the system handles the replication and coordination transparently. However, ensuring strong consistency across the replicas can be more challenging in a leaderless replication model compared to systems with a designated leader. Hence, Amazon DynamoDB is based on a leader-follower architecture, which we discussed in Chapter 1.

Consistent hashing

Consistent hashing is a hashing technique commonly used in distributed systems, including key-value stores, to distribute data across a set of nodes while minimizing the impact of node additions or removals on the overall data distribution. This technique helps ensure high availability, load balancing, and easy scalability in key-value stores and other distributed systems.

In traditional hashing, data is hashed to determine the node responsible for storing or serving it. However, this approach becomes problematic when nodes are added or removed from the system. In such cases, the distribution of data needs to be recalculated, resulting in significant data movement and potential disruptions.

Consistent hashing, shown in Figure 3-3, addresses this issue by introducing a ring-like structure that represents the set of nodes in the system. Each node is assigned a position on the ring using a hash function. Data is also hashed to a position on the ring. The node whose position is the closest clockwise to the data's position becomes responsible for storing or serving that data.

The key advantage of consistent hashing is that when a node is added or removed, only a fraction of the data needs to be remapped to new nodes. Most of the data remains assigned to the same nodes as before, minimizing the movement and disruption of data in the system. This makes consistent hashing highly scalable and efficient in distributed environments.

Furthermore, consistent hashing provides load balancing among nodes since data is evenly distributed around the ring, and nodes tend to have a similar number of data partitions assigned to them. It also allows for easier scaling by adding or removing nodes because the redistribution of data is limited to the affected partitions.

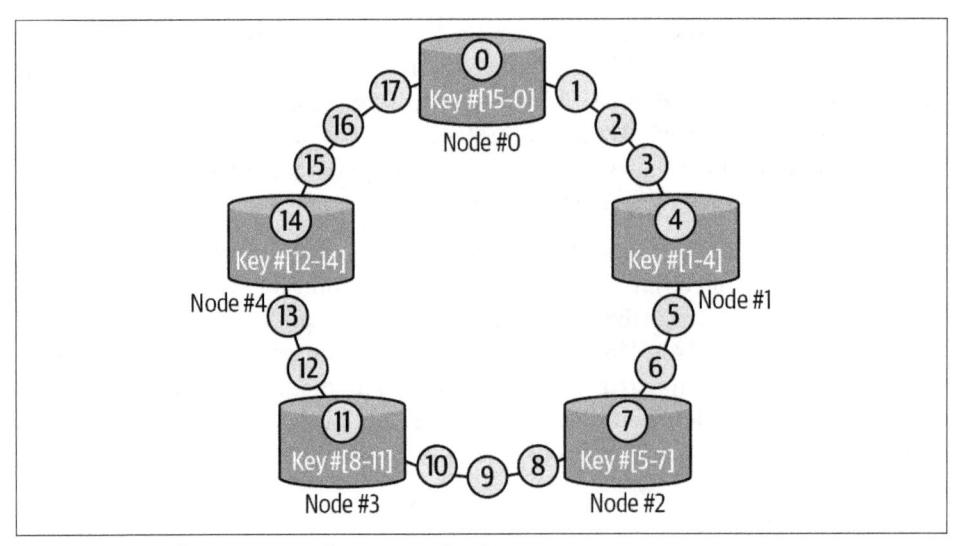

Figure 3-3. Implementation of consistent hashing

Availability in Key-Value Stores

In a distributed key-value store, ensuring high availability is crucial to maintaining system responsiveness and reliability. The following mechanisms are commonly employed to achieve availability in such environments:

Optimistic replication
    Optimistic replication is a technique used to provide availability when there are network partitions or temporary failures. In this approach, multiple replicas of data are maintained across different nodes in the system. When a write operation occurs, the changes are propagated asynchronously to the replicas. Instead of waiting for acknowledgments from all replicas before considering the write operation successful, the system assumes success and continues processing. This optimistic approach reduces latency and allows for continued availability even if some replicas are temporarily unavailable. However, it introduces the possibility of temporary inconsistencies between replicas, which are eventually resolved through background synchronization processes.

Sloppy quorum and last write wins (LWW)
    Sloppy quorum and LWWs are techniques used to achieve availability and eventual consistency during network partitions or replica unavailability. In sloppy quorum, a subset of replicas, rather than the full set, is required to acknowledge a read or write operation. By allowing a relaxed quorum requirement, the system can continue operating even if some replicas are unavailable. However, this relaxation can result in temporary inconsistencies between replicas. To resolve conflicts in write operations, the LWW strategy is often employed. In LWW,

if multiple replicas receive conflicting updates for the same key, the update with the latest timestamp (according to a predefined ordering mechanism) takes precedence. This approach sacrifices strong consistency for availability, ensuring that the most recent write is eventually propagated to all replicas.

Hinted handoff
Hinted handoff is a mechanism used to handle temporary unavailability or network partitions in a distributed key-value store. When a write operation is performed on a replica that cannot immediately communicate with the primary replica, the write is temporarily stored in the form of a "hint." These hints are later delivered to the appropriate replica once it becomes available again. This approach allows for continued availability of write operations, even when there are temporary replica failures. Leveraging hinted handoff ensures that no data is lost and that all updates are eventually applied to the appropriate replicas.

By balancing the trade-offs between availability and consistency, these mechanisms ensure that the system remains responsive and resilient even when there are network partitions, temporary failures, or unavailable replicas.

Advantages, Trade-offs, and Considerations

One of the primary advantages of key-value stores is their ability to deliver high performance and low-latency access to data. Since the data is accessed directly using a key, the retrieval process is highly efficient and typically involves minimal processing overhead. Key-value stores are well suited to use cases where rapid read and write operations are essential, such as caching, session management, and real-time data processing.

While key-value stores offer remarkable scalability and performance benefits, they do come with certain trade-offs. One of the major considerations is the limited querying capabilities. Key-value stores are optimized for simple key-based lookups and lack the advanced querying capabilities provided by relational databases. Moreover, transactions and complex operations involving multiple keys can be challenging to implement in a distributed key-value store without tables, relationships, or defined schemas. Developers typically must handle complex data relationships at the application layer, which can complicate application design.

Key-value stores find extensive use in various domains, including web applications, distributed systems, and caching layers. They excel in scenarios where fast, direct access to data is crucial, such as user session management, user profiles, product catalogs, and real-time analytics.

Dynamo: Key-Value Database

Key-value databases give developers flexible, scalable solutions for managing data in a distributed and highly available manner. One popular key-value store, Dynamo, has gained significant attention and adoption.

Dynamo is a highly available, scalable key-value store developed by Amazon to handle the demanding requirements of its shopping cart service. While Dynamo itself is not open source, its principles have influenced the development of various open source implementations, such as Riak, Voldemort, and Dynomite.

Features of Dynamo include:

Data model
Dynamo follows a simple key-value data model, where each item is uniquely identified by a key. The value associated with the key can be any binary data.

Consistency model
Dynamo uses a tunable eventual consistency model, which means that updates may not be immediately reflected across all replicas.

Query language
Dynamo does not provide a built-in query language but instead relies on simple key-based operations for data access.

High availability
Dynamo prioritizes high availability, ensuring that data remains accessible even when there are failures or network partitions.

Horizontal scalability
Dynamo supports horizontal scaling by distributing data across multiple commodity hardware servers, allowing for increased storage capacity and improved performance with reduced compute cost.

> AWS offers Amazon DynamoDB, which is inspired by the paper on Dynamo (*https://oreil.ly/AbRi9*) and its initial version. We will cover it in more detail in Chapter 10.

The architecture and design of key-value stores prioritize simplicity, scalability, and high-performance data access. Leveraging a straightforward key-value data model and distributed storage, these databases empower organizations to efficiently handle large-scale data management challenges while providing rapid, reliable data-retrieval capabilities. Key-value databases are a valuable tool for tackling modern data-intensive applications.

The next type of nonrelational database is based on the document data model, which stores and manages data in the form of documents.

Document Databases

Document databases are a type of nonrelational database specifically designed for storing, retrieving, and managing semistructured data in the form of documents. They provide a flexible, schemaless approach to data storage, making them ideal for applications with dynamic and evolving data structures. In this section, we will explore the architecture and design considerations of document stores, shedding light on their key features and benefits.

Data Model

At the core of a document store lies the document data model. Instead of organizing data into tables with predefined schemas, document stores store data as self-contained documents analogous to rows in relational databases, typically represented in formats like JSON, BSON, or XML. These documents can have varying structures and can contain nested fields, arrays, and key-value pairs, allowing for hierarchical representation of data. The documents are organized into *collections*, which are analogous to tables in a relational database. The document model provides the ability to store and retrieve complex data structures as a single unit, making it well suited for handling unstructured or semistructured data.

The key components of a document store schema and its architecture are:

Collections
 Collections in a document store are containers that hold related documents. They provide logical groupings of data, supporting the organization and management of data based on its characteristics or purpose. For example, in an ecommerce application, there might be collections for products, orders, and customers. Each collection can have its own set of documents, with each document representing an individual entity or record.

Documents
 Documents are the fundamental unit of data in a document store. A document is a JSON-like structure that stores data as key-value pairs. It represents a single entity or record and can contain nested structures and arrays. Documents within a collection can have different sets of fields, allowing for flexible data structures. This dynamic nature of document stores is particularly advantageous in scenarios where data evolves rapidly or when dealing with diverse and unpredictable data sources. For example, within a "products" collection, each document could have fields like "name," "price," "description," and so on.

Operators
  Document stores provide a rich set of operators, which allow you to query, update, and manipulate data within documents. Common operators include:

  Insert
    Inserts a new document into a collection

  Update
    Modifies an existing document by updating or adding fields

  Delete
    Removes a document from a collection

  Query
    Retrieves documents from a collection based on specified criteria

  Aggregation
    Performs complex data aggregations and transformations on documents, such as grouping, sorting, and aggregating data

Projection
  Projection is a powerful feature in document stores that allows you to retrieve only the desired fields from a document. With projection, you can specify which fields to include or exclude in the result set. Indexing mechanisms, such as secondary indexes, are commonly used to optimize query performance, enabling fast access to the desired documents based on specific fields or criteria. This can significantly reduce network traffic and improve query performance because only the required data is transferred from the database to the client.

In summary, document stores offer a flexible, schemaless approach to data storage and retrieval. Collections group related documents, while documents represent individual entities or records. Operators provide functionality for data manipulation, and projection allows for selective retrieval of fields. The distributed architecture of document stores supports high availability, fault tolerance, and scalability. With their rich features and flexible data model, document stores are well suited for a wide range of use cases, from content management systems to real-time analytics applications.

Availability in Document Stores

The architecture of a document store typically involves a distributed system with multiple nodes. These nodes work together to provide high availability, fault tolerance, and scalability. Each node can handle read and write operations independently, allowing for parallel processing and improved performance. Data within a collection is often partitioned or sharded across multiple nodes to distribute the workload and support horizontal scaling.

Document stores employ various mechanisms to achieve availability:

Replica sets
   A replica set is a group of nodes in a document store that contains multiple copies of the data. Each replica set consists of a primary node and one or more secondary nodes. The primary node is responsible for handling write operations and acting as the primary source of data. Secondary nodes replicate data from the primary node and serve as backups. Replica sets provide fault tolerance by allowing automatic failover in the event of the failure of a primary node.

Primary-secondary node clusters
   In a primary-secondary node cluster architecture, the primary node accepts write operations and maintains the authoritative copy of the data. Secondary nodes replicate the data from the primary node and serve as read replicas. Clients can read from any of the secondary nodes, distributing the read workload and improving read performance. The primary-secondary node cluster architecture ensures that read operations are scalable and can be handled by multiple nodes. In the event of the failure of a primary node diagnosed by the heartbeat mechanism, one of the secondary nodes is promoted to be the new primary, and the cluster continues to operate without data loss.

Heartbeat mechanism
   The heartbeat mechanism monitors the health and status of nodes, detecting failures, initiating failover processes, and promoting secondary nodes as new primaries when needed. It involves regular communication between nodes to detect failures and trigger appropriate actions. Nodes in a document store periodically exchange heartbeat messages to signal their availability. If a node fails to respond within a specified time, it is considered unavailable, and the replica set or cluster takes the action necessary to maintain availability.

Overall, these mechanisms provide fault tolerance, automatic failover, data redundancy, and efficient read scaling. By leveraging these features, document stores can maintain continuous access to data, withstand failures, and deliver consistent, reliable performance to applications and users.

Advantages, Trade-offs, and Considerations

Document stores find extensive use in various application domains, including content management systems, ecommerce platforms, real-time analytics, and mobile app development. They excel in scenarios where flexibility in data modeling, dynamic schema evolution, and efficient querying of complex data structures are paramount. Document stores also facilitate the storage and retrieval of unstructured or semistructured data, making them suitable for scenarios involving user-generated content, sensor data, log files, and social media feeds.

While document stores provide flexibility and scalability, there are trade-offs to consider. The flexibility of the schemaless design can sometimes lead to challenges with data consistency because the enforcement of data integrity constraints may be delegated to the application layer. Additionally, the lack of strong schema enforcement and complex joins can affect certain types of analytical or reporting queries that rely heavily on relationships and aggregations.

In summary, the architecture and design of document stores revolve around the document data model, flexible schemaless storage, distributed scalability, and powerful querying capabilities. By embracing a document-oriented approach, these databases empower organizations to handle semistructured and evolving data with ease, enabling efficient storage, retrieval, and manipulation of complex data structures. Document stores equip data professionals with a versatile tool for managing diverse and dynamic data.

MongoDB: Open Source Document Database

MongoDB (*https://mongodb.com*) is a widely adopted open source document database known for its scalability, performance, and developer-friendly features. It uses a flexible JSON-like document model, allowing developers to store and retrieve data in a schemaless manner. MongoDB supports dynamic schemas, which means that each document in a collection can have its own unique structure.

The features of MongoDB include:

Flexibility
　　MongoDB's schemaless design enables flexible data models and easy adaptation to changing application requirements. It allows developers to handle varying and evolving data structures within the same collection.

Rich query language
　　MongoDB provides a powerful query language with support for complex queries, indexing, and aggregation. It allows developers to express a wide range of query operations and transformations.

Multidocument transactions
　　Transactions in MongoDB adhere to the ACID properties discussed in detail in Chapter 2. MongoDB supports multidocument transactions, enabling developers to work with multiple documents in a single transaction. This is particularly useful in scenarios where data in multiple collections needs to be updated together while maintaining data integrity.

Data consistency models
　　MongoDB supports various consistency models, allowing developers to choose the level of consistency needed for their applications.

Horizontal scalability
MongoDB supports horizontal scaling through sharding, allowing data to be distributed across multiple nodes. This facilitates high performance and provides the ability to handle large data volumes and high traffic loads.

Replication and high availability
MongoDB supports replica sets, which are self-healing clusters that provide data redundancy and automatic failover. Replica sets ensure high availability and fault tolerance by maintaining multiple copies of data.

MongoDB is a popular open source document store with unique features and capabilities. It has a large, active community that provides extensive support, documentation, and a wide range of third-party integrations. MongoDB's flexibility and community support make it suitable for various applications and deployment scenarios, including both on premises and cloud.

> AWS offers Amazon DocumentDB, which is compatible with MongoDB, supports powerful ad hoc queries, and comes with transaction support similar to Amazon DynamoDB's. We will cover it in more detail in Chapter 10.

The next type of nonrelational database is based on a columnar data model that organizes data into column families for efficient storage and retrieval of large volumes of data.

Columnar Databases

Columnar databases or *column-family databases*, also known as *wide-column stores*, are a type of nonrelational database that offer a unique architecture optimized for handling vast amounts of structured and semistructured data. These databases excel at managing large-scale distributed systems, analytics, and use cases requiring fast read and write OLTP performance. In this section, we will explore the architecture and design considerations of wide-column stores, unveiling their key features and advantages.

Data Model

Unlike traditional relational databases that organize data into rows, wide-column stores employ a column-oriented data model, with columns grouped into column families or column groups. In this model, data is stored and retrieved by columns rather than by rows. Each column represents a particular attribute or field, and data values belonging to that attribute are stored contiguously on disk. This design offers significant advantages in terms of query performance because it allows for efficient compression, data skipping, and column-level operations like filtering and aggregation.

Columnar databases employ various compression techniques to improve storage efficiency and query performance. Since each column is stored separately, column-oriented storage allows for better compression ratios. Compression can be applied individually to each column based on its data characteristics, such as data type or redundancy. This not only reduces storage requirements but also improves data access speed by reducing disk I/O and memory footprint.

Flexible schema design

The schema design in a wide column store is flexible, enabling the addition or removal of columns without altering the entire dataset. This flexibility easily adapts to changing business requirements and evolving data models. Schema changes can be performed independently for each column family, providing greater agility in managing data structures.

Keys

Wide-column stores typically use two types of keys, the partition key and the clustering key, which together constitute the composite primary key. The *partition key* is used to distribute data across the nodes in a cluster. It determines the physical location where data is stored. Data is partitioned based on the partition key, and each partition is stored on a separate node. Efficient selection of the partition key is crucial for even data distribution and optimal query performance. The *clustering key* is used to define the order of data within a partition. It allows for efficient sorting and range-based queries within a partition. The clustering key can consist of multiple columns, defining a hierarchical sorting order for the data.

Choosing the appropriate partition and clustering keys is a crucial aspect of designing a wide-column store database. These keys determine how data is distributed, stored, and accessed within the database. The partition key should be chosen on a column with high cardinality, aiming for even data distribution, while the clustering key should be chosen based on the query access pattern of the application, depending on how data is retrieved in a specific order or pattern.

Consistency Levels

Wide-column stores provide different levels of consistency to balance performance and data integrity. They often offer tunable consistency, allowing developers to configure consistency levels on a per-operation basis. This enables the fine-tuning of consistency requirements for specific read and write operations.

Consistency levels in tunable consistency within a wide-column store are based on the concept of the *quorum*, which refers to the minimum number of replicas that need to participate in a read or write operation. The number of replicas required to form a quorum can vary depending on the desired consistency level.

Eventual consistency

Eventual consistency is the weakest level of consistency, allowing for the highest degree of availability and low latency. In wide-column stores, eventual consistency means that replicas are asynchronously updated over time, which can potentially result in temporary data inconsistencies.

For eventual consistency, the quorum requirements can be defined as *any*. In this model, the operation is considered successful as soon as it is applied to at least one replica, without the requirement for acknowledgment or synchronization across all replicas. Over time, the updates are propagated and eventually converge to a consistent state across the system.

Weak consistency

Weak consistency is a less common consistency level that provides a lower level of data integrity compared to strong consistency. In wide-column stores, weak consistency allows for more relaxed requirements, prioritizing availability and low latency over data consistency. For weak consistency, the quorum requirements can be defined as follows:

Quorum
In this model, the consistency level is achieved when a quorum, or a majority of replicas (more than half = $N/2 + 1$), acknowledges the operation. This means that for a successful read or write operation, the data is considered consistent if it is read or written to at least one replica within the quorum. For instance, in a keyspace with three replicas in each of two data centers (totaling six replicas), write requests are sent to all six replicas. If the write request uses a consistency level of quorum, at least four out of the six replicas must acknowledge the write within the timeout for it to be considered successful.

Local quorum
In this model, a local quorum refers to a majority of replicas within the local data center or region. The operation is considered consistent if it is completed within this local quorum.

Strong consistency

Strong consistency provides the highest level of data consistency but may come with increased latency and reduced availability. In wide-column stores, strong consistency ensures that all replicas are synchronously updated and consistent before a response is returned. For strong consistency, the quorum requirements can be defined as:

All
> In this model, the operation must be acknowledged and applied to all replicas in the cluster before it is considered consistent. This means that for a read or write operation to be successful, it must be propagated to and acknowledged by every replica in the system.

Each quorum
> In this model over multiple data centers or regions, each quorum refers to a majority of replicas within each data center or region. The operation is considered consistent when it is completed within each of these quorums.

These examples provide a general understanding of how consistency levels are defined based on quorum in a tunable consistency model within a wide-column store. It's important to note that the specific consistency levels and their corresponding quorum requirements may vary among different wide-column store databases. When selecting a consistency level, it's crucial to consider the trade-offs among consistency, availability, and performance based on the specific requirements of your application and use case.

Wide-column stores offer a flexible data model that allows for dynamic schema evolution and efficient storage of structured and semistructured data. The schema design is adaptable, and keys (partition and clustering) play a crucial role in data distribution and query optimization. Consistency levels provide options for balancing performance and data integrity.

Columnar Store Architecture

The columnar store architecture may vary from one implementation to another, but the core components generally remain the same. The key components of data storage in columnar storage are:

Commit log
> The *commit log* is a write-ahead log that records all write operations performed on the database. It serves as a durable, sequential log of changes made to the data. Whenever a write operation occurs, it is first written to the commit log to ensure that no data is lost in the event of a system failure or crash.

Memtable
> The *memtable* is an in-memory data structure that stores recent write operations before they are flushed to disk. It acts as a write buffer, temporarily holding the data in memory before persisting it to disk in an efficient manner. The memtable is typically structured as an ordered hash table or skip list, allowing for fast write operations. As the memtable fills up, it is periodically flushed to disk, creating SSTables (sorted string tables).

SSTables
> *SSTables* are the on-disk data structure in columnar storage. They are immutable and sorted by key, enabling efficient range queries and compression. Each SSTable contains a set of sorted key-value pairs, where the keys correspond to the row keys and the values represent the columnar data for each key. SSTables are optimized for fast read operations and can be compacted to improve performance and storage efficiency.

Bloom filters
> Columnar storage leverages Bloom filters to ascertain if an SSTable contains data related to a specific partition. Bloom filters are used for index scans but not for range scans. Bloom filters function as probabilistic sets to quickly test whether an element is a member of the set, offering a memory-accuracy trade-off. They are particularly efficient in cases where false positives are acceptable but false negatives are not desired.

Compaction strategies

Compaction is the process of merging and compacting multiple SSTables to improve read performance and manage disk space. Various compaction strategies are employed to balance read and write performance as well as disk space utilization:

Size-tiered compaction
> This strategy groups SSTables into levels based on their size. As SSTables in a level reach a certain threshold, they are merged into a new SSTable in the next level. This reduces the number of SSTables and simplifies data access at the cost of some write amplification.

Leveled compaction
> In this strategy, SSTables are organized into multiple levels, with each level containing SSTables of roughly equal size. SSTables are compacted within each level, and as they progress to higher levels, they are merged with larger SSTables. Leveled compaction offers more balanced read and write performance at the expense of higher disk space overhead.

Time-window compaction
> This strategy is specifically designed for time-series data, where data is organized based on a time window. It allows for efficient expiration of old data by dropping or merging SSTables according to time-based criteria.

Tombstones for soft delete

Tombstones are special markers used for soft deletes in columnar storage. When a row or column is deleted, a tombstone is created to indicate the deletion. Tombstones ensure that deleted data is properly handled during compaction and read operations, maintaining data consistency across SSTables. During compaction, tombstones are used to identify and remove deleted or expired data.

Excessive tombstones in columnar storage can lead to significant increase in garbage collection (GC) pauses during compaction because columnar stores need to process and eliminate these tombstones, slowing data access and increasing latency. Large numbers of tombstones also consume storage space, and querying data in the presence of numerous tombstones can result in slower query performance because the columnar database has to shift through these markers, potentially causing unnecessary overhead and delays in retrieving relevant data. Effective tombstone management is crucial to maintaining the columnar store's performance and responsiveness.

Advantages, Trade-offs, and Considerations

Wide-column stores find widespread use in various domains, particularly in analytics, big data processing, and time-series data. They are well suited for applications that involve complex queries, ad hoc analysis, data warehousing, and high-speed data ingestion. Use cases include log analysis, financial analytics, real-time reporting, Internet of Things (IoT) data processing, and customer behavior analysis.

While wide-column stores offer significant advantages in scalability and query performance, they come with trade-offs. Because of their distributed nature and complex data organization, they often require more advanced data modeling and query optimization compared to traditional relational databases. Wide-column stores may not be as suitable for scenarios that heavily rely on complex joins across multiple tables.

In conclusion, the architecture and design of wide-column stores revolve around the column-oriented data model, distributed scalability, and efficient analytics capabilities. By leveraging the benefits of columnar storage and a flexible schema design, these databases enable organizations to efficiently store, retrieve, and analyze large volumes of structured as well as semistructured data.

Apache Cassandra: Open Source Columnar Database

Apache Cassandra (*https://oreil.ly/6929x*) is a highly scalable, distributed open source columnar database known for its ability to handle massive amounts of structured and semistructured data across multiple commodity servers. It offers a robust architecture and a range of features that make it suitable for high-performance, fault-tolerant applications.

The features of Cassandra include:

Distributed query language
Cassandra uses Cassandra query language (CQL), a query language similar to SQL, to interact with the database. CQL provides a familiar syntax for developers and offers features like data definition, data manipulation, and querying

capabilities. It simplifies data access and supports complex querying, filtering, and sorting operations.

Distributed and decentralized architecture
Cassandra follows a distributed architecture model, employing a peer-to-peer approach. It organizes data across a cluster of nodes, allowing for easy scalability and fault tolerance. Each node in the leaderless cluster can perform read and write operations independently, resulting in a distributed, highly available database system.

Linear scalability
Cassandra's architecture enables linear scalability, meaning it can handle increasing workloads by simply adding more nodes to the cluster. This scalability allows for seamless growth as data volumes and user demand increase, making it a suitable choice for applications with rapidly growing datasets.

High availability and fault tolerance
Cassandra provides built-in mechanisms for high availability and fault tolerance. It uses peer-to-peer replication across nodes, ensuring data redundancy and preventing data loss in the event of node failures. Cassandra automatically replicates data across multiple nodes based on the replication factor, guaranteeing data availability and durability.

Tunable consistency
Cassandra offers tunable consistency, which enables developers to define the level of consistency required for each read and write operation. This flexibility allows for balancing performance and data consistency based on application-specific needs. Developers can configure consistency levels ranging from eventual consistency to strong consistency.

Flexible data replication and data centers
Cassandra allows replication of data across multiple data centers or geographic regions, providing geographical redundancy and disaster-recovery capabilities. It supports multiple replication strategies, including network topology-aware data replication, ensuring data availability and low-latency access in distributed environments.

In summary, Apache Cassandra is an open source columnar database that offers scalability, high availability, fault tolerance, tunable consistency, and support for distributed and decentralized architectures. With its columnar data model, distributed query language, time-series data capabilities, and active community support, Cassandra empowers developers to build robust, scalable applications that can handle massive amounts of data across distributed environments.

> AWS offers Amazon Keyspaces, which is a highly scalable, available, and managed wide-column database service offered as a serverless solution that is compatible with Apache Cassandra. We will cover it in more detail in Chapter 10.

The next type of nonrelational database is based on a graph data model and is well suited for applications that require complex querying and analysis of interconnected data.

Graph Databases

Graph databases are a specialized type of nonrelational database designed to handle highly interconnected data and complex relationships. They excel at storing, querying, and traversing graph-like structures, making them ideal for scenarios involving social networks, recommendation systems, fraud detection, and knowledge graphs. In this section, we will explore the architecture and design considerations of graph stores, uncovering their key features and advantages.

Data Model

At the heart of a graph store lies the graph data model, which represents data as a collection of interconnected nodes (vertices) and relationships (edges). Each node typically corresponds to an entity or an object, while the relationships represent the connections between nodes. Graph databases store these entities, relationships, and associated properties for efficient traversal and querying of the graph structure. The graph data model offers a natural representation of complex, interconnected data, enabling rich and expressive data modeling.

Unlike traditional databases that focus on data entities and their attributes, graph stores prioritize the relationships between entities. Relationships in graph databases can have properties and can be directed or undirected, allowing for various types of connections. The relationship-centric design of graph stores facilitates queries that traverse nodes and relationships to uncover patterns, paths, and insights within the data.

Data Access and Retrieval

Graph stores provide powerful query languages or APIs specifically designed for exploring and querying graph structures. These languages, such as Cypher (used in Neo4j) or Gremlin (used in Apache TinkerPop), provide a declarative, expressive syntax, allowing users to express complex graph patterns, perform graph traversals, and filter and aggregate data based on relationships and properties.

Graph stores employ various indexing techniques to optimize graph traversal and query performance. They typically use indexes on nodes, relationships, or properties to speed up the lookup of specific elements within the graph. Graph databases often utilize caching mechanisms to store frequently accessed graph elements in memory, further improving query response times. These indexing and caching strategies enable graph stores to efficiently handle complex graph traversals and pattern-matching queries.

Advantages, Trade-offs, and Considerations

Graph databases excel in scenarios where understanding and analyzing the relationships between entities are of primary importance. They are particularly well suited for applications that involve complex relationships, network analysis, and recommendation systems. They find extensive use in social networking platforms, fraud-detection systems, recommendation engines, knowledge graphs, and data lineage analysis.

While graph stores offer powerful graph traversal and querying capabilities, they may face challenges when dealing with massive datasets and complex graph patterns. The performance of graph queries heavily depends on the size and structure of the graph, and certain complex queries may require additional optimization techniques. Graph stores also may not be the best choice for scenarios that primarily involve simple tabular data or that require strong transactional capabilities.

In summary, the architecture and design of graph stores revolve around the graph data model, a relationship-centric design, efficient graph traversal and querying, and scalable distributed architectures. By leveraging the power of graph structures and relationships, these databases enable organizations to store, navigate, and uncover valuable insights within highly interconnected datasets.

Neo4j: Open Source Graph Database

Neo4j (*https://neo4j.com*) is a leading open source graph database known for its powerful graph-processing capabilities and intuitive query language. It is designed to efficiently store, manage, and traverse highly connected data, making it ideal for applications that heavily rely on complex relationships and interconnections.

The features of Neo4j include:

Graph data model
    Neo4j is built around the property graph data model, which consists of nodes, relationships, and properties. Nodes represent entities or objects, relationships define connections between nodes, and properties store key-value pairs associated with nodes and relationships. This flexible, expressive data model allows developers to represent and explore complex relationships easily.

Graph query language
   Neo4j uses Cypher, a powerful, intuitive query language specifically designed for graph databases. Cypher allows developers to express complex graph patterns and perform advanced graph traversals using a familiar, human-readable syntax. It provides rich querying capabilities, including filtering, aggregating, and pattern matching, making it easier to extract meaningful insights from highly connected data.

Scalability and performance
   Neo4j offers excellent scalability and performance for graph data processing. It supports horizontal scaling by distributing the graph across multiple machines in a cluster, enabling high throughput and accommodating large-scale deployments. Neo4j's query optimizer efficiently executes queries, leveraging index structures and caching mechanisms to ensure optimal performance even on massive graphs.

ACID compliance
   Neo4j provides strong ACID guarantees to ensure data integrity and reliability. It maintains strict transactional consistency, allowing multiple operations to be grouped into atomic units of work. This ensures that changes made to the graph are durable and consistent, even when there are concurrent operations.

Native graph processing
   Neo4j is designed from the ground up as a native graph database, allowing it to leverage the power of graph-processing algorithms. It provides a wide range of graph-specific operations, such as shortest path calculations, centrality measurements, community detection, and graph analytics. These built-in capabilities enable developers to perform complex graph analysis and traverse relationships efficiently.

Data visualization
   Neo4j provides visualization tools that help users understand the structure of the graph, identify patterns in the graph data, and gain insights into complex relationships. Visualization enhances the intuitive understanding of the data model and aids in decision-making processes.

With its graph data model, powerful Cypher query language, scalability, performance, ACID compliance, native graph-processing capabilities, vibrant community, and visualization tools, Neo4j empowers developers to build sophisticated applications that leverage the power of relationships and graph data. Whether it's used for social networks, recommendation systems, fraud detection, or knowledge graphs, Neo4j provides a robust foundation for graph-based applications.

AWS offers a fully managed graph database service, Amazon Neptune, which we will cover in more detail in Chapter 10.

Conclusion

As we conclude our exploration of nonrelational databases, we can clearly see that the landscape is rich with diversity. Ranging from key-value stores optimized for rapid operations to columnar stores tailored for analytical prowess and document and graph databases catering to flexible data structures and intricate relationships, each type of nonrelational database offers a unique set of capabilities. We did not cover other database types, such as time-series (e.g., InfluxDB), in-memory (e.g., Redis), text-search (e.g., Elasticsearch), vector (e.g., Milvus), geospatial, or ledger databases, but the number of choices is immense. Choosing a database type should be guided by a deep understanding of your application's requirements, workload characteristics, and growth expectations, as in the decision flowchart in Figure 3-4.

In Chapters 2 and 3, we've looked at different kinds of databases, each with its own special abilities. An application may require a relational database as well as a few nonrelational database types to support a specific use case. Think of these databases as different tools in a toolbox to help us manage data in various exciting ways. Sure, using multiple tools means you must learn how to handle each one, but that's OK. Each tool has its job, and it's important to use the right one for the task at hand. For example, you have to put a nail in the wall, and you have a hammer, wrench, screwdriver, and other tools—you'd choose the hammer in that case. So remember to always pick the right tool for the job instead of trying to make one tool do everything or using all the tools—because it just doesn't work that way!

Table 3-1 provides a summary of the comparison of the characteristics of relational and nonrelational stores covered in Chapters 2 and 3.

Table 3-1. Relational versus nonrelational store

Property	Relational store	Nonrelational store
Data model	Follows a strict schema. Data is stored in tables with a well-defined structure. Adding columns to a defined table can be difficult.	Schemaless. Data is stored without a well-defined table structure. Data can be organized as key-value pairs, JSON, documents, graphs, or wide-column formats, depending on the specific NoSQL design.
Hierarchical storage	Not suited for hierarchical data storage.	Best suited for hierarchical or interconnected data storage.
Scalability	Best suited for vertical scaling.	Horizontally scalable. Can employ techniques like sharding to facilitate handling huge amounts of data.

Property	Relational store	Nonrelational store
Joins	Suitable for queries that require a lot of complex joins across multiple tables.	Joins are possible but involve a lot of computational overhead to perform, especially on a distributed database.
CAP theorem	SQL transactions always comply with ACID properties (strong consistency).	NoSQL databases generally follow BASE properties (eventual consistency).

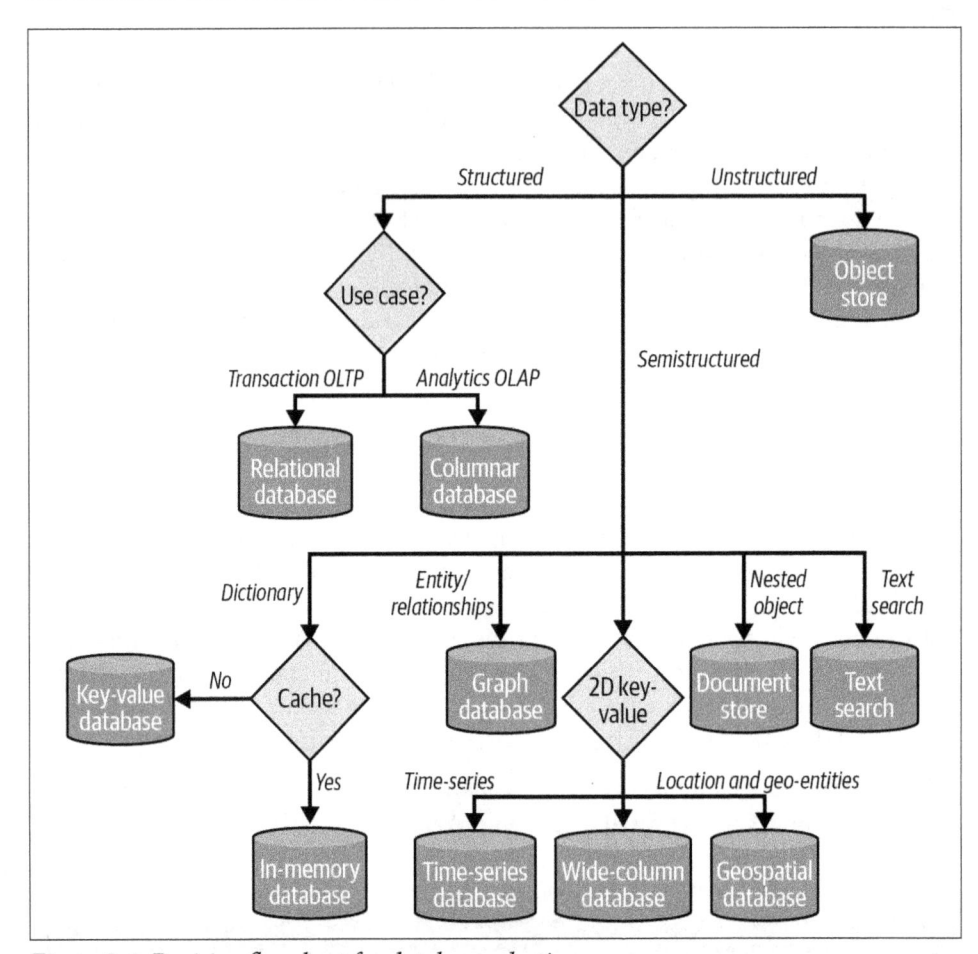

Figure 3-4. Decision flowchart for database selection

We hope you feel equipped with the know-how for using all kinds of databases, along with a basic understanding of which database to choose for which use case. The next chapter will take you on an exploration of caching policies and strategies, which reduce the time required to access frequently accessed data, even from data stores.

CHAPTER 4
Caching Policies and Strategies

In computing, a *cache* is a component or mechanism used to store frequently accessed data or instructions closer to the computing unit, reducing the latency of retrieving the information from slower storage or external resources. In traditional hardware, caches are typically implemented as high-speed, small-capacity memories located closer to the CPU than the main memory. The goal is to improve overall system performance by reducing the time required to access data or instructions.

The concept of caching revolves around the principle of *locality*, which suggests that programs tend to access a relatively small portion of their data or instructions repeatedly. By storing this frequently accessed information in a cache, subsequent access to the same data can be served faster, resulting in improved performance.

When data is accessed from a cache, there are two possible outcomes: cache hit and cache miss. A *cache hit* occurs when the requested data is found in the cache, allowing for fast retrieval without accessing the slower main memory or external resources. A *cache miss* happens when the requested data is not present in the cache, requiring the system to fetch the data from the main memory or external storage. Cache hit rates measure the effectiveness of the cache in serving requests without needing to access slower external storage, while cache miss rates indicate how often the cache fails to serve requested data.

This chapter will cover important information to help you understand how to use data caching effectively. We'll talk about cache eviction policies, which are rules for deciding when to remove data from the cache to make retrieving important data faster. We'll also cover cache invalidation, which ensures the cached data is always correct and matches the real underlying data source. The chapter will discuss caching strategies for both read- and write-intensive applications. And we'll go over how to put caching into action, including where to locate the caches to get the best results.

You'll learn about how caching works and why CDNs are important. Finally, you'll discover two popular open source caching solutions. Let's begin with caching.

Benefits of Caching

Caches play a crucial role in improving system performance and reducing latency for several reasons:

Faster access
> Caches offer faster access times compared to main memory or external storage. Keeping frequently accessed data closer to the CPU can significantly lower cache access times, reducing the time required to fetch the data on average and thus reducing mean access time or latency.

Reduced latency
> Caches decrease latency by reducing the need to access slower storage resources. By serving data from a cache hit, the system avoids the delay associated with fetching data from main memory or external sources, thereby reducing overall latency, which we discussed in detail in Chapter 1.

Bandwidth optimization
> Caches optimize bandwidth usage by reducing the number of requests sent to slower storage. When data is frequently accessed from the cache, that reduces the demand on the memory bus or external interfaces, freeing up resources for other operations.

Improved throughput
> Caches improve overall system throughput by allowing the CPU to access frequently needed data quickly, without waiting for slower storage access. This enables the CPU to perform more computations in a given amount of time.

Amdahl's law and the Pareto distribution provide further insights into the benefits of caching.

Amdahl's law states that the overall speed increase achieved by optimizing a particular component of a system is limited by the fraction of time that component is utilized. Caches, being a critical optimization component, can have a significant impact on overall system performance, especially when the fraction of cache hits is high. Amdahl's law emphasizes the importance of efficient caching to maximize the benefits of performance optimization.

The *Pareto distribution*, also known as the *80/20 rule*, states that a significant portion of the system's workload is driven by a small fraction of the data. Caching aligns well with this distribution by allowing the frequently accessed data to reside in a fast cache, serving the most critical operations efficiently. By focusing caching efforts on the most-accessed data, the Pareto distribution can be leveraged to optimize performance for the most important workloads.

In summary, caches provide faster access to frequently accessed data, reducing latency and improving overall system performance. They optimize bandwidth, increase throughput, and align with principles such as Amdahl's law and the Pareto distribution to maximize performance benefits.

Cache Eviction Policies

Caching plays a crucial role in improving the performance and efficiency of data-retrieval systems by storing frequently accessed data closer to the consumers. Caching policies determine how the cache handles data eviction and replacement when its capacity is reached. Cache eviction policies try to maximize the *cache hit ratio*: the percentage of time the requested item was found in the cache and served. A higher cache hit ratio reduces the need to retrieve data from external storage, resulting in better system performance. In this section, we will explore various caching policies, including Belady's algorithm, queue-based policies, recency-based policies, and frequency-based policies.

Belady's Algorithm

Belady's algorithm is an optimal caching algorithm that evicts the data item that will be used farthest in the future. It requires knowledge of the future access pattern, which is usually impractical to obtain. Belady's algorithm serves as a theoretical benchmark for evaluating the performance of other caching policies.

Queue-Based Policies

Queue-based cache eviction policies involve managing the cache by treating it like a queue. When the cache reaches its capacity, one of the following policies is used to remove data to make space for new data:

First in, first out (FIFO)
 FIFO is a simple caching policy that evicts the oldest data item from the cache. It follows the principle that the first data item inserted into the cache is the first one to be evicted when the cache is full. Note that in traditional FIFO, items are not moved upon access; they are simply added to the queue, when they are inserted in the cache. So once the item is inserted, its position is fixed until it is eventually evicted from the cache. This can lead to premature eviction of items that are still in demand, resulting in the aging problem.

Last in, first out (LIFO)
> LIFO is the opposite of FIFO, where the most recently inserted data item is the first one to be evicted. LIFO does not consider the access pattern and can result in poor cache utilization and eviction decisions.

A real-life use case of FIFO is in print queue management, where FIFO ensures fairness by processing documents in the order they were submitted, evicting the oldest job if the queue gets full.

Recency-Based Policies

Recency-based cache eviction policies focus on the time aspect of data access. These policies prioritize keeping the most recently accessed items in the cache:

Least recently used (LRU)
> LRU is a popular caching policy that evicts the least recently accessed data item from the cache. It assumes that recently accessed items are more likely to be accessed in the near future. LRU requires tracking access timestamps for each item, making it slightly more complex to implement.

Most recently used (MRU)
> MRU evicts the most recently accessed data item from the cache. It assumes that the most recently accessed item is unlikely to be accessed again soon. MRU is effective in scenarios where a small subset of items is frequently accessed and those older items are more likely to be reused.

As a real-life use case example, MRU evicts the most recently accessed pages in web browsers, assuming users are less likely to revisit them immediately and freeing up space for new content.

Frequency-Based Policies

Frequency-based cache eviction policies prioritize retaining items in the cache based on how often they are accessed. The cache replaces items that have been accessed least frequently, assuming that rarely accessed data may not be as critical for performance optimization. Frequency-based policies include:

Least frequently used (LFU)
> LFU evicts the least frequently accessed data item from the cache. It assumes that items with lower access frequency are less likely to be accessed in the future. LFU requires maintaining access frequency counts for each item, which can be memory intensive.

Least frequently recently used (LFRU)
> LFRU combines the concepts of LFU and LRU by considering both the frequency of access and the recency of access. It evicts the item with the lowest frequency count among the least recently used items.

In CDNs that serve frequently accessed static content, LFRU can optimize the cache by balancing recency and frequency. For example, a popular video might be accessed frequently over a short period but become less relevant over time. LFRU would ensure that this video remains in cache as long as it continues to see frequent access while also considering other items that may have gained frequency, making sure that the most valuable content stays available. We will cover CDN architecture in "Content Delivery Networks" on page 108.

Allowlist Policy

An *allowlist policy* for cache replacement is a mechanism that defines a set of prioritized items eligible for retention in a cache when space is limited. Instead of using a traditional cache eviction policy that removes the least recently used or least frequently accessed items, an allowlist policy focuses on explicitly specifying which items should be preserved in the cache. This policy ensures that important or high-priority data remains available, even during periods of cache pressure. By allowing specific items to remain in the cache while evicting others, the allowlist policy optimizes cache utilization and improves performance for critical data access scenarios.

In a web application that serves dynamic content, an allowlist policy can be implemented to retain crucial user-specific data, such as session information or frequently accessed configuration settings. When the cache reaches its capacity, the system prioritizes items on the allowlist, ensuring that critical data remains available while allowing non-allowlisted items to be evicted using a standard eviction strategy like LRU. This mechanism enhances application performance and user experience, particularly during peak usage periods when access to essential data is vital.

Caching policies serve different purposes and exhibit varying performance characteristics based on the access patterns and workload of the system. Choosing the right caching policy depends on the specific requirements and characteristics of the application. By understanding and implementing these caching policies effectively, system designers and developers can optimize cache utilization, improve data-retrieval performance, and enhance the overall user experience. Now, we'll turn to cache invalidation strategies, which are applied after identifying which data to evict based on the cache eviction policies.

Cache Invalidation

Cache invalidation is a crucial aspect of cache management that ensures the cached data remains consistent with the underlying data source. Effective cache invalidation strategies help maintain data integrity and prevent stale or outdated data from being served. The following are four common cache invalidation techniques:

Active invalidation
> Active invalidation involves explicitly removing or invalidating cached data when changes occur in the underlying data source. This approach requires the application or the system to notify or trigger cache invalidation operations. For example, when data is modified or deleted in the data source, the cache is immediately updated or cleared to ensure that subsequent requests fetch the latest data. Active invalidation provides precise control over cache consistency but requires additional overhead to manage the invalidation process effectively.
>
> In a social media application, when a user posts new content, the system actively invalidates the caches of all users' feeds that might contain outdated information. This ensures that everyone sees the most recent updates without delay, providing a fresh and accurate user experience.

Invalidating on modification
> The cache is invalidated when data in the underlying data source is modified. When a modification operation occurs, such as an update or deletion, the cache is notified or flagged to invalidate the corresponding cached data. The next access to the invalidated data triggers a cache miss, and the data is fetched from the data source, ensuring the cache contains the most up-to-date information. This approach minimizes the chances of serving stale data but introduces a slight delay for cache misses during the invalidation process.
>
> In an ecommerce platform, whenever a product's details (such as price, description, or availability) are modified, the corresponding cache entries are invalidated. This prevents users from seeing outdated information and ensures that they always access the latest product data, which is crucial for making purchasing decisions.

Invalidating on read
> The cache is invalidated when the cached data is accessed or the read request is made. Upon receiving a read request, the cache checks if the data is still valid or has expired based on the data version or entity tag (ETag). If the data is expired or flagged as invalid, the cache fetches the latest data from the data source and updates the cache before serving the request. This approach guarantees that fresh data is always served, but it adds latency to each read operation since the cache must validate the data's freshness before responding.

In a news application, when a user reads an article, the system checks if the cached version of that article is still valid. If the article has been updated since it was cached, the cache is invalidated, and the latest version is fetched and served to the user. This guarantees that subsequent readers receive the most current content, especially if updates or corrections are made shortly after the initial publication.

> An *ETag* is a unique identifier assigned to a specific version of a resource on a web server and used for cache validation. When a client requests a resource, it can include the ETag in an `If-None-Match` header to check if the cached version is still valid. If the ETag matches the current version, the server responds with a "304 Not Modified" status, reducing bandwidth usage and improving performance.

Time to live (TTL)

TTL is a cache invalidation technique that associates a time duration with each cached item. When an item is stored in the cache, it is marked with a TTL value indicating how long the item is considered valid. After the TTL period elapses, the cache treats the item as expired, and subsequent requests for the expired item trigger cache misses, prompting the cache to fetch the latest data from the data source. TTL-based cache invalidation provides a simple and automatic way to manage cache freshness, but it may result in serving slightly stale data until the TTL expires.

A weather application may use TTL to cache weather data for a specific duration, such as 30 minutes. After this period, the cached data is considered stale and automatically invalidated, prompting the system to fetch fresh weather information and ensuring that users receive timely, accurate weather updates without overwhelming the data source with requests.

Choosing a cache invalidation strategy depends on factors like the nature of the data, the frequency of updates, the performance requirements, and the desired consistency guarantees. Active invalidation offers precise control but requires active management, invalidating on modification ensures immediate data freshness, invalidating on read guarantees fresh data on every read operation, and TTL-based invalidation provides a time-based expiration mechanism. Understanding the characteristics of the data and the system's requirements helps when selecting the appropriate cache invalidation strategy to maintain data consistency and improve overall performance.

Caching Strategies

Caching strategies define how data is managed and synchronized between the cache and the underlying data source. In this section, we will explore several caching strategies shown in Figure 4-1: cache-aside, read-through, refresh-ahead, write-through, write-around, and write-back.

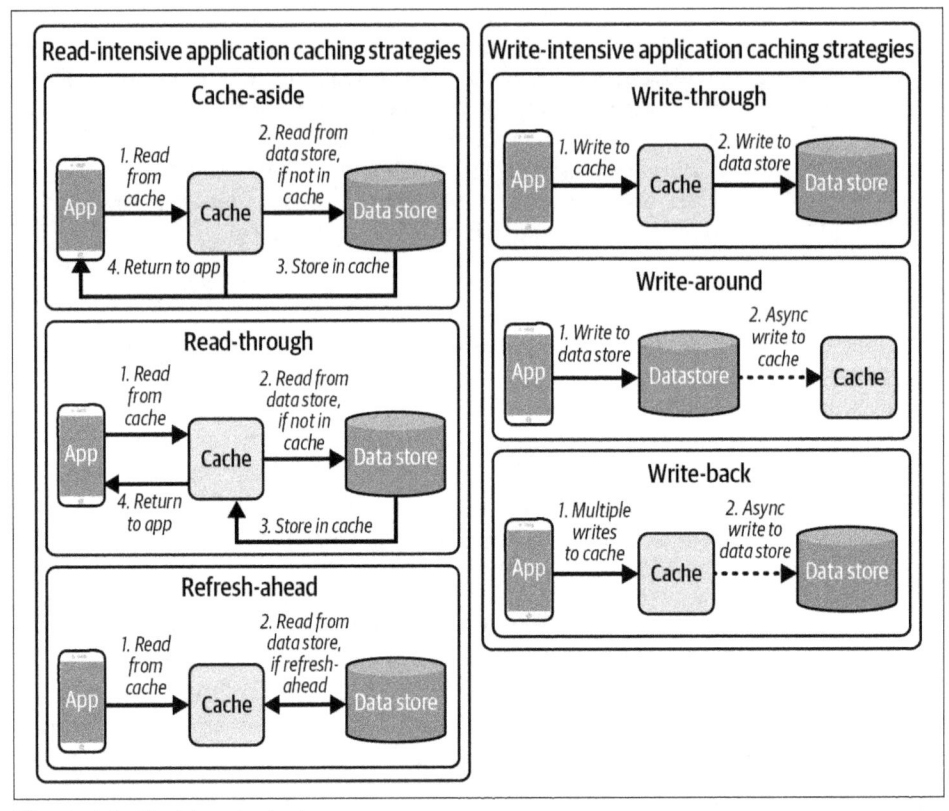

Figure 4-1. Caching strategies

Read-Intensive Strategies

The lefthand side of the diagram displays read-intensive caching strategies, focusing on optimizing the retrieval of data that is frequently read or accessed. The goal of a read-intensive caching strategy is to minimize the latency and improve the overall performance of read operations by serving the cached data directly from memory, which is much faster than fetching it from a slower, more distant data source. This strategy is particularly beneficial for applications where the majority of operations involve reading data rather than updating or writing data. Let's look at these read-intensive caching strategies in more detail.

Cache-aside

The cache-aside caching strategy, also known as *lazy loading*, delegates the responsibility of managing the cache to the application code. When data is requested, the application first checks the cache. If the data is found, it is returned from the cache. If the data is not in the cache, the application retrieves it from the data source, stores it in the cache, and then returns it to the caller. Cache-aside caching offers flexibility because the application has full control over caching decisions, but additional logic to manage the cache is required.

Read-through

The read-through caching strategy retrieves data from the cache if available; otherwise, the cache itself fetches the data from the underlying data source. When a cache miss occurs for a read operation, the cache retrieves the data from the data source, stores it in the cache for future use, and returns the data to the caller. Subsequent read requests for the same data can be served directly from the cache, improving the overall read performance. Unlike the cache-aside strategy, this strategy offloads the responsibility of managing cache lookups from the application, providing a simplified data-retrieval process. While read-through caching enhances read performance once populated, it can initially introduce higher latency during the warm-up period due to cache misses. This can lead to unpredictable P999 latency spikes as the first requests involve longer fetch times from the data source rather than quick retrieval from the cache.

Refresh-ahead

The refresh-ahead caching strategy, also known as *prefetching*, proactively retrieves data from the data source into the cache before it is explicitly requested. The cache anticipates the future need for specific data items and fetches them in advance. By prefetching data, the cache reduces latency for subsequent read requests and improves the overall performance of data retrieval. This strategy results in a better and more predictable P999 latency profile because data is preloaded into the cache. When a user requests the anticipated data, it can be served almost instantly from the cache rather than fetching it from the slower data source. This proactive approach minimizes the likelihood of latency spikes, leading to a more consistent, reliable performance, even under varying load conditions.

Cache warm-up involves preloading data into the cache before it is needed, ensuring that frequently accessed data is readily available. A *cold start* occurs when the cache is empty, requiring the system to fetch data from the underlying source, which leads to higher latency and potential performance bottlenecks as the cache fills. In contrast, a *warm start* involves having data preloaded in the cache, allowing subsequent requests to be served quickly from memory and thereby improving overall application performance.

Write-Intensive Strategies

The righthand side of the diagram in Figure 4-1 displays the write-intensive strategies, focusing on optimizing the storage and management of data that is frequently updated or written. Unlike read-intensive caching, where the focus is on optimizing data retrieval, a write-intensive caching strategy aims to enhance the efficiency of data updates and writes while still maintaining acceptable performance levels. In a write-intensive caching strategy, the cache is designed to handle frequent write operations, ensuring that updated data is stored temporarily in the cache before eventually being synchronized with the underlying data source, such as a database or a remote server, leading to better consistency. This approach can help reduce the load on the primary data store and improve the application's responsiveness by acknowledging write operations more quickly. Let's look at these write-intensive caching strategies in more detail.

Write-through

The write-through caching strategy involves writing data to both the cache and the underlying data source simultaneously. When a write operation occurs, the data is first written to the cache and then immediately propagated to the persistent storage synchronously before the write operation is considered complete. This strategy ensures that the data remains consistent between the cache and the data source. However, it may introduce additional latency due to the synchronous write operations.

Write-around

The write-around caching strategy involves bypassing the cache for write operations. When the application wants to update data, it writes directly to the underlying data source, bypassing the cache. As a result, the written data does not reside in the cache, reducing cache pollution with infrequently accessed data. However, subsequent read operations for the updated data might experience cache misses until the data is fetched again from the data source and cached.

Write-back

The write-back caching strategy allows write operations to be performed directly on the cache, deferring the update to the underlying data source until a later time. When data is modified in the cache, the change is recorded in the cache itself, and the update is eventually propagated to the data source asynchronously on a schedule or when specific conditions are met (e.g., cache eviction or time intervals). Write-back caching provides faster write operations by reducing the number of immediate disk writes.

In addition to improving write latency, write-back caching provides better throughput management, making it capable of handling bursty data traffic. Since write operations are first handled in memory, the system can absorb spikes in write requests without overwhelming the underlying data source. This capability allows for more efficient handling of sudden increases in workload, ensuring that applications remain responsive even during high-demand periods. However, it introduces a potential risk of data loss in the event of a system failure before the changes are flushed to the data source.

Each caching strategy has its own advantages and considerations, and selecting an appropriate strategy depends on the specific requirements and characteristics of the system. By understanding these caching strategies, system designers and developers can make informed decisions to optimize data access and improve the overall performance of their applications.

Cache Deployment

When deploying a cache, various options are available depending on the specific requirements and architecture of the system. There are three common approaches to cache deployment: in-process, interprocess, and remote caching.

In-Process Caching

The cache resides within the same process or application as the requesting component. It is typically implemented as an in-memory data store and is directly accessible by the application or service. In-process caching provides fast data access and low latency. This deployment approach is suitable for scenarios where data sharing and caching requirements are limited to a single application or process.

For example, in web applications, user session data can be cached in memory to quickly retrieve session information without querying the database on each request, allowing for sticky sessions. This is discussed in detail in Chapter 5.

Interprocess Caching

The cache is deployed as a separate process or service that runs alongside the applications or services. It acts as a dedicated caching layer that can be accessed by multiple applications or processes. Applications communicate with the cache using interprocess communication mechanisms such as shared memory, pipes, sockets, or remote procedure calls (RPCs). Interprocess caching improves resource utilization and data consistency across different components. It is well suited for scenarios where data needs to be shared and cached across multiple applications or processes within a single machine.

For example, a financial services application might use Apache Ignite (*https://ignite.apache.org*) to cache transaction data, making it accessible to various components of the application for real-time analytics and reporting. We will cover the design and architecture of a financial application in detail in Chapter 21.

Remote Caching

The cache is deployed as a separate service or cluster that runs on a different machine or location than the requesting components. The cache service is accessed remotely over a network using protocols such as HTTP, TCP/IP, or custom communication protocols. Remote caching can be used to share cached data among different applications or services running on separate machines or even across geographically distributed locations, providing scalability and fault tolerance. Remote caching is suitable for scenarios that require caching data across a distributed system or when the cache needs to be accessed by components running on different machines.

For example, a social media application might use a Redis Cluster (discussed in detail in "Redis" on page 113) to cache user profile information and feed data, ensuring that all application servers can quickly access this information without querying the main database repeatedly. We will cover the design and architecture of a social media application in detail in Chapter 16.

Choosing a Cache Deployment Approach

The choice of cache deployment depends on factors like the scale of the system, performance requirements, data sharing needs, and architectural considerations. These considerations are compared in Table 4-1.

Table 4-1. Comparison of caching-deployment approaches

Approach	Latency	Latency seconds	Description	Use case
In-process caching	Low latency	Microseconds range	In-process caching offers the lowest latency since the cache resides within the same process as the application.	Ideal for scenarios requiring fast access to frequently used data

Approach	Latency	Latency seconds	Description	Use case
Interprocess caching	Moderate latency	Low milliseconds range	Interprocess caching introduces moderate latency due to the need for interprocess communication (IPC) mechanisms.	Suitable for sharing data across multiple applications on the same machine
Remote caching	High latency	Milliseconds	Remote caching has the highest latency since it involves network communication to access a cache that runs on a different machine.	Ideal for distributed applications that require scalability and data sharing across multiple machines

Caching Mechanisms

The following caching mechanisms can be used to improve application performance:

Client-side caching
　Cached data is stored on the client device, typically in the browser's memory or local storage. This mechanism allows web applications to store and retrieve static resources, such as HTML, CSS, JavaScript, and images, directly from the client's device. Client-side caching reduces the need to fetch resources from the server on subsequent requests, leading to faster page-load times and improved user experience.

CDN caching
　Static content is cached on distributed servers that are strategically located across different geographic regions. CDNs serve cached content to users based on their proximity to the CDN server, reducing the latency and load on the origin server. CDN caching is commonly used to cache static files, media assets, and other frequently accessed content, improving the overall performance and scalability of web applications.

Web server caching
　These caching mechanisms are implemented at the server side to store frequently accessed content. When a request is made to the server, it first checks if the requested content is already cached. If found, the server serves the cached content directly, avoiding the need to regenerate the content. Web server caching is effective for static web pages, dynamic content with a long expiration time, and content that is expensive to generate.

Application caching
　Data is cached within the application's memory or in-memory databases. This mechanism is typically used to store frequently accessed data or computation results that are costly to generate or retrieve from other data sources. Application caching improves response times by reducing the need for repeated data retrieval and computation, enhancing the overall performance of the application.

Database caching
   Database caching focuses on improving the performance of database operations by caching frequently accessed data or query results. This mechanism can be implemented at two levels:

   Query-level caching
      Query-level caching stores the results of frequently executed queries in memory. When the same query is executed, the cached result is served instead of querying the database again, reducing database load and improving response times.

   Object-level caching
      Object-level caching caches individual data objects or records retrieved from the database. This mechanism is useful when accessing specific objects frequently or when the database is relatively static. Object-level caching reduces the need for frequent database queries, improving overall application performance.

By employing these caching mechanisms as shown in Figure 4-2, organizations and developers can optimize data retrieval, reduce latency, and improve the scalability and responsiveness of their systems. However, it is essential to carefully consider cache invalidation, cache coherence, and cache management strategies to ensure the consistency and integrity of the cached data.

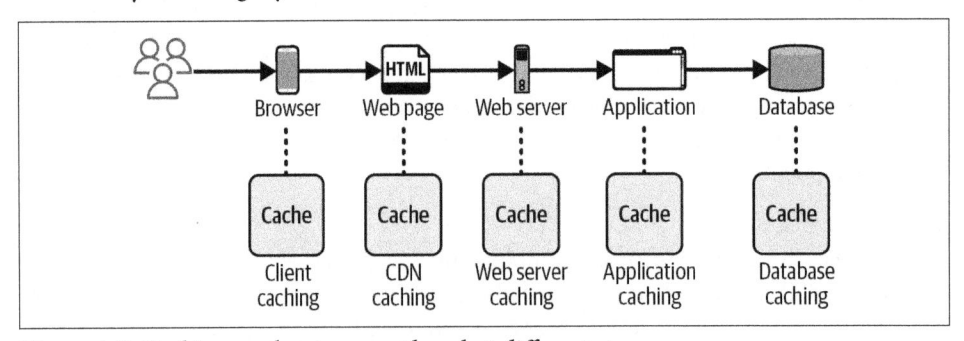

Figure 4-2. Caching mechanisms employed at different stages

Content Delivery Networks

In caching mechanisms, CDNs play a crucial role in improving the performance and availability of web content for end users by caching at edge locations to reduce latency and enhance scalability. CDNs employ various strategies and architectural models to efficiently distribute and cache content across geographically distributed servers. CDNs can be categorized into two main types: push and pull CDNs.

Push CDNs

In a push CDN, content is precached and distributed to edge servers in advance. The CDN provider proactively pushes content to edge locations based on predicted demand or predetermined rules. With push CDNs, content is uploaded only when it is new or changed, reducing traffic while maximizing storage efficiency. This approach ensures faster content delivery because the content is readily available at the edge servers when requested by end users.

Push CDNs are suitable for websites with low traffic or content that doesn't require frequent updates, such as video-streaming platforms like Netflix and Amazon Prime Video (we will cover the design and architecture of these platforms in our use case in Chapter 20 for a streaming service). Instead of regularly pulling content from the server, the content is uploaded to the CDNs once and remains there until changes occur.

Pull CDNs

In a pull CDN, content is cached on demand. The CDN servers pull the content from the origin server when the first user requests it. The content is then cached at the edge servers for subsequent requests, optimizing delivery for future users. The duration for which content is cached is determined by a TTL setting. Pull CDNs minimize storage space on the CDN, but there can be redundant traffic if files are pulled before their expiration, resulting in unnecessary data transfer. Pull CDNs are well suited for websites with high traffic since recently requested content remains on the CDN, evenly distributing the load.

CDN optimization techniques

CDNs employ different optimization techniques to improve the performance of caching at the edge server:

Dynamic content caching optimization
    CDNs face challenges when caching dynamic content that frequently changes based on user interactions or real-time data. To optimize dynamic content caching, CDNs employ various techniques:

Content fragmentation
    Breaking down dynamic content into smaller fragments to enable partial caching and efficient updates

Edge Side Includes (ESI)
    Implementing ESI tags to separate dynamic and static content, allowing dynamic portions to be processed on the fly while caching the static fragments

Content personalization
>Leveraging user profiling and segmentation techniques to cache personalized or user-specific content at the edge servers

Multitier CDN architecture
>Multitier CDN architecture involves distributing content across multiple layers or tiers of edge servers. This approach allows for better scalability, fault tolerance, and improved content delivery to geographically diverse regions. It enables efficient content replication and reduces latency by bringing content closer to end users.

DNS redirection
>CDNs use DNS redirection to direct user requests to the nearest or most suitable edge server based on factors like geographic proximity, network conditions, and server availability, optimizing content delivery and reducing latency.

Client multiplexing
>This technique combines multiple HTTP requests and responses into a single connection between the client and the edge server. This reduces the overhead of establishing multiple connections and improves efficiency, especially for small object requests, resulting in faster content delivery.

Content consistency in CDNs

Ensuring content consistency across multiple edge servers within a CDN is critical for delivering the most up-to-date and accurate content. CDNs employ various methods to maintain content consistency:

Periodic polling
>CDNs periodically poll the origin server to check for updates or changes in content. This ensures that cached content is refreshed to reflect the latest version.

TTL
>CDNs use TTL values, specified in HTTP headers or DNS records, to determine how long cached content remains valid. Once the TTL expires, the CDN fetches updated content from the origin server.

Leases
>CDNs use lease-based mechanisms to control the duration of content caching at the edge servers. Leases define a specific time window during which the content remains valid before requiring renewal or revalidation.

AWS offers Amazon CloudFront, a pull CDN built for high performance, security, and developer convenience, which we will cover in more detail in Chapter 9.

Using a CDN can come with certain drawbacks. CDNs may incur significant costs depending on the amount of traffic, but it's important to compare these costs to the expenses you would incur without utilizing a CDN. If updates are made before the TTL expires, there is the possibility that content may be outdated until it is refreshed on the CDN. CDNs require modifying URLs for static content to point to the CDN, which can be an additional task to manage. Overall, CDNs offer benefits in terms of performance and scalability but require careful consideration of these factors and the specific needs of your website.

Now, we'll look at two popular open source caching solutions to understand their architecture and how they implement the caching concepts discussed in the chapter.

Open Source Caching Solutions

Open source caching solutions have gained popularity because of their efficiency, scalability, and ease of use. Let's take a closer look at Memcached and Redis, two widely adopted open source caching solutions.

Memcached

Memcached is an open source, high-performance caching solution widely used in web applications. It operates as a distributed memory object caching system, storing data in memory across multiple servers. Here are some key features and benefits of Memcached:

Simple and lightweight
    Memcached is designed to be simple, lightweight, and easy to deploy. It focuses solely on caching and provides a straightforward key-value interface for data storage and retrieval.

Horizontal scalability
    Memcached follows a distributed architecture, allowing it to scale horizontally by adding more servers to the cache cluster. This distributed approach ensures high availability, fault tolerance, and improved performance for growing workloads.

Protocol compatibility
    Memcached adheres to a simple protocol that is compatible with various programming languages. This compatibility makes it easy to integrate Memcached into applications developed in different languages.

Transparent caching layer
Memcached operates as a transparent caching layer, sitting between the application and the data source. It helps alleviate database or API load by caching frequently accessed data, reducing the need for repetitive queries.

Cache-aside is the strategy most used with Memcached, allowing applications to manage caching behavior based on usage patterns. The LRU eviction policy is favored for effectively maintaining relevant cached data by evicting the least recently accessed items, ensuring that frequently accessed data remains available.

Memcached's architecture consists of a centralized server that coordinates the storage and retrieval of cached data. When a client sends a request to store or retrieve data, the server handles the request and interacts with the underlying memory allocation strategy.

Memcached follows a multithreaded architecture that enables it to efficiently handle concurrent requests and scale across multiple CPU cores. In this architecture, Memcached utilizes a pool of worker threads that can simultaneously process client requests. Each worker thread is responsible for handling a subset of incoming requests, allowing for parallel execution and improved throughput. This multithreaded approach ensures that Memcached can effectively handle high traffic loads and distribute the processing workload across available CPU resources. By leveraging multiple threads, Memcached can achieve better performance and responsiveness, making it suitable for demanding caching scenarios where high concurrency is a requirement.

In terms of memory allocation, Memcached employs a slab allocation strategy. It divides the allocated memory into fixed-size chunks called *slabs*. Each slab is further divided into smaller units known as *pages*. These pages are then allocated to store individual cache items. The slab allocation strategy allows Memcached to efficiently manage memory by grouping items of similar sizes together. It reduces memory fragmentation and improves memory utilization.

When a new item is added to the cache, Memcached determines the appropriate slab size for the item based on its size. If an existing slab with enough free space is available, the item is stored in that slab. Otherwise, Memcached allocates a new slab from the available memory pool and adds the item to that slab. The slab allocation strategy allows Memcached to store a large number of items in memory while maintaining optimal performance.

Memcached's architecture and memory allocation strategy work together to provide a lightweight, efficient caching solution that can handle high traffic loads and deliver fast data-access times. Memcached effectively leverages memory and employs a scalable architecture, enabling applications to significantly improve performance by caching frequently accessed data in memory.

Redis

Redis, short for Remote Dictionary Server, is a server-based, in-memory data structure store that can serve as a high-performance cache. Unlike traditional databases that rely on iterating, sorting, and ordering rows, Redis organizes data in customizable data structures from the ground up, supporting a wide range of data types, such as strings, bitmaps, bitfields, lists, sets, hashes, geospatial, and hyperlog. This versatility is suited to various caching use cases. Here are some key features and benefits of Redis:

High performance
   Redis is designed for speed, leveraging an in-memory storage model that allows for extremely fast data retrieval and updates. It can handle a massive number of operations per second, making it suitable for high-demand applications.

Persistence options
   Redis provides persistence options that allow data to be stored on disk, ensuring durability even in the event of system restarts. This feature makes Redis suitable for use cases where data needs to be retained beyond system restarts or cache invalidations.

Advanced caching features
   Redis offers advanced caching features, such as expiration times, eviction policies, and automatic cache invalidation based on TTL values. It also supports data partitioning and replication for scalability and fault tolerance. Cache-aside is the most commonly used strategy with Redis, and it supports several eviction policies, such as LRU, LFU, random, and TTL.

Pub/sub and messaging
   Redis includes publish-subscribe (pub/sub) messaging capabilities, enabling real-time messaging and event-driven architectures. This makes it suitable for scenarios involving real-time data updates and notifications.

Redis serves as an in-memory database primarily used as a cache in front of other databases, such as MySQL or PostgreSQL. By leveraging the speed of memory, Redis enhances application performance and reduces the load on the main database. It is particularly useful for storing data that changes infrequently but is frequently requested as well as data that is less critical but undergoes frequent updates. Examples of such data include session or data caches, leaderboard information, and rollup analytics for dashboards.

Redis's architecture is designed for high performance, low latency, and simplicity. It provides a range of deployment options for ensuring high availability based on the requirements and cost constraints.

Availability in Redis deployments

Redis supports different deployment architectures as shown in Figure 4-3, including a single Redis instance, Redis HA (high availability), Redis Sentinel, and Redis Cluster. Each architecture has its trade-offs and is suitable for different use cases and scalability needs.

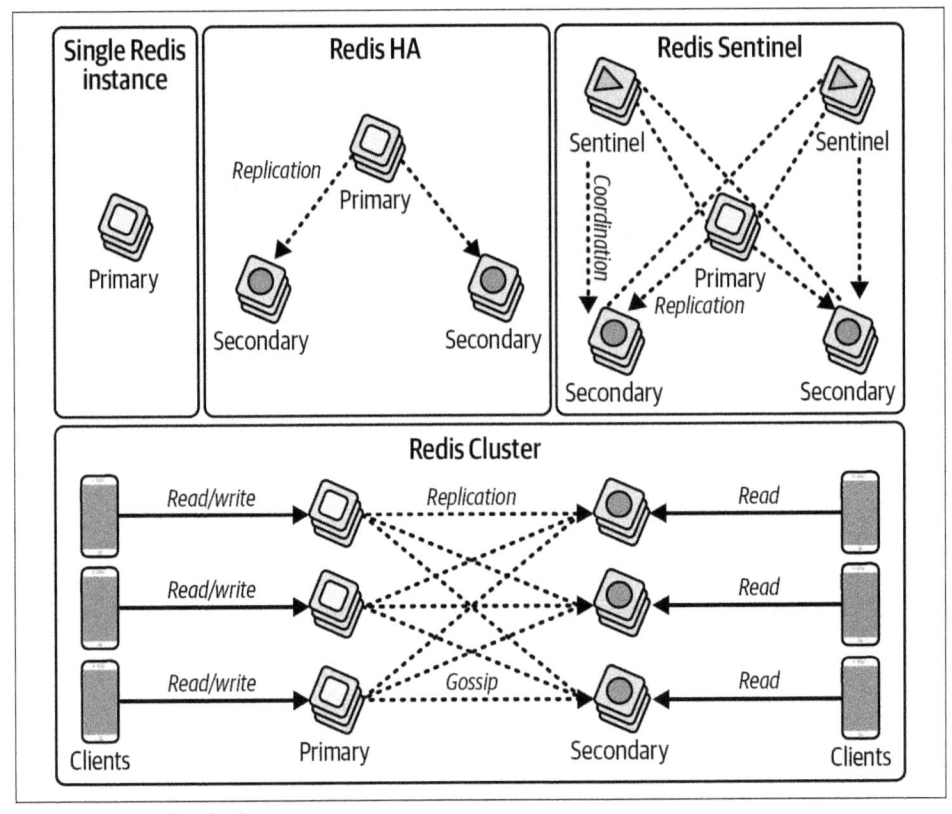

Figure 4-3. Redis deployment setups

In a single Redis instance setup, Redis is deployed as a standalone server. While this is straightforward and suitable for small instances, it lacks fault tolerance. If the instance fails or becomes unavailable, all client calls to Redis will fail, affecting overall system performance.

Redis HA involves deploying a main Redis instance with one or more secondary instances that synchronize with replication. The secondary instances can help scale read operations or provide failover in case the main instance is lost. Replication ID and offset play a crucial role in the synchronization process, allowing secondary instances to catch up with the main instance's data.

Redis Sentinel is a distributed system that ensures high availability for Redis. Sentinel processes coordinate the state and monitor the availability of main and secondary instances. They also serve as a point of discovery for clients, informing them of the current main instance. Sentinel processes can start a failover process if the primary instance becomes unavailable.

Redis Cluster enables horizontal scaling by distributing data across multiple machines or shards. Algorithmic sharding is used to determine which Redis instance (shard) holds a specific key. Redis Cluster employs a hash-slotting mechanism to map data to shards and allows for seamless resharding when adding new instances to the cluster. Gossip Protocol is used in Redis Cluster to maintain cluster health. Nodes constantly communicate to determine the availability of shards and can promote secondary instances to primary if needed.

Durability in Redis deployment

Redis provides two persistence models for data durability: Redis database (RDB) files and append-only files (AOFs). These persistence mechanisms ensure that data is not lost in case of system restarts or crashes.

RDB is the default persistence model in Redis. It periodically creates snapshots of the dataset and saves them as binary RDB files. These files capture the state of the Redis database at a specific point in time. Here are key features of RDB persistence:

Snapshot-based persistence
    RDB persistence works by periodically taking snapshots of the entire dataset and storing them in a file. The frequency of snapshots can be configured.

Efficiency and speed
    RDB files are highly efficient in terms of disk space usage and data loading speed. They are compact and can be loaded back into Redis quickly, making them suitable for scenarios where fast recovery is essential.

Full data recovery
    RDB files provide full data recovery as they contain the entire dataset. In case of system failures, Redis can restore the data by loading the most recent RDB file available.

It's worth noting that RDB files have some limitations. Since they are snapshots, they do not provide real-time durability and may result in data loss if a crash occurs between two snapshot points. Additionally, restoring large RDB files can take time and affect the system's performance during the recovery process.

AOF persistence is an alternative persistence model to RDB files that logs every write operation to an append-only file. AOF captures a sequential log of write operations, enabling Redis to reconstruct the dataset by replaying the log. Here are some key features of AOF persistence:

Write-ahead log
: AOF persists every write operation to the append-only file as a series of commands or raw data. This log can be used to rebuild the dataset from scratch.

Durability and flexibility
: AOF offers more durability than RDB files since it captures every write operation. It provides the ability to recover data up to the last executed command. Moreover, AOF offers different persistence options (such as every write, every second, or both) to balance durability and performance.

Append-only nature
: AOF appends new write operations to the end of the file, ensuring that the original dataset is never modified. This approach protects against data corruption caused by crashes or power failures.

AOF persistence comes with its own considerations. The append-only file can grow larger over time, potentially occupying significant disk space. Redis offers options for AOF file rewriting to compact the log and reduce its size. Additionally, AOF persistence typically has a slightly higher performance overhead compared to RDB files due to the need to write every command to disk.

In practice, Redis users often employ a combination of RDB and AOF persistence based on their specific requirements and trade-offs among performance, durability, and recovery-time objectives. It's important to note that Redis also provides an option to use no persistence (volatile mode) if durability is not a primary concern or if data can be regenerated from an external source in the event of a restart or crash.

> Redis is primarily used for volatile caching, but AWS has introduced Amazon MemoryDB, a Redis-compatible, durable, in-memory database service designed for applications requiring microsecond read and single-digit millisecond write performance. With a focus on data durability and high availability, MemoryDB is ideal for use cases like caching, session management, and real-time analytics. We leave you to explore its features and applications.

Memory management in Redis

Redis leverages forking and copy-on-write (CoW) techniques to facilitate data persistence efficiently within its single-threaded architecture. When Redis performs a snapshot (RDB) or background saving operation, it follows these steps:

1. Redis uses the `fork()` system call to create a child process, which is an identical copy of the parent process. Forking is a lightweight operation as it creates a CoW clone of the parent's memory.
2. Initially, the child process shares the same memory pages with the parent process. However, when either the parent or the child process modifies a memory page, CoW comes into play. Instead of immediately duplicating the modified page, the operating system creates a new copy only when necessary.

By employing CoW, Redis achieves the following benefits:

Memory efficiency
When the child process is initially created, it shares the same memory pages with the parent process. This shared-memory approach consumes minimal additional memory. Only the modified pages are copied when necessary, saving memory resources.

Performance
Since only the modified pages are duplicated, Redis can take advantage of the CoW mechanism to perform persistence operations without incurring a significant performance overhead. This is particularly beneficial for large datasets where copying the entire dataset for persistence would be time-consuming.

Fork safety
Redis uses fork-based persistence to avoid blocking the main event loop during the snapshot process. By forking a child process, the parent process can continue serving client requests while the child process performs the persistence operation independently. This ensures high responsiveness and uninterrupted service.

While forking and CoW provide memory efficiency and performance benefits, there are some drawbacks to consider. Forking can result in increased memory usage during the CoW process if many modified pages need to be duplicated. The fork operation may also be slower on systems with large memory footprints.

Overall, Redis effectively utilizes forking and CoW mechanisms within its single-threaded architecture to achieve efficient data persistence. By employing these techniques, Redis can perform snapshots and background saving operations without significantly affecting its performance or memory usage.

Overall, Redis offers developers a powerful, flexible data storage solution with several deployment options and capabilities.

Both Redis and Memcached are excellent open source caching solutions, each with its own strengths. The choice between them depends on specific requirements and use cases. Redis is suitable for scenarios requiring versatile data structures, persistence, pub/sub messaging, and advanced caching features. Memcached shines in simple, lightweight caching use cases that prioritize scalability and ease of integration.

> AWS offers Amazon ElastiCache, which is compatible with both Redis and Memcached for real-time use cases like caching, session stores, gaming, geospatial services, analytics, and queuing. We will cover it in more detail in Chapter 10.

Conclusion

In this chapter, we have made a comprehensive exploration of the fundamental concepts and strategies that empower efficient data caching. We've covered cache eviction policies, cache invalidation mechanisms, and a plethora of caching strategies, which will equip you with the knowledge to optimize data access and storage. We've delved into caching deployment, learned how strategic placement can maximize impact, and explored the diverse caching mechanisms available. Additionally, we've touched on CDNs and the open source caching solutions Redis and Memcached, which offer robust options for enhancing performance. Incorporating Redis or Memcached into your architecture can significantly improve application performance, reduce response times, and enhance the overall user experience by leveraging the power of in-memory caching.

In the next chapter we will look at scaling and load balancing strategies. Scaling is a pivotal aspect of modern computing that allows systems to handle increased loads gracefully. We will also delve into strategies for load balancing to distribute incoming traffic efficiently. Together, these strategies will empower you to design and maintain high-performing systems that can handle the demands of today's dynamic digital landscape.

CHAPTER 5

Load Balancing Approaches and Techniques

In the quest for scalability and to ensure uninterrupted availability of services, organizations have adopted horizontal and vertical scaling techniques, as discussed in Chapter 1. These methods have addressed some of the scalability challenges, but they do not guarantee continuous service availability. The rapid growth of the internet and the need for modern high-traffic websites to handle hundreds of thousands of concurrent requests necessitate a more robust approach.

When a single server is responsible for handling all incoming requests, it becomes overloaded, which can lead to system failures. To overcome this limitation, we horizontally scale the system. Then, load balancing comes into play to efficiently distribute incoming network traffic across the group of backend servers, often referred to as a *server pool*. This is much like starting up a company on your own and later hiring more people (and distributing the tasks among them) to scale the business.

In this chapter, we will start with understanding different networking components for managing traffic and improving performance. We will then focus on the concept of load balancers (LBs), which play a crucial role in achieving efficient load distribution and ensuring high availability of services. We will delve into the mechanisms of load balancing as well as the various load balancing algorithms employed and their respective strengths and weaknesses. Understanding LBs and their functionality enhances organizations' ability to handle increasing loads, scale their infrastructure, and deliver a seamless experience to their users or clients. Finally, you'll learn about a popular open source load balancing solution. So let's get started with the different networking components.

Networking Components

In the realm of networking and web services, several components play crucial roles in managing and optimizing traffic flow, scaling, enhancing security, and improving performance. Four such components are forward proxies, reverse proxies, LBs, and API gateways, illustrated in Figure 5-1.

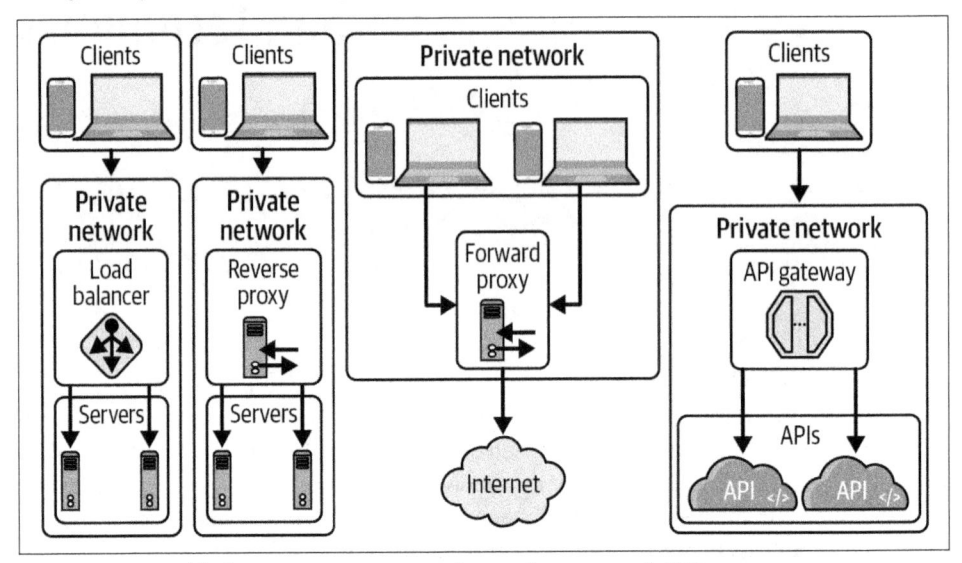

Figure 5-1. Load balancer, reverse proxy, forward proxy, and API gateway

Although they share some similarities, each of these components serves a distinct purpose and operates at a different level within a network architecture. Let's explore the differences between them:

Load balancer
   An LB is a crucial component in network architecture that distributes incoming network traffic across multiple servers to enhance the performance and accessibility of applications, websites, or databases. It plays a dual role: monitoring resource statuses while orchestrating the flow of requests. When a server is unresponsive, is incapable of handling new requests, or exhibits an increased error rate, the LB halts traffic to that server and routes it to another available server. LBs can operate at various layers of the Open Systems Interconnection (OSI) model, including L4 (transport layer) and L7 (application layer), and they use different algorithms to distribute traffic based on factors like server load, response time, and even geographic proximity.

The *OSI model* describes seven layers that computer systems use to communicate over the network, which we will cover in more detail in Chapter 6. AWS offers Elastic Load Balancers (ELBs) in different types as application, network, and gateway LBs, which we will cover in more detail in Chapter 9.

Reverse proxy

A reverse proxy sits as a gateway between the internet and web servers, intercepting incoming requests from clients and routing them to the appropriate backend servers. Reverse proxies are commonly used to improve security by hiding backend server details from clients. They also improve scalability and performance by offloading tasks like Secure Sockets Layer (SSL) termination, content caching, compression, and load balancing from backend servers.

Forward proxy

In contrast to a reverse proxy, a forward proxy acts as an intermediary between client devices and the internet, mediating the traffic in between. When a client sends a request to access a web resource, the request is first intercepted by the forward proxy. The proxy then forwards the request to the internet on behalf of the client. Forward proxies are commonly used to enforce corporate access control policies, filter web content, improve privacy and security by masking client IP addresses, and cache frequently accessed content. Thus, they are often deployed within corporate networks to manage outbound web traffic.

API gateway

An API gateway is a specialized type of reverse proxy acting as a facade that provides a single unified entry point for client applications to access multiple backend services or APIs. API gateways streamline API management by enforcing security policies, rate limiting, authentication, authorization, request and response transformations, protocol translation, and content negotiation. They are commonly used in microservice architectures to abstract complexities and provide a unified interface for client applications. They are useful for managing the API lifecycle, including versioning, documentation, and monitoring.

AWS offers Amazon API Gateway as a fully managed service that makes it easy for developers to create, publish, maintain, monitor, and secure APIs at any scale, which we will cover in more detail in Chapter 9.

Understanding the differences between these networking components is essential for designing robust, scalable, and secure architectures for modern applications and services. Each component plays a distinct role in managing and optimizing traffic flow within a network environment. This chapter will cover load balancing in detail as these other components are integrated along with LBs for additional benefits. Let's first delve into the benefits of load balancing.

Benefits of Load Balancing

Load balancing offers several advantages in the realm of network and application performance:

Scalability
   LBs facilitate the seamless addition and removal of servers to a network, enabling easy scalability as the demand for services grows or decreases. This can be implemented based on autoscaling policies, which we'll discuss in more detail in Chapter 11.

High availability
   With load balancing, applications and websites can maintain high availability by rerouting traffic away from servers that may be temporarily unavailable because of maintenance or other issues.

Enhanced performance
   By spreading incoming traffic across multiple servers, load balancing prevents any single server from becoming overwhelmed. This helps maintain optimal performance (or throughput) and responsiveness (or latency) for users accessing applications or websites.

Improved fault tolerance
   Distributing traffic among multiple servers minimizes the risk of a single point of failure. If one server encounters issues or fails, the LB redirects traffic to healthy servers, maintaining service continuity and leading to high availability.

Optimized resource utilization
   Load balancing ensures that resources are used efficiently by distributing the workload evenly among servers, preventing any from being underutilized or overburdened. The even load distribution can be dependent on the chosen algorithm, but the idea behind an LB is balancing load among all the servers, ensuring their optimal utilization.

Advanced LBs even offer the capability of routing traffic according to users' geographic locations, optimizing performance and adhering to local regulations. Moreover, LBs functioning as reverse proxies can be expanded to serve as a protective shield against specific cyberthreats by scrutinizing incoming traffic and detecting and blocking potentially harmful requests. The feature gaps between services like the LB and the API gateway have narrowed over the years, and the feature set can be very specific to the LB or API gateway solution. We recommend stateless backend servers behind the LB to ensure no data loss when an existing server is removed from the pool. LB deployment strategies also play a pivotal role in ensuring optimal performance, high availability, and efficient resource utilization within complex network architectures.

LB Deployment and Placement Strategies

Load balancing is not just required within a data center network but also can be deployed at both a global and a local scale. The choice between global and local load balancing and the strategic placement of LBs between web servers, application servers, and database servers significantly affect the reliability and responsiveness of distributed systems.

Global Server Load Balancing

Global server load balancing (GSLB) operates at a larger scale, typically by distributing traffic across different data centers or geographical regions. It optimizes the user experience by directing requests to the nearest or most available data center. This strategy is fundamental for serving content to users worldwide, improving performance, and ensuring compliance with regional regulations.

There are three approaches to GSLB:

ADC-based GSLB
    Application delivery controllers (ADCs) are computer network devices in a data center, often part of an application delivery network (ADN) that manages traffic flow to the servers. Some ADCs have a real-time view of the servers and forward requests based on the health and capacity of the data center.

DNS-based GSLB
    GSLB performed by DNS involves analyzing the client's IP location. Whenever a user requests the IP address for a domain name, DNS-based GSLB directs the user to the IP address of the data center geographically nearest to the user's location.

CDN-based GSLB
    GSLB implementation can also be done through CDN, where a global CDN service gathers data from clients' original servers and stores it across a network of servers spread geographically, ensuring swift, dependable distribution of online static content to users across the globe.

Local Load Balancing

In contrast, local load balancing manages traffic within a specific data center or a localized network, functioning akin to reverse proxies. It balances the load among servers within the same geographical region or network segment. This strategy is critical for optimizing internal network traffic, ensuring efficient resource utilization, and maintaining high availability within a specific infrastructure. Clients' requests seamlessly connect to the LB, which operates using a virtual IP (VIP) address.

> A *VIP* is an address not directly tied to a physical machine; instead, multiple machines share the same VIP. If a network interface fails, the packets directed to it are typically lost. However, with a VIP, packets are automatically redirected to a failover machine. Externally, a VIP appears as a singular machine, while internally, a group of machines uses the same address. Typically, DNS queries are answered with VIPs, contributing to seamless rerouting of traffic and ensuring robust failover capabilities.

Normally, an LB operates between the client and the server, receiving incoming network and application traffic and then distributing it among several backend servers using different algorithms. In a three-tier architecture, LBs can be placed between the server instances of the three tiers, as shown in Figure 5-2.

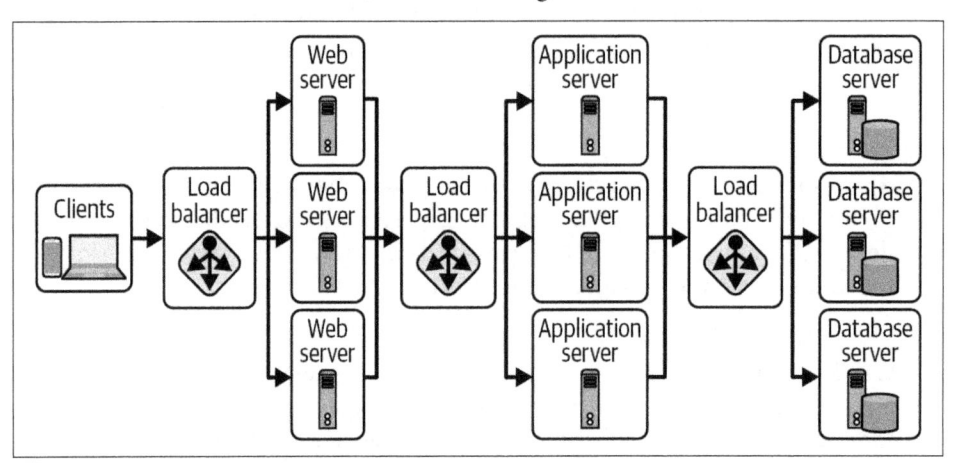

Figure 5-2. Load balancer placements in a three-tier architecture

LBs placed between clients and web servers serve as the entry point for incoming user requests. They distribute web traffic across multiple web servers, optimizing response times and preventing any single server from becoming overwhelmed. This ensures efficient handling of user requests, improving the overall performance and reliability of web-based services.

LBs positioned between web and application servers manage the flow of requests within an application layer. They evenly distribute requests among multiple application servers, ensuring that no single server is overburdened. This setup enhances the scalability, fault tolerance, and performance of applications, effectively handling user interactions and functionalities.

While less common, placing LBs between application and database servers can be beneficial for read-heavy workloads. They can distribute read queries among multiple database servers, optimizing read performance and scaling database operations. Identifying a read versus a write query can be achieved in an application LB (L7) using URL paths, and routing can be done on the same. The routing can also be done based on HTTP methods; for example, `GET /path` is routed to server A and `POST /path` is routed to service B. We'll discuss HTTP methods more in Chapter 6. Load balancing between database servers requires careful consideration because of data consistency and synchronization concerns.

The strategic placement of LBs between different infrastructure layers is crucial for maintaining balance, optimizing resource utilization, and ensuring high availability. Careful consideration of traffic patterns, application requirements, and system architecture is essential for determining the most effective deployment strategy and placement of LBs.

Load balancing as a concept revolves around distributing tasks among available workers, with no single prescribed method of distribution. Consequently, there are multiple load balancing algorithms, each offering a different approach to distributing the workload.

Load Balancing Algorithms

Load balancing algorithms are fundamental to the efficient distribution of incoming traffic across multiple servers. These algorithms can be categorized as static or dynamic. Each offers distinct methods of balancing the load and optimizing resource utilization. Let's explore various load balancing algorithms, their characteristics, and how they influence the distribution of traffic.

Static Load Balancing Algorithms

Static algorithms make load assignments based on existing knowledge of server configurations, disregarding changes in server states at runtime. They are less complex and are typically implemented in a single router or commodity machine where all requests converge. Some well-known static load balancing algorithms include:

Round robin
> This algorithm distributes incoming requests equally among servers in a sequential manner. Each server receives a request in turn, ensuring a balanced workload distribution. However, it doesn't consider server load or response times, potentially leading to uneven resource utilization.

Weighted round robin
   Like round robin, this algorithm assigns different weights to servers based on their capabilities or capacities. The traffic is proportionately divided between the servers based on the weights, making it beneficial for balancing workloads on servers with varying capacities. In most scenarios, though, all the machines in a cluster have identical configurations for consistency, and hence a simple round-robin algorithm is used.

Hash-based algorithms
   These algorithms use specific attributes from the request (like the source IP or content) to generate a hash key, which is then mapped to a server. This ensures that requests with similar attributes are consistently directed to the same server, aiding in session persistence. This algorithm is rarely used because of issues faced when rebalancing servers in the pool: the server mapping needs to be reorganized upon the addition or removal of servers and could lead to some servers getting too much traffic compared to others.

Dynamic Load Balancing Algorithms

Dynamic algorithms make load assignments based on current or recent server states. They engage in communication with servers, incurring communication overhead. Maintaining state information significantly complicates the algorithm's design, resulting in better request-forwarding decisions. Some well-known dynamic load-balancing algorithms include:

Least connections
   Servers with the fewest active connections receive new requests. This algorithm aims to distribute traffic to servers that are less busy, effectively managing the current server load. However, it may not consider server capacity, which can lead to potential load imbalances.

Least response time
   This algorithm directs requests to the server with the quickest response time. It monitors servers' successful response times and channels traffic to the most responsive server, ensuring efficient resource utilization.

Least loaded
   This algorithm assesses the current load on each server and directs new requests to the one with the least load. This dynamic approach ensures efficient resource distribution based on the current server's performance parameters, such as CPU and memory utilization.

Static algorithms have predefined rules for distributing traffic, offering simplicity but potentially leading to uneven server loads. Dynamic algorithms adjust traffic distribution based on real-time server conditions, providing better load balancing but potentially incurring higher processing overhead.

Selecting the appropriate load balancing algorithm depends on the specific requirements of an application or system. Some applications may benefit from static algorithms because of their simplicity, while others, especially those with varying server loads, may find dynamic algorithms more suitable.

Understanding these load balancing algorithms is crucial for optimizing system performance and ensuring the efficient use of resources in diverse network environments. Different scenarios may demand the use of a specific algorithm or a combination of several algorithms to achieve the desired balance in workload distribution.

Session Persistence in LBs

Static and dynamic algorithms must prioritize the health of hosting servers while maintaining a state to store session information for various clients. If session data isn't stored at a lower layer, such as a distributed cache or database, LBs take charge of managing it. In this section, we'll discuss stateful or stateless LBs based on how they handle and manage session information, as shown in Figure 5-3.

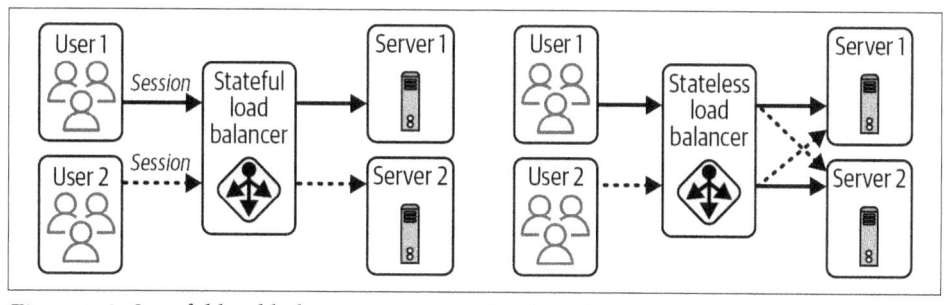

Figure 5-3. Stateful load balancer versus stateless load balancer

Stateful Load Balancers

Stateful LBs, as shown on the left in Figure 5-3, maintain session information, keeping track of the state of each client-server interaction. They store data related to the ongoing sessions, such as session cookies or other session identifiers. This enables the LB to consistently direct subsequent requests from the same client to the server that originally handled the initial request, ensuring session persistence.

Sticky sessions, also known as *session persistence* or *session affinity*, are a mechanism used in load balancing to ensure that a user's requests are consistently directed to the same server within a server farm or a group of servers in stateful load balancing. Sticky sessions achieve this by "sticking" a user's session to a specific server for the duration of their session. After the initial connection, the LB will route subsequent requests from that user to the same server. This can be implemented using various techniques:

Cookie-based session affinity
> The LB uses a session cookie generated during the initial connection to identify and route subsequent requests from the same user to the server indicated in the cookie.

Source IP affinity
> Requests from a particular IP address are consistently directed to the same server. This method can be less effective in scenarios where users are behind network address translation (NAT) or use proxy servers.

Sticky sessions are crucial for maintaining session state, ensuring that all user interactions and data associated with a session remain consistent and available on a specific server, even in a distributed server environment managed by an LB.

The benefits of stateful load balancing include:

Session persistence
> Ensures that all requests from the same client during a session are directed to the same server, maintaining continuity for tasks or interactions that span multiple requests

Efficient handling of stateful applications
> Ideal for applications that require a continuous connection or state information across multiple requests and that should be processed on the same server, such as ecommerce platforms or banking systems

Considerations for stateful load balancing include:

Resource overhead
> Maintaining session information requires additional memory and processing, potentially affecting the LB's performance. This requires extra resources but also saves external resources, such as the database, and it removes the network call to the database, improving the network latency.

Scalability challenges
> The need to maintain the session state across multiple servers can lead to limitations in scaling.

Stateless Load Balancers

Stateless LBs, as shown on the right in Figure 5-3, do not retain session information or state data. Each request is treated independently, and there's no knowledge or tracking of previous interactions between clients and servers. Requests are distributed purely based on the load balancing algorithm without any consideration for session continuity.

The benefits of stateless load balancing include:

Scalability
Stateless LBs are highly scalable because they do not need to maintain session information. Requests can be easily directed to any available server without considering previous interactions.

Simplicity and efficiency
These LBs are generally less complex and can efficiently distribute traffic without the overhead of session management.

The choice between stateful and stateless load balancing depends on the requirements of the application or system. Applications requiring session continuity benefit from stateful LBs, whereas those emphasizing scalability and simplicity are better suited to stateless LBs. A combination of both types is often employed in complex network architectures to address diverse needs.

> Evaluate your business use case before finalizing the solution, but one simple and recommended solution is to use stateless LBs and leverage Redis or a similar data store for session management. We'll discuss a use case for building stateful servers at WhatsApp scale in Chapter 19.

Types of Load Balancers

Understanding the different types of LBs is essential for effectively managing traffic and ensuring seamless application delivery. In this section, we will explore the classification of LBs based on functionality and configuration.

LB Types Based on Functionality

LBs can be categorized based on their functionality into different types, each serving specific needs and requirements. Let's delve into the details of DNS LBs, equal-cost multipath (ECMP) routers, and network and application LBs.

DNS load balancers

DNS LBs distribute traffic at the DNS level by resolving domain names to different IP addresses based on predefined policies, serving as tier-0 LBs. They are easy to set up and can provide basic load balancing functionality but may lack some advanced features compared to L4 and L7 LBs. Some examples of DNS load balancers are Amazon Route 53 and Azure Traffic Manager.

ECMP routers

ECMP routers are a method of load balancing typically used at the network layer as a tier-1 LB. They distribute traffic across multiple paths or links with equal cost, enabling efficient utilization of network resources and providing fault tolerance. ECMP routers operate by hashing packet headers to determine the appropriate path for each packet, ensuring that traffic is evenly distributed among available links. This approach improves network performance and reliability by leveraging multiple paths simultaneously. Some examples of ECMP routers are Cisco Nexus switches and Juniper Networks routers.

Network load balancers (L4 LBs)

Operating at the transport layer (L4) of the OSI model, network LBs handle traffic based on network variables like IP addresses and destination ports. These LBs distribute traffic at the transport level, making routing decisions solely based on network layer information. They primarily handle network-level protocols like IP, TCP, FTP, and UDP. L4 LBs are often implemented as NATs, which distribute traffic among backend servers.

Some features of L4 LBs include:

Session persistence at the IP address level
 L4 LBs can achieve session persistence by maintaining consistency at the IP address level. This ensures that subsequent requests from the same client are directed to the same backend server.

No termination for TCP connections
 Unlike L7 LBs, L4 LBs do not terminate TCP connections. Instead, they forward incoming traffic to backend servers without inspecting the content of the packets. Network LBs are ideal for efficiently managing TCP traffic and are commonly used in scenarios where basic load balancing is sufficient.

L4 LBs operate in the following two modes:

Direct server return (DSR) mode
 In this mode, the TCP connection is established directly between the client and the backend server. The LB changes only the destination MAC address of the packets, allowing backend servers to respond directly to clients. This mode ensures that the LB does not become a bottleneck for outgoing traffic. DSR mode can be useful for scenarios like WebSocket connections and large reply traffic as compared to the request (e.g., downloading an object from Amazon S3).

NAT mode
 Clients connect to the service VIP and the LB forwards packets to backend servers by changing the destination IP address (or DNAT). The LB becomes the

default gateway for backend servers, and all traffic passes through it. This mode limits the output bandwidth to the LB's capacity and hides the backend server information from the clients, enhancing security.

Some examples of network LBs are AWS Network Load Balancer (NLB), Azure Load Balancer, nginx configured as a TCP, and UDP load balancer.

Application load balancers (L7 LBs)

Application LBs operate at the application layer (L7) of the OSI model, enabling them to make routing decisions based on application-specific parameters. These LBs consider factors like HTTP headers, cookies, and content to distribute traffic intelligently, optimizing application performance and enhancing security. Application LBs are well suited for complex applications and environments requiring advanced routing capabilities.

Some features of L7 LBs include:

Distribution based on application layer protocols
L7 LBs distribute requests based on application layer protocols like HTTP. They can further distribute requests based on specific data within the application message and can be used to distribute read and write workloads.

Session persistence with cookies
L7 LBs can achieve session persistence by using cookies to keep track of client sessions. This ensures that subsequent requests from the same client are directed to the same backend server. This can be helpful in scenarios such as ecommerce shopping carts, where a user session is started from wherever the user left off earlier.

Connection termination
To extract HTTP information, L7 LBs terminate the connection at the LB, resulting in two TCP connections: one between the client and the LB and another between the LB and the backend server. One example is SSL/TLS offloading at the load balancer and decrypted traffic being forwarded to the backend servers over HTTP or another protocol. This is helpful for simplifying the processing on backend servers, and backend servers don't need to maintain the SSL certificate for request verification.

Some examples of application LBs are AWS Application Load Balancer (ALB), Azure Application Gateway, and nginx configured as an HTTP LB.

Understanding the differences between these types of LBs is crucial for selecting the appropriate solution based on the specific requirements of your application or infrastructure. Whether you need basic network-level load balancing or advanced application-aware routing, there's an LB type to suit your needs.

LB Types Based on Configuration

LBs can be configured as hardware, as software, or on the cloud. The correct configuration helps with cost-effective scaling, fault tolerance, and seamless integration with your infrastructure, enabling efficient management of traffic and resources. LBs can thus be categorized based on their configuration into two main types: hardware and software.

Hardware LBs

Hardware LBs are physical devices dedicated to load balancing tasks. These appliances require proprietary hardware and are typically deployed in data centers or on-premises environments, operating as standalone units and capable of handling large volumes of concurrent users. While hardware LBs offer high performance and reliability, they can be expensive to procure and maintain. Additionally, their scalability may be limited by the hardware infrastructure. Their configuration can be resource intensive, making them less favorable even for sizable enterprises. Availability might pose challenges because of the need for additional hardware for failover in case of failures. Maintenance and compatibility issues, along with vendor lock-ins, limit their flexibility. Some examples of hardware LBs are F5 BIG-IP Load Balancer, Cisco System Catalyst, and Citrix NetScaler.

Software LBs

Software LBs are implemented as software applications running on standard server hardware or virtual machines. They scale effectively as demands increase, and they ensure availability by enabling the implementation of shadow LBs at minimal extra cost. They offer greater flexibility, scalability, and adaptability than hardware LBs because they can be deployed on commodity hardware or in cloud environments. Software LBs are cost-effective alternatives to hardware solutions and are well suited for dynamic or cloud-based infrastructures. Moreover, these solutions offer predictive analysis to support preparations for future traffic patterns. Some examples of software LBs are HAProxy and nginx.

> In the realm of cloud computing, load balancer as a service (LBaaS) has emerged, where cloud providers offer load balancing services. Users pay according to usage or the service-level agreement (SLA). The key advantages of LBaaSs are ease of use, flexibility, metered costs, and robust auditing and monitoring services, which can enhance business decision making.

Understanding the different types of LBs and their respective characteristics is essential for designing resilient, scalable application architectures. By selecting the appropriate load balancing solution based on functionality and configuration requirements, organizations can optimize resource utilization, enhance application performance, and ensure seamless user experiences.

To close out this chapter, let's dive deeper into one popular open source load balancing solution to understand its details and how it implements the concepts discussed in the chapter.

Nginx: Open Source Load Balancer

Nginx is a high-performance open source web server and reverse proxy server renowned for its efficiency, scalability, and versatility. In addition to its core functionalities as a web server and reverse proxy, nginx serves as a powerful LB, providing advanced capabilities for distributing incoming traffic across multiple backend servers. Nginx's load balancing features include:

L4 and L7 load balancing
  Nginx offers both L4 (transport layer) and L7 (application layer) load balancing capabilities, allowing users to distribute traffic based on various factors, such as IP addresses, TCP/UDP ports, HTTP headers, cookies, and content.

Various load balancing algorithms
  Nginx supports a range of load balancing algorithms to suit different use cases and requirements. These include round robin, least connections, IP hash, and more. Users can configure the desired algorithm to optimize traffic distribution based on factors like server load, response time, and session persistence.

Health checking and failure detection
  Nginx continuously monitors the health of backend servers through configurable health checks. It automatically detects failed or degraded servers and removes them from the load balancing pool, ensuring that traffic is routed only to healthy servers. This proactive approach enhances application availability and reliability.

Dynamic configuration updates
  Nginx allows for dynamic configuration updates, enabling seamless scaling and reconfiguration of load balancing settings without requiring service interruption or manual intervention. This flexibility is particularly beneficial in dynamic or cloud-based environments where infrastructure changes frequently.

Nginx implements the following load balancing concepts, which we discussed in detail in this chapter:

Reverse proxy load balancing
  Nginx serves as a reverse proxy, intercepting incoming client requests and distributing them across multiple backend servers. By offloading tasks like SSL termination, content caching, and compression, nginx enhances security, scalability, and performance of web applications.

HTTP load balancing
> With its comprehensive support for HTTP-based load balancing, nginx can intelligently distribute HTTP requests based on various criteria, such as URL paths, HTTP headers, and cookies. This allows for advanced routing and traffic shaping, improving application performance and user experience.

TCP and UDP load balancing
> Nginx extends its load balancing capabilities beyond HTTP to support TCP and UDP protocols. This enables users to distribute non-HTTP traffic, such as database queries, DNS requests, and gaming traffic, across multiple backend servers, enhancing scalability and reliability for diverse applications.

Session persistence
> Nginx offers session persistence mechanisms to ensure that subsequent requests from the same client are directed to the same backend server. This is achieved through techniques like IP hash load balancing, where requests from a specific client IP address are consistently routed to a particular backend server, maintaining session continuity.

At a high level, configuring nginx as a web server is a matter of defining which URLs it handles and how it processes requests for resources at those URLs. At a lower level, the configuration defines a set of virtual servers that control the processing of requests for particular domains or IP addresses.

Here is what a simple nginx configuration looks like:

```
http {
    upstream backend_servers {
        server 10.0.0.1:8080;
        server 10.0.0.2:8080;
        server 10.0.0.3:8080;
    server 10.0.0.4:8080;
    }

    server {
        listen 80;
        server_name example.com;

        location / {
            proxy_pass http://backend_servers;
            # Additional proxy settings can be configured here
        }
    }
}
```

In this example configuration, nginx is configured as a reverse proxy and LB. Incoming HTTP requests to the domain *example.com* are proxied to a pool of backend servers defined in the upstream block. Nginx distributes the requests across the backend servers using its default round-robin load balancing algorithm.

Nginx shines as a versatile and powerful open source web server, serving as a potent LB. Whether it's managing web applications, API services, or other networked systems, nginx ensures scalability, reliability, and performance optimization for modern distributed architectures.

Conclusion

This chapter provided a comprehensive overview of load balancing, touching on its benefits, deployment strategies, placement techniques, algorithms, session-persistence mechanisms, and various types of LBs distinguished by their functionality and configuration. We've seen how load balancing plays a pivotal role in enhancing system performance, scalability, and fault tolerance, making it an important component of modern system design. Understanding the intricacies of load balancing equips you with the knowledge necessary to architect robust, resilient systems capable of efficiently distributing workloads across resources.

As we transition to the next chapter on communication networks and protocols, we'll embark on a deeper exploration of the underlying mechanisms that facilitate data exchange in distributed systems. Through an examination of the OSI model and synchronous and asynchronous communication types, as well as an analysis of protocols such as RPC, REST, GraphQL, WebRTC, and more, you will gain insight into the diverse landscape of communication technologies. This understanding will be instrumental to designing and implementing effective communication strategies that underpin the seamless operation of interconnected systems for large-scale system design.

CHAPTER 6
Communication Networks and Protocols

How do you know what's going on in someone's mind? You ask them. You might simply say, "I believe something is troubling you, and sharing it might help to take the burden off your mind." This is a simple exchange of words that we call *communication*. There can be different ways to communicate. For example, in this scenario, the conversation might have happened in person or via a messaging application or a phone call in a language you both understand. We very briefly introduced you to the concept of communication in Chapter 1. In this chapter, we'll extend the idea of communication in much more detail.

The internet has changed a lot over time, and many solutions have been built to solve new problems that we encounter while communicating over the internet. It is important that there are guidelines or mechanisms to ensure that people and machines can work with one another. We'll begin our discussion with communication models to strengthen our understanding of communication over the internet adhering to certain rules, which are called *protocols*. You may have seen a lot of keywords floating around, such as TCP, XMPP, WebSockets, WebRTC, HTTP, GraphQL, REST, and so on. It can be very confusing to figure out what these terms mean and in which scenarios they should be used. This chapter will help you gain an understanding of communication-related terms, and we'll identify the correct scenarios for using a particular technology.

Communication Models and Protocols

The first thing that you need to communicate with another person is a common language that you both can understand and use to convey your messages. This common language has a set of rules, generally referred to as *grammar*, and these rules define how you speak and write. A similar analogy applies in machines: for machines to communicate over the internet, they follow certain rules, referred to as *communication protocols*. There are different communication protocols operating at different layers in the communication model. The layers in a communication model represent how data travels from one location to another across the internet in a reliable way. The layers also ensure that data transforms from one form to another so that it can be understood by both humans and machines. We'll talk about two such models—Open Systems Interconnection (OSI) and Transmission Control Protocol and Internet Protocol (TCP/IP)—and then we'll discuss the protocols.

OSI Model

The *OSI model* is a reference model that divides the communication network into seven layers, with each layer responsible for performing a specific job. The top layer is an application layer (L7), and the bottommost layer is a physical layer (L1). L7 corresponds to data on how humans perceive, such as plain English language, and L1 corresponds to data on how machines perceive, such as binary format. For any communication to happen, the data travels through the OSI model layers from top to bottom and bottom to top, as described in Table 6-1.

We'll explore the example protocols in Table 6-1 in the following sections.

Table 6-1. OSI model

Layer number	Layer name	Layer function
Layer 7	Application layer	L7 has direct access to the user data, and the software application relies on it via protocols like HTTP, SMTP, SSH, and so on. This layer is also helpful in service advertisement, such as which services are available over the network to connect.
Layer 6	Presentation layer	This layer is responsible for formatting, encryption, decryption, and compression of data. Formatting ensures that L6 is able to format the data as expected by L7. If the data is in encrypted format, L6 decrypts the data before passing it on to L7 or encrypts the data before passing it on to L5 (if encryption is a requirement). To reduce the data footprint, L6 compresses the data before passing it on to L5.
Layer 5	Session layer	This layer is responsible for the session lifecycle: initiation, maintenance, and termination.
Layer 4	Transportation layer	This layer is responsible for data transport between the devices via protocols like TCP and UDP. It also helps with data buffering, error control, and windowing. It figures out an optimal speed for data communication between the sender and receiver so that a receiver with a slow connection receives the data at the required speed. The extra data can be buffered in a buffer queue so that it can be delivered at the speed needed. In case the buffer queue is full, the new data segments are dropped, referred to as *tail drop*. The layer can request data retransmission if any data segments are lost to ensure reliable connection in the case of the TCP protocol. The windowing feature identifies the amount of data that can be transferred before expecting an acknowledgment from the receiver.
Layer 3	Network layer	This layer is responsible for data transfer between the networks with the help of logical addressing, such as IP addresses. L4 breaks down the data into smaller chunks, called *data packets*, before passing it on to L3.

Layer number	Layer name	Layer function
Layer 2	Data link layer	This layer transfers data between devices, from the incoming network interface to the outgoing network interface, in the form of frames (packets are further broken down into data frames). This layer has two parts: • *Medium access control (MAC)* helps with the physical addressing of devices involved in network communication. The MAC address of any device is globally unique and can identify the device for data delivery. • *Logical link control (LLC)* helps with flow control and error control. The flow and error control in this layer is inside the same network as compared to L3, where it is across different networks.
Layer 1	Physical layer	The data frames from L2 are converted to bit streams (in the form of ones and zeros) in L1. This layer involves the physical devices, such as cables and switches.

In modern-age internet applications, we don't see an OSI model being practically present; it serves only as a reference communication model. In general, internet communications happen via the TCP/IP model. The TCP/IP model layers don't match one-to-one with the OSI model layers, but there are quite a few similarities.

TCP/IP Model

The *TCP/IP model*, also referred to as the *internet protocol suite*, mainly includes TCP, IP, and UDP. The TCP/IP model combines multiple layers of the OSI model into one layer to execute similar functionality; the layers in the two models are compared in Table 6-2.

Table 6-2. Different layers of the OSI and TCP/IP models

OSI model layer	TCP/IP model layer	TCP/IP protocol examples
Application, presentation, session	Application	SMTP, HTTP
Transport	Transport	TCP, UDP
Network	Internet	IP, ICMP
Data link	Data link	IEEE 802.2
Physical	Physical network	Ethernet

> See the RFC documentation (*https://oreil.ly/3nu3W*) for a deeper dive into each of the protocols discussed in this chapter. You can search for the documentation in your favorite search engine with keywords like "TCP protocol RFC documentation." We've linked the TCP documentation (*https://oreil.ly/vZHMC*) for reference.

Different protocols operate at different layers in the communication models. We'll discuss the more general ones to help you gain an understanding of how communication over the internet works, starting with the network layer protocols such as IP, and we'll learn how different protocols are used for specific communication purposes.

Network layer protocols

The most used protocol in the network/internet layer is the *Internet Protocol (IP)*. It is a set of rules responsible for delivering data packets from a source IP address to a destination IP address. (We'll discuss IP addresses and their types more in Chapter 9.) The IP address uniquely identifies the source and destination of data packets across the network and helps routers to route this information from one place to another. Data across the internet is often broken into chunks (referred to as *fragmentation*) to avoid the burden of delivering large packets and to reduce latency. There is also a limit to the maximum size of a packet (1,500 bytes for ethernet) that can be transmitted over the network interface: the *maximum transmission unit (MTU)*.

Each packet in IP protocol contains an IP header and payload. The IP header has the source IP address and the destination IP address, along with any other metadata (such as IP version, packet size, and TTL) required to route the packet. The payload consists of actual data (called *IP datagrams*) that is to be transferred over the network.

Another protocol that operates on this layer is the *Internet Control Message Protocol (ICMP)*. This protocol is generally used for network diagnostics and implementing error mechanisms. For example, to check if Google servers are responding to traffic, we can use the command `ping google.com` (the command output is included here as reference). Let's say the *google.com* URL is not resolved to a server; the router can respond with an ICMP message to the sender:

```
PING google.com (142.250.74.206) 56(84) bytes of data.
64 bytes from fra24s02-in-f14.1e100.net (142.250.74.206): icmp_seq=1 ttl=116
64 bytes from fra24s02-in-f14.1e100.net (142.250.74.206): icmp_seq=2 ttl=116
64 bytes from fra24s02-in-f14.1e100.net (142.250.74.206): icmp_seq=3 ttl=116
```

The network layer protocols in general work in conjunction with transport layer protocols, such as TCP and UDP, for data delivery.

Transmission Control Protocol

The *Transmission Control Protocol (TCP)* is a transport layer protocol that offers reliable communication between sender and receiver with the capability of retransmitting data in case of packet loss. Communication via TCP is initiated between the sender and receiver via a three-way handshake process shown in Figure 6-1. The three-way handshake process is an agreement between the two parties to send and accept the data. The TCP header includes information like the source and destination port numbers, sequence number (identifies how much data is sent during a session), acknowledgment number (used at the receiver end to send an acknowledgment and a request for the next segment), and window (the number of bytes a receiver can accept from a sender).

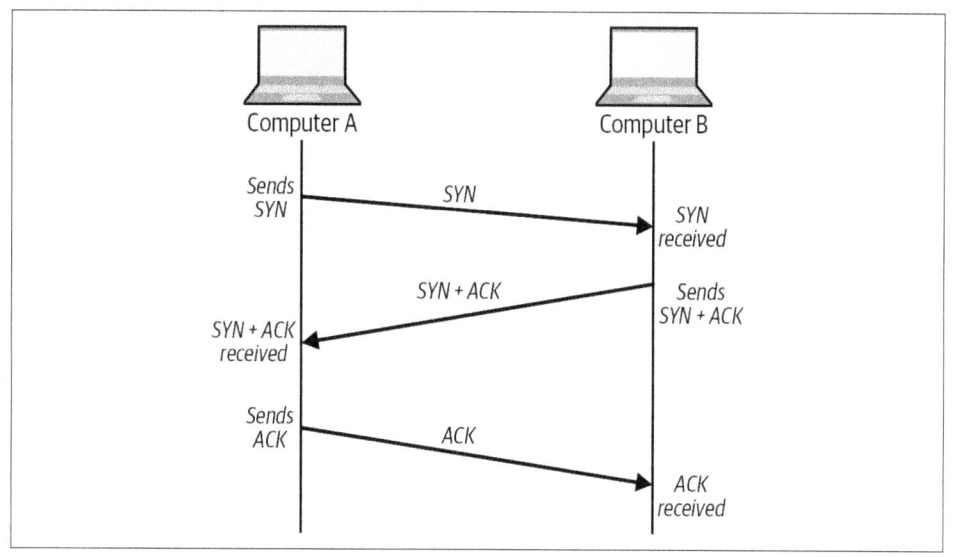

Figure 6-1. TCP three-way handshake process

Once the connection is established after a successful handshake, the protocol needs to figure out the optimal amount of data (window size) that can be transmitted before waiting for an acknowledgment (ACK), ensuring available bandwidth utilization and data transfer without network congestion. This is achieved by two mechanisms: slow start and congestion avoidance (*https://oreil.ly/kNVMG*).

The data transfer begins with a small data size (one segment in a congestion window) —hence the term *slow start*—and the sender gradually increases the window size in an exponential manner (the window is increased by one segment on every ACK). The maximum allowed data transfer size depends on the advertised window size by the receiver. If the allowed internet bandwidth is surpassed, the intermediate router (or the receiver) discards the data packets. Congestion is detected if there are connection timeouts or if duplicate ACKs are received. Congestion avoidance kicks in to deal with these dropped packets, and the congestion window size is halved and set to one segment for timeout scenarios.

We recommend deploying applications in closer vicinity (the same geographic region) to improve performance. Closeness reduces the number of network hops and improves the round trip time (RTT), helping the sender quickly adjust the congestion window size for any congestion occurrence.

A connection has both a source and a destination port for communication. A *port* is a virtual point managed by an OS that defines an entry to or exit from a software application (numbered from 0 to 65535). You can compare them to your personal computer ports, such as USB ports. Each port is responsible for certain types of network communication, and the role is assigned based on the range it falls into. The following are the three divisions of range from 0 to 65535:

Well-known ports
    Ports with numbers from 0 to 1023 are called *well-known ports* (*https://oreil.ly/raByZ*) (also known as *system ports*). These ports are used by system processes and controlled by the Internet Assigned Numbers Authority (IANA) (*https://oreil.ly/MZMMP*). For example, Port 22 is used for Secure Shell (SSH) (*https://oreil.ly/TFmzf*), and Port 80 is used for HTTP (*https://oreil.ly/J5p9j*).

Registered ports
    Ports with numbers from 1024 to 49151 are called *registered ports* (*https://oreil.ly/3QPN1*) (also known as *user ports*). These ports are used by user processes. For example, Port 1194 is used for OpenVPN (*https://oreil.ly/gc6GS*). Both well-known and registered ports are also referred to as *nonephemeral ports* and are assigned by IANA.

Ephemeral ports
    Ports with numbers from 49152 to 65535 are called *ephemeral ports* (also known as *private* or *dynamic ports*). These ports are not controlled by IANA and can be used for private or temporary purposes.

We described the additional work, such as establishing communication or retransmitting lost packets with TCP, that comes with the extra cost of latency. If there are no such requirements, we can go with another transport layer protocol: *User Datagram Protocol (UDP)*.

User Datagram Protocol

Some business use cases where latency (real-time communication) is more important than dropping packets include voice and video calls, live event streaming, gaming, and DNS. The UDP transport protocol is less reliable but faster than TCP and works for these use cases. It is faster because it doesn't involve a three-way handshake process for establishing a connection, and it provides no guarantee of data delivery, so there is no overhead of retries.

The UDP header includes information like the source and destination ports, length, UDP checksum, and data. The UDP header is not as heavy as the TCP header as it holds the minimum data for segment delivery and doesn't provide assurance of the order of segments (data received at the receiver might not be in the same order as sent by the sender). However, not having a three-way handshake between the sender and receiver to start communication can present a security threat. To illustrate how this works, let's first discuss the steps in communicating via UDP:

1. A sender sends a UDP segment to a destination on a specific port.
2. The receiver checks if the request is expected by any application on that port. If yes, then the request is consumed by the application for further processing.
3. If no, the receiver responds with an ICMP packet mentioning that the destination is not reachable.

Given that this processing happens at a large scale, some bad actors can intentionally bombard UDP requests to the server so that server resources are entirely consumed in responding to the requests, causing denial of service to actual traffic. We need to add mechanisms to our systems to mitigate these kinds of issues. One way could be to ignore these requests after a configured threshold by not responding with ICMP messages. The downside of this approach is potentially dropping actual customer requests, but at least we'll be able to keep our system healthy. Another way could be to leverage third-party applications offered by cloud providers, such as AWS Shield (*https://aws.amazon.com/shield*).

Both TCP and UDP serve their purposes, and you should choose based on your business requirements. We prefer TCP for reliability and full-duplex (bidirectional) communications, and UDP for faster response times and unidirectional communications.

The layer operating on top of the network layer is the application layer in the TCP/IP model. Let's dig deeper into a few application layer protocols, starting with HTTP.

Hypertext Transfer Protocol

The world heavily depends on the internet for day-to-day work, and most of this work happens in web browsers and software applications running on mobile devices. Communications over the internet generally follow the client-server model, where a client requests some information (an HTTP request) and the server responds with data (an HTTP response) corresponding to the request on port 80 (port 443 for HTTPS, a secure version of HTTP). To gain more familiarity with how the protocol works, take a look at an example HTTP request for retrieving customer orders based on order ID:

```
GET /api/orders?id=23234555&customerId=dhfsd348e48ddd HTTP/1.1
Host: api.myFoodApp.com
Authorization: Bearer MyAccessToken
User-Agent: MyOnlineFoodOrderApplication/1.0
Accept: application/json
HTTP/1.1 200 OK
Content-Type: application/json
{
  "orderId": "23234555",
```

```
    "customerId": "dhfsd348e48ddd",
    "amount": 199,
    "currency": "INR",
    "items": [
      {
        "product": "Paneer Tikka Masala",
        "quantity": 1,
        "price": 119
      },
      {
        "product": "Tandoori Roti Butter",
        "quantity": 3,
        "price": 80
      }
    ],
    "address": "House 740, 1st Block, Koramangala, Bengaluru",
    "status": "Delivered"
}
```

> The request responses included in this chapter are for illustrative purposes only and were not tested in the production environment.

The HTTP request contains details like the HTTP method (GET in this case), version (1.1), and host specifying where the request is being routed to with the required authentication mechanism. We can specify different HTTP methods (GET, HEAD, POST, PUT, DELETE, CONNECT, OPTIONS, TRACE, PATCH) based on the type of call to the server. The following are the most widely used methods:

GET *method*
: Used to retrieve data without any state modification inside the system (ensures idempotent nature). For example, retrieve order details based on order ID and customer ID.

POST *method*
: Used to create a new resource on the server or send any data for processing and is nonidempotent in nature. For example, place a food order and complete the transaction.

PUT *method*
: Used to update any resource on the server and is idempotent in nature. For example, update the address after placing an order.

DELETE *method*
: Used to remove any resource from the server and is idempotent in nature. For example, delete a saved address entry.

> The POST, PUT, and DELETE method APIs should be idempotent in nature, but the actual nature of the APIs still depends on the developer's code. Follow the general guidelines of idempotent nature based on method type to avoid unintended system behavior.

Next to the HTTP method is the request target specifying the location on the host (server) that the client is trying to access. HTTP has evolved, and the version represents which particular specification the application is using. Older versions are deprecated. The most used versions these days are:

HTTP/1.1
: The most widely used version, HTTP/1.1 offers better support to previous versions, such as reuse of TCP connections to make multiple requests.

HTTP/2
: HTTP/2 optimizes the header to be available in a compressed format (less bandwidth compared to HTTP/1.1), with a single TCP connection for a domain and server push capability to avoid any polling from clients for asynchronous calls (we will elaborate on this in upcoming sections).

HTTP/3
: HTTP/3 improves speed (compared to HTTP/2) by using UDP instead of TCP/IP protocols, also referred to as *QUIC (Quick UDP Internet Connections)* (*https://oreil.ly/uQ7fx*). Therefore, it avoids occasional TCP/IP congestion problems by implementing a congestion control algorithm.

There can be some additional metadata as part of the request, referred to as the *HTTP header*. It can include information like the user agent (where the request is being made from, such as a software application or web browser name), accept (the type of content format expected from the server), and so on.

The HTTP response includes the response to the request (order details for order ID and customer ID). Alongside the response object, it has the HTTP status code. The status code represents what happened with the request. For example, "200 OK" means the request was successfully processed by the server. The status codes range from the 100 series to the 500 series and are listed in Table 6-3.

Table 6-3. HTTP response status codes

Status code series	Status code meaning and examples
100	For informational purposes, such as noting that the server has received the request and it is in processing. • 100: Continue • 101: Switching protocols
200	Notes that the request has been successfully processed by the server. • 200: OK with the response associated with the corresponding request • 201: The request has been processed by the server, and a new resource has been created.
300	The server has redirected the request to another resource for fulfilling it. • 301: The resource has moved permanently to a new location, and the client should update the references on its end. The location header in the response contains the updated URL reference. • 302: The resource has temporarily moved to a new location.
400	There was an issue in the client request that should be rectified before sending it to the server. • 400: The request is not as expected for the server request target. • 401: The request doesn't contain valid credentials for authentication. • 403: The client is not authorized for the request. • 404: The requested resource is not available on the server.
500	The server encountered an error while the request was being processed. • 500: The server encountered some unexpected exception while processing the request. • 503: The server is temporarily unavailable to take client requests.

HTTP is a general protocol for application communications over the internet. Some protocols are designed to solve specific use cases, such as *Simple Mail Transfer Protocol (SMTP)* for email communications.

Simple Mail Transfer Protocol

Email access was directly tied to personal computers in the early days, and an email software application needed to be installed on the computer to download emails for reading. The limitations of this approach included having to own a personal computer (not so common in the early days of the internet), setting up email clients (which could be complex), and synchronizing across the devices. The solution was a web-based email client launched by Hotmail as a free service in 1996.

The software applications interact via application layer protocols like SMTP for email services and forward the communication flow through other layers in the TCP/IP model. The SMTP protocol is used for email communications between two or more parties. Let's look at an example (shown in Figure 6-2) of how a person can send an email via different mail agents.

The SMTP client identifies the mail domain (such as *gmail.com*, *hotmail.com*, etc.) and then establishes a two-way stateful transmission channel to the corresponding

SMTP server(s) to transfer mail. The connection is initiated via SMTP commands, and the server replies to corresponding commands with success or failure. The SMTP server can be the destination of mail delivery, or it can be an intermediate server to forward the mail. When the sender and receiver belong to different domains (for example, email from *gmail.com* to *hotmail.com*), the intermediate server is called a *relay server*.

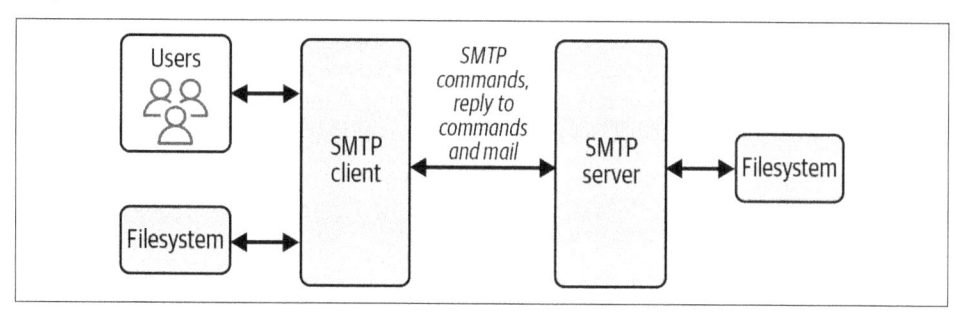

Figure 6-2. Email communication via SMTP

Let's compare this to physical mail delivery: you've gone to the local post office and mailed two letters—one to be delivered in your own town and another to be delivered to a friend in a nearby town. The first letter can be delivered without involving any other post office, but in the case of the second, the letter is transferred to the post office of the nearby town and then delivered to your friend. Because our delivery agents can't directly go to other towns to deliver letters, we require another post office in between—the relay server, in the case of SMTP—to bear this responsibility.

The SMTP server can also behave as a *gateway*, meaning that further transport of mail is carried out with the help of other protocols, not via SMTP. SMTP clients and servers are also referred to as *mail transfer agents (MTAs)* because they offer the mail transfer service. SMTP commands (*https://oreil.ly/rpweI*) are used for communication between the parties, and replies include a success or failure acknowledgment corresponding to the commands sent.

We often add media to emails as attachments, which are not inherently supported by SMTP. For these purposes, we use *Multipurpose Internet Mail Extensions (MIMEs)*. The MIME protocol makes SMTP extensible to support media attachments and conversion of non-ASCII characters to 7-bit ASCII characters (English language alphabets and numbers). Recall that we described ports very briefly when discussing TCP—SMTP operates on Port 25 for plain-text communications and Port 587 for encrypted mail communications.

SMTP essentially operates on a push mechanism, transferring email contents from clients to servers. There are two other protocols, Post Office Protocol (POP) and Internet Message Access Protocol (IMAP), that specifically work on the pull mechanism, retrieving the email from servers to send to user devices. POP connects with the email servers, downloads the content to the local machine, and deletes the emails from the server. IMAP directly reads from servers without downloading content to the local machine or deleting the emails after reading. Both these protocols have their benefits. POP is fast because the message is predownloaded for reading, but since the messages are deleted from the servers, we can't read the same emails on different devices. IMAP allows us to read emails on any number of devices, but it is not as fast as POP.

We've discussed protocols designed specifically for email communications, but email communications are not near real time. Next, we'll move to the *Extensible Messaging and Presence Protocol (XMPP)*, which offers near real-time communication over the internet.

Extensible Messaging and Presence Protocol

XMPP (*https://xmpp.org*) is an instant message protocol based on Extensible Markup Language (XML) with additional features, such as presence information (noting when a user is online or offline) and a contact list (called a *roster*). XMPP helps keep communication near real time among users by streaming XML *stanzas* (a fundamental unit of communication in XMPP with message and recipient information) over a persistent TCP or HTTP connection. XMPP can be operated in a more efficient manner using WebSockets (*https://oreil.ly/4DbrQ*) as a subprotocol (we'll discuss this shortly) instead of HTTP binding (*https://oreil.ly/hlzDp*) since WebSockets are inherently built for bidirectional communications. This protocol can operate in asynchronous fashion as well, which essentially means the recipient user doesn't have to be online. This can be helpful in use cases like notification broadcasting.

The lifecycle of an XMPP connection starts with the client initiating a TCP connection with a server on Port 5222 for plain text and 5223 for encrypted communications. The next steps are:

1. The client sends a stream header to start the negotiation process for stream features, such as authentication mechanisms and encryption methods.

2. After negotiation, the client shares credentials for authentication depending on whether that was agreed to during the negotiation process.

3. The client binds to a resource. This enables unique identification with the use of a Jabber ID, which we'll explain shortly.

4. The client can establish a session (if needed) by sending a session request to a server.

5. Once a session is established, the client shares the presence information with the server. Now the client can request a roster and continue with sending or receiving messages via XML stanzas.

6. As with any other protocol, the connection is terminated at the end of the session once requested by the client and acknowledged by the server.

XMPP is a decentralized protocol—meaning anyone can host XMPP servers—and works like SMTP. Every user has a unique ID referred to as a *Jabber ID* (JID—note that XMPP was previously known as Jabber), which is like an email address. The JID is denoted by a unique user ID along with the domain name (e.g., *myUserId@example.com*). The user may log in from multiple devices, which can be represented by specifying the resource identifier, such as *myUserId@example.com/mobile*.

XMPP is a widely used protocol for chat applications; for example, you may have used or heard about the WhatsApp chat application. WhatsApp is built on top of ejabberd (*https://oreil.ly/7asN1*), an open source software application written in the Erlang programming language (*https://erlang.org*) that operates over XMPP.

Message Queuing Telemetry Transport (MQTT) (*https://oreil.ly/nO5UU*) is another real-time protocol that we'll discuss next.

Message Queuing Telemetry Transport

As its name suggests, MQTT was originally designed for applications to send telemetry data to and from space probes using minimum resources. The MQTT protocol is heavily used for IoT device communication and can support messaging applications as well. MQTT is based on the pub/sub model: users send messages to a topic (publish) and receive them by subscribing to topics. The publishers and subscribers are completely independent of one another, and the pub/sub actions are facilitated by MQTT brokers, as shown in Figure 6-3.

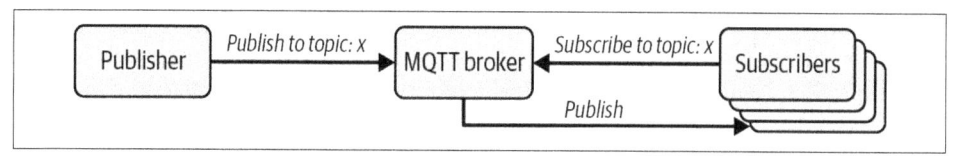

Figure 6-3. MQTT architecture

MQTT supports bidirectional communications between the devices and the cloud and offers multiple quality of service (QoS) (*https://oreil.ly/Ir-vL*) levels for ensuring message delivery guarantees. The QoS levels are defined separately by the publisher (to publish a message to a topic) and the subscriber (to consume a message from a topic). The three QoS levels supported by MQTT are:

At most once—QoS Level 0
    QoS 0 is based on the principle of "fire and forget." The sender publishes a message only once (no retransmission), and the consumer doesn't acknowledge receiving a message for confirmation. QoS Level 0 is simplest to implement as no guarantees need to be ensured for message delivery.

At least once—QoS Level 1
> QoS 1 ensures the message is delivered to the subscriber at least once, so there is a possibility of duplicate messages, and the subscriber should appropriately handle that. The publisher waits for an acknowledgment of message delivery and retransmits the message if the acknowledgment is not received within a certain time frame. This level is intermediary between Level 0 and Level 1 in terms of both reliability and implementation.

Exactly once—QoS Level 2
> QoS 2 guarantees "exactly once" message delivery to the recipients. This is achieved by four-part verification between the publisher and subscriber for every message (thus reducing efficiency and complicating the implementation).

We can select the QoS levels based on the efficiency and reliability requirements. QoS 0 is most efficient but least reliable, while QoS 2 is most reliable but least efficient.

Protocols are essentially a set of rules to establish communication among the involved parties. In the next section, we'll discuss the different communication types available over the internet and how we can use them as necessary for our business needs.

Communication Types

We briefly touched on the general idea of synchronous (sync) and asynchronous (async) communication in Chapter 1. In synchronous communication between two parties, the first party requests some data and then waits for the response from the second party. In the case of asynchronous communication, the first party requests some data but doesn't wait for the response. The second party can respond in the near future via events or any other mechanism. Both the sync and the async modes of communications have their own sets of challenges and benefits, and it's very important that we identify when to use which for our business use cases.

Sync communications are generally preferred for low-latency calls: we're aware that the server will return the response for the corresponding request within the expected time frame and won't take too long. The premise is that if we already know the request is going to take time to process, then we're blocking a system resource at the client's end and not performing any actual work. Note that using async mode doesn't mean the system is latency heavy—the request can be processed as soon as it is consumed by the service here as well. The fundamental difference lies in the method of communication.

With async calls, the response is not immediately returned for a request nor is it returned over the same connection. There are two ways to receive a response in the near future: either the client sends a request to the server again after some time, requesting a response, or the server delivers the response without the client needing to request it. The first mechanism is referred to as a *pull-based* mechanism, and the second is called a *push-based* mechanism.

There can be multiple methods of communication in the pull- and push-based mechanisms. We'll discuss them one by one, beginning with the pull-based approaches—namely, HTTP regular polling and HTTP long polling.

Pull Mechanism: HTTP Polling

Let's take an example of an online food-ordering platform to understand the different kinds of pull mechanisms. Once an order is placed, we want to know its status, such as order preparation is ongoing, a delivery agent is assigned, the delivery agent has picked up the food, the delivery agent is at a particular location, and finally, food is delivered at our doorstep. Table 6-4 lists different approaches that the client application can take to request the latest status of the order from the server application.

Table 6-4. Pull-mechanism approaches

Approach	Approach considerations
HTTP regular polling: 1. Clients ask the server for a recent status at regular intervals, such as five seconds. 2. The server checks the status and responds back.	Clients regularly invoke an API and might not get a response, wasting network bandwidth. We don't recommend this approach for production workloads as it will consume unnecessary resources.
HTTP long polling: 1. Clients ask the server for a recent status at regular intervals, such as one minute. 2. The server responds only if there is a change in status; otherwise, it holds the connection for a fixed interval, such as one minute. 3. The client reestablishes the connection after this interval to check for the most recent status.	This requires fewer server calls compared to HTTP regular polling, reducing overall resource consumption; hence, the approach is an improvement over HTTP regular polling. Implement an exponential strategy in case a response is not received in the first call. For example, you might have seen how Gmail responds when there's no internet connection. First, it tries to connect within 1 second, then within 5 seconds, then 30 seconds, and so on.

The next set of approaches that we're going to discuss are push-based mechanisms, which essentially means that clients don't ask for a response; it's the server's responsibility to send a response once the results are ready.

Push Mechanism: WebSockets

In HTTP long polling, the connection is terminated after a certain time, and then the client reinitiates a connection. But what if we require a persistent connection? WebSockets (*https://oreil.ly/p6xfg*) represent a bidirectional persistent connection (full-duplex communication on a single TCP connection) over HTTP where clients and servers communicate with each other. Once the connection is established between the client and server, the messages can flow to and fro. A popular example for these kinds of requirements is a chat application (architecture details are given in Chapter 19).

Two people (or more, in the case of user groups) interact with each other in real time, so a persistent connection makes more sense here compared to the client application asking for a response again and again.

The WebSocket connection follows a similar flow as TCP. Any connection is started with a handshake process, and then the actual data transfer happens. The handshake process before data transfer ensures the agreement between the client and the server for bidirectional communication. The first step is that the client initiates an HTTP GET call (see the following code snippet) to the host server with the Connection type set as Upgrade and a Sec-WebSocket-Key (random base64-encoded key) (*https://oreil.ly/YrUen*) for ensuring security:

```
GET ws://myChatApp.com/chat HTTP/1.1
Host: myChatApp.com
Connection: Upgrade
Upgrade: websocket
Sec-WebSocket-Version: 13
Sec-WebSocket-Key: q4xkcO32u266gldTuKaSOw==
```

Once the server receives this request, it responds with HTTP status code 101, meaning the protocol is switched from HTTP to WebSocket. This is shown in the following code snippet:

```
HTTP/1.1 101 Switching Protocols
Upgrade: websocket
Connection: Upgrade
Sec-WebSocket-Accept: skjfdPPEKjdksejsl+sdr=
```

The server also responds with Sec-WebSocket-Accept, created by the server by appending a predefined GUID (258EAFA5-E914-47DA-95CA-C5AB0DC85B11, as defined in RFC 6455) to Sec-WebSocket-Key, hashing it to the SHA-1 algorithm (*https://oreil.ly/sZ2hk*) and encoding it to base64.

When the server acknowledgment is received, the WebSocket connection is established for the client and server to communicate with each other. The communication messages can be in textual or binary format following a frame structure. A frame should always be masked before sending to the server—if not, the connection is closed by the server upon receiving an unmasked frame. The masking key is 4 bytes long and should be randomly generated to mask the message payload. The masking key and payload are XOR (*https://oreil.ly/duwH5*) together to generate a masked frame, and the reverse process is performed by the server to retrieve the original payload.

The frame consists of payload data and additional metadata, such as whether the frame is masked or not (denoted by 1 or 0), payload length, and masking key. The payload data is a combination of extension data and application data. The application data consists of the original message, and extension data is an optional field that can help achieve additional capabilities, such as encryption and compression. Finally, the connection between client and server is torn down at the end of the communication.

Now, we might not always have a requirement for bidirectional connection. We may just require a communication channel from server to clients. We'll discuss this idea in the next section, where we elaborate on server-sent events (SSEs).

Push Mechanism: Server-Sent Events

Let's go back to our example of checking the status of an order we placed on an online food-ordering application. SSE can be a feasible approach in this case as the server is responsible for updating the order status and no such input is required from the client's end. The server is not dependent on any message-delivery acknowledgments from clients—if there is such a requirement, SSE might not be the best fit for that use case. SSE is implemented over a long-lived HTTP connection to consume any updates or notifications from the server in text format. We define an EventSource in a client application, which includes the URL of the SSE event stream on the server, and any new event is delivered to this EventSource via the event stream.

> SSE is also used in messenger applications much like WebSockets; for example, BlackBerry Messenger (BBM) and LinkedIn (https://oreil.ly/9zlxR) messaging and live video interactions work on SSE as an underlying technology.

We discussed that the network is not reliable in Chapter 1, and due to this unreliability, a long-lived HTTP connection can always break. In these kinds of scenarios, we need the ability to reestablish the connection from where we left off so as to continue consuming the events from the server. SSE has this capability built in: it can reestablish dropped connections and recover any messages that might have been missed by the clients during the connection issue.

We mentioned that responses in the case of async architectures can be delivered via WebSockets or SSE. Yet another way could be publishing a response to a topic that clients have subscribed to or delivering a response to the HTTP endpoint exposed by the client. This mechanism is widely used for server-to-server communication for callbacks (the response of the API is delivered asynchronously). We'll elaborate on this idea in Chapter 8 while discussing pub/sub architectures, and in Chapter 12 while discussing Amazon Simple Queue Service (SQS) and Amazon Simple Notification Service (SNS).

Up to this point, we've looked at different networking protocols and mechanisms for communication over the internet. With networking protocols, there are common communication standards (protocols or architectural styles) that are generally followed in the client-server architecture. Let's take a closer look at this.

Common Communication Protocol Standards

In the client-server architecture, clients interact with servers to retrieve some information or perform an action on the server. Consider a scenario where each client and server defines its own paradigms for interaction over the internet—it becomes very difficult for software applications to adapt and implement a vast set of paradigms. This can be easier if the client-server calls are commonly defined and everyone uses them. In this section, we'll explain the concept of an *application programming interface (API)* and its multiple types to identify how they suit particular business use case requirements. An API enables two software applications to communicate over the internet using a set of definitions and protocols. We'll start our discussion with RPC and then explore other paradigms.

Remote Procedure Call

Typically, a single machine can't hold all the necessary implementation logic, so part of the code is hosted somewhere else, which may or may not be owned by your company. In the example of fulfilling an order on an online food-ordering application, the frontend application calls the backend service to place an order, the backend service talks with the payment service to process the payment in the desired payment mode, the payment service talks with external providers like a bank or payment gateway (PG) to process the payment, and finally, the order is placed. Now, consider the interaction of our own payment service with a PG: the PG is not owned by us, but we invoke the payment-processing method similarly to how we call any local method in our codebase. This is referred to as *Remote Procedure Call (RPC)*.

A *procedure* is a block of code responsible for executing a specific set of tasks. It can be as simple as a program adding two numbers or, in this case, processing a payment via a PG. RPC means executing this piece of code, aka the procedure, on a remote machine as if it were being executed on your local personal computer or laptop. Now, let's understand why we need such a mechanism and discuss how this remote code execution works.

If the code is hosted on a remote machine, the one definite benefit we get is code reusability and scalability. The code can be shared among multiple clients, offering abstraction to the clients on the code execution, and it is scalable such that the code can be distributed among multiple machines. It additionally abstracts out the network communication for how the local machine interacts with the remote machine to execute a procedure; for a developer, it's similar to any local procedure call. There can be multiple teams in an organization that might own up to hundreds of microservices written in different programming languages. We define the interfaces, and RPC helps with cross-language and platform support by taking on the headache of data marshaling (encoding) and unmarshaling (decoding).

Recall that while discussing the benefits of RPC, we mentioned that the different microservices might be written in different programming languages, so it's not possible to invoke the remote function directly. We need an intermediary that can handle this conversion logic—this is referred to as *stub*. A stub function offers a similar interface as a remote method that clients can invoke, and it internally handles the implementation details, such as network communication and marshaling of method arguments to a message over the network. On the server side, the stub function will unmarshal the message to the arguments as expected by the remote method. Once the method processing is complete, the method response is again marshaled and sent back over the network where the client-side stub function unmarshals it to an object that is readable by the client machine.

The common interface or a contract to specify the remote procedures and data types is defined in the interface definition language (IDL). This interface is language agnostic, meaning it will work with any desired programming language. The IDL is used to generate the stubs used for client communication. Some examples include the Web Services Description Language (WSDL), which is used with Simple Object Access Protocol (SOAP), and the Apache Thrift IDL.

While there are benefits to RPC, there are also downsides since we're operating in a distributed environment. Some of the issues we might face here, which we don't have to consider with local method invocation, are worrying about network latency, handling network failures and retry mechanisms for network calls, and ensuring the interfaces are compatible as systems evolve.

Some examples of RPC include SOAP (*https://oreil.ly/72X4-*), Representational State Transfer (REST), gRPC (*https://grpc.io*), and Thrift (*https://thrift.apache.org*). *SOAP* is a protocol that offers mechanisms to clients and servers for communicating with one another using XML messages. SOAP is not tied to any specific protocol and can be used alongside other protocols, such as HTTP, SMTP, and TCP, although it is mostly used with HTTP. SOAP is relatively complex with its XML-based structure, and it has its own learning curve. You won't find many new use cases being developed via this protocol. Developers tend to lean toward simpler paradigms, such as REST, over SOAP for application development and interaction over the internet.

REST

REST is widely used alongside the HTTP protocol for client-server interactions and uses HTTP methods to implement different CRUD (create, read, update, and delete) operations. REST is a software architectural style, not a protocol like SOAP, and is used extensively for building applications for today's internet.

The following are the guiding principles of the REST design pattern:

- Communication over REST APIs includes the clients, the server, and resources. The *resource* is a fundamental entity that can be uniquely identified by a URL. The clients can interact with the server to perform any operation on these resources via HTTP methods.
- REST operates over a stateless paradigm, meaning the server is not responsible for maintaining the state of older requests. The state maintenance (if required) should be handled by the client, and all relevant information should be part of the HTTP request in order for the server to process it.
- It is possible that responses to particular REST APIs don't change too frequently. In these kinds of scenarios, the responses can be cached at the client's end, at the browser level, or using a CDN or any other caching mechanism.
- There is a uniform interface between the components involved in information transfer following standardized ways for communication. This ensures that it's easy to evolve the capability of the software application. Key factors include unique resource identification, resource update via representations (the client and server communicate to update a resource in formats such as plain text, JSON, XML, or HTML), self-descriptive messages (the server should share relevant information in response in order for it to be processed by the client), and hypermedia as the engine of application state (clients should be able to navigate through the resources via hyperlinks present in the server response).
- Multiple systems can be involved in gathering information. The client is abstracted out from these multiple layer calls inside the system and is only responsible for sending requests to the first layer (such as an LB, API gateway, or any other service endpoint) and gathering a response from it.
- The server can deliver code on demand in the form of scripts in response to client requests, and clients can execute it per requirement.

Note that the APIs following these standards are referred to as *RESTful APIs*.

> We'll explore LBs, API gateways, NAT, IP addresses, and related networking concepts in Chapter 9.

As REST can operate with JSON, it's simple for developers to work with. SOAP is known for its support for advanced security features, typed data, and procedures (SOAP allows RPCs similar to local procedures), but it comes with higher complexity. We can definitely introduce advanced security aspects in REST as well, though that

156 | Chapter 6: Communication Networks and Protocols

requires extra design considerations that SOAP is inherently built to support. As always, it varies from use case to use case, and there is no perfect choice.

The REST architectural pattern operates on a fixed schema defined by the server, but in some cases, we might look for flexibility in the way that the client can define data needs. Let's explore this idea in more detail in the next section where we talk about GraphQL.

GraphQL

GraphQL is an API query language that allows clients to write a query specific to data retrieved on a single API endpoint (unlike REST, where we define endpoints per API). To compare GraphQL with REST, let's look at an example: we want to retrieve a food item's name and description to show items that are available from a particular restaurant on an online food-ordering application. With REST, we'll require an API that can return these exact details or use an API that returns complete information about the food item and shows only the required information on the application (similarly, there can be cases where we need to combine data from multiple APIs). There can be scenarios of overfetching or underfetching data with REST, which can be resolved by the query flexibility offered by GraphQL, in addition to a few other features that we'll discuss shortly. Querying only the required data consumes only the necessary network bandwidth, which can make applications faster on slower networks.

Now that you have a fair idea of GraphQL's advantages over REST, let's dig a little deeper into how it works. GraphQL has a strong type system to define the entities supported via the client's query, which are written in the GraphQL Schema Definition Language (SDL). Let's extend our previous example to show how it can be supported via GraphQL:

```
type Restaurant {
  id: String!
  name: String!
  rating: Float
  foodItems: [FoodItem!]!
}

type FoodItem {
  id: String!
  name: String!
  rating: Float
  isVeg: Boolean!
}
query {
  Restaurant (id: "lsoa34444lsoa") {
    name
    foodItems {
      name
```

```
        description
      }
    }
  }
```

We defined two objects in SDL to support our example: `Restaurant` and `FoodItem` (the exclamation mark [!] denotes a mandatory attribute). To gather data on food items, the query specifies only the attributes required by the client.

> Visit the GraphQL documentation (*https://graphql.org/learn*) for full information on GraphQL.

Moving forward, querying (data read) is not the only capability we need with the APIs; we also need support for operations such as creating, updating, and deleting data (data modification on server data stores). GraphQL supports these operations with a feature called *mutations*. The mutations start with a mutation keyword with syntax similar to GraphQL queries. Let's look at an example mutation of creating a new food item for a restaurant:

```
mutation {
  createFoodItem(name: "Paneer Tikka Masala", isVeg: true) {
    id
    name
  }
}
```

Mutations can also send a response similar to a GraphQL query. Along with performing its main job of data modification, as in the previous example, the mutation will return the ID and name of the newly created food item as part of the response.

We might also be interested in knowing about any new changes happening on the server side. For this, we can leverage technologies such as SSE or WebSockets, which we discussed earlier in this chapter. We can also use GraphQL subscriptions (defined by the `Subscription` keyword), which inherently establish a bidirectional connection to inform us about any new events in near real time, such as if a new food item is created. GraphQL queries, mutations, and subscriptions are defined in the GraphQL schema and offer clients insights into the API capabilities.

One of the benefits of GraphQL over REST is its integration with a single endpoint and the fact that it serves all the API needs with the same API endpoint, instead of multiple endpoints. As our system evolves, it's possible that frontend applications will need to interact with multiple backend applications to gather the necessary data, and each backend application exposes its own GraphQL endpoint. This can be optimized by choosing a GraphQL client like Apollo (*https://apollographql.com*) or

AWS AppSync (which we'll discuss in Chapter 12) to help applications scale with much more ease.

Web Real-Time Communication

People around the world interact with one another over text messaging, voice calls, or video calls. Text messaging is simple to implement and operate compared to voice and video calls. Think of a scenario where you're interacting with your friend on a video call: what do you expect experience-wise from the video-calling application? The primary expectations are that you're able to see your friend clearly and to hear their voice without any lag. WebRTC (which stands for Web Real-Time Communication) offers a mechanism for supporting audio and video communications in web browsers or mobile applications by APIs without requiring installation of any specific plug-ins. It also offers support for file sharing and data exchange between the web services in near real time.

Up to this point, all the protocols or architectural patterns we've discussed have included a server, and we focused our discussion on client-server communication. WebRTC allows direct peer-to-peer connection without any requirement for a server in between. Even though peers can communicate directly, a server can be introduced if the need arises (such as to ensure secure communication). A key consideration to note is that the latency can increase substantially if the number of peers communicating with one another increases to double digits—for example, a voice channel on Discord servers (*https://oreil.ly/u1Ya1*) with a thousand members.

WebRTC is not itself a protocol—it's a tool working on top of multiple protocols to serve our use case. Some APIs offered by WebRTC include RTCPeerConnection for establishing connections between the peers, getUserMedia to access audio and video from a user's device, and RTCDataChannel for bidirectional data exchange between the peers. Let's take a look at how the peer-to-peer connection is established.

For communication over the internet and connecting with another device, we require the IP address and the port number. It becomes difficult if the devices are behind a NAT (more details on this in Chapter 9). In these kinds of scenarios, WebRTC can use Interactive Connectivity Establishment (ICE), which helps figure out the optimal communication route. We don't require ICE if it is not a direct peer-to-peer connection and our system operates on a client-server architecture.

To communicate with any device, we need a unique address. This might not be possible if you're operating inside a private network behind a NAT (all devices in this network will have the same public IP address and are distinguished by assigned private IP address). The Session Traversal Utilities for NAT (STUN) protocol (*https://oreil.ly/ABUGB*) is used if the devices are behind a NAT. Both the peers connect with the STUN server to figure out the IP address, port (allocated by NAT corresponding to the private IP address and port), and type of NAT the device is behind. Once this information is obtained, it will be used as part of the Session Description Protocol (SDP) (*https://oreil.ly/ZTpvz*), as shown in Figure 6-4.

The two peer devices exchange ICE candidates (network address and port) with each other via a signaling mechanism such as SDP. SDP includes information like media type (audio or video), transport protocol (UDP, IP, etc.), media format, remote address, and port for the media.

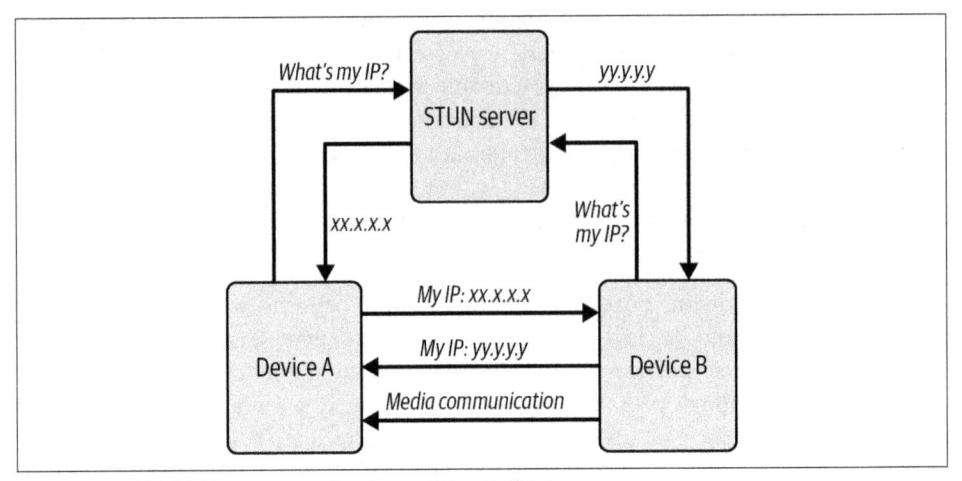

Figure 6-4. WebRTC communication with a STUN server

In some scenarios, direct peer-to-peer connection may not be feasible because of restrictive firewalls and the STUN server fails to do its job. In these scenarios, we can use Traversal Using Relays around NAT (TURN) servers (*https://oreil.ly/VjhcQ*). A TURN server acts as an intermediary between the peers to communicate, where essentially one device sends a message to the TURN server, and then the TURN server relays this to another device. A TURN server can be used singlehandedly to serve the functionality of STUN and relay traffic, but the STUN server is always used as the first point of action. This is because using the TURN server to stream high-quality data is relatively expensive, adding an extra hop into the architecture.

Once the peer-to-peer connection is established, media data can be exchanged in both directions to carry forward the communication. WebRTC is used across the IT industry to support voice and video communications.

Conclusion

The OSI model is a good starting point for understanding data communication over the internet. The device communications we see around us mostly follow the TCP/IP model, with TCP, UDP, and IP being the base protocols for data transport. Multiple protocols are built around them, such as HTTP, SMTP, and XMPP, to serve specific use cases. Determining which protocol makes more sense to implement for your specific use case can be confusing, so it's important to identify the most critical requirements to make your decision. You may also find that combining multiple technologies to meet customer demands is your best option. For example, XMPP is extensively used for text messages, and WebRTC is a preferred choice for audio and video communications. Direct peer-to-peer communication can become complex, particularly when you involve multiuser experiences such as group video or audio calls. Combining these tools can reduce this complexity, bringing the benefits of the text, audio, and video functionality of WebRTC and XMPP together.

We also discussed communication types and which mechanism might make more sense for your implementation. We suggest having your use case requirements in place before trying to compare your options—there may never be a clear winner when designing large-scale distributed systems. We ended our discussion with different communication standards and architectures for how client-server information sharing works across the internet. While we have tried to cover the basic and most widely used communication tools, multiple other protocols or technologies have been designed and built to solve specific use cases that we simply didn't have the room to discuss here.

In the next chapter we'll dig into the concept of containers. Docker and Kubernetes are hot keywords in the industry—it's likely you've already heard of these concepts, which are used to deploy and run your software applications.

CHAPTER 7
Containerization, Orchestration, and Deployments

In recent years, containerization has become a game changer in the world of software development and deployment. Traditional methods of building and deploying applications often faced challenges like inconsistency, lack of portability, and inefficient use of resources. Containerization offers a solution to these problems in a new and effective way.

So what is *containerization*? Simply put, it's a way to package an application along with everything it needs to run—like libraries and dependencies—into a lightweight, portable unit called a *container*. These containers ensure that the application runs the same way no matter where it's deployed, whether that's on a developer's laptop, on a testing server, or in a production environment. This consistency helps developers focus on writing code without worrying about compatibility issues or the complexities of deployment. Docker (*https://docker.com*), one of the most popular tools for containerization, makes it easy to create, share, and run these containers. It streamlines the development process, helping teams work faster and get their applications to market more quickly.

In this chapter, we'll start by explaining the basic concepts of containerization, with a focus on Docker. You'll learn how containers work, how to create them, and how to manage them on a large scale. We'll also touch on more advanced topics, such as managing container images, orchestrating containers with tools like Kubernetes (*https://kubernetes.io*), and deploying applications using modern strategies. By the end of this chapter, you'll have a solid understanding of containerization and how it can improve your approach to system design and software development. Let's dive in and discover how containerization can make your developer operations easier and more efficient!

Evolution of Application Deployment

In the early stages of software deployment, organizations relied on physical servers to run their applications. Each application typically was hosted on a separate physical server, leading to issues with resource allocation and underutilization. For instance, if multiple applications share the same server, one application could monopolize resources, causing performance degradation for others. This approach proved inefficient and expensive as organizations struggled to maintain numerous physical servers. To address the limitations of traditional deployment, virtualization emerged as a game-changing technology.

Virtualization, illustrated in Figure 7-1, enables organizations to run multiple *virtual machines (VMs)* on a single physical server's CPU, thereby maximizing resource utilization and scalability. A VM emulates a physical computer using software. Each VM operates as an isolated instance with its own OS and application stack, ensuring security and isolation between applications. The *hypervisor* acts as a middleman between the host machine and VMs to create virtualized hardware components, including virtual disks, network interfaces, and CPUs. VMs provide strong isolation between applications, but they also require significant overhead in terms of memory, storage, and processing power while introducing complexity associated with managing multiple OS instances.

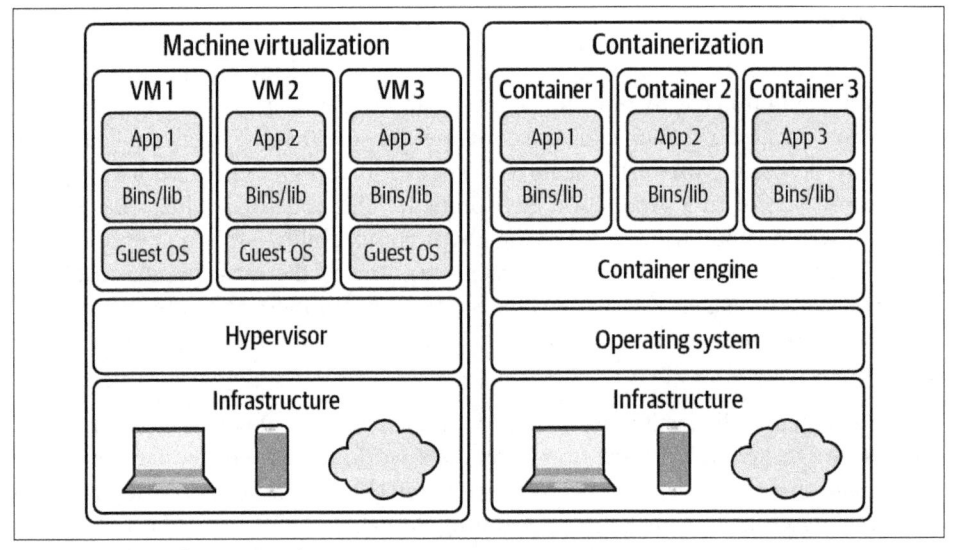

Figure 7-1. Machine virtualization versus containerization

Containers represent the next evolution in deployment technology, offering a lightweight, portable alternative to VMs. Containers, as shown in Figure 7-1, share the host OS kernel and runtime environment, enabling them to be more efficient and agile than VMs. Unlike VMs, which require separate OS instances, containers leverage OS-level virtualization to share the underlying OS kernel, resulting in faster startup times and lower resource overhead.

Both containers and VMs play crucial roles in deploying and executing applications. While they share some similarities in their ability to isolate and encapsulate workloads, containers and VMs differ significantly in their architecture, resource utilization, and deployment characteristics, as described in Table 7-1.

Table 7-1. VMs versus containers

Property	VMs	Containers
Virtualization	Hardware level: VMs emulate physical hardware and provide complete virtualized environments, including a guest OS, on top of a hypervisor layer. Each VM runs its own OS instance independent of the host system and consumes dedicated system resources, such as CPU, memory, and disk space.	OS level: containers leverage OS-level virtualization to provide lightweight, isolated environments for running applications. Each container shares the host OS kernel but maintains separate user space, allowing multiple containers to run concurrently on the same host.
Resource utilization	Less efficient: VMs are less efficient in resource utilization compared to containers because each VM requires its own OS instance, which consumes additional memory, CPU, and disk space.	Highly efficient: containers are highly efficient in terms of resource utilization because they share the host OS kernel and require minimal overhead.
Deployment flexibility	Hypervisor-tied: although VMs provide isolation and encapsulation, they are less flexible in terms of deployment compared to containers. VMs are tied to specific hypervisor platforms and may require additional configuration or conversion steps when migrating between different virtualization platforms.	Portable: containers offer greater deployment flexibility compared to VMs, thanks to their lightweight, portable nature. Containers can be easily moved between different environments, such as development, testing, and production, without modifications.
Overhead	Heavyweight: VMs have larger footprint sizes and may suffer from resource contention when multiple VMs are run on the same host.	Lightweight: containers impose minimal overhead on system resources.
Speed	Slow startup: VMs are typically larger and slower to start compared to containers because of the overhead of running multiple OS instances.	Fast startup: since containers do not need to boot a separate OS instance, they have faster startup times and consume fewer system resources, making them ideal for deploying lightweight, scalable applications.
Performance	Limited: VMs often have limited performance due to overhead from emulating hardware.	Native: containers offer native performance by leveraging the host OS kernel directly.
Security	Fully isolated: VMs offer full isolation at the OS level, which enhances security by minimizing the risk of cross-VM attacks.	Process-level isolation: containers provide process-level isolation within shared OS resources, which requires additional security measures to prevent container escapes and unauthorized access between processes.

Containers and VMs represent distinct approaches to application isolation and deployment in system design. Containers offer lightweight, efficient, portable environments for running applications, whereas VMs provide stronger isolation and compatibility with existing infrastructure. By understanding the differences between containers and VMs, system designers can make informed decisions about which technology to leverage based on their specific requirements and use cases. Whether you are deploying microservice architectures in the cloud or running legacy applications on premises, containers and VMs offer complementary solutions for modern system design and infrastructure management.

Containerization

Now, let's look at some basic concepts around containerization, including Docker, images, the registry, and containers, which form the foundation of containerization.

Docker

Docker is the de facto standard for containerization. It offers a comprehensive platform for building, shipping, and running containers. With Docker, developers can define application environments using Dockerfiles (*https://oreil.ly/w_NP0*), build container images, and deploy applications to any environment seamlessly. Docker provides a rich set of tools and APIs for managing containers, orchestrating distributed applications, and integrating with existing DevOps workflows.

Here is an example of a simple Dockerfile for creating a basic Python web application using Flask framework, which is converted to a Docker image consisting of layers as shown in Figure 7-2:

```
# Use the official Python image from Docker Hub
FROM python:3.9-slim

# Set the working directory in the container
WORKDIR /app

# Copy the current directory contents into the container at /app
COPY . /app

# Install Flask and other dependencies via pip
RUN pip install --no-cache-dir -r requirements.txt

# Expose port 5000 to the outside world
EXPOSE 5000

# Define environment variable
ENV NAME World

# Run app.py when the container launches
CMD ["python", "app.py"]
```

Now, let's understand the Docker images, which are created from the Dockerfiles.

```
Dockerfile                                    Docker image
FROM python:3.9-slim                          Docker image layers
WORKDIR /app
COPY . /app                                      FROM python:3.9-slim
RUN pip install --no-cache-dir -r
requirements.txt             Docker             WORKDIR /app
EXPOSE 5000                   image
                             builder
ENV NAME World                                    COPY . /app

CMD ["python", "app.py"]
                                              RUN pip install --no-cache-dir -r
                                                     requirements.txt

                                                    EXPOSE 5000

                                                   ENV NAME world

                                              CMD ["python", "app.py"]
```

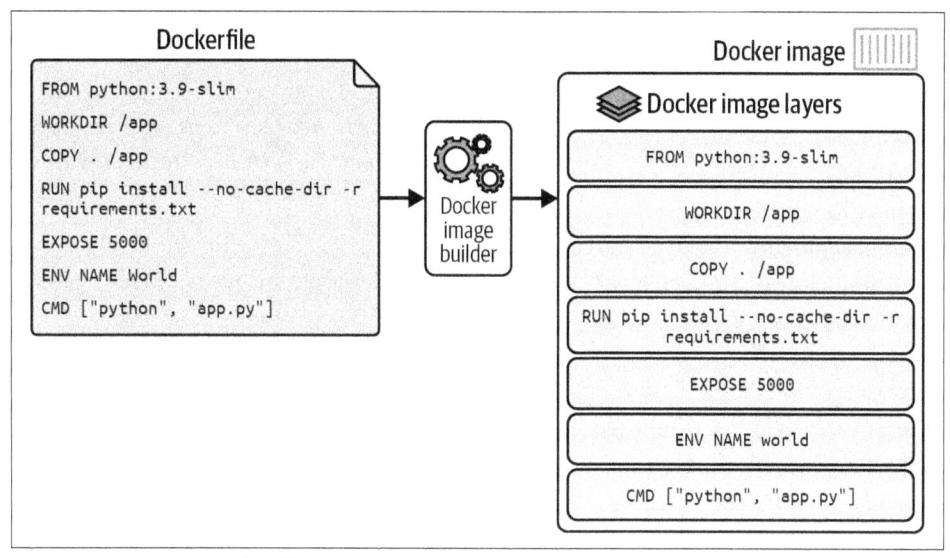

Figure 7-2. From Dockerfile to Docker image

Images

Container images are the building blocks of containerized applications. An *image* is a lightweight, standalone executable package that contains everything needed to run an application, including the application code, runtime, libraries, and dependencies. Images are created from Dockerfiles, which specify the instructions for building the image layer by layer. Docker Hub and other container registries host public and private repositories of prebuilt images, allowing developers to share and distribute containerized applications easily.

At its core, a container image consists of the following elements:

Base image
   The base image serves as the foundation of the container image and provides the runtime environment for the application. It typically includes a minimal OS (such as Alpine Linux or Ubuntu) and essential system libraries and utilities. Base images are optimized for size and security, enabling developers to build lightweight, secure containerized applications.

Application code
   The application code represents the core functionality of the containerized application. It includes the source code, binaries, and dependencies required to execute the application. Application code is bundled into the container image, ensuring that the application behaves consistently across different environments.

Runtime dependencies
> In addition to the application code, container images may include runtime dependencies, such as libraries, frameworks, and runtime environments (e.g., Node.js, Python, Java). These dependencies are essential for executing the application and are packaged into the container image to ensure compatibility and portability.

Configuration files
> Container images may contain configuration files and settings needed to configure and customize the application runtime environment. Configuration files are typically stored in well-defined locations within the container image, allowing the application to be easily configured at runtime.

Container images are composed of multiple layers, each representing a discrete component or modification to the base image. These layers are stacked on top of one another to form the complete container image. The key components of container images are:

Base layer
> The base layer serves as the foundation of the container image and contains the minimal OS and system libraries needed to run the application. The base layer is immutable and provides a clean slate for building and customizing container images.

Intermediate layers
> Intermediate layers represent modifications or additions to the base image, such as installing packages, copying files, or configuring settings. Each intermediate layer is created by a Dockerfile instruction (*https://oreil.ly/krHtG*) (e.g., RUN, COPY, ADD) and contributes to the final state of the container image.

Top layer
> The top layer is the final layer of the container image and contains the application code, runtime dependencies, and configuration files. This layer is read-write and allows changes to be made to the container image at runtime, such as creating or modifying files within the container filesystem.

Building and managing container images is a fundamental aspect of container deployment. Container images can be created and customized using Dockerfiles, declarative files that specify the instructions for building the image layer by layer. Docker provides a set of commands and tools for building and tagging container images and pushing them to container registries, such as Docker Hub (*https://hub.docker.com*) or Amazon Elastic Container Registry (ECR) (*https://aws.amazon.com/ecr*).

Container images should be versioned and tagged appropriately to track changes and ensure consistency across environments. Versioning schemes such as semantic versioning (SemVer) (*https://semver.org*) or date-based versioning can be used to manage container image versions effectively. Additionally, container images should be scanned for vulnerabilities and regularly updated to mitigate security risks and ensure compliance with industry standards.

> We'll cover using Amazon ECR to maintain container images on AWS for deployment on AWS Lambda, Amazon Elastic Container Service (ECS), and Amazon Elastic Kubernetes Service (EKS) in Chapter 11.

The next question that arises is where the container images are stored: in the container registry, which we will look at next.

Registry

The *container registry* serves as the central repository for storing, managing, and distributing container images in a scalable, efficient manner. Container registries serve several key functions. They provide secure, reliable storage for container images, ensuring availability when needed. They enable effective image management through versioning, tagging, and organizing images into repositories. They also facilitate distribution of images across various environments, such as development, testing, and production, ensuring consistency throughout the deployment pipeline. Finally, they enforce access controls and permissions to regulate who can push, pull, and modify images, ensuring security and compliance with organizational policies.

To support the storage, management, and distribution of container images, container registries offer the following capabilities:

Private repositories
    Container registries enable creation of private repositories, which allow organizations to securely store and manage proprietary or sensitive container images behind authentication and access controls.

Tagging and versioning
    Container registries allow developers to tag and version container images, making it easy to track changes, manage dependencies, and ensure consistency across environments.

Scalability and high availability
    Container registries are designed to be highly scalable and available, capable of handling large volumes of container images and supporting continuous integration and continuous deployment (CI/CD) workflows.

Content trust and signing
　　Container registries support content-trust mechanisms such as Docker Content Trust (DCT) (*https://oreil.ly/yKoOc*) or Notary, which allow users to verify the integrity and authenticity of container images through digital signatures.

Integration with CI/CD pipelines
　　Container registries integrate seamlessly with CI/CD pipelines, enabling automated image builds, testing, and deployment workflows.

To maximize the benefits of container registries, organizations should follow best practices for managing and using container images effectively. This includes using private registries whenever possible, especially for proprietary or sensitive applications, to store and manage container images securely. Implementing access controls based on role-based access control (RBAC) policies is essential to restrict access to these images, ensuring that only authorized users can push, pull, and modify them. Automating the process of building, tagging, and pushing container images to the registry through CI/CD pipelines ensures consistency and reliability in the image build process. Regularly scanning container images for vulnerabilities using security scanning tools and addressing any identified issues before deploying images to production are crucial for maintaining security. Additionally, adopting a consistent versioning and tagging strategy for container images helps track changes and manage dependencies, and it allows for easy rollback to previous versions if needed.

Container registries serve as the backbone of the container ecosystem. They provide a centralized, secure repository for storing, managing, and distributing container images. Figure 7-3 illustrates the interaction between the Docker Client, Docker Host, and Docker Registry.

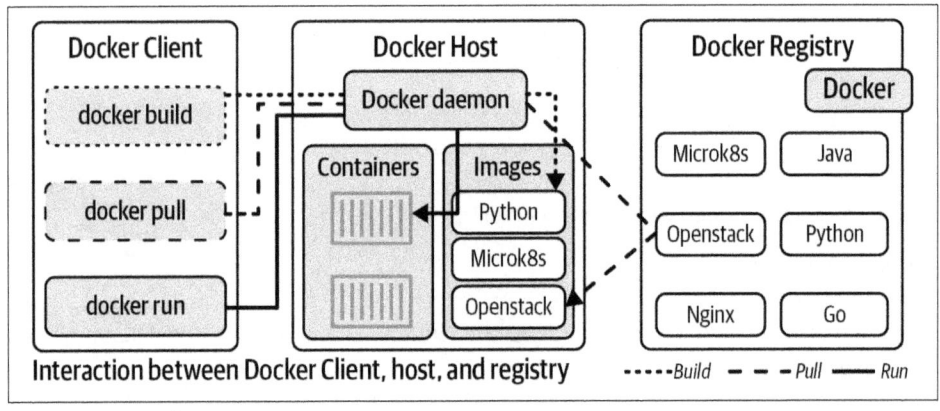

Figure 7-3. Docker ecosystem

The Docker Client is where users build (`docker build`), retrieve (`docker pull`), and run (`docker run`) images. The Docker Host, with its Docker daemon, manages these images and runs containers. The Docker Registry acts as a centralized storage and distribution hub for Docker images, enabling users to push and pull images across different environments. The Docker Registry serves as the backbone of the Docker ecosystem, ensuring consistent, reliable access to container images.

In the next section, we'll explore the lifecycle of containers and the processes that govern their operation.

Containers

In the realm of containerization, understanding the lifecycle of containers, the underlying processes, and the role of container engines like Docker is crucial for efficiently deploying and managing containerized applications. The lifecycle of a container, as shown in Figure 7-4, encompasses several stages from creation to termination, each of which plays a vital role in deploying and executing containerized applications.

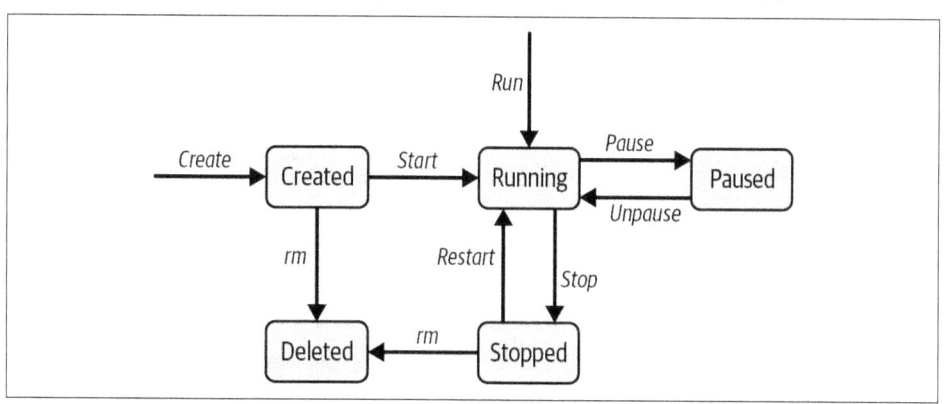

Figure 7-4. Docker container lifecycle

Let's discuss each part of the process:

Image creation
　　The container lifecycle begins with the creation of a container image, which serves as the blueprint for the container. Images are typically created using Dockerfiles, which define the instructions for building the image layer by layer.

Container creation
　　Once an image is built, containers can be instantiated from the image using the docker run command (*https://oreil.ly/fnL5v*). During container creation, the Docker engine allocates resources, such as CPU, memory, and storage, and sets up the container environment based on the image specifications.

Container execution
　　Once created, containers execute the command specified in the image, which typically corresponds to the primary application or service being run. Containers

run in isolation from one another and the host system, ensuring that applications behave predictably and securely.

Container management
During runtime, containers can be managed using various Docker commands, such as `docker start`, `docker stop`, `docker pause`, and `docker restart`. Administrators use these commands to control the lifecycle of containers, including starting, stopping, pausing, and restarting containers as needed.

Container termination
Containers are terminated using the `docker rm` command once they are no longer needed. Container termination releases the allocated resources and removes the container from the host system, ensuring efficient resource utilization.

Within a containerized environment, containers run as isolated processes, each with its own namespace, filesystem, and network stack. Key processes involved in container execution include:

Init process
Each container starts with an init process, which serves as the entry point for the containerized application. The init process typically runs as Process ID (PID) 1 within the container and is responsible for managing other processes and handling signals.

Application processes
Application processes represent the primary functionality of the containerized application and are spawned by the init process. These processes execute within the container environment and interact with the host system and other containers as needed.

Supporting processes
In addition to the application processes, containers may run supporting processes, such as logging daemons, monitoring agents, or service discovery tools. These processes enhance the functionality and reliability of the containerized application and may run alongside or within the same container as the application processes.

Docker engine and runtime

The Docker engine serves as the core component of the Docker platform, providing the functionality for building, running, and managing containers. The Docker engine consists of several key components, as shown in Figure 7-5.

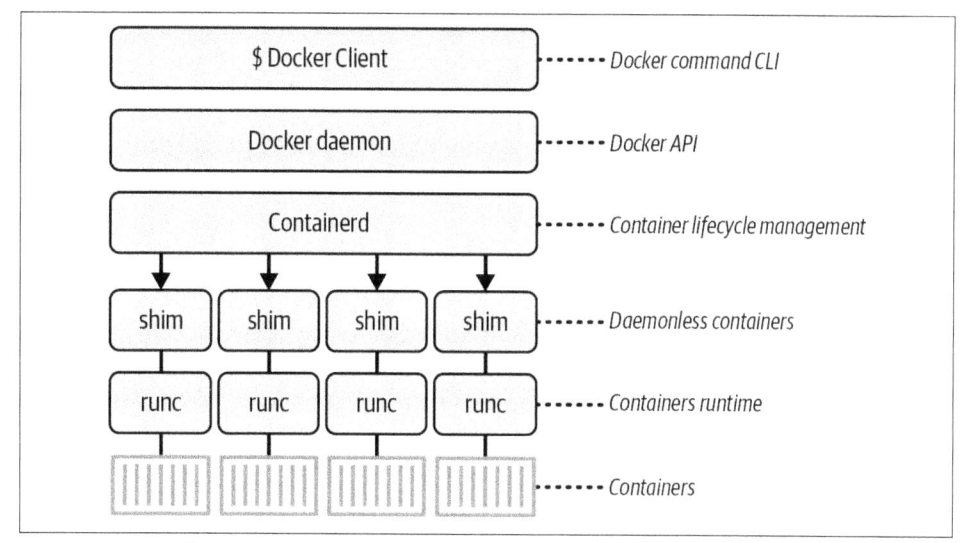

Figure 7-5. Docker engine architecture

The components of the Docker engine are:

Docker daemon
    The Docker daemon (`dockerd`) is the background service that manages container operations, including image and container management, resource allocation, and network configuration. The Docker daemon listens for Docker API requests and executes commands on behalf of clients.

Docker CLI
    The Docker CLI (`docker`) provides a user-friendly interface for interacting with the Docker daemon and performing common container operations, such as building images, creating containers, and managing the container lifecycle.

Containerd
    Containerd is an industry-standard container runtime that serves as the core runtime component of the Docker engine. Containerd manages the execution and lifecycle of containers, including container creation, runtime management, and resource isolation.

Runc
    Runc is a lightweight container runtime that implements the Open Container Initiative (OCI) runtime specification. Runc creates and executes container processes, manages container namespaces and filesystems, and enforces container security policies.

The container lifecycle, processes, and Docker engine play integral roles in the deployment and management of containerized applications. Containerization empowers organizations to embrace cloud native architectures, streamline development workflows, and accelerate digital transformation initiatives, driving innovation and agility in today's dynamic IT landscape.

As organizations increasingly adopt containerization, the need for efficient management and scaling of these containerized applications becomes critical. This is where container orchestration comes into play.

Container Orchestration

Container orchestration platforms, such as Kubernetes, play a pivotal role in managing the deployment and operation of containerized applications at scale. *Kubernetes*, often abbreviated as K8s, is an open source container orchestration platform designed to automate deploying, scaling, and managing containerized applications.

Kubernetes architecture

The Kubernetes architecture (*https://oreil.ly/WoSWJ*), illustrated in Figure 7-6, comprises several key components distributed across a cluster of machines.

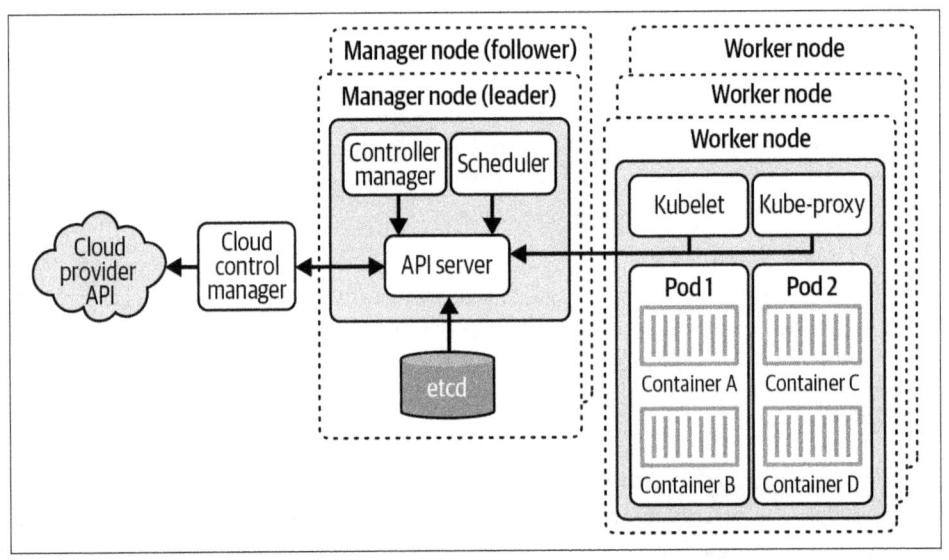

Figure 7-6. Kubernetes architecture

Nodes are the individual machines, physical or virtual, that form the Kubernetes cluster. There are two types of nodes:

Manager or control plane nodes
  These nodes host the control plane components and orchestrate the worker nodes. They manage the cluster's overall state, respond to requests from users

or external systems, and make decisions about when and where to deploy applications.

Worker nodes
Also known as *minions*, these nodes run the actual containerized applications. Each worker node typically runs multiple containers managed by the Kubernetes system.

Control plane nodes consist of several components:

API server
The API server is the central management entity in Kubernetes. It exposes the Kubernetes API, which allows users, management tools, and other parts of the cluster to interact with Kubernetes. It processes REST operations, validates and configures data, and updates the corresponding objects in the cluster's etcd data store.

Scheduler
The scheduler places newly created Pods onto available nodes in the cluster. It considers factors like resource requirements, hardware and software constraints, affinity, anti-affinity, and other policies defined by the user.

Controller manager
The controller manager is a daemon that embeds the core control loops shipped with Kubernetes. These control loops watch the state of the cluster through the API server and work toward the desired state. Examples of controllers include the Node Controller, ReplicaSet Controller, and Deployment Controller.

Etcd
Although not strictly part of the control plane nodes, etcd is a consistent and highly available key-value store used as Kubernetes's backing store for all cluster data. It stores configuration data, state data, and metadata about the cluster.

The worker node components include:

Kubelet
The kubelet is an agent running on each worker node that manages the lifecycle of containers on that node. It receives Pod definitions via various means (such as the API server or local files), ensures that the containers described in those Pod definitions are running and healthy, and reports back to the control plane about the node's health.

Kube-proxy
Kube-proxy is a network proxy that runs on each worker node. It maintains network rules on the host and performs connection forwarding to the appropriate

backend services. It enables the Kubernetes service abstraction by managing network routing for TCP and UDP packets.

The Kubernetes architecture is structured around a control plane that manages the cluster's state and a set of worker nodes that execute the workloads. The interaction between these components ensures efficient deployment and management of containerized applications at scale.

Kubernetes concepts

Let's understand the basic concepts of Kubernetes, which form the foundation of container orchestration:

Pods

A Pod is the smallest deployable unit in Kubernetes, representing one or more containers that share networking and storage resources. Pods encapsulate application components and ensure that they are colocated and coscheduled. Pods are ephemeral and can be scaled up or down or replaced dynamically to meet demand.

Cluster

A Kubernetes cluster consists of one or more control plane nodes and multiple worker nodes (data plane nodes), forming a distributed computing environment for running containerized applications. Clusters provide high availability, fault tolerance, and scalability for containerized workloads, ensuring consistent performance and reliability.

ReplicaSets

ReplicaSets ensure that a specified number of Pod replicas are running at any given time. They maintain the desired state of Pod replicas, scale Pods up or down in response to changes in demand, and ensure fault tolerance and availability.

Services

Services provide network abstraction for accessing Pods within the Kubernetes cluster. They enable load balancing, service discovery, and automatic routing of traffic to Pods based on labels and selectors. Services can be exposed internally within the cluster or externally to the internet.

Deployments

Deployments provide a declarative way to manage application deployments and updates in Kubernetes. Deployments define the desired state of the application, including the number of replicas, the container images, and the rollout strategy. Deployments ensure that the desired state is achieved and maintained, enabling seamless updates and rollbacks.

Volumes
> Volumes provide persistent storage for containers in Kubernetes, allowing data to persist beyond the lifecycle of individual Pods. Volumes enable data sharing between containers, stateful applications, and external storage systems, ensuring data integrity and availability for containerized workloads.

ConfigMaps and secrets
> ConfigMaps and secrets are Kubernetes resources used to store configuration data and sensitive information, such as passwords or API keys, respectively. They provide a centralized, secure way to manage application configuration and secrets, decoupling configuration from container images and enabling dynamic configuration updates.

Jobs
> Jobs are Kubernetes resources used to run batch or intermittent tasks to completion. Jobs ensure that a specified number of Pods complete their tasks successfully before terminating. They are ideal for running tasks such as data processing, backups, or periodic maintenance in Kubernetes clusters.

Resources
> Resources, such as CPU and memory, are allocated to containers based on resource requests and limits specified in Kubernetes manifests. Resource management ensures efficient resource utilization, prevents resource contention, and maintains performance and reliability in Kubernetes clusters.

> We'll cover Amazon EKS, a fully managed Kubernetes service for simplifying the deployment, management, and scaling of containerized applications using Kubernetes on the AWS cloud, in Chapter 11. EKS manages the Kubernetes control plane, including updates, scaling, and availability, which allows you to focus on deploying and managing your applications.

Kubernetes provides a robust, flexible platform for container orchestration, enabling organizations to deploy, scale, and manage containerized applications with ease. By leveraging the Kubernetes architecture and its core components, organizations can build resilient, scalable, and highly available cloud native applications.

Now that you have a solid understanding of Kubernetes and its components, the next step is to explore how these elements are applied in real-world scenarios, particularly in managing application deployments. This leads us to the concept of container deployment strategies.

Container Deployment Strategies

Deployments are the standard way to manage application deployments in Kubernetes. They ensure declarative updates to application deployments, maintain desired replica counts, and handle rollouts and rollbacks efficiently. Deployments automate creating and scaling Pods based on a desired state, making it easy to manage application lifecycles.

Deploying applications in Kubernetes involves more than just rolling out new versions; it requires thoughtful strategies to ensure seamless updates, minimize downtime, and mitigate risks. The following are some common deployment strategies:

Re-creating deployment
    Updating a deployment in Kubernetes involves the re-creation of pods, when existing instances are terminated and replaced with the new versions. This approach proves beneficial when the coexistence of old and new application versions is not feasible. The downtime experienced is contingent on the duration required for the application to halt and restart.

Rolling deployment
    Rolling deployments, the default offering in Kubernetes, aim to minimize cluster downtime by gradually and seamlessly replacing Pods running the old application version with the new one, facilitated by readiness probes. Once the readiness probe confirms the availability of the new application version, the old one is phased out. If issues arise, the deployment can be halted and rolled back to the previous version, averting cluster-wide downtime. However, because Pods are replaced individually, deployments may take time, especially in larger clusters. Suppose a new deployment is initiated before the ongoing one completes. In that case, Kubernetes updates the version to the new deployment's specification, disregarding the previous version wherever it hasn't yet been applied.

> *Readiness probes* monitor the application's readiness state. If a probe fails, traffic is diverted away from the Pod, ensuring it doesn't receive requests until it is ready. These probes are especially useful for applications that require initialization steps before serving traffic or during traffic surges that might overload the app temporarily.

StatefulSet deployments
    StatefulSet deployments are used to deploy stateful applications, such as databases or distributed systems, in Kubernetes. StatefulSets ensure that Pods are consistently named, networked, and persisted across restarts, maintaining data integrity and availability for stateful workloads.

Blue-green deployment
> This strategy involves running two identical production environments, labeled "blue" and "green." At any given time, only one environment serves live traffic, while the other remains idle. When a new version is ready, traffic is routed to the idle environment, allowing for zero-downtime deployments and easy rollback if issues arise.

Serverless deployments
> Also known as *function as a service (FaaS)*, serverless deployments abstract away the infrastructure layer so that developers can focus solely on writing code. Kubernetes provides serverless capabilities through platforms like Knative or AWS Lambda on Kubernetes, enabling developers to deploy event-driven, autoscaling applications without managing the underlying infrastructure.

Canary deployments
> Canary deployments involve gradually rolling out a new version of an application to a subset of users or traffic segments while monitoring for errors or performance issues. These deployments allow for early detection of issues and provide a controlled rollback mechanism if necessary. Kubernetes supports canary deployments through features like traffic splitting and automated rollbacks.

Advanced deployment strategies are essential for managing the complexity of modern cloud native applications in Kubernetes. By leveraging these innovative approaches, organizations can achieve seamless updates, minimize downtime, and deliver exceptional user experiences. Kubernetes integrates seamlessly with infrastructure-as-code (IaC) practices, allowing teams to automate deploying and scaling containerized applications while leveraging a variety of IaC tools to define and manage their infrastructure.

> IaC is a modern approach to managing IT infrastructure through code, enabling automation and consistency in provisioning and configuration. IaC allows teams to define their infrastructure using declarative configuration files, which can be version-controlled and replicated easily, facilitating collaboration and traceability. Some common tools supporting IaC are Terraform (*https://terraform.io*), AWS CloudFormation (*https://aws.amazon.com/cloudformation*), Ansible (*https://ansible.com*), Pulumi (*https://pulumi.com*), Chef (*https://chef.io*), Puppet (*https://puppet.com*), and AWS CDK (*https://oreil.ly/NCJvE*).

Kubernetes fits into the IaC paradigm by enabling the orchestration of containerized applications at scale. With Kubernetes, you can define your entire application environment—containers, networking, storage, and configurations—using declarative YAML files. This allows teams to version-control their infrastructure configurations, replicate environments easily, and automate deployment processes. Kubernetes provides a robust platform for implementing these strategies, empowering teams to deploy, scale, and manage applications with confidence and efficiency.

Changes should be deployed to a test (or staging) environment. Once changes are confirmed in the test environment via manual testing (or automated integrated tests), they can be propagated to the production environment serving real user traffic. Let's discuss this process more in the next section.

CI/CD Pipeline with Gitflow and Automated Deployment Strategies

As the number of software projects within an organization increases, so does the complexity of managing deployments. Manual deployments become prone to errors and require considerable engineering resources to manage, ultimately slowing the development lifecycle. To address this, CI/CD provides an automated flow that reduces operational costs and accelerates deployment from code review to production. Let's dive into the key concepts of CI/CD, starting with code development using Gitflow, and explore the steps for implementing them effectively.

Gitflow Workflow for Branch Management

Gitflow is a branching strategy (*https://oreil.ly/hQ8Pl*) that organizes development, testing, and releases with clear, structured branches. This ensures smooth integrations, well-planned releases, and quick rollouts for bug fixes.

The main branches are:

`main`
 The stable production branch with the latest approved code

`develop`
 The integration branch where features are merged before release

The feature branches are:

`feature/*`
 Created for each new feature or task; merged into `develop` upon completion

`release/*`
 Used for final testing and last-minute adjustments; merged into both `main` and `develop`

`hotfix/*`
 Created from `main` for urgent production fixes; merged into both `main` and `develop`

Developers create a feature branch off `develop`, complete their work, and create a pull request (PR) (*https://oreil.ly/vuqYx*) for merging back to `develop`. Once the code is ready for release, a `release` branch is created from `develop`, tested, and merged into both `main` and `develop`. `Hotfix` branches enable urgent fixes and are created from `main` and merged back to both `main` and `develop` for consistency. The end-to-end flow is shown in Figure 7-7.

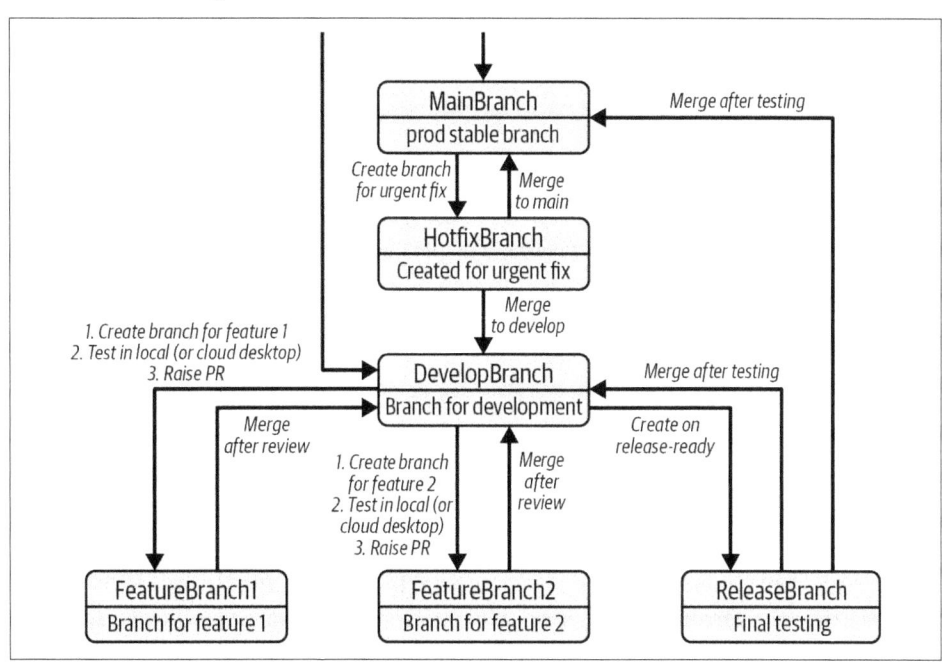

Figure 7-7. Gitflow branching strategy

Continuous Integration

CI aims to integrate code changes from multiple developers into a shared repository multiple times a day. This process ensures that code changes are regularly tested, built, and validated to catch integration issues early.

After developing code in their local or cloud environments, developers create a feature branch for each new feature or fix. Once development is complete, they raise a PR, which includes details about the change, its purpose, and any test cases.

CI then initiates an automated build process to confirm that the code compiles without errors. Automated unit tests run to verify that individual components function correctly. Code quality and lint checks ensure adherence to style and best practices. Automated security tools, such as SonarQube or Amazon CodeGuru, scan for vulnerabilities. Automated code reviews identify potential inefficiencies, and manual reviews offer feedback on logic and potential improvements. If any step fails, feedback is given to the developer, who can then update the code as needed.

Once all CI checks are green, the PR undergoes peer and automated reviews for additional feedback. After any issues are addressed, the PR is approved and merged into the `develop` branch, initiating a postmerge pipeline. In the postmerge pipeline, CI builds and tests the new code to verify seamless integration. For containerized applications, a Docker image is built and prepared for deployment to testing and production environments.

Continuous Deployment

CD is the process that deploys changes to a test environment, staging environment, and finally production after successful CI checks, without requiring manual intervention. CD provides a streamlined, responsive approach to getting code into production quickly, making it easier to roll out features and updates.

After CI is successfully completed, code is deployed to a test environment for further verification, checking that different parts of the application communicate and function correctly with integration tests. Load testing then simulates high traffic to understand performance impact. An approval process may be required for significant changes before proceeding to further environments. Once the testing environment is validated, the changes are promoted to a staging environment. Basic functionality smoke tests ensure readiness for production.

In a canary deployment, updates are rolled out to a small group of users or servers first. Metrics (e.g., error rates, latency) are monitored to ensure stability. If issues are detected, automated rollbacks restore the previous stable version. Once the canary deployment is successful, the update is gradually deployed to the rest of the production environment.

Monitoring and Incident Management

Proactive monitoring and incident response are essential for identifying and addressing issues quickly. For continuous monitoring, tools like CloudWatch, ELK Stack, or Prometheus are used to monitor key metrics (e.g., CPU, memory, request latency) in real time. Dashboards and alerts are set up to track stability and performance. Alerts are integrated with incident management tools (e.g., PagerDuty, Opsgenie) to notify engineers of issues. Automated playbooks provide quick responses to common incidents, ensuring fast recovery.

Conclusion

Containerization has had a significant impact on software development and deployment. In this chapter, we've covered the basics of containerization, explored how Docker works, looked at container images, discussed container registries and runtimes, and learned about using Kubernetes for orchestration and deployment. We also talked about the differences between containers and VMs, highlighting how containers offer more flexibility and scalability. We emphasized the importance of having smaller image sizes, optimizing builds, and managing images efficiently for easier retrieval and deployment. We revealed Kubernetes's powerful architecture, including its key components, such as Pods, clusters, and services. We also explored various deployment strategies, such as blue-green and serverless deployments, to help manage application rollouts and updates smoothly.

As you continue your journey with containerization and orchestration, remember that learning is an ongoing process. Keep experimenting with different deployment strategies, stay up to date with the latest tools and best practices, and always seek ways to improve your deployment workflows.

In the next chapter, we'll shift our focus to architecture design and patterns. We'll explore various architecture patterns for big data, pub/sub models, solution architecture, and more, with use cases ranging from distributed filesystems to distributed message queues. This will equip you with the knowledge to architect large-scale systems for Day N, scaling to millions and beyond.

CHAPTER 8
Architectural Designs and Patterns

In this chapter, we dive into the world of architectural design and patterns. These models and patterns form the backbone of modern software systems. We will explore how these designs support scalability, maintainability, and efficient data handling in diverse applications. This chapter will not only equip you with theoretical foundations but also inspire practical applications and innovations in your system design endeavors.

We begin our journey with *change data capture (CDC)*, a pivotal technique in data architecture used for capturing changes made to data in a database. Then, advancing into the realm of asynchronous communication patterns, we discuss the pub/sub architecture, in which publishers emit events without knowledge of the subscribers' identities. We'll look at how message brokers and message queues manage data flow across systems. Our focus will be on Apache Kafka, a high-throughput distributed messaging system, and we'll illustrate its architecture and use cases for handling large-scale data streams.

In distributed systems, managing service interactions is critical. In this chapter, we will explore key architecture patterns for building scalable, resilient, and maintainable systems in modern cloud environments. We'll compare the choreography (decentralized) and orchestration (centralized) management approaches, examining scenarios where each is most effective. We'll then move on to big data architectures, covering foundational models like lambda, kappa, and data lake architectures, along with the Hadoop Distributed File System (HDFS), a distributed filesystem for handling massive datasets. We'll also look at application architectures, comparing monolithic, N-tier, and microservice structures. Then, we'll delve into event-driven systems, highlighting how they enable communication across decoupled services in response to real-time events.

The chapter concludes with a tour of essential cloud architecture patterns, from resilience techniques like the circuit breaker to transactional strategies like saga orchestration, offering a practical toolkit for robust system design. The architecture patterns in this chapter serve as the blueprints for designing systems for the various use cases covered in Part III.

Change Data Capture

CDC is a sophisticated approach to data integration that tracks and captures changes in data at the source database in real time. This method pushes changes to various destinations, including other databases, data warehouses, or even real-time processing engines. The essence of CDC is its ability to provide fresh data to different parts of an organization, thereby ensuring that all systems reflect the latest information.

The need for real-time data processing drives organizations to adopt CDC. In an era where data is as valuable as oil, having the most updated data can significantly enhance operational efficiency and decision-making capabilities. Traditional batch-processing methods, while reliable, fail to meet the demands for immediacy in today's fast-paced business environments. They often require scheduled downtime and can affect system performance during data extraction, which is not conducive to real-time responsiveness.

In cases where organizations need real-time analytics, CDC can synchronize transactional databases (like an RDBMS) with data warehouses (e.g., Snowflake, Redshift). This allows data pipelines to continuously push fresh data from the transactional system to the warehouse, ensuring up-to-date insights without heavy ETL (extract, transform, and load) batch jobs. We'll explore CDC further in Chapter 16, when we discuss handling the design of new post creation.

CDC offers numerous advantages over batch loading, especially in terms of real-time performance:

Reduced latency
    CDC enables almost instantaneous data updates, allowing businesses to react to changes swiftly, which is crucial for dynamic pricing, stock updates, or personalized customer interactions.

Lower costs and bandwidth usage
    By transmitting only the changes made since the last transfer, CDC minimizes the bandwidth required and reduces the costs associated with data transfer.

Increased system efficiency
    Since CDC captures changes as they occur, it imposes minimal impact on the source systems, avoiding the intensive resource use associated with batch processes.

Software architects can implement CDC using various techniques, each suited to different system architectures and performance requirements:

Audit-column-based CDC

Time-based audit columns are a simple yet powerful method of implementing CDC. Adding timestamp columns such as `created_at` and `updated_at` to database tables makes it possible to track when each record was inserted or last modified. This method is particularly effective for applications that require a historical audit trail of changes. Its primary advantage lies in its simplicity and low overhead since it leverages the inherent capabilities of most RDBMSs.

Log-based CDC

Log-based CDC operates by reading transaction logs maintained by the database. Since these logs are designed to keep a record of all changes for data recovery and integrity, they serve as a reliable source for capturing data changes without additional overhead on the database itself. This method supports near real-time data integration, making it suitable for high-availability systems and those requiring immediate consistency across platforms. Tools like Debezium interface with these logs transparently, providing a seamless flow of data changes into various types of data sinks, such as Kafka and databases.

> An extension of log-based CDC, the stream-based CDC method formats log data into more consumable streams, making it easier for applications to process changes in real time. One such example is Amazon DynamoDB streams for publishing data updates in DynamoDB tables to different sources.

Table deltas

Table deltas involve capturing changes based on the comparison of table snapshots at different times. This approach is straightforward: by periodically taking full snapshots of a table and comparing these snapshots, we can derive the changes. This method might introduce delays and is more resource intensive, however; thus, it is generally suited for systems with lower transaction volumes or where real-time sync is not critical. Despite these drawbacks, it remains a viable option for batch-processing scenarios where system resources and processing windows are appropriately planned.

Trigger-based CDC

Trigger-based CDC uses database triggers to capture changes by automatically executing predefined procedures or SQL commands in response to events (`INSERT, UPDATE, DELETE`) occurring in a table. This method allows for immediate capture and custom handling of data changes, facilitating complex transformations or immediate checks during the data-capture phase. While this method is highly flexible and occurs in real time, managing database triggers can increase the load and complexity, especially in large-scale systems.

In real-world applications, CDC is not just a data integration tool: it is part of a broader strategy to enhance data agility and accessibility across enterprises. With cloud platforms increasingly offering built-in support for CDC, its adoption is becoming more straightforward and accessible. Organizations can leverage CDC to maintain up-to-date data across distributed environments and thus improve analytical capabilities without significant overhead or complexities.

Publisher-Subscriber Architecture

Pub/sub architecture is a foundational model in event-driven programming that facilitates asynchronous communication among different parts of the system. This pattern is vital for applications where components need to interact efficiently without directly being linked to one another, thereby promoting loose coupling and scalable design.

Although it is often conflated with the observer pattern, the pub/sub architecture stands out for its inherent design philosophy and operational dynamics. The core difference between the two lies in the routing mechanism. In the observer design pattern, observers are aware of the subject and can directly register with it to receive updates. Communication is generally synchronous, and all observers are notified simultaneously through direct method calls.

The pub/sub model, on the other hand, abstracts the publisher from the subscribers through a broker or event bus, which handles the transmission of messages or events. The publishers send messages to an event channel without knowing the subscribers' details, which in turn listen to the channel without knowing who the publisher is. This setup enables asynchronous communication and can support complex many-to-many interactions more seamlessly than the observer pattern can.

Pub/sub architectures involve a broker and queue; let's look at those components in more detail.

Message Brokers

Message brokers are key components in pub/sub architectures that manage the transmission of messages between producers (publishers) and consumers (subscribers). They ensure that messages are appropriately routed, maintained, and delivered, even in complex distributed systems.

A typical message broker architecture, as shown in Figure 8-1, involves queues that temporarily store messages and topics that categorize these messages. Publishers send messages to specific topics, while subscribers register their interest in one or more topics. The broker then ensures that messages from the relevant topics are delivered to the appropriate subscribers.

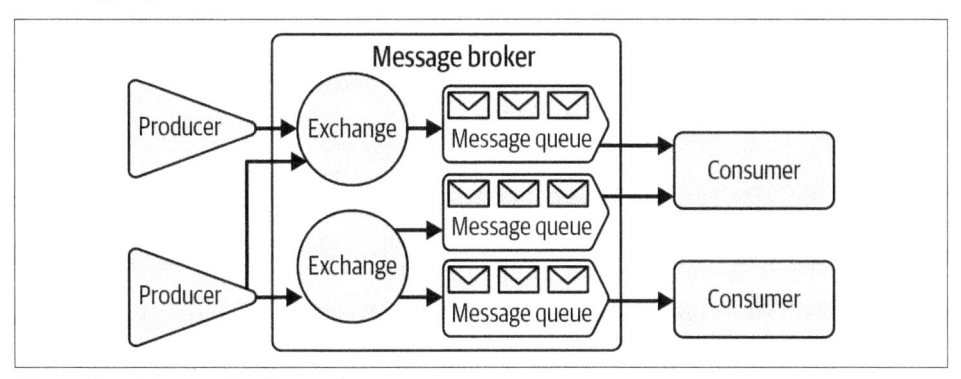

Figure 8-1. Message broker and queues

Advanced Message Queuing Protocol (AMQP) is an open standard for passing messages between applications or organizations with a focus on high interoperability and reliability. AMQP mandates the behavior of the message provider and broker to ensure consistent message delivery, thus making it a favored choice for systems requiring robustness and functional predictability.

Message Queues

Message queues are a fundamental part of the messaging infrastructure that act as a temporary holding pen for messages waiting to be routed from publishers to subscribers, as shown in Figure 8-1.

Apache Kafka, which we'll look at in detail in the last section of this chapter, is a prominent example of a message queue system. It is designed to handle high volumes of data while supporting high-throughput applications. Kafka and similar technologies illustrate the evolving capabilities of message queues in modern system architectures, particularly in handling large-scale, real-time data feeds efficiently.

The pub/sub architecture, facilitated by advanced message brokers and queue systems like Kafka, represents a powerful paradigm for building decoupled, scalable, efficient applications. This architecture not only supports a separation of concerns but also enhances the ability to handle asynchronous communications across different components of a software system. This approach is increasingly relevant in today's distributed systems, where managing data flow efficiently and reliably is more critical than ever.

Choreography and Orchestration

In the design of distributed systems, particularly those employing microservices, methods of managing service interactions—namely, choreography and orchestration—play pivotal roles in defining system behavior and capabilities.

Choreography

Choreography employs a decentralized approach to workflow management. In this model, each service knows what to do and when to do it based on the events it consumes. There is no central coordinator; instead, services perform their duties independently following the event notifications they receive. This method promotes loose coupling as services are designed to react to events rather than direct commands from a central authority. It enhances system scalability and resilience because services operate independently.

The lack of a central controller can make it difficult to enforce certain business rules and to monitor the overall flow of processes. Error handling and debugging can also become more complex because the distributed nature of the architecture scatters log entries and error reports across various services.

A subpattern in choreography is *choreographed asynchronous events*. In this pattern, services emit and consume events through a central message bus, allowing for a loosely coupled system where services operate independently without needing to know the details of one another's operations. This pattern is particularly useful in systems with a high volume of write operations, such as IoT data processing or real-time notification systems.

Advantages include scalability due to the decoupled nature and resilience against service failures as each service can operate autonomously. However, challenges arise in managing the overall system state, making it harder to trace and debug workflows since they are distributed across multiple services. These challenges can be solved by the orchestration paradigm.

> Design problems like ecommerce platforms' order-processing systems and hotel reservation systems can be addressed using choreography between services. We will discuss a similar pattern for managing booking confirmation and payment flow in Chapter 18. The booking system waits for customer payment and reacts to events such as `PaymentProcessed` to confirm the booking with a `BookingConfirmed` event. This event is further used by other services, such as the billing system, to generate an invoice.

Orchestration

Orchestration, in contrast to choreography, relies on a central coordinator, or an *orchestrator*, which controls the interaction between services by making decisions about the process flow, directing different services when to act. This approach simplifies monitoring and managing business logic, which can be advantageous for complex business processes that require precise coordination and strict compliance to workflows. It also simplifies error handling and recovery since the orchestrator can keep track of process states and make decisions accordingly.

> Multiple orchestration solutions are available as open source software and managed services by cloud providers, including Conductor (*https://oreil.ly/50w9A*) and Maestro (*https://oreil.ly/KW-dX*) designed by Netflix, Temporal workflow orchestrator (*https://oreil.ly/2eulB*), AWS Step Functions, and Apache Airflow. We'll discuss Step Functions and Airflow in Chapter 12.

Orchestration can lead to increased coupling between services as they rely on a central point for directions. This can also become a single point of failure, potentially affecting the system's resilience and scalability. Orchestration can be implemented in various patterns, each suited to different workflow requirements and system architectures.

> Design problems like managing a video-upload feature on YouTube and Netflix can be easily managed via orchestration platforms. Each step in the workflow invokes a specific service to perform a task, such as validating, encoding, and distributing video. We'll discuss this in much more detail in Chapter 20.

Orchestrated, synchronous, and sequential pattern

In this pattern, the orchestrator sends synchronous requests to services in a sequential manner, waiting for each response before proceeding to the next step. This approach is suitable for workflows that are complex and involve multiple steps that need to be completed in a specific order, such as ecommerce checkout processes.

Advantages of this pattern include centralized control, which makes managing complex workflows easier, and easier debugging because of the explicit workflow definition in the orchestrator. However, the system can face challenges, such as a single point of failure in the orchestrator and potential performance bottlenecks due to the sequential execution of tasks.

Orchestrated, synchronous, and parallel pattern

Similar to the sequential approach but with parallel execution of independent tasks, this pattern improves performance and reduces latency. It is effective in scenarios where multiple services can be called simultaneously, such as in data-aggregation services.

Advantages of this pattern include improved performance by reducing the overall time to complete workflows and flexibility in managing workflows that involve both parallel and sequential steps. However, challenges can be the increased complexity of managing parallel operations and the risk of resource contention if services are not optimized for parallel execution.

Orchestrated, asynchronous, and sequential pattern

In this pattern, the orchestrator sends asynchronous requests, allowing services to process tasks independently and return results via callbacks or message queues. This approach is ideal for systems with long-running tasks where services need to continue processing without waiting for responses, such as in batch-processing systems.

Advantages of this pattern include better handling of long-running processes without blocking resources and increased system resilience since services can retry operations on failure. However, challenges arise from the increased complexity of managing asynchronous responses and the need for additional mechanisms to handle eventual consistency and failure recovery.

Hybrid orchestration and choreography pattern

This pattern combines the strengths of both choreography and orchestration by using orchestration for explicit workflows and choreography for implicit, event-driven operations. It is useful in complex systems where some workflows require strict control, while others benefit from decentralized execution, such as in large-scale distributed applications.

In a large ecommerce platform, the order-processing service acts as the orchestrator, controlling the main steps of the workflow: verifying payment, reserving inventory, confirming the order, and initiating shipment. This explicit orchestration ensures that the core order workflow remains tightly controlled, with each step executed in a specific order, which is essential for transaction integrity and reliability. Alongside the orchestrated core, various supporting services use a decentralized, event-driven approach. For example, when an order is shipped, an event is emitted. Independent services, like the notification service and the analytics service, listen to this event and perform their respective tasks (sending notifications to the customer and updating delivery statistics) without direct coordination, allowing for flexibility and scalability.

Advantages of this pattern include the flexibility to handle diverse workflow requirements and improved system resilience by leveraging both centralized and decentralized approaches. However, challenges are the complexity of ensuring clear boundaries between orchestrated and choreographed operations and the risk of overlapping responsibilities leading to inefficiencies.

Deciding Between Choreography and Orchestration

The decision to use choreography or orchestration largely depends on specific project requirements. Choreography is better suited to systems where high scalability and resilience are necessary and where business processes can be adequately handled with a decentralized approach. Orchestration is preferable for complex processes requiring tight control and coordination across multiple services, where the business logic is too intricate to be effectively managed through a decentralized approach. Both approaches have their place in system design, and understanding their strengths and limitations is crucial for architects to design solutions that not only meet current needs but also are adaptable to future demands and changes in business processes.

As enterprises continue to generate exponentially growing volumes of data, the big data architectural strategies to store, process, and analyze such vast datasets become increasingly important, so we will look at those in the next section.

Big Data Architecture

Big data architectures are designed to effectively handle the challenge of the 5 Vs of data—volume, velocity, variety, veracity, and value—ensuring that organizations can derive actionable insights and maintain performance scalability. Big data architectures have evolved from traditional databases to large data warehouses and data lakes. We'll discuss three models for modern big data architecture based on how they have evolved.

Lambda Architecture

Lambda architecture, illustrated in Figure 8-2, is a hybrid data-processing model that combines both batch and real-time processing methods.

This architecture is designed to balance latency, throughput, and fault tolerance by processing and presenting data in these three layers:

Batch layer
> This layer handles large volumes of data in batches, processing historical data stored over extended periods. It provides comprehensive and accurate views but with higher latency. The batch layer is responsible for creating precomputed views that store the results of the batch processing.

Speed layer
> For real-time data processing needs, the speed layer processes data as it arrives, ensuring low latency. This layer compensates for the high latency of the batch layer by providing timely—albeit potentially approximate—views.

Serving layer
> The final component, the serving layer, merges output from both the batch and the speed layers to present a coherent view of results to the end users.

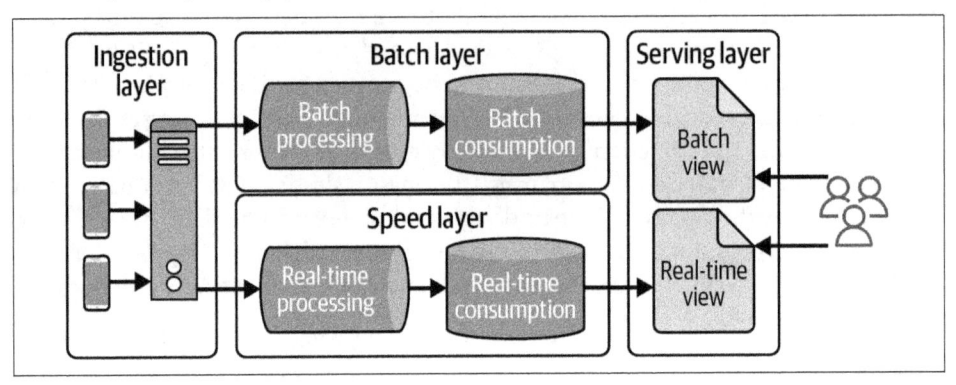

Figure 8-2. Lambda architecture

Lambda architecture is beneficial for scenarios where it is crucial to have a near real-time view of data but also to handle massive datasets that are not feasible to process quickly. The two components—batch and speed layers— introduce an additional complexity of operational management. This limitation can be solved by kappa architecture, which combines both into a single system.

Kappa Architecture

An evolution of lambda architecture, *kappa architecture* simplifies operational complexity by treating all incoming data as a stream. This model, shown in Figure 8-3, proposes using a single processing layer (the stream-processing layer) for both real-time and historical data. By treating all data as a stream, kappa architecture removes the need to maintain two separate codebases and systems for batch and real-time processing, simplifying development and maintenance.

This architecture leverages advanced stream-processing tools that can handle time windowing, event ordering, and state management across potentially unbounded datasets. Kappa architecture is particularly suitable for applications where the input data is naturally streaming or where fast data recency is more critical than computing-intensive, complex batch analytics.

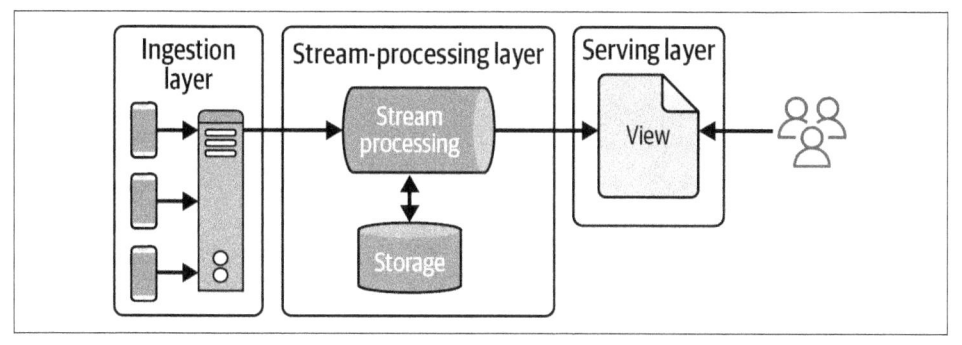

Figure 8-3. Kappa architecture

> The idea here is to simplify the batch and streaming workloads into a single pipeline, but implementation and productionization can vary depending on the organization's use case. Uber leverages kappa architecture (*https://oreil.ly/5sKlo*) to solve multiple problems, such as dynamic ride pricing, fraud detection, and user experience analytics. A single pipeline is designed to address these different use cases with easy switching between batch and streaming workloads.

Data Lake Architecture

Data lakes are centralized repositories designed to store, process, and secure large volumes of structured and unstructured data. Unlike traditional data warehouses, which generally store data in a structured, processed format, data lakes retain vast amounts of raw data in its native format. This approach, illustrated in Figure 8-4, offers a few distinct advantages, including scaling out using low-cost hardware, flexible configuration of the data lake's organization, indexing and processing logic, and storage support for and analysis of a wide variety of data types, including logs, XML, JSON, and binary formats. Data lake architecture not only supports big data storage but also integrates with various big data processing frameworks to enable comprehensive analytics and machine learning directly on the stored data.

> You can also use object storage solutions like Amazon S3 to build data lake architectures. S3 offers easy integration with big data services like Amazon EMR, AWS Glue, and Amazon Athena to run big data workloads. We'll discuss these services in much more detail in Chapter 13.

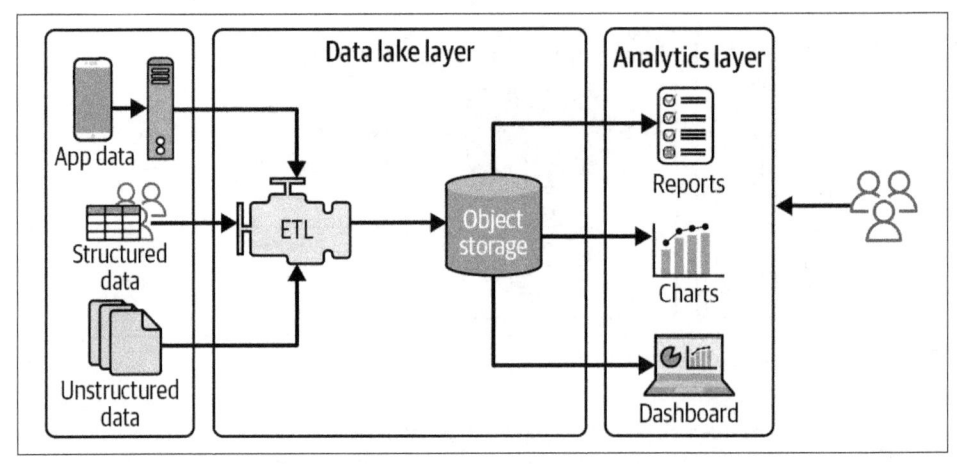

Figure 8-4. Data lake architecture

By implementing big data architectures such as lambda, kappa, and data lake, organizations can effectively manage their data ecosystems to support both current analytical needs and future data-driven initiatives. This ensures that the infrastructure not only meets the technical requirements of big data processing but also aligns with strategic business objectives.

While big data architecture is primarily concerned with processing and managing large volumes of data efficiently, application solution system design focuses on creating systems that meet specific business requirements and integrate various components. The next section will contrast solution architecture designs with the data-centric approaches of big data architecture.

Solution Architecture

Solution architecture has evolved from monolithic architectures to microservices, reflecting shifts in technology and business requirements. This section provides an overview of this evolution and these architectures, exploring their configurations and the principles behind their designs.

Monoliths

In a *monolithic architecture*, shown in Figure 8-5, all components of the software application are tightly integrated and run as a single service. This means that any changes made anywhere in the application can affect the entire system, which simplifies development and deployment processes in the early stages of a product's lifecycle.

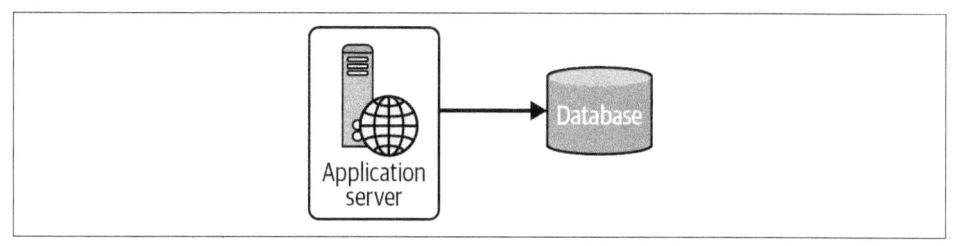

Figure 8-5. Monolithic architecture

Monoliths are straightforward to develop, test, deploy, and scale horizontally since they are a single executable or deployment unit. This is a very big advantage over microservices because the network interactions between different microservices are skipped, which helps reduce latency and provides easier handling of unreliable networks.

However, as applications grow, monoliths can become unwieldy and difficult to understand and modify. Scaling specific functions of the application rather than the entire application can also become challenging. From a scalability standpoint, we recommend keeping the code decoupled and modular so that it can be deployed separately if necessary. Even if the code is deployed in a single repository, modular code architecture allows you to reuse the components or add new features easily, and it maintains the code readability to proper standards. The next section describes this pattern in more detail.

N-tier Architectures

N-tier architectures break an application down into logical layers, each with a specific responsibility. Typically, these include at least three layers: presentation (frontend), business logic (middle-tier), and data management (backend). This is referred to as *three-tier architecture*, illustrated in Figure 8-6.

This architecture enhances maintainability by separating concerns among components, making it easier to manage, update, and scale individual parts of the system without affecting others. This architecture choice provides scalability and flexibility since each layer can be scaled independently according to demand. For instance, the data layer can be scaled up to handle larger data loads without necessarily scaling the presentation layer.

While N-tier architectures provide a significant improvement over monolithic designs by separating concerns, modern applications often require even greater flexibility, scalability, and fault tolerance. This is where microservices come into play.

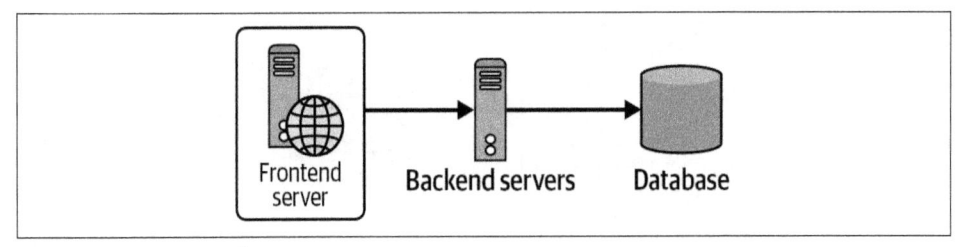

Figure 8-6. N-tier architecture

Microservices

A *microservice architecture*, illustrated in Figure 8-7, takes the principles of N-tier systems further by decomposing them into smaller, loosely coupled services. Each microservice focuses on a single functionality and can be developed, deployed, and scaled independently.

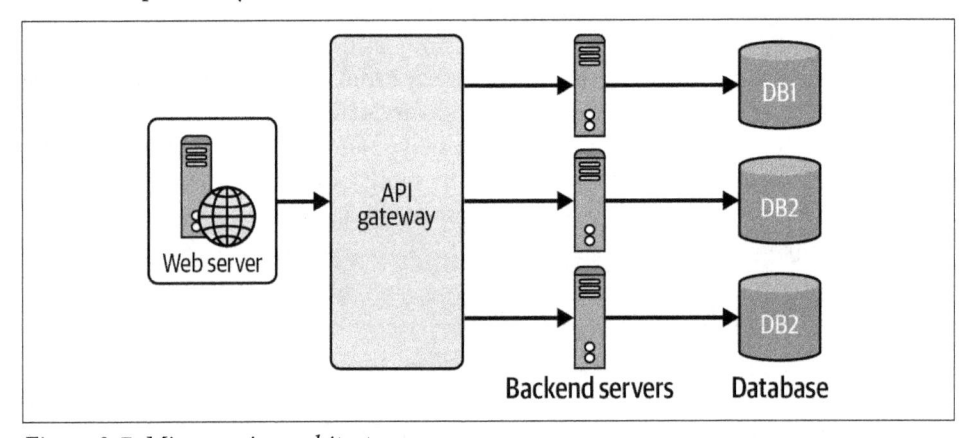

Figure 8-7. Microservice architecture

The microservice architecture offers several benefits and challenges. It gives teams autonomy to develop, test, deploy, and scale services independently, speeding up development cycles and improving fault isolation. It also allows for technology diversity, enabling different services to use the best-suited technology stack for their specific tasks.

However, the decentralized nature of microservices increases the complexity of management and operations, particularly with regard to interservice communications, data consistency, and transaction management. Additionally, service overhead can grow since each service may require its own database, libraries, and dependencies, increasing the resource footprint and management effort.

Transitioning from a monolithic to a microservice architecture may not suit every project or organization and should be approached with a clear understanding of the associated trade-offs. Issues like network latency, message formats, data integrity, and transaction management require robust strategies, such as API gateways, service meshes, and comprehensive logging and monitoring systems, to ensure system reliability and performance. By carefully evaluating the needs of the business and the capabilities of the team, organizations can choose the most appropriate architecture to support their goals, ensuring that their software infrastructure is both effective today and adaptable for future needs.

Another interesting paradigm for implementing application or big data architecture is event-driven architecture (EDA).

Event-Driven Architecture

EDA is a paradigm that orchestrates behavior around the production, detection, and consumption of events. This model offers a dynamic framework for applications to react to various state changes across distributed systems without the tight coupling of components, promoting scalability and responsiveness. We will start with EDA concepts and implementation paradigms and then go into the details of event sourcing specifically.

EDA Concepts and Implementations

An event-driven system enables the components of an application to communicate based on events rather than direct calls or shared-state manipulation. This is often realized by using events as messages that might be persisted until processed. Such systems leverage a state-machine approach. Here are the main concepts in this approach:

State machine
    A mathematical abstraction used to design algorithms based on a behavior model. A state machine reads a set of inputs and changes to a different state based on those inputs.

State
    A description of the status of a system waiting to execute a transition.

Transition
    A change from one state to another. A transition is a set of actions to execute when a condition is fulfilled or an event is received.

Event
    The entity that drives the state changes.

Event-driven state machine
   A state machine is event-driven if the transition from one state to another is triggered by an event or a message (not based on consuming or parsing characters or based on conditions).

Paradigms of Event-Driven Implementations

EDA is about implementing components that communicate via publishing events rather than making, for example, RPC/CRUD calls against one another or manipulating shared state. It's a communication strategy (albeit one that often relies on messages being persisted for fairly long periods until they are consumed). The two major implementation styles for EDA are state-oriented implementation and event sourcing.

State-oriented implementation

This method involves capturing the current state only, focusing on persisting state changes over time. State data is treated as mutable within controlled limits, modified only through defined operations, which makes the system responsive but tightly bound to current state conditions without historical tracking.

Event sourcing

Unlike state-oriented implementations, event sourcing persists each state change as an immutable event. These events are the system's source of truth, from which the current state can be reconstructed. This approach supports historical state reconstruction, auditing, and complex system behaviors like rollback and replay of events to handle errors or system failures.

Event sourcing allows for the following:

Complete rebuilds
   Enables systems to discard and rebuild state from scratch by replaying events

Temporal queries
   Inspects a state at any point in time by reprocessing events up to that moment

Event replays
   Corrects errors by reprocessing events after correcting them or adding new ones

Event-driven systems often use an *event store*, an append-only persistence optimized for storing events in sequence, as a single source of truth about the operations on both the application state and the data. This store ensures that all events are captured immutably, providing a reliable foundation for triggering actions, building projections, or reconstructing past states. These systems decouple data changes from application logic, allowing systems to scale and adapt more flexibly to changing business requirements.

An event-sourced persistence will model the entities as event streams and keep an immutable journal of these event streams. When the entity state or attribute mutates, it produces and saves a new event. When the entity state needs to be restored, all the events for that entity are read, and each event is applied to change the state, reaching the correct final state of the entity. Note that state here is the pure function application of the event stream on the entity.

When implementing event sourcing in event-driven systems, there are several important factors to consider:

Eventual consistency
  Reads may not reflect the most recent writes immediately because of delays in creating materialized views or projections. During the time between event publication and view creation, new events may be added to the event journal.

Event log immutability
  The event log should be immutable, meaning events cannot be updated once written. To correct a previous event, a new event must be added. Any changes to the event schema must be applied consistently across all stored events.

Event ordering and linearity
  Maintaining the correct order of events is crucial for data consistency, especially when multiple publishers are involved. Adding timestamps or incremental identifiers to events can help resolve ordering conflicts.

Consumer idempotency
  Since events might be delivered more than once, consumers must be idempotent, meaning they should be able to handle duplicate events without applying the same update multiple times, which could lead to incorrect state changes.

Snapshotting and materializing
  Regular snapshotting and materializing of events are necessary, especially when dealing with large event streams. This helps manage on-demand queries and ensures efficient access to the current state of the model.

Because of the decentralized control over the application's flow and the distributed nature of event handling, you'll need to keep these practical considerations for eventual consistency in mind and manage the complexity when architecting event-driven systems.

Event-driven architecture represents a paradigm shift from traditional request-driven models, providing a flexible, scalable way to handle asynchronous system behaviors and data flows. This architectural style is particularly well suited to applications where scalability, responsiveness, and robustness are crucial, such as in microservice environments or systems requiring complex business processes and workflows.

> Event sourcing and CDC both track changes in data, but they serve different purposes. Event sourcing captures all changes as events that can re-create or revert the system's state over time, essentially using events as the source of truth. In contrast, CDC primarily focuses on capturing changes made to a database to replicate or integrate data, using the database's transaction logs to record state changes without inherently storing the intent or context of the changes.

Common Cloud Architecture Patterns

In this section, we explore essential cloud architecture patterns that form the backbone of scalable, resilient, maintainable systems in cloud environments. These patterns—ranging from resilience-focused techniques like the circuit breaker to transaction-handling strategies like saga orchestration—will provide you with foundational tools that are especially valuable in the system design use cases presented in Part III. Understanding these patterns will better equip you to apply robust, tested solutions to common challenges in distributed architectures, setting the stage for effective design decisions.

Event-Based Patterns: CQRS and Saga

Event-based architectures leverage the following patterns to manage distributed transactions and operations:

Command query responsibility segregation (CQRS)
    CQRS is an architectural pattern that separates the operations that read data (queries) from the operations that update data (commands) into different interfaces. This separation allows read and write operations to be handled differently, optimizing performance, scalability, and security. For example, read models can be scaled independently from write models, which is particularly beneficial in systems where the number of read operations vastly exceeds the number of write operations.

Saga
    Sagas manage transactions that span multiple services, where each transaction step is paired with a compensating action for rollback if needed. They are based on either choreography or orchestration. In choreography, each service involved in the saga performs its transaction and publishes events that trigger the next steps in other services. In orchestration, a central coordinator (the orchestrator)

directs each step of the saga, managing the sequence and triggering compensating transactions if necessary.

These patterns are crucial in environments where distributed transactions need to be managed across microservices, providing a structure for handling complex operations reliably and efficiently.

Failure-Tolerant Patterns: Circuit Breaker, Retry with Backoff, and Rate Limiter

To enhance system resilience in the face of failures, employ the following patterns:

Circuit breaker
    The circuit breaker pattern prevents a cascade of failures in distributed systems. When a particular service or operation fails to a threshold level, the circuit breaker "trips," and further attempts to invoke the failing service are halted temporarily, thus allowing it to recover and maintain system stability.

Retry with backoff
    Retry with backoff involves reattempting failed operations with increasing delays between attempts, increasing the interval (backoff) progressively with each retry until a maximum number of retries is reached. This pattern is particularly useful when handling transient faults by providing time for the issue to resolve before retrying.

Rate limiter
    The rate limiter pattern controls the number of requests to a service within a specified time frame, preventing the system from being overwhelmed by a high volume of traffic or sudden spikes in demand. Rate limiting can be applied at various levels: per user, per service, or globally across a system. This pattern ensures that services continue to operate smoothly even under heavy load, reducing the likelihood of degraded performance or system crashes due to resource exhaustion.

These patterns work together to prevent cascading failures in distributed systems, ensuring that failures in one part of the system do not lead to widespread outages.

Domain-Based Patterns: Domain-Driven Design and Decompose by Subdomains

The following patterns focus on aligning software design with business objectives:

Domain-driven design (DDD)
    DDD focuses on the core domain logic and its complexity, basing the design on the domain's behavior and logic. This pattern encourages the creation of a domain model that incorporates business rules and behaviors, leading to a more

intuitive correlation between the software and the business requirements it aims to fulfill.

Decompose by subdomains
   Decompose by subdomains builds on DDD in a microservice architecture to divide a system into subdomains, each handling a specific business capability. Each microservice manages a subdomain, which improves maintainability and scalability by allowing the microservice to evolve independently based on its unique business requirements.

These patterns are essential for building modular, scalable systems that can evolve as business needs change.

API Routing Strategies and Patterns

API routing patterns determine how requests are directed within cloud environments to the appropriate services. These patterns are essential to ensuring that requests reach the correct backend systems efficiently and securely. Common routing strategies include:

Hostname routing
   This strategy routes requests to different backend systems based on the hostname in the URL. It is commonly used in scenarios where multiple services are hosted under different subdomains or domains.

Path routing
   This routing pattern uses URL paths to direct requests to specific services or handlers. It allows for clear, organized routing based on the structure of the URL, making it easier to manage and scale services.

HTTP header routing
   In this approach, HTTP headers within the request are leveraged to make routing decisions. This is particularly useful for scenarios like A/B testing, where different user groups are directed to different backend services, or for gradual rollouts of new features.

API routing architecture involves either an API gateway or service mesh in microservice-based systems:

API gateway
   An API gateway acts as a centralized entry point for all client requests, providing a unified interface to a set of backend services. It handles tasks such as request routing, composition, and protocol translation. The API gateway can invoke multiple microservices to fulfill a single client request and aggregate the responses into a cohesive result. This pattern is particularly useful in microservice

architectures as it simplifies client interactions and enhances security by centralizing access control and monitoring.

Service mesh
> Service mesh architecture is an infrastructure layer that manages service-to-service communication within a microservice architecture. It provides advanced routing, load balancing, service discovery, and security features like mutual Transport Layer Security (TLS) authentication and traffic encryption. Unlike API gateways, which handle external client-to-service communication, service mesh focuses on internal service-to-service interactions, ensuring reliable, secure communication within the cloud environment. It is implemented using sidecar proxies that intercept and manage network traffic between services, providing observability and resilience without requiring changes to the application code.

These API routing strategies and patterns, along with the API gateway and service mesh architectures, are foundational to building scalable, secure, and maintainable cloud native applications.

Other Cloud Architecture Patterns

In addition to the essential patterns, several other cloud architecture patterns address specific challenges and enhance system design:

Anticorruption layer
> The ACL serves as a protective barrier that prevents potentially disruptive data or requests from entering a system segment, thereby preserving the integrity of an application's core business model. It acts as a translator between different subsystems or external applications, ensuring that data exchanges do not corrupt the domain model.

Strangler fig pattern
> This pattern is used for gradually transforming legacy systems by replacing specific pieces of functionality with new applications and services. Over time, these new components "strangle" the old system, eventually replacing it entirely.

Transactional outbox
> The transactional outbox pattern is used to ensure reliable messaging between services. When changes are made to the database, records are also added to an "outbox" table within the same transaction. A separate process then sends these messages to the message queue or other destinations, ensuring data consistency across service boundaries.

Sidecar pattern
> The sidecar pattern is commonly used in microservice architectures. It involves deploying an additional container or process alongside a service container,

providing platform-connected services such as monitoring, logging, configuration, and networking capabilities. The sidecar can be written in any language without strong dependency on the main container and thus provides decoupling. This pattern allows for isolating infrastructure concerns from the application, making it cleaner and more modular.

Backend for frontend (BFF)
This pattern involves creating separate backend services tailored for different types of clients, such as desktop browsers and mobile devices. It allows developers to optimize these backend services for specific user interfaces, enhancing the user experience by reducing overfetching or underfetching of data.

Cellular architecture
Cellular architecture involves designing systems as collections of cells, where each cell operates independently but can communicate with other cells. Each cell is self-contained with its own data store and logic, capable of scaling autonomously. This approach is highly resilient since failure in one cell does not affect the others, and it supports evolutionary architecture by allowing each cell to evolve independently.

Each of these patterns provides targeted solutions to common problems in developing and managing cloud native applications, offering pathways to more resilient, flexible, and scalable architectures. Remember, this is not an exhaustive list of architecture patterns, and the list keeps evolving with the latest developments in system design. However, these patterns together offer robust solutions to various architectural challenges that you might face when designing complex systems.

Open Source Distributed Systems Architecture

Distributed systems architecture involves dividing responsibilities across multiple computing nodes to ensure that a system is scalable, fault tolerant, and efficient. In this context, we will explore two core components: distributed filesystems and distributed message queues, with a focus on open source implementations like HDFS for filesystems and Kafka for message queues.

HDFS

HDFS is an open source filesystem designed to run on commodity hardware. It is highly fault tolerant and is designed to be deployed on low-cost hardware. HDFS provides high-throughput access to application data and is suitable for applications that require processing of large datasets. Here are some key features of HDFS:

Distributed storage
HDFS is engineered for scalability, distributing data across multiple nodes in a cluster. It breaks large files into blocks and replicates them across different machines, ensuring data redundancy and availability even in the event of hardware failures.

Fault tolerance
One of the key features of HDFS is its built-in fault tolerance. Data is automatically replicated, typically across three different nodes, ensuring that if one node fails, the data remains accessible from the other nodes. This replication mechanism provides reliability and high availability, making HDFS well suited for large-scale data storage.

Scalability and flexibility
HDFS can scale horizontally by adding more nodes to the cluster, allowing it to manage increasing data volumes without significant changes to the infrastructure. This scalability, combined with its ability to store data in various formats, makes HDFS a flexible solution for a wide range of data-processing needs.

High throughput
HDFS is optimized for high throughput, prioritizing data access speed over low latency. It is designed to handle large datasets with a focus on batch processing, making it ideal for big data applications that involve reading and writing large volumes of data.

Cost-effectiveness
By using commodity hardware, HDFS provides a cost-effective solution for storing and processing large volumes of data.

Integration with Hadoop ecosystem
HDFS is deeply integrated with the broader Hadoop ecosystem, supporting various processing frameworks like MapReduce, Hive, and Spark. This integration allows for seamless data processing and analysis, leveraging HDFS's distributed architecture to perform computations close to the data, which can reduce network bottlenecks and improve efficiency.

> AWS offers Amazon Elastic MapReduce (EMR), a managed service that simplifies running big data frameworks like Hadoop, including HDFS, on the AWS cloud. We will explore it further in Chapter 13. Amazon EMR supports processing vast amounts of data using HDFS (or EMRFS), leveraging its scalability, fault tolerance, and integration with the broader Hadoop ecosystem.

HDFS architecture

The HDFS architecture, shown in Figure 8-8, is built around several key components that work together to provide a distributed, fault-tolerant, scalable filesystem.

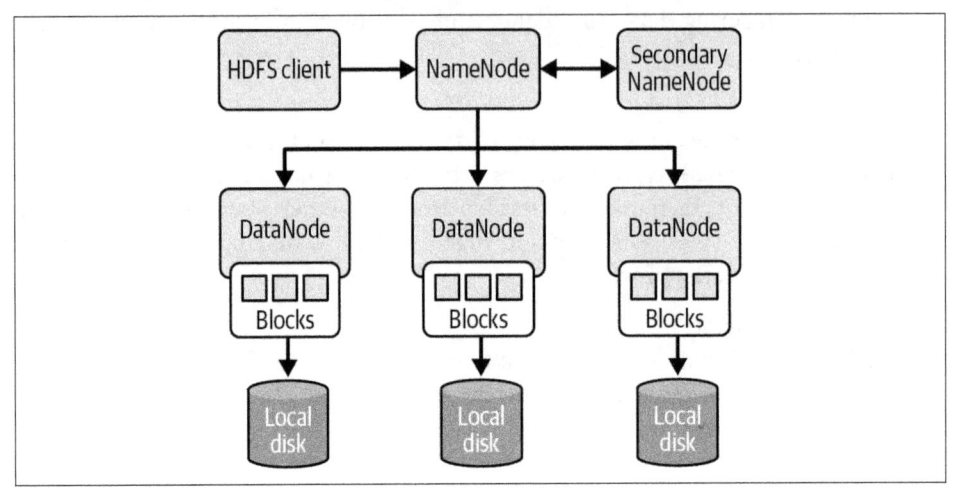

Figure 8-8. HDFS architecture

The components of the HDFS architecture are:

NameNode
 The NameNode is the central component of HDFS, responsible for managing the metadata and namespace of the filesystem. It keeps track of file locations and manages access to files by coordinating the storage across DataNodes. The NameNode is critical for the operation of HDFS; if it fails, the filesystem becomes inaccessible.

DataNodes
 DataNodes are the workers in the HDFS architecture. They store the actual data blocks that make up the files in HDFS. Each DataNode periodically sends heartbeats and block reports to the NameNode, ensuring that the system has an updated view of storage health and availability.

Secondary NameNode
 Despite its name, the secondary NameNode is not a backup for the NameNode. Instead, it works alongside the NameNode to manage the filesystem's metadata. It periodically snapshots the metadata and applies the edit log, which helps reduce the recovery time in case of a NameNode failure.

Blocks
 HDFS stores data in blocks, typically 128 MB in size, which are replicated across multiple DataNodes (usually three) for redundancy. This block-based storage

system enables HDFS to handle large files efficiently, ensuring that even if a DataNode fails, the data remains available from another replica.

When a client wants to read or write a file, it communicates with the NameNode to locate the DataNodes that hold the data blocks. For writing, the NameNode provides a list of DataNodes where the client should write the data blocks. Once written, the DataNodes replicate the blocks to other nodes as directed by the NameNode.

HDFS is rack aware, meaning it understands the physical layout of the nodes across different racks in a data center. The NameNode uses this information to make intelligent decisions about block placement, ensuring that replicas are distributed across different racks. This improves fault tolerance by ensuring that a rack failure doesn't lead to data loss.

HDFS's fault tolerance is achieved through data replication and periodic checks by the NameNode. If a DataNode fails, the NameNode initiates a replication of the affected blocks to other nodes to ensure data availability.

Together, these components and features form a highly reliable, scalable distributed filesystem that is central to the Hadoop ecosystem. HDFS's architecture is designed to handle large-scale data storage and retrieval across thousands of nodes, making it ideal for big data applications.

HDFS plays a critical role within the broader Hadoop ecosystem, offering essential storage capabilities for big data processing. However, when evaluating big data solutions, it's important to consider other platforms as well. While the Hadoop ecosystem provides a comprehensive set of open source tools for managing and processing large datasets, cloud platforms like AWS offer managed services that can simplify deployment and scalability. Let's now compare the Hadoop ecosystem with AWS, highlighting their differences, strengths, and use cases.

Hadoop ecosystem versus AWS

The Hadoop ecosystem is a comprehensive suite of tools designed for distributed data storage and processing across large clusters of computers. The core of Hadoop includes HDFS for scalable storage and MapReduce for parallel processing of large datasets. However, the ecosystem extends far beyond these two components to include tools such as Hive (for SQL-like querying of large datasets), Pig (a high-level scripting language for data analysis), HBase (a NoSQL database for real-time data), and YARN (for resource management). It also includes Apache Spark for in-memory data processing, Oozie for workflow scheduling, and ZooKeeper for distributed coordination.

AWS provides fully managed equivalents for most Hadoop services, eliminating much of the operational overhead. AWS services like Amazon S3 for scalable object storage, Amazon EMR for running Hadoop and Spark clusters, Amazon Athena for interactive query service, and AWS Glue for ETL operations all offer more integrated solutions with scaling, cost management, and security features. Table 8-1 presents a comparison of Hadoop services and their AWS counterparts.

Table 8-1. Hadoop ecosystem versus AWS services

Hadoop ecosystem service	Description	Corresponding AWS service	Comparison
HDFS	Distributed filesystem for large-scale data	Amazon S3/EMRFS (built on top of S3)	S3 is a scalable object store that is easier to manage than HDFS, with pay-as-you-go pricing.
MapReduce	Parallel processing of data	Amazon EMR	EMR supports MapReduce and automates cluster management, offering flexibility in instance types.
Hive	Distributed data warehouse for online analytical processing (OLAP)	Amazon Redshift	Redshift offers a fully managed, petabyte-scale data warehouse that is optimized for OLAP and easier to scale.
Pig	High-level data analysis language	AWS Glue	Glue offers serverless ETL with integrated workflow capabilities, replacing the manual setup of Pig.
Presto	SQL-like querying of large datasets	Amazon Athena	Athena is a serverless query service, allowing SQL queries on S3 without provisioning infrastructure.
HBase	NoSQL database for real-time analytics	HBase on EMR	HBase on EMR provides a managed Hadoop framework similar to the self-managed HBase, which requires manual scaling.
YARN	Resource manager for cluster computing	Amazon EMR/ECS	EMR simplifies YARN management; ECS provides container orchestration, abstracting away cluster management.
ZooKeeper	Coordination for distributed applications	AWS AppConfig	ZooKeeper is used for metadata management in Hadoop and Kafka; AppConfig is used for configuration management on AWS.
Oozie	Workflow scheduling	AWS Step Functions	Step Functions offer serverless orchestration with better integration into AWS services for ETL and workflows, compared to workflow management by Oozie.
Sqoop	Structured data transfer between Hadoop and relational databases	AWS Database Migration Service (DMS)	DMS provides a fully managed service to transfer data from various databases (relational and nonrelational) to the cloud, supporting migrations in real time or as a batch like Sqoop but with additional features for cloud integration.
Flume	Continuous, real-time streaming of unstructured data from various sources into Hadoop	Amazon Kinesis	Kinesis enables real-time data ingestion and processing for analytics and streaming applications, offering a fully managed service compared to Flume's manual setup for streaming.
Spark	In-memory data processing	Spark on Amazon EMR	EMR supports running Spark jobs, offering more flexibility and management options than Hadoop's native Spark setup.

This comparison highlights how AWS provides more integrated, scalable alternatives to traditional Hadoop services, often with reduced operational overhead. We'll be discussing these related AWS services more in Part II.

Apache Kafka: Distributed Message Queue

Apache Kafka is an open source distributed event-streaming platform capable of handling trillions of events a day in real time. As a highly reliable, scalable messaging system, Kafka can process millions of records per second, making it ideal for event-driven architectures, real-time analytics, and complex data pipelines. Here are some key features of Kafka:

Scalability
   Kafka's partitioning mechanism allows it to scale horizontally by distributing data across multiple nodes. This architecture supports high throughput and can handle large volumes of data.

Durability and reliability
   Kafka ensures data durability by persisting messages on disk and replicating them across multiple brokers. This replication guarantees that even in the event of a broker failure, data is not lost.

Fault tolerance
   Kafka is designed to handle failures gracefully. In the event of a broker failure, Kafka's replication mechanism ensures that another broker can take over the failed broker's responsibilities without data loss.

High throughput
   Kafka's design is optimized for high throughput, making it capable of processing millions of records per second. This makes Kafka ideal for real-time data pipelines and event-driven architectures.

Kafka architecture

Figure 8-9 presents Kafka's components and architecture.

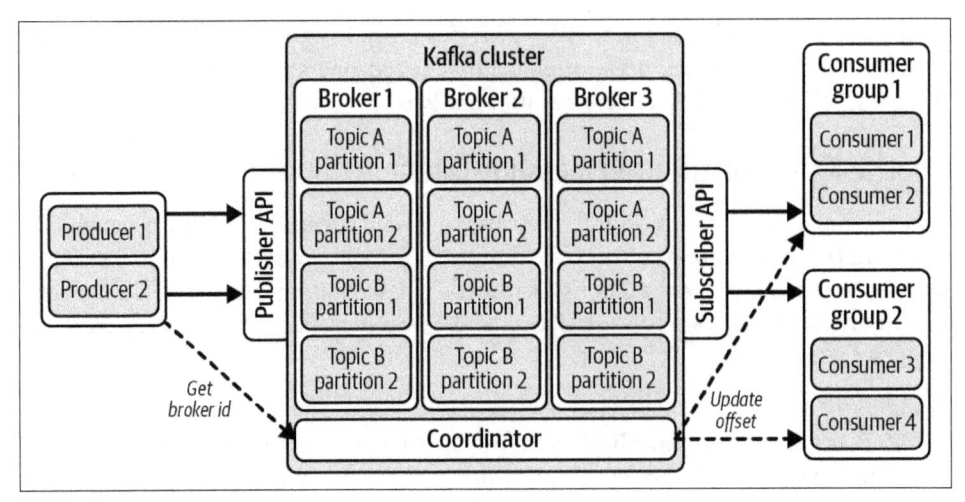

Figure 8-9. Kafka architecture

Let's look at these components in more detail:

Producers
> Producers are responsible for pushing data (records) into Kafka topics. They send data to the Kafka brokers, which manage partitioning and replicating the data across the cluster.

Consumers
> Consumers read data from Kafka topics. They subscribe to one or more topics and consume records in the order they are stored in the partitions.

Schema Registry
> Schema Registry is a service that manages and enforces the schemas used by Kafka producers and consumers. It ensures that data is written in a consistent format, preventing compatibility issues between different versions of data structures as they evolve over time.

Brokers
> Kafka brokers are the servers that manage the persistence and replication of data. Each broker stores data in *partitions*, which are the basic units of scalability in Kafka. Partitions allow Kafka to scale horizontally by distributing data across multiple nodes.

Coordinator
> ZooKeeper used to manage the coordination of Kafka brokers in the cluster. It handled tasks such as leader election for partitions, cluster configuration, and metadata management. Recent versions of Kafka have replaced ZooKeeper with

Apache Kafka Raft (KRaft) (*https://oreil.ly/BBg6D*) for consensus protocol and metadata management.

Topics
A Kafka topic is a category or feed name to which records are stored and published. Topics in Kafka are partitioned to allow data to be distributed across multiple brokers. Each partition is an ordered, immutable sequence of records that is continually appended to a log.

Partitions
Kafka partitions enable parallel processing of records within a topic. Each partition can be hosted on different brokers, allowing Kafka to scale horizontally and handle massive amounts of data. Partitions are also the units of replication in Kafka, ensuring data durability and fault tolerance.

Keys
In Kafka, the key plays a crucial role in determining which partition a record is sent to within a topic. When a producer sends a record, it can specify a key. Kafka uses this key, along with a hashing function, to map the record to a specific partition. This ensures that records with the same key always go to the same partition, preserving the order of records for that key.

> Kafka appends messages to a partition in the exact order they are sent by a producer. If a producer sends message M1 before message M2 to the same partition, M1 will receive a lower offset than M2, ensuring that it appears earlier in the log. It's important to note that this ordering guarantee applies only within individual partitions. Users can manage partitioning strategies to make use of this ordered delivery across different data segments.

Kafka's configuration levels

Kafka offers several configuration levels for fine-tuning the system to meet specific needs:

Replication factor
This level determines the number of copies of a partition that Kafka will maintain across different brokers. Higher replication increases fault tolerance but also requires more storage and network resources.

Acknowledgments
Producers can configure the level of acknowledgment they require from the brokers. For example, a setting of `acks=all` ensures that a message is considered successfully written only when all in-sync replicas acknowledge it, enhancing reliability at the cost of higher latency.

Retention policies
: Kafka allows configuration of how long records are retained in the topics. Retention can be based on time (e.g., seven days) or size (e.g., 100 GB), ensuring that only relevant data is kept for more effective storage management.

Compression
: Message compression in Kafka reduces the amount of data that is transmitted over the network and stored on disk. Different compression algorithms like gzip, snappy, and lz4 can be configured based on the use case.

Kafka provides strong messaging guarantees that ensure the reliable delivery of messages in distributed systems. These guarantees are crucial for maintaining data consistency and integrity across complex data pipelines:

At-most-once delivery
: Messages are delivered to consumers at most once, meaning they may be lost but are never delivered more than once. This is the default setting when no retries or acknowledgments are configured.

At-least-once delivery
: Every message is delivered at least once. This means that even in the event of a failure, the message will eventually reach the consumer, though duplicates may occur. This guarantee is often used when data loss is unacceptable, and duplicate messages can be handled by the application logic. To manage the potential duplicates, applications consuming messages in an at-least-once delivery setup should implement idempotency in their processing logic.

> An operation is *idempotent* if applying it multiple times has the same effect as applying it once. For example, a consumer might keep track of processed message IDs to prevent processing duplicates. This approach ensures that repeated messages do not result in unintended side effects, maintaining data integrity in applications that require precise processing.

Exactly-once delivery
: Exactly-once semantics (EOS) in Kafka ensure that each message is delivered to the consumer exactly once, without any duplicates, even in the face of failures. This is achieved through Kafka's idempotent producers and transactional APIs, which maintain atomicity across multiple partitions and topics. EOS is particularly valuable in systems where data integrity is critical, such as financial transactions.

These messaging guarantees, along with Kafka's robust fault tolerance and scalability, make it a reliable choice for building distributed data streaming and processing systems. Kafka's ability to handle large-scale data streams with low latency has made it a cornerstone in modern distributed systems.

> AWS offers Amazon Managed Streaming for Apache Kafka (MSK) and Amazon Kinesis, which are managed services designed for real-time data streaming. MSK simplifies running Apache Kafka on AWS, while Kinesis provides tools for collecting, processing, and analyzing streaming data. Both services enable scalable, reliable data processing. We will explore them further in Chapter 12.

Comparing HDFS and Kafka

Both HDFS and Kafka are designed to handle large volumes of data efficiently. We compare their features in Table 8-2.

Table 8-2. HDFS versus Kafka

Feature	HDFS	Kafka
Core function	Distributed file storage	Message queue/event-streaming platform
Use case	Big data storage, large-scale processing	Real-time messaging, event sourcing
Data model	Files	Streams of records
Performance	High throughput, optimized for large files	High throughput, optimized for message passing
Scalability	Linear scalability with more nodes	Scales horizontally with topics and partitions
Fault tolerance	Replication across nodes	Replication within and across clusters

Both HDFS and Kafka are powerful open source technologies that cater to specific needs within distributed systems. HDFS is ideal for applications requiring large-scale data storage and processing, while Kafka is suited to applications that need robust, real-time data processing and messaging capabilities. Choosing between HDFS and Kafka depends on your organization's specific data management and processing needs.

Conclusion

The architectural designs and patterns discussed in this chapter provide a comprehensive toolkit for building scalable, maintainable, efficient systems. CDC offers a mechanism for ensuring that data is always up to date across distributed environments, while the pub/sub architecture facilitates decoupled communication between system components. Big data architectures like lambda, kappa, and data lake offer robust solutions for processing and analyzing vast amounts of data. Meanwhile, Kafka and HDFS serve as foundational technologies in distributed systems, each excelling in their domains: real-time event streaming and large-scale data storage, respectively.

By understanding and leveraging the architectural patterns and technologies discussed in the last sections of this chapter, organizations can build systems that not only meet current needs but also are adaptable to future challenges. The flexibility, scalability, and fault tolerance offered by these design patterns ensure that your system architecture can evolve in tandem with growing business demands and technological advancements. Keep in mind that design patterns are constantly changing, and there is no comprehensive list—we've covered only the tip of the iceberg. These architecture patterns are like guidelines that you can follow, but you do not need to completely adhere to them. Use whatever makes sense for your business requirements and do not force a design pattern to your requirements. As technology advances, new patterns and strategies will continue to emerge, shaping the future of system architecture and design.

At this point, we conclude Part I. Part II will dive into the many AWS services, and you'll begin to understand how the concepts that we covered in this part connect to AWS service design and choices.

PART II
Diving Deep into AWS Services

Big and dumb is better.
　—Mark Hill

Part II of this book covers the common AWS network, storage, compute, orchestration, big data and analytics, and machine learning (ML) services. We'll explore the inherent designs and benefits of these managed services. This part also provides guidance for how these services need to be structured in a well-architected framework to build secure, high-performing, resilient, and efficient infrastructure for a variety of applications and workloads.

At the end of Part II, you will:

- Understand the network services offered by AWS and how to use them to build a resilient cloud infrastructure
- Be able to identify the appropriate AWS storage services for different data management needs and use cases
- Learn about the compute services offered by AWS and how to identify the right size and type of resource while keeping the variable cost in check using containers and other serverless offerings for different kinds of workloads
- Use the orchestration services offered by AWS to properly decouple and scale the application on AWS, improving flexibility and performance

- Know what big data and analytics services are offered by AWS to run large-scale jobs and answer queries on large datasets to derive value from your big data
- Discover the ML services offered by AWS and learn how to solve ML business use cases and set up ML pipelines and operations for your business using the managed offerings

Chapter 9 will dive into the fully managed network services that AWS offers. You'll discover how to use them to create a strong, resilient cloud infrastructure. We'll begin with learning how to get started on the AWS cloud. Then, we'll cover basic networking concepts, such as how the internet works, virtual private cloud (VPC), subnets, internet connectivity within and outside the AWS cloud, NAT gateways (a way for your cloud systems to communicate securely with the outside world), Amazon Route 53 (for managing domain names), Amazon CloudFront (to make your web services load faster), AWS Elastic Load Balancer (ELB), and Amazon API Gateway.

Chapter 10 will explore the managed storage services provided by AWS and help you understand how to choose the right storage services for different needs. The chapter will start with Amazon Elastic Block Store (EBS), Amazon Elastic File System (EFS), and Amazon Simple Storage Service (S3) object store and its different classes. The chapter will then cover databases, including Amazon Relational Database Service (RDS), Amazon Aurora, Amazon DynamoDB, Amazon DocumentDB, Amazon Keyspaces, Amazon Timestream, and Amazon Neptune, as well as Amazon ElastiCache, including ElastiCache for Redis and ElastiCache for Memcached.

Chapter 11 will introduce you to the compute services that AWS offers. We'll figure out how to choose the right kind and size of compute resources for different jobs. We'll look at services like Amazon Elastic Compute Cloud (EC2), which is like renting virtual computers in the cloud. Then we'll talk about AWS Lambda, a special kind of on-demand computing that happens in response to events; Amazon Elastic Container Registry (ECR); AWS Fargate for Elastic Container Service (ECS), which manages and deploys containers; and ECS Elastic Kubernetes Service (EKS) cluster for running applications in containers.

Chapter 12 will cover the messaging, orchestration, monitoring, and access management services from AWS. These services help you manage and coordinate different tasks in your software system. We'll talk about Amazon Simple Queue Service (SQS), a way for different parts of your system to communicate indirectly; Amazon Simple Notification Service (SNS) for sending messages; and Amazon Managed Streaming for Apache Kafka (MSK) and Amazon Kinesis, which enable different parts of your system to talk to one another. We'll also explore AWS Step Functions to help you piece together workflows and AWS Managed Workflows to help you manage and monitor workflows. Last, we will cover Amazon CloudWatch for monitoring and debugging your cloud applications, AWS Identity and Access Management (IAM) for authentication and authorization over AWS resources, Amazon Cognito for managing identity pools, and AWS AppSync to orchestrate all AWS services under one GraphQL endpoint.

Chapter 13 will explore AWS's big data, analytics, and ML Services. These services help you work with huge amounts of data and find valuable insights. We'll check out Amazon Redshift, a powerful tool for analyzing data; Amazon Elastic MapReduce (EMR) for processing big data; Amazon Athena for asking questions about your data; AWS Glue for preparing and transforming data; and Amazon QuickSight for creating visual reports. This chapter will also introduce you to the ML services offered by AWS, showing you how to solve ML business use cases and set up ML data pipelines and operations for your business using the managed offerings.

By the end of Part II, you'll have a clear understanding of all these AWS services and how to use them effectively. You'll know how to build a strong, secure cloud infrastructure that can handle different tasks and workloads.

Later, Part III provides several real-world examples of designing systems using AWS cloud computing services. We'll break down different use cases step-by-step in an easy-to-understand way, using the concepts from Part I and the AWS services from Part II for practical implementation.

CHAPTER 9
AWS Network Services

People interact with multiple applications (or with one another) via the internet. We first explored communication network and protocol concepts in Chapter 6; this chapter is an extension of Chapter 6 that will introduce you to the AWS networking services Amazon VPC, Amazon Route 53, AWS Elastic Load Balancer (ELB), Amazon API Gateway, and Amazon CloudFront. The goal is to help you set up your networking infrastructure on the AWS cloud as you learn about the networking concepts related to the different services and how to establish connectivity between them.

Companies used to prefer setting up their own infrastructures in on-premises data centers to make their systems more reliable and safer and to ensure that they operated per business requirements, but that comes with a high cost for infrastructure management. If you are just launching your startup idea, it will likely be too costly for you to set up a personal data center. The cloud provides cost benefits (when analyzing the costs of all the resources and optimizing them to their full potential) along with a lot of flexibility. For example, it's much harder to sell back a physical server that you bought for setting up your personal data center than it is to turn off an Amazon EC2 machine (server) in the AWS cloud.

AWS operates on a shared responsibility model (*https://oreil.ly/L-Dyu*), meaning the customer and AWS work together to make best use of services in a secure and cost-effective way, where AWS is responsible for "security of the cloud" and customers are responsible for "security in the cloud." Before we examine AWS's networking components, let's dig into where these services are located and how they are segregated per customer.

Getting Started with AWS

To start with AWS's cloud computing services, customers need to create an AWS account (*https://oreil.ly/ELJQZ*). This account is a fundamental entity in AWS that provides access to a wide range of services. It holds all the information related to the creation, management, operations, support, and billing of your AWS resources (such as compute instances, storage, networking, etc.). With an AWS account, you can provision and configure resources, monitor usage and costs, set security and access controls, and interact with various AWS services.

It will be very important to identify how many AWS accounts to set up. This will vary from one use case to another and will depend on the scale your organization operates on. The following are some general suggestions to consider when deciding how many AWS accounts to configure:

Complete separation of applications
: Every application is launched in a new AWS account. This option has the benefits of full separation and effective cost management of applications but presents challenges in the form of too much operational cost.

Separation of AWS accounts based on business type
: For example, a cab-booking company operates in domains like cab availability, payments, and analytics. All applications related to a single business will operate in a single account, which has the advantages of correlating applications located near one another, optimizing latency, and offloading requirements of resource setup for service connection among different accounts. These applications can be segregated in Amazon VPCs or availability zones (AZs) depending on the use case.

Separation of AWS accounts based on software domains
: For example, there are separate accounts for networking, monitoring, storage, and security and auditing. This kind of setup provides for easier operations management. For example, all the networking configurations are in a single account that can be managed by the network engineering team.

AWS recommends creating a multiaccount setup to ensure that there is clear division of responsibility while keeping future scaling of systems in mind. For example, separate networking accounts will help keep all networking configurations in a single place, with access only to the networking team. AWS offers the Landing Zone service (*https://oreil.ly/xCpIY*), which provides a baseline to get started with multiaccount architecture, IAM, governance, data security, network design, and logging. AWS Landing Zone can be orchestrated by customers themselves or as a managed service. One such service, AWS Control Tower, can be used to set up initial prescriptive configurations, and further customizations can be made as organizations scale.

AWS Regions

Once you have created an AWS account, you're ready to launch the first server in the cloud. A very intriguing question, though, is: where is this cloud? The AWS cloud operates from a physical location, which might be near you or far from you. AWS defines the geographically distributed locations around the world where it operates data centers as AWS regions (*https://oreil.ly/R4lE5*). For example, the US North Virginia region is called *us-east-1*. Each region is a separate and independent geographic area, isolated from other regions. You can choose the AWS region to launch resources per your business requirements, such as latency constraints or compliance regulations, or for AWS service availability in the region. For example, Netflix architecture has presence in three AWS regions, ensuring high availability even in cases of regional failure. Keeping resources at multiple locations helps build resilient systems, which we touched on in Part I. Amazon provides a complete list of regions available across the globe. There are some global services, such as AWS IAM (*https://aws.amazon.com/iam*), where region selection is not a requirement.

> There is a possibility that not all AWS services are present in your AWS region.

AWS Availability Zones

Customers choose to deploy resources in multiple regions to improve availability, latency, and many other business use cases. A key point to note is that not everyone can afford to replicate resources in multiple AWS regions. Does that mean they must compromise application availability? Cloud providers work on a *shared responsibility model*, which means that to ensure a good run on the cloud, customers and cloud providers must work together. A simple example could be deploying your servers in multiple availability zones (*https://oreil.ly/TC6rf*) instead of just one. That way, even if one AZ goes down, there are servers operational in other AZs to serve the traffic. You can think of a single region as a cluster of data centers and each data center (or combination of data centers) as an availability zone. An AZ is physically isolated from other AZs by meaningful distance, with independent power and cooling and fast, private, fiber-optic, low-latency network connectivity. The purpose of AZs is to provide fault tolerance, resilience, and high availability by allowing you to distribute your applications and data across multiple AZs within a region. AZs are classified with suffixes to region names; for example, *us-east-1a* or *us-east-1b* are AZs within the us-east-1 region.

AWS Local Zones

Consider the following scenario: you are all set to launch your startup for the people of New Delhi, India. The application setup requires single-digit p99.99 latency for API operations, but the nearest AWS region is Mumbai, India. The operations are optimized well, and your use case doesn't allow you to use precached data, such as utilizing a CDN or retrieving data from servers located at a specific AZ. How can you overcome such an issue? This can potentially be solved by placing database instances near customers, which can be achieved via AWS local zones. Local zones enable you to set up infrastructure near your customers, and the infrastructure is connected to an AWS region via a fast-paced network. We'll also discuss potential use of AWS Local Zones in Chapter 21 while designing stock broker application.

AWS local zones are an extension of an AWS region and are designed to bring AWS services with low-latency requirements closer to specific geographic areas. Local zones are geographically separated from their parent regions and are located in metropolitan areas. They provide a subset of AWS services and are primarily intended for latency-sensitive workloads that require proximity to end users or specific on-premises resources. You can check all available locations for local zones (*https://oreil.ly/dQ9pT*) and a list of the supported AWS services (*https://oreil.ly/vKAyW*).

AWS Edge Locations

Imagine that HBO is planning to stream a new season of *Game of Thrones*, and the first episode will be out on an upcoming Sunday morning at 8 A.M. *Game of Thrones* is popular worldwide, and the new episode is expected to be watched by many viewers in multiple countries at the same time. How can HBO ensure the best customer experience via full high-definition video quality with no video buffering? The AWS CDN service Amazon CloudFront can place the content near viewers at locations called *edge locations* so that customers can be served in the minimum time possible.

AWS edge locations are points of presence (PoPs) distributed globally to bring AWS services closer to end users. Edge locations improve the performance of content delivery by acting as caching and content delivery endpoints for CloudFront, thus reducing latency and increasing data-transfer speeds.

You can think of AWS edge locations as data centers that are connected with AWS regions to support fast uploading and downloading of data. Some other services—such as Amazon Route 53, an Amazon DNS service—use the same setup for faster resolution of DNS queries. Figure 9-1 shows the connectivity of users via AWS edge locations to AWS regions.

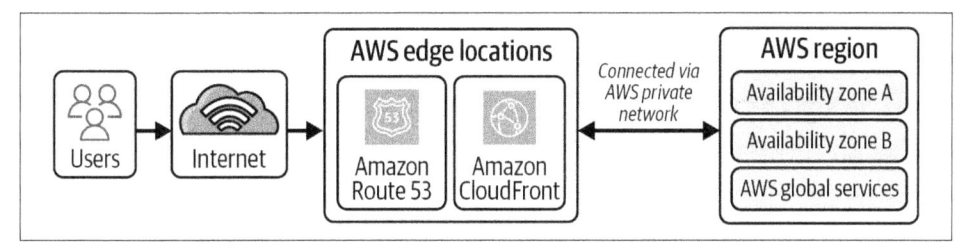

Figure 9-1. Connectivity to an AWS region via an edge location

This high-level view covered how the AWS cloud is set up and made accessible to customers across the globe. Let's jump right into how connectivity can be established with the AWS cloud and the different networking components within it.

Introduction to AWS Networking Services

Figure 9-1 showed how users establish connections to AWS services located within an AWS region. It's important to understand how this accessibility is maintained and how the AWS cloud provides a similar abstraction for your private data center. This section will introduce you to offerings that AWS provides in the context of networking and connectivity.

Amazon VPC

Setting up your own data center could be costly in terms of both monetary costs and operations management. Amazon VPC provides a similar level of infrastructure separation to what you'd have in a personal, private data center. You can think of VPC as your personal data center located inside the AWS cloud.

Amazon's VPC service allows you to create a virtual network in the cloud. It gives you control over your network environment, including selection of an IP address range, creation of subnets, configuration of route tables, and network gateways. VPC enables you to securely launch resources like Amazon EC2 instances, Amazon RDS, and AWS ELBs within a logically isolated section of the AWS cloud.

> This book will not outline the steps in setting up the infrastructure but will focus more on core concepts of AWS. We will provide links to AWS documentation for guidance on setup and recommend you visit the product pages for more details.

A lot of customers use the AWS cloud. Amazon VPC plays a vital role in setting up boundaries between customer resources. AWS accounts come with one default VPC to launch resources, and more VPCs can be created per the use case requirements. There is a default limit of five VPCs per account per region, which can be increased by raising a query with AWS Support Center. We'll dig into VPC in more detail, starting with some basic networking knowledge that will be helpful for making better decisions about how to set up your VPC.

IP addresses

Let's consider a real-world example. You're very excited to meet a new friend in person, and both of you have agreed to meet at Cafe Delhi Heights, Third Floor, 301 and 302, Ambience Mall, Gurugram, India. However, you need a specific location—a table number in this restaurant, not just the restaurant location. This pinpointed location in the networking world is called an *IP address*: a unique string of characters that identifies each computer. Every device should have an IP address to connect with another device on the internet. IP addresses can be of type IPv4 or IPv6.

IPv4. *IPv4* is a 32-bit or 4-byte address space where each byte is represented via decimal numbers (binary octet) and separated by a dot (.), such as 192.168.1.0. How can we identify which destination the traffic should be routed to? How does the postal service deliver mail to your doorstep, or how do you know to meet your new friend at table 21 at Cafe Delhi Heights? Two components are generally required for unique identification. For physical mail, these would be your zip code, postal code, or area PIN code (depending on your country) and your house number, and for meeting your new friend, they would be the restaurant location in Ambience Mall, Gurugram, and the table number inside this restaurant.

Similarly, two components are involved in delivering network packets to your personal computer: a network component (*network ID*) and a host component (*host ID*). For example, your office network will map to a network ID, and your personal computer will map to a host ID.

The division of the number of bits that should be allocated to the network ID and host ID is defined via IP classes, as shown in Figure 9-2. There are in total five IP classes from A to E, out of which Class D is reserved for multitasking and Class E is reserved for research purposes.

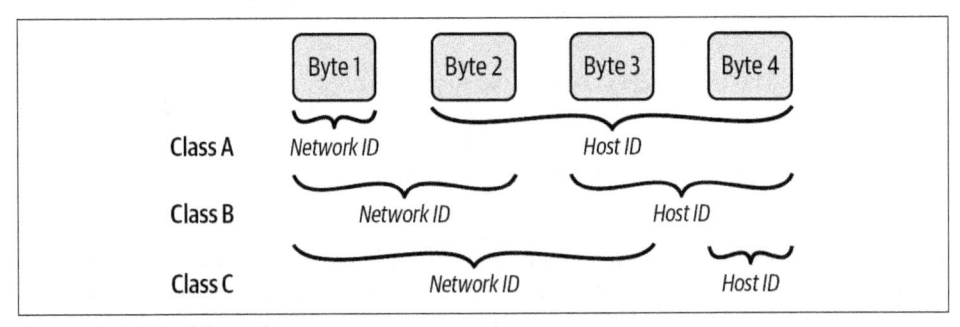

Figure 9-2. IP address classes

One difference between classes A, B, and C is the number of bits assigned to each network ID and host ID. Another is the range of IP addresses that are allowed in each class, which are listed in Table 9-1.

Table 9-1. IPv4 address range by class

IP address class	IP range
Class A	1.0.0.0–127.255.255.255
Class B	128.0.0.0–191.255.255.255
Class C	192.0.0.0–223.255.255.255

Deciding which class suits your specific use case depends on the requirements for the number of networks and number of hosts in a network. For example, Class A provides 126 network IDs and 16,777,214 host IDs, whereas Class C provides 2,097,152 network IDs and 254 host IDs. Division of IP address or network space into network and host address is achieved via subnet masks. Class C addresses are most common for general-purpose use cases, such as home networks and small-business setups.

As the name suggests, *subnets* divide the parent network into subnetworks. The *subnet mask* is the division of the IP address into the network and host address. It is a 32-bit number where host bits are set to 0 and network bits are set to 1. Amazon VPC logically isolates the resources at regional level, and further division into AZs can be achieved via subnets—we'll be exploring this while creating our first VPC in follow-up sections. Figure 9-3 shows an example IPv4 address along with its subnet mask representation.

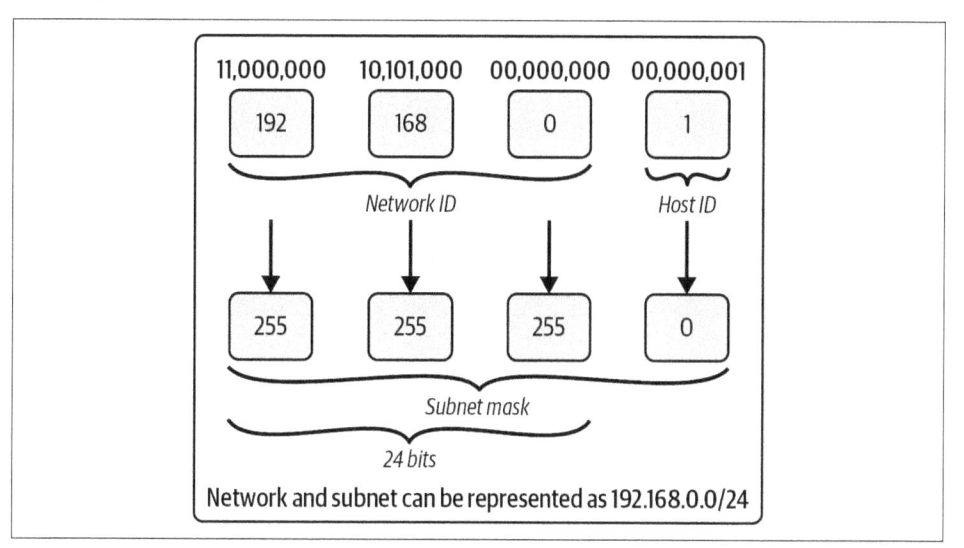

Figure 9-3. Representation of an IPv4 address and subnet mask

A specific problem that arises with IPv4 addresses is the very limited number of addresses available in comparison to the number of devices and networks across the world. The intermittent solution to slow exhaustion of IPv4 addresses is via *Classless Inter-Domain Routing (CIDR)*.

> Keep in mind that the first four IP addresses and last IP address in each subnet CIDR block are reserved for special purposes (*https://oreil.ly/GQvXO*) and therefore can't be assigned to hosts (or resources).

CIDR is a way of representing an IP address and its subnet mask. The classless concept was introduced in 1993 to slow the exhaustion of IPv4 addresses. CIDR helps in varying subnet mask length, skipping standard division via classes. This kind of division optimizes the class space of IP addresses. You can see this represented in Figure 9-4.

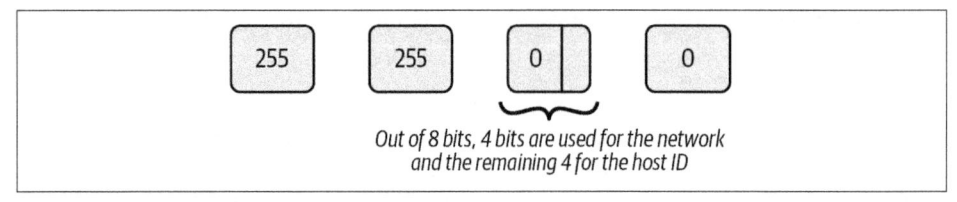

Figure 9-4. Variable length subnet mask

However, the long-term solution is migration to IPv6 addresses.

IPv6. *IPv6* is 128 bits, which provides a much larger network space as compared to 32-bit IPv4 addresses. IPv6 is represented by eight groups of four hexadecimal digits and separated by colons, such as *ab90:cd00:0000:0cef:0123:0000:211f:345d*. Figure 9-5 describes a simple IPv6 notation where the site prefix represents public topology allocated by an ISP or regional internet registry; the subnet ID represents a private topology, which is internal to a specific network; and the interface ID represents a unique device identifier, which is configured via the interface's MAC address using IEEE's extended unique identifier (EUI-64) format.

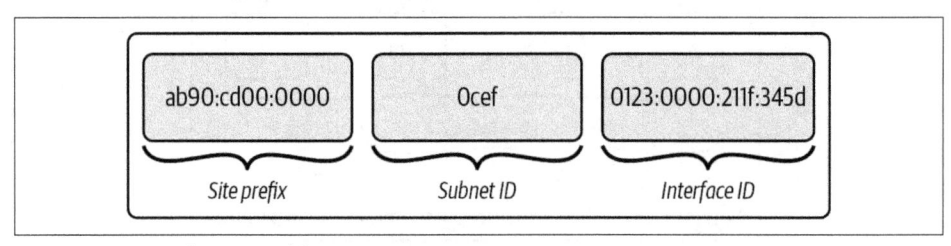

Figure 9-5. Simple IPv6 address representation

Both IPv4 and IPv6 addresses can be further divided into public and private IP addresses based on their visibility. The concept of public-private is used more for IPv4 addresses, considering the limited availability of addresses. We'll be using examples of IPv4 addresses to walk through it.

Private and public IP addresses. Returning to our example, you agreed to meet your friend at a reserved table, number 21, at Cafe Delhi Heights to enjoy the restaurant's positive vibe and food. You got curious and decided to visit the kitchen where this delicious food was prepared, but the restaurant owner denied you access, saying that only specific individuals can go to the kitchen. Here, the kitchen is private space, and the general sitting area is public space. Certainly, there are ways to get to the private space (aka the kitchen in this scenario), which we'll explore in follow-up sections.

Or consider your work-from-home setup: you have a router for WiFi connection, and all your devices (such as your mobile phone, office laptop, personal laptop, etc.) connect with this router to access the internet. If you run a Google search on all the devices for "What's my IP?" you'll get the same IP address. This IP address is called a *public IP address* and is assigned by the ISP. You might wonder how a single IP address can be used by multiple devices for communication; that is where NAT comes in, which we'll discuss more in "NAT gateway" on page 238. Restarting the router might generate a different IP address, but it will still be the same across all the devices connected to the same ISP.

All these devices can connect with one another without going over the internet via *private IP addresses*. The router assigns a private IP address to each device connected to it. Table 9-2 shows the range of addresses allowed for private IP addresses—the rest can all be used for public network space.

Table 9-2. Private IPv4 address space per class

IP address class	IP address range
Class A	10.0.0.0–10.255.255.255
Class B	172.16.0.0–172.31.255.255
Class C	192.168.0.0–192.168.255.255

IP addresses are assigned dynamically from the provided IP address range upon creating an AWS resource. In case there is a requirement to associate specific IP addresses to a resource, we can use elastic IP addresses.

Elastic IP address. An *elastic IP address* is a static, public IPv4 address associated with an AWS account that can be assigned to an Amazon EC2 instance or network interface. This can be used for scenarios requiring a static IP address that should not change over time. For example, an elastic IP address maintains the same IP address if an unhealthy EC2 instance is replaced by a healthy instance.

Note that there is an additional cost associated with elastic IP addresses. They are chargeable and are bought for a specific region; IP addresses of one region are not accessible in other regions.

Creating an Amazon VPC

The networking ideas we discussed in the previous sections will help us set up our first VPC. The VPC wizard asks for the IPv4 CIDR block, IPv6 CIDR block, and tenancy. The IPv4 CIDR block is a required input that must be added to proceed further. The VPC can work in dual mode, operating with both IPv4 and IPv6. The allowed CIDR block for IPv4 is between /16 and /28; for IPv6, it is fixed to /64.

You'll need to consider the following points for the CIDR block:

- Creating a VPC requires an initial IPv4 CIDR block, although you might have a use case to just use an IPv6 address space. VPC supports both IPv4 and IPv6 address spaces in a single VPC, which can be specified during creation.
- The CIDR block should be specified from the RFC 1918 range, and it is recommended to use a private IP address range, although public can also be chosen.
- The size of the CIDR block can't be changed once created. Customers should carefully plan the size of CIDR considering future needs to avoid hurdles or rework in the future. In short, bigger CIDR blocks can be chosen to have more flexibility in the future if you're not able to gather concrete details now.
- The CIDR block should not overlap with existing CIDR blocks associated with VPCs. This is also essential for using services like VPC peering and AWS Direct Connect; the CIDR blocks should not overlap across the VPCs.
- You can associate up to five additional CIDR blocks to a VPC (this is a soft limit and can be adjusted up to 50); the additional CIDR blocks' ranges should be strictly smaller than the primary CIDR block.

> *Soft limit* means the limit is adjustable and can be increased by following AWS Service Quotas or with help of the AWS support team.

Next, we need to consider tenancy. Let's go back to our real-world example. There are two ways to book Cafe Delhi Heights for meeting your new friend. The first option is to book the entire restaurant if this is a top-secret meeting and you don't want any other people there during your booked time. This is called *dedicated tenancy*.

The second option is to reserve a table for two—other available tables can be booked by other people. This is called *shared tenancy*. Because of the cost, it's logical to go with the second option unless there is a specific reason not to, such as a secret meeting. The same concept applies when we request servers from AWS. The instances can run either on shared hardware (other people's instances can run on the same hardware via virtualization) or on dedicated hardware where your instances are separated from other customer's resources, depending on your business needs. This option can be selected at the time of creating the VPC, and all the instances launched in the VPC are created with the same option by default, unless overridden.

> AWS provides multiple tools for creating resources, such as the AWS CLI, and the AWS Cloud Development Kit (CDK), or via the AWS Console. As a beginner, you can start by experimenting with the AWS Console, but as systems scale, we recommend maintaining a code repository to provision any AWS resources, which is popularly known as *infrastructure-as-code (IaC)*. This could help on multiple fronts, such as replicating the same resources in another region or maintaining an infrastructure audit.

The next step in VPC configuration is setting up subnets. Subnets separate resources across multiple AZs.

Subnets

As we've mentioned, *subnet* means a subnetwork: a logical subdivision of the IP address range inside the VPC CIDR block. Why should you divide network space into multiple subnetworks? The general idea of separation of resources per AZ is to ensure high application availability. Each subnet is associated with an AZ within an AWS region. By associating resources to specific subnets, we ensure that resources are launched into that AZ. One interesting fact about mapping subnets to AZs is it can vary from customer to customer: the us-east-1a AZ for you can be us-east-1b for your friend. AWS abstracts out these details from customers to ensure uniform allocation (per availability) of resources.

Each subnet should be assigned a CIDR block similar to the VPC; the CIDR block to be assigned can be the same as the VPC CIDR block or a subset of it. The key point is that the CIDR block across the subnets inside your VPC should not overlap. The first four and the last IP address in each subnet CIDR block are reserved and can't be assigned to resources.

The subnet can be a public subnet or a private subnet, depending on its connectivity to the internet. Public and private subnets look similar; the difference lies in their accessibility to the internet. For example, a web application's servers can be placed in a public subnet so that the application is accessible to the general public via the internet, and the database servers can be placed in a private subnet to limit accessibility from the general public; see Figure 9-6 for reference. You were denied access to the kitchen at Cafe Delhi Heights because it's located in a private space (or private subnet), although you can freely roam in the general sitting area as this is public space or public subnet.

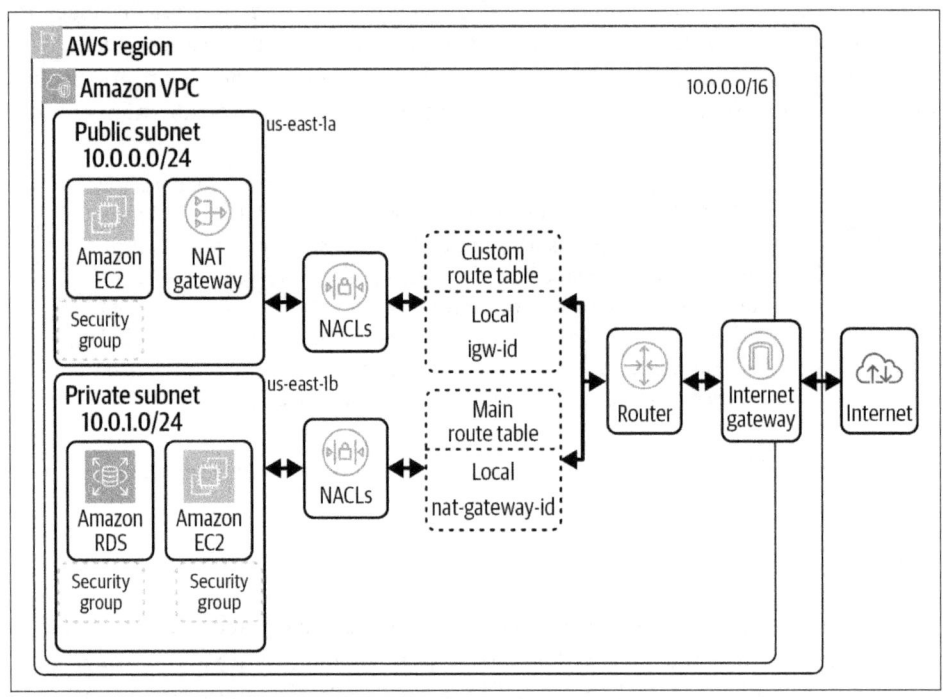

Figure 9-6. Overview of different networking components

The resources in the public subnet can access the internet because of the presence of a direct route to an internet gateway (shown as igw-id in the custom route table in Figure 9-6), whereas resources in the private subnet require a NAT service or a NAT instance to access the internet (nat-gateway-id entry in the route table). Later sections in this chapter will provide more details on network access control lists (NACLs), route tables, the NAT gateway, and the internet gateway. The key point is that the direct route to the internet gateway is the only differentiating factor between public and private subnets. A subnet with resources having a public IPv4 address but no direct route to the internet gateway is called a *private subnet*.

When setting up your VPCs and subnets inside your AWS account, consider these following best practices:

Use multiple subnets
    Create multiple subnets within different AZs to achieve fault tolerance and high availability.

Isolate resources
> Use separate subnets for different types of resources to improve security and network segmentation.

Separate public and private subnets
> Place resources with public access in public subnets and sensitive resources in private subnets.

VPC provides a logically isolated network in the AWS cloud, but how does this network connect with the internet? Or how can internet traffic access the resources located in the subnets? Let's discuss that next.

Internet Connectivity

Routing traffic and securing resources are achieved via components like route tables, internet gateways, and security groups, which we'll focus on in this section.

Route Tables

In the AWS cloud, you just need to configure required routes in the route table; you don't have to worry about setting up a router. A *route table* is a collection of rules, called *routes*, that determine where network traffic from your subnet or gateway is directed. We can assume that AWS internally maintains a router to facilitate this routing.

Every subnet should be associated with a route table, and the main route table is created implicitly to provide private access among the subnets. You should create more custom route tables as required and assign them to subnets—note that the same route table can be associated with multiple subnets. The key consideration here should be to create a route table for clear division of routing responsibility; this helps provide better maintainability and readability of routes by not overcrowding a single route table.

There are two kinds of route tables: main route tables and custom route tables.

The main route table automatically comes with a VPC and by default contains the first entry for local routing in the VPC, which helps resources in different subnets establish connectivity with one another. Every creation of a subnet leads to implicit association to the main route table. If required, customers can create a custom route table and explicitly associate it to a subnet.

You need to consider the following about the main route table:

- It can't be deleted, and a custom route table can't be set as the main route table, though the main route table can be replaced with a custom route table for subnet association.

- You can add additional routes to the main table—our recommendation would be to avoid this and create custom route tables for adding custom routes.
- The configured routes are general-purpose routes and might not be the optimal security configuration for all use cases. Audit the routes before using them in production environments.

Custom route tables don't contain any routes by default and should be updated per the requirements for network traffic routing. Custom route tables can be deleted, unlike the main route table, though there should be no subnet associations for this operation to be successful.

Now that you know the two types of route tables and their purposes, let's see how routes are added and what they look like. There are two important inputs in the route table (see Table 9-3 for an example):

Destination
Added as CIDR; basically, a range of IP addresses that specifies where the network packets should go, such as 10.0.0.0/16

Target
Specifies how the network packets will reach the destination, such as gateway, network interface, or a connection—for example, internet gateway (IGW) for routing traffic to the internet or VPC peering connection

Table 9-3. Route table with internet connectivity via IGW

Destination	Target
VPC CIDR	Local
0.0.0.0/0	igw-id

Route tables direct network traffic in and out of a subnet, but they don't apply any security filters on this traffic. AWS provides software firewalls, security groups (SGs), and NACLs to implement traffic filters, which are useful for controlling the network traffic permissions. These components help control the traffic that can flow in and out of the VPC.

Security Groups

SGs define the rules for the traffic allowed to (and from) the resources. SGs are created at the VPC level and assigned at an instance level, controlling inbound and outbound traffic at the instance level based on protocols, ports, and IP addresses. Your EC2 instance can have one or more SGs. There will always be one SG associated to an instance, and, if not created, a default SG will be associated, which is created at the time of VPC creation.

To secure and limit access for incoming and outgoing traffic to instances, you need to add inbound and outbound rules to your SG. *Inbound rules* define traffic that is allowed to the instance, and *outbound rules* define traffic that is allowed from the instance.

Keep in mind the following facts about SGs:

- SGs are stateful. For example, you fire one request from your personal laptop to an EC2 instance to get some data, and your IP address is added as part of the inbound rules. You'll get a response back even if there are no outbound rules included for your personal laptop. In short, rules allowed in one direction will automatically be allowed in the opposite direction; there is no requirement to explicitly add them.
- You can't delete the default SG. Our recommendation is to create a custom SG as needed. Multiple SGs can be associated to an instance, but you should create SGs keeping future scale in mind. For example, you should avoid duplicate-rules SGs and reuse wherever possible.
- You should only add required access and not overexpose the resources. For example, for SSH connections, only allow Port 22 for a set of IP addresses and not the entire internet.
- SGs don't provide an option to define explicit deny rules. All the rules that don't match the allowed-rules condition are implicitly denied access to resources.

For each rule added as part of the inbound or outbound rules, you'll need to specify the following parameters, as shown in Table 9-4:

Type
This represents the type of traffic. AWS determines the protocol and port range automatically on the basis of the chosen type value. There is also a custom type to add custom values, such as for port range.

Source or destination
The source attribute is added for inbound rules, and the destination attribute is added for outbound rules. Here, you can add specific IP addresses, complete CIDR blocks, or other security groups.

Description
It is helpful to identify why a certain rule is added or what purpose it solves. This is an optional field, but we recommend using it for easy future reference.

Table 9-4. Example SG outbound rule

Type	Protocol	Port range	Destination	Description
SSH	TCP	22	117.212.92.68	Test SSH rule

Network Access Control Lists

NACLs are stateless packet filters that are attached at the subnet level. Unlike SGs, NACLs provide the ability to add, allow, or deny rules for outbound or inbound traffic at the subnet level. You can think of them as an additional layer of security on top of SGs, which block the traffic if SGs are too flexible.

Thinking back to our example of the Cafe Delhi Heights kitchen, imagine there are individual chefs in the kitchen—you may be allowed to enter the kitchen, but a chef may still refuse to talk to you.

There are a few key things you need to remember about NACLs:

- NACLs are stateless. Customers need to add explicit rules for both inbound and outbound traffic to allow or deny actions.
- Amazon VPC comes with a default NACL. The default will be attached to all the subnets inside the VPC, and it allows all inbound/outbound traffic. For fine-grained traffic control, you can create a custom NACL or modify rules in an existing one—our recommendation is to create custom NACLs as needed.
- NACLs define inbound or outbound rules to allow or deny actions. The rules will be evaluated in sequence, and once a particular rule succeeds, all the rules in sequence following it will be skipped. If none of the rules succeed, then a final rule marked as * will evaluate it as a deny action.

For each inbound or outbound rule, you'll need to specify the following parameters, as shown in Table 9-5:

Rule number
    The rule number is the sequence of numbers in which rules are evaluated. It can be numbered from 1 to 32766.

Type
    Type represents the type of traffic. Based on the chosen type, AWS prepopulates the protocol and port range. A custom protocol and port range can also be added per the selected type.

Source
    Source represents inbound rules added as a CIDR block.

Destination
    Destination represents outbound rules added as a CIDR block.

Allow or deny
    For every rule, an explicit action should be added to "allow" or "deny." This action determines if traffic is allowed or denied.

Table 9-5. Example NACL inbound rule

Rule number	Type	Protocol	Port range	Source	Allow/deny
100	All traffic	All	All	0.0.0.0/0	Allow
*	All traffic	All	All	0.0.0.0/0	Deny

Route tables, SGs, and NACLs help you configure routes and network security. To enable the connectivity per the configured routes, AWS offers Internet Gateway or NAT gateway.

Amazon VPC-to-Internet Connectivity

We described VPC as a personal data center in the AWS cloud. How will users establish connectivity with this personal data center, and how will this personal data center connect to the internet? In this section, we'll dig into different AWS components that resolve these connectivity hurdles.

Internet Gateway

In Table 9-3, we showed you a route as destination 0.0.0.0/0 and target as igw-id for allowing internet access to resources. The destination for this route refers to the entire internet, and the target is an IGW identifier.

IGW is an AWS-managed VPC software component that provides a connection between your VPC and the internet. IGW is a highly available, redundant, and horizontally scalable application that is attached to the VPC and can span the subnets in different AZs.

In the context of our Cafe Delhi Heights example, IGW represents the front door to get in or out of the restaurant. Just as you can only go to the public sitting area in the restaurant and can't go inside the kitchen, IGW only connects to resources in public subnets.

Here are a few key points about IGW:

- IGW establishes connectivity in both directions, from internet to VPC and vice versa, using public IP addresses.
- IGW provides NAT support for instances with public IPv4 addresses in the subnet. For traffic leaving for the internet from an instance, IGW makes sure the reply to the request is sent back to a public IPv4 address. For traffic destined for a resource with a public IPv4 address, IGW ensures translation to the instance's private IP address before the traffic is delivered to the VPC.
- IGWs are used in conjunction with route tables to determine the path of network traffic. A route table associated with the VPC directs traffic destined for the

internet to IGW. It acts as the default gateway for outbound traffic and routes it to the appropriate destination.

- IGWs enable VPC resources to communicate with other AWS services, such as Amazon S3 or Amazon DynamoDB, over the internet.
- IGWs are stateless, which means they don't maintain any information about the state of network connections. Each packet is evaluated independently based on routing rules and security settings.
- IGWs are designed to be highly available and scalable. They are automatically replicated across multiple AZs within a region, providing redundancy and fault tolerance.

IGWs establish internet connectivity from public subnets, but how about private subnets? There can be scenarios where private subnet resources require internet access; one such example could be downloading the latest software update. The private subnet to public internet connectivity is achieved via a NAT gateway.

NAT gateway

In our restaurant example, the cooks working in the kitchen asked the head chef if they could collect feedback from customers about the food being served; only the head chef is allowed to interact with customers directly in the main restaurant space, and cooks only work in the kitchen, just to avoid overwhelming the customers or increasing the crowd in the main area.

The role of head chef is served by the NAT gateway for a subnet—it connects instances in a private subnet with the internet via IGW. You can think of the NAT gateway as a bridge between IGW and private instances. IGW requires a public IP for interaction with the internet, and the NAT gateway facilitates that support. This support is available for TCP, UDP, and ICMP protocols.

NAT gateways are AWS-managed network devices that allow resources within private subnets in a VPC to initiate outbound internet connections while preventing direct inbound access from the internet by hiding their private IP addresses. To go a layer deeper, NAT converts a private IP address to a NAT device's public IP address, which is mapped back to the private IP address when a response is returned from the internet. To establish a connection, you need to allocate an Elastic IP (EIP) address and associate it with the NAT gateway. The EIP serves as a static, public IP address that represents the NAT gateway and is used for communication with the internet.

Here are the key things to consider about NAT gateways:

- For high availability, the NAT gateway should be set up at the AZ level so that if an AZ goes down, it doesn't affect traffic-serving capability from other AZs.

- Another reason for NAT gateway division at the AZ level is to avoid packet drops for traffic greater than 10 million packets per second.
- The NAT gateway can't be used by the external internet to initiate connection with instances in a private subnet.
- The NAT gateway provides public (default) and private connectivity. Public is useful for connectivity with the outside internet, whereas private is useful for connecting with other VPCs or on-premises networks.
- The NAT gateway comes with an additional infrastructure cost, unlike IGW, whose pricing depends on traffic flow via IGW.

We have discussed connectivity to personal data centers (meaning VPCs), but there could also be scenarios where we own multiple such data centers. The next section explores different mechanisms available from AWS to create cross-VPC connectivity.

Connectivity Between Amazon VPCs

You may have use cases such as AWS resource integration across VPCs, security, or presence in multiple regions where different components residing in different VPCs need to connect with one another, which could be in the same or in different AWS accounts, while maintaining isolation. To return to our restaurant example, Cafe Delhi Heights is becoming more popular day by day, so the restaurant head opened a new location for the additional customers, but the food is still prepared in the old kitchen. Now there is a requirement to establish good connectivity for faster delivery of food to the newly opened location and in a secure way. Similarly, there can be a need to operate two microservices in different VPCs (or different AWS accounts altogether). For these microservices to communicate in a secure way, AWS provides different connectivity options.

These connectivity options fall mainly under two kinds of relationships: many-to-many and hub-and-spoke. Traffic is managed individually between each VPC in many-to-many VPC relationships, whereas a central resource manages traffic routing between the VPCs in the hub-and-spoke model.

Amazon VPC Peering

VPC peering (*https://oreil.ly/5SQMv*) is based on a many-to-many approach where one VPC peers with another VPC to enable full, bidirectional, private network connectivity. It enables resources in different VPCs to communicate with one another using private IP addresses as if they were in the same network. VPC peering doesn't support transitive dependency and can be a cost-effective interconnectivity method if the number of VPCs is less than 10. As the number of VPCs increases, the mesh can become very complex to manage and operate.

You can manage the connections via route tables, SGs, and NACLs to allow specific resources or subnets to utilize the VPC peering connection. The network packets between the VPCs flow via AWS private network with no bandwidth constraints—no physical hardware is required for this setup; you only pay for the amount of data transfer.

Think of a scenario where all the Cafe Delhi Heights locations have their own bars, but food is prepared at a central location and supplied to the smaller setups. Now, let's extend this example to a system architecture consisting of a web frontend and backend. The connectivity between the backend and frontend tier can be established via VPC peering, assuming both are hosted in separate VPCs. Figure 9-7 shows connectivity between servers running in different VPCs via a VPC peering connection.

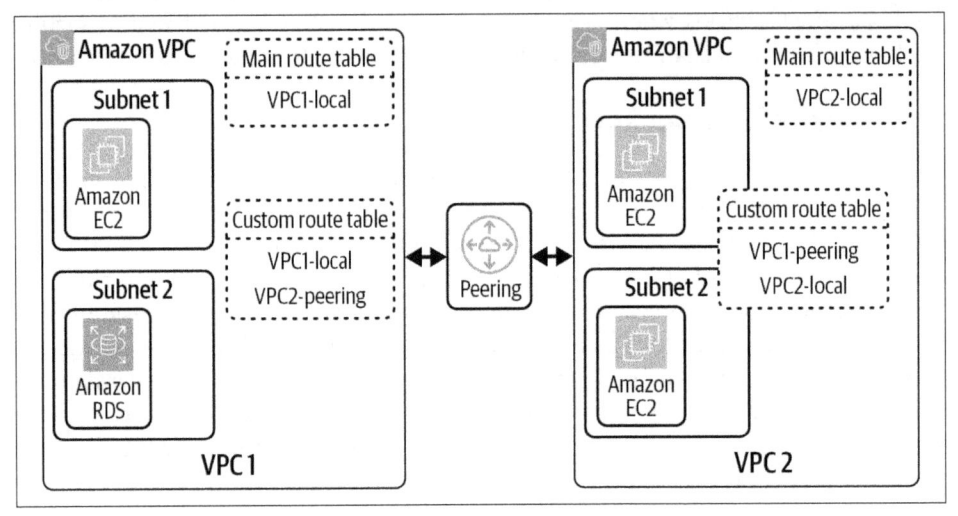

Figure 9-7. VPC peering

There are certain limitations with VPC peering (*https://oreil.ly/mpf8e*) with increasing scale, and it becomes hard to manage the routing configurations between VPCs. To overcome these bottlenecks, AWS offers a service called Transit Gateway.

AWS Transit Gateway

AWS Transit Gateway is a scalable solution to establish connectivity among multiple VPCs, on-premises networks, and other AWS services. Based on the hub-and-spoke model, Transit Gateway is a regional resource that acts as an intermediary to set up all the network routing at a single place via routing tables, be it VPCs or a hybrid connectivity method such as virtual private network (VPN) (*https://aws.amazon.com/vpn*) or AWS Direct Connect.

For better control of networking routes, Transit Gateway can be set up in a separate networking AWS account that network engineers can manage at a centralized location. Figure 9-8 shows Transit Gateway acting as a central resource for providing connectivity among VPCs, Direct Connect, and a VPN connection.

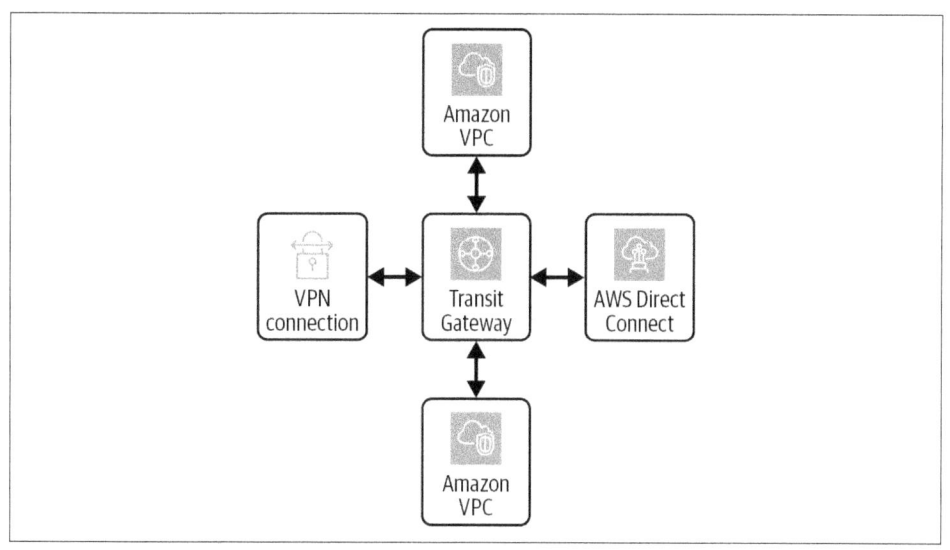

Figure 9-8. AWS Transit Gateway

The key difference between Transit Gateway and VPC peering is scale: Transit Gateway is scalable for connectivity across thousands of VPCs. Other parameters are favorable to VPC peering, such as lower cost, no bandwidth constraints, and reduced latency.

Figure 9-7 shows the frontend and backend tier connectivity via VPC peering in different VPCs. Another solution for this kind of setup is to use PrivateLink.

AWS PrivateLink

AWS PrivateLink privately exposes an application to consumers in another VPC and ensures that traffic flows in an AWS backbone network without going over the internet. The key difference is traffic flow direction: VPC peering provides bidirectional connectivity, but if clients need to serve requests using only private IP addresses, AWS PrivateLink will facilitate this kind of connectivity.

PrivateLink is established between two parties: the one that allows access to its specific service is the *service provider*, and others consuming this service are considered the *consumers*.

To make its service available in a region, the service provider creates an endpoint service, which is mapped with a network load balancer. An application LB can't be directly attached with an endpoint service. The service consumers create VPC endpoints to connect their VPCs to endpoint services by specifying the service name.

As shown in Figure 9-9, the endpoint could be an interface endpoint or a gateway endpoint. An interface endpoint establishes a connection to an endpoint service in another VPC whereas a gateway endpoint connects with Amazon S3 or Amazon DynamoDB using private IP addresses. Another type is a gateway LB, which can be used to manage third-party virtual appliances, such as for compliance (more on LBs shortly).

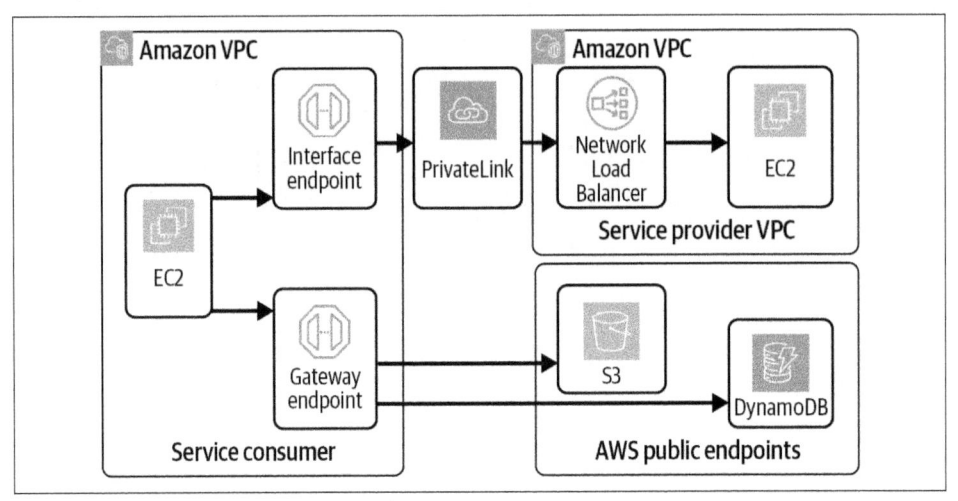

Figure 9-9. Connectivity via endpoint services

> Configuration management and understanding different networking features, such as VPC peering, Transit Gateways, and Private-Links, require expertise. AWS offers VPC Lattice as a managed service to remove all this overhead and simplify application connectivity across VPCs and AWS accounts.

Certain businesses still operate with on-premises data centers. During the process of migrating to the cloud, there can be an intermediary state where some operations are served by on-premises data centers and the rest via AWS cloud computing services. Let's explore different solutions offered by AWS to establish connectivity between these two separate data centers.

Hybrid Connectivity

The current infrastructure of Cafe Delhi Heights is a central location for preparing food and a bar at each separate location. To make our systems more efficient, we're planning to move most of the food preparation to all the locations, but some key dishes will still be prepared at the central location. In this scenario, operations happen at two places—this is what we mean by *hybrid connectivity*.

It could be possible that you started with a personal data center, but over time you decided to move to the AWS cloud. Now, AWS maintains the service infrastructure, but the databases are still managed at an on-premises data center. To support this, there needs to be some mechanism to establish connectivity between on-premises data centers and AWS data centers—that's a VPN.

AWS Virtual Private Network

What mechanism can be used to securely connect on-premises data centers to Amazon VPCs? The service framework that ensures this data security is VPN. Figure 9-10 shows an example connection setup using AWS VPN from a customer data center to a VPC located in an AWS region.

The components of a VPN setup are as follows:

Customer gateway
    A software or hardware component that is set up at the customer's end. These are the device requirements (*https://oreil.ly/SKSOs*).

VPN connection
    A secure, encrypted connection channel between the customer gateway and VPN gateway. Two tunnels are set up to avoid any availability issues due to failure or scheduled maintenance.

VPN gateway
    Present at the AWS side to ensure communication between the VPC and the VPN connection.

The VPN transfers data packets over the internet anonymously. AWS provides another service, Direct Connect, to configure dedicated networks for connectivity.

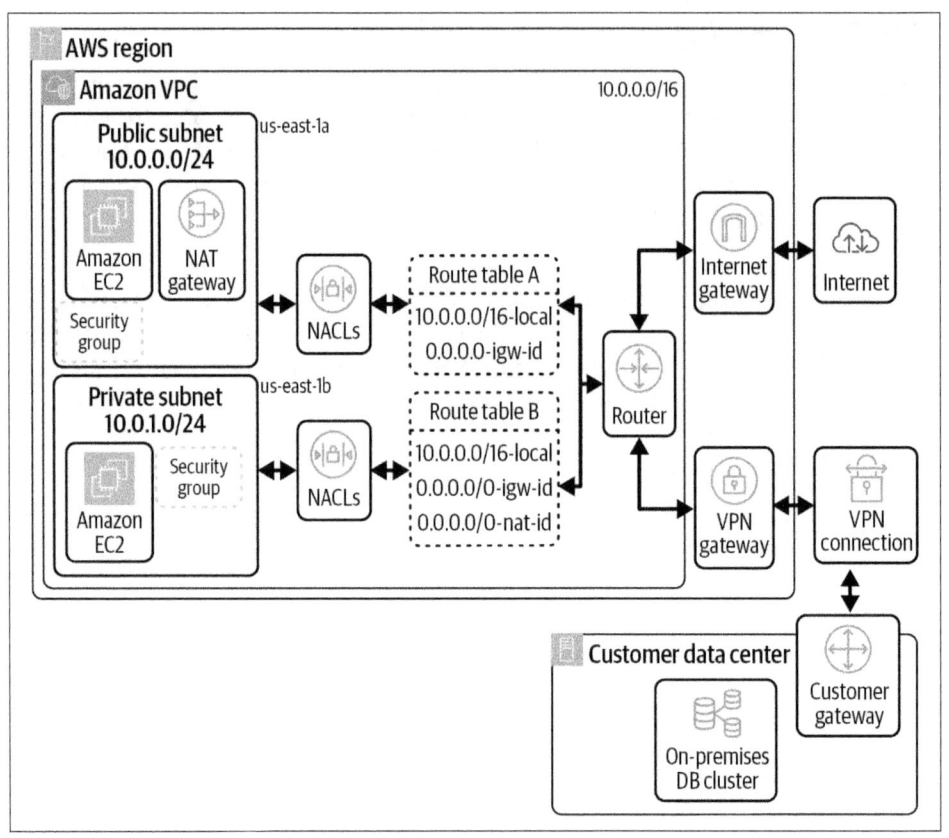

Figure 9-10. VPN connection

AWS Direct Connect

AWS Direct Connect provides the capability of configuring a dedicated network connection (Ethernet fiber-optic cable) for data transfer from the customer data center to a Direct Connect location without using the internet. The Direct Connect location is configured with a router to route the traffic and connect to the AWS backbone network. It provides consistent, high-bandwidth connectivity suitable for large-scale or latency-sensitive workloads. You can use the Direct Connect Resiliency toolkit (*https://oreil.ly/0-HcF*) to ensure maximum availability of connections set up from a personal data center to the Direct Connect location. Figure 9-11 shows an example connection setup from a customer data center to VPC via a Direct Connect location.

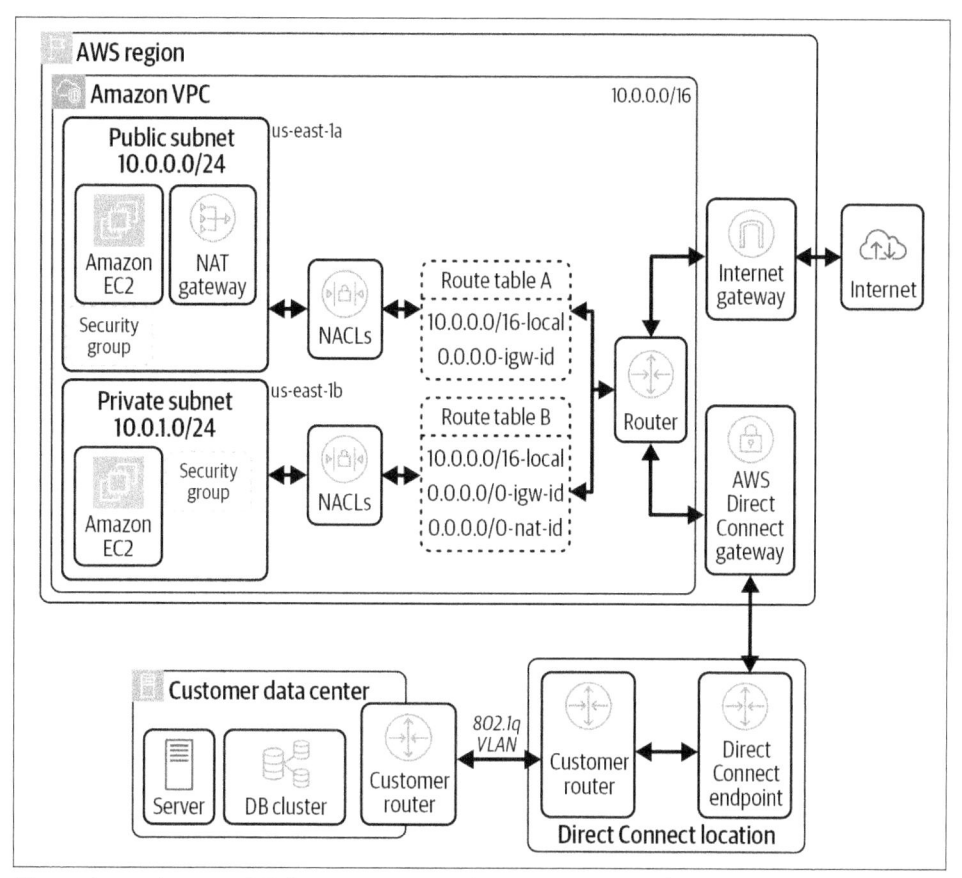

Figure 9-11. Amazon VPC connectivity with an on-premises data center via Direct Connect

The main components are as follows:

Customer router
 Installed at an on-premises data center holding all networking rules, the customer router routes traffic from the data center to the Direct Connect location. The customer router connects with the router at the Direct Connect location via 802.1Q VLAN ethernet cable.

Direct Connect location
 Direct Connect is available worldwide at multiple locations (*https://oreil.ly/AME1w*). You can select a location closest to the on-premises data center to minimize cost and latency. You can check for all networking requirements in the AWS documentation (*https://oreil.ly/sjruP*).

Direct Connect gateway
>The Direct Connect gateway establishes the connection between the VPC and the Direct Connect location via a private virtual interface.

Virtual interface (VIF)
>The VIF is used to set up private, secure connections to required resources such as S3 without going over the internet. You can select public VIF, private VIF, or transit VIF depending on the use case:
>
>- Public VIF connects to AWS resources such as Amazon S3 over public IP addresses.
>- Private VIF connects to AWS resources using their private IP addresses hosted in the Amazon VPC.
>- Transit VIF connects to AWS resources using their private IP addresses hosted in the Amazon VPC through the Transit Gateway.

We have explored many ways that network packets flow inside the Amazon network as well as multiple connectivity options provided by AWS. The rest of the chapter focuses on the entry points for these network packets as applications scale, such as Amazon Route 53, LBs, and Amazon API Gateway. We'll conclude the chapter by discussing Amazon CloudFront, the CDN provided by AWS for placing data content near users to enable faster retrieval.

Amazon Route 53

Amazon Route 53 is a scalable, highly available Domain Name System (DNS) in the AWS ecosystem used for domain registration, DNS routing, and health checking. We began "IP addresses" on page 226 by stating that every device on the internet requires an IP address to establish a connection with other devices, but what if a human is operating one side of a connection? It can be very difficult to remember all the IP addresses—well, unless you have a photographic memory.

Humans are better at remembering names than numbers; it's easier to remember *www.google.com* instead of 142.251.46.174 or to remember Cafe Delhi Heights at Ambience Mall instead of a latitude of 28.525446566084423 and a longitude of 77.09008858115097. DNS makes our lives easier by facilitating conversion from domain names to IP addresses.

We should have a general understanding of what happens when we type *www.google.com* in a web browser to understand data flow on the internet. Figure 9-12 shows how a domain like *www.google.com* is resolved to an IP address and made accessible to end users using Route 53. After the DNS resolution in steps 1 through 5, the browser establishes a TCP connection with Google web servers and sends an HTTP request to the servers (step 6). The server handles the request and sends back an HTTP response as the final step (7). The browser renders this response in the browser tab for further user interactions.

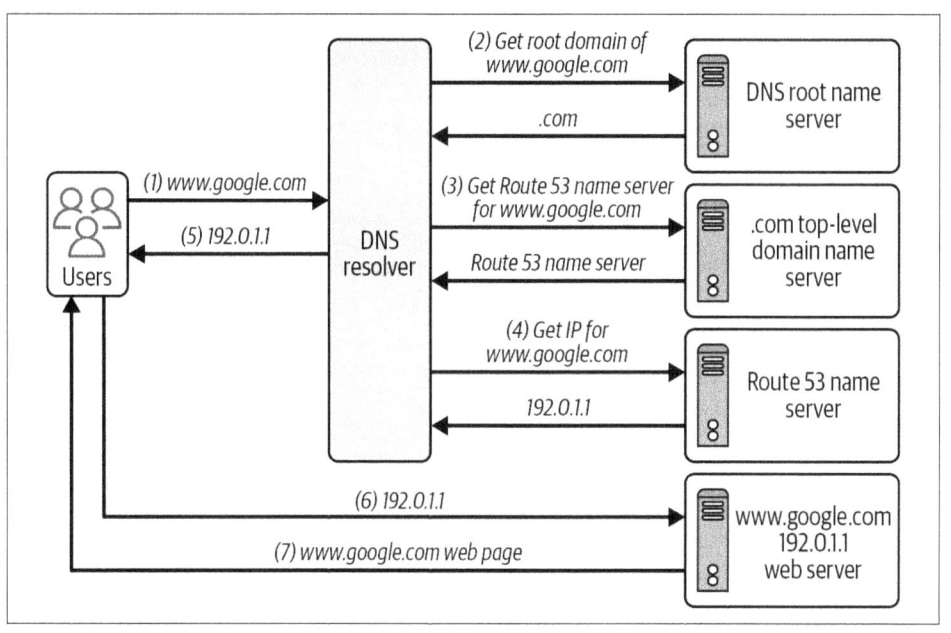

Figure 9-12. DNS resolution via Amazon Route 53

Here are the key considerations for using Amazon Route 53:

- Route 53 can be used to register new domain names, and you can transfer existing DNS to be managed by it.
- You can create, update, and manage your public DNS records via Route 53, along with health checks to monitor the health of applications, web servers, and related resources.
- You can configure routing policies (*https://oreil.ly/FfkRt*) for traffic management on DNS records, specifying how Route 53 responds to queries.
- Route 53 supports various DNS record types, such as A, AAAA, CNAME, mail exchange (MX), TXT, and more, enabling flexible DNS configuration. Alias records (*https://oreil.ly/mhDPH*), a feature specific to Route 53, allows routing of traffic to AWS resources with zero additional cost for the DNS query.
- DNS records of your domain are collectively stored in hosted zones to answer the domain queries.
- Route 53 uses Anycast as its networking and routing technology, which reduces latency by routing requests through the nearest data center and increases availability with multiple servers to respond to traffic instead of just one origin server.

AWS Elastic Load Balancer

As discussed in Chapter 5, LBs improve the availability, scalability, and fault tolerance of applications by distributing traffic across healthy targets. LBs can automatically scale based on traffic patterns and health checks, ensuring optimal performance.

ELB is a managed service that scales for the customer's traffic on the go and provides the following capabilities:

- Distributes the incoming traffic among a pool of resources
- Serves requests without disruption as new resources are added or old ones are removed
- Monitors resource health via ELB-provided health checks

AWS ELB is available as the following types:

Application load balancer (ALB)
    Operates at the application layer (L7) for HTTP, HTTPS, and gRPC protocols

Network load balancer (NLB)
    Operates at the network layer (L4) for TCP, UDP, and TLS protocols

Classic load balancer (CLB)
    Legacy version of an LB that supports both L4 and L7 traffic

Gateway load balancer (GWLB)
    Used as an L3 gateway and L4 LB for the IP protocol

There's a detailed product comparison on AWS (*https://oreil.ly/aMRtW*).

Our recommendation is to take a bottom-up approach by thinking about the base feature requirements for a given workload. These requirements, along with pricing, will help you decide which LB type is best suited to your workload—there are additional features that ELB offers, which will be the cherry on the top. Figure 9-13 shows traffic distribution by ELB to different types of targets.

The following are main components of ELB:

Load balancer
    The LB is a single point of contact from the client's perspective; it can then forward the request to configured listeners.

Listeners
    The listener is a process that checks for the client's request using the configured protocol and port number. The request is forwarded to target groups based on the rules associated with a listener.

Target groups
   Target groups direct traffic to configured targets using the configured port and protocol, such as EC2 instances, IP addresses, and so on.

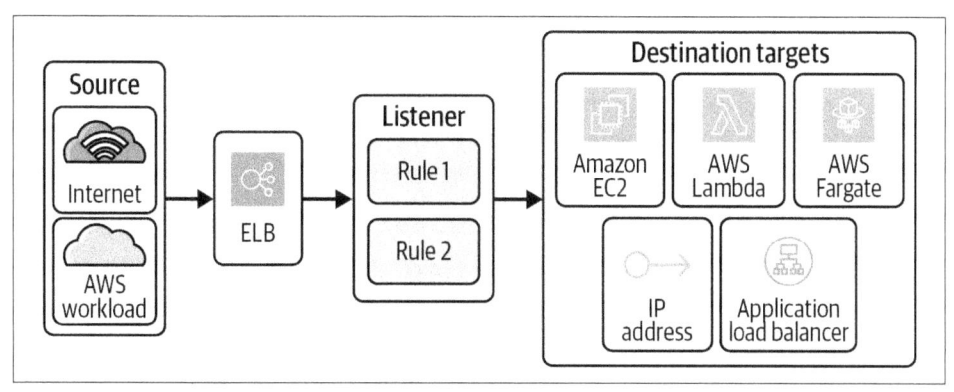

Figure 9-13. AWS ELB configuration

Here are a few key considerations for ELBs:

- An NLB can have targets like an ALB, containers, instances, and IPs. An ALB can have containers, instances, IPs, and Lambdas as targets. A GWLB can have IPs and instances as targets.

- GWLBs are useful in systems like firewalls, intrusion detection and prevention systems, and deep packet inspection systems. They enable customers to deploy, scale, and manage virtual appliances. One example scenario for inspection systems is placing the GWLB between the source and destination for packet analysis and monitoring.

- ALBs don't provide support for private link and static IP addresses for inbound traffic; an NLB is a suitable choice for this use case. In scenarios where additional features of an ALB are a value-add to an NLB or vice versa, an ALB can be used as a target for an NLB to gain benefits from both.

- Since an ALB has request header data, it can support request routing in multiple ways, such as path based, host based, query string parameter based, and source IP address based. In contrast, an NLB can't inspect the HTTP request, which makes it a little lighter in processing compared to an ALB, resulting in reduced latency.

- NLBs are optimized to handle sudden spiky traffic patterns; for ALBs, it's a best practice to inform AWS Support in advance if a traffic spike is expected to preallocate the capacity.

- NLBs support long-lived TCP connections, unlike ALBs. This is helpful in scenarios with requirements like a huge number of persistent connections, such as WebSocket connections for an online gaming application.

- ALBs provide support for AWS Web Application Firewall (WAF) and authentication mechanisms such as Amazon Cognito and OpenID Connect. This offloads the responsibility from the application, making it lighter.
- The LB will reside in a public subnet, and you can host the backend resources in a private subnet, which are not directly accessible to outside traffic.
- Idle timeout configuration for ALB can be set between 1 and 4,000 seconds (the default is 60 seconds), whereas for NLB this configuration is 350 seconds.

Amazon API Gateway

Amazon API Gateway is a fully managed AWS service for creating, publishing, maintaining, monitoring, and securing REST, HTTP, and WebSocket APIs. Consider a scenario where, instead of humans serving your food at Cafe Delhi Heights, robots are deployed to do so. You order by selecting the food items from the kiosk installed at the table, and once the food is prepared, it is served by robots—well, in this scenario, you don't know the food is prepared by robots or humans in the kitchen. That's the beauty of resource abstraction: customers use the API Gateway's published API to perform specific functions at scale, and API Gateway can internally connect with any AWS service, as shown in Figure 9-14.

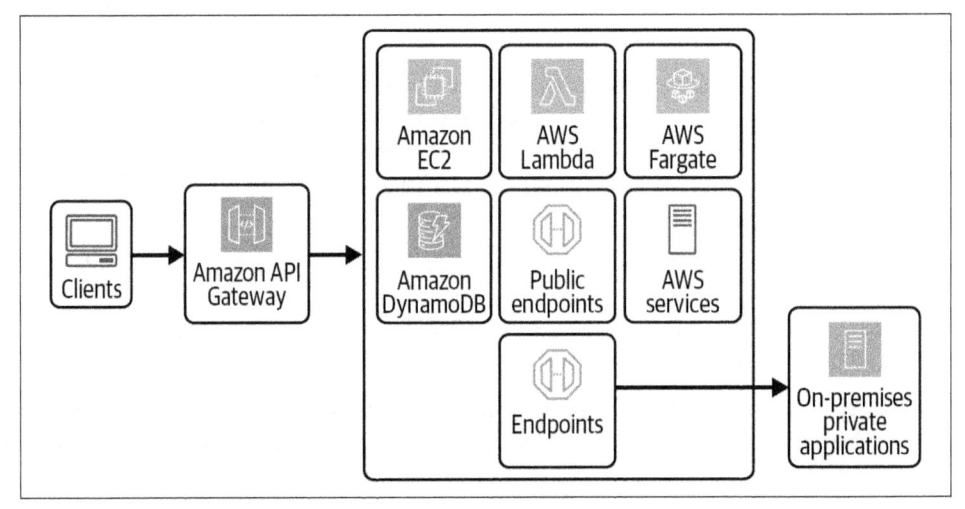

Figure 9-14. Amazon API Gateway connectivity with AWS services

Here are a few key considerations for using API Gateway:

- API Gateway supports both stateless and stateful APIs:
  — REST and HTTP APIs are stateless. They both have the same basic functionality and are HTTP based to support standard methods like GET, PUT, POST,

and so on. REST APIs support some additional features, such as API keys, per-client rate and usage throttling, and request validation.
— WebSocket APIs are stateful. They operate on the basis of the WebSocket protocol with full-duplex client-server communication.
- API Gateway can support authentication via AWS IAM policies, AWS Lambda authorizer functions, and Amazon Cognito user pools.
- API Gateway provides monitoring via CloudWatch and CloudTrail services.
- API Gateway can avoid web exploits like SQL injection via AWS WAF integration.
- API Gateway can directly connect with AWS services like Amazon DynamoDB via service APIs, reducing intermediary infrastructure costs. For example, in a scenario where you retrieve a DynamoDB record using a partition key, the general implementation would be to invoke a Lambda, which then connects with DynamoDB to get the data. API Gateway removes the need for AWS Lambda in between by directly connecting with DynamoDB and serving responses.
- API Gateway doesn't provide health checks for backend resources as ELB does.
- The timeout configuration for REST APIs on API Gateway is between 50 ms and 29 seconds; it is 30 seconds for HTTP APIs. There is a two-hour connection duration for WebSocket APIs, with an idle timeout of 10 minutes.
- API Gateway can be used for cross-account or -region integration; for example, AWS Lambdas are owned by different teams in different AWS accounts per business requirements but are served by an API Gateway in a central AWS account.
- API Gateway supports caching of the endpoint's responses, which reduces traffic to the endpoint and improves latency. TTL for caching can vary from 0 (caching is disabled) to 3,600 seconds, with a default of 300 seconds.

API Gateway and LBs help abstract out backend infrastructure from customers. Now, consider a scenario where a customer's requests hit API Gateway and one of the microservices fetches data from Amazon S3; this operation is definitely latency intensive if the file size is large. The latency can be reduced by placing the content near the customer's location via the AWS CDN service, Amazon CloudFront.

Amazon CloudFront

We briefly touched on two ways Cafe Delhi Heights can manage food preparation and delivery operations: (1) food is prepared at a central location and delivered to smaller storefronts on demand, and (2) kitchens are set up at all the locations. There is definitely an extra cost to setting up kitchens at every location. Another option is to analyze the demands for different food items, prepare the food in advance at a central location, and store it at the smaller outlets ahead of time. This way, the food is prepared at only a single location, and the customers are served at all the outlets in the minimum time possible.

In software systems, a key factor to improving the customer's experience is to serve the request with minimum latency. One potential solution is to replicate infrastructure in multiple AWS regions and use AWS local zones. This solution should be accessed only as a last resort for your business architecture, and latency should not be the key factor in deciding on it. Another cost-effective solution is to cache the content near the customer's location via a CDN, as discussed in Chapter 4. Amazon CloudFront is a worldwide network of data centers called *edge locations* that helps you achieve low latency for serving both static and dynamic content in a secure way via AWS Shield, AWS IAM, AWS WAF, and TLS certificates.

There are a few things to keep in mind:

- CloudFront can be used to serve both static and dynamic content over HTTP or WebSocket protocols. For example, static content placed in S3 buckets or dynamic content generated via any web service, such as running on EC2 servers, can be directly served via CloudFront, as shown in Figure 9-15.

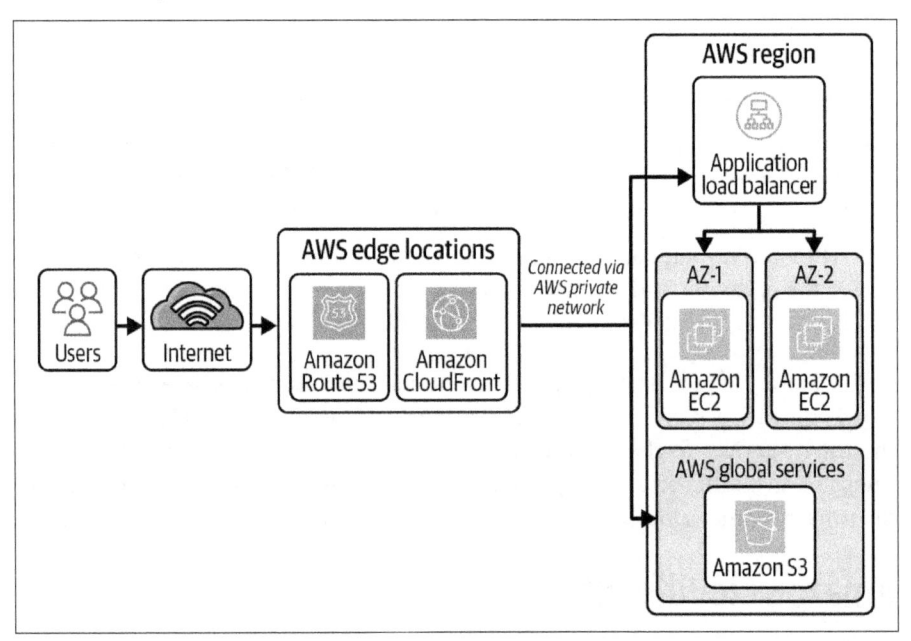

Figure 9-15. Content distribution via Amazon CloudFront

- CloudFront by default integrates with AWS Shield to help avoid distributed denial-of-service (DDos) attacks and can be integrated with AWS WAF for application layer security.

- CloudFront provides encryption both at rest and in transit. Data at edge locations is always stored in encrypted format, and Amazon Certificate Manager or custom certificates can be used for in-transit traffic.
- For ensuring user-level access to content, CloudFront provides options for signed cookies, signed URLs, and georestriction.

In short, CloudFront enables you to cache content near your application users and serve user queries faster.

Conclusion

We began this chapter by getting started with AWS cloud computing services, and then we explored different networking concepts and services that AWS offers to set up a networking infrastructure on the AWS cloud. Since the AWS cloud comes with a plethora of services, it's important to understand how a specific service will solve a problem statement.

It's neither easy nor feasible for everyone to set up their own personal data center, and AWS solves this problem by offering Amazon VPC as a solution. There may be requirements for multiple data centers to connect, and AWS provides different connectivity mechanisms to enable this support. It is also important that only the intended users access the resources hosted in the AWS cloud, which can be ensured by using security mechanisms like security groups, NACLs, and appropriate rules added to the route tables.

Finally, we discussed how the internal resources can be abstracted out from external users by using solutions such as AWS ELB and Amazon API Gateway. AWS also offers a highly scalable DNS service, Amazon Route 53, for managing domain names. Here's a simple example to illustrate using Route 53—we started by using an NLB, and the users hit this endpoint. Later, we realized that an ALB was a more appropriate choice than the NLB. In this situation, there are three options: share the new ALB endpoint with customers, keep the NLB as front-facing to the ALB with the ALB redirecting traffic to the application, or use Amazon Route 53 domain so that the same domain name is accessible to customers with no impact from changes to internal resources.

Data storage solutions are an important consideration when storing and maintaining data in the cloud. In the next chapter, we'll explore different types of AWS storage services, such as DynamoDB, Amazon S3, and relational databases, and we'll discuss each of these services with respect to the use cases they best serve.

CHAPTER 10
AWS Storage Services

Chapters 2 and 3 introduced multiple storage types and solutions. This chapter explores AWS-specific storage services (*https://oreil.ly/a1A_9*), which map to different kinds of storage solutions present in the market. We'll start with traditional storage services like block storage and then move to various kinds of databases used to store data identifying business and technical requirements.

Referring to our example of Cafe Delhi Heights from Chapter 9, the chain of restaurants is going online where customers can look for available food items and place an order. To provide the best customer experience and food-delivery services online, Cafe Delhi Heights will store data such as restaurant images, menus, marketing campaign information, and so forth on AWS storage services. Cafe Delhi Heights has given us the job of making this happen, so let's identify their storage requirements and choose the best AWS storage solution. We need to be able to:

- Store a customer's profile and access details like username and password
- Store food information such as available menu items
- Store different kinds of media, such as images of food items and reviews uploaded by customers
- Perform big data analytics to improve the customer experience, such as separating good and bad reviews
- Create food communities and allow people to interact in social circles
- Search for food items based on multiple identifiers, such as name, restaurant location, and ratings
- Archive application logs and metrics after 90 days and have them persist for a year

AWS storage services enable customers to store, protect, and analyze data without the worry of any operational overhead. We'll discuss storage services in two major sections: cloud storage and databases. We'll start with cloud storage and look at block, file, and object storage services.

Cloud Storage on AWS

AWS offers multiple options for cloud storage: Amazon Elastic Block Store (EBS) as a block storage service, Amazon Elastic File System (EFS) as a file storage service, and Amazon Simple Storage Service (S3) as an object storage service. We discussed the general concepts of these storage options in Chapter 2. In this section, we'll look at the services offered by AWS to support these solutions. Each of these services caters to specific storage requirements, so we'll examine the benefits each can provide in the following sections.

Amazon Elastic Block Store

Amazon EBS (*https://oreil.ly/4vn6V*) is a block storage solution that acts like a physical hard drive attached to a personal computer. EBS can be attached to an Amazon EC2 instance (more on EC2 in Chapter 11) with a lifecycle that is independent of the EC2 instance and is flexible in nature, meaning it allows for configuration modification on live production workloads, such as the ability to:

- Increase size dynamically
- Change provisioned input/output operations per second (IOPS) capacity
- Change volume type

EBS volumes provide access to data stored on disk with minimum latency and are preferred for use cases requiring frequent disk access, such as:

- Creating and maintaining your own database instead of using any services offered by AWS
- Creating OS boot volumes

For use cases that require temporary block storage and better I/O performance than EBS (such as caching, device buffers, etc.), AWS offers another storage solution called an instance store (*https://oreil.ly/gsMeo*) that is directly attached to an instance, unlike EBS, which is network-attached storage. The data in the instance store is wiped out in scenarios such as disk failures and change in the state of an EC2 instance (stop/hibernate/terminate). Instance stores don't come with the flexibility of EBS volumes, such as attaching to any EC2 instance, dynamic increase in size, and the like.

AWS offers a wide range of EBS volumes to choose from based on multiple factors, including cost and performance. Let's look at the scenarios in which to use each kind of volume type:

Solid-state drives (SSDs)
　These volume types, including general-purpose SSDs and provisioned-IOPS SSDs, are optimized for transactional workloads. Their major performance attribute is small I/O size.

Hard disk drives (HDDs)
　These volume types, including throughput-optimized SSDs and cold HDDs, are optimized for large streaming workloads. Their major performance attribute is throughput.

Magnetic disks
　These volume types are mostly suitable for smaller workloads where performance is not a key factor, such as infrequent data access from a storage disk.

Here are few key points about EBS volumes to consider:

- Multiple EBS volumes can be attached to an EC2 instance.
- The scope of the EBS volume is at the AZ level. An EBS volume in us-east-1a can't be attached to an EC2 instance in us-east-1b. We can create point-in-time snapshots (backups) of EBS volumes to enable replication and ensure high availability across AZs or regions.
- EBS volumes were first launched as nonsharing block storage, meaning an EBS volume can't be shared among multiple EC2 instances. AWS launched the Multi-Attach EBS volumes feature (*https://oreil.ly/sup6p*) to allow users to attach a single provisioned-IOPS SSD volume to a max of 16 Nitro-based EC2s (*https://oreil.ly/Yj49e*) in the same AZ for Linux applications.
- EBS volumes are automatically replicated within an AZ to prevent any data loss.

EBS volumes have certain limitations, such as the scope at the AZ level and data sharing across EC2 instances. AWS offers another storage solution, Amazon EFS, to overcome these limitations.

Amazon Elastic File System

EFS (*https://oreil.ly/6Fmlc*) is a shared file system that allows storage sharing across multiple servers placed in a region or at an on-premises data center. EFS is a fully managed, serverless solution that supports all AWS compute platforms, such as Amazon EC2, Amazon ECS, and AWS Lambda. There is no need to preconfigure storage space, and pricing is determined based on the storage space you use for your applications.

Amazon EFS is generally used for business use cases, such as big data analytics, ML workload, and content management. Both the EFS and EBS storage solutions offer low latency for data access, though there are multiple contributing factors in overall performance, such as latency, throughput, and IOPS.

EFS offers multiple storage classes. You can select a storage class that best fits your business needs:

EFS Standard and Standard Infrequent Access (Standard IA)
: Both storage classes provide the highest level of availability across the AZs in an AWS region. EFS Standard is optimal for use cases requiring frequent data access, whereas Standard IA is the better choice for infrequent data access and is a cost-optimal solution. The latency of first byte read or write is higher for the IA storage-class type.

EFS One Zone and One Zone Infrequent Access (One Zone IA)
: One Zone storage classes differ from Standard storage classes in terms of availability and cost. One Zone ensures high availability within a single AZ, whereas Standard spans the AZs within a region. Because of this, One Zone is relatively cheaper. AWS Backup, which replicates the data across three AZs, can be used for better durability.

Cloud is still a relatively new technology for hosting business applications, and there are scenarios where you'll rely on other filesystems, such as Windows File Server. For such use cases, AWS offers a managed service: Amazon FSx (*https://oreil.ly/ldVSO*), which scales automatically without any operational overhead. You can leverage FSx to run popular open source and licensed filesystems without the worry of maintenance or hardware setup. There are two FSx variants that you can select as needed per your use case:

FSx for Windows File Server (https://oreil.ly/fW9na)
: This option is built on Windows Server and is accessible over the Server Message Block (SMB) protocol from Windows, Linux, or MacOS to execute use cases such as data deduplication, end-user file store, and Microsoft Active Directory (AD) integration.

FSx for Lustre (https://oreil.ly/_BuxA)
: Built on a popular high-performance filesystem, Lustre (*https://lustre.org*), this option works well for compute-intensive workloads, such as ML, high-performance computing, and video rendering. It can also be linked with Amazon S3, allowing accessing and processing of data concurrently from the filesystem as well as the S3 API.

Note that a server is required for accessing data from EBS and EFS storage services. S3 is an unlimited storage solution offered by AWS that allows users to directly access the files over the public internet or a private AWS network without requiring a server in between.

Amazon Simple Storage Service

AWS provides Amazon S3 as an unlimited object storage solution. You can use S3 to store and protect data for a wide range of use cases, such as websites, media storage, backups, and big data analytics. S3 stores objects in containers called *buckets*. Here are some key concepts that will deepen your understanding of how to use S3:

Bucket
    A bucket is a container identified by a unique name. You need to specify the bucket name and AWS region while creating the bucket, along with other options, such as versioning support.

Object
    An object is a file that is uploaded to a bucket and identified by a key name that is unique across the bucket. An object in a bucket has exactly one key as an identifier.

Versioning
    S3 allows you to store multiple versions of the same object. This enables users to access any object version and is useful in scenarios like application failure. A unique version ID is associated with each version of the object.

S3 storage classes

The data-storage pattern can vary from use case to use case; therefore, S3 offers multiple storage classes. You can select a storage class based on business requirements, such as: do we need to access the data frequently, or do we require a data archival store?

It's important to identify your business use case and then choose the S3 storage class (*https://oreil.ly/i3Qco*) that best fits to make the most out of S3 with minimum cost. S3 has three storage classes based on the object's access type and redundancy.

Frequently accessed objects. The storage class for frequently accessed objects is preferred for latency-sensitive (at the millisecond level) use cases. There are two subclasses based on required redundancy support:

S3 Standard
    The default storage class when a bucket is created

Reduced redundancy
    Can be chosen for noncritical use cases with reduced redundancy compared to S3 Standard

AWS recommends the S3 storage class over reduced redundancy as it is more cost-effective.

Infrequently accessed objects. The storage class for infrequently accessed objects is preferred for long-lived, infrequently accessed data, such as backups. There are two subclasses based on required redundancy support:

Standard IA
Data is stored redundantly in multiple AZs, so objects are resilient to a loss of AZ.

One Zone IA
Data is stored in a single AZ, so data is less resilient in comparison to Standard IA, which also makes this subclass relatively cheaper. This storage class is preferred if data loss is not critical for business or if data can be re-created in some way.

Archived objects. The storage class for archived objects provides low-cost data-archiving support with a resiliency like the S3 Standard storage class. There are three subclasses based on data-retrieval needs:

S3 Glacier Instant Retrieval
This storage class is useful for rarely accessed data that requires millisecond retrieval. The storage cost is less, and the data-access cost is at the higher end when compared with Standard IA.

S3 Glacier Flexible Retrieval
This storage class is useful for data accessibility within minutes (one to five minutes). This subclass requires a minimum storage duration period of 90 days, so even if data is removed or transitioned before that time, the cost will be calculated for the full 90 days.

S3 Glacier Deep Dive
This storage class is the least costly, requires a minimum storage duration of 180 days, and has a default retrieval time of 12 hours. You can also use the bulk-retrieval option, with data being retrieved within 48 hours.

Lifecycle configurations. Consider a scenario requiring frequent data access for 30 days and infrequent access after that. Such use cases can be satisfied via S3 lifecycle configurations; these configurations are the rules that apply to bucket objects. There are two type of actions that you need to define as part of these configurations:

Transition actions
Define object transition to another storage class, such as move object from Standard to Standard IA storage class after 30 days.

Expiration actions
    Define object expiration. S3 will delete objects automatically once they are expired per the configured rule.

Intelligent tiering. S3 optionally provides intelligent-tiering support such that data is automatically moved to different storage classes without any operational overhead. Here is the lifecycle followed by the objects to be moved to different storage classes:

Frequent access
    Objects uploaded or transitioned to S3 intelligent tiering are stored in the frequent access tier.

Infrequent access
    Objects are moved to the infrequent access tier if they are not accessed for 30 consecutive days.

Archive instant access
    Objects are moved to the archive instant access tier if they are not accessed for 90 consecutive days. S3 provides two optional archive access tiers based on the time period of data access. If activated, data is moved to archive access if it is not accessed for a minimum of 90 consecutive days and moved to deep archive access if it is not accessed for a minimum of 180 consecutive days.

Storage classes store data to S3 based on access patterns or required redundancy support. Another factor to consider is data security while storing objects to S3.

Amazon S3 data security

Objects in an S3 bucket are by default accessible to the owner of the bucket. S3 provides different mechanisms for securing data and configuring access permissions for the S3 bucket and objects:

Encryption
    S3 encrypts all objects by default with server-side encryption (SSE-S3) unless a different encryption option is selected, such as AWS Key Management Service (KMS), referred to as SSE-KMS (*https://oreil.ly/skNNa*). You can also configure client-side encryption for more security.

Object Lock
    Object Lock (*https://oreil.ly/RWgqD*) can be enabled on versioned buckets. Once enabled, objects are stored using a write once, read many (WORM) model, which could be a regulatory requirement for an organization. Object Lock provides an extra protection layer for object changes and helps prevent deleting or overwriting objects for a fixed retention period or indefinitely (referred to as a *legal hold*).

Block off public access
> This option is for setting up and managing centralized control on public access to the bucket. This configuration can also be applied at the account level so that it is reflected for all S3 buckets in the AWS account. In general, it is not a good idea to make a bucket public unless there is a specific business requirement, such as a bucket with publicly accessible media files. You can use Access Analyzer for S3 (*https://oreil.ly/R_H-_*) to identify buckets that grant public access.

IAM policies
> IAM policies (*https://oreil.ly/BWlOg*) grant users or groups read-write access to S3 resources.

Amazon Macie
> Amazon Macie (*https://aws.amazon.com/macie*) identifies and secures sensitive data stored in S3 buckets, such as credit card numbers. It also helps evaluate bucket-level access controls (similar to Access Analyzer), such as publicly accessible buckets.

Access control lists (ACLs)
> S3 ACLs (*https://oreil.ly/wVf4E*) are attached to an S3 bucket or object as subresources to manage access by other users. ACLs are disabled by default, and it is recommended to keep them that way unless there is a requirement to control the access of each object individually. Instead of ACLs, you can rely on policies (*https://oreil.ly/QVffd*) for access control.

Bucket policy
> Bucket policies (*https://oreil.ly/qhwTP*) manage access permissions to an S3 bucket as well as the objects in it. For example, they can allow account A to read objects from an S3 bucket owned by account B. Bucket policies are limited to 20 KB in size.

We have covered different services that allow you to store data with cloud storage and process it like storage on a personal computer. Next, we'll discuss the database services offered by AWS. You should already be familiar with how data is stored in databases from Chapter 2 (relational databases) and Chapter 3 (nonrelational databases).

AWS Databases

AWS offers a range of database services—Amazon RDS, Amazon DynamoDB, Amazon DocumentDB, Amazon ElastiCache, and more—to meet customer requirements for different use cases. These services minimize or completely remove any operational overhead of software and hardware management and enable you to gain the needed scale for your organization. We'll start with the relational database offering, which falls under the umbrella service RDS, with support for Oracle, Microsoft SQL Server, MySQL, PostgreSQL, MariaDB, and Amazon Aurora as database engines.

Amazon RDS

Without Amazon RDS, you have a couple of options when you want to run relational database engines like MySQL or PostgreSQL, which were covered in Chapter 2. Should you want to use, for example, a MySQL database engine on your local machine, you'd need to download the installation package and install it. If you're using AWS cloud computing services, you could install the package on an EC2 machine, but once it's up and running, you'll have to take care of maintaining it, attaching EBS volumes, and so on.

RDS removes all this overhead so that you can just focus on creating a DB instance and start using it with a few clicks. You can follow the steps from the documentation for creating RDS DB instances (*https://oreil.ly/IxH3y*), but a few details are important to keep in mind when creating a database:

Engine type
    You can select the database engine that meets your needs. Once you select a specific engine, you are required to specify some additional configurations, such as edition and engine version.

Templates
    Templates enable you to preselect the setting options while setting up a database. The available templates are production, dev/test, and free tier.

Settings
    Settings include details like DB instance identifier (which is unique across AWS accounts in the region) and credentials settings (username and password).

DB instance class
    The DB instance class determines the computation and memory capacity of an instance. You can select from a list of standard, memory-optimized, and burstable classes (*https://oreil.ly/X87Ed*), depending on your workload's processing and memory requirements.

Storage
    Storage configurations allow you to select a storage type from SSD, HDD, or magnetic disks, and a storage allocation number with autoscaling enabled or disabled.

Availability and durability
    To ensure high availability of production databases, RDS has multi-AZ deployment options for creating a standby instance in different AZs. This helps overcome any database or AZ failure.

Connectivity

Connectivity configurations allow you to select a VPC DB instance. Additional configurations establish connections with DB instances, including the subnet group, the security group, whether the instance is publicly accessible, the AZ, and the database port.

In addition to these options, you can configure settings like backups, monitoring, and maintenance windows.

Amazon also provides its own proprietary database engine, Aurora (*https://oreil.ly/_7Ash*), which is compatible with MySQL and PostgreSQL. Aurora is up to five times faster than MySQL and up to three times faster than PostgreSQL running on the same hardware. It also scales automatically per the application needs. Aurora creates six copies of your data distributed across three AZs and continuously backs it up to S3. Aurora also can replicate data across multiple regions for faster global access. You can use Aurora Serverless for unpredictable workloads or for development purposes when you don't have a requirement to keep DB instances running all the time.

Here are few key considerations regarding Aurora:

- There is no requirement to configure storage requirements as with RDS—this is handled internally by Aurora.
- Aurora Serverless operates based on minimum and maximum Aurora capacity units and not based on instance types like RDS.
- RDS works at the VPC level. Classic RDS can be opened to the public internet or restricted to allow specific IPs to access it from the outside. With Aurora Serverless, you can't provide public access, but you can use the Data API (*https://oreil.ly/40qsr*) or leverage an EC2 machine in the same VPC as Aurora to facilitate the connectivity.
- For data security or to meet compliance requirements for data encryption at rest, RDS (*https://oreil.ly/ZLguz*) and Aurora (*https://oreil.ly/y33pf*) both have the functionality to encrypt DB instances.
- An Aurora DB cluster can consist of up to 15 Aurora replicas (*https://oreil.ly/tiIKU*). The replicas scale and distribute the read workload to multiple instances, ensuring latency-optimized read operations. The read replica is promoted to the writer instance in case the writer instance goes down, increasing overall availability of the Aurora cluster.

RDS is a beneficial service when your business requirements require support for relational structured data with complete compliance with ACID properties. Many modern applications don't have a requirement for strong ACID compliance, full relational support, or fixed schema. NoSQL databases are viable solutions to address these kinds of use cases while also providing scalability, high performance, and no operational overhead. We described multiple types of NoSQL databases in Chapter 3. In this chapter, we will cover the equivalent services offered by AWS for different types of NoSQL databases, starting with Amazon DynamoDB as a key-value database solution.

> To support unlimited compute and storage scaling in relational databases for transactional workloads, AWS has announced Aurora DSQL. Aurora DSQL is a distributed relational database with PostgreSQL compatibility, ACID compliance, and zero maintenance overhead.

Amazon DynamoDB

Amazon DynamoDB is a key-value database designed to provide single-digit millisecond latency for any workload scale. DynamoDB stores data in tables and follows a schemaless design. We discussed the primary key, partition key, and sort key in Chapter 3 in the context of using key-value data stores to uniquely identify items. In DynamoDB architecture, the primary key is represented by a partition key or a combination of a partition key and a sort key. Any queries on data can be performed via the AWS CLI, AWS Console, or AWS Software Development Kit (SDK) in your preferred language. DynamoDB is based on the leader-follower nodes model and internally stores the data on storage nodes called *partitions*.

Here are the keys responsible for data storage on DynamoDB:

Partition key
　The partition key must be specified when the table is created and is used as an input to the internal hash function to determine a physical partition where data should be stored. A request router (RR) component routes the request to a specific partition, as shown in Figure 10-1. RR is a stateless service that consults with the Partition Metadata Service to determine the partition; then, the request is forwarded to a specific partition. The `PUT` request is sent to the leader node, while the `GET` request can be served via the leader or the follower node, depending on the required consistency support.

Sort key
　The sort key is an optional attribute upon table creation. If it is specified, then the primary key is a combination of the partition key and the sort key; otherwise, it's just the partition key. The combination of partition key and sort key should be unique for data storage. All items with the same partition key are stored together on the same physical partition in a sorted order by sort-key value. We recommend creating a DynamoDB table with both the partition key and the sort key per the read/write query patterns that will serve the user requests without the need for global secondary indexes (GSIs).

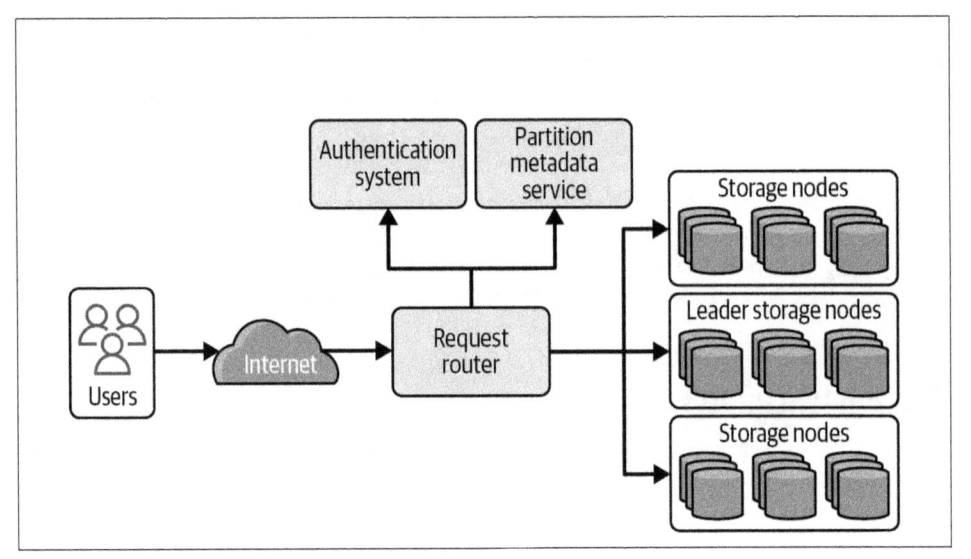

Figure 10-1. DynamoDB internal architecture

DynamoDB is a fully managed service. You don't have to configure any servers or storage space. Instead, you can select from different capacity modes (*https://oreil.ly/ IbKC6*) for allowed reads and writes per specific tables. DynamoDB defines reads and writes as read capacity units (RCUs) and write capacity units (WCUs), respectively, and pricing (*https://oreil.ly/XxmZK*) is based on consumed RCUs and WCUs, along with required consistency or transaction support. Let's understand the available DynamoDB capacity modes:

Provisioned
 Customers can configure specific RCU and WCU values for tables that are to be supported, and DynamoDB internally manages the resources to support this scale. This is the preferred mode for applications with predictable traffic, when you can easily forecast RCU and WCU requirements.

Autoscaling
 For varying workloads with undeterminable, fixed provisioned capacity, you can use autoscaling mode with lower and upper RCU and WCU limits, and DynamoDB automatically scales up or down based on the traffic.

On-demand
 On-demand is a serverless kind of support where you don't need to configure RCU and WCU values. DynamoDB manages the scale in the backend, and we as customers don't have to worry about it. This is the preferred mode for use cases such as tables with unknown workloads or unpredictable application traffic.

The DynamoDB table might be responsible for serving multiple use cases, and not all of these use cases will be performant just with primary key design. DynamoDB provides index support (*https://oreil.ly/bZ5UM*) to speed up queries, which can be created on top of the table as necessary. We can think of a DynamoDB index as a child table that is created by selecting some of the attributes from the main table. DynamoDB supports two types of indexes: local secondary index (LSI) and global secondary index (GSI). The differences between them are listed in Table 10-1.

Table 10-1. Differences between LSIs and GSIs in Amazon DynamoDB

Parameter	LSI	GSI
Lifecycle	The LSI lifecycle is the same as that of the table. It can only be created or deleted along with table creation and deletion.	The GSI lifecycle is independent of the table and can be created or deleted as required.
Primary key schema	The partition key is the same as the base table with a different sort key.	The partition key and the sort key can be different from the base table.
Querying capability	Scoped to the partition as of the base table—hence the term "local"—with an indexed data size limitation of 10 GB.	Queries can span the partitions on base table data— hence the term "global"—with no size limitations.
Provisioned capacity	LSI shares read/write throughput capacity with the base table.	GSI has independent settings for read/write throughput from the base table.
Read consistency	Offers both strong and eventual read consistency.	Offers only eventual read consistency.

As we move from traditional relational databases to a wide variety of modern NoSQL databases, one key difference is transaction support. Transaction is inherently available in SQL-like databases but is not supported in all the NoSQL databases. DynamoDB provides transaction support, and we can choose the specific read and write APIs (*https://oreil.ly/Hr4K-*) if our use case has a requirement for transactions. Another difference is strong consistency support: DynamoDB provides both eventual and strong consistency support (though GSI only supports eventual consistency), and we can specify the required support type (*https://oreil.ly/F0DLV*) as we access the data.

We discussed identifying physical partitions based on the partition key and different capacity modes, which helps us configure read and write throughput for DynamoDB tables. The throughput values apply on a table as a whole and are equally divided among the partitions being created. The partitions have hard limits for allowing 3,000 RCUs and 1,000 WCUs (or a combination of both) per second, and requests are throttled once this limit is breached. Apart from read and write requests, there is a 10-GB upper limit as allowed storage per partition. You should carefully design the schema with an understanding of the query patterns as well as the DynamoDB architecture in mind to avoid breaching these limits.

The partition breaching the defined limits is referred to as *hot partition* (or *hot key*). A partition key can be categorized as hot if it receives disproportionately high read or write (or both) traffic compared to other partitions. Figuring out query patterns is key to coming up with the best feasible schema design for a DynamoDB table. You can use CloudWatch contributor insights (*https://oreil.ly/voj-0*) for debugging and identifying existing hot partitions or most accessed items in DynamoDB tables.

Let's discuss a few best practices for partition key design to avoid hot partition issues in DynamoDB:

- The table schema should be designed with high cardinality of partition keys. This ensures that the data is widespread across the partitions, improving both read and write efficiency.
- DynamoDB APIs (and AWS SDK in general for all AWS services) throw specific exceptions with proper details, and applications can act on these exceptions accordingly. Retry (*https://oreil.ly/mmLFl*) with exponential backoff is one recommended solution if the hot partition issue occurs rarely. For frequent hot partition issues, more detailed analysis should be done to figure out a stable solution.
- Redesigning a table schema with existing data could be too much work and needs to be considered from different angles, such as migration downtime and application code changes. The following are intermittent solutions—or long term, if the use case allows—for read and write throttling due to hot partitions:
  — For reads, a cache (discussed in "Amazon ElastiCache" on page 272) is a recommended solution. The cache can improve the latency and resolve the hot partition issue.
  — For writes (*https://oreil.ly/Z654h*), the solution is to attach a random (or calculated based on logic) suffix to a partition key, such as a number from 1 to 100. The read query will require additional application logic to figure out the actual partition (access all the partitions from 1 to 100 in the case of random logic or a specific partition if the suffix is based on some logic).

Evaluate data-access patterns to make best use of DynamoDB at a lower cost and zero operational burden.

Amazon DocumentDB

Amazon DocumentDB is a document database offered by AWS designed to store and query data as JSON-like documents. A document (*https://oreil.ly/OqK-v*) is structured as a collection of nested key-value pairs and can be useful in scenarios like storing food-item information, such as for Cafe Delhi Heights's online store. Here is a sample document for a customer order:

```
{
  "Name": "Mandeep Singh",
  "orderId": "1234-1234-4567",
  "FoodItems": [
    {
      "itemName": "Biryani",
      "qty": 1
    },
    {
      "itemName": "Nuggets",
      "qty": 2
    }
  ]
}
```

We can add attributes to the food items or remove them without worrying about the fixed schema, as in relational databases. Some other business use cases include content management (*https://oreil.ly/CpG9l*), real-time big data, and user-profile maintenance.

For reference, Table 10-2 compares the terminology associated with DocumentDB with that of relational databases.

Table 10-2. SQL versus Amazon DocumentDB terminology

SQL	Amazon DocumentDB
Table	Collection
Row	Document
Column	Field
Primary key	Object ID

DocumentDB is compatible with MongoDB (*https://mongodb.com*), with support for powerful ad hoc queries, and it comes with transaction support (*https://oreil.ly/czpQE*) similar to DynamoDB's. There are a few functional benefits of DocumentDB over MongoDB, such as transaction support for all CRUD statements, including operations on multiple documents. For all functional differences between MongoDB and DocumentDB, refer to the AWS documentation (*https://oreil.ly/KLy5s*).

Unlike with DynamoDB, we need to specify the instance class (*https://oreil.ly/d-Ek5*) and number of instances for DocumentDB cluster setup. For production systems, we recommend choosing at least three instances for higher availability. The final step is to set up a username and password for authentication and to establish a connection with a DocumentDB cluster.

AWS also provides migration tools (*https://oreil.ly/K_wcP*) such as Database Migration Service (DMS) to facilitate easier migration of MongoDB workloads from on-premises or EC2 servers to DocumentDB.

Amazon Neptune

Going back to our Cafe Delhi Heights scenario, one of the requirements for launching an online restaurant is to create food communities for the customers that allow for tracking things like customers' likes and dislikes of particular food items. Suppose you want to figure out if a food item is liked by everyone in your community, for example.

These kinds of use cases with highly connected data can be stored and queried at scale with AWS's fully managed graph database service, Amazon Neptune. Neptune is optimized to store and map billions of relationships and enable real-time navigation of connections with a millisecond query response time via Apache TinkerPop Gremlin (*https://oreil.ly/dvvYF*) or openCypher (*http://opencypher.org*) for property graph databases and SPARQL (*https://oreil.ly/hr_wX*) for graph databases in Resource Description Framework (RDF) format. AWS recommends consulting the GitHub repository AWS Reference Architectures for Using Graph Databases (*https://oreil.ly/i2v70*) to look into graph data models and use cases, query languages, and sample examples of deployment architectures.

Another example use case for Neptune is to get a clear picture of your cloud infrastructure to see how different services or entities are connected to one another. You may want to know which entities use a particular IAM role, as shown in Figure 10-2, or figure out overpermissive IAM policies with * marked on resource permissions. For example, you may not want all the users in the organization to be able to modify network security groups.

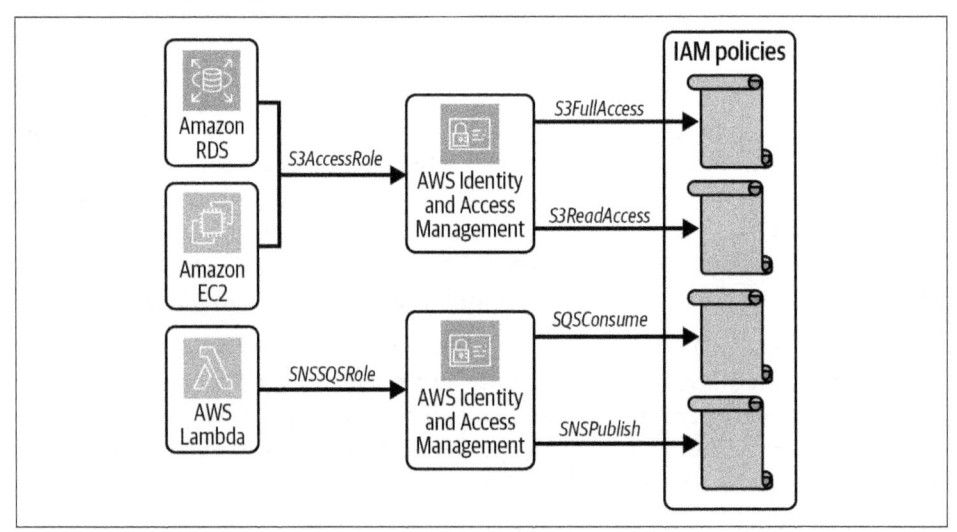

Figure 10-2. Graph representation of IAM role-entities association

For a step-by-step guide to cluster setup, refer to the AWS documentation (*https://oreil.ly/JwbLg*). Now, we'll discuss some points you should be aware of while setting up your graph database cluster.

Compute

The Neptune cluster is launched with a specific instance type that should be selected at the time of creating the cluster. The cluster can have a maximum of one writer instance and up to 15 read replicas; note that writer instances scale vertically, whereas read instances can scale vertically or horizontally. We recommend configuring at least one read replica for higher application availability and better read performance. If a writer instance goes down, the read replica is promoted to writer, and the writer is restarted as a read replica. In case there is only a single writer instance in a cluster, the cluster might be down for a few minutes as it restarts and comes back online.

Neptune also offers a serverless configuration, which can be useful for variable workloads. We can specify an upper capacity limit, and it is used only if needed.

Storage

Neptune stores data six times across three AZs. Neptune's storage layer is independent of the compute layers and scales independently and automatically as necessary. It starts with 10 GB and grows up to 128 TB as data increases.

Traffic distribution

Neptune provides separate writer and reader endpoints. The writer endpoint (called the *cluster endpoint*) points to the primary instance and should be used for write operations and, optionally, read queries. The reader endpoint distributes requests across the read replicas in round-robin fashion and should be used for all read queries. Neptune also provides an *instance endpoint* (an endpoint that connects to a specific DB instance) and a custom endpoint that can be used to represent a set of DB instances. Neptune doesn't offer load balancing functionality on instances. For any such requirement, it should be built into the application code.

Caching

Neptune offers three types of caching support to improve performance:

Buffer cache
    In-memory cache to improve query performance. Neptune allocates two-thirds of memory of instance to cache.

Lookup cache (https://oreil.ly/xkShP)
    An instance-level cache for improving read performance for queries with repetitive lookup of property values or RDF literals. It is enabled by default for R5d

instances (*https://oreil.ly/yo1_9*) (purpose built for workloads processing large workloads in memory) and uses the instance's NVM Express-based (NVMe-based) SSD to store these values for quick access.

Query results cache (https://oreil.ly/GKaKi)
Gremlin read-only query results can be cached to get faster responses upon query rerun. For clearing the cache, you can specify TTL for queries, clear the cache at query level, or clear the entire cache.

Amazon ElastiCache

In-memory databases are extensively used as caching solutions to improve system performance. Amazon ElastiCache is a managed service offered by AWS as a distributed cache environment that works with the Redis and Memcached engines, both covered in detail in Chapter 4. Redis and Memcached are in-memory, key-value caching solutions, but there are associated differences (*https://oreil.ly/OZoO9*), and it's important to figure out which caching engine meets your business requirements. Memcached is a simple key-value caching solution to offload reads from a primary data source with multithreading support. Redis comes with functionalities such as persistence for long-lived data, advanced data types like lists and sets, sorting and ranking datasets in memory, geospatial support, message broker, and more. The following are some key considerations for each of the caching engines available as part of ElastiCache.

Subnet

As noted in Chapter 9, the number of IP addresses available for use are based on subnet CIDR. As a first step in cluster creation, you should create a subnet associated with Amazon VPC with support available for the required number of IP addresses as they are assigned to nodes in the cluster.

Data tiering

Data can be tiered between memory and NVMe SSD storage for optimizing costs and is ideal for applications that regularly access up to 20% data. This support is available with ElastiCache for Redis for the R6gd instance family, and infrequent data is moved to SSD asynchronously once memory (DRAM) is fully utilized, as shown in Figure 10-3. The storage can scale up to 1 PB in a single cluster.

Both Redis and Memcached can be scaled horizontally and vertically. Redis works on the concept of primary node and read replicas and can be launched with two kinds of configurations:

Cluster mode disabled
 There can be a maximum of one primary node and up to five replica nodes. This configuration scales horizontally for reads and vertically for writes.

Cluster mode enabled
 There can be a maximum of 500 nodes and up to 5 replicas associated with each node.

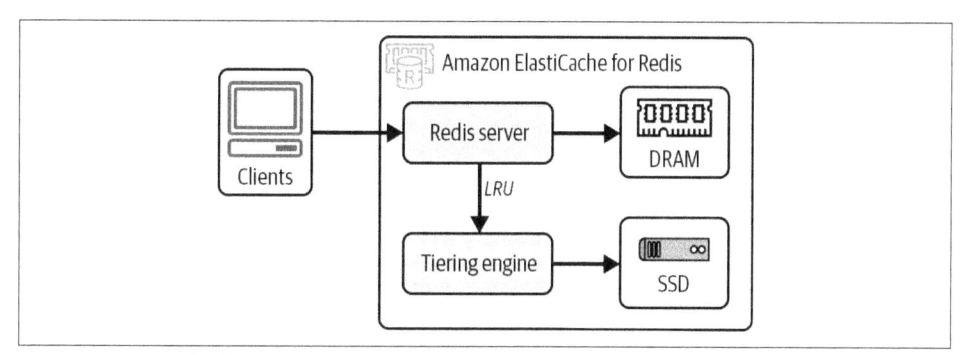

Figure 10-3. Redis data-tiering support

Redundancy and replication

ElastiCache for Redis has multi-AZ deployment (*https://oreil.ly/fkNRY*) support similar to RDS. Whenever a primary node is down, a read replica (one to five read replicas placed in different AZs) is promoted to primary, which ensures high availability even if the entire AZ is down. The replication of data on read replicas also ensures separation of read and write workload.

Multithreading

Redis is a single-threaded process when incoming requests are handled sequentially, while Memcached is multithreaded, meaning it makes good use of larger Amazon EC2 instance sizes with multiple cores.

Persistence

Redis can be used as a standalone database for applications since it supports persistence for long-lived data. Memcached is a pure caching solution that should be used in front of any database, such as RDS, to improve read performance.

Encryption and compliance

Redis supports Payment Card Industry Data Security Standard (PCI DSS), Health Insurance Portability and Accountability Act (HIPAA), and Federal Risk and Authorization Management Program (FedRAMP) requirements as well as encryption capabilities. Memcached doesn't have strong support for authentication and encryption, so the recommendation is to launch Memcached nodes in private subnets with no public connectivity to ensure higher security.

For a step-by-step guide to cluster creation, follow the AWS page for Redis and Memcached (*https://oreil.ly/RgKCB*).

Amazon DynamoDB Accelerator

As discussed, you can use Memcached or Redis to offload your database read queries, such as RDS or DynamoDB. DynamoDB offers a custom in-memory cache offering as well, DynamoDB Accelerator (DAX) (*https://oreil.ly/O7Fad*), to improve read performance. DAX is a cluster of primary node and read replicas that run inside VPC, as shown in Figure 10-4. To access DAX, a DAX client is installed alongside an application on the server that directs the application's DynamoDB API requests to the DAX cluster.

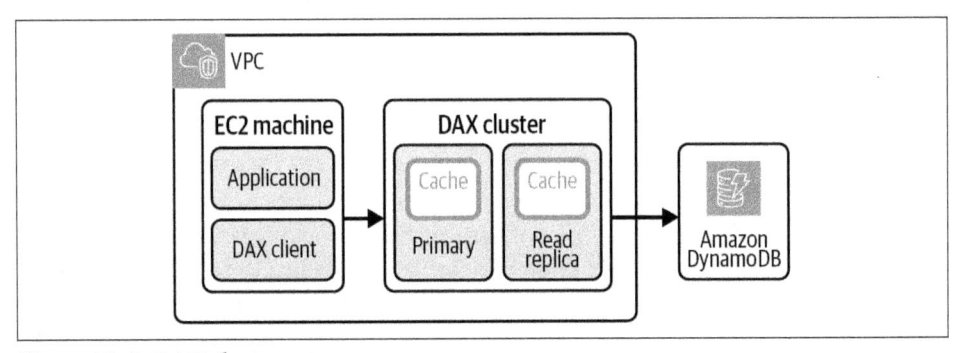

Figure 10-4. DAX cluster setup

Here is how read and write APIs execute in the presence of both the DAX cluster and DynamoDB:

Read APIs
　　The eventually consistent read API calls (GetItem, BatchGetItem, Query, and Scan) are served from DAX. In the scenario of cache miss, the request is passed to DynamoDB to retrieve the response. As DynamoDB returns the result, it also writes the result to the DAX cache on the primary node.

Write APIs
　　For the write API calls (BatchWriteItem, UpdateItem, DeleteItem, and PutItem), data is first written to the DynamoDB table and then to the DAX cluster. The API returns success only if the write is successful on both DynamoDB and DAX.

Amazon OpenSearch

You may want to display search results to users based on the user's search query; in the example of Cafe Delhi Heights, these search results could be a food item, restaurant location, or any supported filters. A search for a food item should return all the restaurant locations serving that item, and a search for a restaurant location should display all dishes served by that location. How can such data be modeled in a database for faster retrieval? For these kinds of business use cases, AWS offers a search database, OpenSearch.

OpenSearch (*https://oreil.ly/S2MvR*) is an open source project derived from Elasticsearch, unlike most of the AWS services, which run on proprietary software. OpenSearch is popular for use cases like full-text search, logs and analytics, ingestion pipelines, and ML. AWS provides OpenSearch dashboards on top of the search engine, which help visualize the data. Here are a few key considerations for the OpenSearch architecture and how we as customers can get the best out of it:

Cluster setup
OpenSearch can work as a single-node or multinode cluster. As this is an open source project, you can also set up your own cluster following these steps (*https://oreil.ly/sQ3dA*). OpenSearch is a managed service that helps you avoid the operational overhead of setup and works on instance-based (cluster manager and data nodes) or serverless mode. AWS recommends setting up an odd number of cluster manager nodes for a production OpenSearch cluster, with a minimum of three nodes. The type of cluster manager node can be decided based on the number of data nodes (*https://oreil.ly/nqOHv*) in your domain, such as setting up m5.large.search or m6g.large.search for a count of 1–10 data nodes. You can skip setting up dedicated cluster manager nodes for development use cases to save costs (one of the data nodes holds cluster manager–node responsibilities), though it is recommended to configure them for production scenarios for better cluster stability and dedicated nodes for cluster management tasks.

Storage
You can select either EBS or instance store volumes to be associated with the instances; the volume types available will depend on the chosen instance type.

Cluster access
For cluster access and networking, you can choose either VPC access or public access. VPC access allows you to operate the cluster inside your VPC as well as to configure subnets, security groups, and IAM roles.

Deployment
OpenSearch enables configuration updates, such as increasing EBS storage space or upgrading the instance type on a live-running cluster. The configurations are

deployed to a new cluster via blue/green deployment (*https://oreil.ly/kW07Y*) to avoid any impact. Perform any such updates during off-peak hours.

Dashboard authentication
OpenSearch provides the option to configure authentication for dashboards via Security Assertion Markup Language (SAML) authentication (*https://oreil.ly/rreMP*) or Amazon Cognito authentication (*https://oreil.ly/_BG_h*).

Amazon Timestream

Amazon Timestream is a fully managed, serverless database service offered for use cases that require time-series data operations, such as DevOps analysis data. Timestream automatically scales to handle trillions of events per day with one-tenth the cost and is up to one thousand times faster than relational databases.

Here are few points to consider for Timestream:

- As Timestream is serverless, it is easy to use with no requirement for analyzing number or type of instances.
- Timestream provides built-in analytics support with interpolation and smoothing functions for identifying trends, patterns, and anomalies using standard SQL.
- Data is encrypted by default with a standard key or a customer-owned KMS key.
- Timestream provides support for data-retention policies based on a configured time and for moving data to different storage tiers per policy. It supports two storage tiers: in-memory tier (preferred for latency-sensitive queries) and magnetic disk tier (preferred for analytical queries).
- Records require timestamps as a mandatory dimension, and data stored to Timestream cannot be deleted or updated. Removal of data should be handled via configuration of retention policies.

Amazon Keyspaces

We discussed wide-column databases in Chapter 3 and then looked at an open source variant, Apache Cassandra. The AWS-managed solution to meet similar requirements is Amazon Keyspaces.

Keyspaces is a highly scalable, available, and managed wide-column database service compatible with the open source Apache Cassandra database. Keyspaces is offered as a serverless service, meaning you don't have to worry about resource provisioning and can simply focus on building your applications. Here a few use cases for which to consider using Keyspaces:

- You want to migrate on-premises Cassandra clusters or clusters running on EC2 instances to a fully managed AWS service. This helps reduce large cluster management overhead, such as managing deployment, figuring out best configurations for your workload like Java virtual machine (JVM) tuning for garbage collection, understanding Cassandra internals, provisioning capacity for expected workloads, upgrading to newer versions, patching and maintaining cluster infrastructure, and so on.

- You have a business requirement to be compatible with open source Cassandra.
- Keyspaces has better integration with AWS services like Amazon CloudWatch for monitoring purposes or AWS IAM for authentication, compared to customers managing them on their own.

Since Keyspaces abstracts out infrastructure management, you don't have access to low-level cluster management control plane APIs. Keyspaces offers two types of capacity modes for tables' read and write workloads similar to DynamoDB: provisioned capacity with autoscaling and on demand. All the data in Keyspaces tables is by default encrypted and replicated in multiple AZs for high availability and durability. Refer to the AWS guide (*https://oreil.ly/LTqIN*) for the functional differences between Cassandra and Keyspaces.

Conclusion

We discussed a wide range of storage services offered by AWS that can be used to fulfill your business needs. "Cloud Storage on AWS" on page 256 focused on primitive storage options, such as block storage, file storage, and object storage, and "AWS Databases" on page 262 covered AWS services offered for relational and nonrelational databases. It's quite important to understand the business use case for choosing the best cost-optimal storage service. To that end, let's take another look at our Cafe Delhi Heights storage requirements. Table 10-3 lists which AWS storage services can be used to fulfill these requirements.

Table 10-3. Storage service identification for Cafe Delhi Heights

Requirement	Storage service
Store customer's profile and access details, such as username and password	Amazon RDS, Amazon Aurora, Amazon ElastiCache as cache on top of persistent store for frequent queries
Store food information, such as available menu items	Amazon DynamoDB, Amazon DocumentDB, Amazon Keyspaces, Amazon OpenSearch
Store different kinds of media, such as images of restaurant food items and customer-uploaded reviews	Amazon S3
Big data analytics to improve the customer experience, such as separating good and bad reviews	Amazon S3, Amazon EFS, Amazon DynamoDB
Create food communities and allow people to interact in social circles	Amazon Neptune

Requirement	Storage service
Search for food items based on multiple identifiers, such as food name, restaurant location, ratings, etc.	Amazon OpenSearch
Application logs and metrics archival after 90 days and persistence for one year	Amazon S3, Amazon OpenSearch

> Refer to Chapters 2 and 3 for general guidelines and a flowchart for choosing a storage solution based on your business use case.

For handling the client requests or processing on data stored on AWS storage services, we require servers or compute platforms. In the next chapter, we'll dive deep into different kinds of compute platforms offered by AWS and discover how we can identify the best option for our business use cases.

CHAPTER 11
AWS Compute Services

You love programming and spend your free time designing and creating new software applications on your personal computer. You recently created an application that converts input images to cartoon images and demoed this to your friend, who happens to be a software engineer at a big tech company. The friend really liked the idea and suggested sharing the application with other people—plus it can help you earn some extra dollars. But how can you achieve this task? How can you make a program running on a personal computer accessible to other people?

For this specific example, you need some mechanism that allows people to send an image to a personal computer and the personal computer to return the output as a cartoon image via the internet. In this scenario, the personal computer is acting as a server. A *server* is nothing but a computer that is running most of the time (i.e., a highly available application), responsible for serving any kind of request. This server can be accessible just to you, to any other computer, or to other users, who all are referred to as *clients*.

Servers are an essential part of any application, and AWS offers multiple compute platforms to run applications. A compute platform in the AWS cloud is a virtual server hosted in an AWS data center that can be accessed over the internet. We'll start our discussion with a compute platform similar to a personal computer called Amazon Elastic Compute Cloud (EC2), and then we'll move on to AWS Lambda and containerization services present in the AWS cloud.

Amazon Elastic Compute Cloud

Amazon EC2 is a scalable virtual server hosting services provided by AWS. We can leverage the EC2 service to create VMs in the AWS cloud with a required set of configurations, such as CPU, memory, storage, networking, and so on. These VMs or virtual computing environments are called *instances*. AWS provides the option to select bare-metal servers or to go with a virtualized environment maintained via hypervisor, which should be determined by identifying your business and compliance requirements. Here are general descriptions of bare-metal and hypervisor servers:

Bare-metal server
: Physical servers dedicated to a single tenant. These servers are helpful for workloads that require direct access to Intel Xeon processor infrastructure, such as Intel virtualization (VT-x) (*https://oreil.ly/f_zl6*), that have a strict compliance requirement, or that need to run a custom hypervisor. For example, you might need to run Oracle Hypervisor instead of Nitro.

Hypervisor
: A virtualization component for running multiple VMs on a single physical server, as shown in Figure 11-1. Hypervisor helps allocate computing resources, such as CPU and memory, to VMs running their own OS and applications. AWS supports two hypervisors based on available instance types: Xen (*https://xenproject.org*) and Nitro (*https://aws.amazon.com/ec2/nitro*). The Nitro system (*https://oreil.ly/n-6xJ*) is a new-generation hypervisor with enhanced security and performance.

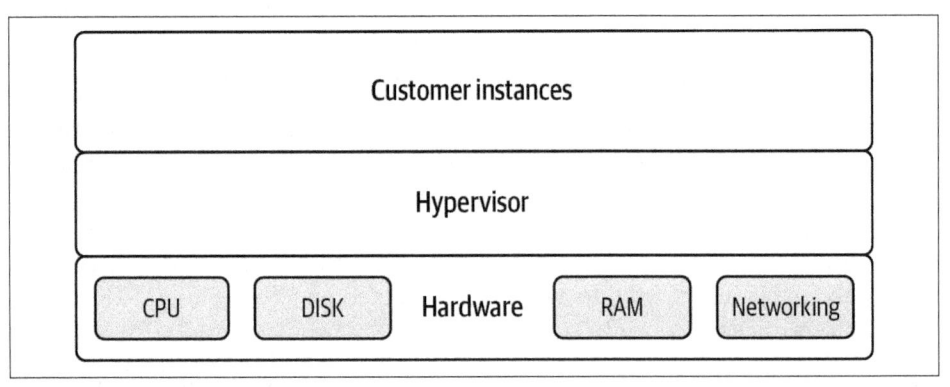

Figure 11-1. Xen hypervisor

Launching and running instances in the AWS cloud is easy and removes the headache of maintaining physical hardware. EC2 instances can be launched with just a few clicks on the AWS Console by following the steps in the AWS documentation (*https://oreil.ly/HH7mS*). The instances are launched with a specific set of configurations that are determined by Amazon Machine Image (AMI).

> One EC2 instance doesn't necessarily map to one physical server in the AWS cloud.

Amazon Machine Image

We can launch an EC2 instance with different configurations, such as the OS, the storage volumes attached to the instance, the install dependencies before instance bootup, custom security configurations, and so on. These configurations can be defined via a preconfigured template called an *AMI*, which enables easy, efficient provisioning of EC2 instances with the desired software stack. Consider a scenario where you as an engineer are responsible for installing security dependencies to all the EC2 instances launched in an organization. One way is to run scripts on these EC2 instances after they are launched, but a more optimal way would be to create a base AMI with all the required dependencies installed. This saves a lot of time and ensures 100% confidence that none of the EC2 instances are missed for the required dependencies.

As customers, we can launch EC2 instances using freely available AMIs from the AWS community, purchase AMIs from third parties such as Red Hat, or create our own custom AMIs depending on our needs. For example, Amazon Linux and Linux 2 AMIs are available free of cost and are fully supported and maintained by AWS. AWS provides a marketplace where users can choose from a wide variety of publicly available AMIs. Here are few considerations for choosing the best AMI for your business use case:

Region
    AMIs are created specific to the region. If an AMI is not available in a specific region, you can copy the AMI (*https://oreil.ly/qR1Qx*) to the required region and use it to launch EC2 instances.

OS and architecture
    EC2 instance runs on an OS, and you can choose from multiple OS flavors (32-bit or 64-bit architectures) supported by AWS (*https://oreil.ly/9ZeBP*).

Launch permissions
    An AMI can be owned by AWS, businesses, or individuals, and it can be made available to the general public, a set of users, or just a single individual.

Root device storage
    AMIs are backed either by Amazon EBS or by an instance store (see Chapter 10 for more details) as root device storage. The root device storage contains the image used to boot the EC2 instance. There are significant differences between these storage choices (*https://oreil.ly/t3DTk*), such as size limit (64 TB for EBS io2 Block Express and 10 GB for instance store), data persistence, and boot time (usually less than one minute for EBS and less than five minutes for instance store).

> You can find the complete details on EC2 instance root device storage in the AWS documentation (*https://oreil.ly/VDXDr*).

The next decision we need to make is the instance type. AWS offers a wide range of instance types based on different capabilities, and we can choose which best suits our requirements.

Instance Type

Hardware requirements can vary from customer to customer, so with this in mind, the EC2 service provides different instance types. *Instance types* define the hardware and performance characteristics of an EC2 instance. We might not always have a concrete answer for which instance type is most suitable. We can start by installing our application on any general-purpose instance and then perform load testing. This will help determine the limits where this specific instance breaks and can eventually help us figure out the instance type and the number of instances needed for the workload.

Different instance types offer varying combinations of CPU, memory, storage, and networking capacities. The following are the different instance type families available:

General-purpose instances
  Suitable for most of the workloads in the industry. They maintain a fine balance between compute, memory, and network resources.

Compute-optimized instances
  Suitable for CPU-intensive workloads, such as high-performance computing, big data analytics, and so on.

Memory-optimized instances
  Suitable for workloads with requirements for large dataset processing in RAM, such as in-memory caches.

Storage-optimized instances
  Suitable for workloads with requirements for high sequential read and write access to large datasets on local storage such as databases.

Accelerated-computing instances
  GPU-based instances that are suitable for workloads with requirements for high-performance computing, computational finance, ML, and so on.

Choosing the appropriate instance type is crucial for achieving optimal performance and cost-efficiency for specific workloads. For updated guidance on instance types and instance families, refer to the AWS page on EC2 instance types (https://oreil.ly/uympU).

Here are some additional considerations to be mindful of when you launch an EC2 instance:

- To establish a connection with an instance after it has launched, you should select a key pair to enable Secure Shell (SSH) access to the instance.
- EC2 instances are launched at the AZ level within a specific region. EC2 allows you to modify default network configurations, such as the VPC instance it should be launched in, the subnet in the VPC, the security group, and so on. These configurations help determine how the connection to launched instances will be established.
- You can choose to assign a public IP to an instance. Public IP assignment allows connections to an instance directly from the public internet, given that you've set the appropriate permissions via either security groups or NACLs.

For running the application at scale, we need a good balance of vertical and horizontal scaling for a number of instances in the entire infrastructure. By looking at usage metrics, we can figure out the minimum number of instances that will be required throughout a longer period. For such scenarios, cost can be reduced by using reserved EC2 instance capacity (https://oreil.ly/v0Tqr) to get up to a 72% discount compared to on-demand instance pricing based on the usage commitment (a one-year or three-year commitment). Note that on-demand instances are instances that we launch as needed from the AWS Console, while we precommit to using EC2 instances for a certain period of time in the case of reserved instances.

There may be use cases where we're not much worried about losing (terminating) an instance while the workload is running or the workload can be resumed later once instances are available in the EC2 pool. For such scenarios, we can leverage something called *spot instances* (https://oreil.ly/Vu_ul).

Spot instances are less expensive than on-demand instances. Let's take an example: assume the us-east-1a AZ has a total capacity of 100 m4.large instances. Out of these 100, half are already in use by customers. Based on AWS historic analysis, 30 instances will be requested by customers shortly as dedicated capacity. In this EC2 pool of 100 instances, 20 instances are left that no one is benefiting from—neither AWS nor its customers. So these instances are made available as spot instances at a lower cost. Customers can request spot instances from this pool for usage. For scenarios like AWS customers requiring more than the 30 available instances, as predicted earlier, any of the spot instances can be turned off and assigned to the requesting customers.

Traffic on applications running on top of EC2 instances can vary across the day, and we might not always require a fixed number of running EC2 instances. For example, the application requires 10 instances at noon but only 2 at midnight. AWS offers an autoscaling feature that automatically adds and removes instances for the application. Let's dive into autoscaling next.

Autoscaling

Autoscaling is an AWS feature that automatically adjusts the number of EC2 instances in the collection in response to changing workload demands. We can create a collection of EC2 instances based on any factor, such as AZ, instance type, and so on. These collections are called *autoscaling groups (ASGs)* when autoscaling is enabled on them. In these groups, we can specify the minimum and maximum number of instances and apply an autoscaling policy for automatically adding and removing the instances within this limit. This helps maintain application performance and availability by dynamically scaling the capacity up or down based on predefined scaling policies.

Autoscaling can be configured to scale based on metrics like CPU utilization, network traffic, or user-defined metrics. It ensures that the application scales seamlessly to handle increased traffic and reduces costs during periods of low demand. Apart from handling scale, autoscaling can ensure that a fixed number of instances are always running in a healthy state (instances are replaced in case of health-check failures). Here is how a new instance is added as a cumulative CPU utilization limit is breached for an ASG (see Figure 11-2):

- For ASG 1, the minimum number of instances configured is one and the maximum is four.
- Assume that the autoscaling policy states that a new instance is added to the group if maximum CPU utilization exceeds 75% for five continuous minutes.
- As the limit is breached, autoscaling kicks in with the desired number of instances going from one to two, and a new EC2 instance is launched.

Large applications in the AWS cloud might be running thousands of EC2 machines to serve customer traffic or internal system processing, and failures are bound to happen. The EC2 instances might go down due to unforeseen hardware failures, and we as customers should have proper mechanisms in place to overcome these failures. There are multiple ways to handle these issues:

- Autoscaling policies to always maintain the desired number of instances within a group
- EC2 instances launched in multiple AZs to withstand AZ failure

- EC2 automatic recovery to relaunch the instance in case of failure; the instance is relaunched with the same configurations, such as instance ID, metadata, attached EBS volumes, private IPs, and EIP addresses

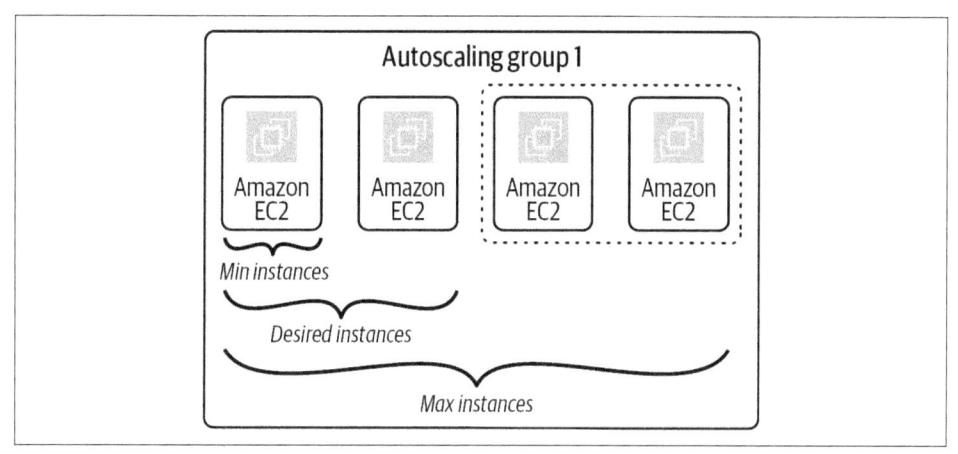

Figure 11-2. Autoscaling

Autoscaling is a great tool for scaling instances up and down, but there is a limit to how quickly the instances are launched to address spiky traffic workloads. Relying on autoscaling for spiky traffic might abruptly cut off application availability; we recommend prescaling of instances for such events (for example, a live cricket match or an NFL event) or setting scaling configurations to a lower number (for example, set instance addition at 60% CPU utilization instead of 80%). To reduce application launch and startup time on new instances, keep the application image size as small as possible and don't include unwanted dependencies.

Apart from configuring the minimum and maximum number of instances in a scaling activity, we can define a cooldown period (*https://oreil.ly/P-eAj*) (the default is 300 seconds). After a scaling activity (launch or termination of an instance), AWS waits for the defined cooldown period before initiating any further scaling activities, ensuring stability of the ASG.

EC2 is the oldest and most widely used service for running applications in the AWS cloud. EC2 provides control over maintaining the software stack and maximum visibility of hardware operations. However, it might not always be a requirement to know how application software is deployed, or you might want to avoid any operational maintenance of systems, such as OS patching. AWS offers serverless services where customers don't need to worry about instance provisioning or capacity planning. *Serverless*, as the name suggests, abstracts out server details and allows us to directly run our workloads. AWS Lambda operates on a serverless model, supporting code execution with the required scale.

AWS Lambda

AWS Lambda is a fully managed, serverless compute service that lets users run code without the overhead of server maintenance. The only thing we need to run our applications on Lambda is code in our preferred language, referred to as *Lambda function*. Lambda supports multiple programming languages and enables rapid development and deployment of event-driven applications. The backend architecture of Lambda is provisioned per function runtime and executed on customer invocation events. Lambda automatically scales the underlying infrastructure to match the workload, providing high availability and reliability. Here are the main concepts relating to the Lambda service that you should understand:

Function
> An application's codebase in your preferred programming language that is supported by Lambda. Function is invoked with the help of a trigger to execute specific logic.

Trigger
> Any resource or configuration that is responsible for invoking Lambda function—for example, invocation (*https://oreil.ly/-lImC*) via the AWS Console or via any AWS services, such as Amazon SQS, Amazon DynamoDB streams, Amazon Kinesis, and so on.

Event
> A custom JSON-formatted document or any other structure specific to an AWS service, such as SNS notification, which is used to pass information to Lambda function for processing.

Lambda execution environment
> Lambda backend infrastructure internally creates a secure, isolated runtime environment for function execution. This runtime environment is called the *execution environment* and is set up with the help of user inputs, such as function language runtime, available memory, and maximum execution time for function (the maximum supported configuration is 15 minutes). The Lambda execution shuts down as the execution time elapses. The execution environment is launched with a specific instruction set architecture, and Lambda offers two types of architectures to determine computer processor type:
>
> - ARM64 with 64-bit ARM architecture for AWS Graviton2 processors (*https://oreil.ly/7FKn0*)
> - x86-64 with 64-bit x86 architecture for x86-based processors
>
> We recommend using ARM64 architecture for cost and performance efficiency over x86.

Deployment package
   The Lambda function code can be deployed via a deployment package in two ways:

   - A *.zip* file with code and its dependencies stored in Amazon S3 with a maximum allowed size of 250 MB. Lambda provides the OS and runtime for function.
   - A container image stored in Amazon ECR with the code and its dependencies and a maximum allowed size of 10 GB. The image should be compatible with OCI (*https://opencontainers.org*) and should include the OS and runtime.

Layers
   Common code, such as utilities or libraries, can be zipped as layers instead of adding them to each Lambda function. Layers can be attached to Lambda for code sharing, reducing the overall Lambda function code bundle size and decreasing the startup time. Layers also support versioning to maintain multiple versions of code libraries and ensure backward compatibility.

Destination
   Another AWS service configured to receive invocation records upon completion (success or failure) of asynchronous Lambda execution. AWS supports standard SQS queue, standard SNS topic, Lambda function, and EventBridge event bus as destinations.

> AWS often adds new language runtimes; check the Lambda documentation (*https://oreil.ly/P9958*) for updated guidance on supported language runtimes.

The way Lambda function should be invoked for processing depends on your use case. Some options include an object addition to an S3 bucket (*https://oreil.ly/I_a1c*) or a weekly schedule via CloudWatch events (*https://oreil.ly/RBbBj*), or you may choose a specific trigger for Lambda invocation. Lambda supports three types of invocation modes (*https://oreil.ly/KbRR1*):

Synchronous invocation
   Synchronous invocation can be achieved in multiple ways: via the Amazon API Gateway, an ALB, the AWS CLI, and so on. In this invocation mode, customers wait for a response until Lambda completes its execution. This is preferred for latency-sensitive workloads with a maximum of a 15-minute execution timeout. In case Lambda is triggered via any AWS service, the execution timeout could be less, such as 29 seconds for API Gateway.

Asynchronous invocation

    Asynchronous invocation can be achieved via S3, SNS, CloudWatch events, and so on. In this invocation mode, the response is returned immediately, and the request is queued by Lambda for processing. It can also be configured to handle retries and direct invocation responses to a configured destination (*https://oreil.ly/RbZ_O*), unlike synchronous mode.

Polling invocation

    This is the preferred mode for stream- or queue-based services, such as DynamoDB streams, Kinesis, SQS queues, or Kafka. In this invocation mode, Lambda polls the AWS service and synchronously invokes Lambda function for processing. The benefit is that AWS doesn't charge customers for message polling; we pay only for Lambda function invocation. The retry mechanism is dependent on the data expiration in the AWS service, such as from one minute to 14 days for an SQS queue.

We mentioned Lambda provision resources on invocation, which could result in more request processing time due to cold-start problems. *Cold start* refers to the time Lambda takes to provision resources and prepare an execution environment involving function code downloaded from S3 or ECR, creating an environment with memory and runtime configurations and executing any initialization code out of the main function code. After this complete setup, Lambda starts serving customer requests. The cold-start time could vary from 100 ms to one second and typically occurs for 1% of total invocations, as analyzed by AWS on production workloads. AWS recommends multiple ways to reduce cold-start problems:

Warm start

    The execution environment is not deleted as soon as the function completes its execution but rather is retained for some time so as to serve continuous requests invoking the same Lambda function. This skips the setup of execution time on each Lambda invocation, which is referred to as a *warm start*. The cold start is not in the customer's hands, and Lambda can create an execution environment on a need basis. For example, Lambda creates a fresh execution environment for concurrent invocation to handle increasing traffic. We can use warm start to our advantage by intentionally invoking Lambda function with dummy input before it serves actual requests. This approach is only recommended for scheduled or low-traffic workloads, not for production environments operating at large scale.

Provisioned concurrency

    Provisioned concurrency ensures that the execution environment is set up in advance, ready to serve requests. For example, Lambda function with a provisioned concurrency of four will create four execution environments in parallel, which can be extremely helpful for functions with a large initialization codebase.

Memory configurations
> AWS provides an option to configure memory for Lambda function that ranges from 128 MB to 10,240 MB. The compute power allocated to Lambda function is proportional to the configured memory, so it is advisable to tune memory settings to improve performance. You can come up with the best memory configuration for your workload by running test runs on Lambda function, or you can explore using the Lambda Power Tuning tool (*https://oreil.ly/URjgH*) for this purpose.

Static initialization optimization
> As Lambda prepares the execution environment, it configures any required connections or downloads code dependencies. A large number of dependencies can definitely add to the cold-start time, so it is recommended to import only required dependencies. If the function codebase becomes too large where such a scenario is not feasible, other avenues can be explored, such as breaking a function into multiple child functions.

SnapStart
> For Java 11 runtime environments, SnapStart improves function startup time by taking an encrypted snapshot of the memory and disk state of the initialized execution environment. The new function invocation resumes its execution from the cached snapshot, thereby improving on the cold-start time.

As mentioned, Lambda supports a variety of invocation modes and scales automatically for required traffic. The key factor when deciding whether to choose Lambda as a compute platform is determining whether you're fine with too much abstraction of infrastructure. Consider: is there a requirement to fine-tune system efficiency at the infrastructure level? Is it OK if there is a latency spike due to cold-start issues? These are some of the questions you should try to answer to make your decision.

We discussed different containerization concepts in Chapter 7. Next, we'll explore how we can use containers as a compute platform and launch our systems on the AWS cloud.

Containerization Services

AWS offers container orchestration for running Docker containers via two services: Amazon Elastic Container Service (ECS) and Amazon Elastic Kubernetes Service (EKS). ECS is a fully managed container orchestration service, whereas EKS is a managed service for running open source Kubernetes on the AWS cloud.

> This section builds on concepts covered in Chapter 7—read that chapter first.

Amazon Elastic Container Service

Amazon ECS is a fully managed, highly available service for managing deployment, operations, and scaling of containerized applications for the required traffic load. ECS integrates with other AWS services, such as Amazon EC2, Amazon ECR, and AWS ELB, to provide a complete container management solution. The following is some important terminology related to Amazon ECS:

Task
  A task is the basic unit of deployment in ECS responsible for running one or more containers, as shown in Figure 11-3.

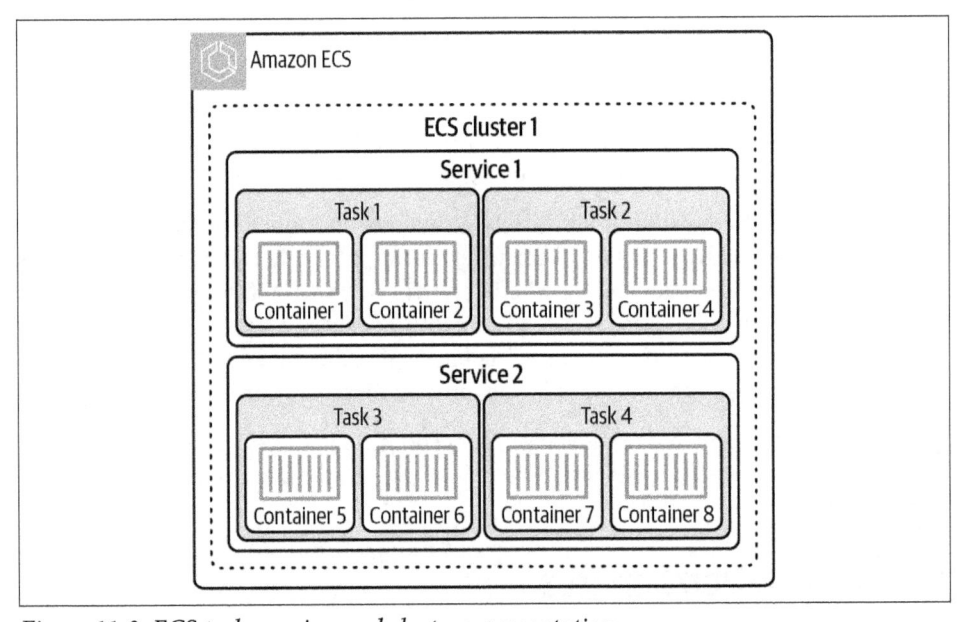

Figure 11-3. ECS task, service, and cluster representation

ECS service
  The ECS service groups identical tasks to scale and monitors them in a single place.

ECS cluster
> The infrastructure is registered to an ECS cluster, which acts as a logical grouping of ECS tasks or services running via ECS Fargate, ECS EC2 launch types, or both types in the single cluster.

Task definitions
> These define various configurations (*https://oreil.ly/tXxnK*) for a task, such as runtime platform, task size, launch type, data volumes, environment variables, container definitions for configurations specific to containers launched within a task, and so on. Task definitions enable you to define complex multicontainer applications and specify how they should be orchestrated. Here is an example with Fargate as the launch option:
>
> ```
> {
>     "family": "fargate-task-definition",
>     "containerDefinitions": [
>         {
>             "image": "AwsAccId.dkr.ecr.us-west-2.amazonaws.com/repository:tag",
>             "name": "my-fargate-application",
>             "portMappings": [
>                 {
>                     "containerPort": 80,
>                     "hostPort": 80,
>                 }
>             ]
>         }
>     ],
>     "essential": true,
>     "cpu": "256",
>     "memory": "512",
>     "executionRoleArn": "arn:aws:iam::AwsAccId:role/ecsTaskExecutionRole",
>     "networkMode": "awsvpc",
>     "runtimePlatform": {
>         "operatingSystemFamily": "LINUX"
>     },
>     "requiresCompatibilities": [
>         "FARGATE"
>     ]
> }
> ```

Amazon Elastic Container Registry
> Amazon ECR (*https://oreil.ly/Mpz-u*) is an AWS-managed container image registry that can be used to push, pull, and manage Docker or OCI images.

Two types of launch options are available with ECS: (1) ECS EC2, where we manage our containers on a fleet of EC2 machines, and (2) ECS Fargate, a serverless option where we hand over complete operational management responsibility to AWS. The key differences between these two deployment options are listed in Table 11-1.

Table 11-1. Amazon ECS launch types

Comparison factor	Amazon ECS EC2	Amazon ECS Fargate
Operational management	The compute layer is managed by customers, such as instance type and number of EC2 instances, application scaling, OS-level patching, and so on. EC2 supports autoscaling to adjust the number of instances based on resource utilization or application demand.	Serverless, meaning customers don't have to worry about server management tasks, such as applying OS security patches. Customers can specify OS, vCPU, memory (*https://oreil.ly/wnfut*), and autoscaling configurations.
Pricing	There is no separate cost for ECS; customers are charged (*https://oreil.ly/eP7lk*) for the running time of EC2 instances plus any storage selection, such as EBS volumes.	Cost (*https://oreil.ly/3P9kW*) is based on vCPU, memory, CPU architecture, and storage selection for ECS tasks or EKS pods, and customers are charged only when container workloads are active.
Business use cases	AWS recommends ECS EC2 for workloads with high CPU or memory requirements, cost-optimization requirements, application requirements for persistent storage access, or compliance and organization requirements to manage infrastructure on your own.	AWS recommends ECS Fargate for large workloads to be optimized for low overheads, small workloads with occasional bursts, and batch workloads.
Limitations	There is extra operational overhead at the customer's end for selecting EC2 instances, maintaining fleets, patching the OS, and so on.	There is no support for graphics processing unit (GPU) and EBS volumes for persistent storage. You can use EFS volumes (*https://oreil.ly/rq5MT*) for persistent storage and bind mounts for ephemeral storage. In short, fewer customizations are available compared to ECS EC2.

ECS seamlessly integrates with other AWS services, such as Amazon CloudWatch for observability, AWS IAM for security and access control, AWS Cloud Map (*https://oreil.ly/Lijc3*), and AWS ALB to provide service discovery and load balancing capabilities. Cloud Map allows users to register and discover services dynamically, making it easier for containers to communicate with one another. ALB provides load balancing across containers, distributing traffic based on configured rules, which helps achieve high availability and scalability.

Here are some additional key benefits of ECS:

Scalability
ECS allows you to scale your containerized applications seamlessly based on demand. It automatically adjusts resources to handle traffic spikes efficiently via autoscaling or serverless compute options.

High availability
ECS ensures high availability of your containers by spreading them across multiple AZs within a region. It automatically recovers failed containers and keeps your applications running smoothly.

Cost-effectiveness
    With ECS, you pay only for the resources you use. It optimizes resource allocation and scales based on actual demand, helping to reduce costs.

Security and compliance
    ECS integrates with AWS IAM, allowing you to control access to your containers and resources. It also provides encryption options for data in transit and at rest.

Amazon EKS is another service that AWS offers for launching applications on containers. Let's explore how it differs from Amazon ECS and in which use cases customers generally prefer to go with EKS instead of ECS.

Amazon Elastic Kubernetes Service

Amazon EKS is a fully managed Kubernetes service that simplifies deploying, managing, and scaling containerized applications using Kubernetes on the AWS cloud. EKS eliminates the need for manual setup and configuration of Kubernetes clusters, so developers can focus on their applications rather than the underlying infrastructure. EKS is available with EKS EC2 and Fargate launch types, similar to ECS.

Now you might wonder: why are there two different containerized services, and how do I decide which is best for my use case? Some of the key benefits of EKS include:

Managed Kubernetes control plane
    EKS manages the Kubernetes cluster control plane, which includes the API server and etcd persistence database (*https://oreil.ly/mlpe1*). This eliminates the administrative overhead of managing and scaling the control plane for the customer, ensuring high availability and a reliability guarantee from AWS.

Multi-AZ support
    EKS supports running Kubernetes clusters across multiple AZs, providing enhanced availability and fault tolerance. With cluster resources distributed across different AZs, applications running on EKS can tolerate failures and continue to operate seamlessly. The EKS control plane runs in three AZs with support for automatic detection and replacement of unhealthy nodes.

Automated Kubernetes version upgrades
    EKS automatically handles Kubernetes version upgrades for the control plane, simplifying the process of staying up to date with the latest features and security patches. This helps ensure that clusters are running on stable, secure Kubernetes versions without requiring manual intervention.

Hybrid deployments
　For highly latency-sensitive workloads, EKS on AWS Outposts (*https://oreil.ly/ D1014*) can be used to operate applications at on-premises data centers. Outposts extends AWS infrastructure, services, and tools to the customer's personal data center, essentially making it feasible to run EKS workloads there.

Integration with AWS services
　EKS seamlessly integrates with various AWS services, enabling developers to leverage the extensive ecosystem of AWS resources and capabilities. It integrates with services like AWS ELB, Amazon VPC, AWS IAM, AWS CloudTrail, and more, providing a unified experience for managing and securing applications.

Scalability and elasticity
　With Amazon EKS, scaling Kubernetes clusters to accommodate increased workloads is effortless. It leverages Amazon EC2 instances and ASGs to dynamically scale worker nodes based on demand, or Fargate launch can be used as a serverless option. This allows applications to handle traffic spikes and change resource requirements seamlessly. We can also leverage EC2 spot instances to reduce the cost of EKS clusters or use GPU-optimized instances for high-performance computing.

Security and compliance
　EKS incorporates several security features to protect applications and data. It integrates with AWS IAM to control access to cluster resources, supports fine-grained network policies using Amazon VPC, and allows encryption of data at rest using AWS KMS. EKS is compliant with various industry regulations, such as System and Organization Controls (SOC) (*https://oreil.ly/qMRt0*), PCI DSS (*https://oreil.ly/oxQW8*), ISO (*https://oreil.ly/VajbI*), FedRAMP Moderate (*https://oreil.ly/UJF8F*), Information Security Registered Assessors Program (IRAP) (*https://oreil.ly/78ggQ*), Cloud Computing Compliance Controls Catalog (C5) (*https://oreil.ly/RjghE*), Korea-Information Security Management System (K-ISMS) (*https://oreil.ly/dhW5D*), Esquema Nacional de Seguridad (ENS) High (*https://oreil.ly/_lbgS*), Outsourced Service Provider's Audit Report (OSPAR) (*https://oreil.ly/aIXj1*), Health Information Trust Alliance Common Security Framework (HITRUST CSF) (*https://oreil.ly/xzijT*), and HIPAA (*https://oreil.ly/ 489qi*).

Monitoring and logging
　EKS provides integrations with popular monitoring and logging services, including Amazon CloudWatch and AWS CloudTrail. These services enable developers to gain insights into cluster performance, monitor resource utilization, and track API calls and events for auditing and troubleshooting purposes.

Ecosystem and community

As an open source platform, Kubernetes has a vibrant ecosystem and community. EKS benefits from this by providing compatibility with Kubernetes-native tools, frameworks, and operators. Developers can leverage these tools to enhance their application's deployment, management, and observability within the EKS environment.

Your love for open source could be just another reason to choose EKS, where you have complete visibility into the ongoing development and the Kubernetes internal architecture. EKS on AWS offers the benefits of both worlds: open source support as well as offloading of management tasks to AWS, along with easier integration with other AWS services.

Conclusion

Selecting a compute platform for launching applications could be a difficult choice, so you should clearly lay out all the application requirements or expectations to help you make a wise decision. There is a philosophy of a "two-way door" decision-making process at Amazon that states, "You can always revert your decision if things are not working out as expected." Similarly, the compute platform can always be reiterated as the application scope or traffic pattern changes for your application. Here are a few recommendations we think will be helpful in deciding on your compute platform:

Flexibility

EC2 offers maximum flexibility to users with customizations at the hardware level in addition to how software applications are deployed. In contrast, AWS Lambda abstracts the resources completely, and customers have to focus only on the code, with restrictions such as a maximum 15-minute invocation time. The higher flexibility of EC2 brings a larger operational overhead for system maintenance, such as OS patching for security issues, figuring out the most efficient instance type for the application, configuring autoscaling policies, deploying applications, and so on.

Learning curve

As we start building and launching applications, familiarity with the platform is another factor to consider. More familiarity means fewer unknowns and quicker application launches. For example, if you're completely new to any compute platform, it's very easy to start with Lambda and launch applications in the minimum time possible since you just have to focus on writing code and skip all the headaches of application deployment and maintenance for the required traffic.

Traffic patterns
: All compute platforms offered by AWS can operate at high scale. You should understand the requirements in hand and why a specific platform will best serve the business use case and provide cost efficiency. For example, EC2 or ECS EC2 provides more hardware control so could be a better choice for high-latency, sensitive operations or GPU-accelerated computing.

Cost
: It's important to consider the cost of resources in the AWS cloud. The pricing model for each of the compute platforms varies, and there is no direct head-to-head comparison. Cost could depend on traffic patterns, size of workload, or resource selection, such as EC2 instance type, ECS Fargate task size, or Lambda memory configuration. Consider operational overhead as well because eventually people will maintain the operations.

While you may not know the best solution right off the bat, don't forget that it's always a two-way-door decision and can be reiterated.

In the next chapter, we'll explore messaging services such as Amazon SQS, Amazon SNS, and Apache Kafka; workflow orchestration services such as AWS Step Functions and Apache Airflow; application health and monitoring services such as AWS CloudWatch; and application security services such as AWS IAM and Amazon Cognito.

CHAPTER 12
AWS Messaging, Orchestration, Monitoring, and Access Management Services

In systems running at a large scale, multiple components interact and coordinate with one another to perform tasks, which is called *orchestration*. This communication and coordination among application components can be managed by different AWS services, and we can pick and choose our services based on our use case. In this chapter, we'll deep dive into core orchestration services like Amazon Simple Notification Service (SNS), which can be used to broadcast messages to multiple subscribers, and AWS Step Functions, which can be used to coordinate and execute different AWS or custom services in a specific order.

We'll begin with a discussion of AWS services that help us achieve the pub/sub design pattern in the AWS cloud environment, such as Amazon Managed Streaming for Apache Kafka (MSK), Amazon Kinesis, Amazon Simple Queue Service (SQS), and Amazon SNS. Then, we'll move on to monitoring, authorization, and authentication services, such as Amazon CloudWatch, AWS IAM, and Amazon Cognito.

Amazon Managed Streaming for Apache Kafka

We discussed pub/sub architecture, message brokers, and message queues in Chapter 8; this chapter introduces several services that AWS offers for designing applications on top of these concepts. Apache Kafka is an open source message broker and event-streaming platform used extensively for designing event-driven architectures. AWS offers a managed service for Apache Kafka, Amazon MSK, to reduce the operational burden. MSK exposes to customers control-plane operations, such as creating, updating, and deleting clusters, and data-plane operations, such as producing and consuming events.

When setting up the MSK cluster (*https://oreil.ly/WVNoA*), you specify the number and type of broker nodes along with the storage capacity in each AZ. A minimum of two AZs must be selected to ensure high cluster availability. MSK automatically detects broker failures and replaces the node with a healthy node with the same IP address. Like many other services in the AWS environment, MSK is offered in two capacity modes: serverless and provisioned. You can choose the serverless option to let AWS worry about infrastructure configuration; the provisioned option allows you to select nodes and storage configurations. Coordination and synchronization among the broker nodes is managed via ZooKeeper (*https://oreil.ly/ws1R8*) nodes, and MSK creates these nodes for us. MSK also supports KRaft mode (*https://oreil.ly/okRt4*) in recent version 3.7.x (*https://oreil.ly/tvuc3*); KRaft can handle the ZooKeeper functionality.

The next set of configurations in setting up the MSK cluster are related to networking, security, and monitoring. You should select AZs and subnets in which brokers should be launched and then define security measures. First, let's discuss how clients can access the MSK cluster:

Unauthenticated access
: As the name suggests, you can allow clients to directly access your cluster without any authentication, though this is not a recommended way to configure access control.

IAM role-based access
: The access to the MSK cluster is managed by IAM roles and associated IAM policies.

SASL/SCRAM authentication
: SASL/SCRAM (*https://oreil.ly/wHKKd*) stands for Simple Authentication and Security Layer/Salted Challenge Response Authentication Mechanism. You essentially use sign-in credentials (username and password) for clients and store them to AWS Secrets Manager (*https://oreil.ly/iR-UB*), associated with a secret resource. This provides a secure method of cluster access, while Secrets Manager takes full responsibility for auditing, updating, and rotating credentials. You can share the same credentials across the clusters as necessary.

TLS authentication
: You can use TLS authentication for client access and store these certificates in AWS Certificate Manager (ACM) (*https://oreil.ly/zaMW2*).

For data security, you can encrypt your data both at rest and in transit. Encryption at rest can be enabled by an AWS-managed or a customer-managed key. For in-transit encryption, you can use TLS encryption for communications within the cluster and use plain-text or TLS encryption or both for communication between the broker and clients.

There can be multiple forms of live-streaming data requiring near real-time analysis. MSK is used for the data ingestion from the sources and then feeds this data to other sources, such as Kinesis Data Firehose (*htttps://oreil.ly/rPRmx*), AWS Lambda, or Apache Flink (*https://oreil.ly/skuxq*), for analysis. Let's discuss the Amazon Kinesis offerings next.

Amazon Kinesis

Amazon Kinesis can serve multiple use cases revolving around streaming, analytics, and ETL. Four subservices are available under the Kinesis umbrella: Kinesis Data Streams (KDS), Kinesis Data Firehose (KDF), Kinesis Data Analytics (KDA), and Kinesis Video Streams (KVS). Let's start with KDS.

Amazon Kinesis Data Streams

To extend the example of capturing real-time user interactions, you have multiple devices operated by users referred to as the *source*. This interaction stream is then ingested and stored by KDS. As the stream is now available in Kinesis, it can be processed based on requirements like Spark on EMR clusters. Finally, the results can be dumped to a destination like DynamoDB, or you can analyze the results with any analytical tool, as shown in Figure 12-1. In short, data streaming on Kinesis enables us to ingest, process, and analyze huge volumes of data at a large scale without any management overhead on our plate.

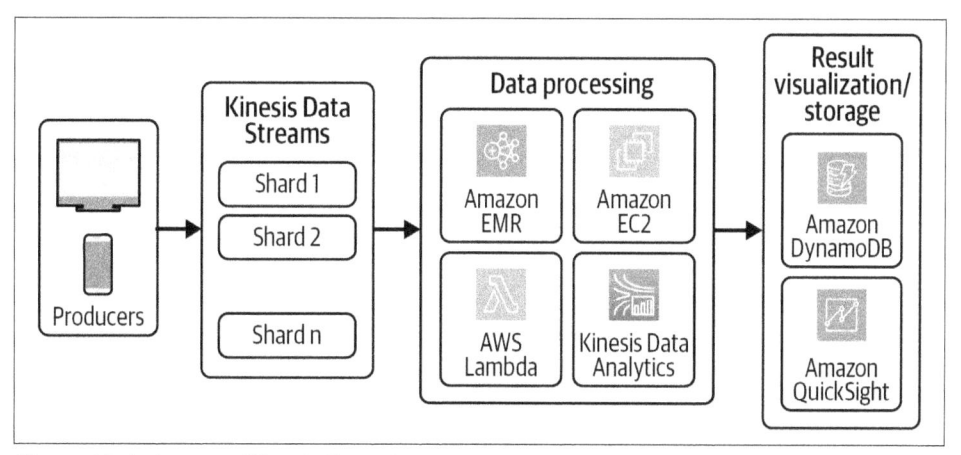

Figure 12-1. Amazon Kinesis Data Streams

A *shard* is the base throughput unit in KDS and is a uniquely identified sequence of data records in a stream. A shard can ingest up to 1 MB per second, supporting up to

1,000 transactions per second (TPS), and it can emit up to 2 MB per second to consumers. Look at alternatives (such as Apache Kafka) if these limitations impact your business use case solution. You can configure a number of shards (*https://oreil.ly/ Qz1eD*) by looking at the supported TPS by a shard and your business use case production and consumption rate. This configuration is required for provisioned mode of KDS. You can also consider on-demand mode, where this overhead is handled by AWS itself and it automatically scales per requirements.

The producers publish data records to data streams, which consist of a sequence number, partition key, and data blob:

Sequence number
Auto-assigned by KDS and is unique per partition key within its shard.

Partition key
Groups data at the shard level, meaning which shard a data record belongs to. The key should be chosen such that it resolves to uniform data distribution across the available shards.

Data blob
An immutable sequence of bytes that consists of the content or information, with a maximum allowed size of 1 MB.

Let's discuss the key considerations for using KDS:

- To address the limitation of 2 MB/s fan-out at a shard level, KDS offers an additional feature: enhanced fan-out (EFO) (*https://oreil.ly/833ah*). This can be used to have a dedicated pipe at each consumer level of shard so as to have 2 MB/s read throughput.

- KDS temporarily stores the data for a time period ranging from 24 hours to seven days; in the same time, it can be replayed for any retry strategies.

- AWS KMS (*https://oreil.ly/pJji-*) can be used to encrypt sensitive data as it enters KDS.

- KDS provides multiple options on shards, such as update number of shards (*https://oreil.ly/T_6WN*), split a shard (*https://oreil.ly/yd5oy*), or merge shards into one (*https://oreil.ly/jQ2OU*). This helps ensure full capacity utilization of a shard. The update shard operation can internally merge the split shards to configure the updated number of shards config. Splitting or merging a shard can be useful if a shard is too "hot" or "cold," meaning it is receiving too much or too little traffic. If the traffic is too high, it makes sense to split it to balance out the traffic; if the traffic is too low, it makes sense to merge the shards to optimize the number of shards.

Amazon MSK, which we discussed in the previous section, also provides streaming capabilities similar to KDS. Finalizing your choice of a particular technology depends on the business use case. No technology is inherently better than the other—every tool has its pros and cons. With this in mind, we'll lay out how these two technologies differ from each other in Table 12-1.

Table 12-1 should be helpful for devising some insights into which solution could be better for any future use cases. Now let's move to another Kinesis offering, KDA, which is useful for analytics purposes in near real time as data is processed via KDS or MSK.

Table 12-1. Amazon MSK and Amazon KDS comparison

Parameter	Amazon MSK	Amazon KDS
Business use cases	The feature gap narrowed between MSK and KDS over time, and the MSK ecosystem evolved to support direct integration with AWS services without the requirement of a connector. For example, MSK topics can be defined as event sources for Lambda (*https://oreil.ly/syb7f*), integration with S3 (*https://oreil.ly/EAF3i*) via KDF, stream consumption in Redshift (*https://oreil.ly/y10TW*), and OpenSearch (*https://oreil.ly/dVTNW*).	Kinesis also offers direct integration with multiple AWS services. The deciding factor for MSK or KDS mostly depends on previous expertise.
Operations	The base logical entity is a partition, and you're required to configure a number of brokers for the cluster launch. The serverless compute option doesn't require customers to configure the number and type of brokers and is fully managed by AWS.	The base logical entity is a shard, and you're required to specify the number of shards as per your workload. There is also an option for on-demand capacity, which doesn't require customers to specify shard configuration and is managed by AWS.
Latency	Messages are available immediately after they are written to the topic. The latency can be at the lower end as compared to KDS.	It offers low latency: data to consumers is available to consume within 200 ms (*https://oreil.ly/9rudG*). With EFO, the latency is relatively lower than 200 ms.
Message ordering	Messages within a topic partition maintain an order.	Events within a single shard maintain an order.
Message delivery	MSK has support for exactly-once message delivery semantics, which could be helpful for streaming financial transactions with no requirement for explicit handling of duplication in the application code.	KDS offers at-least-once message delivery semantics. The application should have a duplicate handling mechanism (*https://oreil.ly/odW2k*) in case the system doesn't expect duplicate records.
Pricing	Cost (*https://oreil.ly/8G1iv*) is based on the number and type of broker instances per hour and the amount of storage allocated to the broker. For a serverless option, the cost is based on the hourly rate of clusters and each partition being created along with the storage required for write and read from the topics.	Customers are charged (*https://oreil.ly/JHlb1*) by the shard and the number of PUT operations to write data into the stream. There is no charge for reading data that is less than seven days old. For an on-demand option, the cost is per GB data written/read from data streams along with the number of streams. There is an additional charge for features like data retention for more than 24 hours and EFO.

Parameter	Amazon MSK	Amazon KDS
Data retention	Data retention can be configured up to the amount of storage available on the brokers. When the requirement is to keep data for more than one year, MSK could be the preferred choice, but look into AWS archival storage solutions as well.	Data is accessible by default up to 24 hours, and that can be increased up to one year.
Migration overhead	MSK could be a great choice if you're already managing the Kafka clusters on your own on Amazon EC2 instances or in an on-premises data center. This helps reduce any migration workload to a different setup for streaming.	Those with no familiarity with any of the services should look for other parameters to decide on a service to meet your business requirements.

Amazon Kinesis Data Analytics

Amazon KDA is a fully managed service for Apache Flink capabilities (*https://oreil.ly/3IWh_*) that puts no overhead on the customer's plate and scales automatically for the desired throughput of incoming data. KDA can process, query, and analyze streaming data in near real time and send it to configured data destinations, such as KDS, MSK, S3, and OpenSearch.

Let's first get a general understanding of Apache Flink before we discuss KDA. Apache Flink is an open source distributed processing engine framework for processing real-time data streams. It supports both bounded and unbounded stream processing. *Bounded* refers to batch processing; *unbounded* refers to processing streaming data in real time. Flink performs stateful computations in memory for low latency. The stateful nature ensures exactly-once processing of streaming data events. Flink ensures that the state is maintained even if the system goes down by asynchronous checkpointing the state to durable storage. It supports SQL and Table APIs (*https://oreil.ly/WwHba*), DataStream APIs (*https://oreil.ly/jEsqs*), and stateful functions (*https://oreil.ly/LiIyC*) for easy access of data. SQL and Table APIs have the most abstraction, while DataStream APIs and stateful functions give more granular control and visibility to customers. It also has language support for Java, Scala, Python, and SQL.

Deployments and infrastructure management can be a huge pain point for customers and requires expertise in Flink's core concepts. KDA is a serverless offering that allows customers to focus on business logic; AWS manages everything end to end. Here are some of the features specific to KDA:

- Because KDA is available in the AWS environment, it offers easy integration with other AWS services, such as Amazon KDS, Amazon MSK, Amazon S3, Amazon OpenSearch, Amazon CloudWatch, Amazon DynamoDB, Amazon KDF, and AWS Glue Schema Registry.
- KDA can be easily integrated with open source tools via Apache Flink connectors (*https://oreil.ly/wcsTj*) and offers support for building custom connectors for use cases that are not supported as of now.

- The integration with the AWS Glue data catalog helps you store and share metadata across multiple applications.
- KDA offers KDA Studio (*https://oreil.ly/yIqMV*), which is a wrapper around Apache Flink SQL and Table APIs to analyze the streaming data in an interactive way via Apache Zeppelin (*https://zeppelin.apache.org*) serverless notebooks. KDA Studio supports the SQL, Scala, and Python languages.

> A *notebook* is a web-based developer interactive environment running in the browser of your choice. Developers can write queries or code in supported languages for different use cases, such as data transformation, visualization, and analysis.

KDA is primarily a fully managed version of Apache Flink, and since it is part of AWS's cloud offerings, you can easily integrate it with other AWS services. Now, let's discuss one more use case where we just have the requirement to load live streaming data to destinations. This requirement is met via Amazon KDF.

Amazon Kinesis Data Firehose

Amazon KDF is a service for delivering live streaming data to different destinations, such as Amazon S3, Amazon OpenSearch, Amazon Redshift, Splunk (*https://oreil.ly/GLF03*), or any custom HTTP/HTTPS endpoints to easily integrate with third-party data storage providers. KDF is a fully managed service, so customers don't have to worry about infrastructure and service maintenance. KDF doesn't offer any storage of its own, so there isn't the feature of replaying messages like in KDS. You can configure KDF to transform data before delivering it. Some built-in transformations are provided by KDF, such as conversion to Apache Parquet format. You can also add your custom transformations using AWS Lambda functions.

The following are some considerations for using KDF:

- The data record sent by the producer to the KDF delivery stream should not exceed 1,000 KB.
- To enhance security and reduce storage space at destination data storage solutions, you can batch, compress, and encrypt the data before loading.
- KDF buffers incoming streaming data to a certain size (buffer size) or certain period (buffer interval) before delivering it to data destinations. The buffer size could range from 1 to 128 MB for S3, from 1 to 100 MB for Amazon OpenSearch, and from 0.2 to 3 MB for AWS Lambda. The buffer interval for all these service integrations can range from 60 to 900 seconds.

- When Amazon Redshift is configured as a data destination, KDF first delivers data to the S3 bucket and then issues a COPY command (*https://oreil.ly/GcX-t*) to load data from the S3 bucket to the Redshift cluster.

- When you select S3 as a delivery destination, you can also enable dynamic partitioning of data. This helps on two fronts: it provides easy access to data in S3 for querying purposes, and it removes the need for partitioning at the source or after the data is stored. You can specify a specific key or an expression evaluated at runtime to identify keys to be used for partitioning.

- When it comes to data delivery to multiple destinations, KDF has a limitation. A single delivery stream can currently deliver data only to a single Amazon Redshift cluster or table, a single S3 bucket, and a single Amazon OpenSearch cluster or index. If there is a requirement to deliver to multiple destinations, a separate delivery stream should be created.

- KDF supports at-least-once data delivery semantics. There is a possibility that data is duplicated at the delivery destination due to retry mechanisms put in place for failure handling.

In short, Amazon KDF is a streaming ETL service fully managed by AWS for customers. Now let's move to another Kinesis offering, the Amazon KVS service.

Amazon Kinesis Video Streams

Amazon KVS is optimized to deliver live streaming video data to AWS in near real time from millions of sources for any processing, such as running ML algorithms or applying custom video processing. KVS can be used for offline batch analytics as well, and it supports other data streams, such as audio, images, and RADAR data.

KVS can be useful in a lot of scenarios (*https://oreil.ly/AoE6A*), so let's take an example of how it can help with building a household security system. When people are not home, it can be useful to get a real-time, continuous feed of what's happening at their homes. To build this, a security company installs the cameras at the home in the desired locations. These cameras act as a source of information and have KVS Producer libraries installed to connect securely with KVS on the AWS cloud. The connection constantly streams the video feed to KVS where the data can optionally be stored or redirected to consumers. The consumers are applications that consume this data, such as a user accessing the feed on a mobile device, which can be helpful in cases like robbery or unannounced visitors. All of this can be achieved in real time.

Here are a few key considerations for using KVS:

- KVS provides durable data storage for configurable retention periods. It automatically encrypts the data at rest and in transit, creating an index over this data based on producer-generated or service-side timestamps for quick and easy access.
- KVS is a fully managed, serverless offering, so customers don't have to worry about infrastructure management or expertise to tune configurations.
- KVS provides a parser library (*htttps://oreil.ly/EW7z3*) that helps consumer applications get data from video streams with very low latency. It can be used in Java applications for Matroska Video (MKV) streams.

Analyze your business requirements and choose the specific Amazon Kinesis offering that best suits your needs.

AWS also offers Amazon SNS and Amazon SQS, which can be used to create topics for publishing events, and these can be consumed by multiple consumers, such as SQS. In Chapter 11, we discussed why customers might prefer Amazon EKS to Amazon ECS for launching their applications. A similar analogy applies here: Kafka is an open source message broker service that can be used in place of a combination of SNS and SQS. The reasons you might choose it are similar as well: you could be migrating your workloads to the AWS cloud or running existing workloads on the AWS cloud, or you just love open source software with its full visibility on development features. Let's move our attention to SQS and SNS for management of topics and queues.

Amazon Simple Queue Service

Chapter 1 introduced you to the concept of asynchronous communication, and Chapter 8 introduced message queues. Amazon SQS is a fully managed AWS queue service that automatically scales according to customer traffic requirements. It is a highly available service that doesn't require any maintenance and deployment work from the customer's end. Some key use cases where SQS stands out include:

Application decoupling
> Two microservices don't interact with each other directly but rather communicate with SQS in between. This avoids any service dependency such that one service being down doesn't affect the other.

Back pressure control
> The client consuming messages from SQS can consume messages at its own rate. The messages in SQS are kept for a maximum of 14 days or per customer configurations.

Let's review the important concepts and key considerations related to Amazon SQS:

Visibility timeout
> The message from the queue is not deleted after it is received by one consumer; instead, it is kept in SQS-owned temporary storage until a timeout setting, referred to as a *visibility timeout*. Once the consumer processes the message, it should tell SQS to delete the message within the visibility timeout. In scenarios set up for no communication until visibility timeout, the message is made available again for other consumers to consume. It can have values ranging from zero seconds to 12 hours.

Retention period
> This is the amount of time the message is kept in the queue if it is not received by any consumers. It can have values ranging from one minute to 14 days.

Dead letter queue (DLQ)
> There may be scenarios where a consumer failed to process a message but you might need the message for use cases like retrying after some time or for debugging purposes. This is where DLQ can help: the consumer can push failed messages to DLQ for any further action at a later time.

Maximum message size
> The maximum allowed message size is 256 KB. This allowed size should be good enough for all standard use cases, but for scenarios with requirements for more than that, consider S3 or DynamoDB. The message can be stored as an S3 or DynamoDB object, which can be referenced in an SQS message.

Message delivery
> Two consumers can't compete for a single message at the same time; only a single thread can process a message at once. This ensures reliability since multiple producers can send messages and multiple consumers can receive messages.

SQS types
> SQS offers two types of queues: standard and FIFO. Standard queues don't guarantee message ordering, while FIFO does. Refer to Table 12-2 for a detailed comparison of the two.

SQS is widely used with SNS to meet message broker requirements without actually maintaining any infrastructure, such as a support use case of messaging fan-out (*https://oreil.ly/JUssx*). For a single message to be delivered to multiple recipients, it can be published to an SNS topic to which multiple SQSs are subscribed. The copy of the message is sent to each SQS, from which it can be independently processed by clients. Now, we'll discuss what use cases SNS solves and how it differs from SQS.

Table 12-2. Standard versus FIFO queues

Comparison parameter	Standard queue	FIFO queue
Message ordering	Message ordering works on the best-effort basis. It is not guaranteed that messages are delivered in the same order that they are received by SQS.	Message ordering is guaranteed.
Throughput	Unlimited throughput; scales per customer needs.	The maximum allowed is 300 TPS. Requests can be batched in a batch of 10, so, essentially, you can achieve a maximum of 3,000 TPS.
Message delivery	Standard queue ensures at-least-once delivery. Messages might be delivered more than once to clients. The application logic should be idempotent to avoid unexpected behavior.	Messages are delivered exactly once.
Cost	Relatively cheaper than FIFO.	About 25% costlier (*https://oreil.ly/96sEJ*) than standard queues.

Amazon Simple Notification Service

Amazon SNS is an intermediary service that enables communication between producers and consumers. A producer publishes a message to an SNS topic, and then SNS forwards this message to all the subscriptions (aka consumers) via a push mechanism. The supported consumers are Amazon KDF streams, Amazon SQS, AWS Lambda, HTTP(S) endpoints, email, mobile push notifications, and mobile text messages.

To explain further, let's return to our Cafe Delhi Heights restaurant example from previous chapters and think about the different offers and coupons we get on our phones. After your phone number is saved to the restaurant's system and you agree to receive text messages, the restaurant sends messages if there are any new offers or discounts. Here, the restaurant is a message producer that publishes messages to discount channels, and we as subscribers get these messages.

We'll compare the main differences between SQS and SNS in Table 12-3.

Table 12-3. Amazon SQS and Amazon SNS comparison

Comparison parameter	Amazon SQS	Amazon SNS
Message delivery mechanism	Application should poll messages from SQS.	SNS pushes messages to its subscribers.
Parallelism	Only a single consumer can access a message at any time, and it's the consumer's responsibility to delete messages from the queue once processed.	SNS pushes messages to all its consumers in parallel, and each consumer can process the message independently.

Comparison parameter	Amazon SQS	Amazon SNS
Message delivery latency	As it's the application's responsibility to poll messages from SQS, the delivery latency depends on the client polling mechanism.	There is no guaranteed latency SLA per documentation. Messages published to SNS topics are delivered to consumers instantaneously (*https://oreil.ly/vhWUg*), with retry policies (*https://oreil.ly/621Zj*) in case of delivery failures.

It's clear that SQS and SNS solve different use cases, and one service should not be seen as a replacement for the other service. Let's explore SNS more now by looking into its important concepts and key considerations:

Message attributes
    Message attributes are optional metadata items that can be sent along with the message body, represented by key, value, and type, with supported types being string, string array, binary, and number. These attributes can be used to take appropriate action on a message without processing the message body. Message attributes can optionally be used to filter messages at the subscriber level. For example, an SNS topic publishes weather-conditions messages for the entire continent of Asia, and it includes the country code in the message attributes. So if the application wants to process only the India-specific messages, it can directly filter out other messages without even reading them.

Message filtering
    You saw one example of how message attributes can be helpful when filtering messages. This is achieved by assigning a filter policy to a topic subscription so that only the intended messages are delivered to subscribers. Filter policies can also be applied on the message body, though the message body should be a well-formed JSON object.

Message durability
    The message received from the publisher is stored across multiple AZs before acknowledging success. This ensures message availability even during AZ downtimes.

Message delivery failure handling
    There can be scenarios when a subscriber is not available to receive messages, so SNS has a retry policy based on the delivery protocol to overcome unavailability issues. In case the message is not delivered even after retries, a DLQ can be configured so that messages are pushed there and can be polled when the system comes back online.

Message security
    To ensure data security or to handle sensitive data, you can enable server-side encryption (*https://oreil.ly/o9GTg*) on SNS topics by specifying an AWS KMS

key. Once enabled, SNS encrypts the received message and stores it in encrypted form. The message is decrypted when it is being forwarded to topic subscribers. This encrypts only the message body, so avoid storing any sensitive information in topic and message metadata.

Message ordering
> To cater to strict message ordering needs and prevent message duplication, SNS supports FIFO topics (*https://oreil.ly/MQQL1*) similar to SQS. You can use standard topics by default if there are no such requirements.

A combination of SQS, Lambda, and SNS is widely used to support event-driven asynchronous architecture (the pub/sub model) and orchestrate simple workflows. If you think about it, KDS offers a similar model where data is published to streams and multiple consumers can consume the data from a stream. The big difference is the near real-time processing offered by the KDS or MSK streaming solution. In the case of the SNS and SQS model, the data should be ingested first to any specific system for analysis, but KDS allows for data analysis as the data is received.

Moving on to use cases with requirements for orchestrating complex workflows in event-driven steps, let's explore AWS's workflow orchestration services.

Workflow Orchestration

AWS offers two workflow orchestration services: AWS Step Functions and Amazon Managed Workflow for Apache Airflow (MWAA). Apache Airflow is more popular and recommended for batch workloads, while Step Functions is suitable for both live streaming and batch workloads (integrated with AWS Batch service (*https://oreil.ly/HJZP9*)). Let's take a simple example of ordering food online from our favorite restaurant—Cafe Delhi Heights. The sequence of steps to place an order after selecting a food item are (1) process the payment, (2) send food-order requests to the restaurant, (3) choose delivery partners, and (4) track delivery, as shown in Figure 12-2.

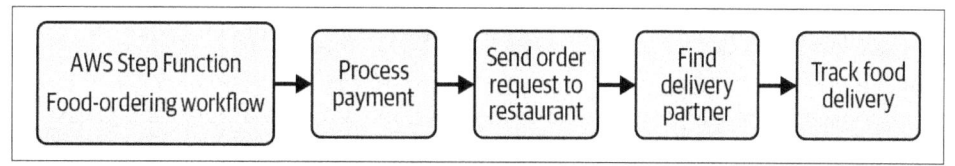

Figure 12-2. Food-ordering workflow

Both of the offered services are fully managed by AWS, so customers can focus on building their applications without worrying about infrastructure maintenance. Increased application reliability is the main benefit of executing application logic in steps because it ensures independent execution (issues in one component don't affect others) and proper failure handling. Step Functions is a proprietary service, while

MWAA is built on top of open source Apache Airflow (*https://airflow.apache.org*). Let's explore both options in more detail.

AWS Step Functions

AWS Step Functions is a fully managed, serverless, and visual workflow orchestration service that helps customers create and run state machines (*https://oreil.ly/OiSuJ*) with ease to coordinate among the distributed application components. Here are some basic terms you need to know to fully understand AWS Step Functions:

State machine
    A state machine represents the orchestration workflow as a sequence of steps, the relationships among them, and their input and output. These steps coordinate among themselves and interact with different components, such as an activity (*https://oreil.ly/5cn_A*), Lambda function, SQS, DynamoDB, or any other service (*https://oreil.ly/Hxp6f*), to complete a specific operation.

Task
    A task is a single state or step in a state machine. The task determines the action to be executed, such as calling Lambda to fetch an object from an S3 bucket and parse it. In short, a single state's responsibility is to take input from the previous state, execute the specified work, and pass on the output to the next state.

Activity
    A task is responsible for performing some work, which can be executed by workers on an EC2 machine, ECS, Lambda function, or any application with the ability to make HTTP connections hosted anywhere. This is enabled by a Step Functions feature called an activity. A Step Functions workflow step waits for activity workers to poll Step Functions for work via the GetActivityTask (*https://oreil.ly/k43zp*) API, complete the work, and send an execution callback to Step Functions via the SendTaskSuccess (*https://oreil.ly/pY1cF*) or SendTaskFailure (*https://oreil.ly/lGLAq*) API. The timeout value to wait for callback can be configured in the task definition per the nature of application and your use case.

You can use Amazon States Language (ASL) (*https://oreil.ly/k40Ag*) or the Step Functions console to create your workflows. ASL is a JSON-based structured language to define workflow states declaratively, as shown in the following code snippet:

```
{
    "Comment": "Amazon States language Example",
    "StartAt": "Hello World",
    "States": {
    "Hello World": {
      "Type": "Task",
      "Resource": "arn:aws:lambda:us-east-1:123456789012:function:HelloWorld",
      "End": true
    }
```

            }
        }

AWS Step Functions always encrypts the data at rest using transparent server-side encryption, and all the data being passed from Step Functions to any integrated services is encrypted using TLS. This ensures protection of our sensitive data without any operational overhead. The action being taken by the state is determined by the type of state. The different state types you can choose from while designing your state machine are:

Pass (https://oreil.ly/huzCU)
> The Pass state doesn't perform any work but just passes its input as its output. This state is mostly useful in state machine debugging and can also be used in transforming input (*https://oreil.ly/MAGAy*) so that transformed data is passed to the following state.

Task (https://oreil.ly/njcoM)
> As we discussed previously, the task essentially performs the work in a state machine. The Task state represents a single unit of work via a Lambda function, an activity, or the API actions of different AWS services.

Choice (https://oreil.ly/0a_OU)
> The Choice state is similar to the `if-else` statement of any programming language. It is a conditional statement that evaluates to true or false to determine further actions to be taken in a state machine.

Wait (https://oreil.ly/UEd0J)
> The Wait state takes a pause action during state machine workflow execution. The timeout value can be a relative value in seconds from the state start time or an absolute time as an exact timestamp.

Succeed (https://oreil.ly/rM-IL)
> The Succeed state is a terminal state to stop workflow execution successfully.

Fail (https://oreil.ly/YCo8l)
> The Fail state is the opposite of the Succeed state; it stops the workflow execution with failure. You can also explicitly catch the failure to take any specific action or just ignore the failure to move on to the following state.

Parallel (https://oreil.ly/Wx6N5)
> The Parallel state adds multiple branches in a state machine. This can help execute independent states in parallel to make workflow processing faster.

Map (https://oreil.ly/WVbbi)
> The Map state runs a set of workflow steps in parallel for each item in the dataset as a JSON array or CSV file. Map state supports inline (*https://oreil.ly/ClldX*)

and distributed modes of operation, and you can select one of them per your requirements:

- Inline mode supports input as a JSON array from the previous step and can run up to 40 concurrent executions; the execution history should not exceed 25,000 entries.
- Distributed mode can support JSON or CSV files stored in Amazon S3 or a JSON array from the previous step. This mode offers high concurrency compared to inline mode and supports up to 10,000 parallel executions without any hard limit on execution history.

> The difference between Parallel and Map state is support for dynamic parallelism. In Parallel state, you define multiple branches to be executed in parallel, while Map state can create parallel child branches dynamically based on input.

You should always be prepared for service disruption and to overcome failure scenarios. In Step Functions, we recommend adding error handling, retry mechanisms (*https://oreil.ly/fDFvd*), redrive mechanisms (*https://oreil.ly/q2DqA*), and alerting mechanisms as applicable for better success of the state machine.

The business requirements vary from use case to use case, such as event-processing volume, system durability, workflow execution time, idempotency, and so on. To address these different requirements, Step Functions is offered in two types: standard and express workflows. A detailed comparison of these two types is provided in Table 12-4.

Table 12-4. Standard and express workflow comparison in AWS Step Functions

Comparison parameter	Standard workflows	Express workflows
Primary use case	Used for long-running workloads (up to one year) and durable and auditable workflows, such as ETL workloads.	Used for short-lived (up to five minutes), high-volume, event-processing workloads, such as streaming data processing.
Execution model	The workflow is executed exactly once unless explicit retry behavior is in place.	Support is available for both synchronous and asynchronous execution models. The execution is at least once for async and at most once for sync workflows. Sync workflows can be invoked from API Gateway or Lambda function or by using the StartSyncExecution (*https://oreil.ly/9dYkk*) API call.
Support for AWS Step Functions activities	Supported with a maximum of one thousand pollers allowed on the same activity Amazon Resource Name (ARN).	Not supported.

Comparison parameter	Standard workflows	Express workflows
Execution history	Maximum of 25,000 entries in the execution event history. To avoid this, you can explore using the distributed-mode Map state or starting a new state machine from Task state to run state machine execution.	No hard limit on the number of events.

> The type selection should be an informed choice as it can't be changed after workflow creation.

You can use the Step Functions console to debug your workflows for failures on any other analysis, such as execution time, input, output, failure reason, or retry mechanism, which helps you diagnose production issues with ease.

Amazon Managed Workflow for Apache Airflow

Apache Airflow (*https://airflow.apache.org*) is an open source tool for programmatically creating, scheduling, and monitoring workflows. The workflows can be created as *Directed Acyclic Graphs (DAGs)* (*https://oreil.ly/ygivw*): a set of tasks executed in one direction without any loops. Apache Airflow uses message queues to orchestrate an arbitrary number of workers to the desired scale. A simple example could be ETL jobs that load data from multiple sources, transform the data, and then save it to a destination data store for analytics and insights.

A simplistic view of Airflow architecture (*https://oreil.ly/MCGeP*) with all the components involved in workflow execution is shown in Figure 12-3. Let's walk through the components:

Scheduler
　　Triggers the scheduled workflows and submits tasks to the executor for execution

Executor (https://oreil.ly/TckXC)
　　A small component of the scheduler that determines the task's execution style, such as sequential or parallel

Web server
　　Powers the user interface

Metadata database (https://oreil.ly/xtsvA)
　　Stores the task and workflow states; you can use PostgreSQL, MySQL, or SQLite as a metadata database

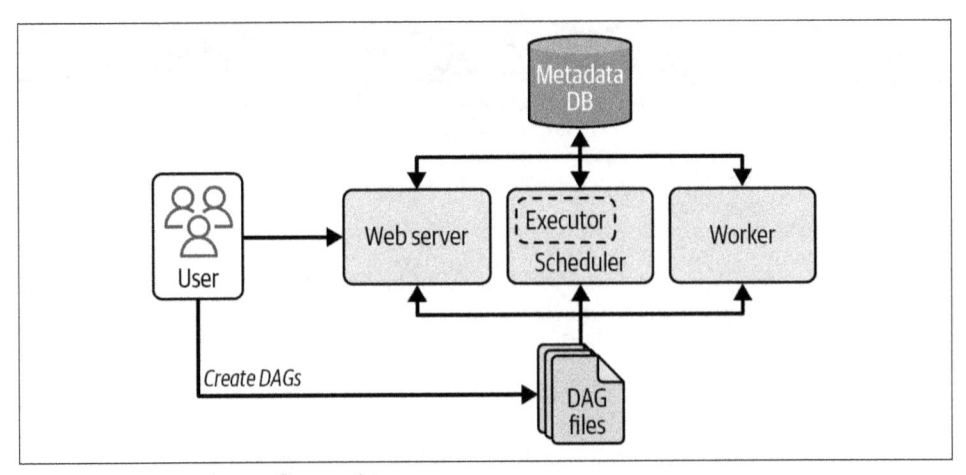

Figure 12-3. Apache Airflow architecture

AWS takes the operational workload of Apache Airflow infrastructure management off the customer's plate and offers Amazon MWAA as a managed service to scale as necessary. Here are some features that distinguish it from open source tools:

Scalability
> You can define the minimum and maximum number of workers for the MWAA environment, and AWS handles the capacity management.

Security
> You can use IAM roles and policies for access management to different AWS services, and all the workers and schedulers run in MWAA's VPC (*https://oreil.ly/dLaXZ*), ensuring private fleet management. All data is encrypted by default using AWS KMS as added security. You can enable private or public access modes as necessary using AWS IAM (*https://oreil.ly/k2TuP*) policies and AWS IAM Identity Center (*https://oreil.ly/ck5no*). Public access mode ensures accessibility to the Apache Airflow server over the internet via a VPC endpoint; private access mode is only accessible in your VPC.

Operations management
> Setup is very easy with a few clicks in the AWS Console, and you don't have to worry about version upgrades or applying any security patches.

Monitoring
> To monitor and analyze MWAA tasks and workflows, you can use Apache Airflow logs and metrics in Amazon CloudWatch.

Logs and metrics capabilities are required for monitoring the health of your applications as well as of AWS resources you're using to create your infrastructure. Let's turn our attention to the CloudWatch service, which offers these features.

Amazon CloudWatch

Launching an application on the AWS cloud infrastructure is the first step, but now you have to ensure the application keeps running, serving customer traffic without any issues. Application metrics help you figure out the state of an application, such as traffic served by the application, API latency, and the health of the infrastructure. Engineers can set up alerts on top of these metrics for detecting anomalies, such as high failure of an API, and then debug the issue by looking at logs and metric graphs.

To monitor application health and debug any issues that occur, AWS offers Amazon CloudWatch. CloudWatch provides storage and search capability on application logs, visualizations of application metrics, and dashboards and alerts for any unexpected application behavior.

Application Logs

As applications run to serve customer requests, logs are generated; these can be custom logs or logs specific to a language runtime. These logs help us debug any issues that have occurred in the system. You can publish logs to CloudWatch in real time for any compute platform you're using and look for specific error logs via CloudWatch's search functionality or the insights feature. Here are some key features and terminology associated with CloudWatch logs:

Log storage
    CloudWatch can act as a central repository for all our application or other AWS service logs. The logs are part of a *log stream*, which is a sequence of log events that share the same source. All the log streams with similar properties, such as source, retention, monitoring, and access control settings, are part of a *log group*. For example, software applications have been set up to create hourly log streams, which means that every hour, a log stream is created like: log_stream_2023_05_15_07 (log_stream_name_year_month_day_hour).

Personally identifiable information (PII) data
    We should avoid logging any PII, such as Social Security numbers, medical histories, and credit card details. This data might be pushed to production by mistake. To detect such logs, CloudWatch can identify and mask (*https://oreil.ly/9IUEv*) the log statement by leveraging pattern matching and ML.

Log search
    You definitely need a search capability on top of your logs to help with debugging. CloudWatch supports multiple filters by following a pattern-matching syntax. You can use these filters to identify specific patterns in logs and publish a metric for them, such as counting the number of ERROR 400 messages for a particular API.

CloudWatch offers log insights as an additional feature for interactive search, analysis, and visualization of log data. You can search in up to 50 log groups in a single request via the supported query language (*https://oreil.ly/ZzgIX*), such as the total number of InternalServerExceptions across five microservice log groups.

For general visualization, such as of CPU utilization or total invocations of an API, where we don't want to run queries to plot graphs on top of the data, an effective method is using CloudWatch metrics and alarms to raise alerts for any unexpected behavior.

Metrics and Alarms

CloudWatch metrics help with application monitoring, enabling users to search and graph metrics and create alarms on top of them. For example, it can plot service custom metrics, such as the number of 500 HTTP error codes, and raise an alarm if the total count of 500 HTTP errors per minute is greater than 10 for a continuous 15 minutes. Let's dig into metrics and alarms in a little more detail.

Metrics

A *metric* is essentially a time-ordered set of data points sent to CloudWatch for visualization. As mentioned previously, the metrics can be AWS resource metrics or custom application metrics. Most AWS services publish some default metrics without charging customers, and you can definitely further tune them as necessary—for example, with minute-level granularity. Like log insights, CloudWatch's metrics insights (*https://oreil.ly/AV2JV*) feature can be used to query and find patterns on different published metrics and create alarms for them. Let's understand some terminology associated with metrics:

Namespace
    A namespace is a root-level identifier to distinguish metrics from one another. For example, EC2 service metrics are captured in the EC2 namespace. We can also create custom namespaces; for example, multiple microservices in a single AWS account can be separated by namespaces.

Dimension
    A dimension is a metric identification property represented by name-value pairs. A single metric can have up to 30 dimensions associated with it. For example, for representing API latency of a specific operation of an application, the namespace is the application name with two dimensions: API name and metric type.

Metric resolution
    You can choose between standard resolution and high resolution, depending on the granularity required for your use case. Metrics are available at a minimum of

one-minute granularity in standard resolution or one-second granularity in high resolution.

Statistics
Statistics can be used for data aggregation over a period of time. A couple of examples are maximum latency and sum of API invocations in the last hour. You can choose from a list of supported statistics (*https://oreil.ly/Vbaih*) according to your business needs, such as maximum, minimum, sample count, sum, average, percentile, and so on. Each statistic also has a unit associated (*https://oreil.ly/6zm-B*) with it, such as count, percentage, or seconds. For example, the average CPU utilization in the last hour would be shown as 75%.

For further analysis, CloudWatch metrics can be streamed to the destination of our choice in near real time in JSON or OpenTelemetry 0.7.0 format (*https://oreil.ly/bBKSR*). A single metric stream can include up to one thousand filters, giving you control over the metrics you want to stream. Some use cases where this could apply include:

- Deliver metrics to Amazon S3 via Amazon KDF delivery stream. This can be useful (along with billing data) for looking for cost optimizations and resource performance.
- Choose third-party service providers as a destination for monitoring and troubleshooting applications.

Metrics are good for visualization and debugging purposes, but for raising an alert or sending a notification based on unexpected behavior, we should set up alarms.

Alarms

Application monitoring is an important aspect of maintaining application health. Alarms monitor application metrics and notify users or other applications to take appropriate action when the configured thresholds are breached. For example, you can take autoscaling action by adding one instance when an application's EC2 CPU utilization is greater than 75% and remove one instance when it is less than 30%. The following are some important things to consider when setting up alarms.

Metric. An alarm is set up on top of a single metric or a math expression on a combination of metrics. To set up an alarm, you should include all metric information, such as metric namespace, metric name, and all dimensions.

Alarm conditions. An alarm is invoked when specific conditions are met, and these conditions are defined by parameters like threshold type, alarm condition, data points to alarm, and missing data treatment. There are two supported types of threshold configurations: static and anomaly detection. Static configuration can be used to configure a specific threshold value on greater than, greater or equal to, lower than, and lower or equal to alarm conditions. Anomaly detection allows a band of values to be used as a threshold, with supported conditions outside of the band (greater than or less than), lower than, and greater than the band. We might not always want to raise an alarm with just one metric data point. This is a configurable property and can be set up per the alarm's requirements.

There can be scenarios when the metric is not pushed to CloudWatch due to application issues or if there was no actual metric to be published for a specific time period. In both these cases, we can define how to treat the missing data. The supported behaviors are missing data being treated as good (within the threshold), bad (breaching the threshold), ignored (maintaining the current alarm state), and missing (transition alarm to insufficient data for alarm condition evaluation).

Configurable actions. The alarm can be in three states: an OK state, an in-alarm state, or insufficient data to evaluate the alarm. The alarm actions can be configured upon transition from one state to another. Supported alarm actions are notification, autoscaling action, EC2 action, and Systems Manager action. The notification action notifies people by sending a message to the SNS topic. The autoscaling action enables you to add or remove instances from an ASG per the alarm threshold. An EC2 action allows actions like rebooting, stopping, terminating, or recovering an EC2 instance. You can also set up a Systems Manager (*https://oreil.ly/HjpND*) action by creating an OpsItem (*https://oreil.ly/vDyz-*), which the operations team can look into and take appropriate action.

You can also create an alarm on top of multiple alarms, referred to as a *composite alarm*. This can help reduce operation noise by configuring the actions on composite alarms and skipping them on child alarms. The composite alarm is invoked based on the configured conditions or rule expressions (*https://oreil.ly/WiEBy*), such as reach alarm state when all child alarms are in alarm state or when any one of them is in alarm state. For example, you could set up a composite alarm on application resource utilization, such as CPU utilization, memory usage, and storage space.

Figure 12-4 illustrates an application architecture in integration with Amazon CloudWatch for all the monitoring needs. The application pushes logs and metrics to AWS via CloudWatch APIs (PutLogEvents (*https://oreil.ly/VUs4l*) and PutMetricData (*https://oreil.ly/6oAhy*)), which can be viewed in the AWS Console for debugging or application monitoring. The alarms are activated upon a state change in a metric based on a certain threshold. Any state in AWS resources is captured by CloudWatch Events.

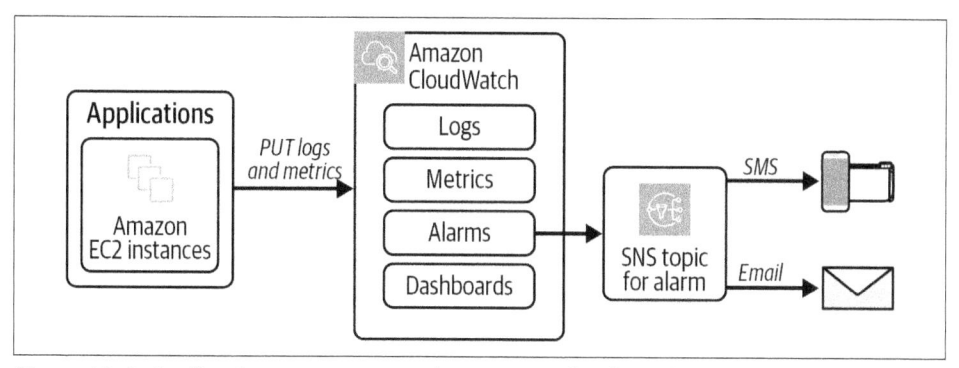

Figure 12-4. Application integration with Amazon CloudWatch

Amazon CloudWatch Events

AWS services or resources transition from one state to another. For example, as you launch an EC2 machine, it transitions from a pending to a running state after its setup and configuration. These state changes can be streamed in near real time via CloudWatch Events to a desired destination so that you can take any appropriate action. Events can also be used to schedule automated actions using cron or rate expressions. For example, for our online food-delivery restaurant, we could run a Lambda function every day at 7 A.M. (similar to cron expressions) to aggregate the previous day's earnings. Some other target destinations include Amazon EC2 instances, Amazon KDS, Amazon ECS tasks, AWS Systems Manager Run Command (*https://oreil.ly/hMGzr*) and Automation (*https://oreil.ly/BHhbm*), Amazon SQS, and Amazon SNS topics.

AWS offers a service similar to CloudWatch Events called Amazon EventBridge. Both services have the same underlying architecture, but EventBridge offers more features to customers. EventBridge provides backward compatibility to CloudWatch Events APIs and works on a similar concept as CloudWatch Events: it receives an event (*https://oreil.ly/ywJKO*) for a state change and applies an associated rule (*https://oreil.ly/1y-28*) to route this event to up to five targets (*https://oreil.ly/Jf_hZ*).

The AWS Console automatically redirects to the EventBridge page upon selection of rules from the CloudWatch console. You can also use the CloudWatch Events page. We recommend using EventBridge for more features, such as event ingestion from software as a service (SaaS) applications. Let's discuss a few of these added benefits in more detail:

Integration with SaaS providers
  A PagerDuty application (*https://pagerduty.com*), for example, can be used to collect data from multiple platforms to provide a unified view that informs team members of any issue occurrence. Let's say that based on a PagerDuty alert, there is a requirement to restart an EC2 machine. This action can be automated

by sending an event to EventBridge, and it can deliver that event action to a specific target. If we remove EventBridge from the picture here, polling and custom webhooks are mostly used to fetch data from third-party providers to our software application. Polling can be compute intensive—you might receive empty responses multiple times—whereas webhooks require communication over the public internet. To address this, EventBridge allows integration with SaaS providers (*https://oreil.ly/gPTU3*) over private AWS networks without exposing the data to the public internet.

Custom event buses
    An event bus provides a way to communicate from event senders to receivers. All events in CloudWatch Events are routed via the default event bus present in the AWS account, whereas EventBridge supports creation of custom event buses (*https://oreil.ly/R9fiJ*) specific to customer workloads and controlled access.

Enhanced rules
    EventBridge allows content-based filtering (*https://oreil.ly/ynz4J*) to filter values in events. This enables you to apply filtering at the EventBridge level, which helps your application to consume only the required event traffic. Additionally, you don't need this filtering logic in your application.

Schema registry
    EventBridge stores schemas for AWS services, integrated SaaS providers, and your custom events, helping with inference during the development process.

CloudWatch is an extremely important AWS service that ensures health monitoring of other AWS services and your custom applications deployed in the AWS cloud environment. Security of AWS services and resources is another important aspect to consider in order to avoid any misuse. The next section explores the AWS IAM service, which you can use for access control mechanisms in your AWS account.

AWS Identity and Access Management

We touched on using IAM in multiple places in this book. IAM enables access control and enforces security measures in terms of authentication and authorization for different AWS resources or your overall AWS account. When you create your AWS account for the first time, you log in via root user credentials (with full administrative access), but when accessing different resources or allowing multiple people to log in and access an AWS account, we recommend you provide only the required access to avoid any misuse. This permissions granularity is defined via IAM users, groups, roles, and policies. For example, a support engineer might have only read-only access to CloudWatch logs, but a DevOps engineer might have access to create new log groups or delete existing log groups.

Before we check out IAM's features and benefits, let's discuss the basic terminology:

Root user
> The root user is the user generated as you create your AWS account with email and password credentials. The root user essentially has all the permissions to perform any action in an AWS account and can't be denied access by any explicit IAM policies. Service control policies (SCPs) (*https://oreil.ly/urNZt*) are organization policies that can be used to limit the permissions of the root user of a member account. Create a separate administrative user to perform day-to-day tasks and using the root credentials for tasks (*https://oreil.ly/XtEH_*) that can be performed only by the root user, such as deleting an account, signing up for AWS GovCloud (US), and registering as a seller.

IAM user
> An IAM user represents a person or service with a specific set of permissions to perform a task. IAM users have long-term credentials and don't expire over time. The credentials can be a username and password for logging in to the AWS Console or a combination of an AWS secret key ID and AWS secret access key for logging programmatically. Avoid creating IAM users and using IAM roles with temporary credentials wherever possible. If creating IAM users is required, update passwords and rotate AWS secret keys (*https://oreil.ly/XyK35*) regularly.

IAM group
> IAM groups group users with the same set of permissions. You can't log in to AWS accounts using group names, but groups make it easy to manage a similar set of users. This can be helpful when managing users with the same permissions by reducing the burden of assigning the same permissions again and again compared to just adding a new user to the group.

IAM role
> An IAM role is similar to an IAM user but is not associated with a specific person or service. A role is temporarily assumed by a person, service, or another AWS account to perform any task. For example, applications running on an EC2 machine will assume a role to make API calls to other resources, such as downloading a file from S3. This ensures temporary access only for the needed time and is automatically revoked after that. IAM roles can be created with restricted access, which helps prevent any unintended changes to the AWS resources environment. We recommend IAM roles over IAM users with temporary access for a limited period. There may be some use cases where IAM users will be explicitly required, such as third-party workloads that are unable to assume IAM roles, AWS CodeCommit access, Amazon Keyspaces access, or any IAM users created for emergency issues; you should ensure multifactor authentication (MFA) (*https://oreil.ly/i_B6d*) in those cases.

IAM policy (hhttps://oreil.ly/Gw-eW)

An IAM policy is a JSON object (apart from the ACL (*https://oreil.ly/FykRj*) policy type, which we discussed in Chapter 10 and is based on an XML structure (*https://oreil.ly/4wmQE*)) representing a set of permissions that is attached to an IAM identity (user, group, or role) or an AWS resource. Recall the example regarding how EC2 can be given access to download objects from S3. For that role to have S3 download permissions, you need to attach an IAM policy like the following:

```
{
  "Version": "2012-10-17",
  "Statement": [
    {
      "Effect": "Allow",
      "Action": ["s3:ListBucket"],
      "Resource": ["arn:aws:s3:::samplebucket"]
    },
    {
      "Effect": "Allow",
      "Action": [
        "s3:GetObject"
      ],
      "Resource": ["arn:aws:s3:::samplebucket/*"]
    }
  ]
}
```

The JSON document of the IAM policy (*https://oreil.ly/YoG29*) essentially contains `Effect` as `Allow` or `Deny`, with `Action` specifying all the resource operations and `Resource` specifying the determined resources, along with additional elements such as `Condition`, `Principal`, and `Sid`.

In Chapter 9, we discussed bringing Cafe Delhi Heights online in relation to different AWS storage services. We've now created an AWS account to host and operate the restaurant online and hired many people to help us out. Everyone contributing to the development and testing of the software applications will require access to the AWS account. There are multiple ways to provide access:

- Share the root credentials with everyone on the team. We don't recommend this option as it provides complete access to everyone. This is not required and might be misused—either knowingly or unknowingly.

- Create IAM users and associate them to groups like developer-group, devops-group, and support-group. This can be considered a preferred option, but there are some downsides, as we discussed previously.

- We might already be managing the team via some identity provider (IdP), such as Google, Facebook, or Amazon. We can create an IAM Identity Provider entity to establish trust between the IdP and the AWS account. This enables all users to assume an IAM role for a limited time with a limited set of permissions without exposing AWS access keys.

As different teams work together, there will always be use cases where one team requires access to an AWS resource in another team's AWS account, or it could be possible that multiple teams own resources in the same account. For these scenarios, access can be managed via trust and permissions policies referred to as *delegation*. The trust policy specifies trusted account members that are allowed to assume a role, and the permission policy specifies what permissions a trusted user has to perform a task.

AWS IAM helps with securing and managing access to different AWS resources. AWS offers another service, Amazon Cognito, for user pool management working as an IdP and many other features for user authentications.

Amazon Cognito

Amazon Cognito is a fully managed, highly scalable customer identity and access management (CIAM) service that enables customers to set up and manage their identity pools for authentication (AuthN) and authorization (AuthZ). Cognito takes complete ownership of managing compute and storage for supporting this. You can use Cognito for new user registrations, existing user logins, guest user maintenance, and access control definition. Let's take a look at a simple example: we want customers of our online restaurant to be able to upload images along with food reviews. To allow customers to upload an image directly to our AWS account's S3 bucket, we can provide temporary write access via Cognito.

> AuthN establishes the identity of an entity, and AuthZ determines what this entity has access to.
>
> In AWS account access terms, AuthN establishes whether you can log in to an AWS account, and AuthZ establishes whether you can access a specific AWS resource.

To understand how Cognito works, you should understand the following concepts:

Identity provider
    An IdP stores and manages users' digital identities. Cognito itself can act as an IdP, and you can integrate it with third-party IdPs like Google, Amazon, and Facebook (supported protocols are OAuth 2.0 (*https://oauth.net/2*), SAML (*https://oreil.ly/_j7xb*), and OpenID (*https://oreil.ly/KU3m5*)). For example, you will likely see Google as a sign-in choice on many applications you use day to day. The IdP is also called the *federated identity* since it can be used across

platforms for user authentication. Creating a trust relationship between AWS and an external IdP is called *federation*.

User pool
　A user pool is a user directory that acts as an IdP. The user records are stored in the user pool directory for users signed in via both Cognito or a third-party integrated IdP. It also supports all the features like signup, forgotten password, login, password lengths and policy, and MFA.

Identity pool
　Identity pools provide temporary credentials for application access for both authenticated and nonauthenticated users by taking valid tokens, such as a JSON Web Token (JWT) or SAML token, as input. The temporary role can be assigned to users based on different tags that you specify. For our example of ordering food online, the users are allowed to look for food and select items without logging into the system, but to place an order, users must be logged in. This can be managed by redirecting to Amazon Cognito Hosted UI once the user clicks "place order" and then redirecting to payments to confirm the order.

User pool Hosted UI
　We need some kind of user interface for users to sign up or log in to our application. Cognito offers a URL hosted by AWS for interaction between users and the application. This interface can include email, password for login, or any integrated third-party IdPs, as shown in Figure 12-5. Once users are authenticated, they are directed to a specific application page specified as a redirect URL. We can also customize the UI page as necessary, such as with a custom logo or CSS.

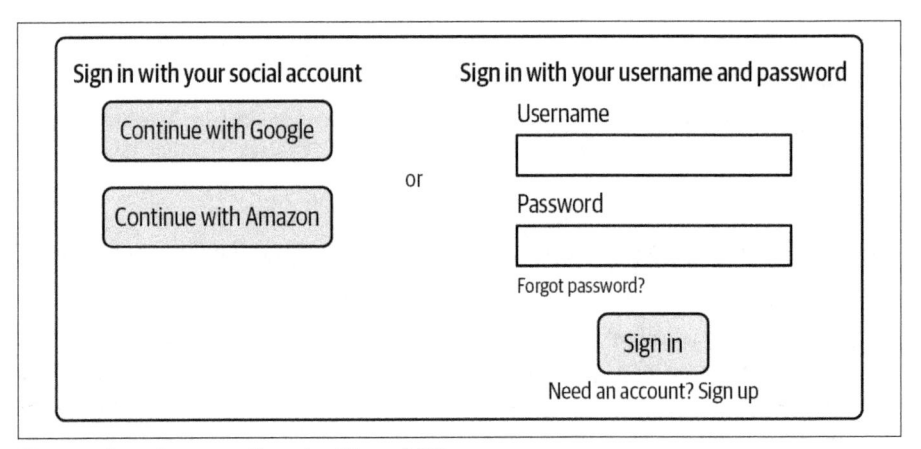

Figure 12-5. Amazon Cognito Hosted UI

Triggers
> You can consume Cognito Events (*https://oreil.ly/j1uvf*), such as user preauthentication or postauthentication, and run AWS Lambda functions based on them via triggers. The Lambda triggers run extra logic for AuthN and AuthZ of users for underlying applications. For example, you can run a custom set of rules for validation, such as noting that the user location for accessing a particular web page should be India before a user can sign up to the application.

Software applications can interact with Cognito for AuthN and AuthZ in different ways:

- Users interact with Cognito via the frontend application to get a token and use the same token in subsequent API calls. The backend application can interact with Cognito via AWS SDK Amazon Cognito APIs to validate those tokens against the users.

- Cognito provides native integration with AmazonAPI Gateway without any customer efforts. When application APIs are offered via AmazonAPI Gateway, manual token verification is not required, and verification can be handled automatically per the configurations.

- To reduce manual setup at your end, you can use AWS Amplify to automatically create the required infrastructure. You can then use AWS SDK to interact with Cognito.

> You can always build a custom AuthN and AuthZ solution on your own instead of using Cognito. We'll compare these options in much more detail in Chapter 16.

Let's get back to our example of using Cognito to assign temporary credentials for uploading an object to Amazon S3. There are essentially two ways of doing this:

S3 presigned URL (https://oreil.ly/IlTgK)
> A presigned URL can be created with specific permissions on an S3 bucket or a specific object—note that the creator of the presigned URL should have the permissions to create it. The one downside of this approach could be predefining the object key name, so to create presigned URLs at runtime, you need some compute layer in between. For example, an AWS Lambda captures the filename from a client, creates an S3 presigned URL, and responds to clients to further upload an object.

Amazon Cognito
> You can use Cognito's identity pools to assign temporary credentials to users and allow them to directly upload files to S3. Using this definitely depends on the kind of use case you're working on as this option requires Cognito setup. It could make our work easier if there is already a setup in place for users' AuthN and AuthZ.

These options can also be used in conjunction as Cognito authenticates users and AWS Lambda handles generation of presigned URLs.

We discussed temporary role assignment based on different tags in identity pools—the role can also be assigned based on token and IAM policy, such that you get the role-related information as part of the token and you can use the same to assign the role. For requirements with dynamic role creation, attributes for access control (*https://oreil.ly/jVBb0*) can be helpful in IAM policies.

With the fast pace of development, AWS really helps by providing services like IAM or Cognito for AuthN and AuthZ so that we don't need to build solutions from the ground up. Yet another service is AWS AppSync to help frontend and backend teams scale independently in the development of APIs at a large scale. Let's look into what AWS AppSync has to offer.

AWS AppSync

To fully understand how AWS AppSync works, first let's consider how food items are displayed to customers on our online food-ordering platform. The frontend application displays the food items along with their prices, restaurant coupons, reviews, and the like. This data is maintained by different applications in a backend microservice architecture. The frontend application has two options: to invoke APIs of each service and gather data or to have a single API that collects data from all these different backend services and returns that data to the frontend.

Recall that we discussed GraphQL in Chapter 6. AppSync is essentially a single GraphQL endpoint that can be used to query multiple databases, microservices, and APIs in a single network call. In our example, we can use AppSync to expose a single endpoint to the frontend, which can gather data from different microservices. AppSync can also be used to create pub/sub APIs to publish notifications to subscribed clients, such as real-time sports updates via fully managed, serverless WebSocket connections.

Here are the base components you should be aware of to start using AppSync:

GraphQL schema
> A data model specifying the query pattern for data retrieval.

Resolvers
>The components that provide a link between the schema and different data sources. They convert the GraphQL payload to the underlying system protocol and execute if there are associated IAM permissions.

Data source
>The data destination from which resolvers can fetch the data using the access credentials, such as Amazon DynamoDB, Amazon RDS, AWS Lambda, and HTTP endpoints. The data sources shown in Figure 12-6 can be present in the same AWS account or in different AWS accounts.

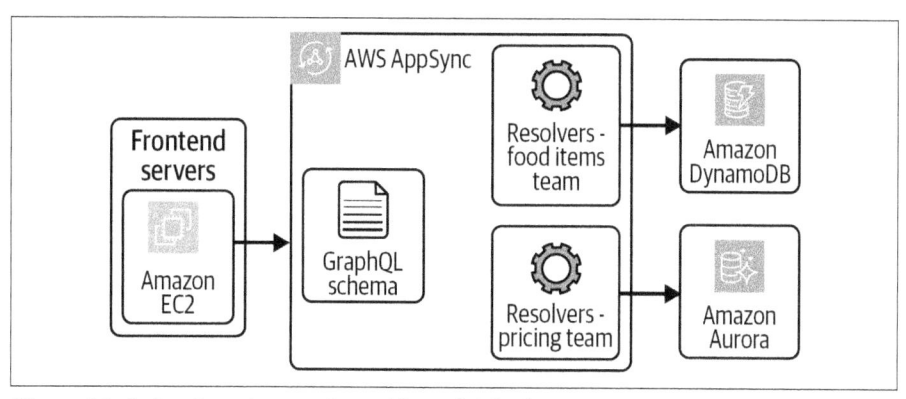

Figure 12-6. AppSync integration with multiple data sources

Merged API
>A single AppSync API constructed from a merge operation of multiple source APIs, GraphQL schemas, resolvers, and data sources. The source APIs can be managed by independent teams, and they can collaborate via the merged API.

Now you might argue, why use AppSync instead of deploying your own GraphQL infrastructure? The primary reason is removing operational overhead for features such as AuthN and AuthZ, caching, and encryption from the customer's plate. AppSync also simplifies building advanced use cases such as chat applications, location-aware notifications, live gaming scoreboards, and offline support along with AWS Amplify (*https://oreil.ly/QyLfn*). To provide these benefits, AppSync is a fully serverless application that offers build-time composition of merged APIs (*https://oreil.ly/UmTf2*) and easy integration with AWS services like AWS WAF, Amazon CloudWatch, Amazon Cognito, and TLS encryption support.

Conclusion

As you know by this point, AWS offers a wide variety of services, and it is very important to understand your business requirements to know how to utilize the best services for your goals. You'll notice that some services have similar features, such as when we compare MSK to SQS-SNS or to KDS.

Or consider that a fully managed serverless application like AWS Step Functions will not give us full visibility into how workflows are orchestrated behind the scenes, but the important question is: do we really need to know that? Because Step Functions is saving us a lot of management and operations costs, with additional debugging capabilities via visual workflows.

We also stressed application monitoring as an important aspect of ensuring high availability and how this can also be achieved by placing metrics, logs, and alarms in Amazon CloudWatch. We then dove into how AuthN and AuthZ services can help secure our applications and how different components in the AWS infrastructure environment can communicate with one another in a secure and restricted way. We recommend following the principle of least privilege: providing the application, user, or another AWS account with only the minimum set of permissions required to perform an operation.

In the next chapter, we'll explore how to launch big data and ML workloads on the AWS cloud and operate at large scale to serve customers.

CHAPTER 13

Big Data, Analytics, and Machine Learning Services

In the world of information technology, data is generated at a huge volume. This data can be just the information of all registered users on online food-ordering applications or real-time user actions captured on the application. Data generated at large volume is referred to as *big data*. If you have a use case to store this data, you can utilize the storage solutions we discussed in Chapter 10 based on your requirements. This chapter focuses on how to process the data at high volume. How can we generate insights out of data already present in storage or live streaming data by running data analytics or ML models on top of it? For example, we might want to determine the most ordered food item based on location or the restaurant with the highest rating in a particular locality.

The first part of this chapter introduces you to AWS big data, live streaming, and analytics services such as Amazon Elastic MapReduce (EMR), AWS Glue, Amazon Athena, Amazon QuickSight, and Amazon Redshift. The second section explores how you can run ML workloads on the AWS cloud and the different services supporting that.

AWS Big Data and Analytics

Information is vital to making business decisions or serving our customers better, but the volume of data is rapidly growing, ranging from terabytes to petabytes (and more). The variety of data is also increasing—data can be in any form. We require specific tools to store and process big data. Traditional tools can become a bottleneck as we can no longer operate on a single machine for data processing. Another challenge is the velocity at which this data is produced: we require tools to consume the data and produce insights from it in near real time to gain maximum output.

In this section, we'll talk about data processing tools like Amazon EMR, AWS Glue, Amazon Athena, and Amazon Redshift, as well as a business intelligence service, Amazon QuickSight.

Amazon Elastic MapReduce

In Chapter 8, we introduced you to big data architecture, multiple concepts underlying it, and open source tools for working with it, such as Hadoop, MapReduce, Spark, Presto, and HDFS. AWS offers managed services that are built directly on top of these open source software applications to get started easily with zero (or minimum) operational overhead. Hadoop open source software is popular for big data processing; Amazon EMR is a managed service for executing data processing frameworks and tools such as MapReduce (*https://oreil.ly/fz6-c*), Apache Spark (*https://spark.apache.org*), Apache Hive (*https://hive.apache.org*), Apache HBase (*https://hbase.apache.org*), and Presto (*https://prestodb.io*).

Setting up and managing large clusters require time and expertise, but EMR makes it easy by offering a managed service where you can launch clusters in minutes and run large data-processing workloads. Open source Hadoop clusters default to HDFS (*https://oreil.ly/3nV3d*) for data storage. You can also explore using different tools available in the community to extend the storage to Amazon S3.

HDFS is tied to the local disks, which disappear once the cluster terminates. Since our use case is processing big data, our storage needs will grow over time, and since HDFS is attached to compute instances, the number of instances will also increase. There is a possibility that our use case has high storage requirements but the compute requirement is relatively less, so we're paying for the compute but not using it at full capacity. This is where the EMR File System (EMRFS) (*https://oreil.ly/82GWO*) can be a better solution.

EMRFS

EMRFS uses Amazon S3 as a filesystem for data processing instead of a local HDFS, so essentially, it's a connector that links EMR clusters to S3. EMRFS ensures streaming of data directly to S3 and uses HDFS as intermediate storage.

Before we dive into EMRFS, understand that it is not a solution to every problem, and you should not see it as a replacement for HDFS. HDFS can still be a better option for jobs with iterative reads on the same dataset or I/O-intensive workloads (meaning workloads that require frequent disk access and retrieval of data over the network since these scenarios could prove to be latency-intensive operations). You can use a combination of S3 and HDFS to address the temporary data storage limitation of HDFS (data is lost on cluster termination) by leveraging tools such as S3DistCP (*https://oreil.ly/fYJ97*) to copy data from S3 to HDFS or from HDFS to S3.

Let's look into some of the benefits that EMRFS offers over traditional HDFS:

- In scenarios when you require the same data to be accessed by multiple clusters, you need to copy data from one cluster to another since HDFS is associated with a single cluster and not shared among all clusters. You can save this cost by using EMRFS as a storage option. EMRFS allows multiple clusters to access the data from the same place, decoupling compute and storage completely, and offers flexibility to scale them independently.
- You might not always require your EMR cluster to be running. So you can terminate the cluster, and storage is maintained in S3, saving compute costs.
- To ensure data availability, HDFS replicates the data at multiple nodes per the replication factor. For example, with a replication factor of three, you'll be paying three times the storage cost. EMRFS is backed by S3, so you don't have to worry about data durability (*https://oreil.ly/JVPs6*) as it is already handled by S3.

These data points provide a clear picture of why EMRFS is a useful utility to consider for storing data. You can get the most out of any tool if you follow certain best practices associated with it. Here are some tips for using EMRFS:

- The data should be partitioned so that the EMR cluster fetches only the data required for processing. This ensures faster data retrieval along with reduced costs.
- The file size should be optimized such that you don't have too many or too few files. As you start using EMRFS, try to avoid files with a size of less than 128 MB because that will ensure fewer calls to S3 along with HDFS requests.
- We also recommend considering data compression, ensuring less usage of storage space on S3. This helps reduce costs on two fronts: storage costs and network costs for data retrieval.
- The data-access patterns can vary based on the use case. You might be interested in only a subset of columns across the columns or a subset of rows across the rows. Apache Parquet (*https://parquet.apache.org*) and Apache ORC (*https://orc.apache.org*) are columnar file formats that give increased read performance to meet the first use case, and Apache Avro (*https://oreil.ly/pSj-M*), a row-optimized file format, is helpful for the latter use case.

Now that you have a good grasp of the concept of EMRFS as a storage option, let's explore other EMR features and specifications.

EMR cluster considerations

The data-processing jobs run on a set of servers, and instance types can be chosen based on workload requirements. As a compute option, you can choose to run an EMR cluster on EC2 instances (*https://oreil.ly/fN_7O*) or EKS (*https://oreil.ly/eCRHT*), or you can go completely serverless (*https://oreil.ly/zIhxj*).

The EMR cluster architecture can have three types of nodes, shown in Figure 13-1:

Primary node
    The primary node is the primary node in the EMR cluster. The primary node uses the YARN resource manager service for application resource management and runs the HDFS NameNode service to track the status of jobs submitted on the cluster along with health monitoring of instance groups.

Core node
    The core nodes run the data daemon for HDFS data storage and the task tracker daemon to perform computation tasks on data. The EMR cluster can have a maximum of one core instance group or instance fleet (*https://oreil.ly/dMjJZ*).

Task node
    Task nodes don't provide data storage—they should be used as extra computation power for the EMR cluster. EMR by default ensures that the application primary of any job runs on the core node to make sure the job doesn't terminate if any of the task nodes are terminated (as in the case of EC2 spot instances). You can configure up to 48 task instance groups depending on the job requirements.

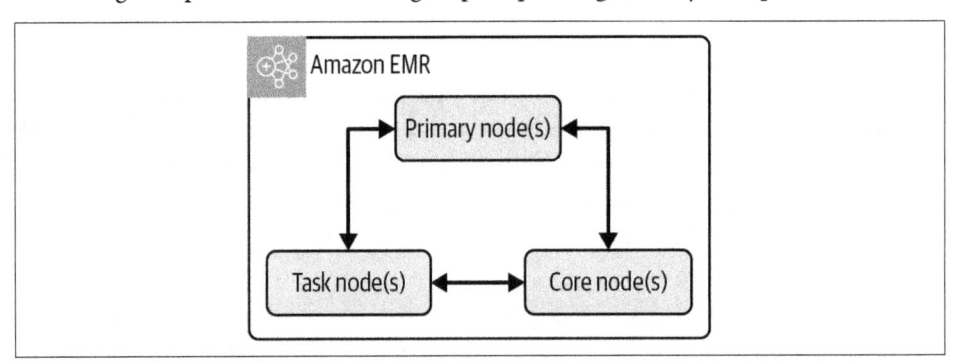

Figure 13-1. EMR cluster nodes

The EMR cluster allows you to choose from the available applications, and it will auto-install all the software without any effort from your end. There may also be a requirement to install custom software or modify a configuration for nodes on EMR nodes. To support this, you can use EMR bootstrap actions (*https://oreil.ly/1_9Y_*), which execute the action after the cluster instances are up.

Depending on the requirements, the EMR cluster can consist of a large number of nodes, which will definitely add to the resource cost incurred from AWS. You can introduce some cost-saving mechanisms:

- EMR provides a configuration to automatically terminate clusters. This ensures the cluster is auto-terminated once the submitted jobs are completed.
- You may have requirements for long-running clusters. If you're sure of the capacity requirements, you can explore reserved instances and AWS saving plans.
- If the EMR workloads are noncritical, you can use EC2 spot instances (discussed in Chapter 11). The spot instances are offered at up to a 90% discount compared to the on-demand instances and can substantially reduce costs. You can also set up clusters with a mix of spot and on-demand instances to ensure the cluster is always up and running while keeping cluster pricing in mind.
- For the variable workloads on long-running clusters, you can use automatic scaling policies on instance groups to add or remove instances.

Before we close our discussion on EMR, let's ponder some considerations for ensuring high reliability of workloads running on EMR clusters:

- The instances in clusters should be spread across AZs to avoid any AZ downtimes. By default, the Hive (*https://oreil.ly/AiOf0*) metastore is stored on the primary node's filesystem. Store the metastore outside the EMR cluster (*https://oreil.ly/FghKi*), such as inside a multi-AZ RDS cluster or Amazon Aurora, to avoid data loss upon cluster termination.
- We recommend using EMR with multiple primary nodes instead of single-primary node. The primary node is a single point of failure, and if it goes down, the entire cluster goes down. Multiple primary node setup provides a safety net.
- Critical data should be kept in S3 instead of a local HDFS to avoid any data dependency issues.
- We recommend EC2 spot instances only for task nodes and not for core nodes. As HDFS is managed by core nodes for data storage, termination of these nodes might lead to data loss.

To address the requirement of spawning EMR clusters at regular intervals, you can leverage Amazon EventBridge and automate the workflow via AWS Step Functions (or Apache Airflow) like so: create an EMR cluster with a specific configuration, submit jobs to the cluster, and once the jobs are complete, terminate the cluster.

In some scenarios, we just care about executing the ETL jobs without worrying about instance or storage management. AWS Glue is a completely serverless data integration application for performing analytical tasks on big data.

AWS Glue

AWS Glue is a data integration service that helps make sense of data with different features. Before digging into these features, let's quickly understand some of the terminology associated with Glue:

Classifier
　A classifier (*https://oreil.ly/wCZ76*) validates whether it can handle the data available in the specific format, and if it can, then it is classified into a `StructType` object. You can use the classifiers offered by Glue or define a custom classifier as needed (*https://oreil.ly/I1Ahs*), such as when a data file is not in a format supported by Glue.

Metadata
　The metadata is the inferred schema by the classifier from the available data in any of the data stores.

Database
　The database is the place where you keep metadata tables. A single table can be associated to a single database only, and in case the database is not specified, Glue uses the default database.

Data catalog
　The data catalog maintains databases, which then consist of one or more metadata tables. These tables can be useful as source and target.

Data crawler
　The data crawler crawls the data from data sources like Amazon S3, figures out the schema via the classifier, and then creates the required tables or partitions in the Glue data catalog. For use cases where the data schema frequently changes, you can run the crawler on a schedule (*https://oreil.ly/xAgEh*), and it automatically figures out modifications since the last run and creates new tables or partitions per the requirements.

Table partitioning
　Partitioning is a way to improve query performance on data. Let's understand it with the help of an example, shown in Figure 13-2. Your application processes sales data and is stored in S3, divided into folders with the parent folder as the year and child folders as months and days. It can have further subfolders, such as hours or minutes, depending on the type and amount of data. If the data is partitioned in such a fashion, it becomes very easy to query for it. Extracting data for February 2022 means going to the folder for Year 2022 and then to the subfolder Month 02, making the query much faster. There can be multiple partition keys for a table, and you can create a partition index (*https://oreil.ly/NNT2o*), a subset of partitions, to avoid loading all the partitions.

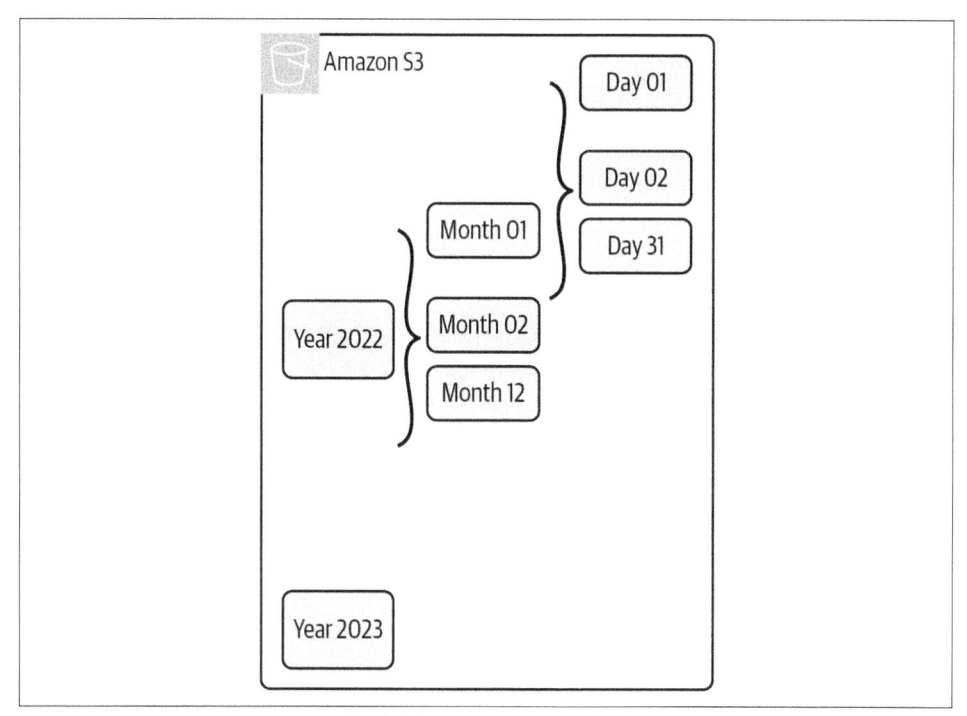

Figure 13-2. Data partitioning by folders in Amazon S3

Data engine
The data engine runs data-processing jobs on top of the data. Glue supports three data engines at the time of writing: AWS Glue for Apache Spark (*https://oreil.ly/HhVFY*), AWS Glue for Ray (*https://oreil.ly/1D89I*), and AWS Glue for Python Shell (*https://oreil.ly/OMzCx*). You can choose one based on your workload requirements:

- With Glue for Apache Spark, you can write ETL code in Python and Scala languages, and the code executes in a distributed environment. The Spark environment on Glue can be assumed as a serverless EMR cluster being operated by AWS. The Spark engine is supported for both batch processing and live streaming data. Glue also addresses a very general problem of disk spilling due to data shuffling (data redistribution within the cluster) by providing a Cloud Shuffle plug-in (*https://oreil.ly/82tDZ*). This plug-in allows you to use S3 or any other object storage in data-spilling situations. The plug-in is available as open source software, so it can be used in custom Spark jobs as well.

- With Glue for Python, a single-node Python engine runs workloads written in Python. It offers default integration with open source libraries like *numpy* or *pandas*, and you can add custom libraries as well. The one problem that customers might face is workload scaling as data grows, which can be resolved by using Glue for Ray (*https://oreil.ly/zdbuC*).

- Glue for Ray allows you to execute Python code in a distributed environment setup and is scalable to hundreds of nodes. This processing engine is based on the open source compute framework Ray (*https://ray.io*), which is extensively used to run Python workloads at large scale, such as deep learning models.

Data processing units (DPUs)
Glue allows customers to configure types of workers to run the data processing jobs, referred to as DPUs. You can analyze your workload requirements (*https://oreil.ly/EHo56*) to find the best configuration of DPUs.

Now, we'll combine our understanding of these different concepts into a simple architecture for how Glue operates, shown in Figure 13-3. Once the structure of the data is created, you can create and run Glue ETL jobs with any data engines of your choice for further visualization and analysis.

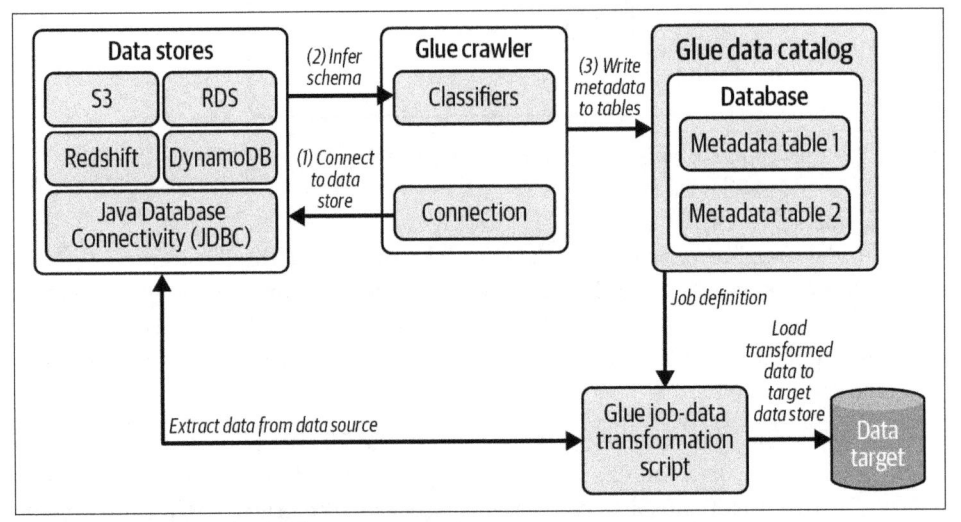

Figure 13-3. AWS Glue architecture overview

Figure 13-3 shows a high-level picture of how Glue manages and runs ETL jobs. We'll now discuss some additional features and offerings of Glue that you can use on an as-needed basis:

Glue Studio
Glue Studio supports visual workflows, built-in transformations, and the Glue Studio notebook. This helps you run tests on the data, and once you're happy with the testing, the code from the notebook can be imported to an ETL job.

Data Quality
> The Data Quality feature (*https://oreil.ly/V1spg*) automatically figures out conditions or logic on which to validate data quality. You can override these as required. Consider an example of sales data: a sales company started its operations in the year 2021, but there is some data with the year marked as 2019. The feature notifies us that this is invalid data and should be scraped out or alerts put on top of it. This feature is available for both data at rest and in transit.

Personally identifiable information
> A validation feature of PII data (*https://oreil.ly/bo4_p*) can be used to detect sensitive data and take any appropriate action, such as masking it.

Autoscaling
> To reduce compute cost and configure an optimal number of DPUs to run Glue jobs, you can leverage the autoscaling feature (*https://oreil.ly/dhP2b*). This will automatically add or remove workers per the workload requirement. You can also configure a maximum number of workers to ensure that Glue doesn't configure workers above a particular limit.

Flex job type
> In Chapter 11, we discussed EC2 spot instances and how they can help reduce overall compute costs. Glue provides similar functionality with the Flex job type (*https://oreil.ly/w91db*), which offers a cost savings of up to 34%. You can leverage this for noncritical workloads.

Scheduling
> There may be use cases where it would be useful to schedule the crawlers or jobs (*https://oreil.ly/5PC-d*) to run at a particular time or on regular intervals. Glue inherently provides support for this. You can also trigger jobs and crawlers on external events via Amazon EventBridge.

Version control
> Glue offers easy integration with GitHub and AWS CodeCommit (*https://oreil.ly/j9fPm*) to manage source version control for your Glue jobs.

Schema registry
> The Glue schema registry (*https://oreil.ly/LpeCM*) is a registry where you can publish your schemas and enforce data-streaming service integrations, such as Amazon MSK, Apache Kafka, Amazon KDS, Amazon KDA, and AWS Lambda.

This long list of features makes it evident that Glue is a powerful ETL service that helps to reduce operational overhead and can operate at a large scale. After learning about EMR and Glue, you might be wondering how the Spark application running on the EMR serverless option differs from Glue Spark. Let's throw some light on this in Table 13-1 as both options seem quite similar.

Table 13-1. Comparison of Amazon EMR serverless and AWS Glue

Parameter	Amazon EMR serverless	AWS Glue
Feature functionality	Data processing and analytics tool that leverages open source software	End-to-end ETL solution with abstraction over software that offers AWS-customized solutions with a focus on data integration, the data catalog, and running transformations on data sources
Operational overhead	Fully managed service	Customers specify the number and type of DPUs
Supported big data applications	Apache Spark and Apache Hive	Apache Spark and Python jobs

Glue and EMR vary on their base functionality, and we as customers should clearly lay out our requirements to choose one for our workloads. Amazon EMR comes with almost all the open source integrations, and we can easily deploy the cluster with these services preinstalled. We discussed some of the reasons you might prefer Glue to EMR; most often, the reasons are operational overhead and system expertise.

Much like EMR and Glue, Amazon Athena is an AWS service that is helpful for querying and analyzing data stored in Amazon S3. You can compare Athena with Presto running on an EMR cluster, which provides similar functionality. The main advantage of such solutions is that data analysis can be performed on raw data without any transformation at the customer's end.

Amazon Athena

Amazon Athena is a fully managed, serverless, big data analysis tool that offers SQL query support on top of data stored in S3. The data analysis doesn't require any transfer of data to other data storage; the data can be directly read from S3 objects and can be queried.

Athena requires that we as customers define the databases and tables with schema. You can do this task manually or leverage the Glue data crawler and Apache Hive metastore (*https://oreil.ly/Lx1qY*) to perform this task for you. Once the database and tables are defined, you can query this data with simple SQL. As you execute the SQL query, Athena internally submits a job that operates in asynchronous fashion, and the response to the query is saved to S3. Additionally, you can integrate Athena with various BI tools (*https://oreil.ly/Apj0y*) for interactive analysis, such as Amazon QuickSight, which we'll discuss in the next section.

Like many other services, Athena's main advantage is that you don't have to worry about infrastructure management. Let's discuss a few other features and considerations for using this service for your data analytics use cases:

Federated query
> We mentioned that Athena is used to query on data stored in S3, but what about data present in other AWS data stores, such as Amazon DynamoDB or on-premises data sources? For these kinds of use cases, Athena offers a feature called federated query (*https://oreil.ly/6Kjbc*). This feature allows you to run SQL queries on a variety of data stores, be they on the AWS cloud or on-premises. Athena achieves this via a Lambda-based data source connector; the connector essentially helps establish a connection and retrieve data. In addition, Athena can have multiple Lambda invocations in parallel to fasten data processing tasks. It is also possible that data won't fit into Lambda memory; to handle this, the data is spilled to S3, avoiding any data loss.

User-defined functions (UDFs)
> UDFs (*https://oreil.ly/SjivZ*) are another feature of Athena supported via the federated query SDK. They allow you to write custom Java code on Lambda and invoke directly from SQL queries to perform any preprocessing or postprocessing tasks on data. Consider a scenario of sensitive data handling: to avoid storing sensitive information to S3 as part of the Athena query response, it is masked via logic executed in UDFs.

ML models
> Athena allows you to use deployed ML models on Amazon SageMaker. You can directly invoke these models in a SQL query (*https://oreil.ly/R81Hk*) for required data analysis. One example could be detecting negative reviews for our online food-ordering platform.

To help with regular scheduling of workflows or invocation based on certain events, we can leverage Amazon EventBridge. For use cases of workflow orchestration and integration with other services, we can utilize AWS Step Functions.

The limitation of using Amazon Athena instead of self-managed Amazon EMR clusters or Amazon Redshift (which we'll discuss shortly) could be the time it takes to execute queries on large datasets, so it might not be the best solution for latency-sensitive operations.

Amazon EMR, AWS Glue, and Amazon Athena are powerful services for big data analytics tasks. Now, let's discuss the AWS-powered business intelligence tool Amazon QuickSight.

Amazon QuickSight

Recall that our online food-ordering application stores data in multiple data stores, such as total orders in a particular region, top-rated restaurants, and most ordered food items. How can we create a unified dashboard connecting to different data stores without providing direct access to data stores to everyone? This can easily be achieved using Amazon QuickSight. QuickSight is a fully managed, serverless business intelligence service offering analytics, visualization, and reporting. It can connect to different kinds of data stores and include them in a single dashboard. The data can include AWS data, third-party data, spreadsheet data, SaaS data, and more.

Here are the key features of and considerations for QuickSight:

- QuickSight essentially enables every user to perform analytics and visualize the data for your use cases with much less expertise. With QuickSight, you don't need to depend on business intelligence teams for your data requests.

- QuickSight is offered in two variants: standard and enterprise (*https://oreil.ly/G8oGk*). The standard edition contains all the features described previously. The enterprise edition includes more advanced capabilities, such as automated and customizable data insights powered by ML and security features, including federated user identities, single sign-on, and encryption at rest. The enterprise edition also helps monetize dashboards via a pay-per-session pricing model. The consumers of the dashboards you've created pay for them per their usage.

- An additional feature is available as part of the enterprise edition: QuickSight Q (*https://oreil.ly/r0C0r*). It is a natural language processing tool where, instead of writing queries, you can directly ask questions like "What are the top five restaurants in Mumbai?"

- QuickSight supports fast advanced calculations to serve data via SPICE (Superfast, Parallel, In-memory Calculation Engine). To use this in-memory data store, you should enable it as part of the database creation or editing process, and you need to configure the required SPICE capacity (*https://oreil.ly/KLg8m*).

We mentioned that QuickSight is helpful for drawing insights, and it can do that for any data source. One such data source is Amazon Redshift.

Amazon Redshift

In simple terms, Amazon Redshift is a data warehousing tool that can act as a data store for data from multiple sources and that lets you run SQL queries at a single place for data analytics. Redshift is an AWS-managed service and can scale to petabytes of data with an elastic scaling (*https://oreil.ly/JXUz6*) option. There is also a serverless option (*https://oreil.ly/ETobh*), which helps you avoid any burden of resource provisioning and workload management.

We'll begin by discussing the architecture of Redshift and then move on to key features offered by this service. Redshift is columnar, PostgreSQL-based storage based on a leader-follower cluster architecture, where the leader acts as a query coordinator that parses and complies the query and then forwards the query to follower (compute) nodes, which work in parallel to gather results. This architecture is shown in

Figure 13-4. There can be from 2 to 128 nodes in a Redshift cluster, and in the case of the serverless option, the entire architecture is abstracted out from customers. The query can be invoked from SQL clients via a Java Database Connectivity (JDBC) (*https://oreil.ly/3_SxR*) or Open Database Connectivity (ODBC) connection (*https://oreil.ly/qXcYO*), or it can use the Data API. The Data API (*https://oreil.ly/90nj2*) offers query execution in both synchronous and asynchronous fashion and can query for results within 24 hours with a query ID.

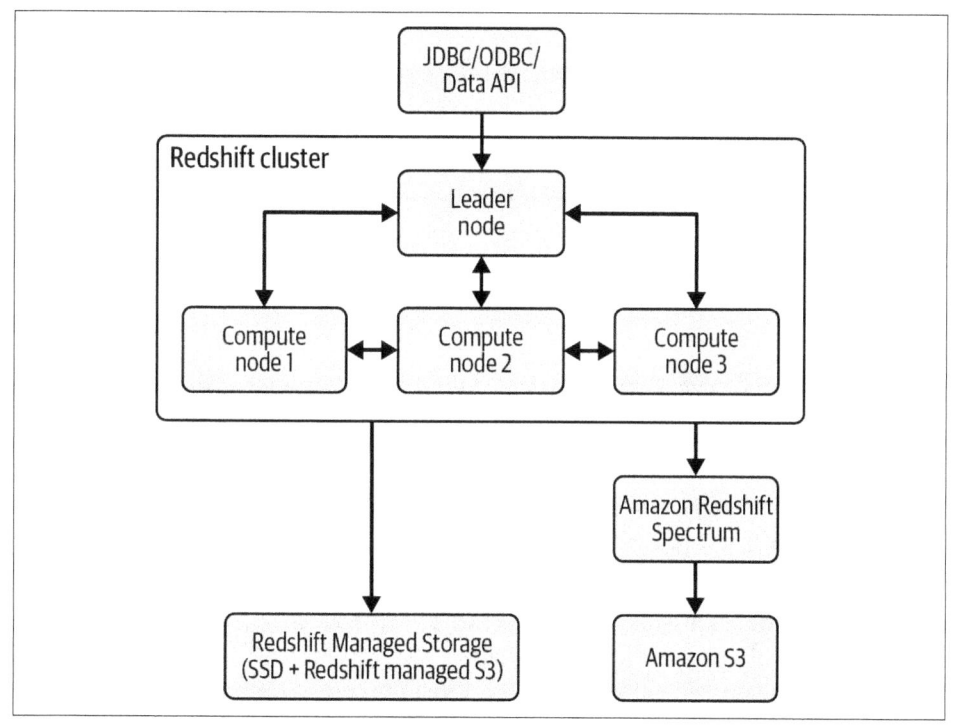

Figure 13-4. Amazon Redshift architecture

With the Redshift architecture, the compute nodes are partitioned into slices, and each slice has its own allocated disk and memory to perform parallel processing. The data is stored in immutable blocks (*https://oreil.ly/TMx2I*). A block consists of column data spanning multiple rows, and a full block can contain millions of values with a size of 1 MB.

To improve query performance over the data blocks, Redshift maintains in-memory metadata information called *zone maps* (*https://oreil.ly/bjhjH*). It stores the minimum and maximum values for a block and effectively prunes the data blocks that don't contain data for a specific query. Zone maps can be optimized using a sort key (*https://oreil.ly/h6cao*), which defines how data is sorted on the physical disk. The sort key works well except in a very few scenarios: when there is only one block per column per slice; when the values within blocks have the same prefix (for strings longer than 8 bytes—Redshift takes the first 8 bytes as a prefix, so sorting won't matter if it's the same); and when the column contains a single distinct value (sorting won't matter since minimum and maximum values are consistent).

To optimize query performance, you can optionally choose to provide a distribution style (*https://oreil.ly/BN5J8*) for data. This ensures that data is evenly distributed across the cluster and that you can make the best out of parallel processing. Redshift supports four distribution styles:

AUTO option (default)
    Redshift chooses the distribution style based on the size of the table data and internally switches among the different distribution styles based on the size.

EVEN option
    Data is distributed across the compute node slices in round-robin fashion by the leader node. This is a recommended option when there are no join operations on the table.

KEY option
    The leader node checks the column value and places it on the compute node slice matching its value.

ALL option
    The entire table data is available on each node. This is only recommended if there are very few insert or update operations on the table.

Redshift offers Redshift Spectrum, which can use S3 as storage; the compute nodes are only responsible for gathering the results. This helps customers directly query the data from S3 without loading it to Redshift clusters. One key consideration here is repeated reads against S3 since the storage doesn't adhere to transactional guarantees.

Redshift also offers Redshift Managed Storage (RMS), which allows customers to scale compute and storage independently. It uses S3 as persistent storage and offers-high speed, SSD-backed, Tier 1 cache support. RMS allows scaling up to 128 TB per instance and up to 16 PB per cluster storage capacity. For scaling further, you can always use S3 as storage.

You can choose from different instance types (*https://oreil.ly/lbvDY*) available for your Redshift cluster. The feature is supported by the new Redshift instance type RA3 (*https://oreil.ly/1iAee*). The other instance types are DC2 (dense compute) with SSD as storage and DS2 (dense storage) with magnetic disks as storage. The DS2 instance types are legacy, and we don't recommend using them for your workloads.

Redshift Spectrum is similar to Athena, where you query on top of the data that sits in S3. The one big difference is you can configure compute, enabling the queries to be much faster. There are additional feature sets for both these services that you should evaluate before choosing one for your workloads:

Materialized views
> Redshift allows you to create materialized views (*https://oreil.ly/L8csr*) from one or more tables to make the queries faster. The materialized views contain pre-compute result sets based on table joins with all or a subset of columns, aggregations, and filters. You can also create materialized views on top of already created materialized views, similar to base tables.

Workload management tools
> Redshift offers workload management (WLM) tools (*https://oreil.ly/Hg1JD*) to separate different query workloads and assign priority so that important queries are executed and less important queries can be throttled or aborted.

Data copying
> You can use the COPY (*https://oreil.ly/pOZQc*) command to load data to Redshift from Amazon S3, Amazon DynamoDB, Amazon EMR, or any remote host accessible via SSH. Support is also available for autocopy (*https://oreil.ly/k1SGb*), which automatically ingests data from Amazon S3 to Redshift clusters.

Data ingestion
> You can integrate Redshift with Amazon MSK or Amazon KDS for ingesting live streaming data and use Informatica Data Loader for Amazon Redshift (*https://oreil.ly/naeCZ*) to access data from on-premises or third-party applications.

Federated query
> You can use Redshift's federated query feature (*https://oreil.ly/OcRRv*) to access live data from external data stores, such as RDS PostgreSQL and MySQL and Aurora PostgreSQL and MySQL, without loading it to Redshift clusters.

Data sharing
> Redshift allows data sharing (*https://oreil.ly/3HIfR*) across the clusters. This helps isolate the read workloads without copying data on multiple clusters.
>
> Redshift provides direct integration (*https://oreil.ly/4rX2L*) with Amazon Aurora so as to avoid any pipeline set up by customers, and the data is directly available in Redshift once it is pushed to Aurora within seconds.
>
> Amazon Redshift Advisor (*https://oreil.ly/u9WgB*) recommends cluster optimizations around query performance and cost savings, such as query-tuning recommendations, deletion of unused clusters, and table data compression.

Redshift is a great tool for data warehousing and analytics use cases scaling to petabytes of data. In the next section, we'll look into different ML services offered by AWS and how they can fit into various use cases.

Machine Learning on AWS

To support ML and AI use cases, AWS offers a range of services (*https://oreil.ly/ AXCws*) from building and running your own ML models to leveraging fully customized applications for specific purposes. For example, Amazon Polly converts text to speech, Amazon Comprehend helps you figure out insights and relationships in unstructured data, and Amazon CodeGuru offers intelligent recommendations to improve code quality. Visit the AWS product pages for the latest updates on their capabilities in the field of AI and ML.

The services can be divided into three broad categories: application services, platform services, and frameworks and hardware solutions. Application services are customized solutions for solving a specific use case. Amazon SageMaker is a platform service that enables you to create your own services by training and deploying ML models. AWS offers different frameworks, such as PyTorch (*https://pytorch.org*), Keras (*https://keras.io*), and TensorFlow (*https://tensorflow.org*), and special hardware with customized CPU (*https://oreil.ly/hGljt*) and GPU (*https://oreil.ly/ACYPT*) to run ML workloads. We'll start our discussion with Amazon SageMaker and then briefly touch on other offerings.

> *Intelligence* refers to our ability to ask questions and provide reasons for the answers to these questions. We call it *AI* when this intelligence is shown by machines. *Machine learning* is a branch of AI representing this intelligence based on previous data and algorithms. This book will not introduce you to ML concepts but rather will explore a few AWS services offering ML capabilities.

Amazon SageMaker

The default benefit we achieve by choosing the AWS cloud is running any service without the worry of infrastructure management. Amazon SageMaker is an AWS-managed service that allows customers to prepare data and build, train, and deploy ML models quickly. SageMaker offers features to complete each of these steps and then finally deploy your models with ease, getting the best out of it with minimal effort:

Prepare data
SageMaker offers tools for initial data preparation that allow you to build on top of the data, such as Data Wrangler (*https://oreil.ly/kdw5W*). Data Wrangler can be added in ML workflows in Amazon SageMaker Studio (*https://oreil.ly/oRElj*) to import, prepare, transform, and identify features and analyze data.

Build
> Customers can use Jupyter notebooks inside SageMaker Studio to build their ML models. AWS offers its own custom-built algorithms that run efficiently on the AWS infrastructure as well as on popular open source frameworks, such as TensorFlow and PyTorch. You can also write custom code if the available solutions don't fit your use case.

Train
> As SageMaker manages all the infrastructure, you don't have to worry about training. You can use the managed infrastructure from storage to compute.

Deploy
> Deployment of ML models is also taken care of by SageMaker. There are multiple ways to deploy a model, and a particular method can be selected based on the use case. We recommend using real-time inference (*https://oreil.ly/SdNn6*) for workloads with low latency requirements, serverless inference (*https://oreil.ly/xsLLb*) as a fully managed solution and for workloads that can tolerate cold-start problems, asynchronous inference (*https://oreil.ly/K1jnb*) for workloads with large payload sizes (up to 1 GB) and near real-time processing requirements, and batch transforms (*https://oreil.ly/1Gpok*) for processing entire datasets.

SageMaker also offers support for A/B testing by enabling multiple ML models behind a single endpoint. A/B testing helps with figuring out how different models are performing and if they are working per expectations.

Depending on your use case, you can decide to use SageMaker for some or all these features when building and deploying your entire pipeline. For example, you can deploy on SageMaker a model that has already been trained on on-premises infrastructure.

SageMaker also offers the following key features:

Clarify
> SageMaker includes multiple features that can help improve your ML models, such as SageMaker Clarify (*https://oreil.ly/5CFmG*). As the name dictates, it detects any potential bias and helps clarify the predictions that the ML models make using a feature-attribution approach.

Debugger
> Metrics are an important tool for visualizing performance. To visualize an ML model's performance, you can use SageMaker Debugger (*https://oreil.ly/G3b5_*). It also can identify system bottlenecks for EC2 instance jobs with metrics like CPU, GPU, GPU memory, network, and data I/O.

Pipelines
> We mentioned that SageMaker helps with the entire cycle, from data preparation to model deployments. As you scale your systems, it's very important that SageMaker is automatically managed to reduce operational overhead. SageMaker Pipelines (*https://oreil.ly/lgPN_*) helps with this automation and with building end-to-end CI/CD pipelines.

Automatic model tuning (AMT)
> The ML model performance can vary based on hyperparameter values. SageMaker AMT (*https://oreil.ly/mPD1Q*) runs the training job multiple times and figures out the best version of the model.

Ground Truth
> It's important to train ML models on good-quality datasets to get the most out of them. SageMaker Ground Truth (*https://oreil.ly/Azeul*) helps automate this process by creating high-quality, labeled datasets. For data-labeling tasks, you can choose the workforce, such as independent contractors, your own private workforce, or vendor companies on AWS Marketplace.

SageMaker is a great tool for building ML solutions on the AWS cloud. Visit the SageMaker documentation (*https://oreil.ly/VFlK7*) for an even deeper dive into its capabilities as we couldn't possibly fit everything into this chapter.

There may be use cases where you don't have the expertise to build your own solutions. In these scenarios, you can leverage different services offered by AWS to solve specific use cases.

AWS ML Application Services

Building ML solutions on your own takes time as well as expertise in a field where you might not want to invest. If you have a general use case for ML, you can use fully managed services by AWS without the worry of building, deploying, and maintaining ML models. Some of these services include:

Amazon CodeWhisperer
> You might be familiar with the concept of pair programming, where two people have a discussion and then code together. Amazon CodeWhisperer (*https://oreil.ly/EnFbX*) is your coding companion and helps you by generating code suggestions ranging from small code snippets to entire functions. It can also flag security issues in code, and it offers suggestions to remediate the raised concerns that can be easily integrated in your favorite code editor.

Amazon Comprehend
> Amazon Comprehend helps with gathering insights from a document or collection of documents. In our example of an online food-ordering application,

customers write reviews about food they ordered. We can use Comprehend to decipher review behavior (positive/negative) or identify which food items are being talked about. Comprehend can identify insights such as entities (person names, places, items, etc.), PII, document languages, sentiment (positive, negative, neutral, or mixed), and more.

Amazon Kendra

Amazon Kendra (*https://oreil.ly/wL4LK*) is an ML-powered search engine on top of structured or unstructured data repositories. It uses natural language processing to determine which document is most relevant to a user's search queries. You use Kendra along with Amazon Lex (*https://oreil.ly/9dBhV*) to build AI chatbots (*https://oreil.ly/aGejD*) for use cases like customer support to resolve user queries on our online food-ordering application.

Amazon Forecast

Amazon Forecast (*https://oreil.ly/pqJWg*) is helpful for accurate time-series forecasts. Consider an example of an online business: how do you predict traffic for an upcoming sale based on historical traffic or what growth looks like if you launch in a new region? Forecast automatically figures out combinations of ML algorithms suitable for your dataset and helps you with the forecasts.

Amazon Rekognition

Amazon Rekognition (*https://oreil.ly/bwstV*) is a recognition service for image and video analysis. This service can power use cases like search over image and video content, face identification and verification, adult content detection, and text extraction from images.

Amazon Transcribe

Amazon Transcribe (*https://oreil.ly/sWm_0*) is a speech-to-text conversion service. In our online food-ordering application example, we might offer a service where customers can submit their feedback via telephone for food items they ordered. Transcribe can help derive valuable insights (*https://oreil.ly/iwSIc*) from such calls. Some other use cases where it can help is converting voice input to text for processing in your systems, converting audio and video content to be searchable by text, and creating subtitles for videos.

These customized offerings provide direct integrations within our applications with minimal effort. As an example, assume that you own a blog-hosting service where users can manage their blogs and share content with their followers. To add text-to-audio functionality, you can either build your own solution or use Amazon Polly for a much faster start. As we've mentioned before, you can always improve on the solutions if your use case changes later or you see any bottlenecks in existing solutions. The key point is time to market: if you start with a custom solution, it might take much more time to launch the service compared to direct integration with a service like Polly.

In the next section, we'll discuss special infrastructure support provided by AWS to build ML workloads.

AWS ML Infrastructure

AWS offers EC2 instances that are specialized to handle ML workloads for both training and inference. These instances include hardware-based accelerators, also referred to as *coprocessors*, to enhance the computing power and perform tasks like graphics processing, floating point number calculations, and data pattern matching in a much more efficient manner compared to software running on general-purpose CPUs. Some examples of accelerators include GPUs (*https://oreil.ly/gMe3N*), field-programmable gate arrays (FPGAs) (*https://oreil.ly/5ouKn*), AWS Inferentia (*https://oreil.ly/0f_9a*), and AWS Trainium (*https://oreil.ly/4Fr45*). Let's talk about the custom solutions offered by AWS to accelerate our ML workloads:

AWS Trainium
   The Amazon EC2 Trainium instances offer up to 50% cost-to-train savings over comparable EC2 instances. These instances are optimized to run deep learning (*https://oreil.ly/iPkt7*) training workloads with native support of different data types, such as FP32, TF32, BF16, FP16, UINT8, and configurable FP8. It supports AWS Neuron SDK, which is natively integrated with PyTorch (*https://oreil.ly/WbC27*) and TensorFlow (*https://oreil.ly/Tbypv*), so existing framework applications can be used with minimal code changes.

AWS Inferentia
   The Amazon EC2 Inferentia instances are designed to run ML inference applications with high throughput and low latency while saving costs when compared to general-purpose EC2 instances. These types of instances offer high-speed connectivity between the accelerators, enabling deployment of billions of parameters across multiple accelerators on Inferentia EC2 instances.

> *Inference* means reaching a conclusion based on logical reasoning and evidence, so *ML inference* essentially means running ML models on live data to get a final answer (or make a prediction). The training is a prephase to inference, where we train ML applications to learn from existing data and then use this intelligence at the time of inference.

The EC2 instances are purpose built to optimize compute-heavy tasks like running large-scale models, natural language processing, speech recognition, and computer vision. You might consider the cost here: if the accelerator in these EC2 instances makes processing so fast, then it would definitely be costly, and you should decide if you can afford such an expenditure. As these instances are specifically designed for ML workloads, they are cost-effective if you compare them to EC2 instances with similar capabilities. For example, Amazon EC2 Inf1 instances (*https://oreil.ly/8J34f*) provide 2.3 times higher throughput and up to 70% lower cost per inference than comparable EC2 instances. The EC2 Inf2 instances (*https://oreil.ly/rtYkL*) are cheaper than Inf1, with four times higher throughput and 10 times lower latency. A very good benefit of using the AWS cloud is that AWS innovates on the behalf of customers. We as customers might have been happy with the performance and cost benefits of Amazon EC2 Inf1 instances, but AWS has now launched a new version with improvements to the existing options.

Conclusion

This chapter introduced you to AWS services that are helpful when building and running big data analytics and ML workloads at any scale. You may often want to use a combination of multiple services to serve your use case best, such as Amazon EMR to process the live streaming data published to Amazon MSK or plotting Amazon Redshift data via Amazon QuickSight. Since AWS provides easy integration with all its services, it is a seamless experience to use any service and fit it into other service components to meet your requirements.

In the second part of this chapter, we looked into AWS ML offerings, which essentially run ML workloads with zero or minimal operational overhead. AWS offers multiple services to solve specific use cases, which help us utilize the capabilities of ML without having vast knowledge of the concepts. For example, imagine building a language translation tool on your own versus using Amazon Translate (*https://aws.amazon.com/translate*). Amazon Translate will reduce the time to market of launching your application with translation capability.

We concluded with several infrastructure options that are specialized to run ML workloads at scale with higher throughput and lower cost when compared to general-purpose comparable hardware.

This is the final chapter in Part II. We're confident that now you can use your understanding of the material covered in Parts I and II to build real-time, large-scale systems. In Part III, we'll walk through use cases for building different systems on the AWS cloud, starting with a URL shortener service.

PART III
System Design Use Cases

Ninety percent of the functionality delivered now is better than 100% of it delivered never.
—Brian Kernighan and P. J. Plauger

Part III of this book covers some common system design use cases and examples, which we will work through together to build and scale on top of AWS cloud computing services. For all the use cases, we'll start with figuring out the system requirements, then move to a deep dive into system components, and finally close the chapter with a deployment view on AWS with Day 0 architecture (minimum viable product for a startup with, say, one thousand customers) and Day N architecture (scaling to millions of customers). Along the way, we'll discuss the bottlenecks that might occur in design, best practices for designing large-scale systems, and comparisons of similar AWS services.

We recommend following the Make It Work, Make It Right, Make It Fast (*https://oreil.ly/_J-U2*) principle, and all the chapters in Part III follow this philosophy. It's good to be optimistic that one day our system will serve one billion active users, but you don't have to build the system from day one to support this scale. The goal of huge scale should never hold you back from launching the product—just make sure the system is extensible enough so that if there is a need in the future, it can be evolved as new users are onboarded and new features are introduced. For example, the following *amazon.com* website screenshot shows the initial launch of the website—there was no point back then in thinking of how to make it work for a billion customers.

Other reasons for redesigning any system could be cost and operational maintenance, such as when Uber started with Amazon DynamoDB to build a ledger store but later moved to its custom-built storage solution, Docstore (*htttps://oreil.ly/KUvJ3*). The same principle applies while we figure out components in any system: the goal should always be to get the system out in the hands of the public and gather feedback. There is no win in overoptimizing the system if we never reach the goal of solving the customers' problems and finally generating revenue from it; after all, everyone is in business to earn money from the designed system or help other people to do so (as with open source projects).

> **Welcome to Amazon.com Books!**
>
> *One million titles, consistently low prices.*
>
> amazon.com — Earth's biggest bookstore
>
> (If you explore just one thing, make it our personal notification service. We think it's very cool!)
>
> **SPOTLIGHT! -- AUGUST 16TH**
> These are the books we love, offered at Amazon.com low prices. The spotlight moves **EVERY** day so please come often.
>
> **ONE MILLION TITLES**
> Search Amazon.com's million title catalog by author, subject, title, keyword, and more... Or take a look at the books we recommend in over 20 categories... Check out our customer reviews and the award winners from the Hugo and Nebula to the Pulitzer and Nobel... and bestsellers are 30% off the publishers list...
>
> **EYES & EDITORS, A PERSONAL NOTIFICATION SERVICE**
> Like to know when that book you want comes out in paperback or when your favorite author releases a new title? Eyes, our tireless, automated search agent, will send you mail. Meanwhile, our human editors are busy previewing galleys and reading advance reviews. They can let you know when especially wonderful works are published in particular genres or subject areas. Come in, meet Eyes, and have it all explained.
>
> **YOUR ACCOUNT**
> Check the status of your orders or change the email address and password you have on file with us. Please note that you **do not** need an account to use the store. The first time you place an order, you will be given the opportunity to create an account.

Every chapter in Part III will follow this general outline:

1. Introduction
   a. Background
   b. Business use case
2. System requirements
   a. Functional and nonfunctional requirements
   b. System scale

3. Starting with the design
   a. Concepts and principles
   b. System components
   c. A rough system design
4. Launching the system on AWS
   a. Day 0 architecture
   b. Scaling to millions and beyond
   c. Day N architecture
5. Conclusion

By the end of Part III, you will:

- Understand the business use case for each system-design problem and how to ask the right questions to evaluate the requirements
- Know how to outline the functional and nonfunctional requirements for the use case and how to estimate the scale requirements for storage, throughput, and latency, which percolate to capacity and cost estimations
- Know how to build the solution with the first principles using system-design basics and how to handle the edge cases and nuances around the design
- Deploy initial solutions on AWS with Day 0 architecture for a minimum viable product and evolve it into a most valuable product
- Scale the architecture to millions of users for Day 1 and beyond on AWS, making it secure, high-performing, resilient, and efficient

We've chosen eight use cases to explore a wide range of problem statements in the industry:

- Imagine a tool that takes long web addresses and turns them into short ones. Chapter 14 will take you into the world of URL shorteners. We'll learn why they're important, what they need to do, and how to build them using AWS. We'll start with a simple setup for a startup and then see how to make it work for millions of users.
- Chapter 15 is all about web crawlers and search engines like Google and Bing. We'll explore how these systems work, what they need to do, and how to create them using AWS. We'll start small and then figure out how to handle a massive amount of data.
- Ever wonder how social networks like Facebook connect people from all over the world? Chapter 16 will cover how to design a social network like Facebook or Instagram and create a newsfeed system to connect people from all over the

world. We'll cover how to make sure people can share and see updates and how to build it all using AWS.

- Online games are a blast, and real-time leaderboards are an important part of these games. Chapter 17 will show you how to design a system for tracking online game scores and ranking players. We'll use AWS to make sure the leaderboards can handle lots of players and updates.
- Planning a vacation and booking the perfect place to stay can feel thrilling, but have you ever thought about the complex system behind the scenes that makes it all work? Chapter 18 will delve into the architecture of an online hotel reservation system, addressing complex requirements like booking conflicts and transaction handling. We'll break down the components and deploy a scalable solution on the AWS cloud.
- Chapter 19 is about designing a chat application that lets people send messages in real time. We'll see how AWS can help us create a seamless, responsive chat experience.
- Relaxing with Netflix is a favorite pastime for many, and Chapter 20 will teach you how to design a system that processes and streams videos smoothly. We'll learn how to onboard video to the system and discover how the videos are streamed smoothly to a variety of devices all over the world without interruptions.
- Chapter 21 looks into designing a system for buying and selling stocks: a stockbroker application. You'll learn how to create a reliable, efficient stockbroker system and deploy it on AWS.

By the end of the book, you'll have a clear understanding of how to tackle different real-world challenges using AWS cloud computing services. You'll know how to design systems that are efficient, reliable, and ready to handle millions of users. So let's dive in and start designing some amazing systems!

CHAPTER 14
Designing a URL Shortener Service

We explored the concept of DNS in Chapter 9, noting that it's easier to remember a website's URL than its IP addresses—but what about the long URLs? It's easy to remember the root part of the URL (for example, *learning.oreilly.com* in *https://learning.oreilly.com/library/view/system-design-on/9781098146887*), but you can easily forget the long URL. We often embed links in text (*https://oreil.ly/SystemDesignOnAWS*) because that increases the readability.

Another way of sharing long URLs is by shortening them. For example, LinkedIn automatically shortens any URL that is part of a post because this helps increase post readability and user interaction. In microblogging applications like Twitter (now known as X), there is a limit on the number of characters in a single post, so to reduce the length of your text, you can shorten any URLs via some URL shortener service such as TinyURL (*https://tinyurl.com/app*) or Bitly (*https://bitly.com*) and attach those to the post instead of the full-length versions.

This chapter explores the design of a URL shortener service and discusses how to deploy the system on the AWS cloud. We'll start our discussion with requirements gathering and expectations from the system. Later, we'll jump into the details of the system.

System Requirements

You should have a clear goal in mind for the problem you need to solve. From there, the next step to design any system, big or small, is to gather the requirements. These requirements include:

- Why is this system needed? What is the business use case this system is solving?
- Who are the users of this system? How many users?

- Is there already a system that you can leverage instead of designing a new system from scratch? Systems like Bitly expose URL-shortening APIs to business customers, so why should we build our own system instead of using Bitly system APIs?
- Is the system's latency critical?

Requirements lists can be huge, and generating them can be time-consuming, but this is a very important step. Many times in Parts I and II, we discussed how to compare two technologies and pick the best solution depending on your understanding of the business use case. It is not possible to weigh the pros and cons of your options if your requirements are not clearly defined. The requirements of any system are usually specified in two categories: functional requirements and nonfunctional requirements (NFRs).

Functional and Nonfunctional Requirements

Functional requirements are the functionalities or features that the system offers to the end users. The main expectations from a URL shortener service are simple:

- The system takes input as a long URL and return a shortened URL.
- The short URL should redirect to the long URL when accessed by any user.

Along with the most critical requirements, you can consider value-add requirements that can be nice to have from a customer's perspective or helpful in deriving business value. Some of these include:

- Custom URL creation support
- Analytics on the URL access patterns, such as the most popular URLs
- Expiration for a URL so that the URL automatically expires and is no longer accessible after a fixed period
- Plug-in-based architecture to ensure extensibility
- APIs exposed to third-party clients so that they can integrate their applications with our system

We should always gather as many requirements as possible about what might be needed, but we shouldn't get so caught up thinking about future expectations that we lose track of current expectations. The additional requirements will help us design our system in an extensible way so that new features can be added without needing to rearchitect the system.

The other type of requirements is nonfunctional. *NFRs* determine the constraints the system operates on and don't directly affect the user feature-wise, but they are important for ensuring the quality of system operations. Here are a few examples:

Security
  To ensure the system is not exploited by bad actors

High availability
  To ensure a high uptime percentage in a year

Observability
  To ensure that appropriate metrics and alerts are in place for constant monitoring of system health

Low latency
  For short URL creation and redirection

Data stores
  Should be durable and ensure correctness of the data for the expiration time configured for a URL. The data should reside in the system until the expiration time or until it is explicitly removed by a user.

Fault tolerance
  Via mechanisms like retry handling

Interoperability in the system architecture
  The system operates at high scale and can be broken into multiple subsystems, so how will different subsystems interact with one another?

These requirements will help us make better decisions while designing the system. Another part of the requirements-gathering step is identifying the scale the system will operate on.

System Scale

Scale refers to the number of users or the traffic we're expecting on the system. We should be able to answer questions such as:

- What is the potential number of user requests per second (RPS) or queries per second (QPS) to generate a short URL?
- How many user requests (or how much load on the system) for redirecting short URLs to long URLs? We should have clarity on both the average and peak load on the system.
- Do we have any idea of the amount of storage required to store the data?

Coming up with scale numbers can be tricky if you're starting out fresh since you might not have 100% accurate data to base these numbers on. In these scenarios, it's OK to make a fair assumption with a balance of not too little and not too much. Let's move ahead with the following assumptions about our requirements:

- Generate short URL from long URL: 1,000 RPS
- Short URL to long URL redirection: 20,000 RPS
- Average duration of URL persistence in system: one year

There are a lot of database solutions in the market. To decide which one is best for our use case, we need to consider another important parameter: total storage space required. Knowing this can help answer questions like:

- What is the expected cost we'll bear if we use Amazon DynamoDB or Amazon Aurora?
- Do we require data partitioning from the start?

Other considerations important for scale could be figuring out an instance type and number of instances for applications deployed on Amazon EC2 instances or memory requirements for AWS Lambda. It's not easy to get the real numbers before putting the system in production and serving actual consumer traffic. Make fair assumptions and then improve further based on learnings.

One key consideration is system load testing; load testing helps you gain confidence that the system can perform as expected (the system is reliable) with increased traffic demands. Let's discuss the storage space requirements next.

Storage Space

The actual storage required will vary depending on the type of data storage solution we use because the data storage and access patterns are different for each database. An approximate calculation of the storage space will depend on the number of URLs, the lengths of the short URLs and long URLs, user metadata, and URL metadata such as expiration time and creation time. The number of URLs generated in a year can be derived from assumed traffic of 1,000 RPS:

> Total URLs in one year = (1,000 requests/second) × 60 (per minute) × 60 (per hour) × 24 (per day) × 365 (per year) ~ 31.53 billion

Before moving further along on storage calculation, we need to figure out the ideal length of a short URL. The length should be such that the system doesn't run out of unique short URLs and should be able to support the required scale of 31.5 billion unique URLs per year. In Chapter 9, we discussed IPv6 addresses as a replacement for

IPv4 addresses because the world is running out of unique IP addresses. We definitely don't want this kind of problem to occur in our URL shortener system, so the length of the URL should be calculated with the proper considerations from the beginning. You might suggest a length of 12 or 15 to be on the safe side, but that defeats the purpose of shortening the URL.

We can think about generating a short URL from the numbers 0–9, as well as the letters a–z and A–Z. What is the maximum number of unique URLs generated for a given length with these 62 unique characters?

Length(1) = 62^1 = 62

Length(6) = 62^6 = 56.8 billion

Length(7) = 62^7 = 3.5 trillion

Length(8) = 62^8 = 218.3 trillion

We can see based on these calculations that the URL system can support the required scale with a URL length of greater than or equal to 6. Considering future scale, we can finalize the URL length as 7.

Now, let's go back to our original question: what is the required storage space? Considering a simple database schema of storing short URLs, long URLs, expiration times, and metadata, we can calculate our storage needs as follows:

Short URL (7 characters) = 7 bytes

Average long URL (100 characters) = 100 bytes

Expiration date (long) = 8 bytes

Average metadata (user IP, user preferences, etc.) = 1 KB

Total ~ 1150 bytes

For simplicity, let's take 1 KB as the storage requirement for a single URL:

Total storage for one year = 31.53 billion × 1 KB = 29.37 TB

The system has additional storage requirements, such as cache to improve query performance, analytics data, and user authentication database (which can be required if the system offers additional capabilities to logged-in users, such as custom URL creation, view analytics, etc.).

With all these requirements in mind, let's move forward with the design of a URL shortener service.

Starting with the Design

We mentioned in the requirements-gathering section that we shouldn't think too far ahead because we don't know what our system will look like in the future or what new features we might introduce to evolve with the market. We should try to keep our systems open-ended so that we can introduce new features with ease when they are actually needed. Figure 14-1 shows the most basic architecture and user interactions for the URL shortener service to meet the defined functional requirements. The users create a short URL corresponding to a long URL using the URL shortener service and then use the same short URL in the web browser (or terminal) to access the URL. The URL shortener service figures out the long URL corresponding to the short URL and redirects the request.

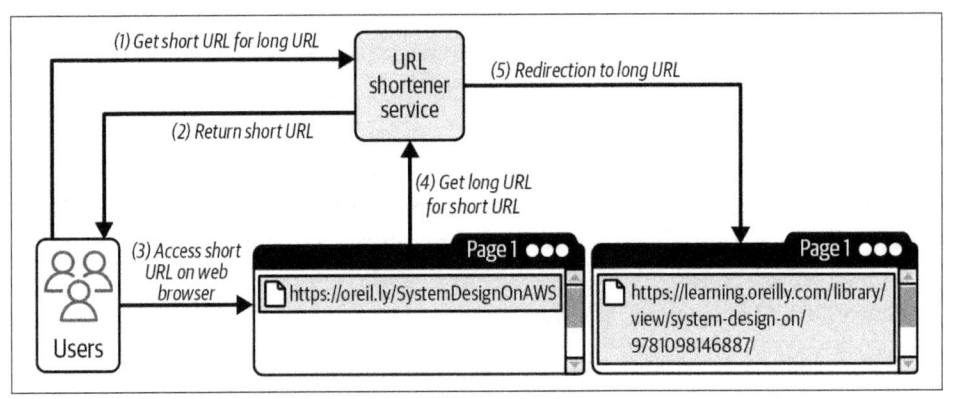

Figure 14-1. User interaction with URL shortener service

The first thing we need to figure out for the design is how a short URL can be generated from a long URL so that it can be optimally stored, supporting faster user-lookup queries.

URL Shortening Algorithm

A long URL can be shortened into a short URL via different algorithms. We'll discuss how some of them can fit our system use case, starting with hashing.

Hashing

Hashing seems to be a viable solution to solve this problem: using a hash function such as MD5, which takes a long URL as input and returns a hash of this long URL as output. The length of the generated hash can be greater than 7, so the system should trim the generated hash to a reduced length. This solution is easy to implement but it has one problem: collision. Two different long URLs could possibly generate the same hash, and even if the hash is different, the truncated length could be the same. At large scale, this can become a frequent problem, making short URL generation a bottleneck.

There are different methods of handling collisions: one possible solution is to take some other set of characters instead of truncating to the first 7 characters. The hash-generation approach also requires a data store lookup (or multiple lookups in the case of collisions), which adds extra latency to the operation, as shown in Figure 14-2.

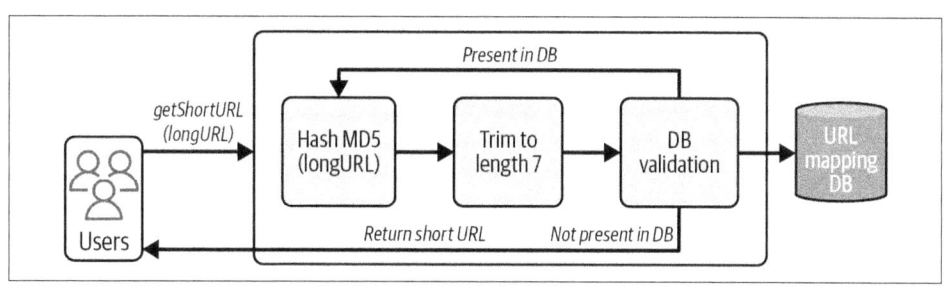

Figure 14-2. Short URL generation by hashing

In short, the hashing solution is not so perfect for our system requirements. Let's think about an option that would avoid the collisions and perhaps also avoid the database lookups to make operation faster.

Unique ID generation

A key point to consider here is that the long URL and short URL don't have to be related—this would essentially be a unique ID generation system, which can map the generated ID to a long URL.

Let's discuss a few approaches for generating unique IDs. The ID can be as simple as a counter incremented every time a new request is received from the users or a feature like AUTO_INCREMENT (*https://oreil.ly/WtqwQ*) from a database. If the system itself (without the involvement of the database) handles the ID generation, we can be sure of solving the problems of both collision handling and avoiding database lookups. Think of it as a server initializing a counter value with "1" and then incrementing it every time a new request arrives. The mapping can be stored to a database, and then the short URL is returned to the user, as shown in Figure 14-3.

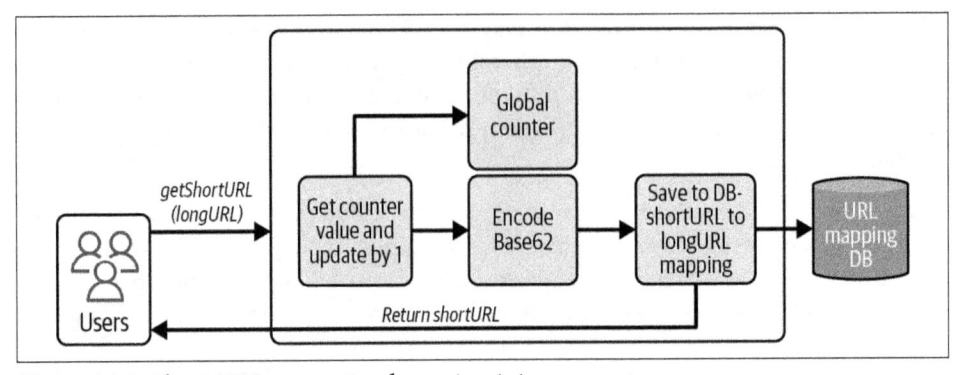

Figure 14-3. Short URL generation by maintaining a counter

The sequence of alphanumeric characters from 0 to 9, a to z, and A to Z when used for encoding is referred to as *base62 encoding*. Note that when using base62 encoding on the counter values (decimal numbers), the short URL will be unique but not always of length 7. For example:

Base62 (1) = 1

Base62 (10) = A

Base62 (61) = z

Base62 (62) = 10

Base62 (63) = 11

Base62 (1000001) = 4C93

To ensure the length is always 7, we can append random characters to the generated base62 value from other character set, which is mutually exclusive of the alphanumeric set (say, _, #, etc.).

We haven't decided on the maintenance of the counter value. The simple solution is to maintain a global counter variable in our application, which is updated after every new short URL generation. But there can be multiple machines on which the application is running, which can lead to a duplicate counter value. Even if there is a single machine, it has a risk of going down, which would make the counter value again start from zero.

To solve this, we can consider maintaining this global counter in a database. This way, it solves the problem of a single machine going down (the counter is not initialized to zero every time) or multiple machines being responsible for URL generation (duplicate counter values across the machines). However, it can also cause issues because we can't allow multiple application threads to access the counter at the same time in order to avoid race conditions, and if we apply a lock (a single machine reads and updates the value), that will increase operation latency.

Let's simplify the entire architecture further to ensure optimal application performance. We can assign additional responsibility to the system of pregenerating the short URLs since they are not dependent on the long URL. This way, multiple machines can utilize the pregenerated IDs (short URLs), solving all the bottlenecks.

Our URL shortener service consists of an additional component responsible for pregeneration of short URLs and keeping them in memory for faster access. An important decision to make here is whether we give this additional responsibility to our URL shortener service or host it as an independent service. (We discussed monolith and microservice architecture in Chapter 8 and the benefits associated with each.)

A single component will ensure comparatively less hardware cost (at least in the beginning) and less latency since there's no requirement for network calls between the services. What you need to consider in order to make the decision here is what value you're getting if this is an independent component instead of hosted as part of the main application. A separate ID generation or key generation service (KGS) can be beneficial for other use cases, and this is an independent responsibility that doesn't have to be tied to the URL shortener service. Given this, we'll go with the idea of hosting a separate service with the responsibility for generating unique keys and passing those on to our URL shortener service when requested, as shown in Figure 14-4.

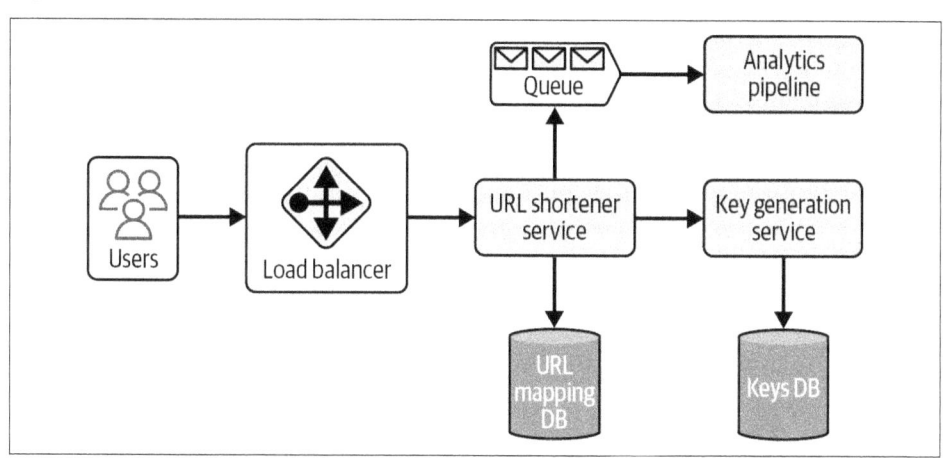

Figure 14-4. URL shortener system architecture

An additional analytics pipeline is included in the architecture. The URL shortener service publishes the events of user activity to the queue, and the analytics pipeline takes care of analyzing and offering insights on the data.

Now, let's look at the KGS in more detail.

Key generation service

The KGS has a simple responsibility of providing unique IDs when requested by our URL shortener service. To ensure traffic control on the KGS as well as make the URL shortener system more efficient, the operation can offer a list of IDs—say, one thousand in a single operation—and the URL shortener service can re-request once these IDs are exhausted. Let's dig a little deeper into how the KGS works: how should these unique IDs be generated?

We can consider using the database's auto-increment feature, such as MySQL's AUTO_INCREMENT or PostgreSQL's SERIAL (*https://oreil.ly/nzd_o*) or SEQUENCE (*https://oreil.ly/HnVc_*). This functionality is applicable for a leader instance (if there are multiple database instances), and it can become a single point of failure for maintenance of IDs, hampering overall system availability. Further, implementing this feature becomes very hard to do in the case of multi-instance database setup, such as horizontally scalable NoSQL databases. We can take inspiration from Flickr's architecture (*https://oreil.ly/uwx2W*), which uses MySQL's auto-increment feature with a REPLACE INTO query to get a globally unique new ID on every new query:

```
CREATE TABLE `Tickets64` (
  `id` bigint(20) unsigned NOT NULL auto_increment,
  `stub` char(1) NOT NULL default '',
  PRIMARY KEY (`id`),
  UNIQUE KEY `stub` (`stub`)
) ENGINE=InnoDB

REPLACE INTO Tickets64 (stub) VALUES ('a');
SELECT LAST_INSERT_ID();
```

To increase system availability and avoid a single point of failure, two database servers are used, starting with an even and odd number and offset as 2 to avoid collision:

```
TicketServer1:
auto-increment-increment = 2
auto-increment-offset = 1

TicketServer2:
auto-increment-increment = 2
auto-increment-offset = 2
```

Further regular snapshots should be taken of these two databases to ensure that a backup is always kept in case of any fatal scenarios. Since only a single row is maintained within a table, we can be sure that the server will not run out of storage space.

Figure 14-5 shows the interaction of the KGS with ticket servers for ID generation.

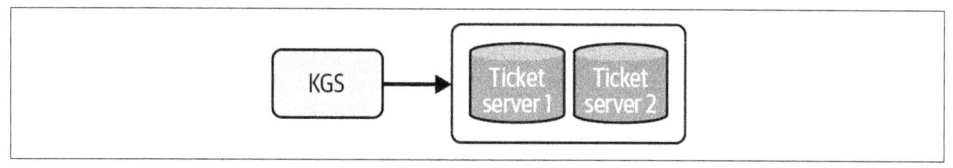

Figure 14-5. Unique ID generation via ticket servers

The two ticket servers generate even and odd IDs, respectively, but this management overhead will increase if the ticket servers are deployed in multiple regions instead of just one. One potential solution to ensure uniqueness across regions could be adding a data center prefix to the short URL, such as a 1 for us-east-1, 2 for eu-west-1, and so on, making the URL eight characters instead of seven.

> In 2010, X proposed another approach for generating 64-bit unique IDs: Snowflake. Snowflake (*https://oreil.ly/ooF5v*) can generate 4,096 unique IDs per millisecond with a combination of timestamp (41 bits for epoch milliseconds timestamp), machine identifier number (10 bits, giving us up to 1,024 machines), and sequence number (12 bits for local counter per machine). The remaining 1 bit is a signed bit always set to 0. This approach won't work directly for our URL shortener because the system always requires a 7-character-length string, but implementation can be built using a similar concept. X used Snowflake because of the requirement for sorting and ensuring ordering guarantees. The URL shortener system does not require creating IDs based on timestamp, so we're free to choose an approach that's easy to implement and maintain the uniqueness.

The KGS can be extended to support multiple types of key generation based on client input in the API or client onboarding configuration. This makes the KGS a single system for generating any kind of identifier. Let's now discuss the APIs that need to be supported by the URL shortener service.

System APIs

APIs help clients integrate with the system to make use of supported functionalities. The URL shortener service should support two main APIs: creating a short URL and retrieving a long URL from a short URL. The following code snippet shows an API signature for creating short URLs:

```
POST /v1/createShortUrl
{
    longUrl,
    customUrl,
```

```
        expiry,
        userMetadata
    }
```

The `longUrl` parameter is mandatory in API requests for generating a short URL. The additional attributes are added to support other functionalities of the application:

customUrl
: Helpful if the user wants to generate a custom URL instead of a random 7-character string. To handle this parameter, the URL shortener service will directly check in the database if the custom URL is already created, and if not, mapping of the custom URL to the long URL will be stored in the database.

expiry
: Enables users to specify a custom expiration for the URL instead of what is defined by the system.

userMetadata
: Used to gather extra information about the user, such as IP address, geographical location, and browser, which helps drive analytics.

> It's possible that the same custom URL could be created by multiple users. Amazon DynamoDB's default PutItem behavior is to update the item if the primary key already exists, but this is not a valid option for the URL shortener system. The PutItem request should contain a condition expression (*https://oreil.ly/wOVmO*) to fail the request for the same custom URL.

The response of the API can be either success or failure. You might remember our discussion of HTTP status codes from Chapter 6—the status codes are helpful for determining the kind of HTTP response the client has received from the server. We should define proper mechanisms for both responses so that the clients can understand the response in failure scenarios and take any further actions, such as retry. The failures can be due to invalid parameters from the client side or some issue at the backend application.

Here is an example of a successful response:

```
HTTP/1.1 200 OK
{
    "shortUrl": "https://oreil.ly/SystemDesignOnAWS"
}
```

Here is an example of a failed response:

```
HTTP/1.1 500 Internal Server Error
{
```

```
    "error": "An error occurred while processing your request"
}
```

As a user creates a short URL and shares it with others or accesses it themself, the API request and response could look something like this:

```
GET v1/getLongUrl
{
    shortUrl,
    userMetadata
}
```

Here is the successful response:

```
HTTP/1.1 302 Found
Location: https://www.oreilly.com/library/view/system-design-on/9781098146887
```

And here is the failed response:

```
HTTP/1.1 404 Not Found
{
    "error": "short url doesn't exist"
}
```

Let's discuss any additional considerations before moving on to the AWS components we will use to deploy the system in production.

System Considerations

By this point, we've proposed two services in the architecture: the URL shortener service and the KGS for supporting end-to-end functionality. The URL shortener service is responsible for short URL generation as well as redirection. The APIs are simple enough to be supported by a single system, but the traffic patterns are quite different for both APIs; the traffic for URL redirection will be much higher than for URL generation.

Imagine a celebrity generating a short URL and sharing it with followers on social media platforms: all of their followers will try to access the URL, increasing overall system traffic. In these kinds of scenarios, we recommend starting with a single system and then evolving if traffic handling becomes a problem.

Separating a system into two components can come with extra overhead, such as a database being accessed from two separate services. The URL shortener service will have both read and write use cases, whereas the URL redirect service will have read use cases on the database. It is generally not a good idea for two services to directly interact with a single database; the most robust solution is to expose the database operations via another service that is responsible for handling all database operations along with cache maintenance. We'll also need to finalize the database choice, given the wide variety of database solutions available on the market.

Database Selection

Multiple factors are involved in selecting the perfect database for a specific use case. We explored different types of databases and compared them in Chapters 2, 3, and 10. Figure 3-4 explains how to navigate through the database choices and finalize on a particular database. Begin with the data type and then look for the needed query patterns by the application. Let's consider the URL shortener service first.

URL shortener service

For the URL shortener service, the data is structured, and the expected query patterns are as follows:

- Get a long URL for a specific short URL.
- Get all URLs for a user in a specific period of time. This is a secondary query pattern and is only required for logged-in users.

These query patterns can be solved by both relational and nonrelational databases, and you can choose based on previous expertise. We recommend a logical partitioning strategy from the start if you choose a relational database for deployment. In the context of this chapter, we'll go ahead with an AWS key-value database: Amazon DynamoDB. There are many benefits of DynamoDB that we get out of the box, such as horizontal scaling, infrastructure management with no worry about scaling up read/write replicas, TTL configuration, and DynamoDB streams for analytics.

> DynamoDB scales horizontally based on customer-configured capacity mode. Begin with the on-demand capacity mode to figure out traffic patterns and then migrate to the provisioned mode if the traffic is predictable. The system can experience throttling issues with both on-demand and provisioned, with autoscaling capacity modes for spiky workloads. Preplanning your capacity is helpful in resolving throttling with provisioned mode (*https://oreil.ly/Z3Ait*), and throttling issues are automatically recovered for on-demand capacity mode (*https://oreil.ly/8Jr1K*). There is also an account-level quota of 40,000 RCUs and WCUs for on-demand; this can be increased by raising a quota increase request on the AWS Console (*https://oreil.ly/7cdFS*).

We can define the DynamoDB partition key and sort key as:

Partition key = {short URL}

Sort key = SU

We can skip defining sort key in the preceding schema because sort key is always a constant string. A constant is suggested because it helps store other entries (apart from long URL mapping) in DynamoDB with partition key as short URL. We'll require GSI for retrieving all URLs created by a user, and we can use the following schema for the same:

Partition key = {userId}

Sort key = u#{timestamp}

The timestamp is included in the sort key to help with retrieving the URLs in a particular time frame. Now, let's discuss the choice of database for the KGS.

KGS

The ID-generation logic is dependent on the ticket servers. Additionally, the KGS should keep some IDs in the buffer to serve the queries faster—but how many IDs should be in the buffer? The logic could be as simple as keeping 10,000 IDs in the buffer, and the number can be tuned based on application traffic. We can utilize an in-memory data store for this purpose, such as Amazon ElastiCache with Redis or Memcached flavor. Redis lists (*https://oreil.ly/kBsUN*) are one way to store IDs.

The KGS doesn't keep an audit history of which IDs are returned to the URL shortener service at particular instances, and we don't have that requirement either. This can be built in if needed, and a cache store will be facilitated on top of a configured persistent data store.

We've discussed the individual components and how the system will operate to serve the requirements. The business aspects of the application are important as well; we want to eventually earn money from our systems. Some examples for revenue generation could be offering URL analytics or a custom URL domain for paid users. Analytics in itself is a big portion of the URL shortener system; the entire end-to-end analytics pipeline is not in the scope of this book. But in the next section, we'll shed some light on how custom domain support can be built into the system.

Custom Domain Support

One of the requirements of the system is to build an extensible system that can expose the APIs to third-party clients—in short, a multitenant system. For example, assume that Google Drive leverages Bitly services to shorten URLs, but Google wants to share custom Google short URLs with users rather than Bitly short URLs.

Enabling custom domain support in the system is somewhat similar to maintaining multiple URL shortener systems, each with different domain names. The important point to consider here is whether the system has virtual (or logical) separation or physical separation. *Physical separation* means deploying multiple systems in parallel, each serving a specific domain, and *virtual separation* means the same system caters to all the clients, with internal code separation or configurations.

> Designing and building multitenant systems requires an extensive thought process on system expectations. This section captures a simplistic version of the thought process.

Let's try to solve this via a single DynamoDB table, which maintains the mappings of short URLs to long URLs. DynamoDB requires a partition key and sort key as part of the primary key, so the system defines:

Partition key = {short URL}

Sort key = {tenant ID}

The `tenant ID` is an identification useful for figuring out different tenants (systems onboarded to the URL shortener system). The `short URL` is created via an API call by the onboarded system, so it is expected to pass the `tenant ID` as part of the request. The `tenant ID` can be created when the system is onboarded, or this can be figured out based on credentials used by the system in the API call. On the get call as well, the `tenant ID` can be derived based on the domain being accessed. The key in the cache store should be created with a combination of `short URL` and `tenant ID` for easy retrievals.

We can definitely create different tables per tenant, but a careful decision should be made based on the number of onboarded systems and their scale of operations. We can take a hybrid approach, often referred to as *cell-based architecture*. Each cell is responsible for serving a set of onboarded tenants, and the system maintains the mapping for which cell serves a particular tenant. Cells can operate independently because they don't share the data between them. Another thing to consider in this architecture is load balancing between the cells; one cell might just onboard a single tenant, but another cell might include 10 tenants, depending on the scale requirements.

We have discussed multiple components and considerations for the URL shortener system. Now, let's combine the components so that they work together, and discuss the launch of the product on the AWS cloud.

Launching the System on AWS

Refer to Figure 14-4 to review the entire system design. In these sections, we'll discuss deploying this proposed system architecture on the AWS cloud. We'll start with Day 0 architecture and use AWS services that are easy to deploy and require less expertise. Then, we'll move on to scaling the architecture.

> To simplify the diagrams, the services introduced in our system design diagrams may not include a load balancer or API gateway to front the application. You can always assume that the service includes an LB or any similar component to distribute load into multiple instances of the application.

Day Zero Architecture

As mentioned, the system should be designed based on the Make It Work, Make It Right, Make It Fast principle, and thinking of those potential 10 million users from the start is not worth it. Day 0 and Day N architecture is a general paradigm followed in Part III. AWS presented a series of sessions (2013 (*https://oreil.ly/youtube-2013*), 2014 (*https://oreil.ly/youtube-2014*), 2015 (*https://oreil.ly/youtube-2015*), 2016 (*https://oreil.ly/youtube-2016*), 2017 (*https://oreil.ly/youtube-2017*), 2018 (*https://oreil.ly/youtube-2018*), 2019 (*https://oreil.ly/youtube-2019*), 2022 (*https://oreil.ly/youtube-2022*), 2023 (*https://oreil.ly/youtube-2023*)) as part of AWS re:Invent, and we want to extract the recommended guidelines and strategies for you to follow to scale from the first user to more than 10 million users.

The general idea is to start with a monolithic application deployed on an EC2 machine with all the components, such as the web server, application execution logic, and database, as shown in Figure 14-6.

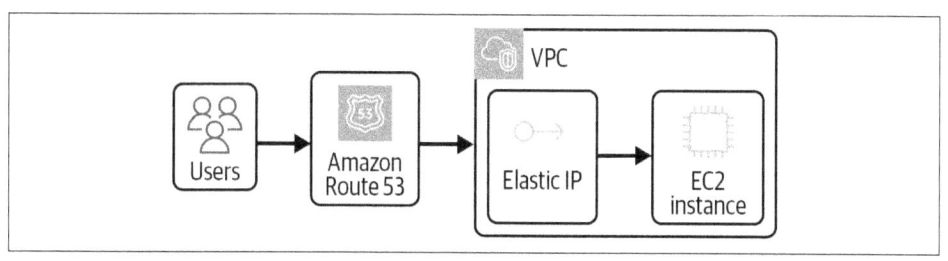

Figure 14-6. Day 0 architecture

This works well for a very few number of users as you roll out the application for experimentation and gather feedback. There are a couple of issues associated with this architecture that should be addressed as the system starts receiving more traffic:

- This is a single application doing everything. It's recommended to avoid putting too many eggs in one basket in order to avoid disruption.

- This has a single point of failure; if the EC2 instance goes down, the application is not available, and user state stored in the database is lost.

A few suggestions to improve the architecture are to separate out the database (with a primary and standby instance (*https://oreil.ly/4oh09*)) and introduce at least two EC2 instances behind an ELB spread across AZs for handling the failover, as shown in Figure 14-7.

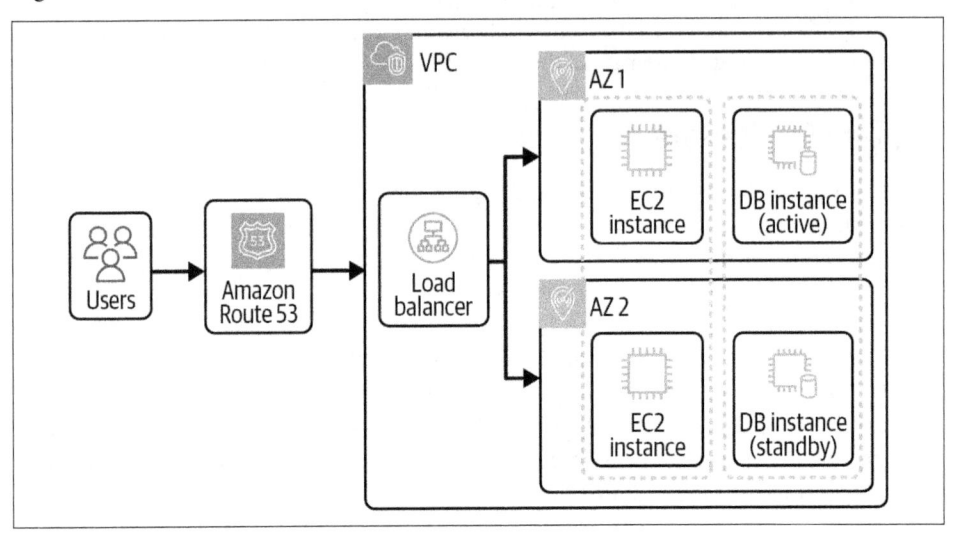

Figure 14-7. Day 0 architecture with improved availability

Spreading the EC2 instances and database instances across multiple AZs makes the architecture more resilient and prevents data loss and downtime. As the user base grows further—say that more than 10,000 customers are accessing the platform regularly—the load on the EC2 instances as well as the database also grows, making them less performant. We can follow these recommendations to scale out the architecture further:

Autoscaling
Introduce autoscaling for EC2 instances. Autoscaling ensures that instances are automatically added or removed based on the traffic without manual intervention.

Database read replicas
The number of read requests (get a long URL for a short URL) are far greater than the number of write requests (short URL creation). Adding read replicas to the database offloads the load from the primary database instance and distributes

the load. The primary instance can focus on the write operations, and all the read traffic can be served by the read replicas in the cluster.

Caching

There are a few URLs that are heavily accessed, so it doesn't make sense to hit the database for the same query again and again. The system can be further optimized by introducing a caching layer in front of the read replicas. The system first checks for short URL mapping in the cache and moves to checking the entry in the database if that is not present. Appropriate expiration policies and cache invalidation strategies (see Chapter 4) should ensure that URLs that are not frequently accessed are moved out of the cache and that data in the cache is fresh and relevant.

The architecture in Figure 14-7 can be improved by integrating these suggestions, as shown in Figure 14-8.

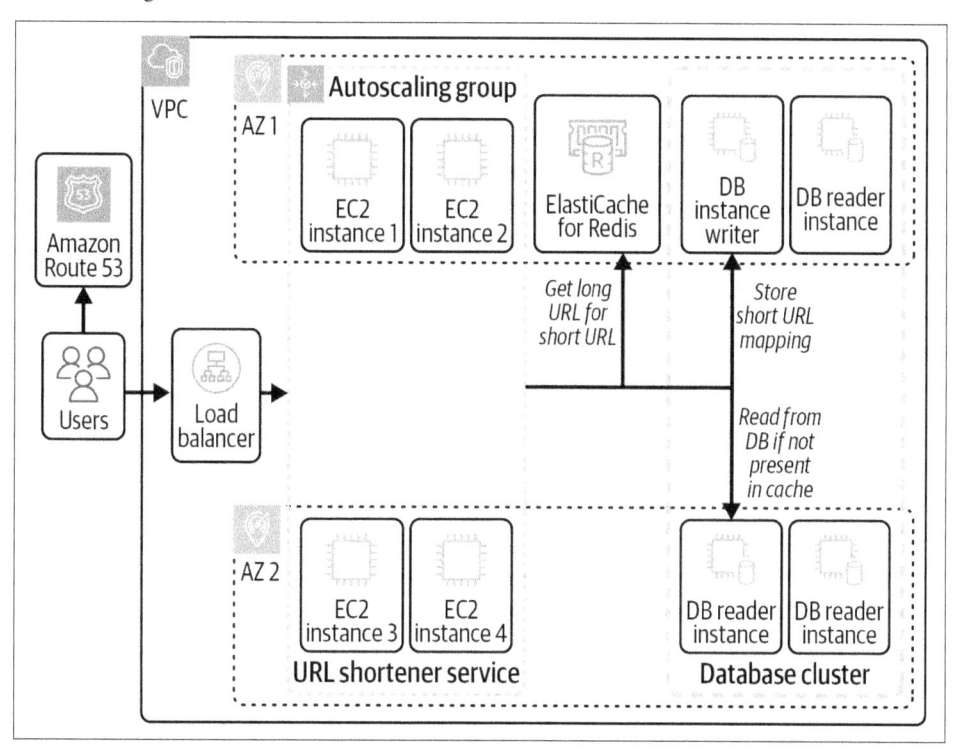

Figure 14-8. Scaling the architecture for more than 10,000 users

We should continuously evaluate the nature of services we're using. Multiple fully managed solutions are available in the AWS cloud (such as Amazon RDS or Amazon Aurora), and we can choose one based on our expertise and the amount of operational overload our organization can bear.

Expecting further growth on the system, we can move the caching layer closer to customers by introducing a CDN (such as Amazon CloudFront). The more frequently accessed short URLs can be directly served from CloudFront instead of hitting the backend servers with the request. CloudFront can also be used to serve any static content for faster load times, such as frontend website components like images, CSS, and JavaScript.

AWS cloud has evolved over the years and has simplified the developer experience to launch products without the need for too much expertise. With so many managed services and serverless offerings available, application deployment has become much easier, with very little to zero maintenance overhead.

A simple software application generally involves three components (or tiers): the frontend, the backend, and the database. For the frontend tier, AWS offers Amplify for building web and mobile applications. AWS Amplify reduces the go-to-market to a large extent by removing a lot of operational overhead with features like authentication, analytics, and push notifications. See the AWS documentation for a full list of features (*https://oreil.ly/YoGVL*).

There are a wide array of compute options on AWS, as discussed in Chapter 11, and we'll choose the simplest deployment option for the Day 0 architecture. One of the options is using AWS Lambda to host the application logic without the worry of infrastructure management, as shown in Figure 14-9.

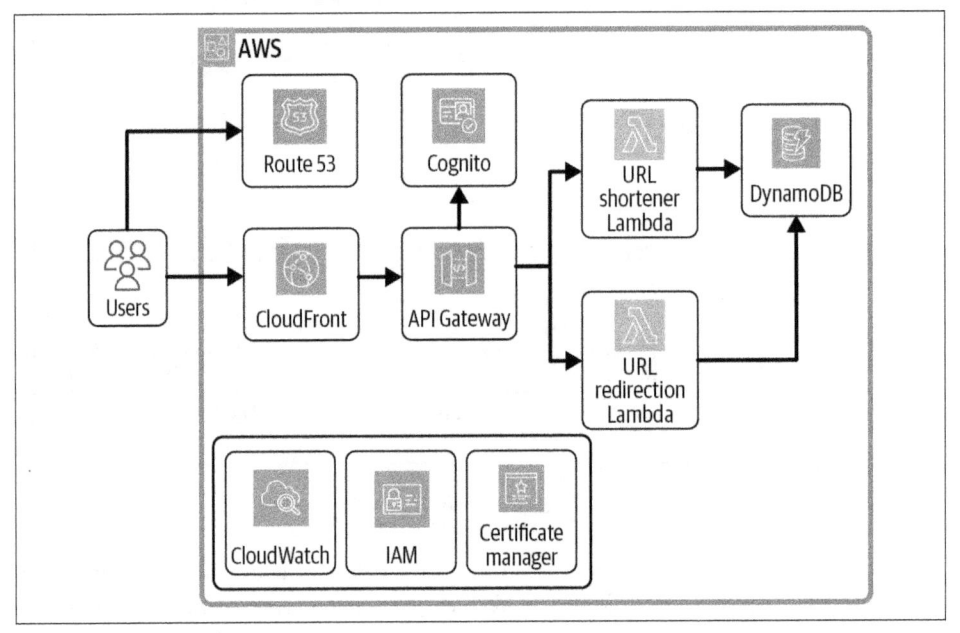

Figure 14-9. URL shortener service on Day 0

As we're proposing to use Lambda for operations on the URL, we can choose to deploy separate Lambdas based on APIs or a single Lambda handling all the operations. Keep separate Lambdas for the different APIs for clear segregation in the application logic. This also helps with moving these API functions to different compute options in the future if needed. The diagram includes some additional services, such as Amazon CloudWatch for monitoring, Amazon Cognito and AWS IAM for authentication and authorization, Amazon VPC to launch the resources, and AWS Certificate Manager for SSL/TLS certificate management.

Another approach for application deployment can be to use the AWS App Runner service (*https://oreil.ly/JaRfp*) to fully manage deployment of containerized web applications or backend API services, as shown in Figure 14-10. App Runner launches all the resources in the VPC managed by AWS itself.

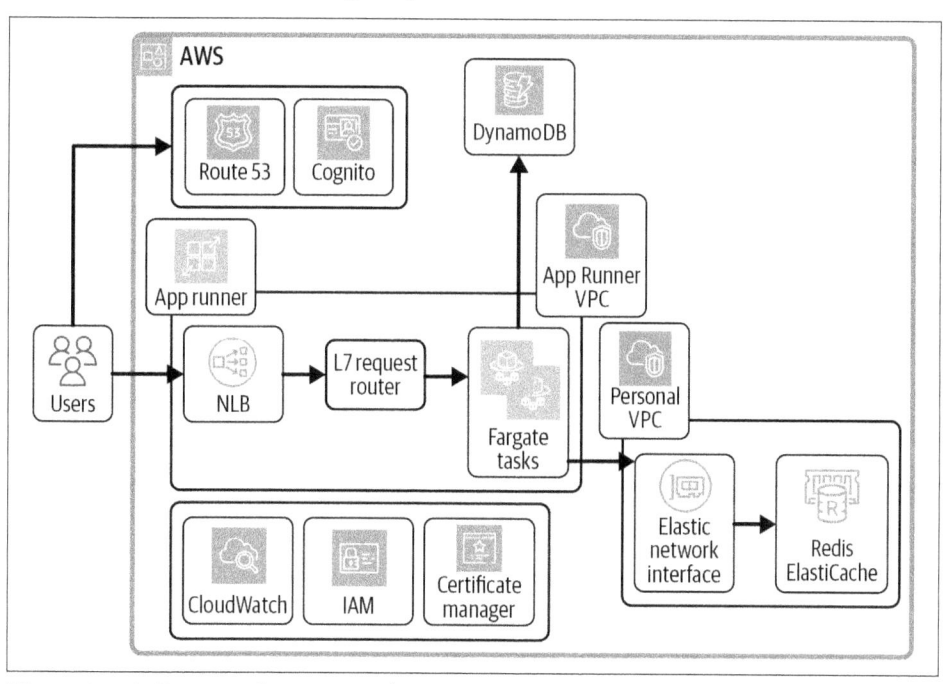

Figure 14-10. Day 0 architecture with AWS App Runner

AWS App Runner abstracts all the components, and customers just need to focus on application development. It is built with a combination of ECS Fargate, autoscaling, ELB, and ECR, and it supports Python, Node.js, Java, Go, Rails, PHP, and .Net as language runtimes. Customers are required to specify a GitHub source code repository or an ECR image, and App Runner takes all the responsibility of application deployment as ECS Fargate tasks. The App Runner CreateService API (*https://oreil.ly/EN17q*) returns a secure URL that can be used to access the service APIs.

Looking at the overall architecture, the user request is routed to the NLB after domain resolution via Route 53 and then forwarded to an application L7 request router, which further redirects to ECS Fargate tasks. We also added Amazon ElastiCache in the diagram to showcase the connectivity (*https://oreil.ly/xCOGs*) between the AWS App Runner VPC and the customer-managed VPC. ElastiCache is helpful for caching the most frequent get calls for mapping short URLs to long URLs and reduces the load on persistent databases with an improvement in the query performance. App Runner can also be configured to accept traffic via a customer-managed personal VPC (a private VPC in an AWS account) by using the AWS PrivateLink endpoint.

There is always the possibility that the Day 0 architecture system will face some bottlenecks as it serves more user traffic and features, so let's now think about how we can scale.

Scaling to Millions and Beyond

With our Day 0 architecture, we try to launch the product without planning too far ahead and choose the technologies we're most familiar with instead of trying out something very new that will include a learning curve. In short, time to market should be minimal. Let's consider the example of a compute platform. There are multiple options, such as AWS Lambda, Amazon EC2, Amazon ECS, and Amazon EKS. If you're most comfortable with Amazon EKS and have prior experience with it, choose that option as a compute platform to start.

We'll now dig deeper into the architectures diagrammed in Figures 14-9 and 14-10 to identify any issues and address them so as to ensure the system's high availability. Let's start our discussion with observability and then move on to the storage and compute counterparts.

Observability

We discussed the importance of metrics and alarms in Chapter 12. To identify bottlenecks, we recommend setting proper metrics and alarms via tools like Amazon CloudWatch and AWS X-Ray. The AWS X-Ray service helps with request tracing in a distributed system architecture as well as figuring out which component is taking more time in processing. As we identify specific components causing issues in the overall system, we can dig deeper to figure out a resolution. Alarms play an important role in identifying critical issues; example alarms could be LONG_URL_REDIRECTION_ERRORS (an alarm is activated if errors are greater than 10 per minute for a continuous five minutes) or SHORT_URL_CREATION_FAILURE (an alarm is activated if the short URL creation API fails above the defined threshold).

Storage layer

The system is using Amazon DynamoDB as a data store to maintain the URL mappings. We don't have to worry about the scaling capabilities of DynamoDB as it is managed completely by AWS. To begin with, we can utilize on-demand capacity mode, and as we figure out traffic patterns, provisioned mode with autoscaling can be used to reduce costs. The application can be launched in multiple AWS regions, and DynamoDB global tables can be used to ensure that data is replicated across the regions. A key consideration for global tables is that there is approximately one second of replication lag between two or more regions (*https://oreil.ly/v1dCW*), so it is possible that a short URL might not be available in another region as soon as it is created.

> At re:Invent 2024, Amazon DynamoDB announced (*https://oreil.ly/ 29MT2*) it was launching support for strong consistency reads in multiregion global tables. The read and write latency tends to be higher compared to eventual consistency but can be useful if strong consistency is a business requirement.

For URLs generated by popular users, the read traffic can be really huge, so there is no point in serving all read queries directly from the database. DynamoDB guarantees single-digit millisecond latency on direct key operations, but to make it even more seamless and bring down latency to microseconds, we can add a caching layer on top of DynamoDB, such as Amazon ElastiCache or Amazon DAX, to improve read performance. The improvement in latency also depends on network latency. Realistically, it could be around 5–10 ms with caching solutions incorporated. The caching layer on top of the database also helps reduce database load and optimize costs.

An key consideration for any system you're designing with DynamoDB as your storage option is justifying the requirement for caching with DAX or ElastiCache—which one should you use? The ideal choice may be DAX since it is specifically built for DynamoDB to improve query read performance, but ElastiCache may be a better choice if the queries are already being served by it for any other use case or if you're more familiar with the technology. This reduces integration effort into newer technology, saving implementation bandwidth. It is always a good idea to perform benchmarking tests to compare two technologies to support a technical decision because, in the end, we need a combination of low latency and a cost-efficient solution. For increased traffic, we recommend distributed cache (such as Redis in cluster mode) to spread out the workload on the cache and increase response times.

> The idea of caching holds true for any database type for serving frequent queries. In addition to these, we should reevaluate the data-access patterns and the possibility of improvement of (for example) slow database queries (or API requests) and query timeout handling. Database federation and sharding also become important with increasing scale in the case of relational databases.

Compute layer

For the compute layer, we preferred AWS Lambda in Figure 14-9 and AWS App Runner in Figure 14-10 to avoid the setup of Amazon EC2 and reduce operational burden, but can Lambda or App Runner scale to millions of customers? Lambda automatically scales per traffic requirements without any customer intervention. However, the problem we might face is p100 latency, which can increase from time to time due to cold-start issues. We discussed a couple of solutions to overcome the cold-start problem in Chapter 11, such as provisioned concurrency, which can help address the latency bottleneck.

App Runner allows a maximum of 25 instances per service and a maximum of 200 concurrent requests per instance, leading to 5,000 concurrent requests per service. See the documentation on AWS limits (*https://oreil.ly/08gMc*) for updated information on service quotas. The limit on the number of requests can become a bottleneck per our scale considerations in "System Scale" on page 357.

> Concurrent requests per instance differ from requests per second. Essentially, an instance can serve 10 requests in a second if an API takes an execution time of 100 ms. We recommend optimization of application code along with keeping an eye on managed services quotas.

A point to consider here is that the limits can be increased in the future by AWS, and this should not prevent us from launching the first version of the product. AWS cloud offerings and open source solutions evolve, and cloud providers innovate on the behalf of their customers, so it is possible that App Runner will be able to support much higher scale with lower cost in the future. Remember that no architecture is considered final, and we can always reevaluate and reiterate in case of any bottlenecks, as shown in the software lifecycle in Figure 14-11.

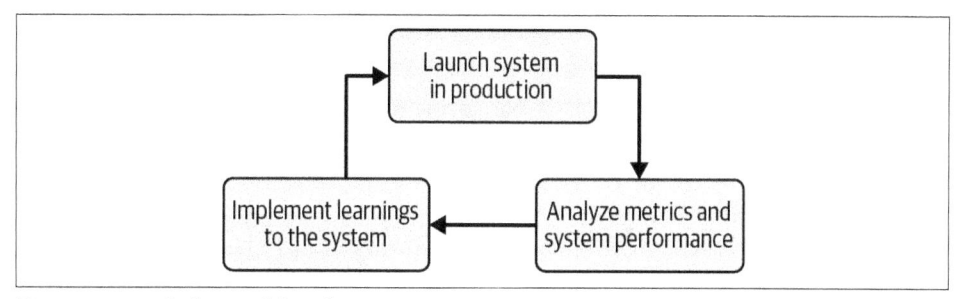

Figure 14-11. Software lifecycle

Here are a few things to consider to scale the compute part of your system:

- Consider migrating to unmanaged versions of services, such as moving to Amazon ECS EC2 from Amazon ECS Fargate, to have more control over hardware configurations. This can prove to be a cheaper alternative in the long run when operating at a huge scale.
- The system will have autoscaling in place to handle any increased load during peak times. The ASGs should be in different AZs to withstand AZ downtimes. In the case of managed systems like ECS Fargate, AWS takes care of deploying the system into multiple AZs to ensure availability. Take this into consideration if you're managing the systems.

Now, let's incorporate all these concepts and present the final architecture on AWS.

Day N Architecture

We're using a single AWS account to host all the services in the architecture—this can be evolved further as necessary to host services in different AWS accounts or to take any other approach of account separation, as we discussed in the section "Getting Started with AWS" on page 222 in Chapter 9. Note that using multiple AWS accounts can increase the cost of data flow across the services, and shared databases can become difficult to manage, though it can make the responsibility of each account simpler with clear boundaries.

Expanding the discussion from Chapter 9, another degree of isolation is at the VPC level. If all the applications are created in the same AWS account, are they present in the same VPC or different VPCs? If they are in the same VPC, are they hosted in the same subnet or in different subnets? The resources should definitely be launched in different subnets (even for a single application) to ensure high availability across the AZs. Launching all applications in a single VPC helps reduce network costs but requires extra care with managing the security of interapplication communications. The rules can be managed by NACLs, and we recommend maintaining a limited number of rules. The rules are evaluated one by one, and a large number of rules can compromise network efficiency by taking more time to evaluate (as compared to all rules being evaluated in parallel).

Our URL shortener system architecture can include five microservices for serving simplistic functional requirements:

Frontend service
: Receives the customer traffic and redirects to specific service VPCs per the operation

URL creator service
: Creates URLs

URL reader service
: Redirects from short URLs to long URLs

KGS
: Generates unique keys to be used as short URLs

Data management service
: A thin layer of CRUD APIs between the databases and services in the architecture. This is introduced into the architecture because the DynamoDB and ElastiCache are accessible to two systems.

Evaluate the architecture from time to time to figure out if the application should be split further (microservice architecture) to address the increasing scale.

Returning to the URL shortener system design, we are looking at a huge scale, so deploying the applications in separate VPCs should ensure proper isolation. Another architecture pattern followed by organizations is deploying multiple microservices on the same EKS cluster (in the same VPC). This makes sense at a limited scale, but in the context of Day N architecture, we recommend using separate EKS clusters (*https://oreil.ly/c9XMm*) for service deployments for complete resource isolation (revisit Chapter 7 for Kubernetes architecture).

> It is not always true that the AWS cloud components can introduce bottlenecks with increasing scale—it could also be the application code introducing bugs and bottlenecks into the system. For example, the DynamoDB key schema worked well on Day 0 but is not performing very well with increased traffic. We can use tools like Amazon CodeGuru Reviewer (*https://oreil.ly/-sTwn*) and Amazon DevOps Guru (*https://oreil.ly/kbPpu*) to identify potential bottlenecks and then work toward resolution.

Figure 14-12 shows the final picture of the architecture of the URL shortener system.

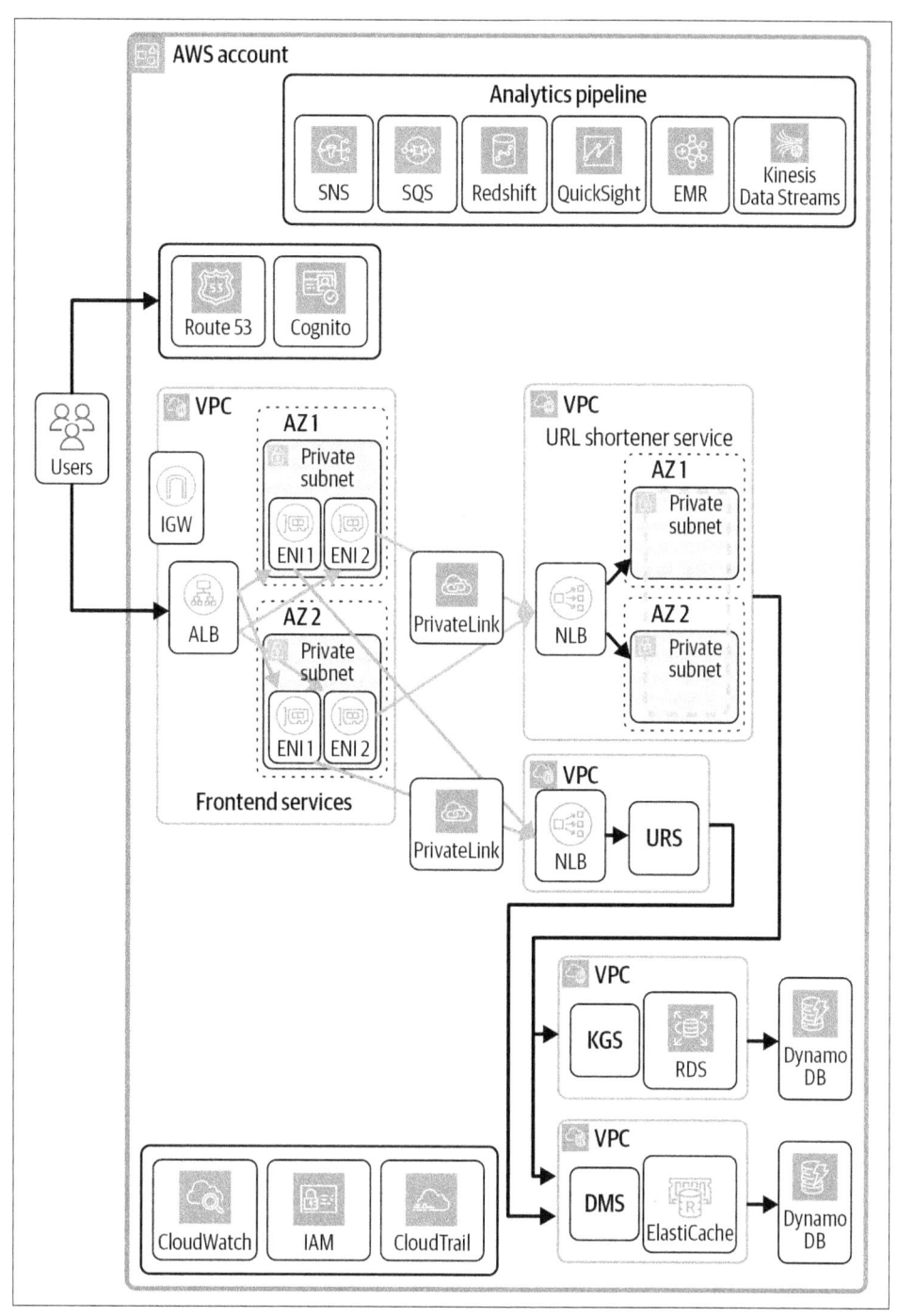

Figure 14-12. URL shortener system

Here are some additional points to keep in mind, which we left out of the diagram to
make it cleaner:

- The public subnet is needed in the frontend service for internet connectivity via
  IGW or putting resources such as bastion host.
- The services residing in different VPCs require a mechanism to connect them
  to one another. AWS Transit Gateways provides bidirectional communication
  between the VPCs; AWS PrivateLinks provides unidirectional communication.
  The CIDR blocks of the VPCs should not overlap in the case of Transit Gateways,
  but PrivateLink doesn't take this into consideration.
- The microservices also interact with AWS services that are present in our owned
  VPC. These services should be accessed via PrivateLink (*https://oreil.ly/ha5qp*)
  instead of NAT gateways. This ensures that the traffic doesn't go over the internet, which adds to application security and minimizes operation latency. NAT
  gateway should only be used when an explicit connection to the internet is
  needed.
- Other ways for microservices running on Amazon ECS to establish communication with one another can be via ECS Service Discovery (*https://oreil.ly/F3hRO*), AWS App Mesh (*https://oreil.ly/wa8D5*), and ECS Service Connect
  (*https://oreil.ly/dg7Iz*).
- Amazon ElastiCache is used as a caching layer on top of DynamoDB to serve
  read queries faster. ElastiCache will remove the least used data per the cache
  eviction policy. We can introduce an additional AWS Lambda function (invoked
  on a DynamoDB data deletion event) to ensure data is removed from the cache
  if it is removed from DynamoDB. This can happen in the case of any custom
  expiration of the short URL by the users. Instead of the Lambda function, we can
  implement a consumer in the data management service itself that can handle this
  responsibility.

> It's possibile that the DDB entry is not deleted at the exact time
> mentioned in TTL (*https://oreil.ly/p23Xd*). Explore alternatives
> if the deletion should happen at exact time specified.

- The architecture presents deployment in a single AWS region. We recommend
  creating all the infrastructure via code for easy replication to other regions if
  required. The system resources are deployed in multiple AZs to ensure increased
  redundancy in case of AZ downtimes.
- The main reason for separating the URL creator service and the URL reader
  service is the huge difference in traffic patterns. A separate service ensures
  independent scaling and clear separation of concern.

- The system architecture should ensure that the increased traffic is from actual users and throttle any unwanted traffic at the API Gateway or ELB level using AWS services like AWS WAF (*https://oreil.ly/zz2xp*) and AWS Shield (*https://oreil.ly/mqEJ8*) or by deploying custom solutions. This can be handled in the frontend service.

This is not an exhaustive list of issues to take care of while serving customers. We will cover additional topics in the rest of Part III. Take a holistic view of the learnings from Part III when deploying systems in production to ensure high standards.

Conclusion

We started off Part III with a URL shortener system, which is a popular problem presented at interviews and a system we commonly use in our daily lives. The gist of any new system design is to start with requirement clarifications and system boundaries. You should clearly know what a system is expected to do and what a system will never do—this helps you make better design decisions.

Once the requirements and scope of the system are finalized, we move on to identifying the high-level components. The scale a system is supposed to serve is an important factor for identifying these components, along with the business use case. A system operational with 10,000 users might not work the same way with 100,000 users. Table 14-1 summarizes scaling the application architecture from zero users to millions of users.

We have moved through multiple possible approaches to building a URL shortener service, discussing the pros and cons of each approach along with potential AWS cloud components we can use. We brought in many of the AWS services we discussed in Part II, and we acknowledge that recognizing which one to choose for your specific use case could be difficult. We recommend choosing a technology that will take the minimum time to understand and deploy—down the line, it can be modified or replaced by another technology if needed.

System design is an iterative process, so start small and enhance your systems on the go as needed. Don't think too far ahead because your priorities may shift after 5 or 10 years. In the next chapter, we'll design a web crawler and search engine system like Google search using AWS components.

Table 14-1. Scaling from zero to millions of users

Step	Why	How	Benefits
Basic monolithic setup	This is the simplest architecture to start with since it consolidates all application components in a single instance.	Deploy the entire application stack (web server, application server, and database) on a single server or instance.	Low initial complexity and cost, making it easy to develop and deploy for small-scale applications
Set up multi-AZ database for high availability	Ensuring database availability across multiple AZs provides resilience against data loss and downtime.	In AWS, for example, you can set up a multi-AZ database using Amazon RDS, which replicates data automatically to a standby in another AZ.	High availability and minimal downtime in the event of a database or AZ failure
Add read replicas to handle increased read traffic	As the application grows, read requests can overload the primary database. Read replicas allow you to offload these requests and distribute the load.	Set up read replicas in the same region or in different regions to improve read performance for users in various geographic areas.	Enhanced read scalability and database performance by handling read requests separately from write operations
Add caching in front of the database	Direct database queries for high-traffic or frequently requested data can result in latency and performance degradation. A cache provides faster data access for repeated queries and reduces database strain.	Choose a cache solution: implement a distributed cache like Redis or Memcached. Integrate with the application: add logic to check the cache for data before querying the database. Manage the cache: use expiration policies to ensure data freshness.	Faster response times, reduced load on the database, and scalability by serving data efficiently
Add multiple EC2 instances and an LB for redundancy and scaling	Distributing the application load across multiple instances prevents single points of failure and improves scalability.	Deploy multiple EC2 instances and place them behind an LB that routes traffic evenly across these instances.	Increased fault tolerance, improved redundancy, and the ability to handle larger volumes of incoming traffic
Implement an ASG for elasticity	Autoscaling adjusts the number of running instances according to demand, optimizing resource usage and costs.	Define scaling policies based on metrics like CPU utilization, traffic, or custom application metrics.	Responsive scaling to meet traffic demand while keeping infrastructure costs manageable
Switch to a managed database service for ease of management	Managing databases can be time intensive, and a managed service like Amazon RDS or Amazon Aurora automates routine tasks, such as backups and scaling.	Migrate to a managed database service compatible with your database engine (e.g., MySQL or PostgreSQL).	Reduced operational overhead, automated maintenance, and simplified scaling options
Move static content to Amazon S3 to reduce server load	Offloading static assets (e.g., images, CSS, JavaScript) to Amazon S3 frees up application servers and reduces bandwidth costs.	Store and serve static files from an S3 bucket, and update application URLs to point to the S3 path for static content.	Lower application server load, high availability, and optimized cost for storing and serving static files
Use a CDN for faster content delivery	A CDN improves content load times by caching and delivering static assets from edge locations close to end users.	Use Amazon CloudFront or another CDN to cache S3-hosted content and distribute it to a global network of edge locations.	Reduced latency, improved load times, and a better user experience, especially for global audiences

Step	Why	How	Benefits
Implement IaC for consistency and automation	IaC tools like Terraform or CloudFormation help manage infrastructure in a version-controlled, reproducible manner.	Define infrastructure components such as EC2 instances, databases, and networks in code, enabling automated deployment and consistency.	Simplified, repeatable infrastructure setup and the ability to deploy consistent environments across development, staging, and production
Set up centralized logging and monitoring	Centralized logging and monitoring enable proactive management of application performance and quick identification of issues.	Use tools like Amazon CloudWatch, ELK Stack, or Datadog to centralize logs and monitor metrics across all components.	Improved visibility, real-time alerts for critical issues, and detailed performance insights for optimized troubleshooting and debugging
Use a distributed cache for frequent data access	For high-traffic applications, caching frequently accessed but less frequently updated data reduces database load and response times.	Implement a distributed cache (such as Redis or Memcached) and adjust the application logic to check the cache for data before querying the database.	Faster response times, reduced database load, and improved scalability by offloading frequently accessed data to a dedicated cache
Refactor into microservices (long-term step)	Breaking down a monolithic application into microservices improves flexibility, scalability, and agility.	Identify specific components or functions that can be refactored into independent services, such as user management or billing, and deploy them separately.	Greater scalability, more efficient resource utilization, and faster development cycles with modular, independently deployable services

CHAPTER 15
Designing a Web Crawler and Search Engine

You have planned a get-together with your loved ones during the holiday season. You love cooking and have decided to cook all the food by yourself, but you don't have the recipes for the dishes you wish to prepare. What is the best possible resolution here? You could ask your friends if they have the recipes or go looking through cookbooks, but a simple yet effective solution is using Google search. Google looks across the internet and finds the best results for how to prepare a specific dish. How does Google go through such a vast sea of information and find the perfect answer? In this chapter, we'll try to figure this out by digging into the architecture of such search systems.

At a high level, the entire system consists of two subsystems: a web crawler and a search engine, as shown in Figure 15-1. A *web crawler* is essentially software responsible for crawling through web content. Content on the internet is growing exponentially, and web crawlers need to regularly crawl the content to maintain the most updated results. The *search engine* sits on top of content accumulated by web crawlers and stores it in such a way that it can look for user-searched keywords in the content and present the most useful results.

With this basic understanding, let's start by gathering the functional and nonfunctional requirements of the proposed system.

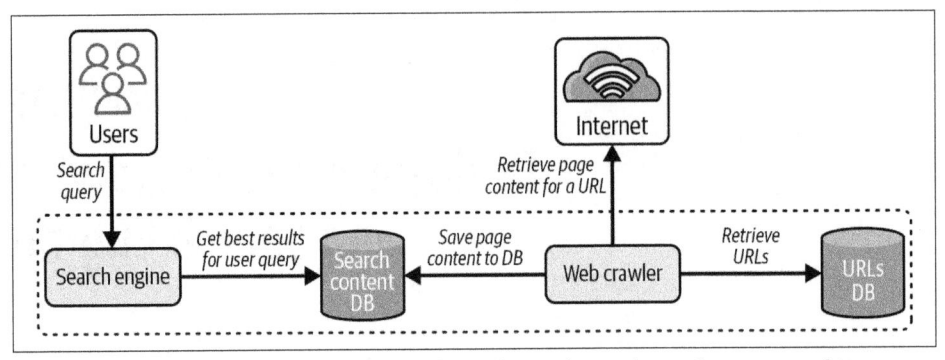

Figure 15-1. Ten-thousand-foot view of the web crawler and search engine architecture

System Requirements

Web crawlers can be used for multiple purposes, so focusing on one use case makes it easy to move in the right direction with our design. For this chapter, content retrieval via search engine is the main problem statement we're trying to solve, but you could also look into other issues, such as web-monitoring tasks like copyright infringement. A web crawler is needed in the system to gather the data, but from the user's perspective, the product is a search engine.

Functional and Nonfunctional Requirements

The functional requirements of the system include:

- Getting the top results (web page title, subtitle, and URL) for a user search query
- Identifying the content freshness rate of the results, which are frequently updated

The NFRs include:

Highly available
    The system can serve user queries most of the time.

Highly reliable
    Queries should be served correctly.

Highly scalable
    The system should be able to handle increasing scale, such as number of webpages and content on those webpages.

Low latency for search queries
    Even with the huge number of pages mapping to a user query, the system should return the most relevant results within milliseconds.

Data freshness
   The underlying storage to serve search queries should be regularly updated.

Data consistency is not highly critical for this use case. A lag in content available on websites and searchable via the search engine is acceptable.

We should also document the system *boundaries*, or what the system is not expected to do. For this use case, that includes:

- The system will not include recommendation and content-relevance algorithms for gathering the search results.
- The search doesn't support near real-time search results—for example, the live score of an ongoing cricket match.

Next, let's jump to the expected scale for this system.

System Scale

The system has two components: the web crawler and the search engine. Both components can be independent systems in themselves, and we'll structure the chapter content to discuss them independently. This makes sense since the requirements of both these systems vary and they are expected to solve different use cases, with the output of one system (the web crawler) being used as input to the other system (the search engine). We'll make some assumptions for each to determine the expected scale of the system.

Web crawler

Important considerations for the web crawler are the number of pages on the web to be crawled and how often these pages need to be crawled. According to a quick Google search, around 1.13 billion websites have been created as of June 2023, and around 200 million of those are active. The web crawler system is only concerned with the active websites. Inside a single website, there can be internal redirects or external redirects to different pages. The external redirects are already counted as part of the 200 million websites, but we need to consider the internal redirects. We'll make assumptions for the average numbers and use the following calculation to determine how much storage we'll need:

Active websites = 200 million

Average pages/website = 50

Total pages = 200 million × 50 = 10 billion

Average page size = 2 MB

Total storage = 2 MB × 10 billion = 20 PB

Web pages can include different forms of content, such as text, images, and videos. The web crawler should only crawl and keep the data that will be used by the search engine. We'll limit the scope of the system to only support text queries in the English language. This will also potentially reduce the storage space—let's say 500 KB per page, amounting to 5 PB of total storage. Another consideration here is the requirement to store the entire page.

> The storage requirement calculated in this book assumes that content is stored in the same format as it is received, but this can certainly vary based on data store selection, data compression algorithms wherever applicable, separate caching data store, and so on.

The content on the internet keeps adding up in the form of new websites and web pages, and the content on existing web pages is constantly updated. The system needs to ensure content freshness so that it stores the most relevant data to offer the ideal search experience.

Let's look into the scale of the search engine system next.

Search engine

What do we estimate the number of requests per second to the search engine system will be? Users open the browser and search with some keywords, and the system should be able to respond with search results that match the search query. Let's consider Google's scale since it is basically the most visited website in the world. Google serves roughly 8.5 billion searches per day (99,000 RPS). To support the search scale, data should be indexed, which requires storage space apart from what we discussed for the web crawler requirements.

We'll work to build a scalable system and talk about key concepts involved in the system, but keep in mind that Google has evolved a lot to support this scale, and it will not be possible to capture all such details in a single chapter. Here are some factors we should consider:

- The search results can vary based on geographical region. For example, a search query with the keywords "latest news" might generate different results in India than it does in the US.
- The system can receive similar search queries from different users, and it should include good caching capabilities to make queries faster.

With these requirements and scale considerations, let's now dig deeper into the design of the system.

Starting with the Design

As we did in "System Requirements" on page 388, we'll discuss the system design analysis for the web crawler and the search engine systems separately. Before we dig deeper into the design, we recommend reading through the Google architecture paper published in 1997 (*http://infolab.stanford.edu/~backrub/google.html*). This paper nicely captures the high-level architecture of web crawler and search engine systems as shown in Figure 15-2 and serves as the starting point for the system-design analysis.

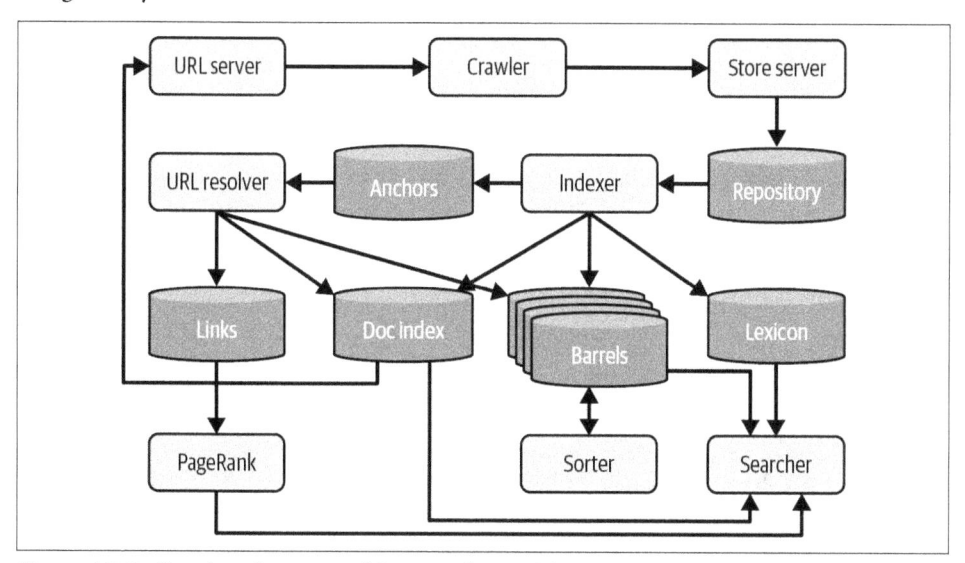

Figure 15-2. Google reference architecture from 1997

Here is a summary of the architecture presented in the technical paper:

1. To start the crawling process, a *URL server* provides a list of URLs to the crawler system to fetch web pages from the internet. Each crawler maintains its own DNS cache for faster lookups.

2. The *store server* receives the web pages gathered by the crawler, and it compresses (using ZLIB compression) (*https://oreil.ly/aPr60*) and stores the HTML content of every web page to a *repository*. The repository data structure is an independent component and can be used to build all the other data structures in the design.

3. The *indexer* reads the web pages from the repository, uncompresses them, and parses the content. The functions performed by the indexer include:

- Parsing of content to ensure removal of any erroneous or unwanted content, such as non-ASCII characters.
- Assigning an identification, called a *doc ID*, to any new URLs (web links) found by parsing the web pages. All the important information about links, such as where the link is pointing from and to and the text of the link, is stored in data structures referred to as *anchors*.
- Converting every word into a *word ID* using an in-memory hash table called a *lexicon*.
- Storing the occurrences of the word IDs in the document in a set of *barrels* in the form of partially sorted forward indexes called *hits*. The hits include the actual word, the position of the word in the document, the approximate font size, and capitalization. These characteristics help determine the relevance of words as compared to other words in the document; for instance, a large font size at the beginning of the document can represent the heading of the document.

4. The *URL resolver* reads the anchor files and converts relative URLs into absolute URLs, which map to the doc IDs, with these additional responsibilities:
   - Putting the anchor text into the forward index barrel associated with the doc ID that the anchor is pointed to
   - Generating a database of links that are pairs of doc IDs; the link database is used to compute page rank for all the documents

5. The sorter sorts the forward barrels (organized by doc ID) by word ID to generate the inverted index for the title, anchor hits, and full text. The sorter further divides a barrel into baskets of short or full barrels based on whether they can fit into main memory.

6. A web server runs the searcher to serve the search queries. To process any search query, it parses the query, converts words into word IDs, seeks to the beginning of the doc list for every word in the search query in the short barrel, finds the document matching all the words, and computes the rank of the document. It then performs the same set of operations on the full barrel. Finally, it sorts the matching rank documents and returns the top one thousand as the response.

> Forward and inverted indexes are terms often used in search use cases. The *forward index* is a mapping of the doc ID to a set of words or keywords. The *inverted index* is an inverse mapping of the forward index containing the mapping from keywords to doc ID.

Designing the Web Crawler

We'll expand on the architecture from the previous section to design a scalable web crawler system. The first thing we'll need to consider is the list of URLs that the system should start with (the *seed URLs*) for crawling the web. How should this list be maintained, and how should it be updated on a regular basis? There is no unified source that can be used to retrieve all the URLs to be used in the seed URL list. The only way to build this list is by starting out with the most-known domains (for example, the one thousand most popular domains) and then constantly updating the list on web crawls. The steps to building this list are:

1. Create a platform for new website owners to submit their site details to make them available for crawling.
2. Retrieve the list of website links or references in the website being crawled.
3. When a user queries for a new website, check this website and add it to the list.

The crawling frequency of the web crawler system is not fixed and can vary from website to website. Historical analysis of the website is one way to determine the crawling frequency. This helps determine if the website is frequently or rarely updated. News websites can be frequently updated with fresh content, but personal websites are usually updated more rarely.

Let's discuss one potential architecture based on web page recrawling at a fixed, regular time interval, as shown in Figure 15-3. The architecture describes a potential implementation idea and has the following steps:

1. The seed URLs database stores the URL with zero TTL or an appropriate TTL so that not all URLs are pushed to the queue at the same time. Implementation of change data capture upon TTL expiration can vary based on database choice; for example, DynamoDB streams can be leveraged.
2. Upon TTL expiration, URLs are pushed to the queue, and the web crawler consumes them.
3. The web crawler retrieves the content of a web page from the internet and sends it for additional processing, such as building indexes.
4. The web crawler saves the URL again to the database with a new TTL. As the web crawler processes the web page content, extra web links are included, which are also pushed to the queue for processing.

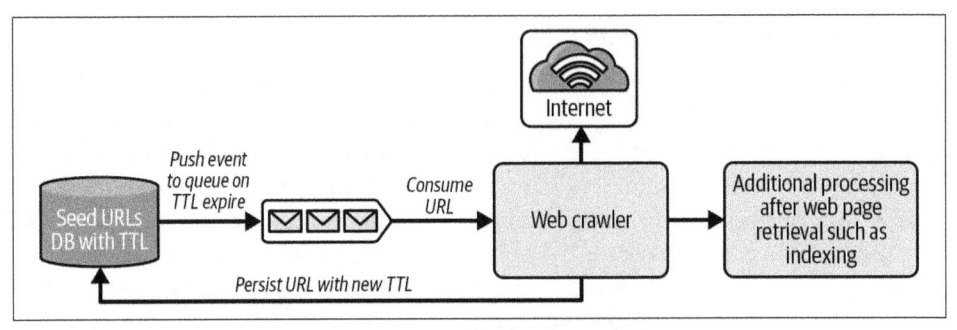

Figure 15-3. Recrawling of web pages based on configured TTL

A web crawler system should have a change-detection algorithm deployed to efficiently figure out if the content is updated without crawling it entirely. Here are few ways to accomplish that:

- ETag (entity tag) (*https://oreil.ly/EvsmZ*) is an HTTP response header that uniquely represents a requested source and is typically a hash of the content. The ETag value can be used to determine if the requested web page has changed. The Last-Modified HTTP response header (*https://oreil.ly/VosmW*) containing the date and time of the last modification is another way of knowing when the resource was last updated.
- Content comparison can validate content modification. However, it is definitely not an efficient process to compare word by word—this is essentially the same as reading the entire web page. A more efficient solution is figuring out specific portions of the page where the content is updated. One such solution is a Merkle tree (discussed in Chapter 3), which efficiently evaluates the updated section; it is generally used by databases like Dynamo (*https://oreil.ly/_Esxg*) to resolve anti-entropy among multiple replicas. Google crawler uses the Simhash algorithm (*https://oreil.ly/Su2gr*) to help figure out content duplication of web pages.
- Occasionally, a website will become popular because a celebrity shared it over social media. The web crawler can detect such traffic surges, then recrawl the website for any content update.

Earlier, we mentioned a queue that can be used to push the URL for a web crawler to consume. The TTL approach based on time is not generally used directly in the large-scale web crawlers because the page to be crawled next can depend on many factors other than TTL. The TTL factor in web crawler terms is referred to as *politeness*, meaning how frequently a crawler fetches content from the web page server. This can happen too often if the URLs referenced in the web page belong to the same domain. Another important factor is figuring out the high-quality pages that need to be crawled as a priority. The system responsible for determining the next URL to be crawled in the web crawler architecture is generally called the *URL frontier*.

Improving the URL frontier

The previous architecture can be extended to address limitations and takes both priority and politeness into consideration. The architecture is referenced from the Mercator web crawler architecture (*https://oreil.ly/qYVwX*) and is shown in Figure 15-4.

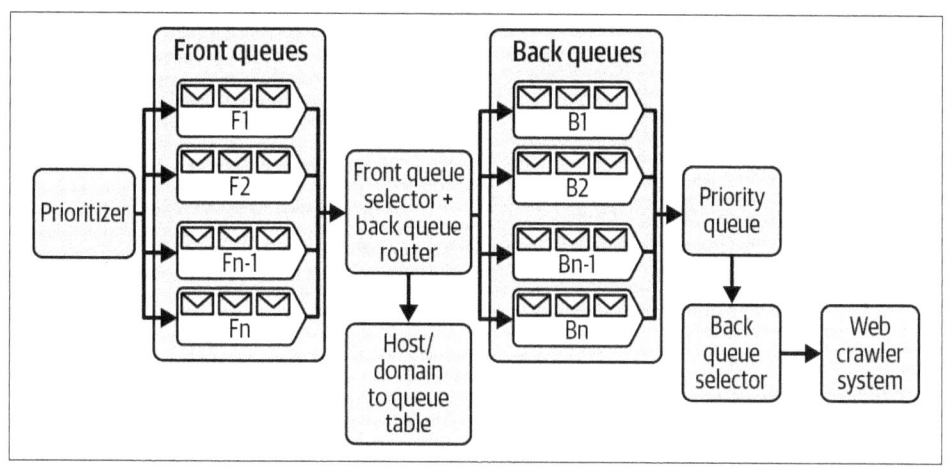

Figure 15-4. URL frontier architecture

The functions of the different components of the URL frontier system are as follows:

Prioritizer and front queues
  The prioritizer and front queues (first in, first out) are responsible for figuring out the priority in which the URL should be crawled by the web crawler system. The prioritizer assigns the priority to the URL from 1 to n, and based on this number, the URL is pushed to a specific front queue. The priority-assigning algorithm can take several factors into consideration, such as percentage change in the web page between two crawls, newness of the web page, user traffic on the page, and more.

Front queue selector and back queue router
  This component is responsible for taking the URLs based on the priority and passing them to the back queues. It maintains an additional database to keep domain-to-back-queue numbers to ensure that the URLs from the same host are served via a single back queue. This is done to make sure that a single domain is called once at most (or per the domain configurations at the search engine level (*https://oreil.ly/sq_Pp*)) by the web crawler.

Back queues
  Back queues enforce politeness of the URL to ensure that the web server is not bombarded too frequently (a single request at a time, with some lag between the requests). The number of back queues should be more than the number of

crawler threads available in the system to ensure that every thread is busy at any given time. This can be configured as three times the number of threads to start and later tuned with proper performance testing of the system.

Priority queue
The priority queue is a heap implementation that stores one entry for each back queue and provides the time at which a particular host (or domain) can be contacted again. The heap is created upon min-heap implementation, and the root element provides the URL that can be contacted first.

Back queue selector
The back queue selector interacts with the heap to take out the root containing the domain with the minimum time and then take out the URL from that particular back queue. Once the URL is crawled by the crawler, the heap is updated with the new time to configure a new politeness value.

The FIFO queues in the architectures keep a fixed number of URLs in the main memory and store most of the URLs on the disk to support a high crawl rate on commodity hardware. Even with the best machines, disk support is required, considering the scale of the internet. The disk-storage algorithms can become a bottleneck for processing a huge number of URLs due to very frequent reads and writes to the disk, as pointed out in the IRLBot research paper (*https://oreil.ly/Pl1eb*), which tested results with 184,000 new URLs generated per second from crawled web pages.

> The current design and implementation of large-scale web crawlers such as Google and Bing are proprietary and are not available to the general public. We referenced several public research papers along with our own knowledge base to ensure that the web crawler system's scalability could support today's internet scale.

IRLBot suggests the disk repository with the update management (DRUM) algorithm as an algorithm for ensuring URL uniqueness. DRUM maintains k memory arrays, each of size M, and k disk buckets (Q_i) and spreads key-value pairs between them based on the key. The data is moved to disk buckets as memory arrays get filled up. For pages with a lot of sub-URLs (in the millions), the politeness rate limiting can become a bottleneck. IRLBot solves this via the spam tracking and avoidance through reputation (STAR) algorithm. The reputation of a page is calculated based on in-degree links from other domain web pages. There is always a possibility that some web pages don't show much relevance because they are new or have fewer in-degree links, but they should also be crawled to ensure that search engines can support any user queries. This is solved by the budget enforcement with anti-spam tactics (BEAST) algorithm. BEAST maintains an additional queue to all such URLs and keeps reevaluating their relevance to figure out when the URLs should be crawled by the web crawler system.

The web crawler system should also ensure that infinite-loop scenarios are avoided while crawling the web. It can happen that a URL is referenced at multiple places in a single web page (or on multiple web pages during a single crawl of the system) or that a URL contains a reference to itself.

URL uniqueness and duplicate detection

The system needs a mechanism for duplicate URL detection. This can be done by having a separate global database across the crawler machines that maintains the list of URLs visited in a single crawl. Since the query to determine whether the URL is a duplicate needs to be fast and doesn't need to be persisted across the crawls, we can use Redis and store the URLs as keys. The Redis cluster can contain TTL policies associated with a URL (which vary from URL to URL) so that the URL is automatically removed from the cache.

Using Bloom filters is another technique for determining whether a URL was visited or not—the key consideration here is the probabilistic nature of Bloom filters. It is possible that the Bloom filter returns yes for an already-crawled URL, causing a recrawl of the URL.

The crawler will also respect any exclusions on the web server configured in a *robots.txt* file. The *robots.txt* file determines whether a web page is allowed for crawling or whether any specific resource is not to be indexed by search engines. On top of exclusions by the web server, there are exclusions maintained by the web crawler to avoid visiting and indexing content from any blocked websites.

Let's combine all the components we discussed to present a final picture of the web crawler system in Figure 15-5. There are a few additional items to consider for the system:

- The crawler is a multiregion deployment, and performance improves if the crawler crawls from the same location where a website is located. Some sites, such as government websites, are blocked from being accessed from other countries, so then it becomes necessary for the crawler to run in the same region where the site is located.
- The crawler mostly uses the HTTP/1.1 protocol version to retrieve web pages. It can use more recent HTTP versions, such as HTTP/2, depending on whether that's supported by the website. The newer version saves computing resources for both the crawler and the website.
- The content on some websites can be so large that the web crawler always upper-caps on the bandwidth consumption. For example, it will only download 15 MB of content and skip the rest of it.

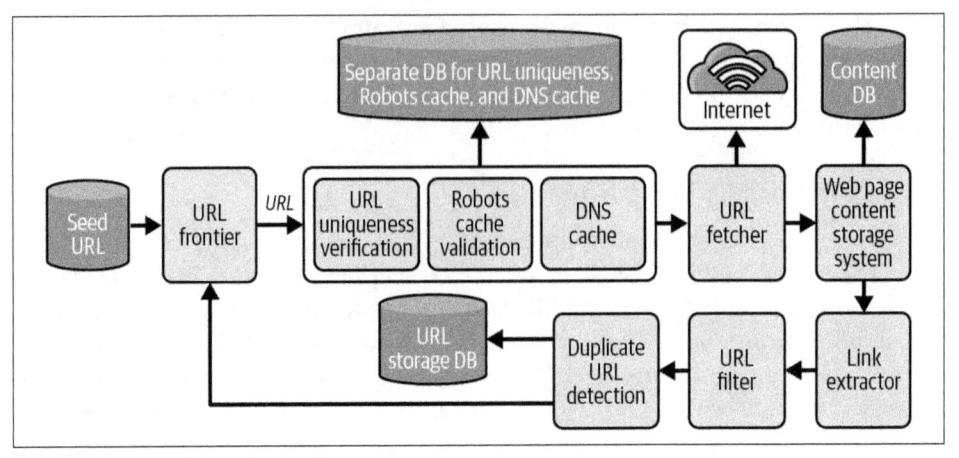

Figure 15-5. Web crawler architecture

The web crawler's job finishes as soon as the web page is downloaded. The search engine system then takes this content as input and indexes it efficiently to serve user search queries. Let's explore the architecture of the search engine system next.

Designing the Search Engine

The search engine system takes a user query as input and provides relevant web pages in response to the query. The web pages are downloaded and stored to a repository (or some kind of database) by the web crawler system, which we discussed in the last section. The search engine should be able to figure out the best matching results for the user search query from this content repository. We'll define a high-level architecture of the search engine system, as shown in Figure 15-6, and then explore each of the components.

After the crawler downloads the web pages to the content store, the *document parser and encoder* is responsible for tasks like parsing the documents and removing unuseful data and then passing the data to the *forward index*. The forward index stores the data, and then it is passed to the *inverted index* for reverse mapping. For any user search query, the query is parsed to the search keywords. The *content relevance system* (such as PageRank) computes the most relevant results and returns them to the user.

You might wonder why we need a forward index in the architecture since the inverted index should be sufficient to serve user queries efficiently, and it's a valid question. The creation of the forward index allows for storing the words as they are parsed from the web page, enabling the inverted index to be a completely independent process that can happen asynchronously. Several different open source solutions have been built to support the inverted-index data structure creation. Let's discuss our options for the search engine system in the next section.

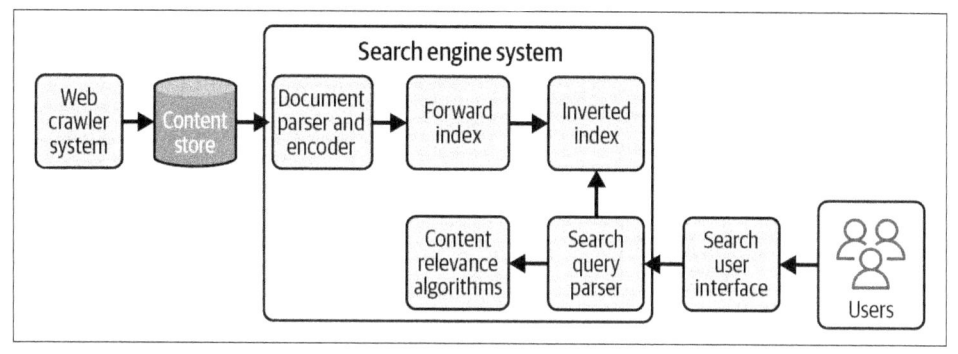

Figure 15-6. High-level architecture of the search engine system

Indexing strategies

We'll start the discussion by exploring the architecture of open source search solutions such as Elasticsearch and Amazon OpenSearch (which we discussed briefly in Chapter 10). Many organizations like Netflix (*https://oreil.ly/GWimh*) use Elasticsearch to build inverted indexes and build search functionality on top of them. Elasticsearch is a nonrelational data store service that can be used to store JSON documents, and Elasticsearch constructs inverted indexes to support search queries on the stored data.

An index is quite similar to an Amazon RDS table. The indexes are further divided into subindexes called *shards* (the shards internally map to the Lucene index (*https://lucene.apache.org*); Elasticsearch is built on top of Lucene). The documents are stored on the shards; a document is like a row in the RDS table. Each shard consists of multiple segments, which are kept in memory (and a transaction log on disk to overcome failures) and are synced to disk in fixed time intervals (referred to as *refresh intervals*). A segment is an immutable data structure and is available for search once it is saved to disk. If a use case requires data to be available for search as soon as it is written, the refresh interval can be configured to a lower value. The smaller segments are merged into a larger segment from time to time, improving the overall search performance (search needs to be performed on a smaller set of segments). We'll discuss shard configurations more in Chapter 18.

To support high availability and read scale, the shards are replicated on multiple data nodes, as shown in Figure 15-7. The data is written to the primary shard on one of the data nodes and then replicated to replica shards asynchronously. The system tries to ensure that primary and replica shards are not colocated on the same data node (given that the Elasticsearch cluster has that number of nodes per the shards configuration).

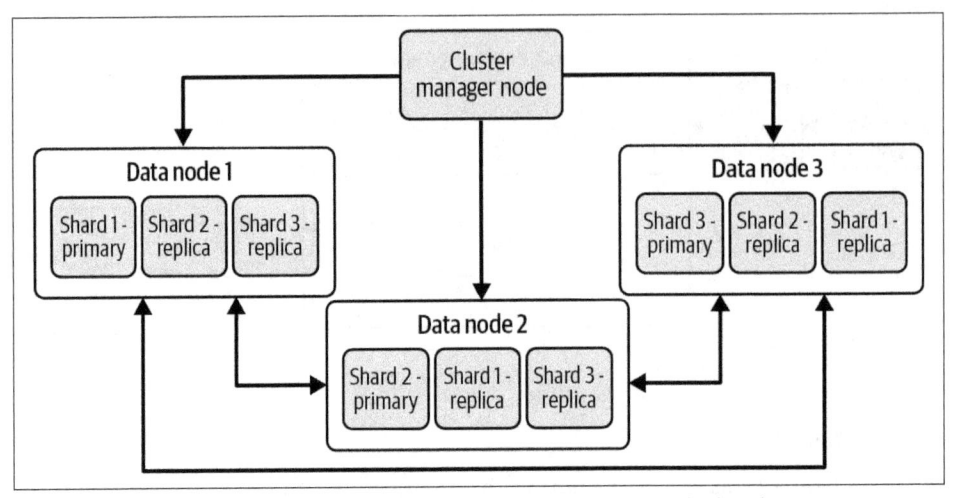

Figure 15-7. Data indexing and replication between Elasticsearch shards

Now take a look at data node 1 in Figure 15-7: it contains primary shard 1 and replicas for shards 2 and 3. The replicas are useful for scaling the read operations without affecting the write performance, but the key consideration here is that all three shards share the same CPU and RAM resources of the data node, where one shard is responsible for writes and the other two for reads. Elasticsearch uses disk to store the indexes and offers multiple caching techniques (*https://oreil.ly/LzJdR*) on top of that to make queries faster.

The reads can be scaled by adding more replicas, but what about the primary shard? If there are issues with a data node consisting of a primary shard, that can affect the indexing performance until the data node is recovered or replaced by some other node, becoming a bottleneck in the overall architecture. In Elasticsearch architecture, the search engine is responsible for indexing the data and uses the same index to support user search queries. This can potentially introduce a bottleneck of one operation affecting the performance of another, meaning reads and writes are happening on the index at the same time. There can be sudden traffic bursts in any one of them that impact the other—for example, a viral search keyword queried by a large number of users in the same timestamp. In Part II, we covered the architecture of multiple AWS services, and the key was decoupling compute and storage in services like Amazon Redshift, Amazon EMR, Amazon Aurora, and so on. Along similar lines, is it possible to architect the system in such a way that both write and read operations can scale independently and are completely decoupled?

To resolve this, we can leverage cloud object storage as intermediary storage where indexing engines can upload the data and search engines can download the data, as shown in Figure 15-8. Multipart upload and download ensure uploading of the large files in chunks to provide better reliability and ease in reuploading or redownloading a smaller chunk if the operation fails. Keep shard sizes relatively small (not too small, to only a few GBs), which helps improve indexing latency. This also makes scaling (adding or removing nodes) search and indexing clusters faster due to the reduction in data-rebalancing overhead.

> We'll discuss optimal shard size for Elasticsearch clusters more in Chapter 18.

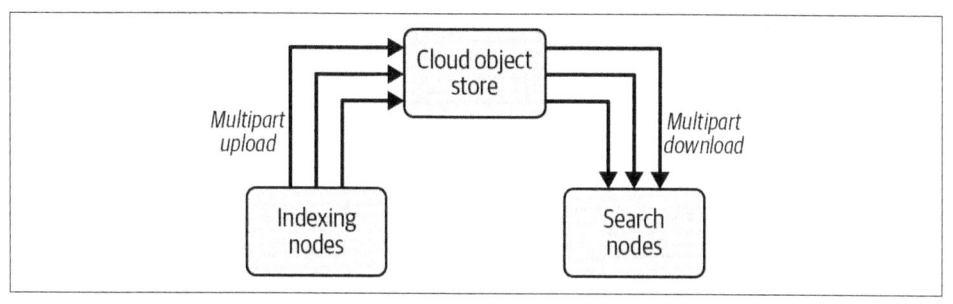

Figure 15-8. Decoupled indexing and search systems

The other benefits of cloud storage options like Amazon S3 are no management overhead of persistent backups and cross-AZ and -region replication. In short, we're getting all the cloud storage availability benefits in the search engine system. It is always a point of discussion: deciding whether to use a cloud provider or to fully manage a custom solution on your own at such a huge scale. There is no foolproof answer, and we recommend reevaluating as your system requirements, cloud-pricing considerations, and need for control over the service evolve.

We ensured that the indexing and search processes can scale independently. Now, to address the indexing-system bottleneck on write operations, the system can use the following mechanisms:

- Write operations should be done in batch or bulk instead of single-write operations for each and every query. This will help reduce load on the system.
- Instead of leader-follower (primary-secondary shard) architecture, the system can be designed to support leader-leader architecture where data is written to multiple primary shards at the same time, with a consensus and quorum algorithms in place. If there is a single leader, there is no requirement for consensus and quorum, so there are trade-offs in both approaches.

We're clear on the fact that we're not using Elasticsearch or Amazon OpenSearch for building the search engine system and that we need a custom solution to build the inverted indexes. The custom solution can be built on top of Apache Lucene library or completely from scratch, depending on further analysis. An inverted index can be really huge given the amount of data, and the system will include a mechanism for dividing the data into multiple machines and clusters. A single huge index cluster is tough to manage compared to multiple small clusters (well, not too small) and can become a bottleneck in the architecture. How should an inverted index be divided into a set of machines? We can represent an inverted index as a mapping from a keyword to the list of doc IDs and the frequency of the word's appearance in the document:

```
Term (key) - {docId, frequency} (value)
Hello - [{doc1, 5}, {doc2, 3}, {doc4, 1}]
World - [{doc1, 5}, {doc3, 4}]
```

There are two approaches to dividing the data here:

Document-based
    All the terms from a document are stored on a single machine, offering the benefit of calculating page relevance easily (if all the words in a search query are present in a single document, the system can retrieve the result from a single machine only). To gather search results, the primary instance forwards the query to all the worker instances and then combines the results to respond to the user queries.

Term-based
    To simply illustrate this, assume the system has extracted 100 terms out of the crawled web pages. These 100 terms are divided into a set of machines: 10 machines with 10 terms each. To respond to search queries, the primary instance can figure out which worker instances to go to; it doesn't need all the workers as in the case of document-based partitioning. The downside of this approach is creating an intersection of search results because the terms corresponding to the same document can reside on different machines and require data transfer over the network.

Based on these trade-offs, we'll choose document-based partitioning to maintain the inverted indexes. Let's discuss scaling of search nodes to facilitate the user read operations next.

Improving search performance

Latency is super critical; it is important that the user queries are answered in submilliseconds. The ideal suggestion is that the search nodes should keep all the data primarily in RAM, meaning all the inverted indexes are cached, but this comes with a cost. Disk is about a hundred times cheaper than RAM, and considering the scale requirements, the cost differentiation between disk and RAM can be huge.

In the case when all the data is kept in main memory, is there a requirement for persistent storage? For any node failures, the data can always be downloaded from cloud storage. It's a tough call to make, and we recommend keeping the inverted indexes as backups in disk storage as well. Yes, they can always be downloaded from cloud storage, but that can take more time compared to local disk seeks.

There are pros and cons associated with any approach we take—whether indexes are completely in memory or disk. We can take a middle ground to keep the majority of indexes in memory (most frequently accessed) with disk as a persistence option. The indexing algorithm will ensure that the data is stored in a manner requiring minimum disk-seek operations (ideally, one). Compression of data then becomes important in case the maximum amount of data resides in the main memory.

Data compression

We discussed the storage space requirements for the web crawler based on a few assumptions in "System Requirements" on page 388. The general idea of compression is that the operations of compressing and then decompressing will add to the latency of both indexing and search. This is because the system is spending some time first compressing and then, at a later stage, decompressing the data to support user search queries. One thing we're 100% sure of is that compression can save storage space.

Given that decompression can severely impact the search latency, we should think about latency a bit more. The search latency is critical in the system; indexing latency is also critical, but we can survive with a little lag because it is saving us the huge storage cost and we're fine with an eventual consistent system. We'll compare the considerations when the inverted index resides on disk versus when it resides completely in memory:

Inverted index in memory
   To process an inverted index list without compression requires two steps: moving data from memory to CPU cache and then processing it. With compression, an extra step of decompressing the data is added. The operation of moving data from memory to CPU cache becomes really fast with compressed data, and decompression takes relatively less time. So essentially, the search-query latency is improved with compression of the data.

Inverted index on disk
   This adds the step of moving the data from disk to main memory, but it performs well because we're moving less data. This increases the search-query evaluation speed, giving us the benefit of low storage cost plus the improved performance with the compression in place in the system.

Taking all of this into consideration, we can see that the search queries are quite faster in responding to user requests with compression in place.

Now think of a scenario when a particular search query becomes popular and the system receives a lot of requests with the same search query—this may become a bottleneck in the search system. To overcome this, the system ensures that autoscaling is in place to replicate the data on more nodes to serve queries. It also maintains a cache layer in the same region as users to serve the same search queries without even hitting the search system's inverted indexes. This ensures that the search system is not affected and that user queries are served reliably and with much less latency. There is definitely an implementation in place to invalidate the regional cache from time to time and maintain the data freshness. As the search engine system creates inverted indexes, it assigns the score to each page to make sure relevant content is served to the users.

Relevance of search results

For any search query, there can be hundreds of search results, and the search engine system should ensure that the results are in a sorted format with high-scoring web pages on top. Here are few factors that contribute to deciding the content relevancy of a web page:

- A web page is assigned a higher score if a lot of other web pages point to it. If some top domain adds the reference to the page as well, it becomes more relevant. For example, a research paper used as a reference on Stanford University's site might hold more value than a research paper quoted on the sites of 10 lesser-known universities.
- The words in the web page title, the heading, a larger font, or any other special characteristics (e.g., embedded links, bold, italics, underlining, etc.) can be given more weight.
- The location of the web page adds to a score in the sense that a web page could be very relevant in the US but not so relevant in India.
- The search engine prioritizes positive content instead of negative content in top search results unless the search query explicitly evaluates to the negative content.

Many more attributes can be used to determine a page rank, but we'll close the search engine discussion here and move on to launching the system on the AWS cloud.

Launching the System on AWS

As we did in Chapter 14, we'll follow the policy of quickly setting up the application and choosing AWS services that require no or minimum expertise. Then, we'll tackle issues as we understand more about how the overall system is functioning and the expectations of the users.

Day 0 Architecture

The Day 0 architecture is based on an AWS blog post (*https://oreil.ly/EqgHU*) about scaling up a serverless web crawler and search engine. The entire process of the web crawler system can be broken down into a series of steps, and it essentially keeps repeating these steps until the list of URLs is crawled. To break the workflow into steps, AWS Step Functions (discussed in Chapter 12) is a great choice of service on the AWS cloud. Figure 15-9 shows the state machine representing how the web crawler downloads web pages.

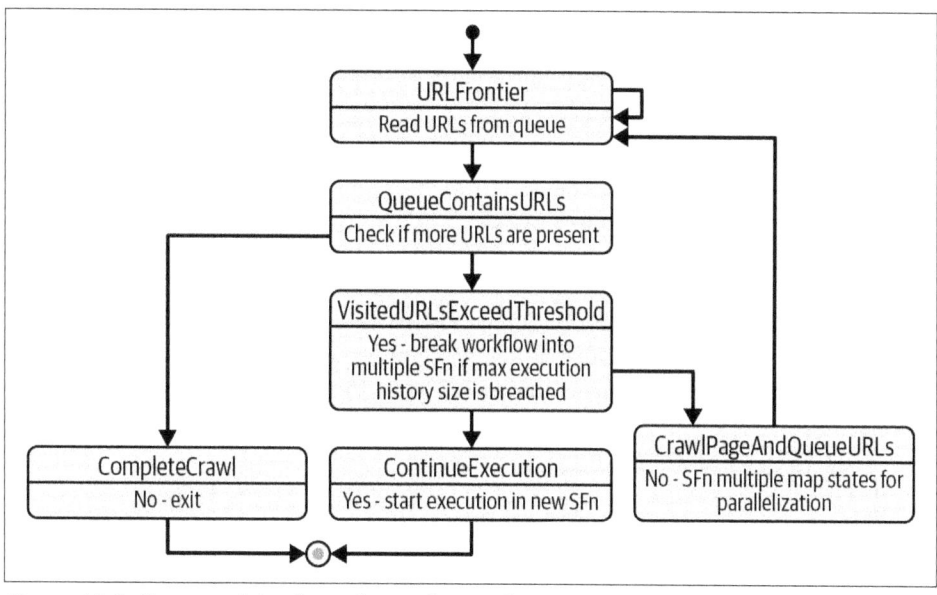

Figure 15-9. State machine for web crawler implementation

All the states in the state machine can be executed as separate Lambda functions and use Step Functions map states for parallelization. There is also a requirement to store the URLs, which can be passed along between the states for evaluation, such as if the URL is already crawled or if there are more URLs to be crawled. Since the list of URLs is huge, it's not possible to pass between the states using Step Functions alone—the system requires persistent storage. For database choices, the system doesn't require any relations or strong consistency across the data, so a nonrelational service like Amazon DynamoDB or Amazon Keyspaces can be an ideal choice here. The system stores the available URLs and any related metadata and requires direct key operations on these URLs. We recommend using a database based on previous expertise here as neither of these two choices stands out clearly. For illustrative purposes, in this chapter we'll use DynamoDB.

The system essentially requires two tables. One is a building block of the URL frontier system to store URLs and is used across the crawls. Another is created at the start of the state machine and deleted at the termination of the state machine; this table stores the URLs crawled during the ongoing crawl to ensure that a single URL is not crawled multiple times.

Once the web page is crawled by the crawler system, it needs a repository database to dump all the web page content. For such use cases, Amazon S3 is the preferred choice for storing the data, and it can be used in the second step of the architecture as a search engine to consume this data and index it. Building a custom search engine is a big task that requires an end-to-end thought process, but to deploy the system quickly, we can use Amazon Kendra, which we introduced very briefly in Chapter 13.

Kendra is a fully managed service offering intelligent search capabilities. It is widely used as an enterprise search solution and is often targeted to build a custom search engine on top of internal documentation in multiple places, such as Slack, Google Drive, relational databases, Confluence docs, and so on. It offers connectors (*https://oreil.ly/POkCo*) to connect with these different data sources and will automatically build a search solution on top of them. As the crawled web page data is stored to S3, the S3 connector (*https://oreil.ly/atbYQ*) can be used to configure S3 as a data source to Kendra. The entire architecture of the web crawler and search engine system after combining all these components is shown in Figure 15-10.

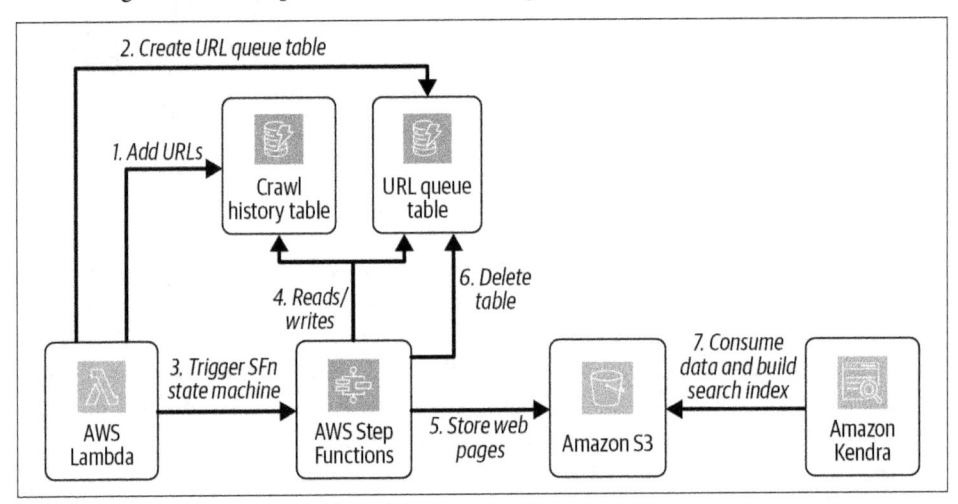

Figure 15-10. Web crawler and search engine architecture

Interestingly, Kendra also offers a web crawler as a connector (*https://oreil.ly/jRr_s*), so we won't even require the web crawler part of the architecture. All we need to do is provide the seed URLs, and Kendra can crawl the websites and index them to support the search on top of that. Let's now look at any limitations the system can face as it scales to serve more and more traffic.

Scaling to Millions and Beyond

If you ignore infrastructure cost on the AWS cloud for a while, can you think of any limitations in the architecture explained in the previous section? Ideally, the architecture uses AWS serverless components, so the components should automatically scale up and down according to the nature of the traffic without any user interference.

Possible limitations include:

- AWS Step Functions can face higher latency and quota limitations. This was addressed by suggesting multiple Step Functions and usage of map states.
- AWS Lambda as a compute option scales automatically per the provided memory configurations. The cold start is not much of an issue because the system can survive a little lag, but we can still leverage a few of the options, such as provisioned capacity, to speed up the process of downloading web pages a little.
- Amazon DynamoDB is a fully managed service that scales indefinitely to support the storage requirements. One point of consideration here is the hard limit for RCU and WCU consumption on a single partition: it should exceed the limit of 1,000 WCUs and 3,000 RCUs or else the requests are throttled. The DynamoDB table is created with the partition key as a URL. Considering that one RCU is consumed for one request, the system can breach this limit if the following situation occurs: a URL is referenced in a lot of web pages, and the web crawler is working concurrently on more than 3,000 URLs. The positive side of this could be that even if the requests are throttled, we can assume the URL is already present in the DynamoDB table and safely skip it (the request was throttled because the partition is present in the DynamoDB). The problem that can surface is retrieval of additional attributes associated with a URL.
- We can consider latency as one parameter on URL retrieval from DynamoDB since there is no caching introduced in the system. Further, the system doesn't store robots cache and DNS cache, which adds to the overall latency of calls to web servers.
- The web page content is stored in S3, which offers unlimited storage and automatically replicates the data for high availability, so there's no bottleneck there.
- Amazon Kendra is a fully managed service, so we don't control how data is stored or what capacity is offered to the customers. The service offers fixed capacity (*https://oreil.ly/jS1wH*) for storage and queries to the customers, and it can be further incremented with the help of AWS support. This control is

often preferred at the customer's end if the system needs to support a huge scale because that makes it easy to custom-build the software according to need.

If your system is operating at Google's scale, or even one-tenth of this scale, it makes sense to manage the implementation on your own instead of relying on managed services like Kendra. This saves cost along with offering fine-tuned control over low-level configurations of the system.

> We're not discouraging you from using AWS managed services—they are great and save a lot of time when building software without requiring any operational burden and expertise on your end. Evaluate your system architecture from time to time and deciding what works best for you.

In Day 0 architecture, we used Kendra to help with the search engine functionalities. Now, let's figure out which microservices can replace Kendra (referencing the functionality from Figure 15-10) and build the architecture from the ground up:

Text-preprocessing service
   This service takes care of text filtering and removes unwanted stop words, and it then creates a forward index with a relevant set of words. This is not a straightforward implementation of direct removal of words and can include multiple options to consider. For example, you can perform a Google search on entire sentences by entering them in double quotes (and to support these search queries, the system needs to index the entire sentence).

Inverted index creation service
   This service is responsible for taking input as a forward index and creating an inverted index for the content. The inverted indexes are uploaded to S3 and downloaded by the inverted index reader service.

Inverted index reader service
   This service downloads the inverted indexes and handles the read queries from the search keyword parser service.

Content relevance service
   This service is responsible for hosting algorithms to get the most relevant content for given search keywords. There can be multiple services for content relevance, and each can work on different sets of criteria, such as geographical proximity or personal user interests.

Search keyword parser service
   This service parses the user input into a set of keywords for further use by the content relevance service and inverted index reader service. The results are combined and returned to the frontend service.

Frontend service
> This service takes actions on user requests, such as applying rate limiting and discarding unwanted traffic. It is essentially a gatekeeper service that forwards only actual traffic to backend services.

A lot of things can happen in the system, and the system should be resilient to handle the fault scenarios gracefully. You can build confidence by intentionally breaking the production environment on known parameters and seeing if the system can handle the faults. This practice is called *chaos engineering*: the discipline of experimenting on a system to build confidence in the system's capability to withstand turbulent conditions in production. The experiment can be as simple as an EC2 instance being down; is it replaced by another one? In the AWS cloud environment, you could use AWS Fault Injection Service (FIS) (*https://aws.amazon.com/fis*). A lot of open source alternatives are also available for running these experiments.

Now, let's incorporate all the components and complete the final architecture on AWS.

Day N Architecture

You can definitely start with a single AWS account, but for Day N architecture, we recommend breaking the architecture into subcomponents with proper resource isolation—as we already did in the previous sections. To start, let's assume there are two teams in the organization that independently own the web crawler and search engine systems (there can be more, such as teams that own ML initiatives, infrastructure management teams, or subteams for the web crawler and search engine systems). Both teams deploy their architectures into separate AWS accounts managed under the parent AWS account.

There are no strict guidelines for how many AWS accounts you should have. Different organizations take different approaches based on their requirements. For example, it is very common for organizations to have separate accounts for each microservice (and even different AWS accounts at the regional level for multiregion deployment of critical services), while some organizations keep a single AWS account to manage all the resources across the microservices. In Chapter 14, we mentioned that having multiple AWS accounts can increase data-flow costs, but it simplifies certain other things, such as billing, complete resource isolation, and development flexibility for teams.

As in previous sections, we'll now present the final architecture broken down into two subsystems, starting with the web crawler.

Web crawler

Let's revisit Figure 15-5 and figure out the AWS services and resources that can be used to deploy the suggested architecture on the AWS cloud, starting with the multiple databases used. The web crawler research papers suggest different data structure implementations to store and reference the data, though we'll evaluate if existing storage options on AWS can suffice for the use case in Table 15-1.

Table 15-1. Web crawler data stores

Use case	AWS service	Comments
Seed URL	DynamoDB	The URL frontier system takes the URLs from this system to begin the crawling process. DynamoDB is a preferred choice because it maintains a direct mapping (key-value pair from the URL to additional metadata) with no requirements for data relationships and strong consistency over the database indexes.
URL storage and URL uniqueness	DynamoDB	This stores all the lists of the URLs that the system finds during the crawling of web pages. The URLs are added to this database after checking if they are not already present.
URL filter	DynamoDB	This database maintains the blocked URLs that the crawler system doesn't want to crawl.
Robots cache	DynamoDB and/or ElastiCache	Both of these caching solutions help save time during the crawls. ElastiCache can be used alone as well as to improve the latency with disk persistence (to recover data in case of node failures).
DNS cache	DynamoDB and/or ElastiCache	The robots cache helps the system figure out any exclusions on subsequent crawls even before crawling. The DNS cache maintains the IP address of the web server without making the round trip to the internet.
Webpage content	S3 and DynamoDB	S3 is an object storage solution that is a preferred choice for storing content like text files, images, videos, and the like, so we can use it to store the web pages. DynamoDB can store any metadata, such as URL-to-S3 file paths for web page content (which is helpful across the web page crawls).

Implementing the URL frontier system requires queues for URL processing so that it can push URLs to the queues and they can be consumed by the web crawler system for further processing. We'll leverage a combination of Amazon SQS and Amazon SNS for this purpose; Amazon MSK can be used for the same purpose as well. The URL frontier publishes URLs to a single SNS topic, and it can route subscribed SQS FIFO queues based on priority attributes in the message. The URL fetcher system requires an additional NAT gateway and internet gateway to communicate with the internet to retrieve the web pages.

The entire crawler processing is essentially a sequence of steps, and it makes sense to use a state machine such as AWS Step Functions or Amazon MWAA (discussed in Chapter 12) at a large scale as well. We can definitely build our own state machines, but using these AWS services helps us leverage the built-in debugging features along with the error-handling mechanisms. The web crawler system architecture fits an event-driven system well: a system completes its processing and announces the completion status; the other system takes this output as input and begins its processing and so on. We can also achieve this via an SNS-SQS architecture instead of Step Functions. We compared choreography and orchestration design patterns in Chapter 8, and the same is applicable here: orchestration (AWS Step Functions) can be preferable to choreography (SQS-SNS) because of additional built-in features of AWS Step Functions, such as error handling and ease of debugging.

Selecting compute options is another important factor for application deployment, and we recommend taking the learnings from Chapter 11 for different types of compute. In short, there is no perfect answer, and we try to take a middle ground by choosing the Amazon EKS EC2 deployment option. We consider this a middle ground based on our previous experience with the technologies and traffic analysis or quota limits enforced by AWS. As in Chapter 14, for better resource isolation we'll deploy the microservices in different VPCs and use a separate Amazon EKS cluster for each of the microservices, as shown in Figure 15-11.

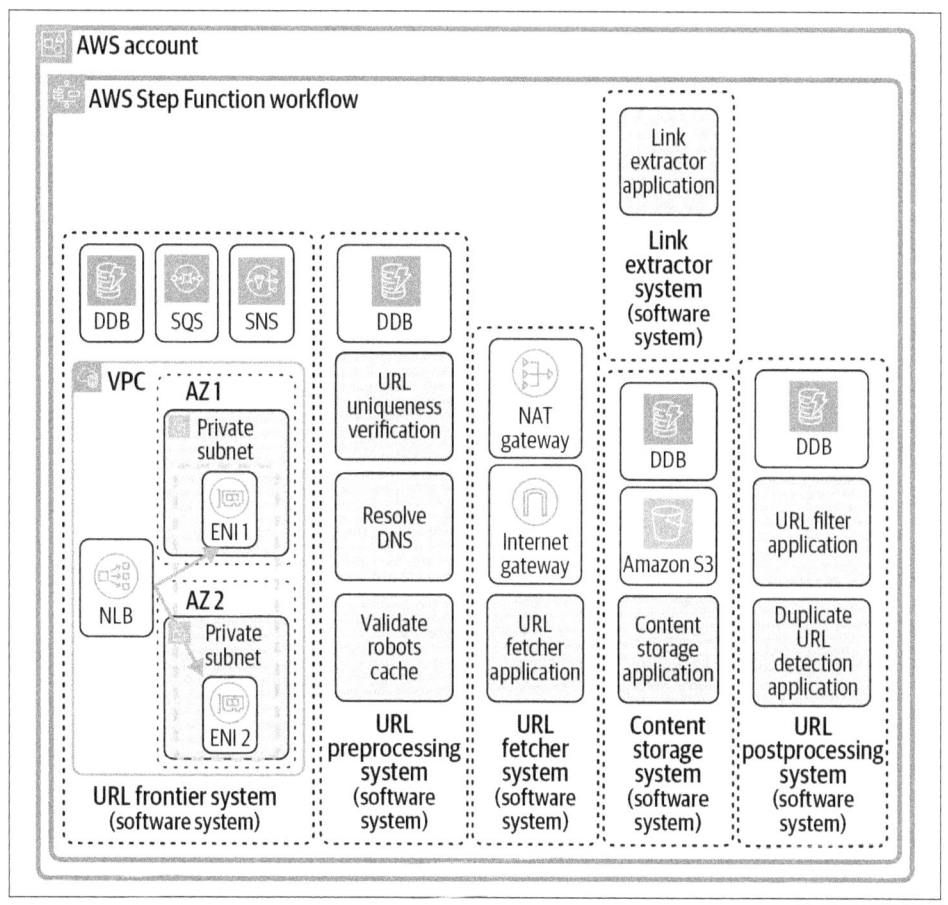

Figure 15-11. Web crawler architecture

> AWS services for monitoring, managing access, and logging are not included in the architecture to keep the diagram less cluttered. Assume them as part of any architecture for overall observability.

As the web pages are ingested into the content storage system, the web crawler system notifies the search engine system about the new content. Upon receiving this notification, the search engine system begins its processing of the creation of indexes. We'll discuss the AWS architecture of the search engine system next.

Search engine

We described the high-level architecture of the search engine system in Figure 15-6 and microservices in "Scaling to Millions and Beyond" on page 407. We'll go with a framework similar to the web crawler system for application deployment. For creating forward and inverted indexes, we won't be relying on any of the AWS services, such as Amazon OpenSearch for search functionality; instead, we'll create custom solutions following the guidelines laid out in "Designing the Search Engine" on page 398. Figures 15-12 and 15-13 illustrate the search engine system's architecture on the AWS cloud.

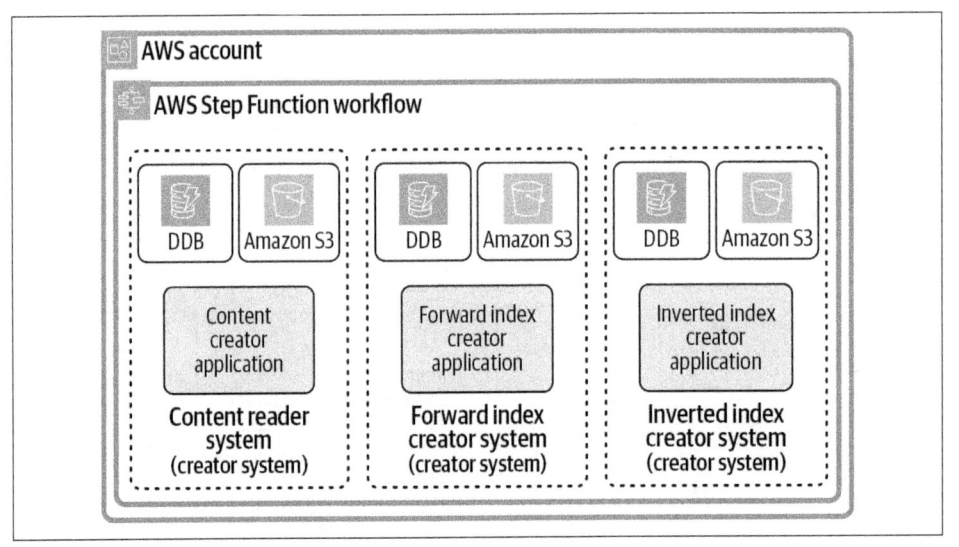

Figure 15-12. Search engine architecture for inverted index creation

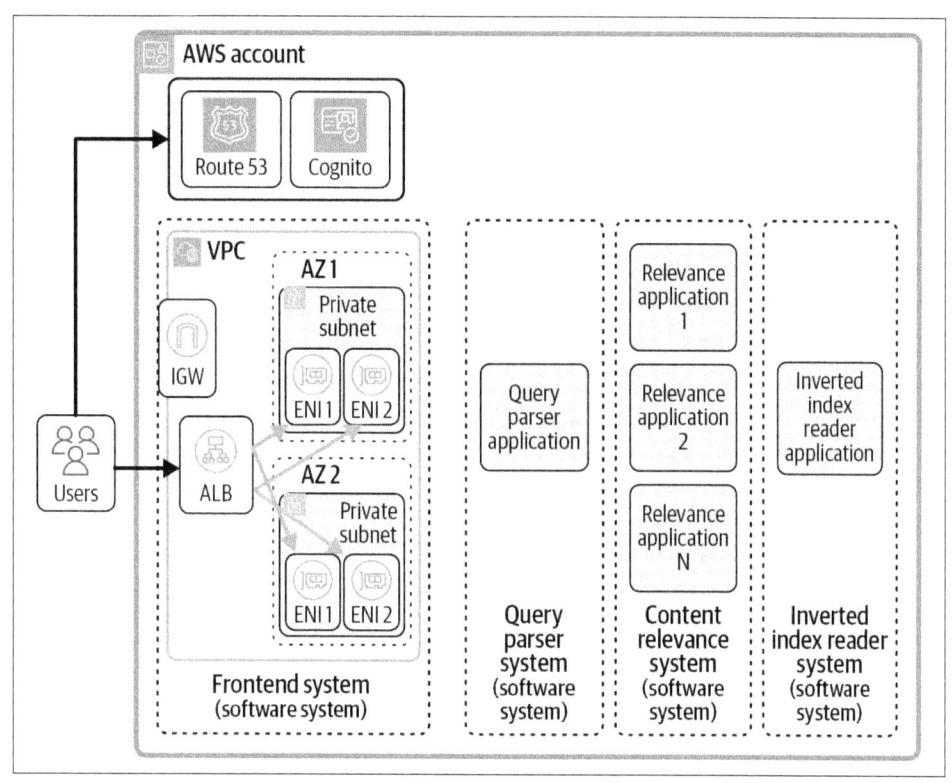

Figure 15-13. Search engine system for serving user queries

The *content reader application* reads the content from a repository stored by the web crawler system, performs preprocessing actions, and makes the content ready for forward index creation. We'll use S3 to store large files like web pages and forward and inverted indexes and use them across the system. Amazon DynamoDB is used for any metadata storage requirements in the architecture. The *forward index creator system* constructs forward indexes using the output from the previous step, which is used as input to the *inverted index creator system* to construct inverted indexes.

The *inverted index reader application* downloads the inverted indexes created by the inverted index creator system and allows reads on top of them. The *content relevance system* consists of multiple applications to figure out the relevance of search results and can use services such as Amazon SageMaker for running any ML algorithms. The *frontend system* takes in user queries, preprocesses them with the help of *the query parser system,* and then returns results with the help of the relevance and reader systems.

Conclusion

Web crawler and search engine systems are complex architectures and require a lot of iteration to crawl the web efficiently and present the most relevant search results to the users. Content relevance algorithms hold a very important place in search engines because users care about good search results only and nothing else. This is true for any system design—as long as we're able to serve users in the best way possible, nothing else matters. Design decisions should include user inputs as concrete functional requirements.

Over the years, multiple papers have been published on distributed web crawlers and search engines, and we recommend reading them before implementing one of your own. This will help you avoid reinventing the wheel, and you can take inspiration from work that has already been done. We made some critical comparisons while choosing a technology for the system architecture, such as in-memory inverted indexes versus on-disk inverted indexes and using Amazon OpenSearch versus building custom solutions. Create a list of pros and cons mapping to your system requirements to finalize on a solution from all the available choices.

In the next chapter, we'll take design decisions to architect a social networking system like Facebook or LinkedIn.

CHAPTER 16
Designing a Social Network and Newsfeed System

Social network websites like Twitter (now X), Instagram, and LinkedIn have become vital parts of people's lives, with most users utilizing them to share information with other people. This information, often referred to as a *post* on each platform, can be shared as text, images, videos, emojis, and more.

Social networking websites offer a variety of features, and we'll specifically dig deeper into the design of the newsfeed (or *user timeline*—we'll use both these terms interchangeably) component of the system. *Newsfeed* refers to the stream of posts and updates published by other users that a user typically sees as soon as they log into a social media app. Users can interact with these posts via emoji or text responses, or even by sharing the posts on their own feed. The newsfeed for each website can be derived based on different factors. We'll start our discussion with the system requirements and then proceed to identifying system components to support these requirements. We'll end the chapter with the potential architecture for our social network newsfeed system on the AWS cloud.

System Requirements

Social networking websites offer a variety of features, such as posts that are shared (text, images, videos), a built-in chat messenger, user stories that typically expire in 24 hours, and more. Each feature can be an independent system—for example, the chat messenger, which we'll discuss in Chapter 19. For now, let's dig into the functional and nonfunctional requirements of our newsfeed system.

Functional and Nonfunctional Requirements

As mentioned before, social networking websites offer a lot of features, so we'll limit the scope of the design to architect just some of these features for our site. The most important functional requirement in the context of this chapter is reflecting the newsfeed to the user. The newsfeed can be based on a single parameter or a combination of factors, including:

- All posts associated with a particular hashtag, topic, or location
- All posts published by the people a user is following
- All posts liked or shared by the people a user is following
- All posts derived based on a user's past interests or assigned priority (for example, breaking news). This involves an ML component, so we'll skip the details because of space constraints.

Our system will create a newsfeed for a user based on people and topics (or hashtags) that the user chooses to follow. We'll also discuss hashtag-based storage and retrieval of posts (keyword-based search) to some extent in this chapter.

To support the newsfeed feature, the system should inherently support these functional requirements:

- A user onboards to the system and follows (or unfollows) people or topics based on personal interests.
- A user can make posts (for example, uploading photos in Instagram or posting a text-based post on X).
- APIs are exposed for retrieving data, which can be useful for monetizing the site. We won't discuss this requirement in detail, but the idea is for developers to use APIs such as search with keywords or to be able to stream the data of all new posts to interested clients.

Here are the NFRs for the system:

- The system should be highly available and fault-tolerant to support all of the functional requirements.
- Eventual consistency is fine for reflecting posts in the newsfeed. There is acceptable lag between when posts are published by a user and when those posts are reflected in followers' timelines.
- Keyword search requests should be fast and latency sensitive.

Let's discuss the scale of the system next.

System Scale

The number of users interacting with one another on social networking websites like X and Facebook is huge, and our system architecture should handle this increasing scale. Let's make some assumptions about the scale the system needs to support, starting with the write traffic:

Number of new posts every second = 10,000

Photos uploaded every second = 800

Videos uploaded every second = 200

Average number of followers per user = 1,000

Maximum number of followers for a user account = 200 million

The read traffic is relatively large compared to the write traffic, so we'll make these assumptions about the scale:

Number of monthly active users on platform = 500 million

User timeline retrieval every second = 100,000

User-interaction traffic, such as liking posts, can be huge; the numbers are in the millions per second. We'll skip that storage-requirement calculation in this chapter; this can be calculated with scale numbers similar to how we handled it in the previous two chapters.

Now that we have finalized the requirements and have clarity on the scale we need to support, let's begin our thought process by identifying key components of the system and presenting the overall picture of the system design.

Starting with the Design

We'll not go into depth on onboarding users to the platform as the onboarding system in the entire architecture basically takes care of this. A user onboards with their personal information and then starts following people and topics. Let's talk a little bit about the storage of follower-following entities so as to ensure that the read queries become efficient. For example, if a user makes a post, that post should be sent to all the user's followers; we need to ensure that the system can retrieve this follower list quickly and send notifications or populate user timelines.

Relationships between users can be established at multiple levels, not just one-to-one, such as friends of friends, locations, shared interests, and so on. For example, LinkedIn suggests people connections (*https://oreil.ly/3X8gm*) as first, second, and third degree: first degree represents people you're directly connected with, second degree represents a mutual connection, and third degree represents all the user relationships apart from first and second degree. To manage these relationships among users, social networking websites generally leverage graph databases, which we discussed in Chapters 3 and 10.

We'll define a *user graph service* to manage the user relationships in a graph database. The user graph service can be used in real time by other services to retrieve user followings.

Now, let's talk about the system architecture to handle new post ingestion (creation of new posts by users).

Handling New Posts

The crux of social networking websites is users sharing information with other people. This helps define the goal of the *user post service*: store posts in such a way that they are sent to other users in near real time. Let's reiterate the functional requirements of the system:

- Allow users to publish new posts and share them with people who are following them.
- Depending on country or company regulations, post validation is incorporated into the system. Validation can include no hate-speech content, not favoring any political agenda, input sanitization to avoid issues like SQL injection, and the like.

Instead of handling validation by the user post service, this responsibility can be given to a frontend service or the *user gateway service*. The user gateway service runs generic validations (not specific to underlying services) along with other functionalities, such as rate limiting, user authorization and authentication, and request blocking for bad actors.

The way that the user post service storage handles this depends on how the user timeline is built; it can be either a push or a pull mechanism:

Push mechanism
    The user post service retrieves all followers of a user, builds their timelines, and stores them in a data store. As the user comes online, the user's timeline can be served directly from the data store.

Pull mechanism
    The user timeline is built in real time. As the user comes online, the system checks for new posts by people followed by the user and delivers them to the user's timeline.

To decide on the approach that would be most beneficial, let's consider two potential users: user A with 100 followers (a standard user) and user B with 100 million followers (a celebrity user). The push mechanism can work well for users who fall into the user A category, but this would be a lot of ingestion work for celebrity users. The complexity really adds up if the post is tagged with another celebrity or if one celebrity replies to another on the post (X reposts). The push approach makes writes complex (O(n) operation where n is number of followers) in favor of optimizing reads (O(1) operation). The pull mechanism is preferred for celebrity users, and the posts are retrieved in real time while constructing the user timelines.

> It's worth noting here that if a user follows a lot of celebrity users only and the user timeline is served directly from disk instead of a precomputed cache, then posts will take a relatively longer time to show up in the newsfeed. This is a little hit we can take on customer experience in favor of reducing system complexity. To improve customer experience, social networking websites save older data on the app itself, which is shown on the next visit with background sync in progress to retrieve the latest feed.

To make the best of both worlds, we can build a hybrid approach to serve both buckets of users. The user timeline is built consisting of all posts from normal users, and celebrity-user posts are appended in real time while retrieving the user timeline. Let's talk about the steps in this hybrid architecture in some more detail:

1. A user with 10,000+ followers publishes a post with a unique post identifier, the *post ID*. The post ID is saved to a persistent database like MySQL. We touched on X's Snowflake in Chapter 14; it can be used here to generate unique post IDs sorted by timestamp.

2. The user post service retrieves all the active follower user IDs from the user graph service to build a timeline in a cache data store for faster retrieval. The cache data store (Redis, for example) stores only the timelines for active users (such as those who last accessed the platform within the past 30 days) and to a certain limit (at the utmost, 30 posts, for example). The rest of the posts are served directly from the on-disk database, and the cache is updated accordingly.

3. The cache data store stores only the post IDs against the user IDs. The key-value structure could be something like the key as the user ID and the values as a list (`postId`, `postedBy`, and `postType`). The additional metadata associated with the post, such as the user's profile picture, likes on the post, and replies associated with the post, can be served independently from a different cache or persistent storage.

4. The *user timeline service* can directly serve the results from the cache data store for active users and from the on-disk persistent database for inactive users (the cache is updated with the recent timeline once the user becomes active again).

Additional components might be involved here, such as ranking and sorting posts depending on the publishing time or user interests, embedding advertisements between posts, and much more. The user timeline service talks to different services (the user service for user information, the post service for post content, and the ranking service for post ranks) and delivers merged results to the user timeline.

Figure 16-1 captures the architecture of what happens behind the scenes when a new post is published by a user. We've introduced a post workflow orchestration component in the architecture, which is invoked by CDC events once the post is saved to the database and works in asynchronous mode. The orchestration component builds the user's timeline in cache, and the same new post event can be consumed by the search service to offer search functionality on tags or keywords (more on this in later sections). X works on a similar architecture, which can be referenced from a high-level system diagram published by Elon Musk (*https://oreil.ly/T4_DO*) and the real-time delivery architecture presented at the QCon conference (*https://oreil.ly/Rzb3e*).

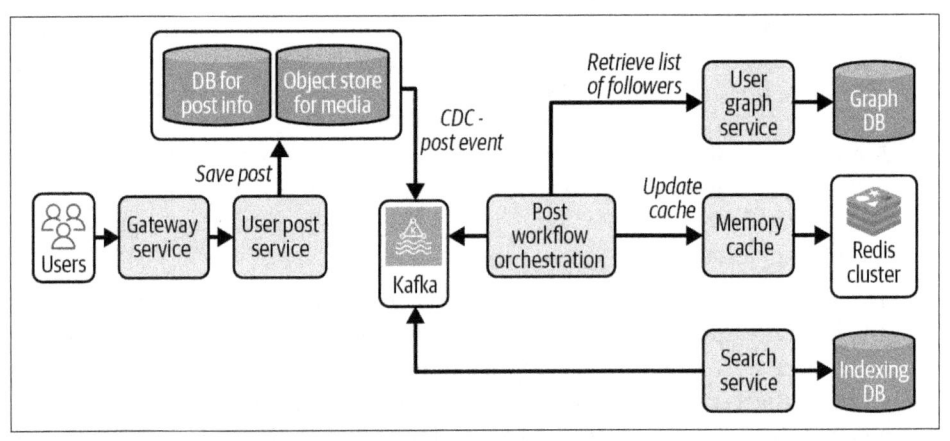

Figure 16-1. New post creation architecture

Let's dig deeper into the database choice for the user post service.

User post service databases

The user post service leverages two databases to store the post information: one for storing a post's structured content (post ID, created by, media metadata) and the other for media content (images and videos). Object storage, such as S3, can be used for storing media content. There is a high probability that the same media is shared by multiple people, and the system should be optimized to handle duplicate content. A simple way to do this could be creating a hash for media content; any new media uploaded is checked against already uploaded media. We'll talk more about this in Chapter 19 when we cover the chat application architecture. Another point of consideration is caching media content at edge locations (by leveraging solutions like Amazon CloudFront) to optimize downloads. This helps on two fronts: reducing calls to the user post service and reducing latency for media downloads.

Let's explore both relational and nonrelational kinds of databases to serve the required use case. We can start by identifying the query patterns and expectations from the database engine, which should narrow down the choice. Table 16-1 lists both the read and write query patterns for the user post service.

Table 16-1. User post service query patterns

Write	Read
Store posts for a user	Read all posts by a user
Store comments against a post	Read all/paginated comments for a post
Store counters (number of likes, reshares) against a post	Get number of likes for a post
Store a list (user ID) of who liked the post; the like type can vary (smile, thumbs up, love, laughter)	Get a list of users who liked the post

Both read and write queries are straightforward and can be satisfied by either database choice: a relational database like PostgreSQL (with sharding to support the scale) or a NoSQL database like Amazon DynamoDB or Amazon Keyspaces (compatible with Apache Cassandra). The data in DynamoDB should be stored in a way that makes the read queries efficient, as shown in Table 16-2.

Table 16-2. Amazon DynamoDB with user post service read queries

Read query	Schema
Read all posts by a user	PK = u#{userId}#post SK = p#{postId}
Read all comments for a post	PK = p#{postId}#comments SK = c#{commentId}
Get number of likes for a post	PK = p#{postId}#likeCount SK = {count}
Get list of users who liked the post	PK = p#{postId}#likeList SK = u#{userId}
Get number of likes for a comment	PK = p#{postId}#c#{commentId}#likeCount SK = {count}

If a user creates a large number of posts over time and we're interested in only the most recent, the post ID should either be generated in Snowflake fashion, or it should include a timestamp in the sort key itself, similar to t#{epochTime}#p#{postId} if the post ID is a completely random identifier. Snowflake is our preferred approach because the system requires an implementation for generating unique post IDs at a huge scale.

> The size of data for a single partition in Amazon DynamoDB is limited to 10 GB, and the defined schema uses the user ID as a partition key. This means we're assuming that the number of users won't exceed this limit. The size of a single row is 0.5 KB (with a limit of 400 characters on the lengths of posts), so the maximum number of posts that a user can create is about 20 million.

We mentioned that relational databases, such as PostgreSQL, could also be used to store user posts, as shown in Figure 16-2.

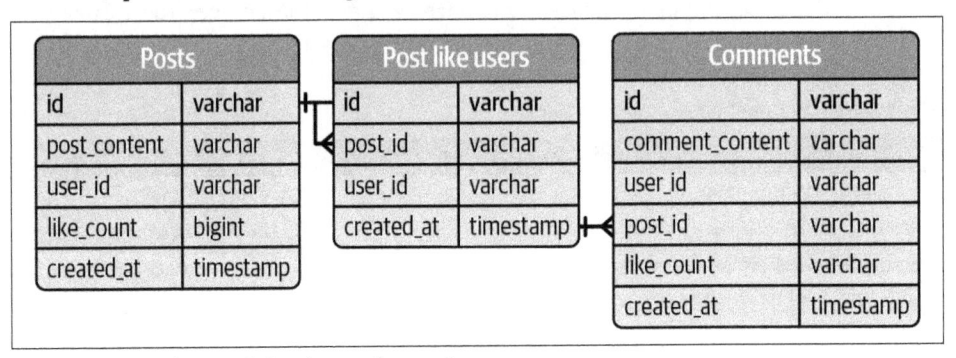

Posts	
id	varchar
post_content	varchar
user_id	varchar
like_count	bigint
created_at	timestamp

Post like users	
id	varchar
post_id	varchar
user_id	varchar
created_at	timestamp

Comments	
id	varchar
comment_content	varchar
user_id	varchar
post_id	varchar
like_count	varchar
created_at	timestamp

Figure 16-2. Relational database schema for user posts

The post_id column of the "post like users" and "comments" tables are referenced to the ID of the "posts" table. To support the query pattern of fetching all the comments against a post, an index can be created on post_id for fast retrieval. Considering the scale of the system, the database should be partitioned to support horizontal scaling. We need to figure out a key based on which data can be partitioned into multiple partitions. Consider partitioning logic in the database from the start, if feasible, even though there might not be a requirement for it. The data can be logically partitioned and moved to different physical partitions on a need basis.

For logical partitioning, we recommend a logic similar to how Redis has a hash slot implementation (discussed in Chapter 4). Instagram deploys a similar mechanism for ID generation (*https://oreil.ly/r-Ny5*) and for managing logical and physical partitioning by leveraging PostgreSQL features. Another point to note here is that we might be using a relational database, but there is no requirement for strong consistency on features, like managing the number of likes or reflecting all the comments published on a post. These read queries can be eventually consistent to ensure optimal customer experience.

We mentioned the post workflow orchestration system responsible for fan-out of all posts to the followers and storing them in memory cache. Let's discuss what goes on behind the scenes in this system and how it scales well for a large number of upcoming posts.

Post workflow orchestration and memory cache

The post workflow orchestration is an async layer that comes into the picture once the post from a user is saved to a persistent database. We recommended Redis as a memory cache data store in Figure 16-1 to cache user timelines. Let's evaluate more on the data store choice here.

Our primary reason for suggesting Redis is lower latency to serve user queries because data is stored in memory. Redis is faster when compared to any of the on-disk solutions, such as MySQL, Amazon DynamoDB, Cassandra, and the like, which makes it an ideal choice. Another point to note here is the data size requirement—it's quite huge given the system scale numbers, and this can add to the cost. Is it worth considering databases like DynamoDB or Cassandra? DynamoDB offers automatic horizontal scaling and consistent single-digit millisecond latency at any scale, so it could be a good choice. The final answer to this dilemma is both yes and no, much like any other system design decision we make.

In the context of this chapter, we'll rely on Redis in cluster mode to serve a timeline-caching use case. Revisit Chapter 4 to refresh your understanding of the Redis cluster architecture and how it helps with horizontal scaling (*https://oreil.ly/2UIIc*) with increasing data. We can leverage Redis's list data structure (*https://oreil.ly/gkog_*) commands like `RPUSHX` (*https://oreil.ly/WVd7H*) to always append the entry to the end of the list if the user ID is present in the list (cache only for active users), and `LTRIM` (*https://oreil.ly/pxXzZ*) to keep a fixed-size list of post IDs.

Another point to note here with regard to the post workflow orchestrator is pushing the data to the Redis cluster. Assuming every user has an average of 1,000 followers and the system receives 100 posts per second, the number of calls to Redis becomes 100,000. However, the actual number of posts is much larger than 100, and the number of calls to Redis can become a bottleneck in terms of latency and I/O consumption. The ideal approach to solve this kind of problem is batching requests. Redis pipelining (*https://oreil.ly/mbjLa*) can be used to club multiple requests together, gain the benefits of request batching, and address this bottleneck. The bulk requests can be parallelized as well for further optimization.

Cache invalidation becomes important for any caching solution we might use. In case a user unfollows someone, the cache should be updated to remove the entry. This again should work in an asynchronous way: any changes in the graph service database are consumed by other components in the architecture and handled per the use case.

The memory cache is the first data store to look for to build a user timeline, so let's discuss that more in the next section.

User timeline service

Figure 16-3 captures the user timeline service, showing how it gathers data from different components in the architecture to build the user timeline. Memory cache is the first point of lookup for precomputed posts, and additional celebrity posts are retrieved from the user post service. The post ranking service helps with the final sorting and merging of results based on the rank. The query to the user graph service varies based on whether the user is active or not. For active users, the user graph service is queried only to retrieve celebrity users followed by the user, and for nonactive users, the entire list is retrieved and the timeline is built from the on-disk data store.

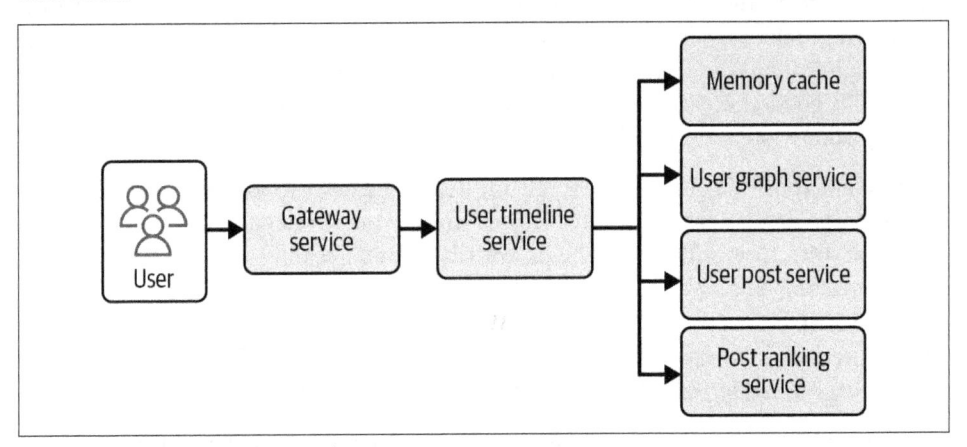

Figure 16-3. User timeline architecture

This architecture assumes that no real-time updates are sent to the user applications and that the timeline is updated upon the page refresh. For supporting the requirement of pushing new posts in real time to user timelines, we can explore persistent connections with the user devices. We'll discuss persistent bidirectional connections in Chapter 19 when we look at the chat application architecture.

We talked about using graph databases for user connections, and we've built a basic understanding of graph databases in previous chapters of this book. Let's dig a little deeper into the architecture of a user graph service and how it works at scale to store so many connections among the users.

Managing User Connections

The base storage requirement is to manage the followers of each user, essentially managing relationships between the users. Relational databases like MySQL are typically a good choice, so you may be wondering why we recommended a graph database in previous sections. The reason is that the nature of the relations and complex queries need to be served in very low latency—for example, figuring out all the users who follow celebrity A and celebrity B and figuring out second-degree connections for LinkedIn (or mutual friends for Facebook). All of these use cases are well served by a graph database.

The responsibility of the user graph service is to manage all the relationships. We just mentioned a user-to-user connection relationship, but the relationship can be of any type. Taking the example of LinkedIn, here are a few relationships that can exist between different entities:

CONNECTED_TO
    User-to-user connections

WORKS_AT
    The user's current organization

WORKED_AT
    The user's past organizations

HAS_SKILL
    The user's skill set

The user graph service exposes APIs to different services for managing any kind of relationships and publishes events for relationship updates that other services can act on.

Keyword or hashtag search is another functional requirement expected from the system. Let's take a look at the search service for serving any search queries performed by the users.

Search Service

What generally comes to mind when we hear the phrase "search use cases" is *indexing*: leveraging inverted index solutions like Elasticsearch to offer search functionality for types of keywords. Searching is a general functionality needed in most systems; we discussed searching in Chapter 15 while building a search engine, and we will return to it in Chapter 18 when we build a hotel reservation system.

As a reminder, here is the search functionality required by the social networking system:

- Retrieve all posts associated with a specific keyword or hashtag. The posts can be further sorted based on location, timestamp, user interests, and so on.

- Search media content (images and videos). In the backend, the system might be generating keywords when media is uploaded. The tags can be system generated or added by the users.

X uses an in-house solution called EarlyBird (an optimized Lucene index) to support searching. The search service aggregator gathers data from all the instances of Early-Bird matching to the search query. Pagination becomes essential for such use cases because the number of results matching a search query can be huge. We'll discuss Elasticsearch optimal configurations like shard size in Chapter 18; the same strategy can be leveraged here to build a search system.

The use cases for searching are many, and there is a need to define the boundaries of what a system is built to support. For example, search for "breakfast recipes" in Instagram, and it presents different types of results in defined sections: "for you" (search results relevant for the user); account names with a breakfast item as the identifier; audio, or music associated with breakfast; tags, or keywords with a breakfast name; and places and reels targeted around "breakfast" as a keyword. Now notice that this search is very fast (along with offering you type-ahead search options), and all these results are rendered very quickly. The amount of data stored on Instagram servers is huge, so the indexing strategy should be quite efficient to power the search functionality at scale.

Figure 16-1 includes invocation of the search service upon any new post creation. The *search service ingestor* component ingests the data into an indexing data store, which is made available via read APIs (*search service aggregator*), as shown in Figure 16-4. The *media metadata extractor service* is an ML component that extracts metadata from images and videos, such as image object (person, location, food item) and location properties if the location is included (location name and location type, such as ocean beach or mountains).

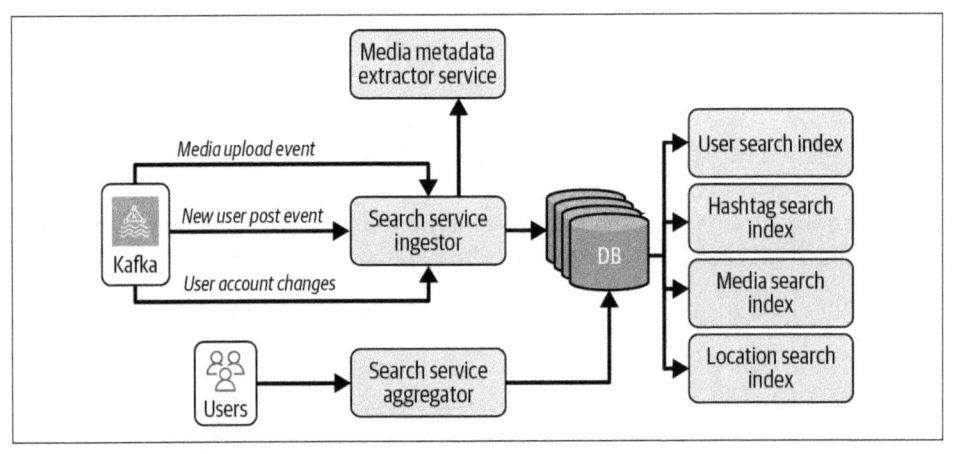

Figure 16-4. Search service

We'll discuss the idea of GraphQL federations for the property search architecture in Chapter 18; a similar implementation can be applied here in the search service aggregator component. The search service aggregator retrieves the results from multiple available indexes based on the query and returns them to the users after ranking them based on relevancy.

With all these insights in mind, let's move to deployment of these components on the AWS cloud.

Launching the System on AWS

The most important consideration for deploying a social networking website is user interaction availability. We should consider how to ensure this when choosing any AWS service. We spent a good amount of time on building systems for handling new posts to make sure the user read paths are optimal. Another consideration for the nature of the system is eventually consistent behavior, giving us the ability to improve on cost and latency. We'll start with the Day 0 architecture of the system and then try to scale for a larger user base.

Day 0 Architecture

We'll design a very basic system to support requirements like uploading of posts by users and ensuring that followers can see these posts in their timelines. The DynamoDB schema (*https://oreil.ly/x3zGg*) from Table 16-2 can be extended to include user information and followers, as shown in Table 16-3.

Table 16-3. User information in Amazon DynamoDB

Query pattern	Schema
User information with counters (number of followers, following, posts)	PK = u#{userId} SK = count
User followers	PK = u#{userId}#followers SK = u#{followerUserId}
User following	PK = u#{userId}#following SK = u#{followingUserId}

A single DynamoDB table serves our storage needs and supports all of the query patterns. We can build the keyword search functionality on top of DynamoDB by streaming the user post data to an Amazon OpenSearch cluster via DynamoDB streams, as shown in Figure 16-5.

This architecture comprises multiple AWS Lambda functions to serve different use cases, as is evident from their names. The transformation Lambda converts DynamoDB data objects to an OpenSearch schema and makes them available for search. This doesn't introduce a separate caching layer, but we can add that as and when required in the form of Amazon DAX or Amazon ElastiCache. We can use Amazon SNS and Amazon SES to deliver notifications to the users, and we can integrate monitoring tools like Amazon CloudWatch for application monitoring and issue debugging.

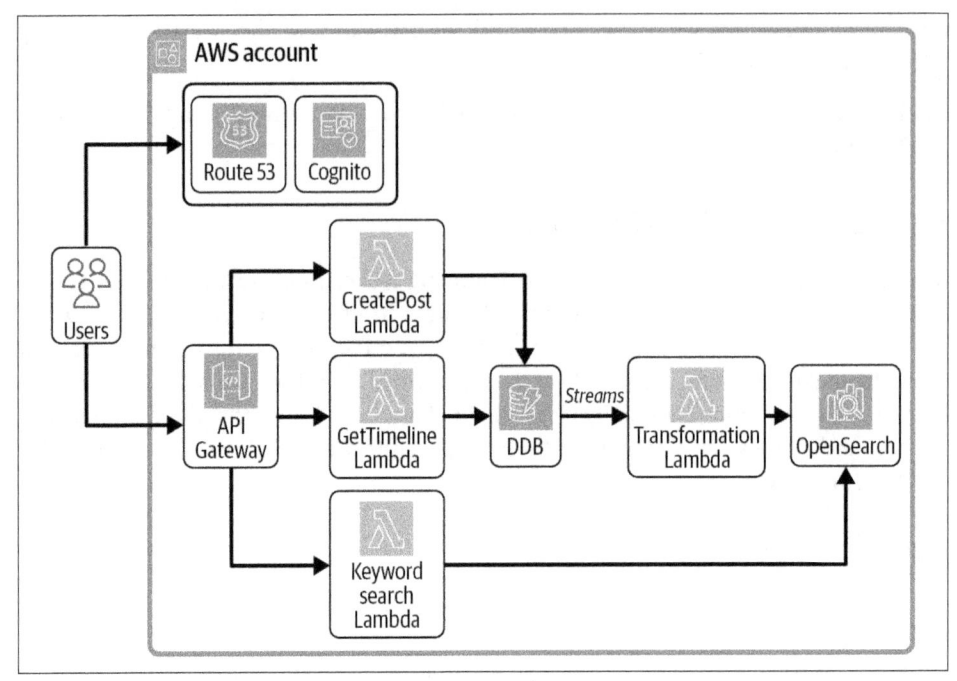

Figure 16-5. Social networking website Day 0 architecture

We skipped the analytics pipeline entirely in the Day 0 architecture; it could be helpful for running complex queries to derive data insights with tools like Amazon Redshift and Amazon QuickSight. The integration can be like data ingestion to an Amazon OpenSearch cluster; a separate Lambda can convert the data to a Redshift schema and save it to the cluster.

Scaling to Millions and Beyond

The scale of social networking websites is huge, and delivering a fast, reliable user experience is of utmost importance. We'll explore many considerations for scaling the architecture throughout the rest of this book, and we recommend taking learnings from all of them. We have already included scalable architecture as part of Figures 16-1 and 16-3; in this section, we'll discuss scaling the architecture further on AWS. Let's start with a few of the storage choices we have made previously in this chapter.

Storage on DynamoDB

Table 16-3 shows the DynamoDB schema for storing a user's information, such as the users that they are following and their followers. We introduced the concept of hot keys in "Amazon DynamoDB" on page 265 in Chapter 10 and made some recommendations to resolve this issue. The suggested DynamoDB schema uses user ID as the partition key, meaning the following and followers data should fit into the limit of 10 GB per user. Some potential problems that can occur with scale, especially for celebrity users, include:

Partition storage limit
> Assuming a storage requirement of 100 bytes for keeping a single follower's data, a celebrity user can have approximately 107 million followers before breaching the 10 GB limit. Revisit Chapter 10 for recommendations on partitioning the data further for a partition that has already been created.

Read and write capacity limit
> DynamoDB throttles the request if a partition has a hard limit of 3,000 RCUs or 1,000 WCUs (or both). The throttling can affect the read/write for count operations that we suggested for managing following and followers count in Table 16-3. This can happen if the user's followers increase or decrease in a spiky workload situation, such as a celebrity gaining popularity after a big endorsement or a falling out of favor due to a public backlash. The problem statement is similar to managing the number of likes for a post or the number of comments on a post. The guiding principle for serving this requirement is eventual consistency. Instead of direct writes to the table, the data should be persisted with a messaging queue in between, and reads should be served from the cache instead of directly hitting the table, as shown in Figure 16-6.

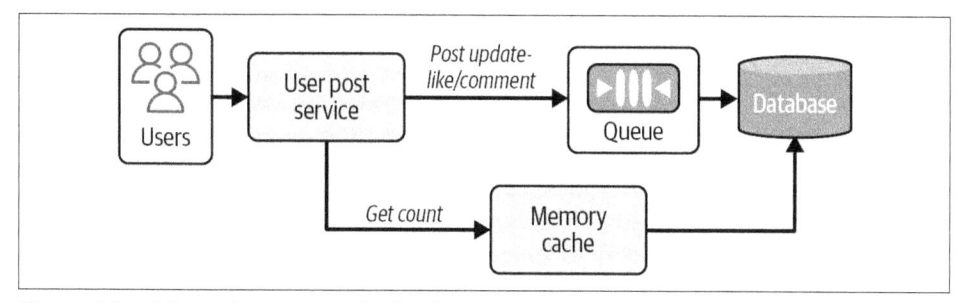

Figure 16-6. Managing count at high volume

We've showcased the user post service in the context of managing the likes count, and a similar pattern is applicable for the number of followers. The write operation can be optimized further by batching multiple requests together; instead of incrementing the like count by one every time, multiple requests can be batched together and updated in one go, reducing database workload.

We discussed the push versus pull mechanism for celebrity users in the context of post creation in "Handling New Posts" on page 418. A similar design problem occurs for the comments published against a post at high scale.

Scaling post comments

We're fine with eventual consistency for the read paths, so the recommendation is comments served using memory cache and in paginated form. An important point to address is that when a user publishes a comment, they should see it with causal consistency, as discussed in Chapter 1. The comment should not disappear due to eventual consistency; this could create confusion about whether it was successfully posted.

One way to address this problem is by handling this behavior in the frontend application (user app or web browser). The application makes an API call to the server for publishing a comment. Upon a successful API response, the comment is cached on the app itself and shown at the top. This is the simplest implementation for a smooth user experience, and a similar design is followed by the social media platforms for the user timeline. The application caches the content on local devices until the response is updated from the servers.

Skip the idea of handling it on the user app for a while—let's think how this can be addressed at the database level. This discussion is important for making decisions in similar problems statements. So the issue is that the user should see a consistent view of data on the application. The simplest implementation is directing all the queries to the leader node where writes are happening (or specifying ConsistentRead (*https://oreil.ly/OKMVD*) as true in the DynamoDB API), but this increases the load on the database. A helpful idea in this situation is "read your write" consistency.

To achieve "read your write" consistency, the user should be tied to the leader node (or enable consistent reads for required operations) for the time being, depending on the time taken for the data replication in the database cluster. Synchronous replication is another way to ensure that all the database nodes have the same view, but it comes with a huge latency cost and is not recommended for write-heavy use cases.

Let's also talk a little bit about reads. The ratio of content producers to consumers is very skewed; the scale of reads is exponentially high compared to the writes. Social platforms generally work on the principle of live comments, meaning that comments are pushed to user devices automatically without refreshing the app or web browser. To support this design, either a user device continuously polls for new updates or the server pushes the updates automatically. A poll-based approach can work at a smaller scale, but it can become a bottleneck with increasing scale. A continuous poll (it should be less than five seconds for near real-time behavior) can overload the backend servers and is not a recommended approach. A system with a push-based approach figures out which viewers are looking at the content and sends the updates to their devices.

The requirement is similar to group messaging for chat applications and is generally solved by managing persistent connections with users' devices. We'll dive deep into chat application design in Chapter 19, with all the architectural nitty-gritty, but let's discuss a shorter way to push comments to all the interested viewers for a particular post, illustrated in Figure 16-7.

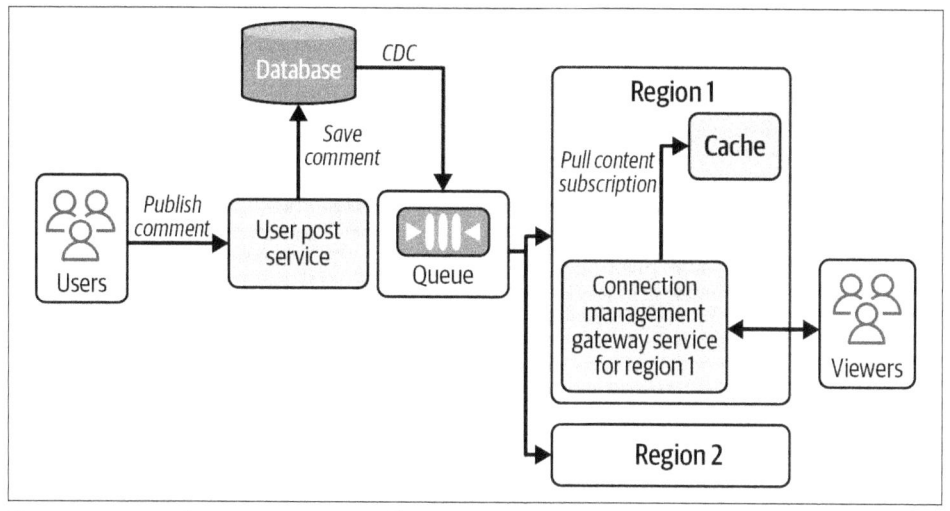

Figure 16-7. Pushing comments to all viewers

Once a comment is published by a user, it is saved locally in the regional database. There is asynchronous replication as well for database writes in one more region for data redundancy, which is discussed in "Multiregion deployments" on page 438. The comment is pushed to the queue for fanning out to all the regions. The regional deployment of the gateway service figures out all the users subscribed to a post and routes the comment to all the user devices.

The authentication and authorization system is another critical component for any system we design. Let's discuss it in the context of scaling the system for millions of customers.

Scaling the authentication system

We'll specifically focus on AuthN and AuthZ and discuss Amazon Cognito scalability and whether it's a good idea to use it at our proposed scale instead of developing a custom solution. We introduced Cognito's offerings and related concepts in Chapter 12, and see that chapter to get the most out of the comparison discussion here. The main idea behind choosing managed services such as Cognito is removing the entire development and operational burden from your plate and letting AWS manage the service end to end.

Security solutions are hard to build and require expertise to build them right because even though the application is operating at a lower scale, you can't compromise on customers' personal data. Table 16-4 compares various aspects of Cognito and a custom authentication service.

Table 16-4. Amazon Cognito versus a custom authentication solution

Comparison aspect	Amazon Cognito	Custom solution
Security features	Cognito comes with multiple features for AuthN and AuthZ, as discussed in Chapter 12.	Cognito allows customization to a great extent, but you still don't have end-to-end flexibility over how the system works internally.
Security expertise	Building solutions to secure your systems takes expertise, and Cognito helps take that off your plate. You don't have to worry about security features and scalability; you can simply focus on the business logic of the software.	Custom solutions require security expertise to build an end-to-end solution. If there is a limitation to using Cognito in any of the aspects, there is an option to build the auth application by self-hosting open source software like Keycloak (*https://keycloak.org*) and amending the code per custom needs.
Operations: managing compute and storage	Cognito scales automatically as needed, and no user intervention is required.	The custom solution requires proper scaling strategies as the business grows.
Compliance regulations, such as HIPAA and PCI DSS	Cognito is compliant with these standards.	The compliance requirements need to be inherently built in custom solutions. While Cognito supports multiple compliance regulations, if any country compliance isn't supported, then custom solutions make more sense.
Multiregion availability	Cognito doesn't offer multiregion support out of the box, which adds extra overhead at the customer's end for managing multiregion users.	Custom solutions can be deployed or replicated across the required regions as needed.
Integration with AWS services	Cognito makes it very easy to integrate with other AWS services, such as Amazon API Gateway and AWS ALB.	Integration requires additional effort for a custom solution.
Migration to another cloud provider, going entirely on-premises, or migrating to a different auth service	Migration can be very tricky with cloud-specific auth solutions. The migration requires figuring out the auth service in another cloud, and it's often a major headache to migrate existing users to a new cloud. Cognito doesn't allow export of user passwords and becomes a bottleneck in migration (you can get around it by authenticating a user via Cognito and forcing them to reset the password; this can work well with active users but is not straightforward for inactive users).	A custom application is easy to migrate to different clouds as long as the compute and storage solutions are cloud agnostic. The extra effort is needed only in situations like moving from Amazon DynamoDB in the AWS cloud to Spanner in the Google cloud (*https://oreil.ly/09MkQ*).

Go through this comparison and identify which aspects best match your needs.

Session management is one of the features we require so that the user doesn't have to go through authentication flow again and again. JWTs (*https://jwt.io/introduction*) are a way to make session management easier. The idea is that once a user is authenticated by the system, subsequent calls to the system should not require AuthN and

AuthZ to speed up the operations (depending on the system architecture, authentication might require talking to an auth service or performing a database lookup to validate the user credentials). JWTs allow users to create a token once they are authenticated for the first time. Subsequent calls to the system are required to pass on this token, and the system validates the user based on this token. This operation is done in memory of the application servers and speeds up the API operations; the API can skip the authorization against specific resources and just focus on executing application logic.

This looks great, but there is no such thing as a free lunch, so what's the catch? The catch is the token expiration time: assume the token expiration is set to five minutes, but the user logs out within one minute. In these scenarios, the token can be misused by man-in-the-middle attacks for the next four minutes, opening the system to security threats. Redis has documented this potential threat in its engineering blog (*https://oreil.ly/_ZVlw*) and recommends using traditional database lookups for user authentication and limiting JWT to service-to-service communications.

We know we keep repeating the phrase "It depends on the business use case," but this holds true here as well. Evaluate the requirements of the system and not blindly settling on any technology. For example, don't assume JWT is a bad choice after reading the previous paragraph; every technology has pros and cons.

We have talked about building Day 0 and Day N architecture in all the chapters in Part III thus far, but this comes with migration effort, so let's discuss a few strategies for planning this better.

Moving from Day 0 to Day N

As companies grow over time, their engineering teams create optimizations on top of existing software or develop new software altogether to support the scale and system features. This should be evaluated from time and time and can heavily depend on the business use case you're trying to solve. Social networking giants like X and Facebook have built multiple technologies to support scale and have made some of them open source. See the documentation of these software applications (refer to the engineering blogs of the companies) to understand the problem statement and solution and gain a deeper understanding of different components in the architecture.

For example, X has developed FlockDB (*https://oreil.ly/vWCwr*) for distributed graph storage, Gizzard (*https://oreil.ly/Op19k*) for managing data partitioning, and Manhattan (*https://oreil.ly/LKb5U*) as a multitenant distributed graph database. Similarly, Facebook has developed Unicorn (*https://oreil.ly/VfVNu*) for searching trillions of edges in the social graph (Instagram uses Unicorn to power the search infrastructure (*https://oreil.ly/q629S*)) and Haystack (*https://oreil.ly/6sRm5*) as object storage for multimedia content, and it has optimized Memcached (*https://oreil.ly/FxOeZ*) for caching at Facebook scale. You can find similar innovations from other companies as well. For example, LinkedIn built its in-house graph database called LIquid (*https://oreil.ly/3X8gm*) to support multidegree connections.

Once an improved system is built, the traffic should be seamlessly transitioned to this new system without affecting end users. The strategy of migration can vary depending on multiple factors, such as the following:

- Migration happens with downtime, and the application is not available in a certain time window. The migration process becomes much more complex if it should be completed without any downtime.
- Whether the system is stateless or stateful: stateless systems are relatively easier to migrate as there is no state saved on the server instance and it is maintained in a database on a different hardware machine. Stateful systems maintain a backend system and database on a single hardware machine. We'll discuss an example of a stateful system in Chapter 19.

Let's discuss different strategies we can follow for smooth migration.

Traffic replication on the new system. We need a mechanism for gaining confidence in the working of the new system, and the best way is to put this system to work. The work for the system is serving actual production traffic. Once developer or quality assurance testing is completed, the system should be tested against real production traffic, as shown in Figure 16-8.

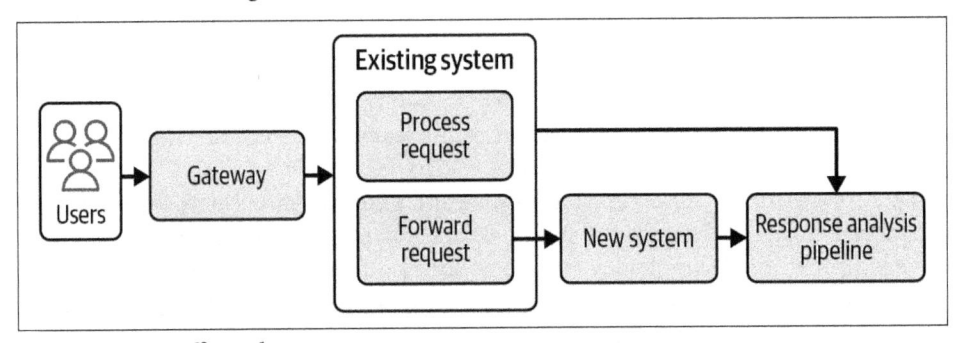

Figure 16-8. Traffic replication on a new system

The existing system both processes the request and forwards the same request to the new system. The *response analysis pipeline* compares these two responses and generates metrics for verification. To ensure the same process can be leveraged by other teams in the organization, we can create a separate service component responsible for replaying the traffic to the new system and verify the results.

Note that the customers are still served by the existing system; the new system is just working in parallel for confidence. To start, the new system is exposed to a portion of the production system and is gradually scaled for all the production traffic. Any issues encountered are fixed along the way.

Actual system migration. Once we're sure the new system is working as expected, we can expose the new system to serve the actual production traffic. This is again done in stages to ensure smooth migration; a strategy for user-facing applications is shown in Figure 16-9.

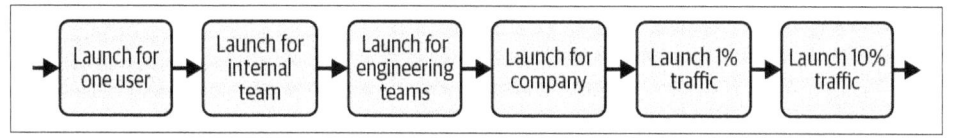

→ Launch for one user → Launch for internal team → Launch for engineering teams → Launch for company → Launch 1% traffic → Launch 10% traffic →

Figure 16-9. Rollout strategy for a user-facing application

A/B testing is a popular strategy that works in a similar fashion. You design experiments and divide the traffic accordingly based on traffic division logic; one such logic is shown in Figure 16-8.

Once the application works well with a limited set of user groups, we can move to a percentage-wise rollout. We can start with as little as 1% of the traffic and gradually move to 10%, 30%, 50%, and so on. After a 100% rollout of the new system, we recommend letting it run for about two weeks and then deciding when to turn off the old system.

Migration is a relatively easier process if no database migration is involved, but if this is not the case, let's discuss some recommendations to handle that.

Database migration. Database migration can involve moving from an older data model to a newer data model on the same database engine or a data-model upgrade and a change of database engine, such as moving from PostgreSQL to DynamoDB.

Here are a few tips for a smooth database migration:

- The older data needs to be moved to a newer database model. This can be done by offline batch loads using a transformation layer, which converts older model data to newer model data.
- During the migration window, the system should follow a dual write strategy. This means the data should be written to both databases.
- The read strategy is also dual. This means the system reads data from both the databases. An extra verification layer can be added that compares the data from both databases for validation. This holds true if the database migration is only involved within the same system; if there is an entirely new architecture

with a different database, the verification can happen at the API request level, as discussed in previous sections.

The last step for any type of migration is clearing up the old resources. The old architecture should be tiered down to remove any operational burden and save the cost of unused resources.

Day N Architecture

The scope of building a user timeline can grow over time and can include additional posts based on interests, location, or any other particular parameters. The primary requirement for building a timeline is to show all posts from the people a user is following, and additional components can be added as the system evolves. The Day N architecture based on all the discussion in this chapter is presented in Figure 16-10.

We skipped Amazon CloudFront in the architecture diagram for simplification, but the idea is to serve media content from a CDN instead of downloading it directly from the S3 bucket. We'll discuss multiple content distribution strategies as part of Chapter 20. We touched on the orchestration component in Chapter 15, and we can use the same reference here.

We should identify the critical components of the system for operating and for serving the users; ranking the posts at user level or adding more posts are extras that we're building to keep users engaged. Let's elaborate more on this idea and how it can help achieve high availability for the systems in the overall architecture.

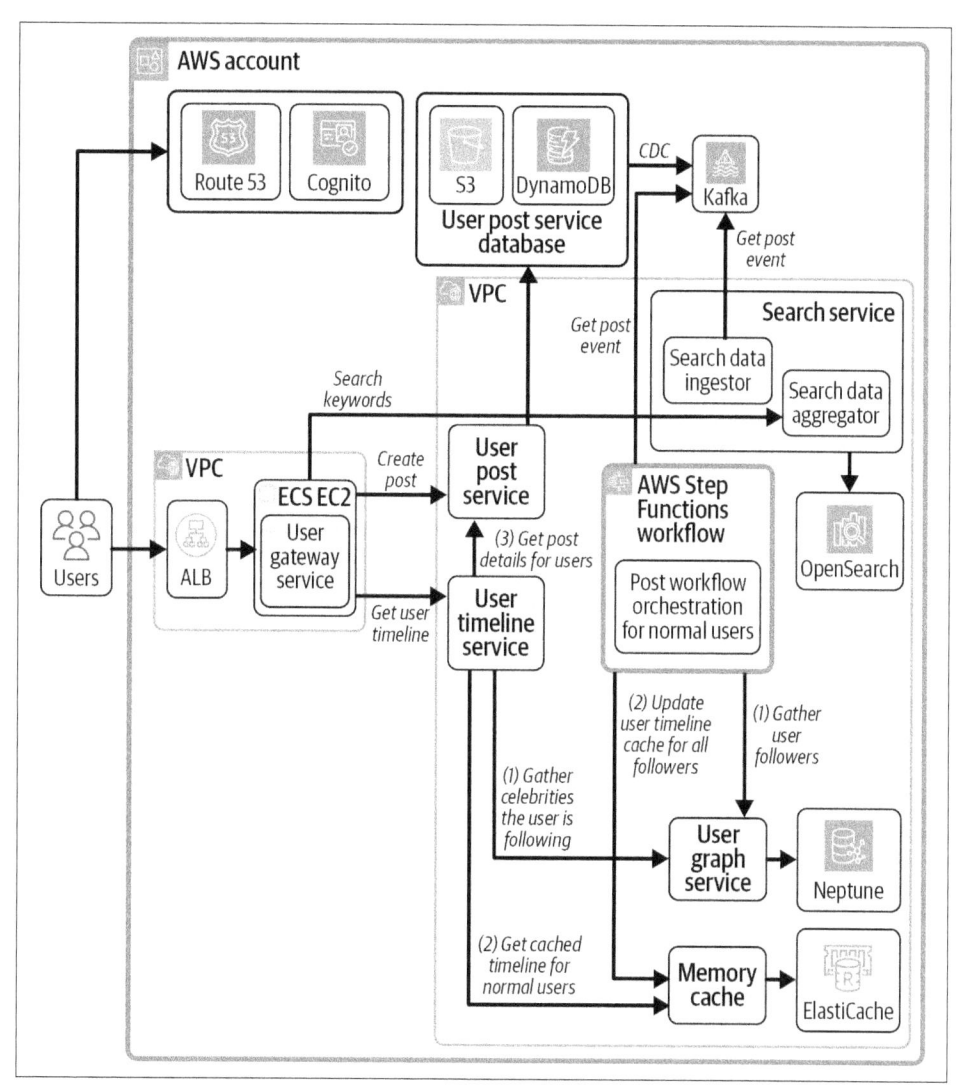

Figure 16-10. Day N architecture

High availability of system

In case of any unforeseen instances, such as cloud provider services going down or increased load due to a retry storm with newly introduced code, the system architecture should ensure that end users are least impacted. We should perform multiple levels of testing from time to time to ensure that the issues are identified beforehand, but let's discuss some recommendations for how to plan better if this situation does occur.

The first recommendation involves identifying the criticality of the application. All the subsystems in the architecture are assigned a certain level of priority; for example Amazon follows a tier structure: Tier 1 means a highly critical system with direct impact on the customer, Tier 2 means a medium-critical system with medium impact (for example, an order is delayed by one day but is still delivered), and Tier 3 means a low-critical system that provides an add-on experience. This division helps Amazon focus only on Tier 1 systems in case of downtime and further makes it mandatory for these systems to go through extra steps of testing before any new changes are made live.

Another suggestion in the same vein involves identifying requests that need to be processed based on priority and dropping nonpriority requests. Let's take an example from Netflix's systems (*https://oreil.ly/7Hi6Z*). Two types of requests are sent to the API gateway: playback requests and telemetry requests. Telemetry requests send the health metrics from the user devices, which are helpful for improving the user experience, but playback requests are most critical because they serve the content. Based on the health metrics, a system state can be identified beforehand, and the gateway drops the request instead of building up the request queue of the system.

An important consideration for large systems is deployment across regions. Let's discuss multiregion deployments in more detail.

Multiregion deployments

Managing an application on such a large scale comes with a lot of challenges, and expanding the application to multiple regions brings a new set of issues. There can be different reasons why companies choose this kind of deployment strategy:

- Following compliance regulations, where the data of one country's users should reside in the same country's data center
- Increasing application resiliency so that the service operates without disruptions even if a cloud region goes down entirely
- Bringing applications nearer to the end users so that requests can be served faster

Let's assume the application is deployed in two AWS regions, and both serve the customer traffic depending on the geolocation of the customer. If one of the region's services are impacted, the traffic is shifted to the functional region, and the customer experience is not affected, as shown in Figure 16-11.

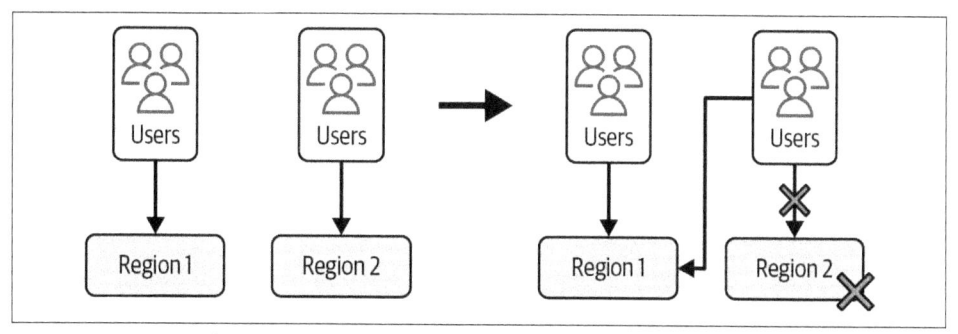

Figure 16-11. Traffic switch upon region failure

Here are a few important considerations for service deployment in multiple regions:

- Both regions are completely functional and can independently serve the customer traffic. There are no common services between the regions.
- The services are stateless, and the state is maintained only at the database layer. The information stored in the databases is continuously replicated to another region asynchronously (because user requests should not be affected due to replication lag). Either the database replication is inherently supported by the database, such as with DynamoDB global tables (*https://oreil.ly/hZONb*) and the global data store for ElastiCache Redis (*https://oreil.ly/mJ4KM*), or you should implement it on your own if support is not available in the database.
- Service deployments across the regions should be in sync with automation as much as possible. Additionally, consider keeping a buffer window between the same deployment on multiple regions. This helps identify any issues in one region before changes are propagated to another region.

In the scenario of region downtime, traffic should be shifted to another region, as shown in Figure 16-11. We recommend shifting this traffic gradually rather than in one go to avoid disruptions in another region due to increased traffic. The thundering herd problem (*https://oreil.ly/w3FV9*) can arise if all the clients switch to another region at the same time. Random jitter should be introduced in the client devices for API invocation to the server.

Serving some users is better than serving none. For region failures, consider a load-shedding strategy to drop a percentage of requests to manage the load on a single region. The systems can eventually be scaled in the single region to serve all the traffic.

Conclusion

Along with identifying system requirements and boundaries, it is very important to figure out user behavior and traffic patterns for how users interact with the platform. Our social networking system has two kinds of users—normal users with fewer followers and celebrity users with followers in the millions—and we segregated these two types for optimal design when building the user timeline.

We also surfaced multiple examples of systems, starting with a simple architecture and then moving to a more complex one as new requirements come up or as the system scales for more users. One such example is managing the user relationships in databases like MySQL and later moving to a graph database to optimally figure out indirect relationships (such as the second-degree connections in LinkedIn). The same analogy applies to choosing a cloud provider service versus building the entire service on your own, as we described in our comparison of Cognito and a custom authentication solution.

In the next chapter, we'll explore the design of another real-time system: an online gaming leadership board in multiplayer games. This chapter will introduce you to concepts around designing low-latency systems with multiple concurrent users playing at the same time.

CHAPTER 17
Designing an Online Game Leaderboard

Online gaming has surged in popularity over the past decade, becoming a global phenomenon that connects millions of players across the world. Games like *Fortnite*, *League of Legends*, *Dota*, and *Call of Duty* have not only provided entertainment but also fostered competitive communities where players continuously strive to improve their skills. A central feature that amplifies this competitive spirit is the *leaderboard*: a system that ranks players based on their performance.

Leaderboards serve as a tangible measure of achievement, motivating players to climb the ranks and outperform their peers. They enhance player engagement by offering clear goals and fostering a sense of community and rivalry. However, behind the simple interface of a leaderboard lies a complex system that must efficiently handle real-time data processing, massive user bases, and the demand for instantaneous updates.

In this chapter, we will delve into the design and architecture of an online game leaderboard system. We'll focus on building a scalable, efficient, real-time ranking system using AWS services. Starting with the foundational requirements, we'll explore how to architect a solution that can grow from supporting a few thousand players to millions worldwide. By building the solution from first principles, we'll create a Day 0 architecture suitable for a startup. Finally, we'll explore strategies to scale the system to handle millions of users, addressing potential bottlenecks and leveraging AWS services effectively. By the end of this chapter, you'll have a comprehensive understanding of how to design a robust online game leaderboard system on AWS that is capable of delivering a seamless, engaging experience to players around the globe.

System Requirements

The requirements center on enhancing player engagement and fostering a competitive community within an online multiplayer game. The leaderboard system is integral to this goal, serving not only as a measure of individual achievement but also as a social platform where players can compare their performance against friends and rivals globally. Let's look at the functional and nonfunctional requirements of our game leaderboard system.

Functional and Nonfunctional Requirements

In modern gaming, the most important functional requirement is that the leaderboards are updated in real time, reflecting players' achievements as they happen. This immediacy is crucial; it heightens the competitive atmosphere and motivates players to continue playing to improve their rankings.

From a business perspective, the leaderboard system supports several critical objectives:

Player retention
By providing immediate and accurate feedback on performance, the leaderboard incentivizes players to continue engaging with the game to improve their rankings.

Community building
Leaderboards foster a sense of community and healthy rivalry, encouraging players to interact and compete with one another.

Monetization opportunities
The leaderboard can be tied to in-game rewards, achievements, or special events, providing additional incentives for players to engage with the game and potentially spend on in-game purchases.

Data insights
The leaderboard system can offer valuable analytics on player behavior and performance trends, informing future game development and marketing strategies.

Leaderboards are not just a feature but a fundamental component that can make or break the gaming experience. In games like the *Battle Royale* titles or massively multiplayer online role-playing games (MMORPGs), leaderboards can be global, regional, or even segmented by specific in-game events or seasons. The system must handle the following critical tasks to meet these expectations:

Real-time score processing
As players achieve milestones, complete levels, or defeat opponents, their scores should be processed and reflected on the leaderboard instantly.

Accurate ranking
> The system should accurately rank players based on scores, implementing tie-breaking criteria to ensure fairness. It must also support dynamic filtering, allowing players to view global, regional, or event-based rankings.

Filtering and segmentation
> Players should be able to view leaderboards based on various criteria like global standings, friends' scores, or time-specific leaderboards (daily, weekly, monthly).

In-game notifications
> Real-time notifications should be integrated to inform players of ranking changes, new milestones, or other significant events, enhancing engagement.

Designing a leaderboard system that can handle the immense scale and the demand for real-time updates is a complex challenge. It involves managing high volumes of data, ensuring low latency for both reads and writes, and maintaining data consistency across distributed systems—all while providing a seamless experience to the end user.

The system should meet the following NFRs to ensure a smooth and competitive player experience:

Real-time updates
> Players expect near-instant updates to their scores on the leaderboard, necessitating low-latency write and read operations. Write latency should be under one second, while read latency for leaderboard retrievals should be less than 100 ms.

Consistency
> The system should maintain eventual consistency across distributed servers, ensuring that players see accurate and up-to-date rankings.

High availability
> The system must maintain 24-7 availability, with redundant architecture to handle failures without affecting user experience.

Scalability
> The system should handle fluctuating player volumes, from a few during off-peak times to millions during global events or tournaments. It should be able to scale horizontally, enabling seamless expansion as player engagement grows.

Low latency
> Both write and read operations must be optimized to ensure a low-latency experience. Network communication between servers and clients should be efficient, minimizing delay.

System Scale

Understanding the scale at which the system needs to operate is essential for making informed design decisions. Let's explore the scale considerations in terms of storage, bandwidth, throughput, and latency.

Storage requirements

The storage solution must accommodate the growing amount of data, including player profiles, scores, game statistics, and historical data. Let's calculate estimates for one thousand players, each potentially submitting multiple scores per day.

The assumptions are:

> Average submissions per player per day = 5
>
> Average storage record size = 500 bytes (player ID, score, timestamp, and metadata)

With these assumptions, the storage requirement for one thousand players can be calculated as:

> Daily data ingestion = 1,000 players × 5 submissions/player × 500 bytes = 2.5 MB/day
>
> Monthly data storage = 2.5 MB/day × 30 days = 75 MB/month

Calculate storage requirements for 10 million players with the same assumptions:

> Daily data ingestion = 107 players × 5 submissions/player × 500 bytes = 25 GB/day
>
> Monthly data storage = 25 GB/day × 30 days = 750 GB/month
>
> Annual data storage = 750 GB/month × 12 months = 9 TB/year

Configure the following data retention policies for older data to optimize costs:

Historical data
> Decide how long to retain historical scores. For example, keep data for one year before archiving.

Archiving
> Move older data to cost-effective storage solutions like Amazon S3 Glacier or Infrequent access tiers.

We also suggest using data compression techniques where applicable to reduce the data footprint.

Bandwidth and throughput

The system must handle a high number of read and write requests per second, especially during peak gaming hours.

The requirements for write operations (score submissions) are:

> Peak write rate per second assuming 1% of total players (10⁷ players × 1% = 100,000 players) submit scores simultaneously and submissions occur over a 10-minute window = 100,000 submissions ÷ 600 seconds ≈ 167 writes/sec
>
> Peak write rate (tournaments) = 1,000 writes per second

The requirements for read operations (leaderboard retrievals) are:

> Assuming each player checks the leaderboard twice a day = 10⁷ players × 2 retrievals/player = 20 million retrievals/day
>
> Average read requests per second = 20 million retrievals/day ÷ 86,400 seconds/day ≈ 231 reads/sec

We take networking solutions for granted and assume they work out of the box because of the multiple serverless offerings by AWS and the easy configuration management of all the services. We discussed multiple distributed system fallacies in Chapter 1, and most of them are related to management of computer networks. We often assume the network is reliable and secure with zero latency and infinite available bandwidth, but this is not the case. We should always take into consideration the required network bandwidth for our business use case. Let's calculate this for an online gaming leaderboard:

> Average payload size = retrieval of 100 entries at 1 KB per entry = 100 entries × 1 KB = 100 KB
>
> Bandwidth for reads = 231 reads/sec × 100 KB = 23.1 MB/sec
>
> Bandwidth for writes = 167 writes/sec × 500 bytes = 83.5 KB/sec

We've gathered the system requirements and gotten an idea of the scale the architecture needs to support. Let's dive into the design.

Starting with the Design

Designing a robust, scalable online game leaderboard system requires a deep understanding of fundamental concepts and principles for distributed systems, data modeling, and concurrency control. By applying these first principles, we can create an architecture that not only meets the current requirements but also is flexible enough to adapt to future needs.

Concepts and Principles

We'll discuss different principles and try to figure out a direction for breaking the problem into smaller parts, starting with data modeling. We'll also touch on other factors, such as latency and consistency.

Data modeling

At the heart of our leaderboard system lies the need for efficient data structures capable of handling sorting and ranking operations at scale. These are the major aspects of data modeling:

Efficient sorting and ranking
> We need data structures that allow quick insertion, deletion, and retrieval while maintaining order based on player scores. Using sorted data structures like skip lists (*https://oreil.ly/HsHKU*) or balanced binary search trees (*https://oreil.ly/2nhBb*) can be beneficial. In-memory data stores like Redis sorted sets (*https://oreil.ly/Q1hJN*) provide built-in support for these operations with high performance.

Schema design
> The database schema should support various querying patterns, including filtering by region, friends, or time frames. Denormalization may be employed to optimize read performance, sacrificing some storage efficiency for speed.

Latency

Low latency is one of the requirements for a smooth user experience with the system. A write latency of 500 ms is an acceptable number. Multiple factors can affect the latency, such as network delays, database write times, and implementation logic processing overhead. For optimizing the write operations, we recommend asynchronous processing and batch writes wherever feasible.

Similarly, we decided 100 ms was an acceptable read latency in "System Requirements" on page 442. Some factors that can affect read latency include data retrieval time, sorting algorithms, and network transmission. We can leverage in-memory caching and efficient data-retrieval methods as an optimization strategy to fix the potential bottlenecks. Users are located worldwide, and solutions like CDN and multiregion deployments can help reduce the overall latency.

Eventual consistency

Balancing the need for real-time updates with system performance may involve accepting eventual consistency in certain components since strong consistency can affect performance and availability. For leaderboards, slight delays in updates are often acceptable, making eventual consistency a viable option.

Choosing the right consistency model depends on the specific use case even with the eventual consistency option. For example, we discussed "reads your write" consistency in Chapter 16, and that might be important for displaying a player's own score immediately after it is submitted.

Data partitioning and sharding

We discussed sharding and partitioning in Chapter 2: these are important with increasing data. Distributing data effectively prevents bottlenecks and allows the system to scale horizontally.

There are two possible partitioning strategies:

By player ID
    Distribute data based on player IDs to ensure even load distribution.

By region
    Partition data by geographic region to reduce latency and comply with data-residency laws.

Selecting an appropriate shard key is vital. It should ensure an even distribution of data and workload. Examples include using a hash of the player ID or combining multiple fields like region and player ID. The system should be capable of rebalancing shards dynamically to handle changes in data distribution or workload. Consistent hashing algorithms are used to distribute data evenly and handle dynamic scaling.

Sorting algorithms

Efficient sorting is crucial for maintaining accurate rankings, especially with large datasets. For small datasets, in-memory sorting algorithms like quicksort or heapsort can be sufficient. With datasets that cannot fit into memory, external merge sort (*https://oreil.ly/FR1be*) allows sorting by dividing the data into manageable chunks. For incremental updates, instead of re-sorting the entire dataset upon each new score submission, algorithms that support incremental updates can improve efficiency.

Caching strategies

Implementing caching mechanisms is vital to reduce latency and offload read traffic from the database. Use in-memory data stores like Redis to cache frequently accessed data, such as top leaderboard entries. Define strategies for cache expiration and invalidation to ensure data freshness.

Based on these concepts and principles, let's compose a rough system design that stitches the basic components together.

A Rough System Design

A high-level system design that meets our requirements is shown in Figure 17-1.

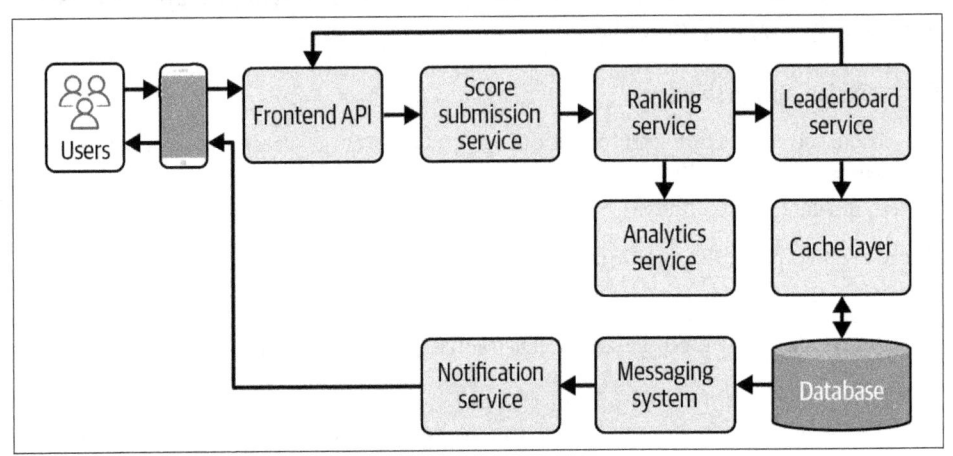

Figure 17-1. Online game leaderboard system architecture

Let's review each piece of this architecture in more detail.

Score submission service

The *score submission service* handles incoming score submissions from players with the following features:

API endpoints
    Provide secure endpoints for game clients to submit scores

Input validation
    Ensures that the submitted scores are valid and not tampered with

Authentication and authorization
    Verify the identity of the player and ensure that they have the right to submit a score

Asynchronous processing
> Uses a messaging system to queue score updates for processing, allowing the service to respond quickly to the client

The client can have "reads your write" consistency with sticky sessions for the server node, with synchronous response and asynchronous processing to queue score updates for other server nodes for other players to view.

Ranking service

The *ranking service* is responsible for calculating player rankings based on the scores with the following features:

Real-time processing
> Updates rankings as new scores are processed

Efficient data structures
> Use data structures that support quick ranking operations, such as sorted sets in Redis

Tie-breaking logic
> Implements rules to handle players with identical scores, such as using submission timestamps as tiebreakers

Leaderboard service

The *leaderboard service* provides the interface for retrieving leaderboard data with the following features:

API endpoints
> Allows clients to request leaderboards with various filters (global, regional, friends)

Pagination
> Supports pagination to handle leaderboards with large numbers of entries

Cache utilization
> Retrieves data from the cache layer to minimize latency

Database

The database stores player scores, profiles, and other relevant data with the following components:

Primary storage
> A NoSQL database like Amazon DynamoDB can handle high write throughput and scale horizontally.

Data partitioning
  Shards data based on player ID or region to distribute the load.

Indexes
  Secondary indexes are created to support various querying patterns.

Data backups and replication
  The data is replicated across multiple nodes for faster response times, and backups are maintained for recovery mechanisms.

Cache layer

The *cache layer* improves read performance by storing frequently accessed data in memory with the following features:

In-memory store
  Uses Redis for its sorted set data structure, which is ideal for ranking

Data expiration policies
  Define when cached data should be refreshed or invalidated to ensure accuracy

Distributed cache
  Employs a cluster of cache servers to handle the load and provide redundancy

Messaging system

The *messaging system* handles asynchronous communication between services with the following features:

Message queues
  Implement queues using systems like Amazon SQS or Apache Kafka to decouple score submissions from processing.

Event-driven architecture
  Services react to events, such as new score submissions, to trigger necessary actions like updating rankings.

Scalability
  The messaging system should scale to handle spikes in message volume during peak times.

Frontend API

The *frontend API* acts as the gateway between game clients and backend services as follows:

Load balancing
  Uses load balancers to distribute incoming requests evenly

Security measures
    Implements SSL/TLS for secure communication and protects against common web vulnerabilities

Rate limiting
    Prevents abuse by limiting the number of requests a client can make in a given time frame; the requests are throttled in case the limit is breached

Additional components

Along with the core functionalities, the following services need to be added to the overall system:

Monitoring and logging
    Implements tools like Amazon CloudWatch to monitor system performance and troubleshoot issues.

Analytics service
    Collects data on player behavior and system performance for business insights; this can be a planned component that can be built as part of scaling the architecture to Day N.

Notification service
    Sends in-game notifications to players when their rankings change using services like Amazon SNS.

With the rough system design in place, the next step involves launching the system on AWS. This process will leverage various AWS services to ensure scalability, reliability, and performance optimization across all components of the application.

Launching the System on AWS

Having established the foundational principles and requirements for our online game leaderboard system, we can now begin designing the initial architecture on AWS. For a startup with approximately a thousand players, the system doesn't need to be overly complex. However, it should be designed with scalability in mind to accommodate future growth seamlessly.

Day 0 Architecture

Our Day 0 architecture focuses on simplicity and cost-effectiveness while ensuring that the core functionalities—score submission, real-time leaderboard updates, and data retrieval—are efficiently handled. The architecture leverages several AWS services to meet these needs:

Amazon API Gateway
    Acts as the entry point for all client requests, providing a secure, scalable API endpoint

AWS Lambda functions
    Handle stateless compute tasks for processing score submissions and retrieving leaderboard data

Amazon DynamoDB
    Serves as the primary data store for player scores, profiles, and metadata

Amazon ElastiCache for Redis
    Implements an in-memory caching layer to store frequently accessed leaderboard entries for quick retrieval

Amazon SQS
    Manages asynchronous processing of score updates and decouples components for better scalability

Amazon SNS
    Facilitates in-game notifications when a player's ranking changes

Figure 17-2 illustrates the Day 0 architecture for our online game leaderboard system.

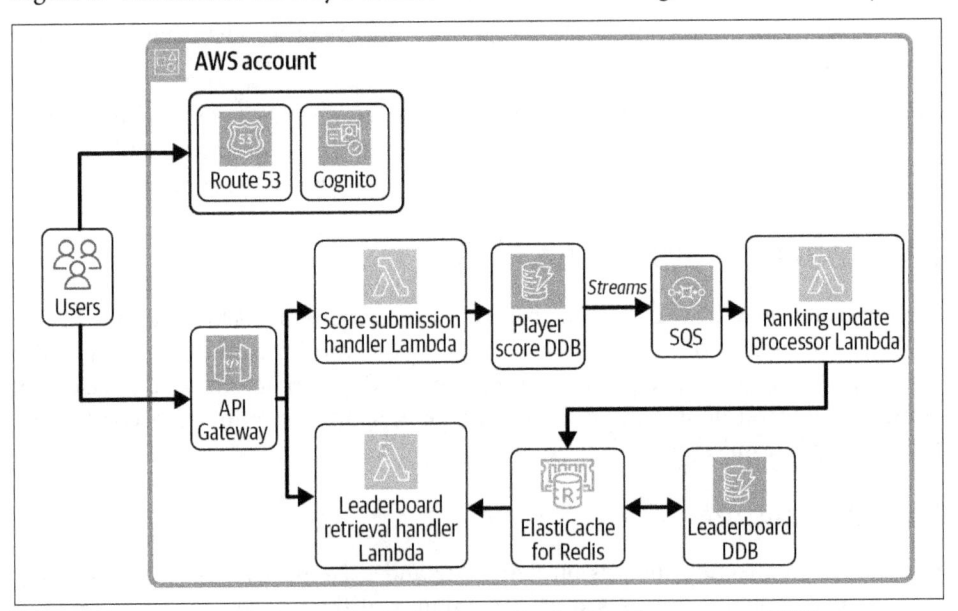

Figure 17-2. Day 0 architecture for online game leaderboard system on AWS

Let's delve into how each component functions within the architecture and how they interact to fulfill our system's requirements. Table 17-1 describes the different Lambda functions and their purposes.

Table 17-1. Lambda functions in the system architecture

Lambda function	Triggered by	Operations
Score submission handler	Amazon API Gateway when a player submits a score	Validates the incoming score data Writes the score to Amazon DynamoDB Sends a message to an SQS queue for asynchronous processing
Leaderboard retrieval handler	Amazon API Gateway when a player requests leaderboard data	Checks ElastiCache (Redis) for cached leaderboard data If cached data is not available or outdated, retrieves data from DynamoDB, updates the cache, and returns the data to the client
Ranking update processor	Messages in the SQS queue	Processes score submissions from the queue Refreshes relevant leaderboard caches in ElastiCache Updates rankings in DynamoDB Publishes notifications to SNS if a player's ranking has changed significantly

We decided to use DynamoDB to store player scores, profiles, and rankings. Table 17-2 lists the different tables and suggested schema. We could very well use a single-table design to store all the entities, as discussed in the previous use case chapters.

Table 17-2. Amazon DynamoDB schema

Table name	Partition key	Sort key	Additional attributes
Player Scores table	Player ID	Timestamp or game session ID	Score, metadata, region, etc.
Leaderboard table	Leaderboard type (e.g., global, regional) with leaderboard ID, such as Global#{leaderboardId}	Rank (inverted for descending order)	Player ID, score, etc.

We're also using Amazon ElastiCache for Redis as a caching and processing layer to reduce read latency for frequently accessed data with the following features:

Leaderboard data cache
    Stores the top *N* leaderboard entries to serve quick read requests

Sorted sets
    Utilizes Redis sorted sets to maintain ordered lists of players based on their scores

Cache invalidation
    Implements strategies to refresh or invalidate cached data when updates occur

Performance
    Offers submillisecond latency for read operations

> In place of Amazon ElastiCache and Amazon DynamoDB in the Day 0 architecture, we can use Amazon RDS to store the players' data and use a combination of indexes and an `ORDER BY` query to retrieve the leaderboard.

In addition, SQS facilitates asynchronous processing of score submissions and decouples the score submission from the ranking update process. SNS is used to send notifications to players when significant events occur, such as changes in rankings. SNS receives notifications from the ranking update processor and forwards them to subscribed endpoints, such as mobile push notifications, email, or SMS. Table 17-3 describes flows in the architecture to summarize how the different components interact to achieve the needed functionality.

Table 17-3. Implementation flows in the system architecture

Flow name	Flow details
Score submission flow	The game client submits a score via the API Gateway. The API Gateway invokes the score submission handler Lambda function. The Lambda function validates the score and writes it to DynamoDB. A message is sent to the SQS queue for asynchronous ranking updates.
Ranking update flow	The ranking update processor Lambda function is triggered by messages in the SQS queue. It reads the new scores from DynamoDB. Rankings are recalculated, and the Leaderboard table in DynamoDB is updated. Relevant entries in ElastiCache are refreshed to reflect the new rankings. Notifications are sent via SNS if necessary.
Leaderboard retrieval flow	The game client requests leaderboard data via the API Gateway. The API Gateway invokes the leaderboard retrieval handler Lambda function. The Lambda function first checks ElastiCache for the requested data. If the data is not available or stale, it retrieves the information from DynamoDB, updates the cache, and returns the data to the client.

Now, let's examine potential issues that might occur in the current architecture and suggestions for scaling it to millions of users.

Scaling to Millions and Beyond

As our online game gains popularity and the player base grows from thousands to millions, our system architecture must evolve to handle the increased load while maintaining low latency and high availability. Scaling the leaderboard system involves identifying potential bottlenecks, optimizing components for high throughput, and leveraging AWS services designed for large-scale operations. Let's discuss different areas for improvement of the architecture, starting with the compute for deploying the systems.

Compute

Lambda as a compute option removes all the operational burden, but since it is fully managed, there are limited configuration options. There are certain limitations for allowed quota, but we can resolve them by requesting a higher concurrency limit from AWS or implementing efficient batching and throttling mechanisms within the application logic. Revisit "AWS Lambda" on page 286 in Chapter 11 for resolutions to problems like cold start with Lambda.

As the system grows, moving from Lambda functions to containerized services using AWS Fargate or Amazon ECS with EC2 might provide better performance and control. We discussed ECS in Chapter 11, but let's reiterate some of the benefits we can achieve with it:

Fine-grained resource management
    Allocate specific CPU and memory resources based on workload requirements

Persistent connections
    Maintain persistent connections to databases and caches, reducing connection overhead

Customization
    Customize runtime environments and optimize for specific application needs

We recommend configuring autoscaling policies for the compute resources, such as automatically adjusting the number of ECS tasks based on resource utilization. This helps handle scaling in and scaling out, and you pay for resources only when they are needed.

Another important consideration is storage for scaling out the architecture, which we'll discuss next.

Storage

DynamoDB is an infinitely scalable database, and we recommend designing optimal query patterns to avoid issues like hot partitions and maintain submillisecond latency of DynamoDB invocations. We also recommend leveraging DynamoDB capabilities like on-demand capacity mode and provisioned capacity mode with autoscaling to avoid request throttling.

Caching and prefetching data become important mostly at peak hours for improving latency when retrieving leaderboard data. We discussed multiregion deployments in Chapter 16, and they can be leveraged here as well to increase resiliency and reduce application latency. Some other recommendations include:

- Employing techniques discussed in Chapter 4 like cache-aside or write-through caching, which can improve data freshness and access speed
- Distributing data across multiple Redis nodes with Redis cluster mode, allowing the cluster to store more data and handle higher throughput, which adds more shards to the cluster to increase capacity and enhances the fault tolerance via automatic failovers to replicas
- Using Global Datastore for cross-region replication of cached data, similar to DynamoDB global tables

We've leveraged the leaderboard retrieval handler Lambda to support user read queries. Let's discuss some improvements on this.

Scaling data retrieval

The logic for data updates is dependent on the fact that the user app is requesting leaderboard updates continuously. This is not scalable and can add to server loads. The more efficient approach here is to push the data from the server to the user devices instead of all the user devices pulling the data.

We discussed a similar architecture in "Scaling post comments" on page 430 in Chapter 16 that can be used here as well. We recommend using persistent connections for such use cases, which we also touch on in Chapters 6 and 19. We can have a custom implementation to manage these connections, as we do in Chapter 19, or we can leverage AWS AppSync for managed GraphQL service-to-pubs real-time updates to the clients over WebSocket connections.

We came up with the storage and bandwidth calculations based on read and write traffic assumptions. We can now use this information to calculate the cost that will be incurred to deploy the solution on the AWS cloud. One factor we often skip when developing software systems is the overall cost; instead, we just look at the cloud provider bills. Let's discuss the *total cost of ownership (TCO)* with respect to building any solution.

Total cost of ownership

The TCO is the cost associated with operating a product throughout its lifecycle. There are multiple components of TCO, as shown in Figure 17-3, and each component has an associated cost. We should understand each component to get a complete view of the cost for building and launching a product, starting with the initial costs.

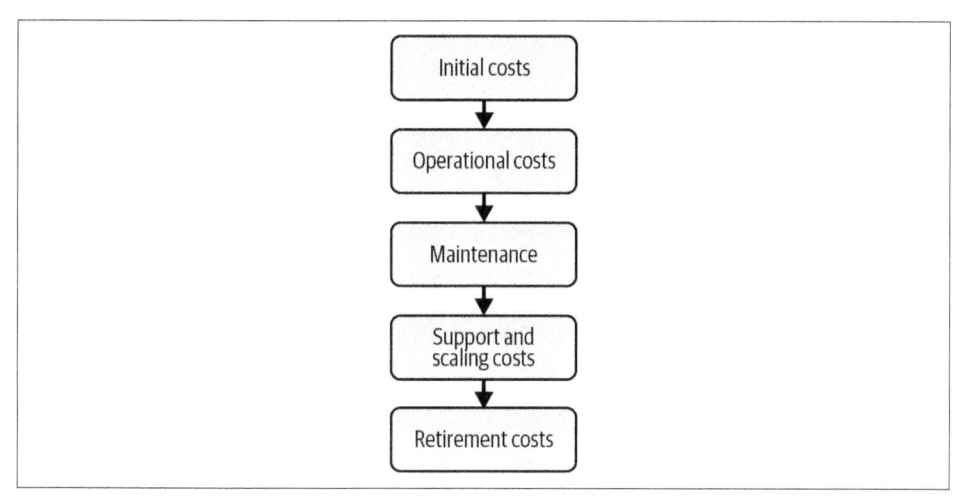

Figure 17-3. Product lifecycle in the context of TCO

Initial costs. As you plan the initial software launch, there is a setup cost for software operations. This includes cloud provider costs for infrastructure (such as EC2, Lambda, etc.), networking (such as NAT gateway), AuthN and AuthZ (such as Cognito), security (such as Shield or WAF) and CI/CD (such as CodePipeline for continuous software delivery and GitHub or CodeCommit for hosting code with version control). There can also be costs related to security and compliance certifications or other services used from a cloud provider depending on the needs, such as Redshift for analytics and CloudWatch for monitoring.

Apart from direct costs paid to a cloud provider or other vendors, there are indirect expenses associated with the launch of the software, such as hiring DevOps engineers to help with infrastructure deployment and software engineers to design and write the business logic code. If the newly designed software is replacing existing software, there is the added cost of building intermediary solutions for traffic and data migration.

We recommend using freely available tools for forecasting the expenses to be incurred depending on the system scale calculations, such as the AWS Pricing Calculator (*https://calculator.aws/#*). Take the AWS region into consideration when calculating the costs since the prices of different AWS services vary based on the region. We will try to calculate the cost on AWS for the suggested scale given in "System Scale" on page 444. Note that these example costs are calculated using the Pricing Calculator and are for reference only.

For the storage cost calculation, we used a storage requirement of 750 GB/month, an average read TPS of 231, and an average write TPS of 167. Let's calculate the cost of DynamoDB with these numbers for the us-east-1 region and on-demand capacity mode selection. The total cost comes out to be $812 per month (note that we have not included costs for additional features, such as backups, DynamoDB streams, and GSIs):

Average item size (all attributes): 500 Byte = 0.48828125 KB

Total storage requirement = 750 GB

Total data storage cost = 750 GB × $0.25 = $187.50

DynamoDB data storage cost (monthly): $187.50

Monthly write cost (monthly): $548.60

Monthly read cost (monthly): $75.88

In the Day N architecture (see Figure 17-4 in that section), the system exposes APIs via API Gateway for the write traffic and leverages AWS AppSync for reads. Let's calculate the cost for API Gateway. The total cost comes out to be $1,462 per month, assuming a single REST API for writes and without any caching capability (*https://oreil.ly/sSFHn*) to cache the responses:

Average write TPS = 167

Total monthly write requests = (167 × 60 × 60 × 24 × 365)/12 = 438,876,000 total REST API requests

Tiered price for: 438,876,000 requests

333,000,000 requests × $0.0000035 = $1,165.50

105,876,000 requests × $0.0000028 = $296.45

Total tier cost: $1,165.50 + $296.45 = $1,461.9528

For networking infrastructure on the AWS cloud, there is no direct cost associated with the creation of the VPC, and the pricing depends on the associated features we use, such as:

NAT gateways
: The pricing depends on the number of NAT gateways and the data processed per NAT gateway. For example, a $38 cost is incurred for one NAT gateway processing 100 GB data per month in the us-east-1 region.

Outbound data transfer
: The outbound data transfer pricing depends on where the data is transferred. For example, it costs $9 to transfer 100 GB per month to the internet, and the cost is zero for transferring to CloudFront.

Similarly, we can calculate pricing for other services being used in the architecture. Let's discuss operational costs next.

Operational costs. Once you launch the software, it runs continuously to serve customer traffic (or the build for any organization's use case). You pay for running this software in the cloud for existing or newly increasing traffic. Here are a few examples of AWS services used in the architecture:

- Amazon CloudWatch for storing logs and metrics
- Data storage cost with managed services
- Introduction of capabilities to expand the infrastructure with scale

> You pay based on instance size with RDS, but you can also choose a pay-as-you-go pricing model to pay only for the actual usage with solutions like Amazon DynamoDB and Amazon Aurora Serverless. There can be additional costs associated with storage, such as managing backups in Amazon S3 and data caching in Amazon ElastiCache. We often skip these calculations in the beginning, but they add up as the system scales.

Other operational costs include improving the existing software to resolve any existing tech debts or introducing new features.

Maintenance costs. We've discussed multiple options for deploying software applications with respect to compute and databases. We can choose to deploy the entire architecture on bare-metal servers or to use AWS managed services like Lambda and DynamoDB. This aspect of management falls under maintenance costs, as do system upgrades (security vulnerability fixes or newer version upgrades of software dependencies).

We've also discussed AWS managed services that are automatically deployed in multiple AZs, removing the headache of disaster management from the customer. We recommend selecting services based on previous expertise; for example, if there is already a team managing infrastructure for other applications in the company, the same team can manage infrastructure for the new applications.

Support and scaling costs. We strive for 100% application availability, but this doesn't really happen in the real world, and errors are bound to happen. The system might be completely down or not working per the expectations of some of the customers. Generally, the organization has incident management mechanisms to address such queries. Some examples of these mechanisms include answering user queries via AI chatbots and raising incident tickets for the engineering team (or support team) to look into. There is a cost associated with maintaining these end-to-end mechanisms, such as paying Atlassian for Jira (ticket lifecycle) (*https://oreil.ly/Xqjnn*) and Opsgenie (on-call and alert management) (*https://oreil.ly/-RdYD*). Apart from all this, there is someone dedicating time to look into these issues, which incurs costs to the organization.

We design systems with the hope that they will be used by millions of customers (in an iterative way), but the system demands additional infrastructure to support the scale. The scaling costs can also be considered part of operational costs since scaling is needed for system operations. Increasing scale can be supported in two ways:

- The existing infrastructure is expanded by adding more servers.
- The existing system becomes a bottleneck and requires a rearchitecture to scale further.

Both of these approaches have costs associated with them, and regular examinations into the reasons for system bottlenecks can help you decide which solution works best.

Retirement costs. We mentioned that the existing system can become a bottleneck, so we plan for redesigning the system. Sunsetting an existing system and moving to the new system comes with migration costs. We discussed strategies for moving from Day 0 architecture to Day N architecture in Chapter 16.

We should take a holistic view to figure out the costs associated with a system to avoid any surprises. Returning to the system architecture discussion, we'll look at the Day N architecture for our system next.

Day N Architecture

Scaling the system requires reevaluating each component to ensure that it can handle the projected load. Figure 17-4 illustrates the scaled architecture for our online game leaderboard system.

To ensure that the online game leaderboard system is robust, scalable, and capable of handling millions of users with high performance, low latency, and strong security, it's critical to adopt best practices across various architecture components. Let's discuss implementation in Redis first.

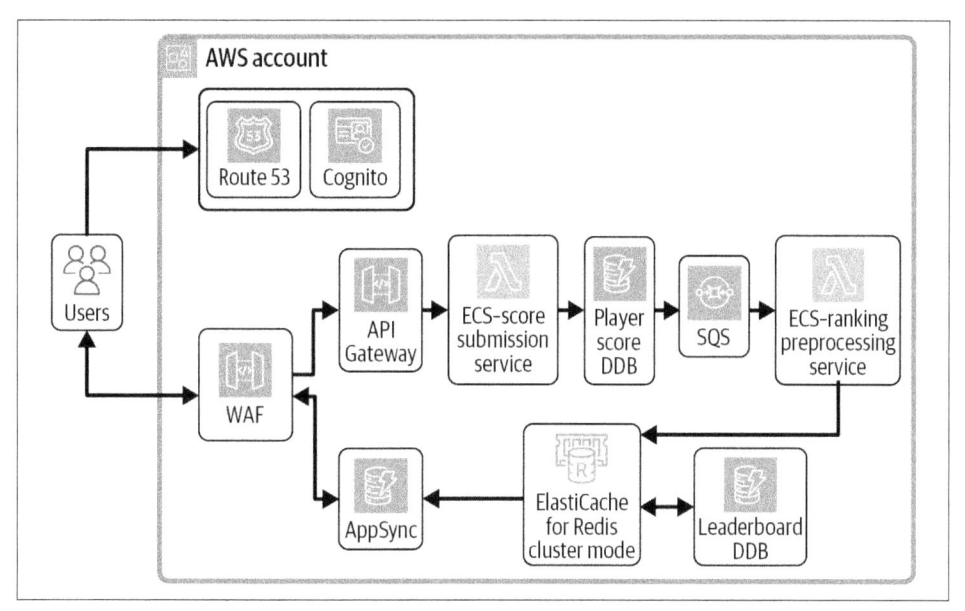

Figure 17-4. Scaled architecture for online game leaderboard system on AWS

Scaling Redis

In-memory data stores like Redis should also be sharded by leveraging Redis Cluster, allowing data to spread across multiple nodes. This setup ensures that requests are balanced and that read and write operations are processed efficiently. The ranking in the leaderboard is calculated using sorted sets in Redis based on scores that are processed and submitted by the score submission service, picked from the SQS queue. Redis will operate as a single node in the Day 0 architecture but can be set up as Redis HA or Redis Cluster with a primary-secondary setup to handle large leaderboard sorted sets. The primary will serve as a sticky server for the involved players for "read your write" consistency; the secondary will be updated using replication, leading to eventual consistency. You can review Redis's setup for distributed handling in Chapter 4.

Redis sorted sets can efficiently store and manage leaderboard data and allow it to be queried for a high volume of player scores in the Day N architecture. Here is how it will work:

- Each time a user submits a new score, it's added to a Redis sorted set using the command `ZADD <leaderboardId> <score> <userId>`.
- To retrieve and display the leaderboard's top one hundred users, use `ZREVRANGE <leaderboardId> 0 99`, which retrieves the highest scores efficiently, even with millions of users and updates per minute.
- To get a specific user's rank, call `ZRANK <leaderboardId> <userId>`, which provides the user's current position based on score.

Redis sorted sets allow for more than just top scores or global rank; you can also show scores of users near a specific user's rank, creating a localized leaderboard view.

Now, let's discuss a few general recommendations for the architecture to ensure smooth operations and optimal performance.

System considerations

An effective caching strategy is key to reducing latency and enhancing read performance. We advise using hierarchical caching that includes multiple layers, such as client-side caching, edge caching with services like Amazon CloudFront, and server-side caching with Amazon ElastiCache. The server-side caching can be divided into further layers, such as request level caching accessible over a lifetime of user request, instance level (or kubernetes pod level) caching accessible to all the requests of an server instance and distributed caching accessible to all the requests across the application instances. This multilayered caching ensures that the most frequently accessed data is served quickly, thereby reducing the load on primary databases and improving user experience.

By implementing these scaling strategies and best practices, we can design an online game leaderboard system that will be well equipped to handle millions of users while maintaining high performance, low latency, and robust security. Leveraging AWS's scalable services allows us to focus on delivering an exceptional gaming experience, confident that the underlying infrastructure can support the demands of a global player base.

Be sure to set up monitoring and logging for CPU usage, memory consumption, error rates, and latency alerts, as well as anomaly detection to identify unusual patterns using CloudWatch. For security, conduct regular access reviews to verify that IAM policies and access logs are up to date and reflect current needs.

Last, for disaster recovery, the system should define an RPO and an RTO, which outline the acceptable limits for data loss and downtime, respectively, and should be tested with recovery procedures to ensure these SLAs. Enable point-in-time recovery for continuous backups of Amazon DynamoDB and schedule automatic snapshots of Redis data on Amazon ElastiCache.

Conclusion

Designing an online game leaderboard system requires a careful balance between technical requirements and an understanding of player behavior. By starting with a simple architecture and progressively optimizing it, we can build a system capable of scaling from thousands to millions of users while maintaining low latency and high availability. Throughout this chapter, we emphasized the importance of efficient data modeling, scalable storage solutions, and effective leveraging of AWS services.

We explored how to evolve our architecture as the system grows, transitioning from basic components like AWS Lambda and Amazon DynamoDB to more advanced solutions, such as DynamoDB global tables, Redis clusters, and containerized services. This progression mirrors how systems often start simply and adapt over time to meet new requirements and handle increased load. By applying best practices, such as proper data partitioning, caching strategies, and continuous monitoring, we ensure the system remains robust and efficient.

Security and disaster recovery were integral to our design, emphasizing the need for fine-grained access controls, data encryption, and multiregion failover strategies. Leveraging AWS's scalable infrastructure and services allows us to focus on delivering an engaging user experience, confident that the underlying system can support a global player base.

In the next chapter, we'll delve into designing a hotel reservation system.

CHAPTER 18
Designing a Hotel Reservation System

We love to travel and often use online hotel reservation systems such as Booking.com, agoda, and Airbnb to book our stays in advance. In this chapter, we'll dive deep into the underlying design of reservation systems for hotel rooms (or any other type of place to stay—we'll use the term *property* here). The reservation system should show listed properties in a particular area and allow users to book rooms for a specific period of time. When designing such systems, consider that there are a lot of edge cases the system should adhere to, such as how to handle double payments and the fact that the same room should not be bookable by multiple people for the same time frame. We'll work on figuring out all such scenarios and finalizing the overall system architecture.

We'll start the discussion with requirement clarifications and our expectations for the system, close on the design by breaking the overall booking system into multiple subsystems, and then conclude the discussion by identifying AWS services useful for deploying this type of system on the AWS cloud.

System Requirements

The most important requirement is quite simple: allow customers to book a room for their future stays. We'll start with a few clarifications:

- The system is responsible for onboarding a single hotel chain or any property onto the system to list the rooms. The system allows properties to onboard and add the rooms with amenities.

- We need to determine who will accept the payments from the users. Does the system accept the payments on the property owners' behalf, or will users directly pay at the property? This is an important requirement to consider because if users directly pay to the property owner, the system doesn't have to take into account the payment lifecycle. But this can detract from the experience for property owners since the customers can book rooms and never show up. To ensure that both users and owners are happy, the system leaves it to owners to decide the mode of payment and any other policies specific to the property.

- Will the system offer any recommendations for visiting nearby attractions near the booked property? No—this feature would definitely be a value-add for the users (along with other features, such as a trip planner), but we'll skip it and keep the scope limited. The system can have external integrations that offer this service.

- The property may have been listed on multiple reservations systems, so we need to determine how the system ensures that availability is updated if it is booked on another system. This can either be automated in some way in which another system sends the updates to our system or the property owner will need to update the property. It is difficult to integrate given all the different reservation platforms (not to mention that the platforms might not support the integration), so we'll rely on owners to update the property status. We'll discuss one edge case of double bookings in this scenario while working on the design.

- We also need to consider dynamic pricing: can the room prices vary based on booking rate, occasion, or any other factor? The architecture should give independence to the owners to determine a fixed price and manage it on their own or leave the decision to the booking system by providing maximum and minimum room prices. We won't go deep into ML algorithms, but we'll discuss a general strategy for supporting dynamic pricing in the system.

We'll finalize the functional and nonfunctional requirements of the system next based on these clarifications.

Functional and Nonfunctional Requirements

The system has two types of users: property owners and customers who book these properties for a certain period of time.

The functional requirements the system should support in the context of property owners are:

- Onboard them to the system with personal details, payment settlement details, and so forth
- List one or more of their properties with details like number and type of rooms, pricing structure, images of the property, and additional benefits
- Update the details, such as available number of rooms, price, and images
- View the status of current and past bookings, user reviews, earnings, and the like

For the users booking a property, the functional requirements are:

- Search for properties in a geographical location for a particular checkin and checkout date-range selection. There can be additional filters for search, such as the property rating (e.g., four stars, five stars), whether pets are allowed, the cancellation policy, and whether breakfast is included.
- Book a room and pay for the room (if that is the property's policy—properties will also have the option to have the user pay at the property with a minimal deposit).
- Update the booking. Possible updates can include selecting new dates, adding more rooms, updating checkin and checkout timing, making a payment, adding room service, and booking spa treatments.
- View current and past bookings.
- Cancel the booking. The payment details on this will depend on the property. Are free cancellations allowed? Or will the user be charged some amount? How are refunds handled?
- Add reviews after the stay. The system restricts the users to add reviews only after the stay is completed at the booked property.

The following NFRs should be ensured by the system:

- The system should overall have high availability and reliability.
- There is strong consistency for bookings and payments. A booking state should be reflected on all reservation systems in the same status.
- The search system should present the list of properties with very low latency.
- The system is responsible only for property reservations, but it should not be limited in any way from supporting other types of reservations, such as flights and rental cars. The system should be extensible and should not require major redesign to support these requirements.
- Fault tolerance in the system ensures that double bookings or payments are primarily avoided and are handled gracefully if they do occur.

System scale is another important factor when making design decisions. We'll work with the scale numbers approximated in the next section.

System Scale

Like the functional requirements, the system scale can be divided into two parts: the number of properties listed on the system and the number of users searching for properties and booking them. Note that the numbers used in this section are based on assumptions, not on any concrete data source. We recommend studying your use case to come up with the initial numbers, and later you can plan for scale.

The assumptions we made for determining scale are as follows:

Number of properties = 10 million worldwide

Average number of properties per location = 500

Average number of rooms per property = 100

Total rooms worldwide = 10 million × 100 = 1 billion

Average stay at a property = 2 days

The scale for searching properties on the platform can be completely different from stays that are actually booked—let's use these estimates for the design:

Search rate = 20 million/day = 250 requests/second

Active users on platform = 100 million

Actual bookings = 10% of searches = 2 million/day = 25 requests/second

We can also calculate approximate storage requirements, which might add value when selecting the data store for the architecture. The system maintains user information, property information, and bookings information:

Storage space for room details {room ID, type, facilities, minimum rate, maximum rate, dimensions} = 500 bytes

Storage space for property details {property ID, address, number of rooms, facilities} = 500 bytes

Average 50 reviews per property and 500 bytes per review {review content, stars, user ID} = 50 × 500 Bytes = 25 KB

Total storage space per property = 500 bytes + 100 × 500 bytes + 25 KB = 75 KB

Storage space for all properties = 10 million × 75 KB ~ 715 GB

Storage space for property media (images and videos) with an average 10 images per property of 1 KB each = 10 KB × 10 million ~ 100 GB

Property media data storage is relatively less since the rate at which properties are added is much lower than the number of bookings per day. We'll calculate the booking storage requirements next:

Storage space per one booking {guest details, booking details, total amount} = 1 KB

Total storage space = 1 KB × 2 million = 2 GB/day = 730 GB/year

With all this in mind, let's start designing the architecture of the reservation system.

Starting with the Design

The property reservation system is similar to the web crawler and search engine system we discussed in Chapter 15. Property owners listing their properties are like web crawlers gathering data from websites. In both these cases, the system stores this data, which is made available to the users for searching later. Therefore, we know that property data from property owners should be stored in such a way that the search is faster on top of data, and we'll leverage the inverted index data structure to facilitate the search.

Before we look more into the storage part of our use case, let's break the system into three high-level parts, shown in Figure 18-1: onboarding of properties, searching for properties, and booking a property.

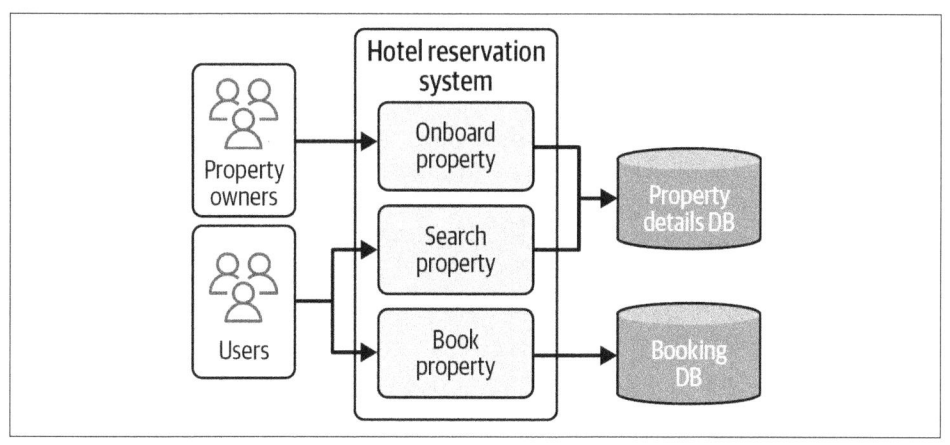

Figure 18-1. High-level view of the property reservation system

Property Onboarding Architecture

The simplest requirement of the onboarding system is to collect data from the property owners and store it in such a fashion that searching on top of this data is fast. This can be broken down into steps in a workflow-like system with each step taking certain kinds of inputs, as shown in Figure 18-2.

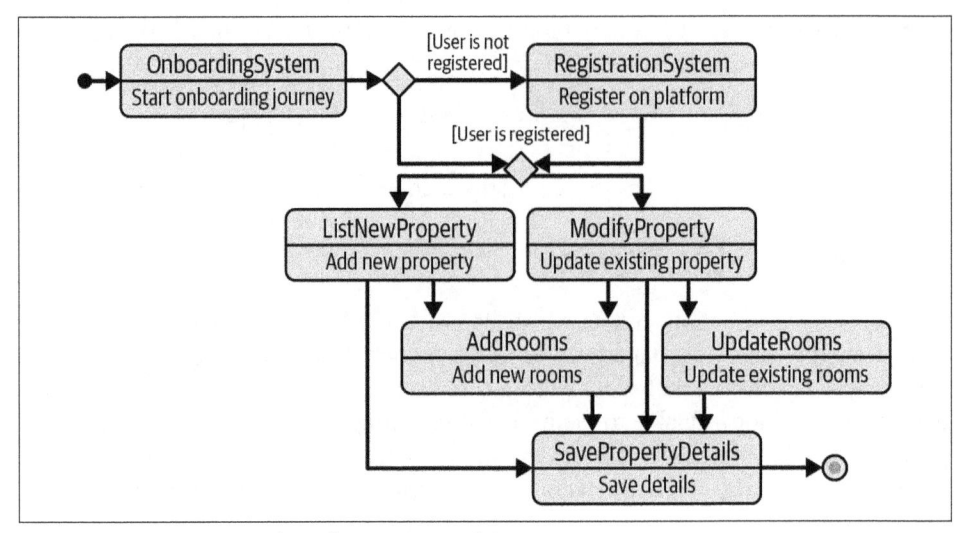

Figure 18-2. Property onboarding state machine

We skipped some of the states to keep the state machine small, such as adding property restrictions, price details, images, and the like. The state machine can be implemented with workflow engines like AWS Step Functions.

The choice of database to store the property details is another key decision we need to make. The data definitely has relational properties: properties are listed for a city, a property contains rooms, and bookings are created for these rooms. So we can explore the idea of using relational databases here. The relations could be a property table that is associated with tables like property address, property rooms, property reviews, and property facilities. The property rooms can be further associated with room facilities and room prices. This is just a suggested schema for Day 0 architecture, and details like pricing and reviews can be maintained by a completely independent system as the system scales.

An additional benefit we get from RDBMS is strong ACID support, but this might require extra effort to implement data-partitioning techniques as the data grows. The system requires strongly consistent support for available rooms on a property to ensure that bookings are confirmed only for available rooms. On the subject of partitioning, if the system has separate databases for properties and bookings, the required storage space is not that large, and it can be managed via Amazon Aurora distributed storage.

For Aurora (*https://oreil.ly/Hr35Z*), the storage space for a cluster could scale up to 128 TB (for all PostgreSQL versions and versions 2, 2.09, 3, and higher for MySQL) and 64 TB (for lower engine versions), which is quite a high storage space number. We'll also be discussing Aurora with limitless storage in "Scaling to Millions and Beyond" on page 493.

In case partitioning is needed, one technique could be dividing the data based on property IDs, and the routing layer in front can figure out exactly where the data resides. We recommend not fully normalizing the data in tables and avoiding complex join operations. This can help optimize query performance (at the cost of storing duplicate data among the tables), and even if the joins are used, the query should be written in a way that joins are applied after data filtering. It is much like query expression versus filter expression on DynamoDB tables data. The filter expression is applied after the data is collected, so it doesn't help if the final data retrieved is a large set or small set—the time taken is the same.

Let's think more about whether we should use solutions like DynamoDB, which can improve scalability and performance by avoiding joins, parallel querying, and out-of-the-box horizontal scaling. The partition key is the property ID, and we can define multiple sort keys to store different attributes associated with a property, as shown in Table 18-1.

Table 18-1. Sort keys for storing property details in Amazon DynamoDB

Sort key	Comments
PY	The main property object with other details like address, facilities, and so on.
PY#IMG#{imageId}	Image details of property images. This can just maintain the Amazon S3 link where the image is stored. Similar sort keys can be created to support different media types.
PY#R#PY#R#{roomId}	This uniquely identifies a room object.
PY#R#{roomType}	This contains different room properties based on room type.
PY#R#{roomType}#{imageId}	Image details based on room type.

You can keep other details as necessary per your requirements, such as food menus, a history of updates to property details, and so on. We can conclude that both RDBMS and DynamoDB are feasible solutions for storing and accessing the property information. One of the sort keys from Table 18-1 is PY#R#{roomType}#{imageId}: the image ID represents a location identifier where the image is being stored, such as an Amazon S3 URL (we discussed Amazon S3 in Chapter 10).

Once the property details are stored in a database, we need a system to offer a search feature on this data. Let's discuss the architecture of the property search next.

Property Search Architecture

The key parameter for any search query is location. Once a user selects a location, the system should be able to present a list of properties in that location. The user can apply more filters to refine the results, such as type of property, whether pets are allowed, or if breakfast is included. The database we created in the previous section is not directly helpful for offering the search capability unless we create different GSIs (in the case of DynamoDB or RDBMS indexes) to support all of the filter query patterns efficiently. The GSI approach can become complex as more and more filters are introduced into the search criteria. A better solution is to leverage search solutions like Elasticsearch or Amazon OpenSearch.

The architectures of these solutions that we explored in Chapter 15 can be useful for serving our property-booking-search use case here. Apart from offering search over fixed search parameters, Elasticsearch can power search queries with fuzzy text. The data from the properties database can be published to the queue as CDC events and then converted into Elasticsearch-compatible schema and persisted, as shown in Figure 18-3.

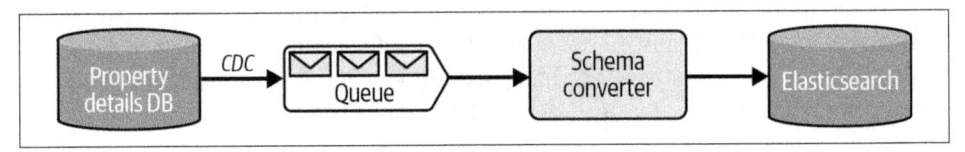

Figure 18-3. Data persistence in Elasticsearch from the database via CDC

The system might also require combining data from two data stores because we need the capability of strong consistency for availability of rooms on a property, and this information is stored in a strongly consistent database. The search can be broken down into two steps:

1. Retrieve properties from the Elasticsearch cluster based on the search criteria.
2. Check these properties against their availability from a strongly consistent database.

There is also a possibility that the search is facilitated by multiple teams and is hosted on separate Elasticsearch clusters or any other database solution. This makes a perfect use case for using GraphQL federations—refer to Chapter 6 for more information on GraphQL and to Chapter 12 for AWS AppSync (a managed GraphQL federation service). The search service can be an independent wrapper that talks to different services and gathers the properties' data based on customer filters.

> Yet another solution is having the application run filters on data in memory instead of using too many indexes on a database or Elasticsearch. This means the application retrieves the data for a location from the database and then runs additional filters on top of this data. This is not a recommended approach in this scenario but can be considered in similar scenarios with less data retrieved on the wire. The number of properties for a particular location could be huge and can become a bottleneck.

We described usage of a strongly consistent database for checking the room availability. We can take a different approach that serves results from an eventually consistent database, making queries much faster, while checking for room availability in a strongly consistent database in parallel but not waiting for these results to merge. Results are merged later in the frontend application if room availability is not the same in both data stores.

There are trade-offs in any approach that we take here; another approach could be waiting for results from the strongly consistent database only if the room availability is minimal (for example, if there are only two rooms left); otherwise, serve the results from only the eventually consistent database.

> The room availability check is to ensure that rooms are booked only if they are available. Organizations take different approaches to solve this problem. One completely different approach taken here is to allow overbooking of rooms based on analysis of past room cancellations at a particular property. This helps simplify the problem scope and ensure that rooms are never vacant.

Let's dig a little bit more into Elasticsearch's underlying architecture (in addition to what we discussed in Chapter 15) and strategies to come up with the Elasticsearch configuration.

Elasticsearch configuration and scaling

As you know, scalability is an important aspect of the system requirements. In Chapter 15, we discussed multiple approaches to scale read and write independently; those approaches apply here as well. In this chapter, let's focus specifically on scalability of Elasticsearch clusters to support increasing reads and writes and a hot nodes issue (a few of the nodes handle all the read/write requests, and the rest of them sit idle). You can change the Elasticsearch shard configurations later, but that requires reindexing of data, which is a costly operation on a system running in production. The shard size should be average (not too small and not too large); the general recommendation is to keep the shard size between 10 GB and 30 GB with critical search latency use cases and between 30 GB and 50 GB for write-heavy workloads such as log analytics.

> We often assume that sharding is done to solve the problem of storage. *Sharding* is more of a general term referring to breaking the workloads into multiple resources to solve a bottleneck or combination of bottlenecks from storage, compute, network, performance, and reliability.

A smaller shard leads to the creation of smaller segments, and too many smaller segments add to the management overhead for hardware resources. Smaller shards offer room for more concurrent queries but can also lead to a lot of queries being queued up at a shard level for increasing traffic. In short, a smaller set of large shards is better than a larger number of smaller shards. Similarly, a very large shard should be avoided to reduce the data-rebalancing overhead on node failures.

> For use cases with requirements for data deletion (such as storing logs in a time-based fashion), we recommend deleting the indexes and not the documents. The indexes are removed from the disk as soon as they are deleted, but this is not the case with documents. The documents are marked for soft delete (causing deleted documents to consume resources as well) and are actually deleted on the segment merge. This is similar to the tombstones problem in Cassandra discussed in Chapter 3.

Coming back to the number of shards that should be configured for an Elasticsearch cluster index, the shard size depends on the actual data size and the expected growth, so first let's figure out the storage requirements (*https://oreil.ly/lNKqz*), and then we'll move to the number of shards. The total storage space depends on the size of the source data, number of replicas, indexing overhead, operating system reserved space, and service maintenance overhead:

- We should configure a minimum of one replica to prevent data loss. The replicas will also help improve search query performance. Each replica contains the full copy of an index, and we'll keep two replicas to start in our system architecture.
- The data is stored in a specific data structure format, and in general, the total size of the source data and index is 110% of the source data.
- The operating system reserves 5% of space for its own processes.
- The OpenSearch service (or Elasticsearch service) reserves space for different operations, such as segment merges, logs, and so on. This is 20% of the storage space for each instance (up to 20 GB) in the case of the OpenSearch service.

We can estimate required storage based on these inputs:

$$\text{Minimum storage requirement} = \frac{\text{Source data} \times (1 + \text{number of replicas}) \times (1 + \text{indexing overhead})}{(1 - \text{Linux reserved space}) \times (1 - \text{OpenSearch Service overhead})}$$

Minimum storage requirement = Source data × (1 + number of replicas) × 1.45
Storage for our system = 715 GB × (1 + 2) × 1.45 = 3.1 TB

Similarly, the formula to calculate the approximate number of shards is:

Number of shards = (Source data + room to grow) × (1 + indexing overhead) / Desired shard size

Number of shards for our system with 2x growth = (715 GB + 715 GB) × 1.1 / 30 = 53

Space required by each shard with current storage requirement = 715 × 1.1 / 53 ~ 15 GB

If you notice here, the shard size falls into the recommended size of 10–30 GB for critical search latency use cases. Referring to the calculation, we can also identify the type of instance that should be used in the cluster setup. Follow an iterative approach for figuring out the instance types and monitoring the metrics to come up with the best possible configuration.

> Horizontal scaling (adding new data nodes) of Elasticsearch will not help with query performance if the shard size is too large because the data partitions where data is written or queried are still large. We can employ application layer logic in these scenarios by creating new indexes (once the index size exceeds a threshold value), which keeps the shard size within the limit even with growing data. Further, an index alias (*https://oreil.ly/Ooky_*) can be created to point to all of these indexes and aggregate the search results.

We mentioned GraphQL federation at the start of this section. Let's elaborate more on how it fits into the reservation system architecture for the property search use case.

GraphQL federation for search

The response to any search request by customers should be a list of properties with each property associated with additional information, such as property details, rating, price for the selected date range (the property might have different types of rooms available, and the system can reflect the pricing for the most popular room types), and property tags (such as free breakfast or pets allowed). All of this information is collected from different systems and then shown collectively on the web UI as in Figure 18-4.

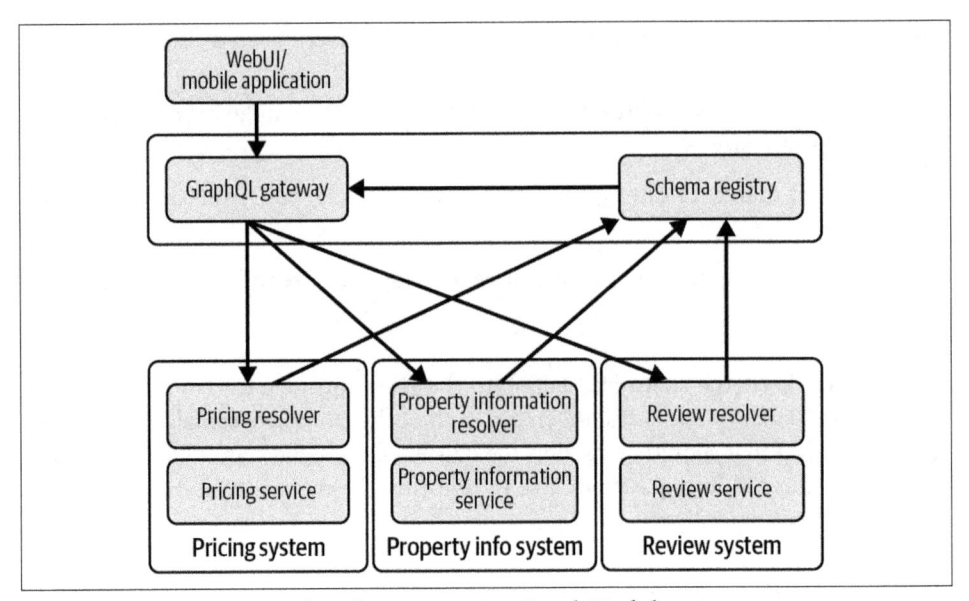

Figure 18-4. Property search architecture using GraphQL federation

The definitions of *resolvers* and *schema registry* match what we discussed in "AWS AppSync" on page 326 in Chapter 12. Booking.com (*https://oreil.ly/yOUjA*) systems leverage Apollo (*https://apollographql.com*) as their GraphQL federation solution, and the schema is fetched from different resolvers every 10 seconds by default. To remove complete dependency from Apollo servers and reduce frequent schema fetches, the schema is cached, and the cache is updated upon new schema build webhook events from Apollo.

> A *webhook* is a callback sent from a source system to a destination system to facilitate event-driven communication among multiple systems. For example, as soon as the customer booking is completed, the backend system posts an HTTP payload to the frontend system endpoint, and the same is reflected to the customer on the web UI.

We described search functionality on the basis of a location keyword in the Elasticsearch cluster. For example, if a user searches for "Goa," then the search results should include properties from Goa, a state in India. Similarly, if a user searches for "Jaipur," then the search results should include properties from Jaipur, a city in India. The search keyword can be anything from the location data, such as locality, town, city, state, and country.

Other features offered by booking systems are to search for properties by enabling your current location and to look for points of interest near the booked property. This can be solved by a concept called *Geohash* (https://oreil.ly/go11H).

Exploring points of interests

Geohash is helpful for encoding latitudes and longitudes into an alphanumeric string. Assume the world has a large two-dimensional grid. Geohash is created by recursively dividing it into smaller grids, as shown in Figure 18-5.

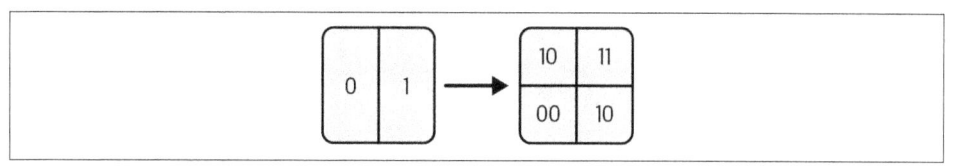

Figure 18-5. Geohash representation

The length of the Geohash determines the precision of any location: a longer string means more precision because the grid is divided multiple times and represents a smaller subsection of the entire world. The shared prefix in Geohashes represents proximity of two locations, so they can be used to efficiently figure out the closest locations to a searched location. To get the surrounding places, we can remove one last character from the Geohash to get a grid that is one level higher and use the prefix to figure out the surrounding places.

> The world is not uniform, and some places are more densely populated than others. Our algorithm should take this into consideration and can divide the grids into smaller levels so that they contain a smaller number of locations (for example, divide the grid further if it has more than two hundred locations). It doesn't really make sense to divide the grid containing the ocean because there will be no locations of interest, whereas it would be very helpful in densely populated New York City.

Another way of representing location is using trees. The most popular implementation is quadtree (Booking.com leverages quadtree to implement its points-of-interest feature (https://oreil.ly/YbjHj)), which works on a similar concept as Geohash. A particular grid is constantly divided into four subparts until the area has the desired number of places. One method of figuring out nearby places is to keep pointers to parent nodes; we can go one level up and get all the child nodes that are in the surrounding area. Another way is to maintain the links between the child nodes via data structures, such as a doubly linked list.

> Redis offers a geospatial feature (*https://oreil.ly/mqz_O*) that allows users to store the location coordinates and then query for nearby locations in a given radius.

The system additionally caches the search results to improve the query performance. The results can be cached in solutions like Redis, and media content (e.g., property images) can be cached in CDN solutions like Amazon CloudFront.

In the next section, we'll discuss the architecture details of property booking.

Property Booking Architecture

The next step after property search is actually booking rooms at the selected property from the search results. A simplistic view of a booking flow is shown in Figure 18-6. The payment system and booking flow go through different states, which we'll discuss in detail now.

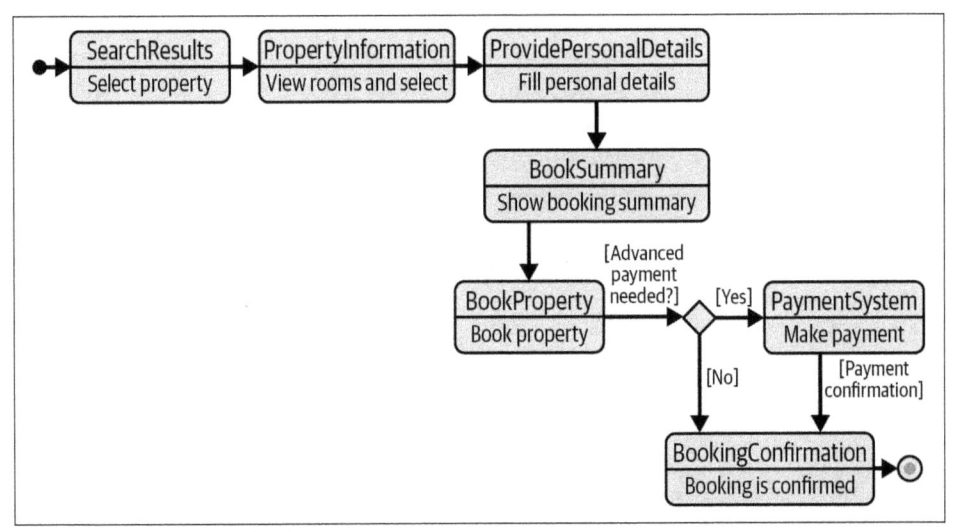

Figure 18-6. Property booking state machine

The booking transitions from one state to another and is needed to determine the current state of the booking. Figure 18-7 shows a minimal state diagram to represent different states and transitions between them for end-to-end booking flow. The booking state machine is initiated when the user moves to the BookProperty state from Figure 18-6. Note that the payment states will be managed separately by the payment system and are independent from the booking system.

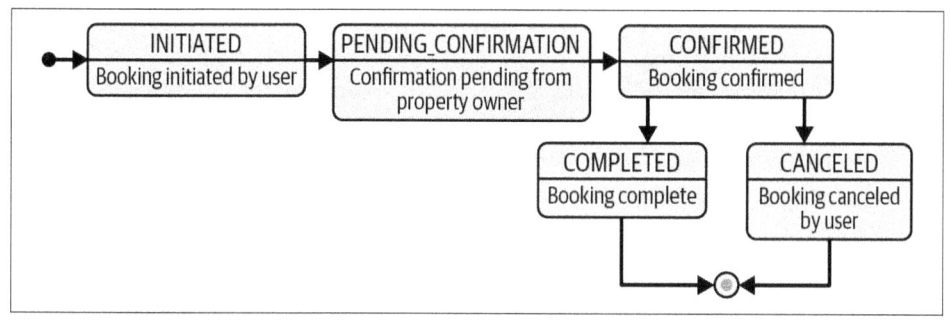

Figure 18-7. Booking states

The transition from PENDING_CONFIRMATION to CONFIRMED states can vary from property to property in the sense that some properties require payment confirmation before confirming the booking. Let's now talk about storing the booking information in a data store.

Data store selection

The booking system creates a booking as shown in Figure 18-6 and stores this information in a data store. We explored relational databases like Amazon Aurora and Amazon DynamoDB for the property onboarding architecture, and we'll do the same for our booking architecture.

A key consideration here is that customers are mostly interested in current ongoing bookings and rarely look for past bookings. A general design decision in these kinds of scenarios could be maintaining two data stores: one for recent data with consistent reads and the other for past historical data. Gojek (*https://oreil.ly/rj4i4*) has a similar implementation: active bookings are stored in PostgreSQL, and the data is partitioned weekly with the help of the PostgreSQL partitions feature (*https://oreil.ly/rL_Ov*), as shown in the following code snippet:

```
CREATE TABLE bookings (
    booking_number PRIMARY KEY,
    customer_id,
    booking_details,
    created_at_timestamp,
    start_date,
    end_date,
    booking_status,
    payment_id
) PARTITION BY RANGE(created_at_timestamp)
```

The older partitions are archived with the help of a scheduler job, and this architecture serves 120,000 requests per minute.

A point to note here is that room bookings can be created well in advance and don't really directly compare to Gojek's architecture, where bookings are mostly done in the present. So can we really take inspiration from this architecture? This design decision can help with real-time bookings, such as a cab-booking service, but not so much in our use case. However, we can still explore the idea of two data stores. The system should persist the older bookings if they are removed from the active database, and we can use a similar approach as diagrammed in Figure 18-3. Instead of keeping just the active bookings, we can make the archival time a little longer (such as one year) and ensure that the data is removed completely after one year from the main database.

> Much like the case of the Elasticsearch indexes that we've discussed, we recommend handling deletion of data partition-wise. The data is soft deleted in the case of PostgreSQL, and regular vacuum processes (*https://oreil.ly/bOt6E*) are required to actually clean the data from the disk, hampering the performance of the database. If we use Amazon DynamoDB as the main data store, the TTL feature can be leveraged to automatically clear out the data after a fixed timestamp.

To finalize on the data store selection, we need a strongly consistent database to ensure the correct status of bookings at all times. In "System Scale" on page 467, we calculated 2 million bookings per day (25 RPS) and storage space as 730 GB per year. This storage requirement can be easily supported by vertical scaling of the Amazon Aurora database and doesn't present any bottleneck, so we'll design the solution with Aurora as the database.

> Amazon DynamoDB can also support strongly consistent behavior, but this is limited to primary key attributes and the LSI. We should be clear on query patterns beforehand to avoid any issues at a later point: unknown query patterns can add to the cost as well as eventual consistency behavior (with GSIs) in the future.

In addition to the bookings table (shared in the previous code snippet), the database will have tables like booking_history (to store the status transitions of particular bookings, which is helpful for auditing purposes), booking_payments, and so on.

A very common and intriguing question that comes to mind is what happens if there is only a single room left and multiple users are trying to book that same room at exactly the same time? Let's discuss this in the next section.

Handling concurrent bookings

There are different ways to handle the double-booking scenario, but first let's understand if there actually is a need to handle this. The systems definitely need help from the property owners (or systems) to resolve ambiguity on bookings because even if the concurrency is handled well in our system, it can occur that the same property is booked on multiple booking platforms. A key point to note is that we can always overbook the rooms based on certain criteria, such as past cancellations. Also, as evident from Figure 18-6, the room is confirmed only after a confirmation is received from the property owner, so we don't require any special handling there.

Although we don't require specific handling for our use case, we'll discuss a few ways that systems handle multiple concurrent requests (for example, multiple users trying to book the same seat for a movie ticket or trying to book the same room at the same property). The idea is to use locks to block the seat or room for a certain time interval, which allows the user to finish the booking. If the user doesn't complete the booking within the fixed time, then it is made available again for other users.

> A *lock* is a technique used in software engineering to gain access to a resource for a specific time frame so that nobody else accesses it for that particular time.

Booking rooms consists of two steps: check the availability of the room (read operation) and book the room (update the availability of the room to false). The lock can be acquired at either of these steps; acquiring the lock at the read step is called *pessimistic locking*, and acquiring it at the update step is called *optimistic locking*. We can use these two types of concurrency techniques to gain access to a room for a particular property:

Pessimistic concurrency technique
    Pessimistic locking requires acquiring a lock at read, and the lock is only released after the operation is completed. Until the lock is acquired, other requests wait for it, which can obviously cause a bottleneck if the number of requests waiting is too large.

Optimistic concurrency technique
    Optimistic locking allows multiple user requests to read and update the data simultaneously. In case of any conflict on the update operation, the data is not committed, and the user is notified accordingly. This can be implemented by enabling versioning on the data: the version number is incremented on every update, and the most recent update should have a higher version number than the previous update. Amazon DynamoDB offers different mechanisms (*https://oreil.ly/kpaJq*) to support optimistic concurrency, and DynamoDBVersionAttribute annotation (*https://oreil.ly/nzR7A*) is one of the ways to implement it.

Returning to the earlier idea of booking a movie ticket and holding the seat for the time being, the lock can be introduced by keeping an entry in the database (e.g., HOLD_FOR_ID) against the user ID, and the time field HOLD_START_AT_TIME keeps the timestamp value (e.g., 20 minutes). Once the timestamp value is breached, the hold is canceled. This can be easily implemented with Redis as the backend data store with the following steps:

1. The user finalizes the seat (or room) and proceeds to payment. The system stores an entry against the seat entity with an expiration (or TTL). The system uses Redis SET with EX (set with expiration seconds) and NX (set if not present) options to store the key 'seat_{theatreId}_{showId}_{seatId}'. There can be more identifiers depending on the data storage pattern.

2. If the user completes the payment, the key is removed from Redis using the DEL operation. If the key is not deleted, Redis removes it automatically after the configured expiration time.

This implementation works well with a single Redis instance, but addition and deletion become tricky with Redis clusters (or any other distributed system solution). Redis recommends the Redlock algorithm (*https://oreil.ly/0qz6J*) for proper implementation in distributed environments. Additionally, we recommend using open source Redis libraries like Jedis (*https://github.com/redis/jedis*) or Lettuce (*https://github.com/redis/lettuce*) for easier integration.

The system also supports booking cancellations. For this, the system updates the booking status, notifies the property owner, and initiates the payment refund if the customer was charged earlier. Further, the system should adhere to idempotent behavior and solve the problem of the same room being booked twice by the same user (or the user being charged twice for the same room). We'll discuss this in more detail in the next section along with processing booking payments.

Payment processing architecture

Different payment solutions are used in different countries, and there can be different compliance regulations for each country. For example, PayPal is heavily used in the US, while Unified Payments Interface (UPI) (*https://oreil.ly/d3xnu*) is quite popular in India but not in other countries. The payment system's core responsibility is to allow customers to pay via their preferred payment option and record the payment (pay-in system). The payment system is also responsible for reconciling the payments from third-party payment gateway solutions, such as Razorpay or PayPal, and making those payments to the property owners (pay-out system) after taking out the booking commission. The core payment system stays the same for both pay-in and pay-out, and debitFrom and CreditTo attributes are associated with payment changes.

The system should adhere to these additional requirements:

- For a single stay, the booking can be modified by the user, such as increasing the number of days or adding property benefits like lunch and dinner.

- The payment options can increase over time, and they can vary from one location to another.
- It goes without saying (but we're going to say it) that customers should be charged only once for a smooth payment experience.

The high-level view of the system to manage the end-to-end payment lifecycle is shown in Figure 18-8.

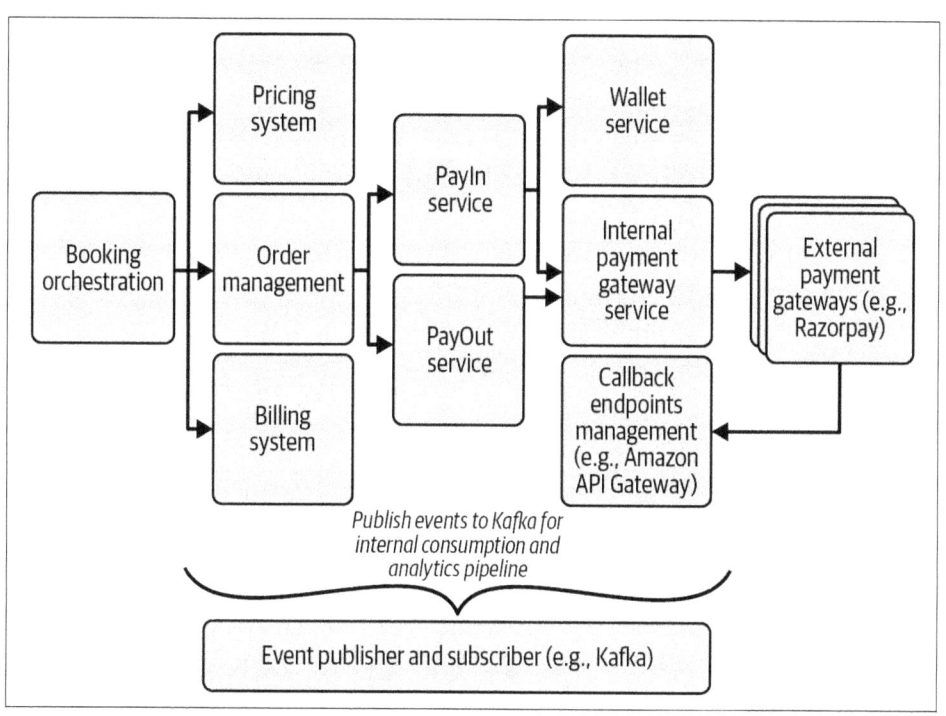

Figure 18-8. Booking payment system architecture

Here are the components of the architecture:

Booking orchestration
    Performs all the booking-related work. Once the user details and property details are gathered, the payment orchestration system (referred to as *order management*) takes care of the entire cycle of pay-in and pay-out.

Pricing system
    Responsible for derivation of prices for the rooms.

Billing system
    Generates invoices.

Order management
: The reason for the extra order management layer is to support the system requirement of booking modifications. A single order can consist of multiple payments associated with one booking. The order construct also simplifies the pay-out system by tying it to the same order booking system that payment was received against.

Wallet service
: Manages the wallet provided to the customers. The wallet can include the rewards earned by customers on bookings, any refunds that are transferred to the wallet, or a custom amount added to the wallet from any payment method. The wallet could be helpful if the payment methods are not working so that the booking can be processed by deducting the amount from the wallet.

PayIn service
: Responsible for customer payments: from customer to booking system or from booking system to customer (in the case of refunds). The customer can pay with an internal wallet or gift card managed by the wallet service or via other payment solutions, such as debit cards facilitated by external payment gateways. A single payment can be a combination of a wallet and external payment gateway as well.

PayOut service
: Handles the logic of settling the payments with property owners. This system deducts the booking platform commission and transfers the rest to the property owner's account.

Reconciliation system
: For any payment system, there is a requirement of an additional reconciliation system, ensuring that the debits and credits for all payments are balanced, no discrepancy is created, and transaction integrity is maintained throughout the payment lifecycle (and will flag a discrepancy if it arises). The reconciliation system operates based on inputs from internal and external systems, such as callbacks from internal and external payment systems, settlement reports from banking partners, payment status inquiry APIs, and the like.

All the payments processed via the payment system go through a set of states and eventually reach a terminal state, such as SUCCESS, FAILURE, REFUND, or CANCELED. The intermediate payments state could be PAYMENT_CREATED, PROCESSING, and so on. The database also stores the responses from external payment gateways in case of payment failures to provide proper insights to the users for why the payment processing failed. Ensuring consistent and idempotent behavior is important for transactional systems, so let's dig a little deeper into this.

Idempotent behavior ensures that the response of the API is the same irrespective of the time at which it is invoked, and it avoids any double payments (i.e., the customer is charged twice or the property host is paid twice). We recommend ensuring idempotency by maintaining a unique idempotency identifier; Airbnb leverages its own custom-built Orpheus general-purpose idempotency library (*https://oreil.ly/w13DT*) for guaranteeing idempotent APIs. Here is a summary of the Airbnb payments architecture, which we can take inspiration from:

- Every client request includes an idempotency key, which helps with uniquely determining duplicate requests. For Amazon DynamoDB transactional requests, we can leverage the clientToken feature (*https://oreil.ly/348GA*). The clientToken is valid for a 10-minute time window and ensures idempotent behavior for the same requests.

- Each payment is divided into three sections: pre-RPC, RPC, and post-RPC. Pre-RPC is a payment initiation call, and a transaction is recorded in the database with intent. The RPC step is actual processing of the payment and includes the call to an external payment partner to process the payment. The final post-RPC step includes handling the response or callbacks from external partners and recording them in the database. The key consideration here is separating database and external network calls; the database calls are made only in the first and final steps, and external network calls are made only in the RPC step. A simple implementation is shown in Figure 18-9.

- The exceptions are categorized as retryable and nonretryable for the clients to determine if the request can be retried. There is also a retryable window configured at the Orpheus end for each request to avoid a blast of retries to the system from clients.

- The requests are handled only by the primary instance of the database, which is sharded by the idempotency key to support the scale.

As shown in the diagram in Figure 18-9, the responsibility of identifier generation can fall on either the client or the payment processing system. For example, the payment acknowledgment ID can be generated by the payment system and sent to an external partner, or the identifier is sent in response to a process payment call. We recommend generating the identifier at the client side if there is a single payment call as the identifier is helpful for inquiring about the payment status or reconciling the payment via received callbacks. The drawback of this approach could be external clients responsible for generating a primary payment attribute; that's where dividing the processing into two steps—pre-RPC and RPC—is helpful.

Room prices generally vary depending on the availability, time of booking, and many other factors. We'll not go into too much depth, but let's gather some general ideas for how dynamic pricing components can be added into the system.

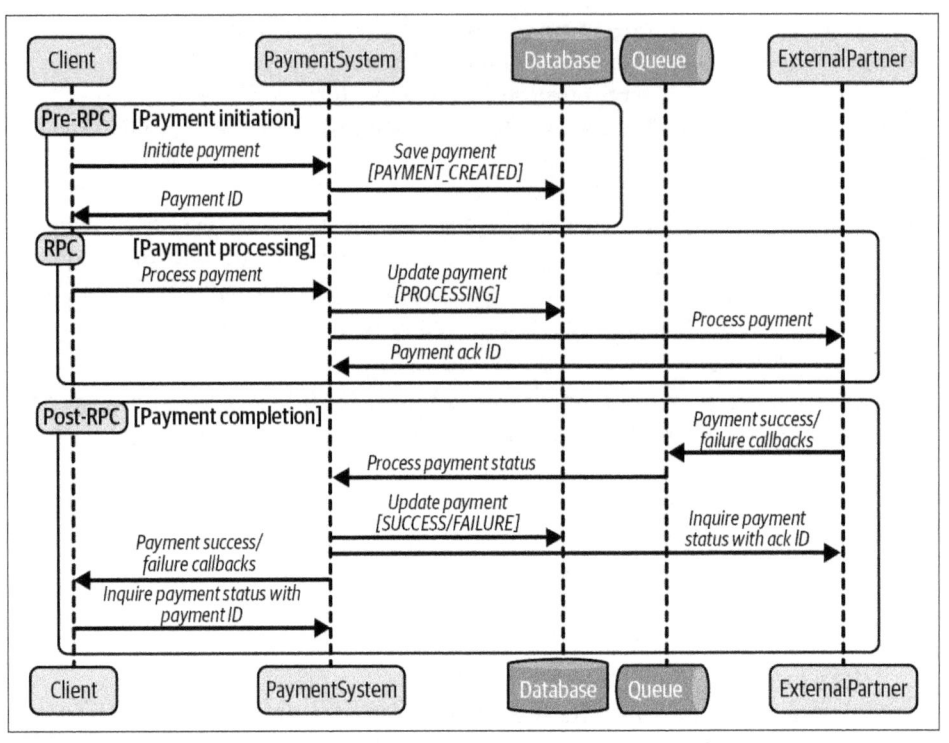

Figure 18-9. Payment processing in three steps: pre-RPC, RPC, and post-RPC

Dynamic pricing in the system

Booking platforms in general don't keep a static price. The price is adjusted based on multiple factors, such as location, date-range selection, the number of days of the stay, and the popularity of the property. The booking and search systems continuously publish the consumer data via event streams for the pricing system to consume and run ML inferences to come up with prices. The pricing system database is continuously updated in the background based on the ML inferences and custom price (or price range) shared by the property owners. Figure 18-10 shows a reference architecture for the dynamic pricing system.

We've used Amazon S3 to store raw data received from different sources (booking, search, and external sources). Amazon SageMaker Feature Store is another service that can be used as a repository to store all the pricing features.

The pricing system has two independent scaling layers, and we can plan to deploy these layers separately or in the same system depending on the workload served by the system. The first is completely asynchronous and responsible for consuming the events and updating the pricing structure, and the second is the read layer for different systems to get the most recent price of a property.

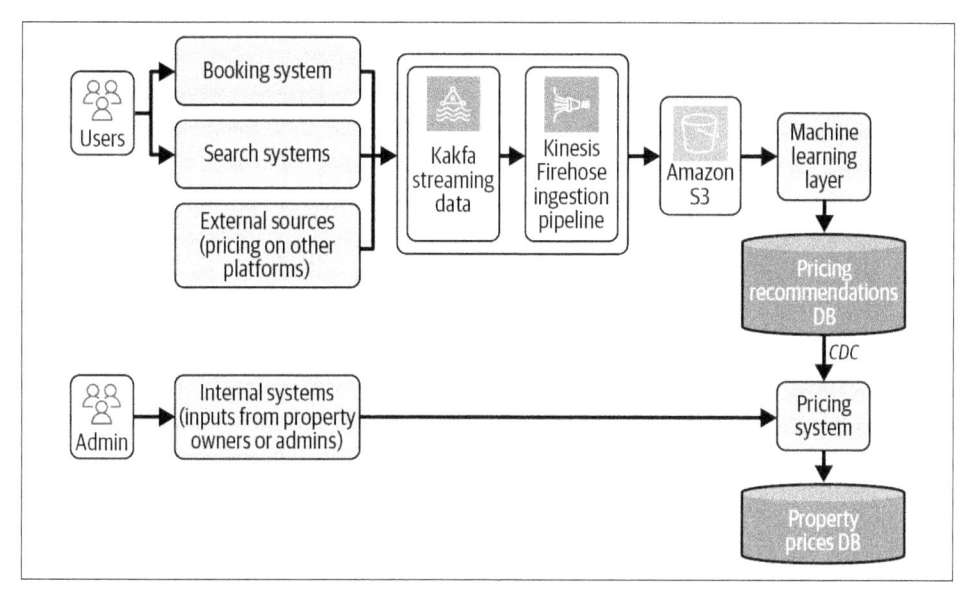

Figure 18-10. Dynamic pricing system

> Given that the price can continuously update in the system, the booking system should ensure that a price is locked for a user for a fixed period of time (e.g., 10 minutes). This avoids the bad customer experience of the price updating once the user proceeds to pay for the booking. Another point to note here is that the price shown to multiple users for the same property at the same time can be different and depends on the pricing structure followed by the business.

There are multiple subsystems inside the property booking system, and we should focus some attention on the way they communicate. Does all communication happen synchronously, or can we leverage message queues in some of them? For interaction between the payments system and booking system, it makes sense to include a combination of both. This is because the payment system in itself can take time for payment processing, so the booking system should just initiate a payment request and then receive an acknowledgment that payment has begun. The payments system publishes the payment status lifecycle, and the booking system can depend on that to figure out the latest status of the payment.

> Queues help decouple two systems and make the rate of publishing and consuming events independent. However, the system should not work with an assumption that queue size can grow infinitely and that any number of messages can be published without consumption (or that the rate of publishing versus consumption varies by a large ratio). This is often solved either by reducing the rate of publishing (referred to as *back pressure*) or by having the queue drop messages based on certain criteria (e.g., messages older than a day are deleted).

As the booking system consumes the events from the payment system (or any other system following this communication paradigm in the architecture), there is a possibility of out-of-order events, events being missed, and duplicate events. Now either it is guaranteed by the queue system that none of these issues will happen or it should be handled by the event-consuming system. Apache Kafka supports exactly-once semantics (*https://oreil.ly/QXLFx*) and event ordering (*https://oreil.ly/zNKBb*) on a single partition (or group IDs in Amazon SQS). This can also be handled in the booking system as follows:

- The system checks for the most recent status from the database before updating the status.
- There is a possibility that the system receives a terminal status before an intermediate status. In this case, the system should discard the events if a payment has already reached terminal state.
- The system has a built-in inquiry mechanism to call the payment system to check for the most recent payment system. This makes the booking system independent and works even if some of the events are missed in the payment callbacks.

We have discussed multiple components in the property booking architecture. Users create a booking, make the payment, and spend their time at the property. The next step is user reviews. The booking system notifies users to ask about their experience at the property and they leave a review, which we'll discuss in the next section.

Property Reviews Architecture

Reviews are associated with a property and a user. The system can ask some predefined questions about the stay (How would you rate the staff? Is it a good value for the price? How was the food?) and allow for generic feedback notes. Generally, the booking systems also implement ML algorithms to determine the type of experience based on the feedback note and improve other user search criteria by running multiple analytics pipelines.

Like the search system, the reviews system is very read heavy. Customers search for properties, look for reviews, and then decide whether to book a specific property.

The read traffic is proportional to search system traffic, whereas write traffic is proportional to property-booking traffic (we can assume 10% of users who book a property actually provide a review of their stay). Here are some search criteria that a review system should support:

- Get all the reviews of the property.
- Get reviews of the property based on any provided text filter, such as reviews associated with food, bathrooms, or room size or reviews for a specific time range.

In essence, we require text search for the user reviews as well as some of the supported features. Elasticsearch (or Amazon OpenSearch) is suitable for such use cases, and we can leverage the same to support the read use cases. But what about the write traffic on the system? A review is stored against a user and a property, and only one review is allowed per user per stay against a particular property. We're fine with eventual consistency on the reviews data for fetching the reviews, but there should definitely be a strongly consistent behavior from a single-user perspective to make sure there's one review per user.

Let's take an example of an Amazon DynamoDB schema to support the write use case, which serves as a source of truth for review data:

Partition key = {propertyId}

Sort key = {userId}

The data is always queried from the Elasticsearch cluster, and we don't have to worry about hot keys concerning too many reviews associated with a single property. However, the queries should always be paginated to get a fixed number of results from DynamoDB, Elasticsearch, or any other data store used in a particular architecture. The simplistic architecture of property reviews shown in Figure 18-11 is as follows:

Reviews system
    Allows users to add a review for their stay on a property. The database layer of the system streams this review to be used by the read layer. The reviews are also consumed by the analytics pipeline to figure out the popularity of the property; this can also be the input for the pricing system to decide the price based on reviews.

Reviews system read layer
    Retrieves reviews for any property per the filters provided by the users from the Elasticsearch cluster.

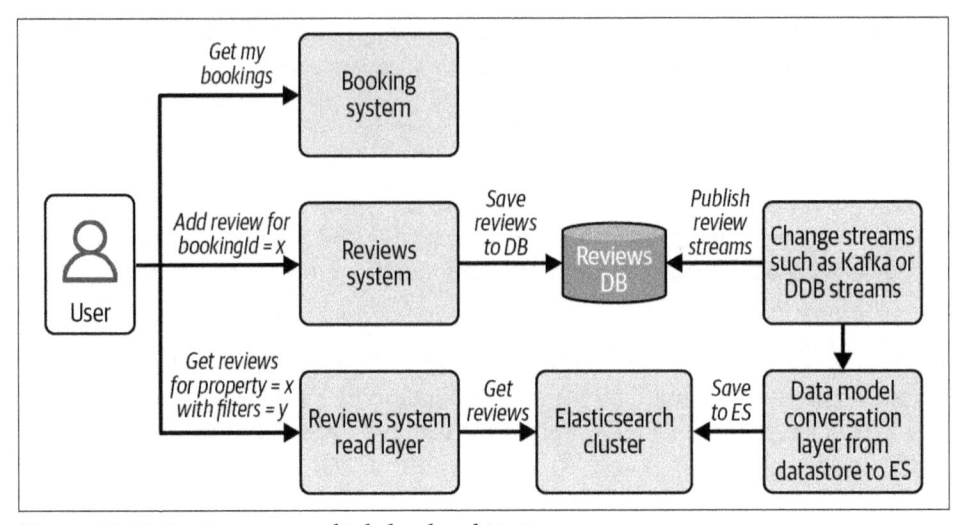

Figure 18-11. Reviews system high-level architecture

With all the details we gathered about the overall booking system, let's determine which AWS technologies to leverage for launching the system on the AWS cloud.

Launching the System on AWS

As with the discussion of the system design, we'll break the system into subparts and design the deployment view of the systems in Day 0 and Day N architectures. Horizontal scaling comes out of the box for the nonrelational databases, and users don't really have to worry about it. For relational databases, users will need to tweak the application code and manage the horizontal scaling on their end. We'll discuss the Aurora Limitless database architecture as part of this section to explore how customers can offload the management overhead and let AWS manage the horizontal scaling of relational databases. Let's start the discussion with the Day 0 architecture of the overall booking system.

Day 0 Architecture

We'll take inspiration from the AWS tech blog (*https://oreil.ly/bOLz0*) and break the design into multiple components for cleaner architecture diagrams, starting with the property onboarding system. The system architecture uses Amazon API Gateway to expose all the create and update APIs, and the authentication is managed by Amazon Cognito user pools. Amazon Route 53 provides a unique domain for users to interact with, which internally resolves to the API Gateway endpoint. AWS Lambda is used as the backend for managing all the property configurations, and it further interacts with three data stores: two Amazon S3 buckets and one Amazon DynamoDB table. The first S3 bucket is used to store any media content, such as property and room images, and the second S3 bucket is used for publishing all of the configurations in static format.

Any newly published configurations to S3 with respect to properties (addition or removal) and their pricing are consumed by the search system to facilitate property search by the users. DynamoDB stores the property information based on the schema we discussed in "Property Onboarding Architecture" on page 469. The architecture is shown in Figure 18-12.

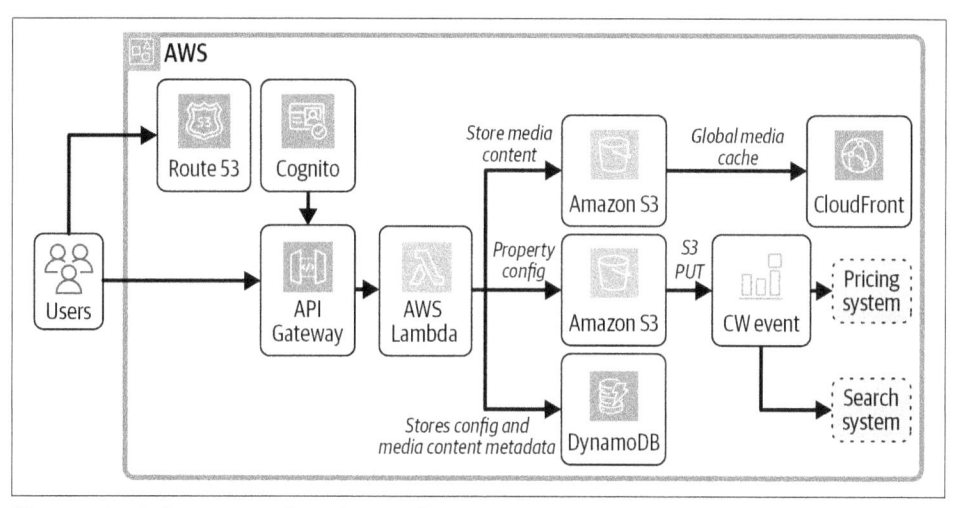

Figure 18-12. Property onboarding architecture on AWS

Room availability is continuously updated by the property owners and in the booking system. A key consideration to note is whether we can utilize DynamoDB streams to publish data to the pricing and search systems. We can, definitely, but the data is modeled in different ways to support multiple search use cases, and it is not the best idea to consume all the modeled data by the different systems. A single static config can be consumed by these systems and modeled per their requirements, which makes the overall architecture simple to operate.

The second subsystem is a search system allowing users to look for properties along with their prices and available rooms at a particular location. Users don't have to be logged in to search for a property, so authentication is optional. In case users are logged in, this information can be used to show more recommendations in the future. Additionally, the system can integrate with Amazon Location Service to offer capabilities like maps and points of interest. The properties are reflected in the search results based on the combination of two sets of databases: in the first, the property should be in the vicinity of the user-searched location using the Geohash database and should incorporate search filters using Elasticsearch, and the second maintains the availability of rooms at the property. The system also emits events for property searches for the properties having the most interest in a date range, and the pricing system can adjust the pricing of the properties accordingly. The high-level architecture of the property search system is shown in Figure 18-13.

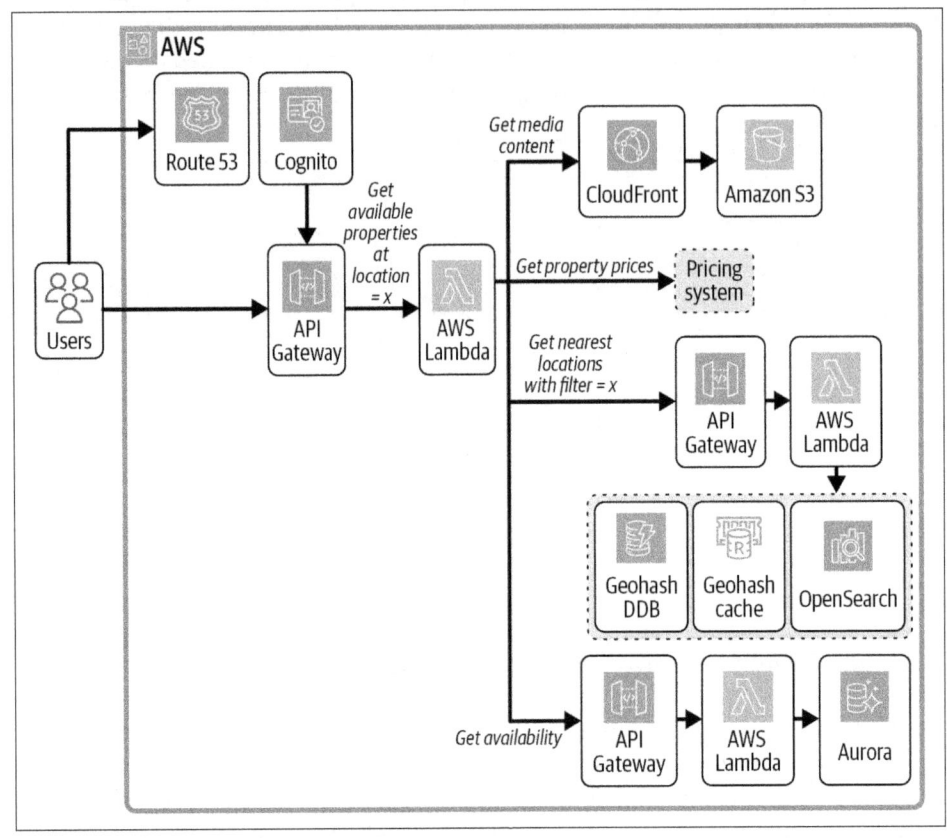

Figure 18-13. Property search architecture on AWS

The next system is a booking system allowing users to book a selected property from the search results. The booking system essentially books an available room, informs the property owner to take confirmation, processes the payment if needed, and finally marks the booking status per the response from the property owner. The architecture of the booking system is shown in Figure 18-14.

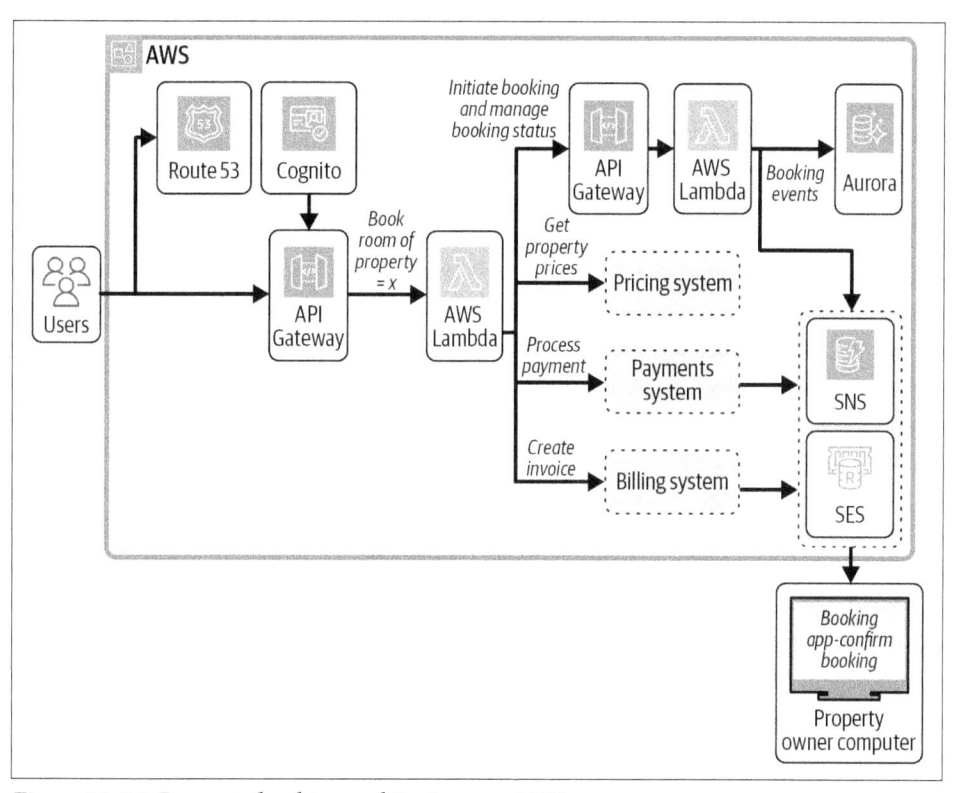

Figure 18-14. Property booking architecture on AWS

We have heavily used AWS serverless technologies in all the architectures described in this section. Let's further evaluate these different systems when scaling to a huge number of customers.

Scaling to Millions and Beyond

Using serverless solutions doesn't directly mean that they don't scale, but they can add to the cost as the traffic increases. The cost of AWS services is justified because customers don't have any operations management overhead. We'll start by looking at Amazon Aurora to figure out if it can meet increasing storage requirements. Per the storage-requirements calculations, the systems should be good to handle the required load since Aurora's storage capacity is 128 TB (up to 64 TB for older engine versions). Aurora shared storage scales in 10 GB segments up to 128 TB, and on top of this storage, we can introduce multiple read replicas (up to 15) and vertically scale the writer instance to handle increasing load, as shown in Figure 18-15.

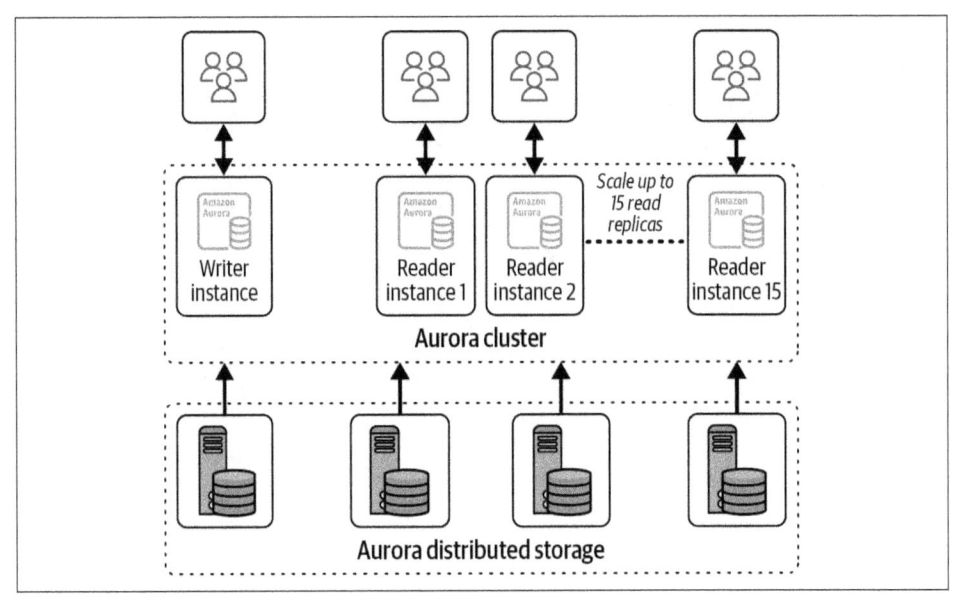

Figure 18-15. Scaling in an Amazon Aurora cluster

Beyond 128 TB in customer-managed Aurora clusters, the sharding on storage should be implemented by the customer. This can also be handed over to AWS using Aurora Serverless as compute, which offers Aurora Limitless Database capability (*https://oreil.ly/0ZNmJ*). This feature is helpful for managing millions of write transactions per second and petabytes of data with no sharding overhead on the customer's plate.

> We compared Amazon RDS and Aurora in Chapter 10 to some extent. Some additional operational challenges in RDS can be solved by migrating to Aurora. Some of these challenges include RDS taking around a day to create and restore read replicas for big clusters and needing to warm up the disk layer of RDS. These challenges are solved by offering an independent distributed storage layer in Aurora clusters.

Now, let's talk a little bit about the architecture of Aurora Limitless Database—the key distinction here is scaling the writes both vertically and horizontally. The user talks to a single writer endpoint, which internally communicates with multiple distributed transaction routers. These routers are responsible for ensuring the consistency and isolation properties of the database, scaling vertically to an extent, and then scaling horizontally to manage the load. The transaction routers store the metadata about the table schema and mapping tables key ranges to further figure out the shards where data should be kept.

There can be three types of tables on Aurora Limitless Database: sharded, standard, and reference. Standard tables are the default tables created in nonsharded Aurora clusters. The sharded tables are partitioned via hash-based partitioning by taking the hash of the shard key to 64 bits, and the ranges of 64 bit space are assigned to the shards. The reference tables can be the small tables for any use cases that don't share the shard key and are kept on each and every shard. All the related tables are colocated on the same shard to ensure minimum latency on data join operations. The data access shards store the sharded key space and the reference tables. These shards are also responsible for performing local transaction logic (global transaction logic across the shards is handled by transaction routers), local planning, and query execution.

The data access shards are further backed by Aurora's distributed storage layer to ensure data durability and high availability, as shown in Figure 18-16.

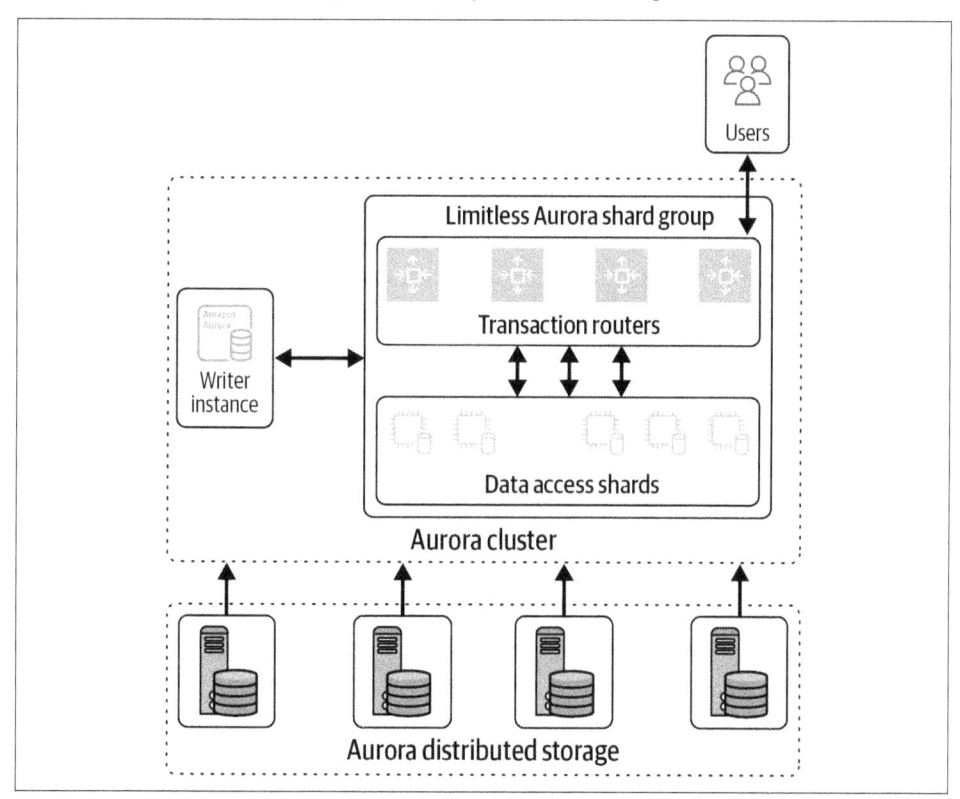

Figure 18-16. Amazon Aurora Limitless Database architecture

Aurora internally divides the shards further into slices (colocated data is present on the same slices). This makes relocation tasks easy on horizontal scaling and offers intrashard parallelism capability to improve query performances. This is quite similar to data division into virtual nodes in a physical node's consistent hashing ring, which we discussed in Chapter 3.

Aurora automatically takes care of high availability and durability by replicating the data across the AZs. For the transaction routers layer, any transaction router that goes down is automatically replaced by another one, and the requests can be handled by other instances. For the data access shards layers, the shards store the data, so there is downtime associated if any of these shards goes down. Aurora provides compute redundancy configuration as 0, 1, and 2 to replicate the shards across the AZs: 0 means there is no replication across the AZs, and 2 means a shard is replicated across two AZs.

The relational databases offer ACID properties out of the box for a single-instance deployment, but for a distributed environment, this support should be managed in the custom application logic. This is offered by the Aurora Limitless Database out of the box. Let's understand how transactions work in a distributed setup of nodes acting as shards. There can be two scenarios for executing multiple queries in a single transaction: all the queries access the same shard, or they access different shards. The same shard query is committed via one-phase commit, and two-phase commit is used for multishard transactions.

Time synchronization is another problem for multishard transactions, but this is solved using Amazon EC2's time-sync service and Aurora's custom implementation of bounded clocks. A SQL statement is sent to a transaction router and then is forwarded to different data access shards, but the time of delivery could be different, causing a time-sync issue on transaction commits. This can become a problem while restoring the data from snapshots (as a single data snapshot is created combining multiple shards) because of inconsistent data. The EC2 time-sync service offers three entries of time: current approximate time, earliest possible time, and latest possible time. The time is always within the earliest and latest possible time range, so the shards agree on one time (with microsecond precision), which has been passed by all of them.

We discussed all these details regarding Aurora Limitless Database to give us an idea of the extra work required for implementing the sharding on our own, adhering to basic relational database features. For the compute part in various architectures, we used AWS Lambda heavily in the Day 0 architecture of different systems. AWS Lambda can be used at scale or replaced by other compute options based on the comparisons we did in Chapters 10 and 14. The choices of database and compute always boil down to determining how each technology fits into your specific use case.

We often use Amazon API Gateway with AWS Lambda and then switch to ELBs with Amazon EC2 or container services. We covered the general idea of these services in Chapter 9, discussing their differences and similarities. Unless you're looking for specific API Gateway features, we recommend choosing ELB over API Gateway for application deployment.

Let's move to our Day N architecture next.

Day N Architecture

Let's think about which things we want to change in the Day 0 architecture if it has to be scaled to millions of users. In "Starting with the Design" on page 469, we discussed multiple components and breaking down the entire system into subcomponents. We also covered sharding mechanisms with Amazon Aurora in the previous section. We pretty much divided the system responsibility into subsystems in the Day 0 architecture, though we preferred most of the serverless offerings of AWS.

We also looked at multiple examples in previous chapters for moving from AWS Lambda to Amazon EC2 or Amazon EKS to support the Day N architecture. Note that we're not saying that serverless solutions don't scale or that they are too costly in all the scenarios. For example, Amazon DynamoDB works well at a huge scale and has predictable costs for defined query patterns. Along similar lines, Amazon Aurora Limitless Database is designed to support large-scale sharded databases, so it would be incorrect to say that we should manage infrastructure as scale grows. We recommend carefully evaluating your design choices and finalizing a choice with the least pain points.

Our architecture will also need a notification system to update customers about what's happening with their bookings. We used a combination of Amazon SNS and Amazon SES to send notifications to customers in the Day 0 architecture (refer to Figure 18-14). This can be further extended to integrate more notification channels, such as WhatsApp, mobile phone push notifications, and so on. Additionally, this system is used for marketing campaigns and sends different kinds of notifications to users. To implement all these features, an independent component in the system architecture can be included to take care of notification delivery and management. We can choose to club the same set of services (e.g., pay-in and pay-out microservices in the payments architecture) on the same EKS cluster, which should save some costs there. Reiterating from the previous chapters, it's not necessary to make the components independent if you don't foresee a need for that.

All the applications in the property reservation architecture are accessible via the frontend service. The frontend system is an application responsible for handling the user traffic for various operations and redirecting it to a specific application, such as user authentication, property onboarding, property search, booking, reviews, and so on.

A simplistic view of the booking system is shown in Figure 18-17 with all the different components discussed in previous sections.

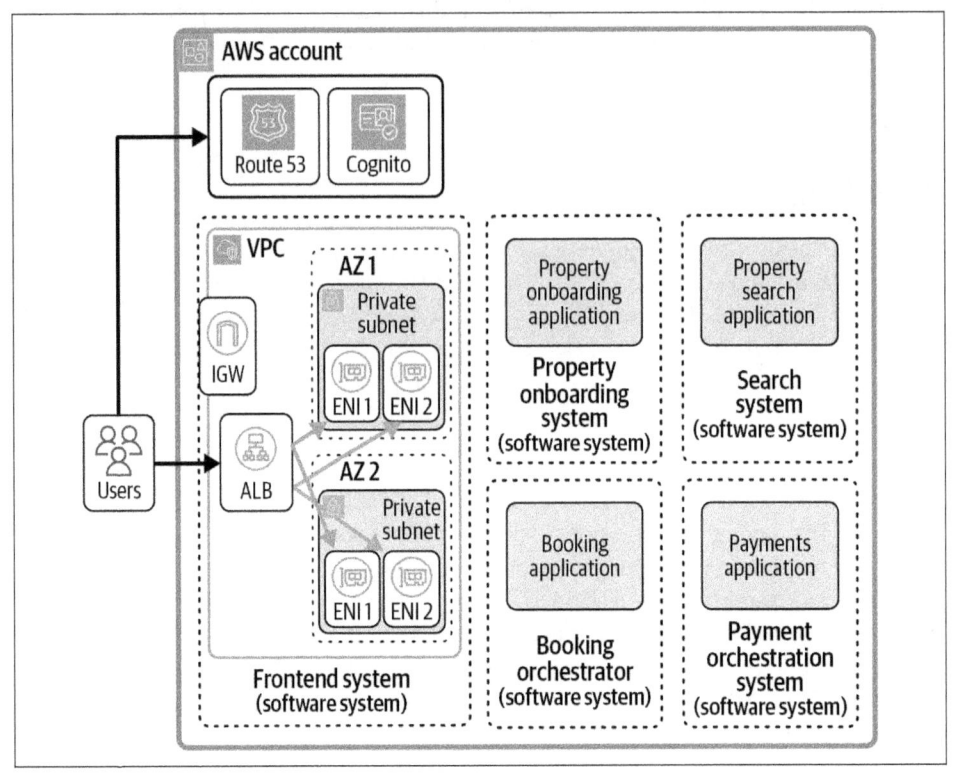

Figure 18-17. Property reservation system Day N architecture

In the architecture, we included all the services in a single AWS account for diagram clarity. We can also divide the AWS accounts based on business verticals, which will require additional networking infrastructure configurations for cross-account communication.

Conclusion

Implementation of any system end to end involves handling a lot of internal use cases, and you should limit the scope of the problem statement to close in on the discussion. We tried to take a similar approach with all the architectures in this part of the book: identifying the scope and then going into depth on it.

In this chapter, we identified a few of the systems in the overall booking architecture and figured out the design and the AWS services that would be beneficial for launching the application. We decided that both Amazon DynamoDB and Amazon Aurora can be useful in our property onboarding system design. This is an important takeaway: it often happens that multiple services will meet your requirements. We recommend evaluating your options primarily on three factors if this happens: your previous expertise on any service, the operational overhead, and the cost you're paying to AWS for service usage.

Remember, on Day 0, we make a lot of assumptions, but we learn over time by observing the system's behavior in production. With these observations in mind, we should reevaluate whether the system should be broken into more subparts for scaling for the system's and the team's operations.

One of the requirements in a booking system could be offering a communications channel between property owners and the customers after a booking. This allows customers to directly interact with hosts for any special requests. In the next chapter, we'll introduce you to the design of such chat applications and how they operate at high scale.

CHAPTER 19
Designing a Chat Application

In Chapter 6, we explored multiple networking protocols and communication mechanisms for building near real-time messaging platforms. Messaging applications are widely used across the globe. The application can be standalone, such as WhatsApp or Telegram, or it can be integrated as a feature inside social networking apps like LinkedIn or Instagram. In this chapter, we'll learn how to design large-scale messaging applications to offer fast communication in near real time. We'll also discuss the underlying architecture of WhatsApp messenger, which serves a huge number of concurrent users. Let's begin with the system requirements of a chat application.

System Requirements

A messaging application can support a wide variety of features, but to keep it simple, we will choose to build a limited set of functionalities and skip features like voice and video calling. Let's finalize the requirements to answer these questions:

What kinds of communication are supported by the application?
   The application offers one-to-one messaging, group messaging, and broadcast messaging. A broadcast is different from group messaging in that only a subset of users can send messages in the broadcast channel.

What type of content will be supported by the application?
   The application allows users to share text messages, images, videos, and documents. The next question that arises is whether there is a limit to the video file size. To avoid large media uploads, the system limits the file size to 100 MB.

Does the application store all the messages on its end, or are messages deleted once they are delivered to the users?
   We'll build a system like WhatsApp that can delete the messages from the server once the messages are delivered to the users.

Will the system include read receipts?
   Reflecting the user last seen and read receipts for any messages sent is a good feature to have. The read receipts can include messages sent to the application server, delivered to the user, and read by the user.

Does the system support end-to-end encryption of messages?
   Encryption ensures that the messages can be read only by the sender and the receiver, which maintains their security. We'll skip the implementation details of encryption support, but the system will not be limited in any way from offering this support in the future.

Is there a limit on the number of members in a group or for message broadcasts?
   We'll limit the system to 1,024 members for a group and for broadcast messages. In broadcast channels, only people with admin access can message, and the rest of the group can only view the message. We're not imposing any limits on the number of people who can be admins—note that if everyone is an admin, then the broadcast channel essentially behaves as a group.

Does the application support features apart from messaging, such as voice calls, video calls, or sharing status updates (like Instagram stories) with the users?
   The application focuses just on the chat functionality and doesn't support any extra features.

Let's turn to the functional and nonfunctional requirements of the system.

Functional and Nonfunctional Requirements

The functional features supported by the chat application are:

- The application supports one-to-one, group, and broadcast messages.
- Text, images, videos, and documents are supported as media types for communication among the users.
- A user should be able to see active status (online/offline) and last seen of any person from their contacts.
- Read receipts should be shown for sent, delivered, and read messages.
- There are push notifications on users' mobile devices for their received messages.

Let's discuss the NFRs next:

- The communication should be near real time with minimum possible latency.
- The system should be highly available and able to operate at increasing scale.

- The system should be able to store chat messages until they are delivered to recipients.

We'll make some assumptions and try to come up with an expected scale for the system in the next section.

System Scale

For the scale that needs to be supported by the system, we can make assumptions based on the scale served by the WhatsApp chat application:

Number of monthly active users = 3 billion

Messages sent = 100 billion/day = 1.2 million/second

Text, images, videos sent every day = 90 billion text, 8 billion images, 2 billion videos

The chat application supports both one-to-one and group messaging. The write-to-read-ratio is approximately 1:1 for direct messaging between two users, and it will be skewed in the case of group messaging. There are no stats available for the number of groups on the WhatsApp platform, so let's take a rough number of one billion. There are generally very few active users sending messages in the groups, and the remaining users are readers only; a good assumption for the read-to-write ratio is 90:10.

The numbers indicate the large number of concurrent users that the system is required to handle, and the system should be horizontally scalable to work without hiccups for peak overloads. The number of connections that a single server can handle highly depends on the choice of implementation and should be figured out with proper load testing. We'll go into more detail on the implementation next.

Starting with the Design

In a very simplistic view of a chat application, a user sends a message to the chat server with the intended recipient, and the chat server delivers this message to the receiver as shown in Figure 19-1. The chat message might be intermittently stored in the database in case the user is not connected to the internet.

The first step before communication can begin between users is registering the user and determining who they can send messages to. This can completely vary from use case to use case; for example, you need a person's registered phone number for communication over WhatsApp and an Instagram handle for communication over Instagram. Here, we'll take our cues from WhatsApp and use the phone number as a unique identifier for user registration. The user is verified via a phone number, and reregistration is required if their phone number changes. The user service can be responsible for registering a user and later for authentication of the user to send and receive messages.

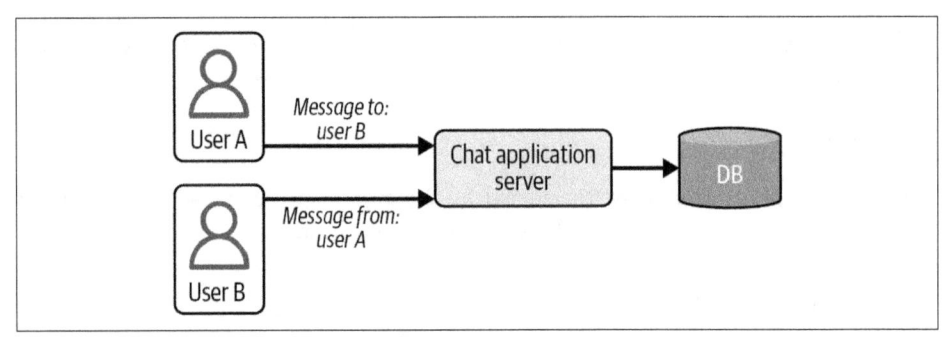

Figure 19-1. High-level overview of chat application

Now, let's look at the messaging architecture and figure out details like optimal networking protocol and message storage selection.

Messaging Architecture

A very important requirement for messaging systems is near real-time behavior: the communication should be instant, as if two people are talking face-to-face. To support this, it is critical to identify the networking protocol (or technology). Some popular protocols are XMPP and MQTT. Refer to Chapter 6 for the architectural details of these protocols. Let's try to figure out the benefits associated with each of these protocols.

Protocol selection

Based on the discussion from Chapter 6, the chat system requires implementation of WebSockets for maintaining a persistent connection between the users and the chat servers. The other mechanisms for retrieving new messages (such as polling) from the chat server are latency and resource-intensive operations (see "Scaling post comments" on page 430 in Chapter 16). Since a persistent connection is maintained, the protocol must be lightweight to ensure that resource consumption by devices is minimum (saving internet usage and battery life).

> Another important point to consider for fast messaging over the network is message payload size, which can heavily depend on the data format. The payload in JSON format can be bulky; one solution to reduce it could be data compression, and another involves using data formats like Thrift or Protocol Buffers (Protobuf).

Assume a user connects to the internet and the chat application establishes a connection with the chat server over HTTPS. There can be two possible approaches here:

- The first call pulls all the user's messages since they were last online and then establishes a persistent bidirectional connection to receive any delta updates.
- The first call registers the user on the chat server, and then all messages (since they were offline or new messages) are sent over a persistent bidirectional connection.

Both the MQTT and XMPP protocols are widely used by different messaging applications to support a large scale of users: MQTT is used by Facebook Messenger, and XMPP is used by WhatsApp. XMPP is inherently built to support messaging, and MQTT is built especially for machine-to-machine communication in resource-constrained environments. Both protocols are lightweight, but MQTT is relatively lighter and operates on the transport layer. XMPP is more feature rich in terms of messaging architecture as compared to MQTT but requires more resources for operating.

There is also the option of not using either XMPP or MQTT but instead relying on a pure WebSocket connection over HTTPS between the client devices and the server. This will definitely introduce additional work on the system's end, which could have been inherently supported by a particular protocol, such as user presence information in the case of XMPP. These protocols can also work with persistent connections, and it is a good idea to use them in order to gain their inherent properties and build on top of them. We'll now try to figure out the system architectural details for building one-to-one chat functionality.

Direct messaging

In the previous section, we mentioned keeping a bidirectional persistent connection between the user and the chat application server. For a user to send a message to another user, the system should be able to figure out which particular server (from the pool of servers) holds the connection for that user. Message delivery from user A to user B can be completed in this series of steps, shown in Figure 19-2:

1. User A sends a connection request to the chat frontend service once the device is online.
2. The chat frontend service authenticates the user by forwarding the request to the user service.
3. The system establishes a persistent connection with the user device and stores an entry in the database of the server ID assigned to the user device.
4. Steps 1 and 2 occur for user B.

5. User A sends a message to the chat frontend service with user B as the intended recipient.
6. The system checks for the server ID assigned to user B from the database in case user B is online and sends the message to user B's device.
7. Once the message is delivered to user B's device, the system sends an acknowledgment over the same persistent bidirectional connection, which is forwarded to user A's device. The message-read acknowledgment works in the same way.

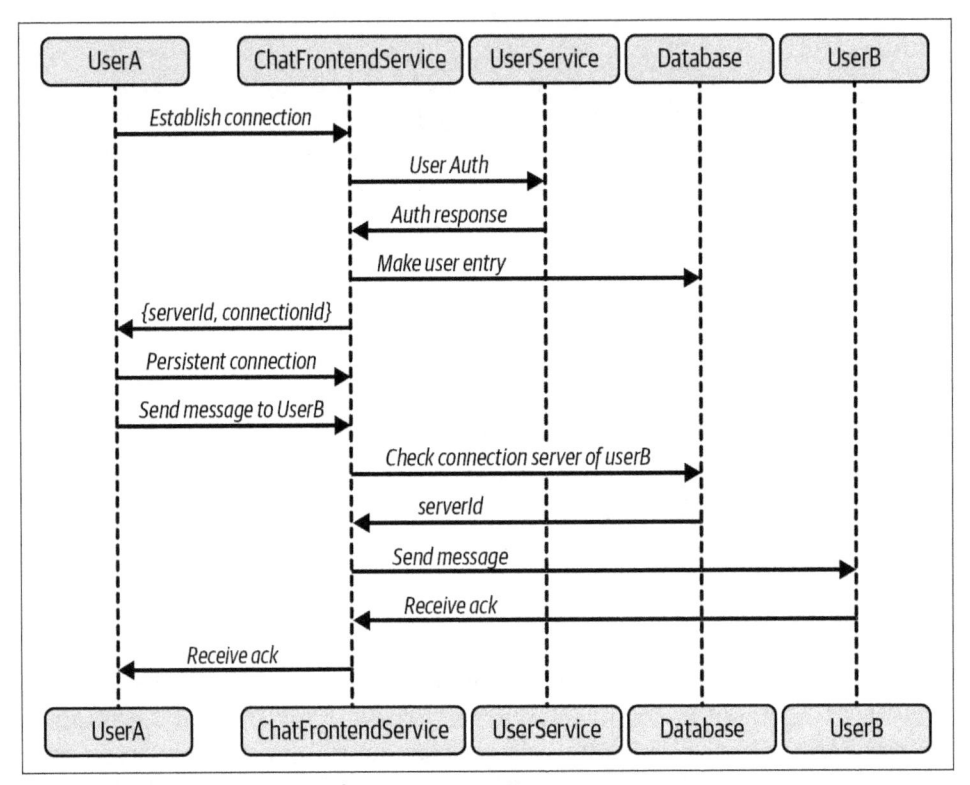

Figure 19-2. Direct messaging between two users

When both users who are communicating are online, there is no requirement for message storage, and the message can be delivered directly to the intended recipient. In case the recipient is offline, the system maintains an independent offline component to store the messages for the time being. The database of user IDs to server IDs also includes information noting if the user is online or when the user was last active. This can be served with a simple key-value database, such as Amazon DynamoDB or Amazon ElastiCache with Redis storing metadata information for users, as shown in Figure 19-3. In a nutshell, we need a connection management mechanism for a very high number of concurrent users and to figure out a way to manage the users to different servers efficiently.

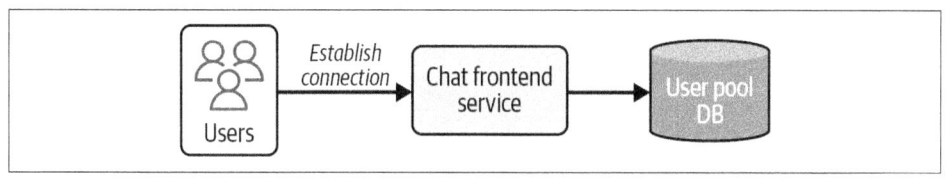

Figure 19-3. Connection user pool management service

> The system should be able to handle network interruptions. Let's say the internet is jittery, which causes the connection with the server to drop intermittently. This can lead to continuous fluctuation of a user's presence status between online and offline. The system can handle this via periodic heartbeats at a fixed interval with the user device to make sure the device is still connected with the chat server.

The user connection should be managed by a thread or process on the running server, and to ensure a single server can support a huge number of connections, the process/thread should be lightweight. The OS processes are not really lightweight, so we'll explore some alternatives on top of them to help with this implementation in the system architecture.

The *actor model* is a conceptual model proposed to support large numbers of connections concurrently with minimal resources. The actor model can be inherently supported by the programming language, or we can use available frameworks or libraries built for the programming language. We'll talk about the Erlang programming language with support for the actor model as Erlang processes in the "WhatsApp Architecture" section. There are similar implementations in other languages, such as goroutines in Go (*https://oreil.ly/-LAGk*), coroutines in Kotlin (*https://oreil.ly/qMyvF*), and virtual threads in Java (*https://oreil.ly/trZ4o*).

The actor model can be helpful for managing a large number of user connections. Akka (*https://oreil.ly/toJyG*) is one of the actor model implementations for the Java and Scala programming languages, and Play framework (*https://oreil.ly/ya6Rg*) is a utility that can be used to manage implementation of the Akka actor model with WebSockets to facilitate the messaging functionality. Using these frameworks in software programs helps us build the applications on top of the actor model and reduces our work since we don't have to build everything from scratch.

Here are the characteristics of the actor model:

- An *actor* is a very small object and acts as a fundamental unit of computation in the system.
- Each actor is isolated and doesn't share memory with other actors. This feature helps with managing the concurrent connections very easily without a requirement of explicit locking for resources.
- Each actor has a designated mailbox (FIFO queue) to receive messages from other actors that serves as a communication channel between the actors.
- An actor is associated with a state and behavior. The behavior defines the state modification logic upon receiving a new message.
- Actors are completely decoupled to work asynchronously and handle one message at a time. To perform the required work, an actor is assigned a lightweight thread to modify the state based on behavior definition from the message. The great thing about this architectural pattern is that threads are not blocked for the entire request execution (as in synchronous systems). The thread is free as soon as work by the actor is complete, and the thread can be assigned to other actors. This allows the system to create a lot more actors (with the same hardware configurations) and execute them with fewer threads, optimizing the overall resource utilization of the system.
- An actor can create child actors and supervise them with the operation (act as a supervisor actor). The supervision handles failures at the topmost layer in case work being executed fails for some reason.

The ratio of the number of actors to threads can vary by a huge proportion on a single machine. In reference to the chat application architecture, each actor is responsible for holding one persistent connection with a user device, but a thread is assigned to the actor only when a message is being sent to the device. The first connection between users is established as a simple HTTPS call from the user device, and then it is converted to persistent connection. The chat frontend service stores the configuration of which particular instance is being assigned to the user from the pool.

A machine may go down while it's managing the user connections. There should be an efficient mechanism to reestablish the connection with user devices without having much impact on the chat application and user experience. This requires spawning a new machine, reestablishing user connections, and updating the user mapping database with a new instance. The establishment of a new connection can be built inside the client application to check for the persistent connection (in case the device is connected to the internet), and if the connection is dropped, the client can initiate a new connection with the server, and the server accordingly reassigns a new actor on a machine and updates the user mapping database.

The one-to-one message functionality can be extended to group and broadcast messages with one difference: the chat frontend service forwards the message request from the user to the group service, and then this service fans out the messages to the group members. In case some users from the group are not available, messages should be kept in the transient storage until the users come back online.

> The system doesn't continuously check for a user's online status; rather, it relies on the user's initial ping to establish connection. Upon establishing the first connection, the system checks for any new messages from when the user was offline and delivers them if there's anything present in the database.

Let's move on to discuss our data store requirements for storing messages and multimedia for offline users.

Message storage

The system supports text, image, and video formats. An object storage data store such as Amazon S3 is a good choice for storing large media files like images, videos, or any other types of documents. For text messaging and references to media files, we can use more structured databases, such as RDBMS or any NoSQL solution. The requirements for the database are simple:

- Store messages in such a way that they can be retrieved once the user is connected to the chat servers. This should serve all kinds of messaging: one-to-one, group, and broadcast.
- Messages should be stored with acknowledgment receipts until the messages are seen by the recipient.

The data should be stored in the database in such a way that the reads are very fast, meaning the system should be able to retrieve all the direct, group, and broadcast chats for a user in the minimum time possible. The storage requirements can be met by both relational databases and NoSQL solutions, such as Amazon DynamoDB. We can identify relationships among the data, such as a message is associated with a user or group, a user can be part of one or more groups, a user is registered with a device, a user has a list of contacts, and so on. Both relational and NoSQL databases meet the storage requirements since the system doesn't require any specific set of constraints offered by a particular database.

One system requirement is deleting messages from the database once they are successfully delivered to users. The choice of database should be able to efficiently perform the deletion process. As pointed out in Chapter 18, data is not actually removed from the disk upon the delete operation but rather is cleaned with the help of regular vacuum processes. To manage the deletion process more effectively, we can try to figure out if data can be partitioned based on the time range so that the entire set of older data can be removed by deleting the partition. The key consideration for the chat application use case could be deleting the data at regular intervals, such as on a weekly or monthly basis, rather than firing the delete query for every message once it is delivered to the user. The deletion process should also take care of deleting unwanted media from the object storage. WhatsApp follows a rather simple architecture for transient message storage using the files—we'll discuss this approach in later sections of this chapter.

The message storage aspect is quite interesting in the case of group messaging. We mentioned that the system stores a copy of messages associated with a user and the user can fetch these messages once they are online, but is this really a requirement for group messaging? Keeping a copy of the same message for each user is overkill and requires much more storage space. Instead, the system should keep a single copy of a message in the context of a group, and the message ID (the unique identifier of the message) can be used as a reference for message sharing, much like media sharing. This consideration becomes critical if the messages are stored on the server forever, but the system proposed in this chapter can still live with it as the messages are stored only for the time that the users are not connected to the chat application.

Now, let's discuss multimedia management in the chat application.

Multimedia system

The chat application supports image and video sharing along with texts. This can be managed by a completely independent component (a media service) to upload and download the media content, and the reference URL of the media can be used as part of messaging. For any request to share media content, the request is sent to the media service, and it returns a reference URL for where the image is uploaded (the same reference URL is used by recipients to download the media content). The reference URL is sent via text messaging following the same principles we discussed in "Direct messaging" on page 505.

Additionally, the media content is pushed to CDNs for faster downloads. On big events like sports events or holidays, it can absolutely happen that the same media content is forwarded by a wide range of users, and storing the content again and again requires a lot of storage space. Media compression is the first technique for saving storage space on devices and allows for faster download and uploads. The compression should not reduce the media quality drastically, and a balance should be kept between saving storage space and maintaining the quality of content.

To further optimize the overall systems, we can follow a simplistic approach to create a hash of media content before storing the image to object storage, such as Amazon S3. The system checks if a hash is already available in the media database and returns the already created reference URL if a hash is available. In case the hash is not present in the database, the system creates a media hash, uploads the media content to object storage, and returns the reference URL (after storing the media hash and reference URL in the database). The system puts a maximum limit on the size of content shared, but it could be the case that multiple short videos are created from the bigger video and are shared among the users. In this case, the computed hash will be different, and the system will store both the big video and the short videos created from the bigger video. A better approach here could be to divide the video into multiple chunks (such as 500 KB each) and then compare the chunks hash with already stored chunks in the data store. We'll discuss breaking a larger video into smaller chunks more in Chapter 20.

The WhatsApp chat application is built in the Erlang programming language on top of Ejabberd open source software. Erlang is a functional programming language with built-in support of actors and is specifically designed to handle a huge number of concurrent connections. Let's talk a little about the WhatsApp architecture with Erlang.

WhatsApp Architecture with Erlang

Ejabberd is open source software specifically designed to support building near real-time chat applications. The software is built in Erlang and can be deployed as an XMPP server. Here is the list of features offered by Ejabberd out of the box, which also covers the defined functional requirements for our system:

- Support for one-to-one and group messaging
- Support for user last activity, user presence status, and typing indicator
- Support for the user's contact list along with their presence status
- Support for message delivery receipts
- Support for sharing media content such as images, videos, and the like

Ejabberd offers a modular architecture and can easily be extended to meet any specific business requirements. Because Ejabberd is built on top of the Erlang programming language, it can use the language's inherent support for message passing and concurrency. Ejabberd software can support more than two million concurrent users (*https://oreil.ly/n1xBl*) on a single machine, which is a great milestone and makes it ideal for managing large connection pools, saving the infrastructure costs. You can read additional use cases built on top of Ejabberd (*https://oreil.ly/uu7JQ*).

Erlang offers lightweight processes with very minimal resources as compared to processes from other programming languages. Most languages use the OS processes and threads for program execution, but Erlang creates its own independent processes in the user space that are not bound to kernel threads (or OS processes) in any way. Erlang uses BEAM (originally Bogdan's Erlang Abstract Machine) as a VM to schedule and run the programs in the Erlang runtime environment. To compare BEAM with JVM, JVM maps its threads with the OS threads, and the OS takes the responsibility of thread scheduling. With Erlang, the scheduling is fully managed by BEAM to optimize the overall working of the system.

On top of all its other benefits, Erlang inherently supports hot-swap deployments, allowing users to upgrade the code without worrying about any impact. *Hot-swap deployment* means you can deploy new code on a production running server without any downtime or hampering the existing connections.

Now, let's look at the overall system architecture of WhatsApp.

System architecture

The WhatsApp architecture is very similar to what we already went over in previous sections. User devices establish a session with the chat daemons (similar to the frontend service in "Direct messaging" on page 505) and web daemons managed by two separate frontend systems. Chat daemons are responsible for handling connections from mobile devices, and web daemons are responsible for handling connections from WhatsApp web clients. In addition to the two frontend systems, a separate system handles the media uploads and downloads from the users, and the media URL is used as a reference during chat communication. The chat and web daemons further connect with different backend Erlang clusters that are fully decoupled from one another to perform tasks like:

- Connecting with the user service to authenticate the user
- Connecting with the offline service to retrieve any messages pending for the user to be delivered

All the chat frontend nodes are fully interconnected with one another (fully mesh network topology), and messages are directly transferred between the users if they're online, without the intervention of backend services. The mapping of users specific to the chat frontend server is maintained by the session service, and the user can reinitiate the connection in case the connection is dropped from either the user's or the server's end. Management of group relationships is handled by the group service, and push notifications are handled by the notification push service. The media servers are implemented on top of another Erlang open source software application, YAWS (Yet Another Web Server) (*https://oreil.ly/MLwFE*). The overall architecture is shown in Figure 19-4.

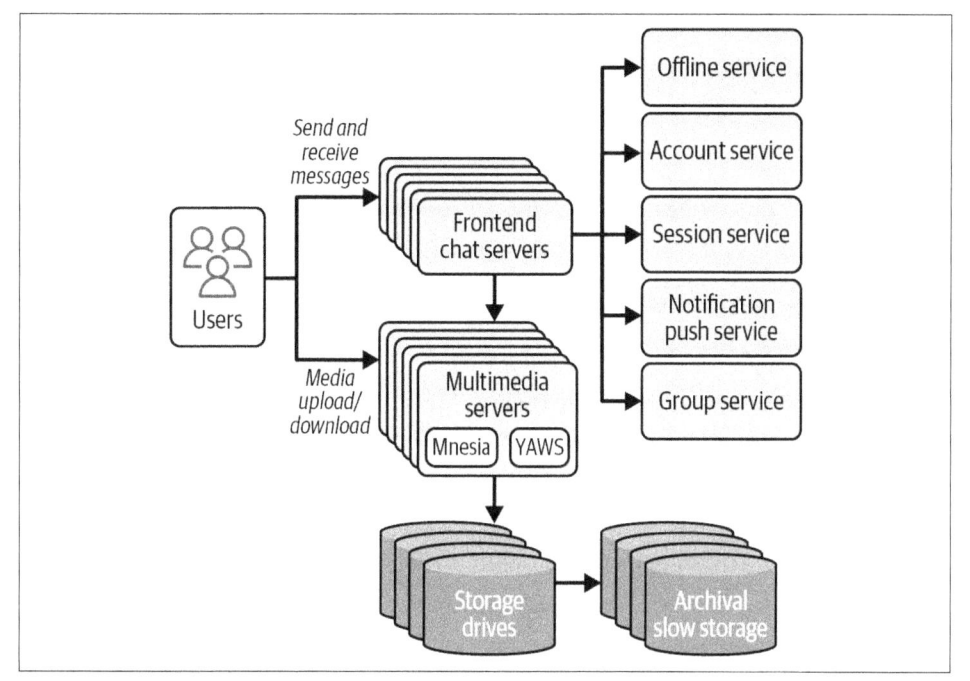

Figure 19-4. WhatsApp architecture

The multimedia system works similarly to what we discussed in the "Multimedia system" on page 510. We mentioned that the media content is deleted once the acknowledgment is received from all the recipients, but the WhatsApp system also configures some delay since there is always the possibility that once a user receives the images or video files, they will forward the messages to their friends and so on. Configuring some delay for deleting the media can save having to reupload it from the user devices and help optimize the overall performance of the system. This also saves bandwidth from the user's end.

> There is a possibility that clients will drop off in the middle of the media-uploading process and therefore only parts of the media file are uploaded to the system. The multimedia system should keep a separate cleaning mechanism to clear out such files from the data store.

There are a lot of different kinds of mobile phones, and each one supports different formats of multimedia content. To ensure a good user experience, the multimedia system transcodes the media file into different formats (more on this in Chapter 20) and delivers it to the user based on their device.

There are also database offerings that are exclusively written in Erlang. Let's discuss use cases for Mnesia and other storage solutions that are used in the WhatsApp architecture.

Databases

Mnesia (*https://oreil.ly/Ooa-g*) is a relational database, and Erlang term storage (ETS) (*https://oreil.ly/nsJ-o*) is an in-memory data store for faster lookups; both are purpose built for Erlang. WhatsApp heavily uses both these data stores for its storage requirements. Let's discuss some of the benefits that Mnesia offers as compared to traditional relational databases like MySQL:

- If the application is written in Erlang, Mnesia offers real-time data lookup by allowing data storage in the same memory space as the application.
- The data objects stored in the database and the Erlang application code are exactly the same, removing the need for data transformation.
- Mnesia allows dynamic reconfiguration of objects at runtime.
- The distributed nature of the Mnesia database provides high fault tolerance.

WhatsApp uses Mnesia as a data store to store all kinds of data, such as account and user profile information, group memberships, and media references and transcodings. WhatsApp deploys the database on the same cluster as the application code (note that they are moving to remote databases as part of the migration to Facebook infrastructure). Deployment of databases on the same instances as the application makes the system stateful and is generally not recommended to ensure easier recovery from system faults, but let's talk about some of the benefits of databases and applications running on the same cluster instance.

For an independent remote database, we need to handle connectivity between application code and the database layer as well as routing, failovers, consistency, and reduced infrastructure management. This is not much of a bottleneck because of multiple offerings by cloud providers and makes the management task a piece of cake. In the Erlang cluster, the data is stored in Mnesia in smaller parts called *islands*. An island is a set of hosts that all share one schema, and each island consists of data from two hosts to provide redundancy in the form of primary and secondary partitions. The partitioning of data is created based on key-to-node mapping, much like how it's handled in Amazon DynamoDB based on the partition key, as shown in Figure 19-5.

The partitions are managed by Erlang gen_server deployment (*https://oreil.ly/pNmBg*). The Erlang gen_server module offers the base functionality of client-server architecture. The client calls the server via an API, and the server acts on the client request and responds.

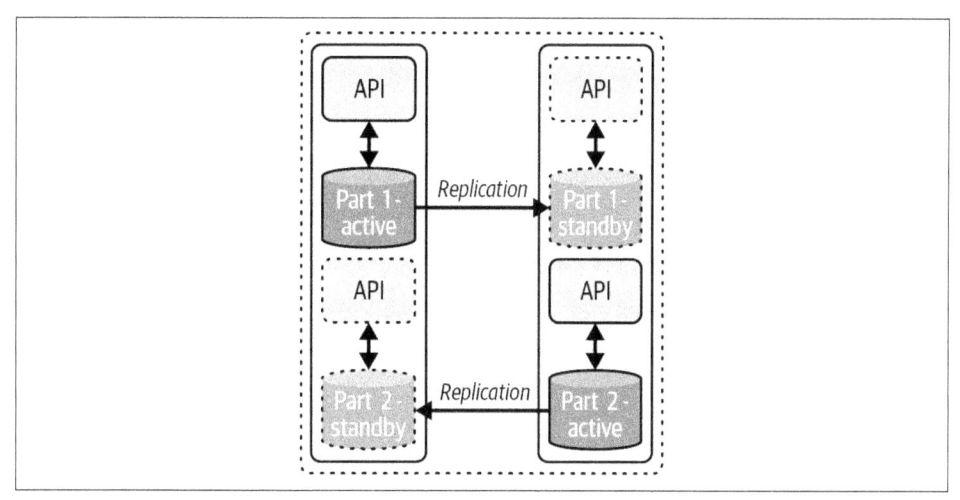

Figure 19-5. Island architecture

In previous sections, we mentioned using transient stores to store messages and media content in case users are offline. The lifecycle of data on the transient store is managed via the offline service. We can utilize the object stores provided by the cloud providers to store this kind of data, such as Amazon S3, but in the case of WhatsApp, the entire data store is in house, managed on the SSD and spinning disks. The storage drives are managed via the JBOD (Just a Bunch of Disks) system. JBOD allows multiple disks to be combined into one representation, and we can access the disks from the software as a single disk. Here are the implementation details for the transient message store:

- The messages corresponding to a user are stored on an append-only file, and the file is deleted once the messages are delivered to the user. The AOF file is like a mailbox that holds letters until they are picked up. The AOF files are kept on the storage partition dedicated to a set of users.
- The media files are stored in the directories, and the references are maintained in the Mnesia database.
- To ensure data redundancy, the data is stored on two parallel storage partitions. The messages are stored in two parallel files on the filesystem. Once the user comes back online, the offline system retrieves the file from both the storage partitions, combines the messages, removes any duplicates, and then sends the messages to the user's device.

Images are stored on the SSD for faster storage and retrieval, and videos are stored on the slower spinning disks. In case the images are not delivered to the recipients within a specific threshold timeframe, they are moved to a slower storage solution to optimize the overall storage costs. The references should be updated in the databases when the files are moved from one location to another. As the messages are not persisted indefinitely at the server side, they are stored on the client device in a local SQLite database.

In the next section, we'll design and deploy the chat application architecture on the AWS cloud.

Launching the System on AWS

We discussed a couple of new concepts in this chapter around maintaining a persistent connection with user devices and offering near real-time behavior. In previous sections, we talked about a scalable architecture for designing a chat application, but we'll start with a much simpler architecture in the Day 0 architecture, and later we'll add enhancements. We'll try to leverage fully managed services to reduce the time to market of the chat application. Later, we'll figure out any potential bottlenecks and make amendments to the design to overcome those limitations.

Day 0 Architecture

We explored AWS AppSync and the idea of fully managed, serverless WebSockets connections in Chapter 12. The chat application requires persistent bidirectional connections, and AppSync is a good candidate to facilitate this requirement. This feature allows us to remove any work related to managing the frontend service responsible for connection management. We skipped user signups and further authentication in the system design section—Amazon Cognito can be leveraged for this functionality. For signups specifically, the authentication is based on a one-time password (OTP) on mobile phones. This is not offered out of the box in Cognito, so we'll need a custom implementation for this feature.

To build the Day 0 architecture of the chat application, we can reference AWS shared blog posts on using AppSync (*https://oreil.ly/4AVQR*) and Amazon ElastiCache for Redis (*https://oreil.ly/w8oB1*). Both of these posts include code samples for launching the application stack on the AWS cloud. The architecture with AppSync is illustrated in Figure 19-6. Users interact via Cognito for authentication, which then makes a user entry in the DynamoDB table. AppSync establishes a direct connection with databases to store message and media content via persistent WebSocket connections. We can create separate AWS Lambda handlers for managing information for groups, notifications, user contacts, and the like.

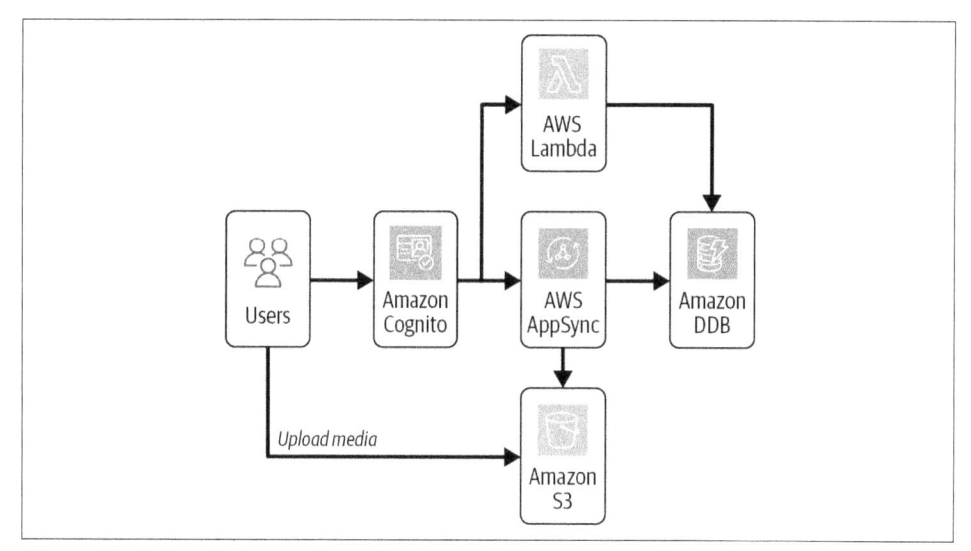

Figure 19-6. Day 0 chat application architecture

Figure 19-6 is a simplistic view of the deployment. The DynamoDB in the architecture proposes a multitable design (separate tables for storing users, messages, and groups) instead of the generally recommended single-table design (*https://oreil.ly/ 1HxLa*) to store all the entities. The DynamoDB multitable design (*https://oreil.ly/ Zi8qJ*) (a separate table for each core entity in the GraphQL schema) is generally recommended for GraphQL implementations due to the fact that clients can fire arbitrary requests for data retrieval and the query access patterns are not entirely fixed. The GraphQL resolvers logic can become quite complex with the single-table design, but you can always choose a combination of both if that suits your requirements best.

The Day 0 architecture we chose here is focused on using AWS-managed serverless services to reduce time to market and operational overhead. Evaluate open source software like Ejabberd for Day 0 architecture and deploying it on Amazon EC2 or containerization services.

To scale the system to a large set of concurrent users, we can always invest time in figuring out the challenges and fixing them. In the next section, we discuss such challenges and how we can resolve them to scale the system to millions and beyond.

Scaling to Millions and Beyond

A chat application is a very user-heavy use case, and it should cater to an increasing user base without impacting the availability and performance of the app. The number of network connections is huge, so one important consideration in the architecture is congestion control. *Congestion* basically means the system is bombarded with more requests than it can actually handle, making the system use all of its resources without performing any actual work of serving the requests. This situation is similar to road traffic: the actual distance covered by a vehicle reduces as the number of vehicles on the road increases.

Congestion handling

Here are some mechanisms that are useful for detecting and controlling the congestion problem:

Graceful degradation
> Once the system realizes it's not possible to serve all the requests successfully, it should be able to drop some of the requests to clear the clutter. The mechanism of dropping the requests can vary from use case to use case; the system can discard all the new requests or discard the older requests based on some set expiration. It is always better to serve some requests than to serve nothing at all. You might have seen dog photos on *amazon.com* whenever Amazon is unable to fulfill a request—this is one way to return a custom error page if the system is overloaded with user requests. In the context of AWS services, the rate limiting on specific thresholds can be implemented with the help of AWS WAF. The system should be able to knock out malicious unwanted traffic, which can be done with tools like AWS WAF and AWS Shield.

Retry, but not too much
> Both client applications and users use retry as a common solution if there's no response within a certain time frame or if they receive an error response from the server application. Users do this by refreshing the browser web page. To avoid a storm of retries, the client should be informed with proper error message details to determine if it's worth retrying the request. Further, the retry should be allowed based on the number of successful requests—for example, only allow one retry if there are one hundred successful requests (retries just with exponential backoffs are not helpful in these scenarios). Another mechanism for independent processing of requests could be decoupling systems by introducing a queue in between, such as SQS. This enables producers to publish requests and consumers to consume the requests at their own rates without overloading the system.

System testing
> The system should be tested for its functionality beyond the expected load, and there should be proper operational mechanisms (metrics, alarms, dashboards, and runbooks) set up to identify and fix the issues. The system should also be chaos tested with tools like Amazon FIS (*https://aws.amazon.com/fis*) to identify any loopholes in worst-case scenarios, such as an entire AZ going down or CPU utilization bumping to 100%.

We used AWS AppSync for managing WebSocket connections in the Day 0 architecture. Per the AWS documentation, there is no hard limit on the number of WebSocket connections, and it should scale with the increasing scale. There are some other AWS services offering WebSocket support; let's discuss them in the next section.

WebSocket management services

AWS has enabled the WebSocket feature in multiple AWS services. The other options apart from AppSync for managing WebSockets are Amazon API Gateway, AWS IoT Core (*https://oreil.ly/ZAqwS*), and load balancer (*https://oreil.ly/0HoSh*) services. Some key considerations in the context of building chat applications are listed in Table 19-1.

Table 19-1. API Gateway, IoT Core, and ELB comparison

Key factor	Amazon API Gateway	AWS IoT Core	ELB
Definition	Creates and manages REST, HTTP, and WebSocket APIs at any scale	Enables IoT devices to securely connect with cloud applications and other devices	Distributes incoming traffic across multiple targets (revisit Chapter 9 for more about ELB and API Gateway)
Support for persistent connections	WebSocket APIs support (*https://oreil.ly/tQMEP*)	MQTT over WebSocket support	Both ALB and NLB allow a connection upgrade to the WebSocket type (*https://oreil.ly/uKpq1*)
Document reference for chat application	Building a chat application with the WebSocket API, DynamoDB, and Lambda	Building a chat application with AWS IoT Core via MQTT over WebSocket	No specific documentation by AWS, but the concept is similar to using WebSockets for persistent connections

There are many other differences between these services, and they offer different benefits. Review the updated guidance on their product pages to help you determine if they meet your business requirements. For a scale as big as WhatsApp, consider managing the system on your own to gain more control over your configurations than you would have with managed services.

AppSync doesn't have any server management overhead, so we don't have to worry about scaling up and down. In case we decide to deploy a frontend service to manage the WebSocket connections, we should come up with our ideal instance configurations and the maximum number of connections that can be supported by one instance. The best approach for estimating this number is load testing the system and accordingly tuning the configurations.

We discussed the idea of multiregion deployments in Chapter 16, and this becomes important for chat application scale as well. Let's discuss the messaging architecture in the context of systems deployed in multiple regions.

Multiregion deployment of messaging systems

With multiregion deployment, users communicating with one another can be located in different regions and connected to separate regions. For such use cases, interregion communication should be incorporated in a latency-effective manner. AWS regions are connected with one another on a dedicated network, so we don't have to worry about handling the region connectivity infrastructure. Chapter 16 focused on the idea that the data of all the users is replicated in the regions, but we may choose to optimize to store user data in only two regions (for redundancy and handling regional failures) instead of all of them. This means that data should be sent to another region for serving the user query because the data is not locally persisted.

Let's take an example of one-to-one messaging between two users located in different geographies: chat servers will connect them to different regional servers. Here are two mechanisms we can explore for connectivity across the regions:

- The send message notification (message from user A to user B) is published to every region; the consumer in every region figures out if the intended recipient belongs to the region. If yes, then it will deliver the message if the user is online or persist the message to the offline system for future delivery.
- A global data store is used for ElastiCache Redis for session service. The global data store helps figure out the exact region a user is connected to, and a message is sent to a specific region only.

For either of these two approaches to work, we need a user registry to figure out the primary region for a user; this is also important for handling offline-user message delivery. We can very well leverage DynamoDB global tables for this use case.

To summarize, we recommend using a global data store for ElastiCache to figure out a user's region if the user is online and deliver the message directly. If a user is not found, use DynamoDB to identify the user region, and the message is handled by the offline system.

With this understanding, let's move to the Day N architecture.

Day N Architecture

Figure 19-4 shows the WhatsApp architecture, a very simple architecture that is able to serve billions of messages every day. The infrastructure is managed in house and deployed on bare-metal servers.

We'll try to leverage AWS components to deploy the systems and meet the data storage requirements. The architecture uses Amazon ECS for deploying services, and we use DynamoDB as a database in most of the applications. As mentioned in "Message storage" on page 509, both relational and nonrelational databases meet the system requirements, and you can choose a solution based on previous expertise. Aurora Serverless Limitless Database discussed in Chapter 18 is one option for managed relational databases, but you should definitely consider managing the database on your own for fine-tuning of configurations at WhatsApp scale. Figure 19-7 illustrates what our own chat app architecture might look like when deployed on the AWS cloud.

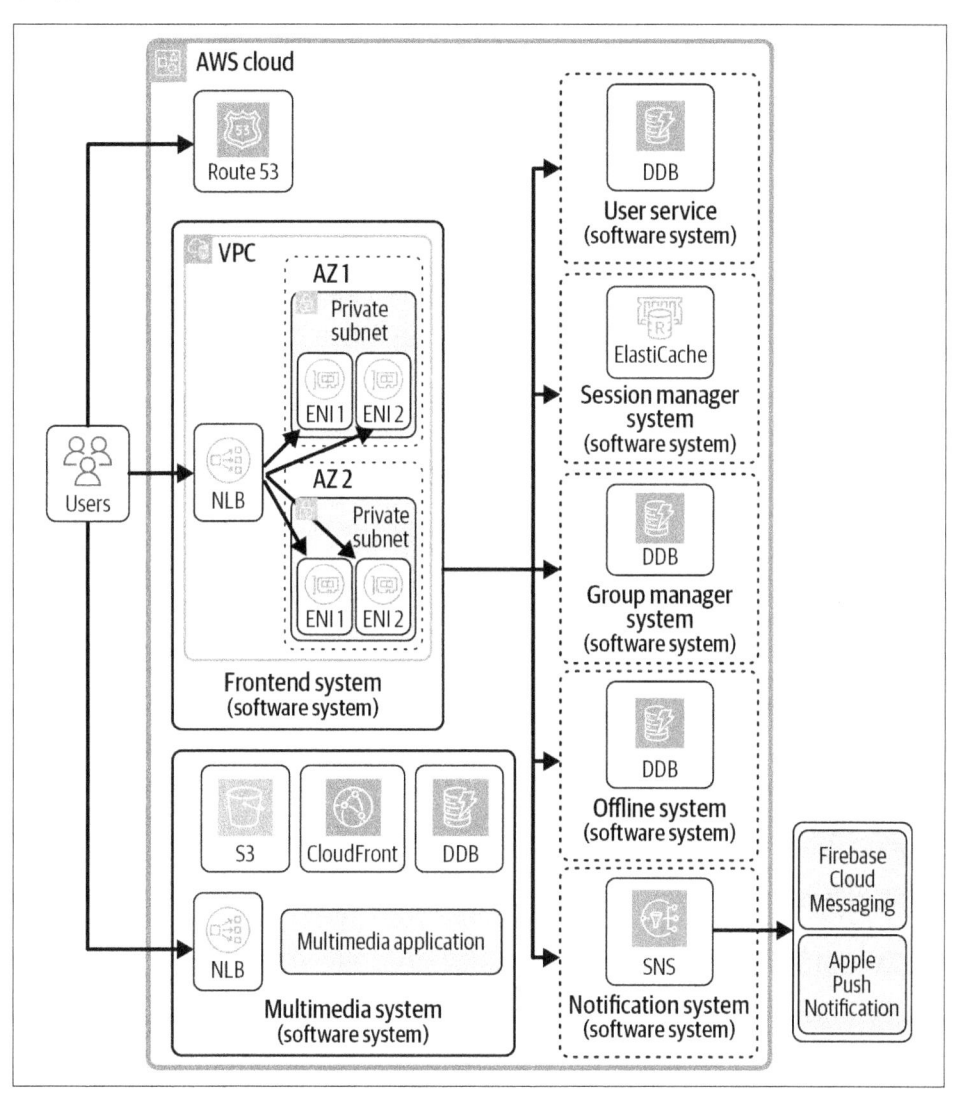

Figure 19-7. Chat application Day N architecture

Here's a summary of the different components from the system architecture:

Frontend system
  Gateway layer for user connections. It works in conjunction with the session manager system to store user device connectivity information with available servers.

Multimedia system
> Uses a combination of Amazon S3 and Amazon CloudFront for media storage and caching capabilities. The multimedia system also uses DynamoDB to store the metadata of media content. The multimedia system works like the video-ingestion pipeline that we will discuss in Chapter 20 for content ingestion into the system and then delivery to users in an efficient manner.

User service
> Responsible for user authentication and maintaining account information.

Notification system
> Delivers notifications to user devices for new messages by using Amazon SNS. Amazon SNS (*https://oreil.ly/YIShz*) sends the notification to Firebase Cloud Messaging (FCM) servers for Android devices and Apple Push Notification (APN) servers for Apple devices. We've kept a very simplistic view of the notification service to limit the scope of this chapter; read company engineering blogs on this topic (e.g., Uber's blog post (*https://oreil.ly/mhkeW*) on optimization of push notifications) to see how it works at a huge scale.

Offline system
> Stores and manages the message when the user device is not connected to the frontend system.

Groups manager system
> Maintains all the group-related information and delivers messages to group members.

The logging and monitoring components are not shown in the architecture diagram, but having them in place is important. We can leverage AWS services like Amazon CloudWatch for storing logs and set up metrics and alerts for visualization and health monitoring.

Conclusion

The WhatsApp architecture is based on one simple principle: "just enough engineering." Simple architectures scale well and require fewer people to manage the systems and the underlying infrastructure. To start with—as we've done in previous chapters—we recommend leveraging cloud provider services to launch and manage the solutions, which can reduce the overall time to market. You can move to different solutions if the need arises.

The choice of language, networking protocol, and implementation paradigm is important for large-scale applications and should be carefully evaluated before application launch. Moving from one programming language to another can prove to be a big pain point once the system is already serving a large user base—it can definitely be achieved, but it's much easier to take that into consideration from the start (with whatever data points you have at that time).

Load testing and chaos engineering are important techniques for figuring out system bottlenecks and identifying system limits. Keep metrics and alarms from day one to monitor system performance. System CPU utilization being at 100% doesn't mean the system is always busy working; there is the possibility of congestion as well, so load testing always helps to decipher these scenarios.

In this chapter, we started talking about uploading video and transcoding it to different formats. We'll discuss this in much more detail in the next chapter.

CHAPTER 20
Designing a Video-Processing Pipeline for a Streaming Service

We talked about video uploads and downloads between users on a messaging application in Chapter 19. To ensure optimal customer experience, there are certain steps we need to take in this video-uploading process, such as compression to reduce the size and transcoding to support different media formats and a wide variety of devices. In this chapter, we'll focus on building a video-processing pipeline for streaming services like Netflix, Amazon Prime Video, and YouTube. As always, we'll start with the system requirements and then dive into the details of the different steps involved. The main goal of our design decisions throughout the chapter will be for the video content to be available to viewers in the optimal quality and the minimum time possible. We'll conclude the chapter by deploying the system on the AWS cloud using AWS media services, and we'll also touch on some considerations for live streaming large-scale events, such as Thursday Night Football in the US and cricket matches in India.

System Requirements

The most important requirement of the system is that the video uploaded from production houses (in the case of Netflix or Amazon Prime Video) or users (in the case of YouTube) should be processed in such a way that it is easily accessible to viewers later. The system design will be applicable to any system involving video processing, but we'll use examples from Netflix's system.

There are a few considerations we need to clarify before defining the functional requirements of the system:

Does the system limit the size of the file being uploaded?
> There is no hard limit on the file size since video files can be quite large if shot in 4K resolution, so the system doesn't enforce any size constraints.

Should the system be designed keeping live streaming, video on demand (VoD), or both in mind?
> We'll focus the discussion on VoD as the main feature of the video-processing pipeline and spend some time on live streaming in the AWS Day 0 architecture discussion.

Can the system support the wide variety of devices that users own, such as Smart TVs, Android phones, iPhones, and tablets?
> The system should be able to stream video content to all device types in the most optimal quality possible.

Can the system implement different ML and analytics components for recommendations?
> The scope of this chapter is limited to not include ML components in the system architecture.

Let's talk about the functional and nonfunctional requirements of the system next.

Functional and Nonfunctional Requirements

Based on the considerations we just covered, we can expect the system to offer the following functional requirements:

- The system allows production houses to upload the media content.
- Video should be available to viewers in different formats per their devices and in different qualities per internet connectivity.
- Videos should be available to viewers in the minimum time possible without too much buffering involved.

Here are the NFRs supported by the system:

- Data should be durable—the system shouldn't lose any data during execution of the video-processing pipeline.
- The system should be extensible to support any type of encoding in the future.
- Availability is important for the application but not 100% critical. The customers are the production studios uploading the videos, so they can be asked to upload at a later point.

Let's talk about system scale next.

System Scale

The key parameter for system scale is the amount of storage space needed to store the content uploaded by video production houses. Along with the original video files, the system creates replicas of the content in compressed form to support different device types and internet bandwidth availability (we'll cover more details about the architecture in later sections). The content is further processed by breaking it into smaller chunks, so we should be able to come up with optimal server configurations to deploy the end-to-end infrastructure.

According to Netflix stats (*https://oreil.ly/k6CJx*), there are more than 18,000 titles on the platform. The number is much larger for platforms like YouTube, where users can upload their own videos. YouTube consists of close to 14 billion videos at the time of this writing, and the number continues to increase year by year. There is one notable difference between YouTube and Netflix: the quality of video uploads. Netflix requires content production houses to upload ultra-high-quality videos, but there is no such enforcement on YouTube. Of course, both platforms have different audiences and use cases.

Let's figure out the storage numbers for our own system based on the assumptions that the system has 30,000 titles and it adds 5,000 new titles every year. The titles can be a combination of movies and TV series (or web series) with multiple episodes. We'll assume a ratio of 90:10 for movies to TV series, with one series consisting of an average of 10 episodes (there is the possibility of multiple seasons as well). The storage space heavily depends on the type of camera devices used for shooting the video, so we'll pick an average there:

> Total number of videos = 27,000 movies + 3,000 × 10 episodes from series
>
> Average length of video = 90 minutes
>
> Average size of original video = 50 GB

Videos are encoded into different formats to compress them so that they are around a thousand times smaller (*https://oreil.ly/5aRko*), contributing to an average size of 50 MB per video. Apart from our main video storage, we need storage for databases to maintain the metadata, such as where the videos are kept in the object storage and other properties related to the content. Of course, the actual video content occupies the major chunk of storage space.

We also need to figure out how frequently the content is accessed from the data storage location. This is important in terms of cloud storage solutions like Amazon S3 where the pricing depends on data transfer rates as well as storage space. For example, Netflix has built a storage wrapper called MezzFS (*https://oreil.ly/hbHO1*) over S3 to reduce download speeds and costs for frequent data access.

Let's start with the design of the video-processing pipeline.

Starting with the Design

The first step in designing our video-processing pipeline (which we'll call our *ingestion system* hereafter) is uploading videos created by production houses. A video uploader is a platform for production houses to upload their content and then track progress to know when the content is actually available for viewing. The videos are generally shot with high-quality cameras, which means the file sizes are relatively large. The uploads should be resumable from the client's end to ensure that the video uploads resume from wherever they left off in case of network issues. This functionality is quite similar to how uploads work on systems like Google Drive.

> Netflix publishes timely engineering blogs (*https://netflixtechblog.com*) to share their architecture and learnings. The content in this chapter is influenced by Netflix's video-processing blogs; read the blogs for an end-to-end understanding of Netflix's systems.

The clients are allowed to upload additional metadata along with the source video, such as video thumbnails, video tags, audio tags, and so on. Once the ingestion system has the video, the system runs a video inspection to make sure the video meets the system-defined constraints. If the quality constraints are not met, the production house is asked to reupload the video source files. The inspection is done on the source file by breaking the file into multiple chunks and then inspecting them independently for faster processing, as shown in Figure 20-1.

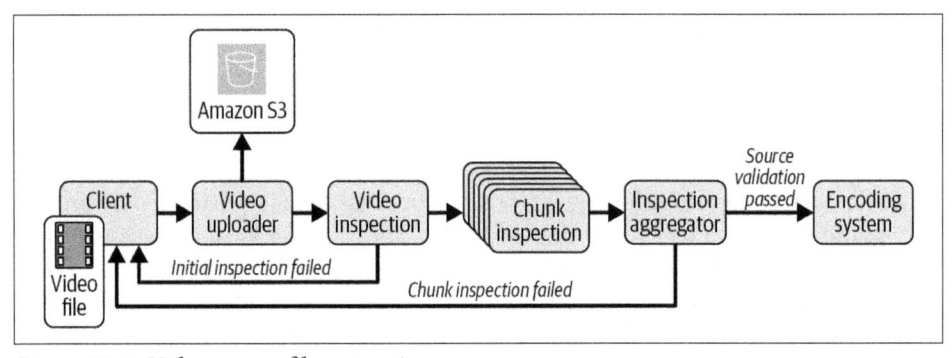

Figure 20-1. Video source file inspection

A key consideration you might have also realized here is that the entire system works in asynchronous fashion in a series of steps (steps can be sequential or parallel per the use case). Let's first identify the key steps in the pipeline and then explore each one:

Video encoding
> To support various kinds of devices and internet bandwidth availability, the video is encoded into different formats and qualities. All of these encoded videos are stored on the servers, and the customers can be served per their requirements.

Video-quality validation
> Quality validation is done after each step in the pipeline to ensure that viewer experience is not impacted.

Content indexing
> As the content is processed, multiple tasks are done in parallel, such as extracting images to be used as thumbnails later, extracting various content parameters, and creating an index for offering search capability to users.

Video distribution
> The final step is video distribution to users. The video content is cached near user locations using CDNs and served to the users upon request.

Let's talk about each of these steps in more detail, starting with video encoding.

Video Encoding

Before we can dig into video encoding, first you need to understand the term *codec*. Short for compressor/decompressor, codec is a specific algorithm or technique used to compress a video (reducing its size) and later to decompress it when it is actually viewed. We'll discuss codec in the context of video files, but it's a general technique and can be applied to any type of file. Some examples of codecs include H.264/ Advanced Video Coding (AVC), High Efficiency Video Coding (HEVC), and VP9. These codecs require a video container (such as *.mp4*, *.avi*, *.mov*, etc.) to host the encoded video. Video container formats can vary from device to device. To ensure that the videos can be played on all types of devices, the system should create copies of the videos in all these formats.

Two things apart from format that we need to take into consideration are the video resolution and the bitrate. *Bitrate* means the number of bits used per second, which helps determine the speed at which chunks can be served on a user's device from system servers (or CDNs if the content is cached at a nearby location). To take an example of MP4 format, the following are the replicas of the video maintained by the system to serve to customers:

- High quality (high bitrate): 4K, 1080p, 720p
- Medium quality (medium bitrate): 1080p, 720p, 480p
- Low quality (low bitrate): 720p, 480p, 360p, 144p

You may have realized that the system needs to perform a lot of work and definitely needs some parallelization in the processing to make it faster. To work in parallel and make the system more efficient, the source video is broken into small chunks after initial inspection of the video. Creating chunks of the video also makes failure handling easy during the encoding process because the system can easily retry for a smaller chunk, but it is resource- and time-consuming to retry for the entire video.

Let's consider what our logic should be for breaking the video into chunks. Should the logic be as simple as dividing the video into 30-second chunks, or do we need some special algorithm to decide the chunk size? Let's dig a little deeper into this. For the moment, forget about the encoding pipeline and think of how content is served to the end users. The goal is to serve the best-quality video with the minimum possible bandwidth. Netflix systems employ multiple mechanisms, such as title-based encoding (*https://oreil.ly/GNpH5*) and shot-based encoding (*https://oreil.ly/wYgb5*), to ensure that maximum-quality videos are served to users at a lower bandwidth usage. Shot-based encoding improves the overall compression efficiency and is a successor to title-based encoding.

Once the encoding process is completed for all the video chunks, they are independently validated for video quality, sent for encoding again if validation fails, and finally reassembled to perform the quality checks against the source video, as shown in Figure 20-2. The final encoded video is around one thousand times smaller than the source video.

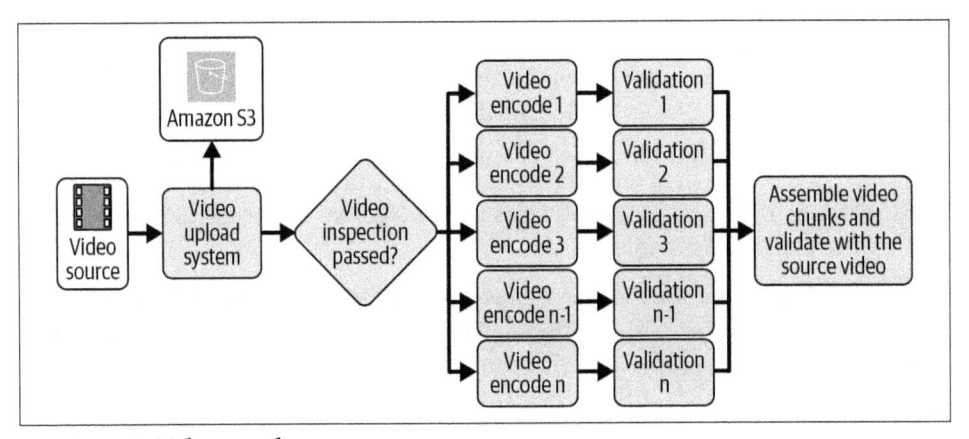

Figure 20-2. Video encoding

The video-encoding system is invoked whenever a new video is uploaded to the system. It can also be used to reencode the video in case more codecs are introduced to support newer devices or some innovation is done in video technology.

Validations for quality are done at every step in the pipeline, so let's talk about validation techniques next.

Video-Quality Validation

Video-quality validation is done at every step, and appropriate actions are taken to restore the video quality if necessary, but the most important video-validation metric is the rating given by the viewer. This rating is the most actionable metric for passing the video-validation test.

The validation logic becomes quite important for the encoded videos because these are the final videos used for streaming. The system validates that every generated encoding meets quality expectations. There is a possibility that frame issues were introduced during the parallel chunk encoding, such as incorrect frame boundaries or duplicate or dropped frames.

After the base validation against the encoded and source video, the system tries to evaluate the viewer's perception if the video was streamed to the user. *Video Multimethod Assessment Fusion (VMAF)* (*https://oreil.ly/0ZCNO*) is one such validation technique deployed by Netflix. VMAF is a perceptual quality assessment algorithm that generates the quality score from the viewer's perspective, such as how a user would rate the video while viewing. Netflix or any streaming platform wants to ensure optimal viewing experience given the network bandwidth and device constraints. VMAF helps generate quality scores based on all these constraints. Accordingly, we can look for optimizations for further improvements. The whole point of validation at every step of the pipeline is failing fast or detecting issues at the earliest possible moment. This ensures optimal viewer experience and reduces the operational burden on engineers.

The other important factor in quality validation is gathering actual metrics of customer behavior on the device when content is played. The media player running on the customer device captures metrics like times between subsequent delivery of video chunks, error rates, buffer rates, playback start, pause, close, and any custom user actions. These metrics are streamed from the user's device to the backend analytics system for complete analysis of user behavior and helps fine-tune the quality-control software. The real-time metrics also help us figure out issues with content delivery when the user is streaming a particular video. For example, if there is a high buffer rate on one edge location, then the next set of video chunks are requested from another edge location, which we'll talk about more in "Content Distribution" on page 532. First, let's discuss content indexing.

Content Indexing

The video should be available for user search. Let's take an example of the movie *The Dark Knight*: the movie should be reflected in the search results if the customers search via any of the keywords, such as the title itself, the director Christopher Nolan, or any of the actors, like Christian Bale or Heath Ledger. Content indexing is done based on a combination of data provided by the production houses and data generated by the system.

The first service that comes to our mind for data indexing is Elasticsearch, which is a great solution when it comes to offering search capabilities. The data should be indexed in Elasticsearch in such a way that users can search via any parameter associated with a video. We discussed Elasticsearch as a solution in Chapters 15 and 18; revisit those chapters to review. In the context of Netflix systems (*https://oreil.ly/ ojJsB*), the search capability is built with Elasticsearch and GraphQL federations, and independent teams can own their own criteria for search.

Let's discuss content distribution next.

Content Distribution

Once the videos are encoded, the video chunks are stored in the object storage, such as Amazon S3, and should be available for user consumption. To ensure that content reaches the audience with minimum latency, the content is distributed to users' nearby locations via CDNs. Let's take one step back and discuss storage on the system servers; then, we'll talk about Netflix's proprietary CDN solution, Open Connect.

Let's think from a user's standpoint about how the user will receive video streams once they press play for a specific video. The encoded video chunks are stored in S3, but we need some kind of metadata layer to store this mapping that can be used later to figure out the locations of videos. Digital rights management (DRM) protection is added to the video chunks, and then the packaged stream is generated from the video chunks for storage.

> DRM protection helps avoid piracy and copyright theft of any type of content. The content is basically encrypted with specific keys, and only the authenticated users can access the content.

The videos are also sent to the CDN based on region and past analysis of where the content can be viewed by the users. The CDN locations for the cached video content are maintained in a metadata store, which is useful for serving the user queries at a later point. Netflix heavily uses the Cassandra database for such requirements. Our system doesn't require any relational database capabilities, so we can choose a NoSQL solution like Cassandra or DynamoDB for easier operations. AWS offers Amazon CloudFront as a CDN offering, and similar capabilities are offered by other cloud providers. Netflix takes it to the next level, moving the data much closer to the viewers by placing the content in the ISP's location on their devices, which are referred to as Open Connect Appliances (OCAs) (*https://oreil.ly/A55XK*). Placing content in the ISP's location benefits both the ISP and Netflix because the bandwidth usage is reduced for fetching the same content over the internet again and again.

There is always a possibility that some users will try to watch rarely accessed movies or TV series, and the content might not be cached on the OCAs in these cases. For these scenarios, the content is moved at that point of time to the user's nearby location, and the first few frames can take additional time to be visible on the user's device.

To summarize the overall architecture, the video encoding service pushes the chunks to S3 and the metadata to Cassandra. The cache management service manages the content distribution to OCAs at different locations. From the user's perspective, once the user clicks the play button for any video, the user's device connects with the play service to gather the video chunks. The play service determines client details, such as type of device and network conditions, to figure out what type of video chunks should be streamed to the device. The steering service determines the OCAs based on information from the play service and constructs the URLs for the user connections. The user's device receives these URLs in response and connects with the OCAs to begin video streaming. The client device runs adaptive streaming algorithms to select the best video chunk based on the available network bandwidth. Figure 20-3 shows a high-level view of content distribution by the system and retrieval by the viewers.

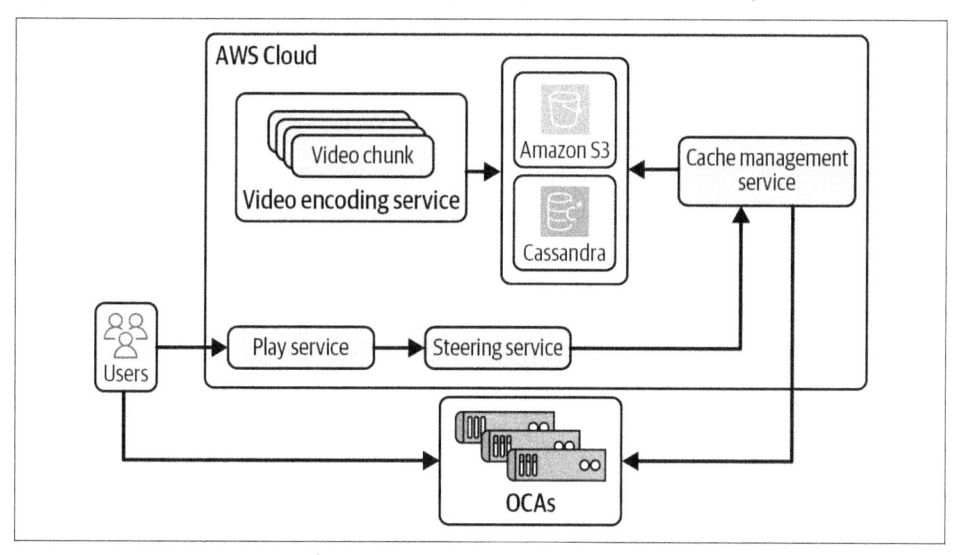

Figure 20-3. Open Connect data storage and retrieval

We've discussed the pipeline in parts; now let's combine all the steps to come up with the final system architecture and its deployment on the AWS cloud.

Launching the System on AWS

At a high level, the system is a combination of steps that are executed in sequence and are dependent on the output of the previous step. We discussed a similar architecture in Chapter 15 for the web crawler system; the video-processing system also fits into the criteria of orchestration systems. We can leverage any orchestration frameworks to manage the end-to-end working of the system. Every step in the orchestration cycle is stateless and idempotent, meaning the system doesn't maintain any state of previous executions and always returns the exact same output for the same input. Let's start the discussion with the Day 0 architecture.

Day 0 Architecture

In Part II, we explored multiple AWS services that can meet customers' requirements for different business use cases. As always, we'll try to use fully managed AWS services to launch the system quickly, so let's figure out which services would be helpful in the different steps of the pipeline for our streaming service. To manage the end-to-end orchestration, we can leverage AWS Step Functions as discussed in Chapter 12, and the storage requirements can be fulfilled by S3 and DynamoDB.

> We've used DynamoDB extensively in Part III for storage requirements since it fits into most of the use cases. In most of the scenarios, multiple databases can fulfill the use case, and we recommend checking out other offerings as well (such as Amazon Keyspaces) based on your expertise.

AWS offers multiple services to support live video streaming (*https://oreil.ly/CNnt_*), and the most important service for building a video-processing pipeline is AWS Elemental MediaConvert. This service converts source video into multiple formats and makes them available for streaming on different kinds of devices—a core video-encoding task. Elemental MediaConvert takes input as source video, encodes the video into different formats, and stores the encoded videos to S3. For faster streaming, we can leverage Amazon CloudFront as a CDN solution to store videos near users' locations.

To elaborate on the overall architecture, shown in Figure 20-4, the video upload system supports video uploading from users and stores videos in S3. Elemental MediaConvert takes videos from S3, converts them into different formats, and again stores the encoded videos to S3. To ensure that content is made available to users based on their locations and interests, the cache management service pushes the content to CloudFront. The entire encoding pipeline is managed by Step Functions, and we'll leverage DynamoDB for metadata storage.

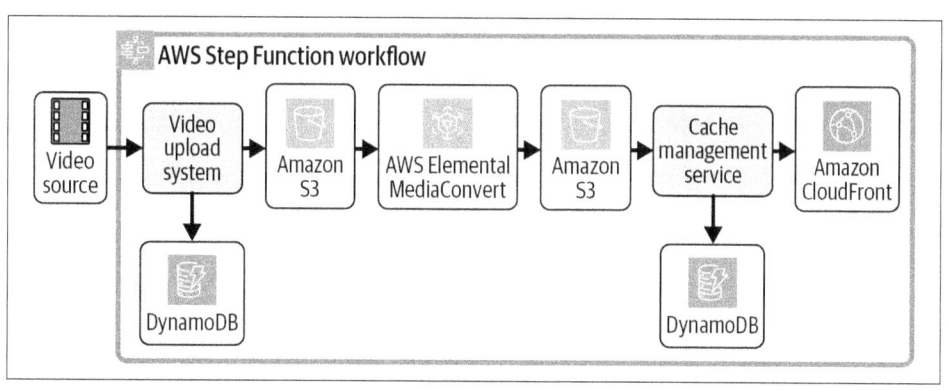

Figure 20-4. Day 0 architecture

We discussed DRM protection in "Content Distribution" on page 532 and why it's critical for video-streaming services. AWS Elemental MediaPackage services (*https://aws.amazon.com/mediapackage*) can help with protecting content and distributing it to CloudFront.

Now, let's look at the architecture for managing live streaming events with AWS managed services. The video is uploaded directly from the video production sources using AWS Elemental MediaLive. As mentioned, video content produced from high-quality cameras consumes a lot of storage space, and it can take a long time to upload such videos for distribution. The latency is critical in the case of live streaming, and the upload time should be as minimal as possible (Amazon Prime Video targets less than 10 seconds of latency for streaming Thursday Night Football). Elemental MediaLive plays a critical role in achieving low latency and offers video encoding and compression at the source. The high-quality video content is encoded at the source in real time and then uploaded to the cloud for further processing and distribution.

The next technology used for faster uploads is AWS Direct Connect, which ensures that the video streams are uploaded via the AWS global network and don't face the congestion challenges of the public internet. Visit Chapter 9 to refresh your understanding of Direct Connect and similar networking services.

Once the video stream reaches the AWS cloud, it is consumed by Elemental MediaPackage for content protection and delivery. MediaPackage helps with manifest creation of the video, content protection via DRM such as Google Widevine and Microsoft PlayReady, and content consumption per the device type, such as HTTP Live Streaming (HLS) for Apple devices and MPEG-DASH for Android devices. The content is stored to S3 as origin and then distributed via the CloudFront service to the end viewers. The architecture with live streaming using AWS services is shown in Figure 20-5.

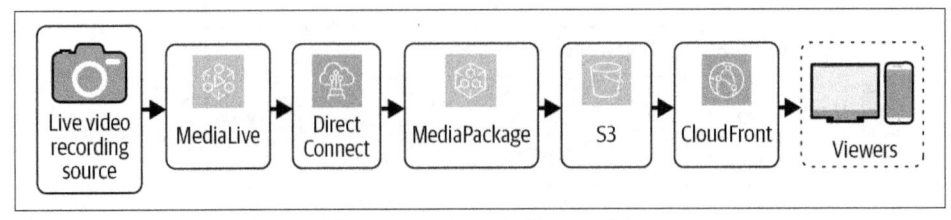

Figure 20-5. Live streaming video-processing pipeline architecture

In Figure 20-5, we used S3 as a video storage solution. AWS offers the Elemental MediaStore service, which is specifically designed and optimized to store media content and serve the live content with low latency.

Now, let's scale the Day 0 architecture of the video-processing pipeline.

Scaling to Millions and Beyond

The most important parameter for scaling the video-processing pipeline is execution time. The system should be able to encode and validate the videos in the minimum possible time and make the videos available for streaming to different device types.

Let's start with the uppermost layer of the architecture shown in Figure 20-4. We already discussed the scalability of AWS Step Functions in Chapter 15; it doesn't present any specific bottleneck in scaling. The only point of consideration here is cost. Step Functions pricing is based on the number of state transitions and the type of Step Function (more details are provided in Chapter 12), and the cost can grow significantly as the amount of content being loaded onto the system increases over time. Start with Step Functions to get retries and better debugging capabilities out of the box; later, you can evaluate whether you need a custom orchestration workflow engine.

Another managed service we used in the architecture is Elemental MediaConvert for video encoding. It is designed to operate at high scale, and there are no limits enforced by AWS, but the consideration here is control needed for operations. It is a great solution to start with, but you're dependent on AWS for encoding decisions. We discussed in previous sections that the video chunk size is not fixed but is optimized based on the video type, and the case of running validations is similar. Keeping this in house helps you fully control the implementation logic and removes the dependency on AWS services.

We broke down the video-processing pipeline into a series of steps in "Starting with the Design" on page 528. All these steps are executed by independent microservices. This ensures that the services can be scaled and bring in innovation without affecting or blocking other components. We can take a reference from the Netflix architecture (*https://oreil.ly/dDOwG*) for dividing components based on the operations. The following is a list of services, each responsible for a specific set of tasks:

Video upload service
> This service handles the video uploads from the content production houses and persists them to S3.

Video inspection service
> This service breaks the videos received from the production houses into chunks, inspects the chunks, and flags any issues. This service also extracts metadata from the video chunks, which is used in later stages of the pipeline.

Complexity analysis service
> This service runs analysis on the source video to figure out the optimal encoding recipe. It also communicates with the video encoding and quality services for preencoding (*https://oreil.ly/dRsBV*) and quality operations, respectively. The results of the encoding and quality services are persisted so that they can be used in later stages of the pipeline.

Ladder generation service
> This service receives the complexity data from the complexity analysis service and creates a bitrate ladder for a given encoding family (H.264, AV1, etc.). The complexity analysis and ladder generation services work together to generate the final encoding recipes, which are later used by the video encoding service.

Video encoding service
> This service takes the source video and encoding recipes as input and generates encoded video in the output.

Video validation service
> This service runs validations on the encoded video. The validation is done based on expectations specified against the video, such as attributes in the encoding recipe and conformance requirements from the codec specification. *Conformance* in terms of codec means whether the codec meets defined standards or not.

Video quality service
> This service computes quality scores (VMAF) by comparing the source video and the encoded video.

All the services are shown in Figure 20-6. They are managed by a workflow orchestrator for their operations. The workflow orchestrator (such as Netflix Conductor (*https://github.com/Netflix/conductor*) and Maestro (*https://github.com/Netflix/maestro*)) sends the required input to a specific service and gathers the output to pass it along to other services in the needed format. The output can be as simple as small metadata or it can be a large file, and accordingly, the workflow orchestrator can decide how the data is shared to other services. For example, the large file can be dumped to S3, and the URL can be shared to the corresponding service.

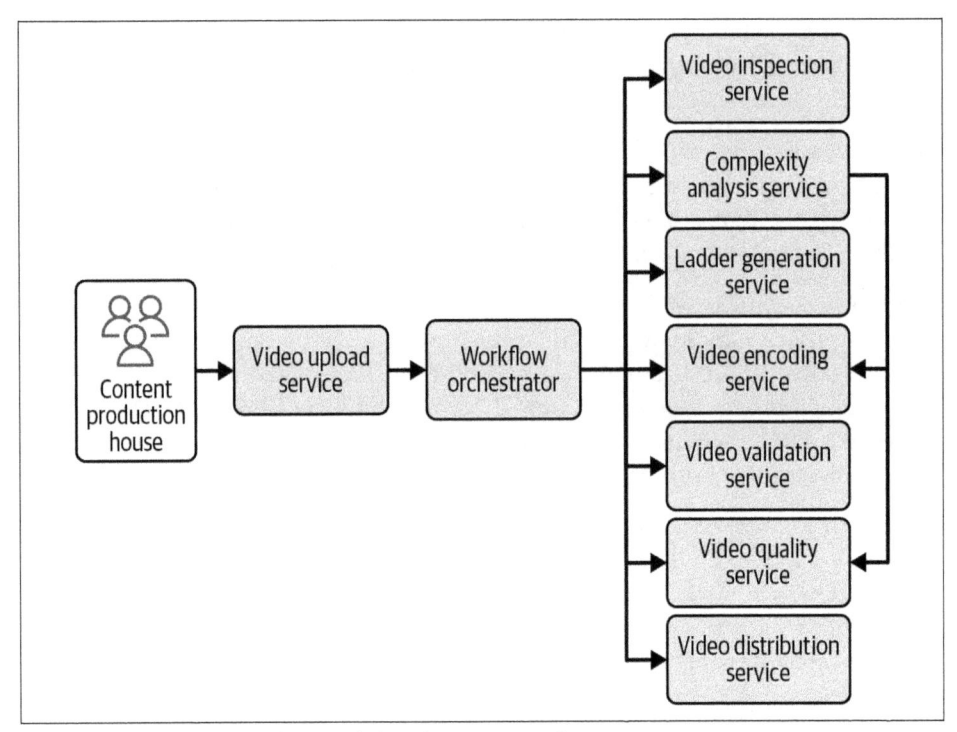

Figure 20-6. Video encoding and distribution at scale

The video distribution services take the encoded videos, apply the packaging, and store them to S3. The videos only make sense if they are combined; this data is maintained in a manifest stored in a metadata database, such as Cassandra or DynamoDB. The cache management service has the responsibility of distributing the data to users' nearby locations and continuously monitoring the correctness and health of the CDN instances (OCAs, in Netflix's case). Developing and deploying an architecture similar to Netflix-managed OCAs can bring with it a lot of operational overhead, and we recommend looking into cloud offerings like Amazon CloudFront for content caching. CloudFront is deployed at AWS-managed edge locations in all the major cities and is used by a lot of customers (*https://oreil.ly/HvP8w*) in the media industry.

Origin Shield is another feature offered as part of CloudFront to improve its caching capabilities. As the name suggests, *Origin Shield* is an additional layer (or shield) in the front of the origin storage, which is helpful for improving the cache hit ratio and reducing the load on the origin. The first points of contact for users via CloudFront are the edge locations, or PoPs. If data is not cached at the edge locations, the request tries to retrieve data from regional caches—also called *regional edge caches (RECs)*—and finally from the origin if data is missing at the RECs as well. Once the origin shield is introduced, it acts as the caching layer between the origin and other RECs so that if the data is not cached at an REC, it is retrieved from the origin shield, as shown in Figure 20-7. In a nutshell, the frequently accessed data from the users (the video chunks) is cached at the edge locations, and users are served upon request.

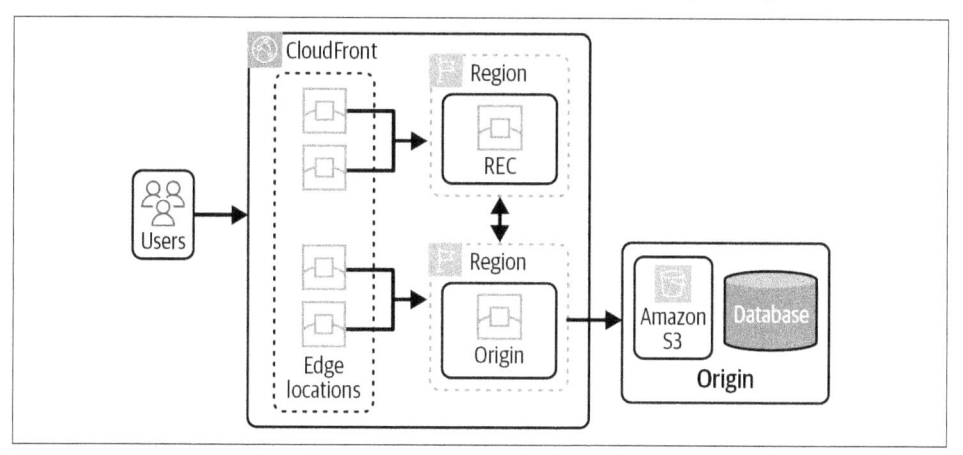

Figure 20-7. Amazon CloudFront with Origin Shield

Let's think more about high-traffic scenarios for content consumption. Streaming video content from an edge location to the user's location consumes a lot of internet bandwidth, and if the number of users is too large, the high traffic can cause network congestion. Network congestion can lead to degradation in video quality. An architecture like OCAs helps take the content one step closer to the user's location. There are two other steps we can take to avoid network-congestion scenarios:

- Work with ISPs so that their internal networks are scaled enough and high traffic requirements don't create network congestion inside their networks.
- Deploy caching appliances inside the ISPs' networks. The video content is cached on the caching appliances and streamed to user devices on request. This architecture really helps in huge live streaming events: the backend system essentially sends a single stream to the ISP, and then the ISP fans it out to all the connected devices.

The video streams up to the CloudFront edge locations and are delivered on a dedicated AWS backbone network away from usual internet traffic—making them much faster—and then a dedicated peering connection can be established with the ISPs to avoid any network congestion. CloudFront also launched embedded PoPs (*https://oreil.ly/AXqrt*) to directly cache the content at the ISPs' facilities similar to Netflix-managed OCAs. The embedded PoPs are designed to have low power consumption and 128 TB of storage per appliance, and they offer high throughput of up to 70 Gbps.

One of the important aspects for application deployment and management is monitoring—this is needed from Day 0 to ensure good system health. We have touched on using Amazon CloudWatch and its features for managing application logs, metrics, and alerts. The architecture presented in Figure 20-6 consists of multiple microservices, and problems can occur in any of them. An orchestration system like AWS Step Functions helps with figuring out the exact step where the state machine failed using error messages.

With respect to the general architecture of systems, the request to a front-facing application can span multiple systems in the distributed environment to gather a response. Proper request tracing in a distributed environment makes debugging issues easier and faster. This becomes very important when we want to figure out any streaming issues later down the line—the engineers will need to debug multiple services, making it very difficult to coordinate across the teams. We can use tools like AWS X-Ray (*https://oreil.ly/1MZ0c*), Zipkin (*https://zipkin.io*), and OpenTracing (*https://opentracing.io*) to trace the application requests in a distributed system architecture. The key design principle in implementing distributed tracing is using the same *request ID* (a unique identifier to process a request received by service) across the applications. An application should pass the request ID as part of headers, and the receiving service should use it for processing the request.

Day N Architecture

We'll expand on the ideas in the previous section to get a view of the deployment of microservices in the AWS cloud. The architecture of the video-processing pipeline will be similar to the architectures discussed in Chapter 15, using AWS Step Functions to orchestrate the workflows with an additional video-upload component to trigger the workflow. Let's expand the architecture from Figure 20-6 with the following steps for end-to-end orchestration on AWS:

1. Content production houses upload videos via the video upload service, which saves the video file to S3.

2. Upload completion on S3 triggers the Step Functions workflow to invoke a series of microservices to perform specific actions. The event trigger can be configured using Amazon EventBridge (*https://oreil.ly/ovFRd*) on S3 "object created" actions.

3. The first service invoked is the video inspection service, and then other services, such as the complexity analysis and video encoding services, are invoked as described previously. The output of these services is used as a trigger point for invoking the next service.

Figure 20-8 shows all the microservices of the video-processing pipeline in a single EKS cluster. There is no hard recommendation for choosing separate EKS clusters versus a single cluster; it heavily depends on factors like scale, need for separation, and compliance constraints, as discussed in Chapter 14. The diagram shows a simple deployment representation for clarity, but the service EKS Pods are deployed in different AZs with autoscaling enabled to ensure the reliability and availability of the system. Considering Netflix or YouTube's scale for content production, we recommend hosting separate EKS clusters because they will be owned by independent teams and this will ensure maximum resource separation.

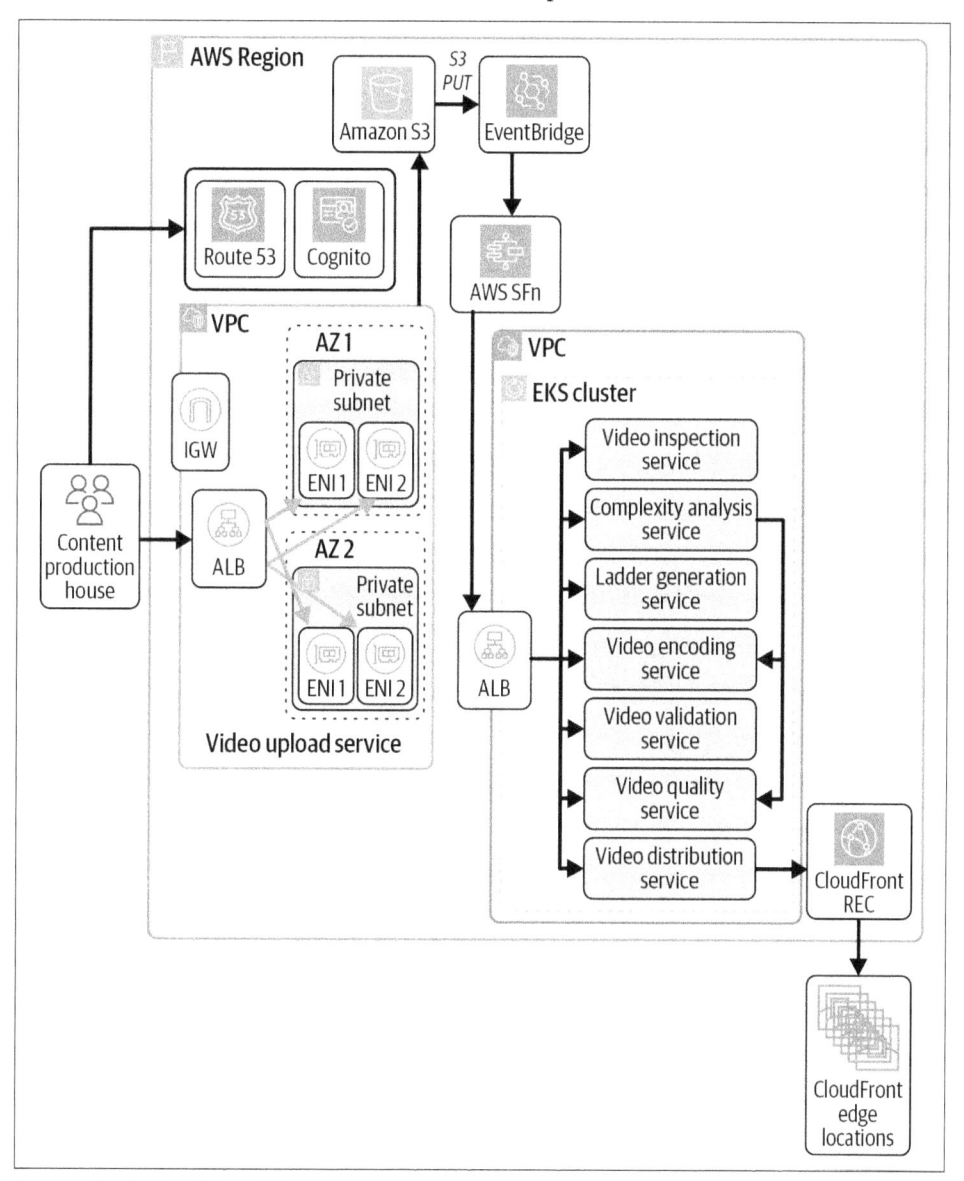

Figure 20-8. Day N architecture

Another paradigm followed for the EKS deployments is creating separate namespaces to deploy the services. Creating different namespaces gives a clear boundary for resource separation used by the services, although the overall control plane still uses the common resource pool. Revisit Chapter 7 for more insights into Kubernetes architecture.

Conclusion

This chapter discussed the architecture of video-processing or ingestion systems for platforms that produce online content, such as Netflix, Amazon Prime Video, and YouTube. The most important takeaway from our review of the overall architecture, which should be applied as a general principle for architecting any new system, is fail-fast behavior. If the system can identify issues at the earliest stage possible, that reduces the touchpoints in the overall system and makes debugging much faster. We've implemented quality checks in all stages of the video-processing pipeline to ensure optimal quality of video.

In Chapter 1, we discussed fallacies in making assumptions about distributed systems, such as infinite network bandwidth availability. Architectures like the video-processing pipeline and content distribution at a large scale lead us to think about these fallacies in more depth. For example, the problem of network congestion is solved by moving content to the user's nearest possible location and storing it there for distribution.

This chapter introduced you to an asynchronous, event-driven system where execution latency to the milliseconds level is important but not critical. In the next chapter, we'll explore the architecture of an online stock-trading application, which is a real-time, latency-critical system.

CHAPTER 21
Designing an Online Stock-Trading Platform

There are a lot of online platforms available to help you invest money in stocks, such as Robinhood, Zerodha, and Groww. These platforms, called *stockbrokers*, work as intermediaries between stock exchanges and users. *Stock exchanges* are marketplaces where stocks are bought and sold. A few examples include the New York Stock Exchange (NYSE) in the US and the National Stock Exchange (NSE) of India. Figure 21-1 illustrates the interaction between the user, the stockbroker, and the stock exchange.

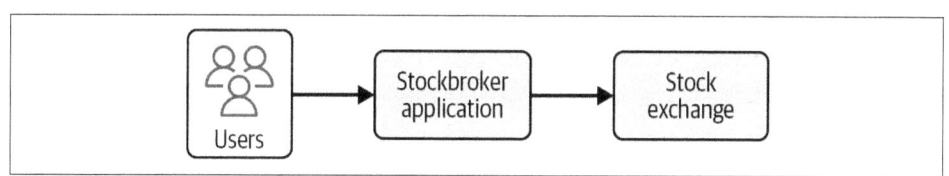

Figure 21-1. Users, stockbrokers, and stock exchange

Buying or selling a stock is called an *order*. The order is executed on the customer's behalf by the stockbroker. In a nutshell, you give money to a stockbroker to buy or sell a particular stock, and the broker talks to the stock exchange to execute the order.

> This chapter focuses on the design of a stockbroker application, not a stock exchange application. Trading stocks is a complicated topic, and we don't suggest referring to this chapter as a guide to stock trading but rather as a technical deep dive into the underlying system architecture.

We recommend surfing through a stockbroker application if you've never had a chance to help understand the application features so that you can determine the system requirements of our stockbroker application. Let's move to those system requirements next.

System Requirements

A stockbroker application offers a wide range of features, but this chapter focuses on the core functionality of buying and selling stocks. The buying and selling of any stock is generally referred to as *order execution* in the trading world. Let's start with the functional and nonfunctional requirements of the system, and then we'll discuss the expected scale.

Functional and Nonfunctional Requirements

The core feature of any stockbroker application is buying and selling stocks. There are some additional features we need to offer to customers to help them make decisions regarding trading stocks. The application only allows buying and selling of stocks during the trading hours of the stock exchange, which generally are six to seven hours of the day. For example, the trading hours for the Nasdaq stock exchange are 9:30 A.M. to 4:00 P.M. EST.

Here is the list of functional requirements that the system should support:

- Users can search by stock name or company name. For example, the stock for Amazon.com, Inc. is listed with the name AMZN on the Nasdaq stock exchange.
- The stock price should be updated in real time with other relevant details, such as average trade price, last opening and closing price, and so on.
- Users can buy new stocks and sell existing stocks.
- Users can view candlestick charts (*https://oreil.ly/2Zmsr*) of any stock over the requested time period.
- Users can view their portfolios with profit and loss (P&L) overall and for individual stocks.

The NFRs of the system are also very critical and should be taken into consideration during the system design. Here is the list of NFRs that the system should ensure:

- The system should be highly available and able to withstand hardware failures or data center downtimes.
- The system should be highly scalable to cater to increasing traffic.
- The system should be highly reliable and durable. There should not be any loss of messages, such as order execution and responses from stock exchange systems.

- The system should operate at submillisecond (< 100 ms) latency for market order executions.
- Strong consistency support is needed in the overall system operations.

System Scale

The system operates and interacts with customers heavily during trading hours. During off-market hours, the system runs other jobs, such as gathering the trades of the day from the exchanges and sending executed trade details to the customers. We'll take Zerodha's scale numbers (*https://oreil.ly/MNrS7*) as our base and add to it to take into account future growth:

> Number of active users on platform = 50 million
>
> Number of users actually executing trades = 10 million
>
> Average number of trades per user = 2
>
> Number of trades per day = 20 million

The 50 million active users are viewing the live stock prices and checking their portfolios, so at any time the system must serve read queries for this set of users. The number of stock-price updates delivered to users per second on average by the broker system is three (for Level 2 data, discussed more in "Designing a Stock Tick System" on page 546). For 50 million active users, the system delivers 150 million stock updates every second.

The number of companies listed on the stock exchange varies based on the country and exchange. Here are a few numbers we can take as reference:

> NSE, India ~ 2,300 (*https://oreil.ly/AclUg*)
>
> Nasdaq, US ~ 3,300 (*https://oreil.ly/HdGGf*)
>
> NYSE, US ~ 2,800 (*https://oreil.ly/0--Nf*)

You can assume that the number of public companies doesn't grow exponentially and that only a very few companies are added from time to time. We'll move to the design of the system next, keeping these requirements and scale considerations in mind.

Starting with the Design

Like the web crawler and search engine (Chapter 15) and the hotel reservation system (Chapter 18), the stock-trading platform consists of two systems. One system ingests the data from exchange platforms for live stock pricing, and another system executes customer orders. We'll first talk about data ingestion to support delivering live and historical stock prices to end users and then move to our system design for buying and selling stocks.

Designing a Stock Tick System

Stock tick means the price change of a stock; the broker system captures price changes from the exchange system and streams them to users watching the stocks. The price change is streamed in near real time without any delays to help customers make decisions regarding whether to buy or sell stocks. The architecture is a mirror image of Figure 21-1, where the exchange system streams the data, and then the brokerage application consumes it and further streams it to the end customers.

In "System Scale" on page 545, we assumed that 20 million trades are executed per day on the broker application. There can be multiple such platforms where users are executing trades, and then there are HFT firms for executing automated trading at a high frequency. The point is that the number of trades executed on a stock exchange platform is really huge (take a look at historical data for NSE India (*https://oreil.ly/cgSm4*) and Nasdaq (*https://oreil.ly/3RgCG*)), and consuming all this data inside a brokerage application requires a lot of resources. Further, broker applications need to pay a specific amount to exchange platforms for market-data consumption.

Keep in mind that most customers don't require data for every order executed on the exchange platform if we leave HFTs out of the picture: the primary reason is that the user will not be able to comprehend these vast amounts of live data to make decisions without the help of computer algorithms, and stock exchanges charge fees to deliver this data via a well-designed networking infrastructure. To cater to this, stock exchanges generally offer different types of data streams based on the amount of data needed. Taking an example of NSE India (*https://oreil.ly/gMJ2C*) (similar levels are offered by other exchange platforms, such as Nasdaq (*https://oreil.ly/I2LDC*)), the real-time data is offered at four levels: levels 1–3 and tick-by-tick (TBT). Level 1 provides the best bid and ask price; level 2 provides market depth data up to five best bid and ask prices; level 3 provides market depth data up to the 20 best bid and ask prices; and TBT provides a full order book (all the orders executed on the exchange platform).

> The *bid price* is the highest price a buyer is willing to pay for a specific number of shares of a stock at a particular time. The *ask price* refers to the lowest price at which a seller agrees to sell a stock.

We'll limit the scope of architecture in this chapter to level 1–3 data consumption, considering the system design requirements of a broker application and not an HFT.

SSEs and WebSockets, which we discussed in Chapter 6, are good choices for data consumption from stock exchanges. There is no standard communication protocol used by all the stock exchanges—it varies from one exchange to another—but one of the popular protocols is the Financial Information eXchange (FIX) protocol (*https://oreil.ly/ve_Mi*). The means used for data delivery can also vary from exchange to exchange. Here are a few of the possible methods for delivering market data:

Cloud subscription
> The exchange allows clients to subscribe to its endpoints and receive the data. The endpoint could be a persistent or one-way connection (depending on the exchange).

Direct connection
> The exchange offers server racks in its facility, and clients can place hardware in colocated (referred to as *colo*) locations with exchange servers. The client hardware at the exchange facility is connected to a client's on-premises data center to directly receive the data. With NSE India (*https://oreil.ly/OqXiD*), for example, Zerodha's broker application (*https://oreil.ly/ng5GT*) delivers level 3 data to customers by consuming the TBT data, converting it to level 3, and then streaming it to the user application.

Vendor connection
> A direct connection might not be cost-effective for all consumers. These consumers can leverage vendor integrations and achieve similar functionality. For example, LSEG Data & Analytics (*https://oreil.ly/9CY74*) is integrated with more than five hundred global exchanges to deliver TBT data.

The exchanges also offer snapshots of historical data to broker applications, which can be used for use cases like candlestick charts.

Now, let's talk about how the broker application's backend systems make sense of this data and stream it to the front-facing application for viewing. The flow is similar to the data stream delivery between the stock exchanges and brokers. We can think of this architecture in two parts: live stock tick data and historical stock market data.

Live stock ticks

Latency is critical when delivering live stock ticks to the end customers: the data should be presented to the viewers as soon as it is available from the stock exchanges. This architecture is similar to the messaging architecture in Chapter 19; the only difference is the broker system is the one that is sending messages to users instead of users exchanging messages with one another. Ordering of messages is also important. The technological solution should ensure that the data is reflected to users in the order in which it arrived.

The stock updates are consumed by the stock tick consumer service (STCS), one of the backend services in the broker architecture. The STCS is a very lightweight service responsible for forwarding the updates received from exchange systems to internal backend services. Message forwarding is done asynchronously by publishing the updates to Kafka. In the broker architecture, two systems will consume these updates: the live stock tick system and the historical stock tick system (discussed in the next section). Kafka can handle the expected scale and provides message ordering, guaranteeing that we can meet one of our system requirements. An additional event-ordering mechanism can be built into the client application where the application can discard any old events based on event sequencing.

The stock live ticker service (SLTS) consumes messages from Kafka and delivers them to the end users in real time. The SLTS maintains persistent connections with end user devices and works similarly to the frontend chat servers in the chat application architecture discussed in Chapter 19. The SLTS contains two in-memory tables: one maintaining the stock prices and the other listing users interested in a specific stock. An interesting point to note here is that there are multiple price entries associated with a single stock (depending on the data depth supported by the system) and updated in near real time. These use cases can be solved by using data structures like balanced trees and priority queues of fixed length or by leveraging Redis sorted sets.

The stock price table is a global key-value store accessible to all the servers of the SLTS, and connection data is maintained locally by each server, as shown in Figure 21-2.

Let's talk a little about persistent connections between user devices and SLTS servers. Once the user is authenticated on the application, a persistent connection is established, and a connection ID is generated for the user device. This connection ID is handled by one of the SLTS servers. The server keeps an in-memory table mapping the stock name to a list of connection IDs interested in the stock. If there are any faults on the SLTS server, the user device establishes a new connection with a new connection ID, and a server is assigned to the user for receiving stock updates. A connection ID is managed by a lightweight thread or process of the system, and a single SLTS server is capable of handling thousands (on the order of 100,000) of such connections (benchmarking should be done to figure out the maximum connections that a single server can support). The lightweight thread can be managed by programming-language-specific constructs, such as Akka actors for JVM languages (or recently launched Java virtual threads), goroutines in Go, or processes in Erlang.

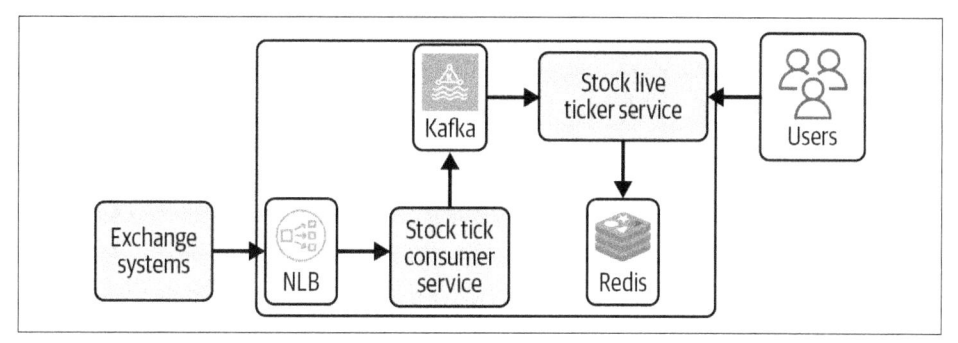

Figure 21-2. Live stock ticks architecture

The live stock updates have these steps: the exchange publishes a stock update; the STCS ingests the update and publishes it to Kafka; the SLTS updates the stock price to a global key-value store (such as Redis); and the SLTS checks for a connection ID interested in the stock and sends the updates to the users' devices. Thinking ahead, there can be two optimizations possible in the SLTS architecture:

- The SLTS is responsible for two actions: persisting the stock price updates to the global key-value store and maintaining the persistent connections with user devices. We can break this into two service deployments: a Kafka consumer is responsible for consuming the update and updating the stock price, and another service is responsible for delivering the stock updates to end user devices.

- The number of stocks listed on the stock exchange is limited, and we can keep a copy of stock prices in memory on the SLTS server. The idea is to keep a hot cache on top of a Redis cache for inferring the stock prices and making the system faster overall. Redis acts as a persistent data store, and the application servers can retrieve the data from Redis on restarts or when a new server is added to the pool.

The live stock ticks delivered to users calculate the P&L of user's stocks in real time and update the dashboard. Now, let's look into deriving historical market data for the users.

Historical stock ticks

The consumer of the historical stock tick service (HSTS) consumes the stock price updates from Kafka and then stores them to the database. The use case of the HSTS is to serve the historical price of a particular stock, so the data should be stored in a database such that we're able to figure out the stock price at any particular timestamp. We discussed the Amazon Timestream database in Chapter 10; it is the most feasible choice for such use cases. A lot of other time-series database choices are available in the market, such as InfluxDB and ClickHouse, and you should make your choice based on previous expertise and building a proof of concept for your use case. Like SLTS, the HSTS has two service deployments: one for writing stock price updates and another for serving the user read queries.

Most of the read queries served to the system are for a recent time period, such as one day or one week. There are fewer queries as the period increases to lengths such as one month, one year, or greater than a year. For this kind of query pattern, data archival becomes important to reduce costs associated with older data infrequently accessed by users. Data archival is available inherently in the Timestream database (*https://oreil.ly/BFP2b*), and we don't need to configure any manual processes. Timestream comes with two storage tiers: memory store and magnetic store. The memory store can be used to serve the most recent queries. After the configured time period, the data is automatically moved to the magnetic store. We can also configure a retention period on the magnetic store; the data is permanently deleted from the magnetic store after this time.

The user checks for current stock prices and historical trends and then can choose to sell existing stocks or buy new stocks. This is handled by the order management system (OMS).

Designing the Order Management System

We already described the order as a stock buy or sell operation. The OMS converts user interest (stock buy or sell) to an order request and forwards it to the exchange system for execution. The OMS runs a set of prevalidations to ensure that all compliance regulations are met before the request is sent to the exchange system. The validation system or risk management system (RMS) runs as a separate service to ensure independent operations and scaling. The high-level picture of order execution through the OMS is shown in Figure 21-3.

The responsibility of the OMS can vary depending on the country where the broker application is operating. Here are two segments in which the OMS can operate:

- The OMS creates an order request based on user input and passes it to the stock exchange for execution. The exchange system takes responsibility for matching this order against another order (a buy order matched against a sell order; reference the order-matching algorithm (*https://oreil.ly/QrmY8*) used by NSE India) and completing it.
- The OMS can match the order from the user pool and then forward the matched order to the exchange system.

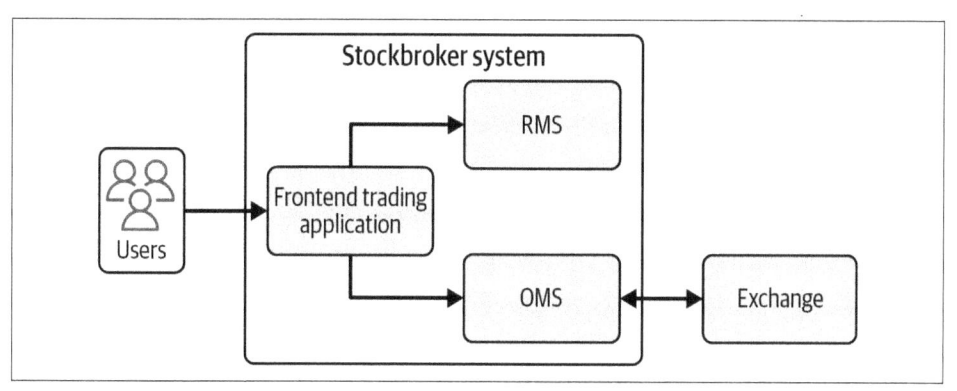

Figure 21-3. Order execution

The OMS can be self-hosted by the broker system, or third-party solutions can be leveraged. For example, Zerodha (*https://oreil.ly/s4z1Q*) uses a combination of self-hosted and third-party OMSs provided by Refinitiv. The third-party OMS generally offers a combination of features, including RMS and connectivity to the exchange systems from the broker systems' data centers. Let's take a look at an example architecture at Zerodha (*https://oreil.ly/Um_TS*) to understand end-to-end connectivity using AWS, an on-premises data center, and the exchange system. The users connect to systems via Cloudflare CDN to place orders on a frontend trading application. The trading application communicates with other backend services (such as request validation) and the OMS on an on-premises data center via AWS Direct Connect for faster communication. The on-premises data center communicates with the exchange systems over a dedicated leased line for final order execution, as shown in Figure 21-4.

The broker backend application also creates an internal order, which maps to the order created by the exchange system. This internal order maintains a reference to the external exchange order and other relevant details, such as payment details for order processing. The internal order is created with a unique identifier and helps with ensuring idempotency of the request (no duplicate order execution). The stock exchange system replies with acknowledgment of the request being received, and further updates are sent asynchronously for actions taken against the order.

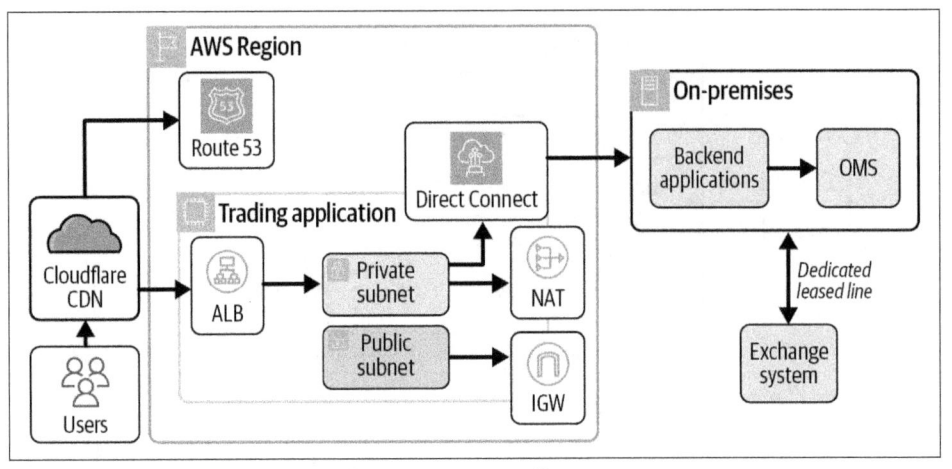

Figure 21-4. Order execution architecture at Zerodha

In the previous sections, we discussed the choices of database as Redis for live stock prices and a time-series database for serving historical stock price charts. Here are the data store requirements for the internal OMS:

- Create an entry in the database for an order before execution.
- Update the entry after acknowledgment is received from the exchange system with details like the order status, timestamp, amount executed by the exchange system (the amount can vary between the time the order was initiated on the broker application and the time the order actually got executed by the exchange system), and exchange order reference.

The database should comply with ACID properties and be scalable to handle a high write load (the system is write heavy as compared to reads). Here are a few of the use cases for reads and writes to the database:

- Create a reference order for an order made by the user.
- Check the status of an order.
- Fetch the user's *tradebook* (all the orders processed on behalf of the user by the broker system).
- When an order is moved to user *holdings* (stocks bought by a user) after a fixed time interval (which varies from exchange to exchange), exchange systems generally share files with the details. The system bulk loads this data to the database.
- This is also applicable to orders placed in advance and executed later based on the type (*https://oreil.ly/q4CS4*): market, limit, or stop-loss.

The latency is critical for live order execution, so database I/O reduction is the key to resolving this. An in-memory data store like Redis is used for end-to-end order execution, and the system in parallel persists this data to a disk data store like PostgreSQL. We've explored using Amazon DynamoDB for transactional workloads in previous chapters, and we can very well use that here as well. DynamoDB offers predictable response times for point queries on the primary key. In case you choose a nondistributed relational data store, we recommend database sharding, considering the scale requirements we finalized. To start, you can create logical database partitions (*https://oreil.ly/NuGmV*) and then move to actual physical partitions when the need arises. For the stockbroker application, the partitioning can be based on the time range, such as weekly or monthly.

Low latency is one of the NFRs we discussed in "System Requirements" on page 544. As mentioned previously, the stockbroker application doesn't target microsecond-magnitude latency like HFT firms do. Latency should definitely be in the submilliseconds, though, so that users don't see delays when viewing the stock prices. Let's discuss a few of the aspects related to ultra-low-latency systems.

Designing Ultra-Low-Latency Systems

Achieving extremely low latency like HFTs do is not feasible for broker applications due to the way the systems are architected. The broker applications connect to users on the public network as opposed to any dedicated network, which adds extra latency in data delivery. In the context of HFT system requirements, the system should be able to ingest TBT market data, run some algorithms to figure out an action (buy a stock, sell a stock, or no action), and execute an order per the evaluation. This whole process should take the minimum possible time to achieve maximum market gains.

The HFT system's architecture is similar to direct connectivity between broker application on-premises data centers and exchange systems over a dedicated network. Let's discuss a few of the techniques that HFTs employ to achieve ultra-low latency in systems, starting with network connectivity between different components.

Network connectivity

There is dedicated network connectivity between HFT systems and the exchange systems to avoid any issues related to network bandwidth. The exchange system requires that the leased lines used have the same capabilities for all the HFTs to ensure fairness among all the firms. The HFT backend system consists of multiple microservices, and there is connectivity involved in these services as well.

A network call to another service could add to the latency, so this is not a feasible approach; the microservices should be executed in shared memory for ultra-fast processing. Aeron clusters (*https://oreil.ly/mMOpf*) and Chronicle queues (*https://oreil.ly/vcH9n*) are a couple of the solutions that can be used to achieve this in a fault-tolerant manner. Another consideration for low-latency systems is managing hardware resources for executing programs. The program thread should not wait for resources or get blocked on any other thread for execution. To solve this, HFT software systems tend to rely on single-threaded systems with no thread-synchronization requirements.

> Evaluate business use cases carefully to figure out the most feasible architecture. A single-threaded execution makes sense for HFT software systems, while huge lightweight threads are helpful in chat systems (refer to Chapter 19).

These are some of the ways to improve network connectivity among HFT systems. The next important consideration is the choice of programming language; some languages offer inherently faster code execution compared to others, and that becomes very important for latency-critical applications.

Programming language

The design can be incredibly good, but if the programming language does other stuff along with code execution, then it adds to the latency. One such popular example of additional work is GC. We talked about how GC can affect system performance in previous chapters, such as tombstones in Apache Cassandra, and you need to figure out a way to get around this for languages like Java. The idea is to have maximum control over how the code is being executed on the hardware to optimize to a magnitude of microseconds. This ideology is similar to using AWS fully managed services versus taking the operational overhead on your own plate. To avoid GC issues, you can choose programming languages like C and C++, but they come with memory-management overhead.

There are pros and cons associated with all programming languages that will need thorough analysis before choosing one. For example, if we go ahead with a JVM language like Java, the GC issues can be addressed with the following techniques:

- Leverage technologies such as Azul Platform Prime (*https://oreil.ly/EsBvK*) that inherently improve the Java code efficiency.

- Introduce programming techniques that don't require GC, such as using *off-heap memory* (memory allocated to the OS outside the purview of JVM), warming up the code before the market opens, or preallocating memory to the pool (no allocation or deletion requirement at runtime). Preallocation is much like using an already established persistent connection instead of reinitiating a TCP handshake every time.

There are other choices, such as FPGA and application-specific integrated circuit (ASIC), which are faster than Java or C++, but these choices are difficult to program and come with their own set of problems. For example, FPGA takes between around 30 minutes and 30 hours for compilation, depending on the program's complexity and the machine type, increasing the deployment time for any critical bug fixes.

The best architectures perform well on the best hardware, so choosing hardware configurations is equally as important as making software architecture decisions. A lot of options are available from the cloud providers to run HFT software, such as Amazon EC2 z1d instances for fast single-threaded execution.

Once you've viewed the stocks based on live stock ticks and historical stocks charts and placed an order, the next action is viewing your P&L dashboard and other analytics on top of it.

Building the P&L Dashboard

The P&L dashboard shows the user's stock holdings at any point in time, which consists of the P&L of each individual stock as well as the overall portfolio. The P&L dashboard should also be updated in real time based on the stock ticks we discussed in "Live stock ticks" on page 547. The real-time update logic can be handled in the client-facing application itself based on the events received over the persistent connection.

The P&L dashboard is derived data from the order execution database (the user tradebook). The idea is to maintain this separately as user holdings instead of computing it at runtime because it is frequently accessed by the users. The calculation of P&L is pretty simple and can be done in these two steps:

1. Get all the stock holdings of a user.
2. Subtract the summation of all the sell orders from the summation of all the buy orders for each of these stocks.

The logic is simple, but the trades can span years; for example, you sell 50% of your stock holdings, which were bought five years ago. This makes derivation of data difficult and is the main reason to perform the operation during off-market hours. One important point to note here is that users' holdings don't change throughout the day but are settled at the end of the day by the exchange systems.

Let's illustrate a simplified schema with Amazon DynamoDB. The following schema is a simple example that gets all stocks for the `userId` with their P&L:

Partition key = {userId}

Sort key for overall P&L = PL

Sort key for each stock = S#{stockName}

We can also maintain the overall P&L in the same table by keeping the same partition key and distinguishing the sort key by an additional prefix.

This schema is for illustrative purposes only. The same table may consist of other entities to solve different query patterns. Older data can be archived to S3 (*https:// oreil.ly/_gavV*) based on configured TTL or moved to DynamoDB standard IA (*https://oreil.ly/Q_IMx*) from standard mode, optimizing the storage costs. Standard IA has increased read and write costs, but again it is designed for infrequent access and achieves 60% cost optimization on storage.

We can create similar tables in RDBMS as well to support all the P&L use cases. Taking an example from the Zerodha broker application (*https://oreil.ly/9Cqck*), the console application (the service responsible for handling P&L) creates a PostgreSQL caching layer on top of the primary PostgreSQL database (bulk updated based on files received from the exchange at the end of the day during off-market hours). The caching PostgreSQL creates millions of tables for the users to maintain their holdings, which are updated every day based on the trades completed for the day.

> The AWS blog (*https://oreil.ly/acXV1*) describes how Zerodha systems perform P&L calculations during off-market hours using the AWS Batch service. Batch is a fully managed batch computing service to schedule and run heavy workloads on a range of AWS compute services: Amazon EC2, Amazon ECS, and Amazon EKS.

Different analytics are also offered by the broker application, and they can best be served by using an analytical database like Amazon Redshift and building a dashboard with solutions like Metabase (*https://metabase.com*) or Amazon QuickSight. The key consideration for analytical queries is that we can survive with a little lag in serving the response, but it should not be too large (less than five seconds).

Now, let's move to the deployment of the architectures we discussed on the AWS cloud.

Launching the System on AWS

We took various architecture references in the previous sections from Zerodha's systems. Zerodha self-hosts most of its services on bare-metal EC2 instances for full control over infrastructure tuning and management. As we have reiterated, every decision in the system-design process is a trade-off, and it's important that you understand the reasoning for how a decision aligns with the business use case. An important consideration in systems like online broker applications is that there are compliance regulations in place that should be adhered to from day one. We'll start with the Day 0 architecture on the AWS cloud to launch the systems quickly and then move toward scaling and coming up with a highly scalable architecture.

Day 0 Architecture

The Day 0 architecture should be modular such that compliance regulations can be easily addressed and don't become a blocker in software development. Another benefit of modular architecture is breaking a single service into multiple microservices later down the line with ease. We explored using AWS AppSync in Chapter 19 for creating persistent connections and supporting delivery of user messages in near real time. The broker application has a requirement for delivering stock ticks, so a similar implementation can be used here.

The system requirements state that the system is heavily accessed by the users during market hours, and then the customer-facing traffic drops exponentially. AppSync automatically scales per the required connections and doesn't require a manual intervention (refer to the AWS blog (*https://oreil.ly/Ys_IU*) for implementation using AppSync and Amazon MSK). The systems leverage third-party systems like LSEG Data & Analytics (*https://oreil.ly/hxetH*) for consumption of live market data. The market data streams are consumed at an NLB endpoint and distributed among the Amazon ECS Fargate tasks. The ECS Fargate ingestors publish this data to MSK, which is streamed to AppSync for data delivery to users over persistent connections. The market data from MSK is also consumed by another stock ticker consumer for ingestion to an Amazon Timestream database to serve historical market data queries. There are separate modules for ingesting the data and serving user queries, as shown in Figure 21-5.

The next part is allowing users to place an order for a stock listed on the exchange. The Day 0 architecture should also be built keeping low latency in mind—it may not be as low as 50–100 ms but should definitely be under one second. The broker system leverages the third-party OMS, such as Refinitiv (acquired by LSEG), and uses AWS Direct Connect for communication between applications hosted in the AWS cloud and Refinitiv servers. The internal trading service handles the user's order request, validates the request via the rule management service, and forwards the request to the Refinitiv OMS upon validation. The OMS talks with the exchange systems for order matching and execution, as shown in Figure 21-6. The acknowledgment to this request is captured and reflected to the customer.

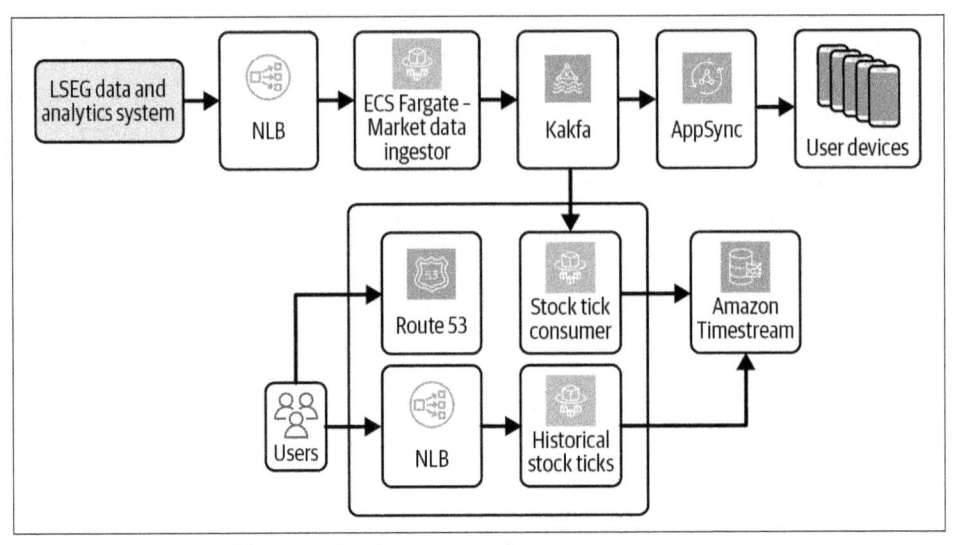

Figure 21-5. Live and historical ticks Day 0 architecture

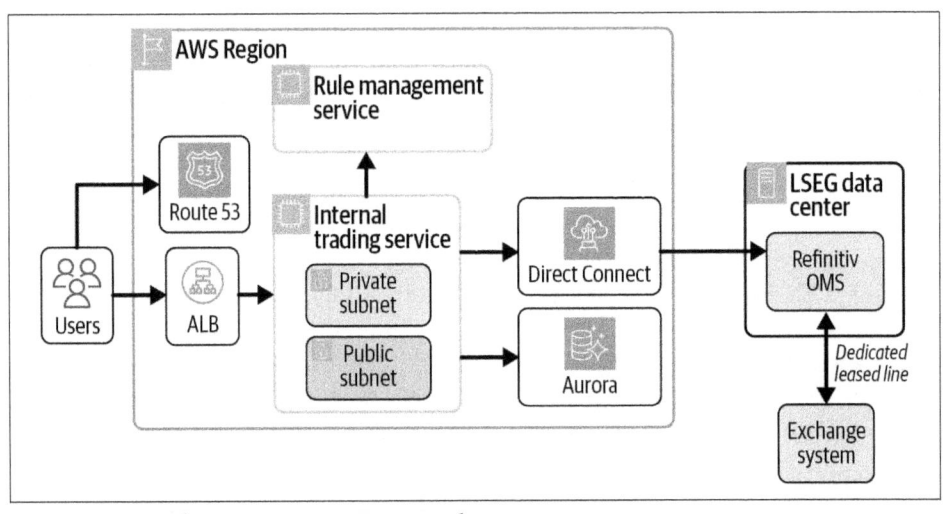

Figure 21-6. Order management Day 0 architecture

The internal trading service uses Amazon Aurora to persist the order entries and publishes events for the order status to be consumed by services like the dashboard service (responsible for computing user P&L and other analytics). The dashboard service uses Amazon Redshift to offer different kinds of analytics.

Scaling to Millions and Beyond

The customer-facing traffic mostly occurs during market hours, so autoscaling plays an important role in saving overall infrastructure costs. Apart from the customer traffic, multiple offline jobs run during off-market hours, such as sending PDFs to users (*https://oreil.ly/uWADr*) for trades done during the day, settling orders based on files received from exchange systems, and calculating users' P&Ls after the settlement cycle. These jobs are not latency critical and can be performed at their own pace, keeping a balance of cost and execution time.

A key consideration for ensuring low latency is keeping the systems in close vicinity (less physical distance). For example, the trading application should be close to the end users to reduce the network hops for connections; the OMS should be close to the exchange systems for faster order execution; and the backend applications should be colocated, avoiding network hops.

Here are some other considerations for ensuring low latency for the customer-facing systems:

Prewarm infrastructure
　　AWS offers scheduled scaling capability (*https://oreil.ly/seC87*), allowing the system to autoscale based on a configured clock time. This ensures that the system is ready to serve the traffic and requests don't wait in a queue for execution. AWS also provides warm pools (*https://oreil.ly/81ETm*) for applications that take a longer boot time and could be useful for autoscaling quickly for any unplanned sudden traffic burst or hardware failures on running systems. We recommend keeping the application binary to the absolute minimum, keeping it lightweight (fewer external dependencies and small module-based services) without overburdening it with a lot of implementation logic.

Cross-AZ deployments
　　We generally recommend deploying the infrastructure across the AZs in a region for higher application reliability and to withstand AZ downtimes, but this can add to the latency. For example, an internal trading service instance in us-east-1a connects with an RMS instance in us-east-1b for validation; this could have been faster if both services were located in the same AZ. This is only recommended for services with requirements for very low latency because the AWS AZs and regions are connected by dedicated networks, and by default, it takes very little time (this is similar to an EC2 instance connecting with an instance store versus EBS volumes). The system should have a disaster-recovery mechanism for AZ or region downtimes.

VPC connectivity

The VPC can span multiple AZs and host the infrastructure in different AZs based on the subnet, as we discussed in Chapter 9. Let's say we decide to host the infrastructure in a single AZ: do the applications span multiple VPCs or belong to the same VPC? Hosting in a single VPC can be an ideal scenario for minimum latency with the assumption that multiple VPCs (in the same or separate AWS accounts) are needed for clear division. The VPC connectivity becomes important for such scenarios, and we recommend VPC peering over AWS Transit Gateways to reduce a network hop and decrease latency.

EC2 placement groups

There are multiple server racks in the AZ, and the different microservices can be present on different racks, adding to the latency. AWS offers an EC2 placement groups feature (*https://oreil.ly/ptzF0*), which ensures that the EC2 machines allocated to you belong to the same server rack. This strategy goes against the general recommendation of spreading out the hardware to avoid correlated failures, but it makes sense for achieving low latency in systems. If the applications are deployed on multiple racks to increase resiliency, the system architecture should ensure that there is no cross-rack connectivity and each microservice has its binary deployed on all the racks. To avoid system downtimes, the disaster-recovery strategy becomes important, such as multiple on-premises data centers deployed with AWS Outposts.

Hardware selection

AWS offers a wide range of instance types, and choosing the best for the workload determines the execution latency; we recommend proper benchmarking to come up with the best instance configurations. EBS volumes used for the workload play equally important roles, and AWS Nitro SSD volumes (*https://oreil.ly/jDWRG*) are helpful in achieving submillisecond latency.

Data caching

Database reads can introduce I/O bottlenecks, adding to the execution latency. In-memory data stores can be more helpful for achieving low latency. These data stores can be used as a caching layer on top of persistent disk stores or used as a primary data store (with a disk-persistence option to avoid data loss) for hot paths such as order execution. We also recommend using Amazon CloudFront wherever feasible for caching the content near the end users.

AWS edge infrastructure

We mentioned that latency can be reduced by reducing the distance, but one of the places we don't have control is the public internet. Customers connecting to broker application servers through the public internet can introduce unwanted network latency; this can be further reduced by using AWS Local Zones (discussed in Chapter 9). Local Zones enable us to place the infrastructure much closer to the customers compared to AWS regions and are very helpful in latency-sensitive applications. AWS Wavelength (*https://oreil.ly/esCO2*) is another edge infrastructure that is helpful for deploying infrastructure to the edge of the telecommunication carrier's 5G networks. This allows for faster communication with 5G-enabled devices. We might not be able to get the best out of it at present, but this will be helpful in the future when most devices are 5G enabled. There is a possibility that Local and Wavelength Zones are still not near the end customers; for these use cases, AWS Outposts is the solution. AWS Outposts allow customers to extend the AWS infrastructure to their on-premises data centers and connect directly to AWS regions using AWS Direct Connect.

We've discussed multiple ways to optimize latency via the AWS infrastructure here. Regular evaluation of the software will help you identify the processes consuming more execution time. Figuring out the exact places where the software is taking more time can help identify a path forward and fix the issue. For example, you might want to denormalize the data to avoid unnecessary joins and improve the query performance; consider using Protobuf or Simple Binary Encoding (SBE) instead of JSON/XML to transfer payload over the network. Another general recommendation for ensuring overall system health is to avoid any deployments or infrastructure-configuration modifications (unless it is a critical requirement) during market hours.

Looking back at the architectures in Figures 21-5 and 21-6, we can see that we skipped some functionalities and focused on only the core components of how users buy and sell stocks. Other components include the following:

User onboarding service
Onboards the user to the stockbroker based on country and stock exchange compliance. This service is similar to the property onboarding architecture discussed in Chapter 18 where the user is onboarding in a set of steps, so we can leverage solutions like Step Functions.

Payments service
Handles fund transfers from the user's preferred payment option to a broker account, which can later be used to buy stocks. This service also transfers funds back to the user's account if stocks are sold or if the user-added funds stay in the broker account too long (per the country's compliance regulations).

User authentication service
Authenticates the user requests for all the operations that can be performed on the broker application.

The stock exchanges share the market order updates at the end of the day with the broker application via different mechanisms. The mechanism can be a callback posted on our system endpoint or a file with all the data. This can vary from exchange to exchange. The broker system takes the following actions based on the updates received from the exchange systems:

- Compute P&L for the users.
- Update the user tradebook.
- Notify users of the trades executed for the day.

It's important to note that the stockbroker application can offer stock listings from different stock exchange platforms. The network connectivity will be somewhat similar, but the rules that the RMS holds or the deployment of the OMS can be different. We recommend operating under the assumption that the stock exchange platforms can vary, such as in the ways that the exchange and broker systems communicate; the broker system gathers market updates from the exchange systems; and the orders are executed. This will help you address any specific future tasks for different stock exchange systems. We'll design the system in the next section keeping separate deployments for the RMS and OMS mapped to a stock exchange.

To also help with scale, developer dependency should be minimized with respect to operations tasks, such as adding or modifying rules in the RMS. The RMS should expose a portal for the operations team to access and modify the rule set. Additionally, the system should have some type of mechanism for testing these rules in the staging environment before they can be moved to the production environment (with a percentage-based rollout strategy). The storage solution maintaining the rules should keep versions of the rule configs as they are modified over time. Any created order should have a rule-config version associated with it. This helps create an audit history to verify the rules executed by the system for successful validation before allowing a trade to happen.

Let's move to Day N architecture on the AWS cloud next.

Day N Architecture

In the Day 0 architecture, we used Refinitiv and LSEG as placeholder systems for the OMS and for retrieving live market data needs. The third-party systems are ideally designed for the scale. These systems are used for illustrative purposes only, and we don't recommend integrating these systems in your architecture. Analyze different solutions available in the industry (or developing a custom solution) to determine what works best for your organization. Involvement of on-premises data centers in the overall architecture also depends on the country and stock exchange compliance regulations. Some stock exchanges restrict the broker applications to only connect to stock exchanges from an on-premises data center via dedicated leased lines (as in Figure 21-4).

To start scaling the system to more live, concurrent users, we'll split the architecture discussion into two parts: the system serving live and historical market data and the system responsible for executing orders.

Market data delivery

For the requirements of both the live market data and the order execution systems, we'll rely on the colocation space offered by the stock exchanges (e.g., Nasdaq (*https://oreil.ly/wgocP*)). This will help reduce overall network hops, optimizing latency and removing dependency on third-party vendors wherever possible. Further, streaming TBT market data to all the clients consumes a lot of bandwidth, so ideally, exchanges stream up to level 2 data (approximately three ticks per second). For use cases to serve level 3 and TBT data, broker applications are required to host their servers in colocation space and consume the TBT data streams.

The broker server colocated in the stock exchange data center consumes the TBT market data, transforms the TBT data to level 3 data, compresses the level 3 data, and streams the data to an on-premises data center via a dedicated leased line. From the on-premises data center, the data is streamed to AWS regions via AWS Direct Connect and delivered to users via the SLTS over a persistent WebSocket connection. The on-premises data center is introduced in between with the assumption that the stock exchange mandates this per regulations. In case this is not mandated, the data can be streamed from the stock exchange to the AWS region directly via Direct Connect. The overall architecture with live and historical stock ticks is shown in Figure 21-7; networking components like gateways, LBs, and the edge cache are skipped to keep the diagram simple.

In this architecture, we assumed that the stock exchange servers are hosted in a self-managed data center. Nowadays, stock exchanges are also migrating to the cloud to host the infrastructure and reduce operational burden. Even with on-premises data centers, stock exchanges are trying to leverage services like AWS Local Zones, which can help achieve the benefits of the cloud in the self-hosted data centers.

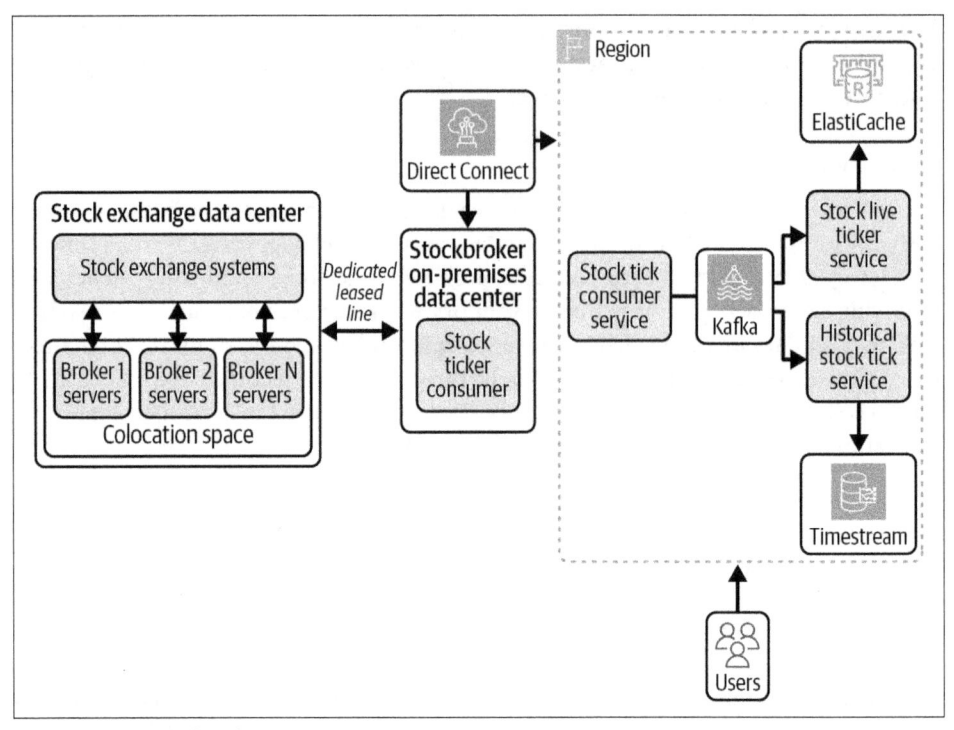

Figure 21-7. Stock ticker system

Market order execution

The flow of requests in market order execution systems is opposite the flow in market data delivery systems. The request starts with the user, with an intent to execute an order. The stockbroker system validates the request for execution and forwards the request to the stock exchange system upon successful validation. The architecture will be similar to Figure 21-6 with some improvements, such as the OMS can be owned by the broker application instead of relying on third-party vendors. We already recommended including a separate deployment per stock exchange for the systems with behavior specific to each stock exchange. An additional component from Figure 21-6 will be an offline data orchestrator to work asynchronously for updates received from the stock exchange system at the end of the day for the trades executed.

The stock exchange is not guaranteed to send the response of order execution against the same request, so we should think about introducing a queue before the OMS. The broker application, upon receiving the request, runs the set of rules to identify if the order can be executed and publishes the request to the OMS queue. The OMS polls the messages from the queue and forwards to the stock exchange system for actual order matching. The Day N architecture is shown in Figure 21-8.

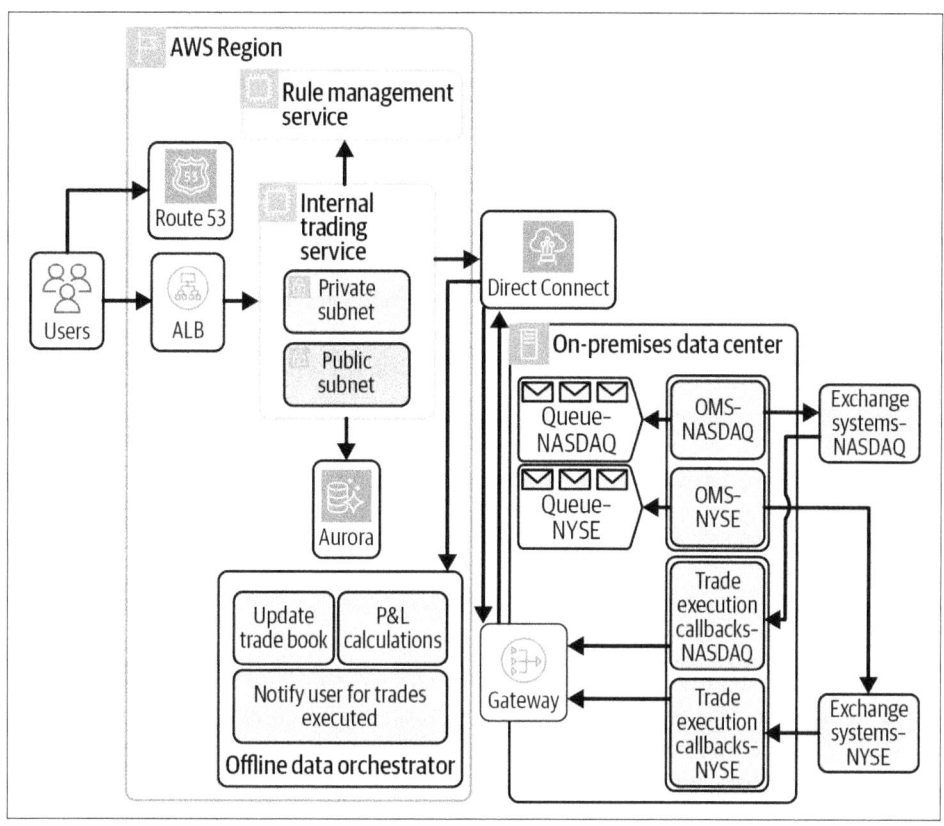

Figure 21-8. Market order execution architecture

We discussed improving execution latency in "Scaling to Millions and Beyond" on page 559; system resiliency is another important consideration for overall success.

System resilience

The system should be able to operate even in the case of hardware failures and recover without any downtimes. The general recommendation to improve resiliency of applications is to deploy in multiple AZs and regions. Most AWS-managed services take care of this by default; for example, Amazon Aurora persists two copies of each write operation in three AZs.

We generally deploy the infrastructure across the AZs of an AWS region, and it by default takes care of issues like AZ downtimes (which rarely happen). With respect to stockbroker applications, we discussed using on-premises data centers or AWS local zones for infrastructure hosting, which brings the maintenance overhead onto our plate.

Follow these recommendations to improve system resiliency:

- To avoid issues in a server rack, keep a duplicate server rack with the same set of services so that the system can default to another server rack in case of failures.
- If the entire data center goes down, the system should be able to operate from a different data center. The other data center can again be on-premises or systems deployed in one of the AZs of an AWS region. With the assumption that these scenarios rarely happen, our recommendation is to host the same set of services in the AWS region, and traffic can be served from there for any issues. The important thing to consider here is active database replication to refer to the current state of ongoing orders and continue the operations from other data centers.
- Figure 21-8 shows one OMS per stock exchange. There is a further possibility of sharding the workload, removing the single point of failure. Each sharded OMS has independent connectivity with the stock exchange network, increasing the overall availability of the system.

Conclusion

Choosing infrastructure and technology is equally as important as writing software; a perfectly written software application can perform badly if inappropriate technology for deployment is selected. The focus of Part III has been on identifying the requirements and the business use case to finalize a solution.

We gathered multiple suggestions and optimizations that we can do at the software and infrastructure levels for improving the execution latency of systems. There are very few ultra-low-latency business use cases, and they require specific solutions. We recommend having maximum control of the software and hardware for these use cases. Every decision with software and hardware configurations becomes important with ultra-low-latency systems, so we don't recommend fully managed services for these use cases. The reason is simple: the fully managed services are designed for all general-purpose use cases, but you have very specific requirements. The fully managed service might be bundled with 10 features, but you just need one with full control.

Let's look at an example of self-hosting versus using cloud-managed services and compare it to cooking your own food versus hiring a cook (or ordering online, eating out, etc.) for preparing meals. Cooking food (or self-hosting software) gives you full control to the lowest of the configurations. If you hire a cook, you can buy groceries or spices, but you can't control the cooking speed, chopping style, quantity of spices —and the list goes on. This is the same with managed services: you may be able to specify RAM size and number of vCPUs (or any other configuration depending on the service), but you don't have the control to tune the software at the OS or hardware level.

I (Mandeep) cook my own food. I like the process, and it doesn't take much time because I have gained expertise over time. People are really surprised when they learn that I cook my own meals, and I get a lot of questions about time management. This is also an issue with self-hosting—you might get worried about engineering-bandwidth requirements for managing the systems, the learning curve, how to handle system downtimes, and so on, but these are not issues most of the time. The theme of this entire book is making sure you evaluate your business use cases before making a decision. If you're able to justify the decision of using managed services, then go ahead with it. For example, I cook food almost every day but take a break from cooking and save some time for other interests by ordering biryani (*https://oreil.ly/G_OZY*) from Zomato (an online food-ordering platform in India similar to DoorDash in the US) every Sunday afternoon.

It's not possible to cover each and every aspect of AWS systems within the scope of this book. Think about what we've talked about throughout the book and applying what you've learned to the systems that you're designing or that you aspire to design. We hope this book has helped enhance your understanding of system design in the AWS cloud and wish you the very best for your future system-design decisions.

Index

Symbols
80/20 rule, 96

A
abstract syntax tree (AST), 48
abstraction, 6
access control
    Cognito, 323-326
    IAM, 320-323
access control lists (ACLs), 262
accounts (AWS), creating, 222
ACID model, 43-44, 70
ACLs (access control lists), 262
active cache invalidation, 100
active-active failover pattern, 16
active-passive failover pattern, 16
activities (in Step Functions), 310
actor model, 507-509
ADCs (application delivery controllers), 123
Advanced Message Queuing Protocol (AMQP), 189
AI (artificial intelligence), 344
Airflow, 313-314
alarm conditions, 317
alarms, 317-318
ALB (application load balancer), 131, 248
algorithms for load balancing, 125-127
allowlist policies, 99
Amazon Machine Image (AMI), 281-282
Amazon States Language (ASL), 310
Amazon VPC (see VPC service)
Amazon Web Services (see AWS)
Amdahl's law, 96
AMI (Amazon Machine Image), 281-282

Amplify, 374
AMQP (Advanced Message Queuing Protocol), 189
analytics (see big data analytics)
anticorruption layer, 205
AOFs (append-only files), 115-116
Apache Airflow, 313-314
Apache Cassandra, 88-89
Apache Kafka (see Kafka)
API Gateway (AWS), 121, 250-251
API gateways, 121, 204
API routing patterns, 204-205
API servers, 175
APIs (application programming interfaces), 154
    GraphQL, 157-159
    RESTful, 155-157
    for URL shortener service, 365-367
    WebRTC, 159-160
App Runner, 375, 378
append-only files (AOFs), 115-116
application caching, 107
application code, 167
application delivery controllers (ADCs), 123
application deployment
    CI/CD pipeline, 180-182
    container deployment strategies, 178-180
    evolution of, 164-166
application layer protocols, 143-150
application load balancer (ALB), 131, 248
application logs, 315
application processes, 172
application programming interfaces (see APIs)
AppSync, 326-327, 516
architectural designs and patterns

569

big data, 193-196
CDC (change data capture), 186-188
choreography, 190, 193
cloud, 202-206
distributed systems, 206-215
    HDFS, 206-209, 215
    Kafka, 211-215
EDA (event-driven architecture), 199-202
orchestration, 191-193
pub/sub model, 188-189
solution, 196-199
archived objects storage class, 260
artificial intelligence (AI), 344
ASGs (autoscaling groups), 284
ask prices (stocks), 546
ASL (Amazon States Language), 310
AST (abstract syntax tree), 48
asynchronous checkpointing, 23
asynchronous communication, 8, 150-153
asynchronous invocation, 288
asynchronous orchestration patterns, 192
asynchronous replication, 62-63
at-least-once delivery, 214
at-most-once delivery, 214
Athena, 338-339
atomicity, 43
audit-column-based CDC, 187
Aurora, 264, 470, 493-497
Aurora DSQL, 265
Aurora Limitless Database, 494-496
authentication
    Cognito, 323-326
    IAM, 320-323
    for social network, 431-433
auto-increment feature (databases), 364
autoscaling, 284-285
autoscaling groups (ASGs), 284
availability, 13-18
    consistency versus, 28-30
    in document stores, 80
    ensuring, 15
    in key-value stores, 76-77
    measuring, 13-14
    of nonrelational databases, 69
    patterns, 16-18
    in Redis, 114-115
    reliability and, 20
    sequential systems versus parallel systems, 14-15
    in social network use case, 437
availability zones (AWS), 223
AWS (Amazon Web Services)
    account creation, 222
    availability zones, 223
    cloud storage services, 256-262
    compute services
        choosing, 295-296
        containerization (see containerization)
        EC2, 279-285
        Lambda, 286-289
    database services, 262-277
        Aurora, 264, 470, 493-497
        DocumentDB, 268-269
        DynamoDB, 265-268
        ElastiCache, 272-274
        Keyspaces, 276-277
        Neptune, 270-272
        OpenSearch, 275-276
        RDS, 263-265
        Timestream, 276
    edge locations, 224
    Hadoop ecosystem versus, 209-211
    local zones, 224
    networking services (see networking services (AWS))
    regions, 223
    shared responsibility model, 221, 223

B

B+ trees, 51-52
back queue routers, 395
back queue selectors, 396
back queues, 395
backend for frontend (BFF), 206
bandwidth, 27, 445
bare-metal servers, 280
base image, 167
BASE principles, 69-70
base62 encoding, 362
Belady's algorithm, 97
benchmarking, 52
BFF (backend for frontend), 206
bid prices (stocks), 546
big data analytics
    Athena, 338-339
    EMR (Elastic MapReduce), 330-333
    Glue, 334-338
    QuickSight, 339-340

Redshift, 340-343
big data architectures, 193-196
bitrate, 529
block-based storage, 36, 37-38, 256-257
blocks (HDFS), 208
Bloom filters, 87
blue-green deployments, 179
boundaries, system, 389
bounded stream processing, 302
branch management, 180
Brewer's theorem (see CAP theorem)
brokers, 212
bucket policies, 262
buckets, 259
buffer managers, 48

C

cache hit, 95
cache layer, 450
cache managers, 49
cache miss, 95
cache warm-up, 104
cache, definition of, 95
cache-aside caching strategy, 103
caching
    benefits of, 96-97
    CDNs (content delivery networks), 108-111
    deployment strategies, 105-106
    with ElastiCache, 272-274
    eviction policies, 97-99
    invalidation policies, 100-101
    mechanisms for, 107-108
    in Neptune, 271
    in online game leaderboard, 448
    open source solutions, 111-118
    strategies for, 102-105
callbacks, 8
canary deployments, 179
candidate keys, 46
CAP theorem, 28-30
capacity modes (DynamoDB), 266
Cassandra, 88-89
catalogs, 50
causal consistency, 11
CD (continuous deployment), 182
CDC (change data capture), 186-188, 202
CDN-based GSLB, 123
CDNs (content delivery networks), 107, 108-111, 532

cell-based architecture, 370
cellular architecture, 206
change data capture (CDC), 186-188, 202
chaos engineering, 409
chat applications
    use case, 501-523
        architecture design, 503-511
        Day 0 architecture, 516-520
        Day N architecture, 520-522
        direct messaging, 505-509
        media content storage, 510-511
        message storage, 509-510
        protocol selection, 504-505
        system requirements, 501-503
        WhatsApp architecture, 511-516
    with WebSockets, 151-153
    XMPP, 148-149, 504-505
checkpointing, 23-24
choosing
    compute services, 295-296
    databases, 93
        for chat application, 509-510
        for hotel reservation system, 479-480
        for URL shortener service, 368-369
        for user post service, 420-422
    protocols for chat application, 504-505
choreographed asynchronous events, 190
choreography, 190, 193
CI (continuous integration), 181
CI/CD pipeline, 180-182
CIDR (Classless Inter-Domain Routing), 228
CIDR blocks, 230-231
circuit breaker pattern, 203
classic load balancer (CLB), 248
classifiers (Glue), 334
Classless Inter-Domain Routing (CIDR), 228
CLB (classic load balancer), 248
client multiplexing, 110
client-side caching, 107
clients, 279
cloud architecture patterns, 202-206
cloud computing services (see networking services (AWS))
cloud storage services (AWS), 256-262
    EBS (Elastic Block Store), 256-257
    EFS (Elastic File System), 257-259
    S3 (Simple Storage Service), 259-262
cloud-managed services, self-hosting versus, 566

Index | 571

CloudFront, 111, 224, 251-253, 538-539
CloudWatch, 315-320
    alarms, 317-318
    application logs, 315
    events, 319-320
    metrics, 316-317
cluster endpoints, 271
clustering keys in column-family stores, 84
clusters, 176, 331-333
codecs, 529
CodeWhisperer, 346
Cognito, 323-326, 431
cold start, 104, 288
collections, 79
collisions, 360-361
column-family stores, 69, 83-90
    advantages and trade-offs, 88
    Apache Cassandra, 88-89
    architecture, 86-88
    consistency levels, 84-86
    data model, 83-84
    Keyspaces, 276-277
columns (in relational databases), 40
command query responsibility segregation (CQRS), 202
comment publication (social network use case), 430-431
commit logs, 86
communication, 6-8, 137, 221
    (see also networking services (AWS))
    asynchronous, 8, 150-153
    OSI model, 138-139
    protocol standards, 154-160
        GraphQL, 157-159
        REST, 155-157
        RPC, 154-155
        WebRTC, 159-160
    protocols, 138
    pub/sub model, 188-189
        Kinesis, 299-305
        MSK (Managed Streaming for Apache Kafka), 297-299
        SNS (Simple Notification Service), 307-309
        SQS (Simple Queue Service), 305-306
    pull-based mechanisms, 151
    push-based mechanisms, 151-153
    synchronous, 7, 150
    TCP/IP model, 139-150
        application layer protocols, 143-150
        network layer protocols, 140
        transport layer protocols, 140-143
compaction strategies, 87
complexity of distributed systems, 12
composite alarms, 318
Comprehend, 346
compression, 403-404
compute services (AWS)
    choosing, 295-296
    containerization (see containerization)
    EC2, 279-285
    Lambda, 286-289
    for online game leaderboard, 455
    for URL shortener service, 378-379
concurrency control managers, 49
concurrency in hotel reservation system, 480-482
ConfigMaps, 177
configurable alarm actions, 318
configuration files, 168
configuration levels (Kafka), 213
configuration-based load balancers, 132-133
conflict resolution, 9
congestion, 517
congestion avoidance, 141, 145, 518-519, 539
consensus protocols, 9
consistency, 8-12, 44
    availability versus, 28-30
    in CDNs, 110
    in column-family stores, 84-86
    consistency spectrum model, 10-12
    in data storage systems, 9-10
    in distributed systems, 8
    in online game leaderboard, 447
consistency spectrum model, 10-12
consistent hashing, 75
constraints, 42
consumers, 212, 241
container images, 167-169
container registries, 169-171
containerd, 173
containerization, 163
    deployment strategies, 178-180
    Docker, 166-174
        container lifecycle, 171-172
        Docker engine, 172-174
        images, 167-169
        registries, 169-171

ECS (Elastic Container Service), 290-293
EKS (Elastic Kubernetes Service), 293-295
Kubernetes, 174-177
containers, 163
    deployment strategies, 178-180
    lifecycle, 171-172
    orchestration, 174-177
    VMs versus, 164-166
content consistency in CDNs, 110
content delivery networks (see CDNs)
content distribution, 532
content fragmentation, 109
content indexing, 531-532
content personalization, 110
continuous deployment (CD), 182
continuous integration (CI), 181
control plane nodes, 174
controller managers, 175
cookie-based session affinity, 128
cooldown periods, 285
coprocessors, 348
copy-on-write (CoW), 116-118
core nodes, 332
CoW (copy-on-write), 116-118
CQRS (command query responsibility segregation), 202
cross-VPC connectivity, 239-242
custom domain support for URL shortener service, 369-370

D

DAGs (Directed Acyclic Graphs), 313
dashboards (QuickSight), 339-340
data catalogs, 334
data compression, 403-404
data control language (DCL), 43
data copying, 343
data crawlers, 334
data definition language (DDL), 43
data dictionaries, 50
data engines, 335
data ingestion, 343
data lakes, 195-196
data manipulation language (DML), 43
data modeling, 446
data processing units (DPUs), 336
data replication, 9
data retrieval, 456
data security (S3), 261-262

data sharing, 343
data storage systems
    cloud storage services (AWS), 256-262
    consistency in, 9-10
    formats of, 36-39
    for hotel reservation system, 479-480
    for media content, 510-511
    nonrelational databases (see nonrelational databases)
    relational databases (see relational databases)
data streaming
    KDA (Kinesis Data Analytics), 302-303
    KDF (Kinesis Data Firehose), 303-304
    KDS (Kinesis Data Streams), 299-301
    KVS (Kinesis Video Streams), 304-305
data tiering, 272
data versioning, 10
database caching, 108
database management systems (DBMS), 39-40
    open source RDBMS, 63-65
    RDBMS architecture, 47-50
databases, 39-40
    auto-increment feature, 364
    AWS, 262-277
        DocumentDB, 268-269
        DynamoDB, 265-268
        ElastiCache, 272-274
        Keyspaces, 276-277
        Neptune, 270-272
        OpenSearch, 275-276
        RDS, 263-265
        Timestream, 276
    choosing, 93
        for chat application, 509-510
        for hotel reservation system, 479-480
        for URL shortener service, 368-369
        for user post service, 420-422
    Glue, 334
    migration, 435
    nonrelational (see nonrelational databases)
    for online game leaderboard, 449-450
    for order management system, 552
    for property onboarding architecture, 470-471
    relational (see relational databases)
    for WhatsApp, 514-516
DataNodes, 208
DAX (DynamoDB Accelerator), 274

Day 0 architecture
    for chat application, 516-520
    for hotel reservation system, 490-497
    for online game leaderboard, 451-460
    for social network, 427-436
    for stockbroker application, 557-562
    for URL shortener service, 371-379
    for video processing, 534-540
    for web crawler/search engine, 405-409
Day N architecture
    for chat application, 520-522
    for hotel reservation system, 497-498
    for online game leaderboard, 460-463
    for social network, 436-439
    for stockbroker application, 562-566
    for URL shortener service, 379-383
    for video processing, 540-542
    for web crawler/search engine, 409-413
DBMS (database management systems), 39-40
    open source RDBMS, 63-65
    RDBMS architecture, 47-50
DCL (data control language), 43
DDD (domain-driven design), 203
DDL (data definition language), 43
dead letter queue (DLQ), 306
decompose by subdomains pattern, 204
dedicated tenancy, 230
delegation, 323
DELETE method, 145
DeleteItem operation (key-value stores), 73
deleting indexes, 474
denormalization, 53-54
dependencies, 168
deployment
    CI/CD pipeline, 180-182
    container deployment strategies, 178-180
    evolution of, 164-166
    Kubernetes, 176
deployment packages, 287
deployment strategies
    for caches, 105-106
    Kubernetes, 178-180
    for load balancers, 123-125
designs (see architectural designs and patterns)
destinations (Lambda), 287
digital rights management (DRM), 532
dimensions (of metrics), 316
Direct Connect, 244-246, 535
direct messaging, 505-509

Directed Acyclic Graphs (DAGs), 313
disaster recovery, 59
distributed systems, 206-215
    complexity and consistency, 12
    consistency in, 8
    fallacies of, 24-26
    HDFS, 206-209, 215
    Kafka, 211-215
distribution styles (Redshift), 342
DLQ (dead letter queue), 306
DML (data manipulation language), 43
DNS (Domain Name System), 246-247
DNS load balancers, 129
DNS redirection, 110
DNS-based GSLB, 123
Docker, 163, 166-174
    container lifecycle, 171-172
    images, 167-169
    registries, 169-171
Docker CLI, 173
Docker Client, 170
Docker daemon, 173
Docker engine, 172-174
Docker Host, 170
Docker Registry, 170
Dockerfiles, 166
document stores, 68, 79-83
    advantages and trade-offs, 81
    availability, 80
    data model, 79-80
    DocumentDB, 83, 268-269
    MongoDB, 82-83
DocumentDB, 83, 268-269
documents, 79
Domain Name System (DNS), 246-247
domain-based patterns, 203
domain-driven design (DDD), 203
DPUs (data processing units), 336
DRM (digital rights management), 532
duplicate detection for URLs, 397-398
durability, 44
    in Redis, 115-116
dynamic content caching optimization, 109
dynamic load balancing algorithms, 126-127
dynamic pricing, 486-488
Dynamo, 78
DynamoDB, 265-268
    for chat application, 517
    limitations of, 422

for online game leaderboard, 453, 455
for property onboarding architecture, 471
scaling, 368
for social network, 428-429
for social network, 427
for URL shortener service, 368, 377
for user post service, 421
for web crawler/search engine, 407
DynamoDB Accelerator (DAX), 274

E

EBS (Elastic Block Store), 38, 256-257
EC2 (Elastic Compute Cloud), 279-285
    AMIs, 281-282
    autoscaling, 284-285
    block-based storage, 38
    file-based storage, 37
    instance types, 282-284
    for machine learning, 348
    placement groups, 560
    for URL shortener service, 371-373
ECMP (equal-cost multipath) routers, 130
ECR (Elastic Container Registry), 291
ECS (Elastic Container Service), 290-293, 455
EDA (event-driven architecture), 199-202
edge locations (AWS), 224, 252
edge side include (ESI) tags, 109
EFS (Elastic File System), 37, 257-259
Ejabberd, 511
EKS (Elastic Kubernetes Service), 177, 293-295
Elastic Block Store (EBS), 38, 256-257
Elastic Compute Cloud (see EC2)
Elastic Container Registry (ECR), 291
Elastic Container Service (ECS), 290-293, 455
Elastic File System (EFS), 37, 257-259
elastic IP addresses, 229
Elastic Kubernetes Service (EKS), 177, 293-295
Elastic Load Balancers (ELBs), 121, 248-250
Elastic MapReduce (EMR), 207, 330-333, 338
ElastiCache, 118, 272-274, 376, 453
Elasticsearch, 472-475
ELBs (Elastic Load Balancers), 121, 248-250
Elemental MediaConvert, 534
Elemental MediaLive, 535
Elemental MediaPackage, 535
Elemental MediaStore, 536
email communications (SMTP), 146-148
EMR (Elastic MapReduce), 207, 330-333, 338
EMRFS (EMR File System), 330-331

encoding, 529-530
encryption, 261, 273, 308
EOS (exactly-once semantics), 214
ephemeral ports, 142
equal-cost multipath (ECMP) routers, 130
ER model, 45
Erlang, 511-516
Erlang term storage (ETS), 514
ESI (edge side include) tags, 109
ETags, 101, 394
etcd, 175
ETS (Erlang term storage), 514
event sourcing, 200-202
event stores, 200
event-driven architecture (EDA), 199-202
event-driven state machines, 200
EventBridge, 319-320
events, 199, 286, 319-320
eventual consistency, 11, 85, 447
eviction policies for caches, 97-99
exactly-once semantics (EOS), 214
execution engines, 48
execution environment, 286
execution plans, 48
Extensible Messaging and Presence Protocol
    (XMPP), 148-149, 504-505

F

FaaS (function as a service), 179
failover patterns, 16
failure-tolerant patterns, 203
fault tolerance, 15, 22-24, 69
federated query, 339, 343
fields (in relational databases), 40
FIFO (first-in, first-out) caching policy, 97
FIFO (first-in, first-out) queues, 306, 396
file-based storage, 36, 257
filesystems
    EMRFS, 330-331
    HDFS, 206-209, 215
first-in, first-out (FIFO) caching policy, 97
first-in, first-out (FIFO) queues, 306, 396
fixed topology fallacy, 25
flexible schema design
    in column-family stores, 84
    nonrelational databases, 68
Flink, 302-303
Forecast, 347
foreign keys, 41, 47

Index | 575

forking, 116-118
forward indexes, 392
forward proxies, 121
fragmentation, 140
frequency-based cache eviction policies, 98-99
frequently accessed objects storage class, 259
front queue selectors, 395
front queues, 395
frontend API, 450
FSx for Lustre, 258
FSx for Windows File Server, 258
function (Lambda), 286
function as a service (FaaS), 179
functional requirements
    chat application, 502
    hotel reservation system, 466-467
    online game leaderboard, 442-443
    social network, 416
    stockbroker application, 544
    URL shortener service, 356
    video processing, 526
    web crawler/search engine, 388
functionality-based load balancers, 129-131

G

game use case (see online game leaderboard use case)
gateway load balancer (GWLB), 248
gateways, 147
Geohash, 477
GET method, 144
GetItem operation (key-value stores), 73
Gitflow, 180
global secondary indexes (GSIs), 267
global server load balancing (GSLB), 123
Glue, 334-338
graph databases, 69, 90-93, 270-272
GraphQL, 157-159, 326-327, 475-476
GSIs (global secondary indexes), 267
GSLB (global server load balancing), 123
GWLB (gateway load balancer), 248

H

Hadoop Distributed File System (HDFS), 206-209, 215, 330-331
Hadoop ecosystem
    AWS versus, 209-211
    HDFS integration, 207
handshake process, 152

hard disk drives (HDDs), 257
hardware load balancers, 132
hash partitioning, 55-56
hash-based algorithms, 126
hashing, 360-361
HDDs (hard disk drives), 257
HDFS (Hadoop Distributed File System), 206-209, 215, 330-331
heartbeat mechanism, 81
HFT (high-frequency trading), 545, 553-555
high availability, 28, 59, 69
high-frequency trading (HFT), 545, 553-555
hinted handoff, 77
historical stock tick service, 549-550
homogeneous network fallacy, 26
horizontal partitioning, 55
horizontal scaling, 21
host ID, 226
hostname routing, 204
hot partitions/hot keys, 268
hot spots, 56
hot-swap deployment, 512
hotel reservation system use case, 465-499
    architecture design, 469-490
        payment processing architecture, 482-485
        property booking architecture, 478-488
        property onboarding architecture, 469-471
        property reviews architecture, 488-490
        property search architecture, 471-478
    Day 0 architecture, 490-497
    Day N architecture, 497-498
    system requirements, 465-469
HTTP (Hypertext Transfer Protocol), 143-146
HTTP header routing, 204
HTTP headers, 145
HTTP polling, 151
HTTP response status codes, 145-146, 366
HTTP/1.1, 145
HTTP/2, 145
HTTP/3, 145
hybrid connectivity, 243-246
hybrid orchestration and choreography pattern, 192
Hypertext Transfer Protocol (HTTP), 143-146
hypervisors, 164, 280

I

IaC (infrastructure-as-code), 179, 231
IAM (Identity and Access Management), 262, 320-323
ICE (Interactive Connectivity Establishment), 159
ICMP (Internet Control Message Protocol), 140
idempotence, 214, 484-485
Identity and Access Management (IAM), 262, 320-323
identity pools, 324
identity providers (IdPs), 323
IDL (interface definition language), 155
IdPs (identity providers), 323
IGW (Internet Gateway), 232, 237-238
images (Docker), 167-169
IMAP (Internet Message Access Protocol), 147
in-memory databases (see caching)
in-process caching, 105
inbound rules, 235
incident management, 182
index aliases, 475
index support, 267
indexes, 42, 50-52
    deleting, 474
    key-value stores, 71
    search engine use case, 399-404
    video processing, 531-532
inference, 348
Inferentia, 348
infinite bandwidth fallacy, 25
infrastructure-as-code (IaC), 179, 231
infrequently accessed objects storage class, 260
ingestion system (see video processing use case)
init process, 172
initial costs (in TCO), 457-459
instance endpoints, 271
instance stores, 256
instances, 280
    autoscaling, 284-285
    launching, 281-282
    types of, 282-284
intelligence, 344
intelligent tiering, 261
Interactive Connectivity Establishment (ICE), 159
interface definition language (IDL), 155
internet connectivity
    NACLs, 236-237
    route tables, 233-234
    security groups, 234-235
    to VPC service, 237-239
Internet Control Message Protocol (ICMP), 140
Internet Gateway (IGW), 232, 237-238
Internet Message Access Protocol (IMAP), 147
Internet Protocol (IP), 140
internet protocol suite (see TCP/IP model)
interprocess caching, 106
invalidation policies for caches, 100-101
inverted indexes, 392, 402-404
IP (Internet Protocol), 140
IP addresses, 140, 226-230
    elastic, 229
    IPv4, 226-228
    IPv6, 228
    private, 229
    public, 229
IP datagrams, 140
IP headers, 140
IPv4, 226-228
IPv6, 228
IRLBot research paper, 396
islands (in Erlang clusters), 514
isolation, 31, 44

J

Jabber ID (JID), 149
jobs (Kubernetes), 177

K

Kafka, 189, 211-215, 297
kappa architecture, 194
KDA (Kinesis Data Analytics), 302-303
KDF (Kinesis Data Firehose), 303-304
KDS (Kinesis Data Streams), 299-301
Kendra, 347, 406, 407
key generation service, 364-365, 369
key-value stores, 69, 71-78
    access and retrieval operations, 73
    advantages and trade-offs, 77
    availability, 76-77
    data model, 71-73
    Dynamo, 78
    DynamoDB, 265-268
    scaling, 73-75
keys, 46-47
    candidate, 46
    in column-family stores, 84

in DynamoDB, 265
foreign, 41, 47
Kafka, 213
in key-value stores, 71-73
primary, 41, 46
Keyspaces, 90, 276-277
Kinesis, 215, 299-305
Kinesis Data Analytics (KDA), 302-303
Kinesis Data Firehose (KDF), 303-304
Kinesis Data Streams (KDS), 299-301
Kinesis Video Streams (KVS), 304-305
KISS (Keep It Simple, Silly), 32
KRaft (Apache Kafka Raft), 212
kube-proxy, 175
kubelets, 175
Kubernetes, 174-177
  deployment strategies, 178-180
  EKS (Elastic Kubernetes Service), 293-295
KVS (Kinesis Video Streams), 304-305

L

Lambda, 286-289
  for online game leaderboard, 453, 455
  for URL shortener service, 375, 378
  for web crawler/search engine, 407
lambda architecture, 193-194
Landing Zone, 222
last in, first out (LIFO), 98
last write wins (LWW), 76
latency, 59
  in online game leaderboard, 446
  programming languages and, 554
  in search engine, 402-404
  in stockbroker application, 559-561
  throughput versus, 27-28
  ultra-low, 545, 553-555
launching
  ECS launch types, 291
  instances, 281-282
layers (Lambda), 287
LBaaS (load balancer as a service), 132
LBs (load balancers), 120
  ALB (application load balancer), 131, 248
  CLB (classic load balancer), 248
  deployment and placement strategies, 123-125
  ELB (Elastic Load Balancer), 248-250
  GWLB (gateway load balancer), 248
  Nginx, 133-135

NLB (network load balancer), 130-131, 248
session persistence, 127-129
types of, 129-133
leaderboard service, 449
leaderboards (see online game leaderboard use case)
leaderless replication, 74-75
least connections algorithms, 126
least frequently recently used (LFRU), 99
least frequently used (LFU), 98
least loaded algorithms, 126
least recently used (LRU), 98
least response time algorithms, 126
leveled compaction, 87
Lex, 347
LFRU (least frequently recently used), 99
LFU (least frequently used), 98
lifecycle configurations, 260
LIFO (last in, first out), 98
listeners, 248
live stock ticks architecture, 547-549
live streaming services (see video processing use case)
load balancer as a service (LBaaS), 132
load balancers (LBs), 120
  ALB (application load balancer), 131, 248
  CLB (classic load balancer), 248
  deployment and placement strategies, 123-125
  GWLB (gateway load balancer), 248
  Nginx, 133-135
  NLB (network load balancer), 130-131, 248
  session persistence, 127-129
  types of, 129-133
load balancing, 15
  algorithms, 125-127
  benefits of, 122-123
  deployment and placement strategies, 123-125
  in Neptune, 271
  with Nginx, 133-135
  session persistence, 127-129
  types of load balancers, 129-133
load distribution, 59
local load balancing, 123-125
local quorum, 85
local secondary indexes (LSIs), 267
local zones (AWS), 224, 560
locality, 95

location searches, 477-478
locking, 10, 480-482
locks, 481
log-based CDC, 187
logical database schema design, 40-42
logs, 315
LRU (least recently used), 98
LSI (local secondary indexes), 267
lucidity, 22
LWW (last write wins), 76

M

machine learning, 344-349
Macie, 262
magnetic disks, 257
mail transfer agents (MTAs), 147
maintainability, 21
maintenance costs (in TCO), 459
Make it Work, Make it Right, Make it Fast principle, 351, 371
Managed Streaming for Apache Kafka (MSK), 215, 297-299, 301
Managed Workflow for Apache Airflow (MWAA), 313-314
manager nodes, 174
materialized views, 343
maximum message size, 306
maximum transmission unit (MTU), 140
mean time between failures (MTBF), 19
mean time to repair (MTTR), 19
measuring
　availability, 13-14
　performance, 32-33
　reliability, 19-20
media content storage, 510-511, 513
Memcached, 111-112, 272
memory capacity, time-space trade-offs, 27
memory management in Redis, 116-118
MemoryDB, 116
memtables, 86
Merkle trees, 75, 394
message attributes, 308
message brokers, 188-189
message delivery failure handling, 308
message durability, 308
message filtering, 308
message ordering, 309
message queues, 189
　Kafka, 211-215
　SQS (Simple Queue Service), 305-306
Message Queuing Telemetry Transport (MQTT), 149-150, 504-505
message security, 308
messaging guarantees (Kafka), 214
messaging system, 450, 501
　(see also chat applications)
metadata, 334
metadata repositories, 50
metrics, 32, 316-317
microservices, 198-199
migration costs (in TCO), 460
migration of social network system, 433-436
MIME (Multipurpose Internet Mail Extensions), 147
minions, 175
ML (machine learning), 344-349
Mnesia, 514
modifiability, 22
modification, invalidation on, 100
modular systems, 31
MongoDB, 82-83, 269
monitoring, 182
　with CloudWatch, 315-320
　URL shortener service, 376
monoliths, 196-197
monotonic read consistency, 10, 11
most recently used (MRU), 98
MQTT (Message Queuing Telemetry Transport), 149-150, 504-505
MRU (most recently used), 98
MSK (Managed Streaming for Apache Kafka), 215, 297-299, 301
MTAs (mail transfer agents), 147
MTBF (mean time between failures), 19
MTTR (mean time to repair), 19
MTU (maximum transmission unit), 140
multileader replication, 17, 60
Multipurpose Internet Mail Extensions (MIME), 147
multiregion deployments
　in chat application, 519
　in social network use case, 438-439
multitenant systems for URL shortener service, 369-370
multithreading, 273
multitier CDN architecture, 110
mutations, 158

MWAA (Managed Workflow for Apache Airflow), 313-314
MySQL, 63-65

N

N-tier architectures, 197
NACLs (network access control lists), 236-237
NameNodes, 208
namespaces, 316
NAT gateways, 238-239
Neo4j, 91-92
Neptune, 93, 270-272
network access control lists (NACLs), 236-237
network ID, 226
network layer protocols, 140
network load balancers (NLBs), 130-131, 248
networking components, 120-122
networking services (AWS)
    API Gateway, 250-251
    CloudFront, 251-253
    ELB (Elastic Load Balancer), 248-250
    in high-frequency trading (HFT), 553-554
    internet connectivity
        NACLs, 236-237
        route tables, 233-234
        security groups, 234-235
        to VPC service, 237-239
    Route 53 (DNS services), 246-247
    VPC service, 225-233
        creating VPC, 230-231
        cross-VPC connectivity, 239-242
        hybrid connectivity, 243-246
        internet connectivity to, 237-239
        IP addresses, 226-230
        subnets, 231-233
newsfeeds, 415
    (see also social network use case)
NFRs (see nonfunctional requirements)
Nginx, 133-135
NLBs (network load balancers), 130-131, 248
nodes, 174
nonfunctional requirements
    chat application, 502
    hotel reservation system, 467
    online game leaderboard, 443
    social network, 416
    stockbroker application, 544-545
    URL shortener service, 357
    video processing, 526

    web crawler/search engine, 388-389
nonrelational databases
    availability and fault tolerance, 69
    BASE principles, 69-70
    column-family stores, 69, 83-90
        advantages and trade-offs, 88
        Apache Cassandra, 88-89
        architecture, 86-88
        consistency levels, 84-86
        data model, 83-84
        Keyspaces, 276-277
    document stores, 68, 79-83
        advantages and trade-offs, 81
        availability, 80
        data model, 79-80
        DocumentDB, 268-269
        MongoDB, 82-83
    graph databases, 69, 90-93, 270-272
    key-value stores, 69, 71-78
        access and retrieval operations, 73
        advantages and trade-offs, 77
        availability, 76-77
        data model, 71-73
        Dynamo, 78
        DynamoDB, 265-268
        scaling, 73-75
    relational databases, compared, 94
    scalability, 69
    schema flexibility, 68
normalization, 45-46
NoSQL databases (see nonrelational databases)
notebooks, 303

O

object lock, 261
object-based storage, 36, 38-39, 259-262
object-level caching, 108
objects (S3), 259
observability, 33, 376
online game leaderboard use case, 441-463
    architecture design, 446-451
    Day 0 architecture, 451-460
    Day N architecture, 460-463
    system requirements, 442-445
open source caching solutions, 111-118
open source distributed systems architecture, 206-215
    HDFS, 206-209, 215
    Kafka, 211-215

open source load balancers, 133-135
open source RDBMS, 63-65
Open Systems Interconnection (see OSI model)
OpenSearch, 275-276
operability, 22
operational costs (in TCO), 459
operators, 80
optimistic locking, 481
optimistic replication, 76
optimizing
    CDNs, 109-110
    relational databases, 50-54
orchestration, 174-177, 191-193, 297
    Kinesis, 299-305
    MSK (Managed Streaming for Apache Kafka), 297-299
    SNS (Simple Notification Service), 307-309
    in social network use case, 420, 423
    SQS (Simple Queue Service), 305-306
    workflow orchestration, 309-314
orchestrators, 191
order management system design, 550-553, 564-565
Origin Shield, 538-539
OSI model, 121, 138-139
outbound rules, 235
Outposts, 561

P

P&L dashboard design, 555-556
PACELC theorem, 29
pages (in Memcached), 112
parallel systems, availability, 14-15
Pareto distribution, 96
partition keys
    in column-family stores, 84
    in DynamoDB, 265
    in key-value stores, 72
partitioning, 54-56, 334, 447
partitions (Kafka), 213
path routing, 204
patterns (see architectural designs and patterns)
patterns of availability, 16-18
payload, 140
payment processing architecture (hotel reservation system), 482-485
peer-to-peer connections, 159-160
performance, 50
    (see also optimizing)
    measuring, 32-33
    replication and, 59
    scalability versus, 28
persistence, 273
    in event sourcing, 201
    in load balancers, 127-129
    in Redis, 115-116
    in stock tick system, 548
    WebSockets, 151-153
personally identifiable information (PII), 315
pessimistic locking, 481
physical separation, 369
PII (personally identifiable information), 315
placement strategies for load balancers, 123-125
Pods, 176
politeness, 394
polling invocation, 288
Polly, 347
POP (Post Office Protocol), 147
ports, 142
POST method, 144
Post Office Protocol (POP), 147
post workflow orchestration (social network use case), 420, 423
PostgreSQL, 64-65
posts, handling in social network use case, 418-424
primary indexes, 51
primary keys
    in DynamoDB, 265
    in key-value stores, 72
    in relational databases, 41, 46
primary nodes, 332
primary-secondary node clusters, 81
prioritizers, 395
priority queues, 396
private IP addresses, 229
private subnets, 231-233, 238-239
PrivateLink, 241-242
procedures, 154
processing time, 27
producers, 212
profiling, 52
Profit & Loss dashboard design, 555-556
programming languages, latency and, 554
projection, 80
property booking architecture (hotel reservation system), 478-488, 492-493

property onboarding architecture (hotel reservation system), 469-471, 491
property reviews architecture (hotel reservation system), 488-490
property search architecture (hotel reservation system), 471-478, 491-492
protocols, 137, 138
 application layer, 143-150
 choosing for chat application, 504-505
 communications standards, 154-160
  GraphQL, 157-159
  REST, 155-157
  RPC, 154-155
  WebRTC, 159-160
 network layer, 140
 transport layer, 140-143
provisioned concurrency, 288
pub/sub (publisher-subscriber) architecture, 188-189
 Kinesis, 299-305
 MSK (Managed Streaming for Apache Kafka), 297-299
 SNS (Simple Notification Service), 307-309
 SQS (Simple Queue Service), 305-306
public access (S3), 262
public IP addresses, 229
public subnets, 231-233, 237-238
pull CDNs, 109
pull-based communication mechanisms, 151, 418
push CDNs, 109
push-based communication mechanisms, 151-153, 307-309, 418
PUT method, 144
PutItem operation (key-value stores), 73

Q

QoS (quality of service) levels (in MQTT), 149
quadtree, 477
quality of service (QoS) levels (in MQTT), 149
query federation, 54
query optimizers, 48
query parsers, 48
query processors, 48
query-level caching, 108
queue-based cache eviction policies, 97-98
queues, 488
QUIC (Quick UDP Internet Connections), 145
QuickSight, 339-340

quorums, 74, 85

R

range keys in key-value stores, 72
range partitioning, 56
ranking service, 449
rate limiter pattern, 203
RCUs (read capacity units), 266
RDB (Redis database) files, 115-116
RDBMS (relational database management systems)
 architecture, 47-50
 open source, 63-65
RDS (Relational Database Service), 65, 263-265
re-creating deployments, 178
read capacity units (RCUs), 266
read, invalidation on, 100-101
read-intensive caching strategies, 102-104
read-through caching strategy, 103
readiness probes, 178
real-time communications, 501
 (see also chat applications)
 MQTT, 149-150, 504-505
 WebRTC, 159-160
 XMPP, 148-149, 504-505
recency-based cache eviction policies, 98
records (in relational databases), 40
recovery managers, 49
recovery point objective (RPO), 23
recovery time objective (RTO), 24
RECs (regional edge caches), 538
Redis, 113-118, 272
 availability in, 114-115
 benefits of, 113
 durability in, 115-116
 memory management in, 116-118
 scaling, 461-462
 in social network use case, 423
Redshift, 340-343
Redshift Managed Storage (RMS), 342
Redshift Spectrum, 342
redundancy, 15, 273
refresh intervals, 399
refresh-ahead caching strategy, 103
regional edge caches (RECs), 538
regions (AWS), 223
registered ports, 142
registries (Docker), 169-171
Rekognition, 347

Relational Database Service (RDS), 65, 263-265
relational databases
    ACID model, 43-44
    database management system architecture,
        47-50
    ER model, 45
    keys, 46-47
    logical schema design, 40-42
    nonrelational databases, compared, 94
    object-level caching, 108
    optimizing, 50-54
    for property onboarding architecture,
        470-471
    query optimizers, 48
    query parsers, 48
    query processors, 48
    query-level caching, 108
    RDS, 263-265
    relationships in, 40, 45
    scaling, 54-63
    schema normalization, 45-46
    SQL, 42-43
    for user post service, 422
relational model, 40
relationships (in relational databases), 40, 45
relay servers, 147
relevance of search results, 404
reliability, 19-20
reliable network fallacy, 24
remote caching, 106
Remote Procedure Call (RPC), 154-155
replica nodes, 8
replica sets, 81
ReplicaSets, 176
replication, 59-63, 273
replication patterns, 17-18
replication-based fault tolerance, 22
Representational State Transfer (REST),
    155-157
resiliency, 59, 565
resolution (of metrics), 316
resources (Kubernetes), 177
response time, 27
REST (Representational State Transfer),
    155-157
retention periods, 306
retirement costs (in TCO), 460
retry with backoff pattern, 203
reverse proxies, 121

RMS (Redshift Managed Storage), 342
rolling deployments, 178
root users, 321
rosters, 148
round robin algorithms, 125
Route 53, 246-247
route tables, 233-234
rows (in relational databases), 40
RPC (Remote Procedure Call), 154-155
RPO (recovery point objective), 23
RTO (recovery time objective), 24
runc, 173
runtime dependencies, 168

S

S3 (Simple Storage Service), 39, 259-262
sagas, 202
SageMaker, 344-346
SASL/SCRAM (Simple Authentication and
    Security Layer/Salted Challenge Response
    Authentication Mechanism), 298
scalability, 20-21, 351
    with AppSync, 326-327
    autoscaling, 284-285
    horizontal scaling, 21
    of nonrelational databases, 69
    performance versus, 28
    replication and, 59
    vertical scaling, 20
scale (of system)
    chat application, 503
    hotel reservation system, 467-469
    online game leaderboard, 444-445
    search engine, 390
    social network, 417
    stockbroker application, 545
    URL shortener service, 357-358
    video processing, 527
    web crawler, 389-390
scaling
    Day 0 architecture (see Day 0 architecture)
    Day N architecture (see Day N architecture)
    in DynamoDB, 368
    Elasticsearch, 473-475
    key-value stores, 73-75
    Redis, 461-462
    relational databases, 54-63
    for URL shortener service, 383
scaling costs (in TCO), 459

Index | 583

schedulers, 175
schema design
    in chat application, 503-516
    in column-family stores, 84
    in hotel reservation system, 469-490
    key-value stores, 71
    nonrelational databases, 68
    in online game leaderboard, 446-451
    relational databases, 40-42
    in social network system, 417-427
    in stockbroker application, 545-556
    in URL shortener service, 360
    in video processing, 528-533
    in web crawler/search engine, 391-404
schema normalization, 45-46
Schema Registry, 212
score submission service, 448-449
SDP (Session Description Protocol), 160
search databases (OpenSearch), 275-276
search engine use case, 387-414
    architecture design, 398-404
    Day 0 architecture, 405-409
    Day N architecture, 412-413
    system requirements, 388-391
search engines, 387
search result relevance, 404
search service
    in hotel reservation system, 471-478
    in social network use case, 425-427
    in video processing use case, 531-532
secondary indexes, 51
secondary NameNodes, 208
secrets, 177
Secrets Manager, 298
secure network fallacy, 25
security
    of messages, 308
    S3, 261-262
security groups, 234-235
security managers, 50
seed URLs, 393
self-hosting, cloud-managed services versus, 566
sequential systems, availability, 14-15
server pools, 119
server-sent events (SSEs), 153
serverless deployments, 179
servers, 279
service mesh architecture, 205

service providers, 241
service-level objectives (SLOs), 20
services (Kubernetes), 176
session affinity, 127
Session Description Protocol (SDP), 160
session persistence in load balancers, 127-129
Session Traversal Utilities for NAT (STUN) protocol, 159-160
sharding, 57, 447, 473
shards, 299-300, 399
shared responsibility model, 221, 223
shared tenancy, 230
sidecar pattern, 205
Simple Authentication and Security Layer/Salted Challenge Response Authentication Mechanism (SASL/SCRAM), 298
Simple Mail Transfer Protocol (SMTP), 146-148
Simple Notification Service (SNS), 307-309, 454
Simple Object Access Protocol (SOAP), 155
Simple Queue Service (SQS), 305-306, 454
Simple Storage Service (S3), 39, 259-262
simplicity, 32
single administrator fallacy, 25
single-leader replication, 17, 60
size-tiered compaction, 87
slabs (in Memcached), 112
sloppy quorum, 76
SLOs (service-level objectives), 20
slow start, 141
SLTS (stock live ticker service), 547-549
SMTP (Simple Mail Transfer Protocol), 146-148
SnapStart, 289
Snowflake, 365
SNS (Simple Notification Service), 307-309, 454
SOAP (Simple Object Access Protocol), 155
social network use case, 415-440
    Day 0 architecture, 427-436
    Day N architecture, 436-439
    migration for scalability, 433-436
    search service, 425-427
    system requirements, 415-417
    user post service design, 418-424
    user relationship design, 417-418, 424-425
soft deletes, 87
soft limit, 230
software deployment (see application deployment)

software load balancers, 132
solid-state drives (SSDs), 257
solution architecture, 196-199
sort keys
    in DynamoDB, 265
    in key-value stores, 72
sorting algorithms, 447
source IP affinity, 128
sources (KDS), 299
spot instances, 283
SQL (structured query language), 42-43
SQL tuning, 52-53
SQS (Simple Queue Service), 305-306, 454
SSDs (solid-state drives), 257
SSEs (server-sent events), 153
SSTables, 87
standard queues, 306
stanzas, 148
state, 199
state machines, 199, 310-312
state-oriented EDA implementations, 200
stateful load balancers, 127-128
StatefulSet deployments, 178
stateless load balancers, 128-129
static initialization optimization (Lambda), 289
static load balancing algorithms, 125-126
statistics, 317
STCS (stock tick consumer service), 548
Step Functions, 310-313, 407, 536
sticky sessions, 127
stock exchanges, 543
stock live ticker service (SLTS), 547-549
stock tick consumer service (STCS), 548
stock tick system design, 546-550, 563
stockbroker application use case, 543-566
    Day 0 architecture, 557-562
    Day N architecture, 562-566
    order management system design, 550-553, 564-565
    P&L dashboard design, 555-556
    stock tick system design, 546-550, 563
    system requirements, 544-545
    ultra-low latency system design, 553-555
storage capacity
    online game leaderboard, 444-445, 455
    time-space trade-offs, 27
    URL shortener service, 358-360
storage classes
    EFS, 258
    S3, 259-261
storage drivers, 36
storage engines, 48
storage systems (see data storage systems)
strangler fig pattern, 205
stream-based CDC, 187
streaming services (see video processing use case)
strong consistency, 10, 28, 85
structured query language (SQL), 42-43
stub functions, 155
STUN (Session Traversal Utilities for NAT) protocol, 159-160
subnet masks, 227
subnets, 227, 231-233, 272
support costs (in TCO), 459
supporting processes, 172
synchronous checkpointing, 23
synchronous communication, 7, 150
synchronous invocation, 287
synchronous orchestration patterns, 191-192
synchronous replication, 61-62
system boundaries, 389
system design, 185
    (see also architectural designs and patterns)
    AWS Well-Architected Framework, 26
    concepts
        availability, 13-18
        communication, 6-8
        consistency, 8-12
        fault tolerance, 22-24
        maintainability, 21
        reliability, 19-20
        scalability, 20-21
    fallacies of distributed systems, 24-26
    goals of, 352
    guidelines, 31-34
    trade-offs, 26-30
    use cases (see use cases)

T

table deltas, 187
table partitioning, 334
tables (in relational databases), 40
target groups, 249
task nodes, 332
tasks (ECS), 290-291
tasks (Step Functions), 310
TCL (transaction control language), 43

TCO (total cost of ownership), 456-460
TCP (Transmission Control Protocol), 140-142
TCP/IP model, 139-150
    application layer protocols, 143-150
    network layer protocols, 140
    transport layer protocols, 140-143
tenancy, 230
"there is no such thing as a free lunch", 33
throughput
    latency versus, 27-28
    online game leaderboard, 445
time synchronization, 496
time to live (TTL), 101, 394
time-space trade-offs, 27
time-window compaction, 87
Timestream, 276, 549
tombstones, 87
topics (Kafka), 213
total cost of ownership (TCO), 456-460
trade-offs guideline, 33
Trainium, 348
transaction control language (TCL), 43
transaction managers, 49
transaction support, 267
transactional outbox pattern, 205
transactions, 42
Transcribe, 347
Transit Gateway, 240-241
transitions, 199
Transmission Control Protocol (TCP), 140-142
transport layer protocols, 140-143
Traversal Using Relays around NAT (TURN)
    servers, 160
trigger-based CDC, 187
triggers, 286, 325
TTL (time to live), 101, 394
tunable consistency, 11
TURN (Traversal Using Relays around NAT)
    servers, 160

U

UDFs (user-defined functions), 339
UDP (User Datagram Protocol), 142-143
ultra-low latency, 545, 553-555
unbounded stream processing, 302
unique ID generation, 361-363
UpdateItem operation (key-value stores), 73
URL duplicate detection, 397-398
URL frontier, 395-397

URL shortener service use case, 355-383
    algorithms for, 360-365
    APIs for, 365-367
    architecture design, 360
    custom domain support, 369-370
    database selection, 368-369
    Day 0 architecture, 371-379
    Day N architecture, 379-383
    scaling overview, 383
    system requirements, 355-360
use cases
    chat application, 501-523
        architecture design, 503-511
        Day 0 architecture, 516-520
        Day N architecture, 520-522
        direct messaging, 505-509
        media content storage, 510-511
        message storage, 509-510
        protocol selection, 504-505
        system requirements, 501-503
        WhatsApp architecture, 511-516
    hotel reservation system, 465-499
        architecture design, 469-490
        Day 0 architecture, 490-497
        Day N architecture, 497-498
        system requirements, 465-469
    online game leaderboard, 441-463
        architecture design, 446-451
        Day 0 architecture, 451-460
        Day N architecture, 460-463
        system requirements, 442-445
    social network, 415-440
        Day 0 architecture, 427-436
        Day N architecture, 436-439
        migration for scalability, 433-436
        search service, 425-427
        system requirements, 415-417
        user post service design, 418-424
        user relationship design, 417-418, 424-425
    stockbroker application, 543-566
        Day 0 architecture, 557-562
        Day N architecture, 562-566
        order management system design, 550-553, 564-565
        P&L dashboard design, 555-556
        stock tick system design, 546-550, 563
        system requirements, 544-545
        ultra-low latency system design, 553-555

as system design guideline, 33
URL shortener service, 355-383
    algorithms for, 360-365
    APIs for, 365-367
    architecture design, 360
    custom domain support, 369-370
    database selection, 368-369
    Day 0 architecture, 371-379
    Day N architecture, 379-383
    scaling overview, 383
    system requirements, 355-360
video processing, 525-542
    architecture design, 528-529, 533
    content distribution, 532
    content indexing, 531-532
    Day 0 architecture, 534-540
    Day N architecture, 540-542
    scaling architecture, 536-540
    system requirements, 525-527
    video encoding process, 529-530
    video-quality validation, 531
web crawler/search engine, 387-414
    architecture design, 391-404
    Day 0 architecture, 405-409
    Day N architecture, 409-413
    system requirements, 388-391
user connections, 505-509
User Datagram Protocol (UDP), 142-143
user gateway service, 418
user graph service, 418, 425
user pool hosted UIs, 324
user pools, 324
user post service design (social network use case), 418-424
user relationship design (social network use case), 417-418, 424-425
user timeline service, 420, 424
user timelines, 415
    (see also social network use case)
user-defined functions (UDFs), 339

V
versioning, 169, 259
vertical partitioning, 55
vertical scaling, 20
video encoding, 529-530
Video Multimethod Assessment Fusion (VMAF), 531
video processing use case, 525-542

    (see also media content storage)
    architecture design, 528-529, 533
    content distribution, 532
    content indexing, 531-532
    Day 0 architecture, 534-540
    Day N architecture, 540-542
    scaling architecture, 536-540
    system requirements, 525-527
    video encoding process, 529-530
    video-quality validation, 531
video streaming, 304-305
video-quality validation, 531
views, 42
VIF (virtual interface), 246
VIP (virtual IP) addresses, 124
virtual interface (VIF), 246
virtual machines (VMs), containers versus, 164-166
virtual private clouds (see VPC service)
virtual private networks (VPNs), 243
virtual separation, 369
virtualization, 164
visibility timeouts, 306
VMAF (Video Multimethod Assessment Fusion), 531
VMs (virtual machines), containers versus, 164-166
volumes (EBS), 257
volumes (Kubernetes), 177
VPC Lattice, 242
VPC peering, 239-240
VPC service, 225-233
    creating VPC, 230-231
    cross-VPC connectivity, 239-242
    hybrid connectivity, 243-246
    internet connectivity to, 237-239
    IP addresses, 226-230
    subnets, 231-233
    for URL shortener service, 379
VPNs (virtual private networks), 243

W
warm start, 104, 288
Wavelength, 561
WCUs (write capacity units), 266
weak consistency, 85
web crawler use case, 387-414
    architecture design, 393-398
    Day 0 architecture, 405-409

Day N architecture, 410-412
    system requirements, 388-391
web crawlers, 387
web server caching, 107
webhooks, 476
WebRTC (Web Real-Time Communication), 159-160
WebSockets, 148, 151-153, 519
weighted round robin algorithms, 126
Well-Architected Framework (AWS), 26
well-known ports, 142
WhatsApp, 511-516
wide-column stores (see column-family stores)
WLM (workload management) tools, 343
worker nodes, 175
workflow orchestration, 309-314
workload management (WLM) tools, 343
write capacity units (WCUs), 266
write-ahead logging, 9
write-around caching strategy, 104
write-back caching strategy, 105
write-through caching strategy, 104

X

X-Ray, 376
XMPP (Extensible Messaging and Presence Protocol), 148-149, 504-505

Z

zero latency fallacy, 24
zero transport cost fallacy, 25
zone maps, 341
ZooKeeper, 212

About the Authors

Jayanth Kumar is a published poet, a technical architect (AWS Solutions Architect Professional), an entrepreneur, an engineering leader, and an assistant professor too.

He earned his bachelor's degree from IIT Bombay and his master's degree from UCLA in Computer Science departments. He formerly held the positions of software engineer at SAP Germany and SAP Silicon Valley. Later, as an entrepreneur, he held the positions of Head of Engineering at Goodhealth, Engineering Manager at Delhivery, and Software Development Manager at Amazon. These challenging experiences made him grow not just into Technology but also into People, Processes and Product leadership.

He always seeks to challenge himself with new learning opportunities and focuses on building robust mechanisms and systems that will stand the test of the time.

Find him on LinkedIn (*https://www.linkedin.com/in/jaykmr*) and his personal blog (*https://jaykmr.com*).

Mandeep Singh is an educator and software engineer with a strong passion for building simple, scalable systems. A graduate from the Army Institute of Technology, he has held various engineering roles at Amazon, Jupiter, and Kyndryl. His experience spans multiple domains, including cloud infrastructure modernization, ecommerce logistics and compliance, and payment systems.

He supports the learning and development of others by sharing lessons on Cloud and System Design on his YouTube channel and LinkedIn. Outside of work, he enjoys morning runs, weight lifting, cooking, and spending time with his family in the serene ambience of his hometown.

Find him on LinkedIn (*https://www.linkedin.com/in/msdeep14*) and YouTube (*https://www.youtube.com/c/MsDeepSingh*).

Colophon

The animal on the cover of *System Design on AWS* is a western spectre dragonfly (*Boyeria irene*). The species is found in Western Europe and North Africa. They have an eye-catching brown and green pattern on their bodies and reddish legs. The western spectre has an IUCN conservation status of Least Concern. Many of the animals on O'Reilly covers are endangered; all of them are important to the world.

The cover illustration is by Karen Montgomery, based on an antique line engraving from *Histoire Naturelle*. The series design is by Edie Freedman, Ellie Volckhausen, and Karen Montgomery. The cover fonts are Gilroy Semibold and Guardian Sans. The text font is Adobe Minion Pro; the heading font is Adobe Myriad Condensed; and the code font is Dalton Maag's Ubuntu Mono.

O'REILLY®

Learn from experts.
Become one yourself.

60,000+ titles | Live events with experts | Role-based courses
Interactive learning | Certification preparation

Try the O'Reilly learning platform free for 10 days.